Women's Property Rights Under CEDAW

Women's Property Rights Under CEDAW

JOSÉ E. ALVAREZ
AND
JUDITH BAUDER

OXFORD
UNIVERSITY PRESS

Oxford University Press is a department of the University of Oxford. It furthers the University's
objective of excellence in research, scholarship, and education by publishing worldwide.
Oxford is a registered trade mark of Oxford University Press in the UK and certain other countries.

Published in the United States of America by Oxford University Press
198 Madison Avenue, New York, NY 10016, United States of America.

© Oxford University Press 2024

All rights reserved. No part of this publication may be reproduced, stored in a retrieval system, or
transmitted, in any form or by any means, without the prior permission in writing of Oxford University
Press, or as expressly permitted by law, by license, or under terms agreed with the appropriate reproduction
rights organization. Inquiries concerning reproduction outside the scope of the above should be sent to the
Rights Department, Oxford University Press, at the address above.

You must not circulate this work in any other form
and you must impose this same condition on any acquirer.

Library of Congress Cataloging-in-Publication Data
Names: Alvarez, José E., author. | Bauder, Judith, author.
Title: Women's property rights under CEDAW / José E. Alvarez & Judith Bauder.
Description: New York : Oxford University Press, 2024. |
Includes bibliographical references and index.
Identifiers: LCCN 2023040385 (print) | LCCN 2023040386 (ebook) |
ISBN 9780197751879 (hardback) | ISBN 9780197751893 (updf) |
ISBN 9780197751886 (epub) | ISBN 9780197751909 (digital online)
Subjects: LCSH: Convention on the Elimination of All Forms of Discrimination against
Women (1979 December 18) | Right of property. | Women (International law) |
Women—Legal status, laws, etc. | Women's rights.
Classification: LCC K3243.A41979 A48 2024 (print) | LCC K3243.A41979 (ebook) |
DDC 346.04/32082—dc23/eng/20231003
LC record available at https://lccn.loc.gov/2023040385
LC ebook record available at https://lccn.loc.gov/2023040386

DOI: 10.1093/oso/9780197751879.001.0001

Printed by Integrated Books International, United States of America

Note to Readers

This publication is designed to provide accurate and authoritative information in regard to the subject
matter covered. It is based upon sources believed to be accurate and reliable and is intended to be
current as of the time it was written. It is sold with the understanding that the publisher is not engaged
in rendering legal, accounting, or other professional services. If legal advice or other expert assistance is
required, the services of a competent professional person should be sought. Also, to confirm that the
information has not been affected or changed by recent developments, traditional legal research
techniques should be used, including checking primary sources where appropriate.

*(Based on the Declaration of Principles jointly adopted by a Committee of the
American Bar Association and a Committee of Publishers and Associations.)*

You may order this or any other Oxford University Press publication
by visiting the Oxford University Press website at www.oup.com.

Contents

Preface and Acknowledgments xv
Foreword by Hilary Charlesworth and Christine Chinkin xix

1. Introduction 1
   1.1 Realities and Challenges 1
   1.2 International Property Rights in Context 11
   1.3 The Origins of "Property" in CEDAW 20
   1.4 CEDAW's Property Provisions 23
   1.5 The Organization of This Book 26

2. The CEDAW Committee's Property Jurisprudence 31
   2.1 Introduction 31
   2.2 The Committee's Authority as an Interpreter of the Convention 33
   2.3 The Committee's Procedures and Output on Property Rights 35
       2.3.1 General Recommendations 36
       2.3.2 Communications 38
       2.3.3 Inquiry Reports 41
       2.3.4 Concluding Observations 42
       2.3.5 Follow-Up Procedures 45
            2.3.5.1 Follow-Up on Communications 46
            2.3.5.2 Follow-Up on Inquiry Reports 46
            2.3.5.3 Follow-Up on Concluding Observations 46
   2.4 Property Rights in Marriage and Family Relations 47
       2.4.1 The Convention and General Recommendations 47
            2.4.1.1 Articles 15 and 16(1)(h) 47
            2.4.1.2 GRs 21 and 29 on Women's Property Rights in Family Relations 47
            2.4.1.3 GRs on Intersectional Discrimination on Women's Property Rights in Family Relations 52
       2.4.2 Communications 54
            2.4.2.1 Cecilia Kell v. Canada 54
            2.4.2.2 E.S. and S.C. v. United Republic of Tanzania 59
       2.4.3 Concluding Observations 63
            2.4.3.1 Equal Legal Capacity to Administer and Manage Property 63
            2.4.3.2 Control over Marital Property 64
            2.4.3.3 Joint Ownership of Marital Property 64
            2.4.3.4 Equal Division of Marital Property 65

		2.4.3.5 Recognition and Distribution of Joint Marital Property	66
		2.4.3.6 Separate Property	67
		2.4.3.7 Intestate Succession and Inheritance	68
		2.4.3.8 Property Rights in Different Types of Family Relations	69
		2.4.3.9 The Impact of Intersectional Discrimination on Women's Property	71
		2.4.3.10 Elimination of Discriminatory Legal Provisions	71
2.5	Property Rights in the Context of Civil and Political Rights		73
	2.5.1	The Convention and General Recommendations	73
		2.5.1.1 Article 7 and GR 23 on Women in Political and Public Life	73
		2.5.1.2 Article 9 and GR 32 on Refugee Status, Asylum, Nationality, and Statelessness of Women	74
		2.5.1.3 Article 15 and GR 33 on Women's Access to Justice	74
	2.5.2	Concluding Observations	76
		2.5.2.1 Property Rights, Identity Documents, and Citizenship	76
		2.5.2.2 Access to Justice and Property Rights	77
2.6	Land Rights		77
	2.6.1	Convention and General Recommendations	77
		2.6.1.1 Article 14(2)(g) and Article 13's Chapeau	78
		2.6.1.2 GR 34 on Rural Women	78
		2.6.1.3 GR 37 on Climate Change	82
		2.6.1.4 GR 39 on the Rights of Indigenous Women and Girls	82
	2.6.2	Concluding Observations	87
		2.6.2.1 Rural Women's Disenfranchisement of Land and Property Rights	88
		2.6.2.2 Land Registration	89
		2.6.2.3 Access to Agricultural Land as a Source of Livelihood	90
		2.6.2.4 Combating Poverty Through Providing for Land Ownership and Land Use	90
		2.6.2.5 Land-Grabbing, Development Projects, and Indigenous Women's Land Rights	91
		2.6.2.6 Participation in Decision-Making Process on Land Policies	92
		2.6.2.7 Elimination of Discriminatory Legislation, Policies, and Practices	93
		2.6.2.8 Visibility and Awareness Raising About Land Rights	93
		2.6.2.9 Temporary Special Measures	94
		2.6.2.10 Land Rights in Conflict Situations	94
2.7	Housing Rights		95
	2.7.1	Convention and General Recommendations	95
		2.7.1.1 Article 14(2)(h) and Article 13's Chapeau	95
		2.7.1.2 GR 27 on Older Women, GR 34 on Rural Women, and GR 37 on Climate Change	95

	2.7.2	Communications	97
		2.7.2.1 L.A. et al. v. North Macedonia and S.N. and E.R. v. North Macedonia	97
	2.7.3	Concluding Observations	101
		2.7.3.1 Intersectional Discrimination Affecting Women's Housing Rights	101
		2.7.3.2 Economic Precarity and Housing Rights	103
		2.7.3.3 Development Projects and Housing Rights	104
		2.7.3.4 Impact of Disasters and Conflict Situations on Housing	104
		2.7.3.5 Temporary Special Measures	105
2.8	Intellectual Property and Seed Rights		105
	2.8.1	The Convention and General Recommendations	105
		2.8.1.1 Article 14(2)(g)	106
		2.8.1.2 GR 34 on Rural Women and GR 39 on Indigenous Women	106
	2.8.2	Concluding Observations	108
		2.8.2.1 Intellectual Property Rights and Economic Empowerment	108
		2.8.2.2 Rights to Seeds	108
2.9	Access to Financial Credit and Economic Empowerment		109
	2.9.1	Convention and General Recommendations	109
		2.9.1.1 Article 13(b) and Article 14(2)(g)	109
		2.9.1.2 GR 21 on Family Relations	109
		2.9.1.3 GR 27 on Older Women	110
		2.9.1.4 GR 34 on Rural Women	110
		2.9.1.5 GR 37 on Climate Change	111
		2.9.1.6 GR 38 on Trafficking in Women and Girls	111
		2.9.1.7 GR 39 on Indigenous Women	112
	2.9.2	Concluding Observations	112
		2.9.2.1 Access to Financial Services	112
		2.9.2.2 Access to Financial Credit to Promote Women's Economic Empowerment	113
		2.9.2.3 Access to Microcredit for Poverty Reduction	114
		2.9.2.4 Intersectionality and Economic Empowerment	114
2.10	Rights to Social Benefits		115
	2.10.1	The Convention and General Recommendations	115
		2.10.1.1 Articles 11, 13, and 14	116
		2.10.1.2 GRs on Social Benefits in the Context of Unpaid Care Work in Families and Informal Work in Family Enterprises	116
		2.10.1.3 GRs on Social Benefits in the Context of Informal Employment	117
		2.10.1.4 GRs on Pension Benefits and Survivorship Benefits	118

	2.10.2 Communications	119
	2.10.2.1 Ms. Dung Thi Thuy Nguyen v. The Netherlands	120
	2.10.2.2 Elisabeth de Blok et al. v. The Netherlands	123
	2.10.2.3 Natalia Ciobanu v. Republic of Moldova	125
	2.10.2.4 V.P. v. Belarus	129
	2.10.3 Concluding Observations	132
	2.10.3.1 Social Security in the Informal Sector	133
	2.10.3.2 Women Domestic Workers	135
	2.10.3.3 Self-Employed Women	135
	2.10.3.4 Pension Benefits and Survivorship Benefits	136
	2.10.3.5 Unemployment Benefits	136
	2.10.3.6 Maternity Benefits and Paid Maternity Leave	137
	2.10.3.7 Discriminatory Social Security Legislation and Temporary Special Measures	137
	2.10.3.8 Intersectional Discrimination and Access to Social Security Benefits	137
	2.10.3.9 Importing Standards from ILO Conventions	139
2.11	Gender-Based Violence and Property Rights	139
	2.11.1 The Convention and General Recommendations	140
	2.11.1.1 The Prohibition of Gender-Based Violence and the Link to Property	140
	2.11.1.2 Gender-Based Violence in Family Relations	142
	2.11.1.3 Harmful Economic Activities and Human Trafficking as Forms of Gender-Based Violence	142
	2.11.1.4 The Regulation of Private Actors and Limitation of Their Property Rights in the Face of Gender-Based Violence as Part of State Parties' Due Diligence Obligations	143
	2.11.1.5 Intervention in Private Property Rights as a Protective Measure in Domestic Violence Situations	145
	2.11.1.6 Access to Housing, Land, and Shelter in Gender-Based Violence Situations	145
	2.11.1.7 Gender-Based Violence as a Form of Intersectional Discrimination	145
	2.11.2 Communications	146
	2.11.2.1 Ms. A.T. v. Hungary	147
	2.11.2.2 Şahide Goekce v. Austria	150
	2.11.2.3 Yildirim v. Austria	150
	2.11.2.4 V.K. v. Bulgaria	151
	2.11.2.5 J.I. v. Finland	152
	2.11.2.6 S.T. v. Russian Federation	153
	2.11.3 Inquiry Reports	153
	2.11.3.1 Inquiry Concerning Canada	153
	2.11.3.1.1 Context and Facts	154

			2.11.3.1.2 Legal Assessment of Human Rights Violations	154
		2.11.3.2	*Inquiry Concerning South Africa*	155
			2.11.3.2.1 Legal Framework and Facts	155
			2.11.3.2.2 Legal Findings and Recommendations	156
	2.11.4	Concluding Observations		159
		2.11.4.1	*Property-Grabbing and Economic Violence*	159
		2.11.4.2	*State's Due Diligence Obligations Entail a Limitation on Perpetrator's Private Property Rights*	160
		2.11.4.3	*Protection and Eviction Orders*	160
		2.11.4.4	*Shelter*	161

3. Critiques of the CEDAW Regime, International Law, and International Human Rights — 163
   3.1 Feminist Critiques: Then and Now — 163
       3.1.1 Early Critiques of CEDAW — 163
       3.1.2 Continuing Critiques of CEDAW — 167
   3.2 Criticisms of International Law and International Human Rights — 173

4. Re-engendering Property — 187
   Introduction — 187
   4.1 Lesson One: The CEDAW's Interpretation Evolves over Time — 190
   4.2 Lesson Two: CEDAW's Property Jurisprudence Does Not Reflect a "Neo-Liberal" Agenda as That Term Is Most Commonly Defined — 196
       4.2.1 Private Property and Titling — 197
       4.2.2 Commodification — 202
       4.2.3 Privatization, Business Deregulation, and Support for Economic Globalization — 203
   4.3 Lesson Three: Beware Universalizing Concepts and Binary Arguments—Whether Expressed by CEDAW's Defenders or Its Critics — 209
   4.4 Lesson Four: Many Other Criticisms of the CEDAW Regime Need Nuance — 213
       4.4.1 The Public/Private Divide — 214
       4.4.2 Intersectionality — 215
       4.4.3 Marginalization — 218
       4.4.4 Root Causes — 219
       4.4.5 Structural Change — 225
   4.5 Lesson Five: CEDAW's Supranational Security Is Necessary — 228

5. Two Separate Worlds: Foreign Investors' Property vs. Women's Property Rights Under CEDAW — 235
   5.1 Introduction — 235

5.2	Explaining the Relative Prominence of International Investment Law	238
5.3	Two Approaches to Defining Protected Property	244
5.4	Distinct State Obligations Other Than the Duty Not to Discriminate	247
5.5	Distinct Approaches to Discrimination	249
5.6	Distinct Territorial and Jurisdictional Scope	252
5.7	Distinct Sources of Authority	253
5.8	Distinct Approaches to Derogation	256
5.9	Distinct Remedies Subject to Distinct Enforcement	258
5.10	Comparing the Two Regimes: A Hypothetical	265
5.11	Conclusions	273

6. Unity Within Diversity: Comparisons with the ICCPR and the ICESCR — 281
    - 6.1 Introduction — 281
    - 6.2 Property and Equality in the ICCPR Framework — 281
        - 6.2.1 The ICCPR's Equality Framework — 281
        - 6.2.2 Women's Equality — 284
        - 6.2.3 The Meaning of Discrimination — 285
        - 6.2.4 Women's Property Rights — 287
        - 6.2.5 Marital Status and Social Security — 289
        - 6.2.6 Forced Eviction — 293
        - 6.2.7 Remedial Approach — 296
    - 6.3 ICESCR — 300
        - 6.3.1 The ICESCR's Equality Framework — 300
        - 6.3.2 Women's Equality and Property Rights — 301
        - 6.3.3 The Right to Housing and Forced Evictions — 304
        - 6.3.4 Other Rights Relating to Property — 311
        - 6.3.5 Remedial Framework — 314
    - 6.4 Conclusions — 316
        - 6.4.1 Blurring Distinctions, Emerging Commonalities — 316
        - 6.4.2 Common Due Diligence Obligations? — 321
        - 6.4.3 Toward Comparative International Property Rights Law — 324
        - 6.4.4 CEDAW's Added Value — 329

7. Taking Women's Property Rights Seriously — 335
    - 7.1 Why CEDAW's Jurisprudence Is About "Property" and Is "Progressive" — 335
    - 7.2 Why CEDAW's Property Jurisprudence Remains a Work in Progress — 346
        - 7.2.1 Flawed Outputs — 346
        - 7.2.2 Substantive Lacunae — 352
        - 7.2.3 Institutional Constraints and Challenges — 360
    - 7.3 Does CEDAW's Property Jurisprudence Matter? — 362
    - 7.4 Beyond *A Room of One's Own* — 365

Afterword by E. Tendayi Achiume 369
Appendices: The CEDAW Committee's Output Engaging with
   Property Rights 373
   (1) Relevant CEDAW Provisions 373
   (2) State Reservations to Property-Relating CEDAW Provisions 375
   (3) Withdrawn State Reservations to Property-Relating CEDAW
       Provisions 376
   (4) The CEDAW Committee's General Recommendations
       Addressing Property Rights 381
   (5) The CEDAW Committee's Views on Communications
       Addressing Property Rights 383
   (6) The CEDAW Committee's Inquiry Reports Addressing
       Property Rights 385
Select Bibliography 387
Index 397

Summary Contents

Preface and Acknowledgments   xv
Foreword by Hilary Charlesworth and Christine Chinkin   xix

1. Introduction   1
2. The CEDAW Committee's Property Jurisprudence   31
3. Critiques of the CEDAW Regime, International Law, and International Human Rights   163
4. Re-engendering Property   187
5. Two Separate Worlds: Foreign Investors' Property vs. Women's Property Rights Under CEDAW   235
6. Unity Within Diversity: Comparisons with the ICCPR and the ICESCR   281
7. Taking Women's Property Rights Seriously   335

Afterword by E. Tendayi Achiume   369
Appendices: The CEDAW Committee's Output Engaging with Property Rights   373
Select Bibliography   387
Index   397

Preface and Acknowledgments

We start with a caveat. The use of the terms "women" and "men" in this book does not suggest that the authors do not appreciate a nonbinary understanding of gender. Gender is a social construct. The binary understanding of gender is in the process of being overcome. However, because the gender binary has been built into legal institutions and infrastructure, including in the Convention on the Elimination of All Forms of Discrimination against Women (CEDAW), retaining this terminology makes sense given the purposes of this book, even if, as this book demonstrates, the CEDAW Committee is making inroads on that binary. Moreover, even if an increasing number of countries in the world have departed from this dichotomous understanding of gender, the infrastructure that has used the gender binary underpins many legal institutions like property. Thus, terms like "women" and "men" are used in this book to demonstrate these longstanding gender parities. Retaining the category of "women" in this book given the preceding reasons does not foreclose a nonbinary understanding of gender that existed even at the time when CEDAW was drafted.[1]

This book emerges from frustration and a desire to take the underlying issues of inequality seriously. Despite the widely reported concerns with the gendered distribution of wealth and property around the world, the work of the foremost global treaty body charged with doing something about it remains something of a secret. Even some feminist equal rights activists are not aware that CEDAW includes significant provisions to protect the property rights of women or that its treaty body has been interpreting those provisions for some forty years. This book seeks to raise awareness of the CEDAW Committee's jurisprudence on this issue and put it in a broader context. It seeks, in the words of Hilary Charlesworth, to expand the "referential universe"[2] of those who speak, often disparagingly, of *the* international law of property. The CEDAW regime's reconceptualization of traditional notions of property needs to be included in future conversations about what equality, discrimination, and development mean.

---

[1] For a similar justification for the retention of the terms "women" and "men," *see* Chen Chao-ju, *Only Paradoxes to Offer? Family-Friendly Policies and Feminist Challenges to Marital Status Discrimination in Taiwan and the US* 4 (Nov. 2022) (unpublished working paper) (on file with the New York University School of law & National Taiwan University).

[2] Hilary Charlesworth, *Prefiguring Feminist Judgment in International Law, in* FEMINIST JUDGEMENTS IN INTERNATIONAL LAW 479, 492 (Loveday Hodson & Troy Lavers eds., 2019).

The book aspires to reach a variety of readers with very different backgrounds, including human rights academics and advocates, general international lawyers or specialists in international investment law or critical theory, government officials, and experts in institutions, including the UN system. This varied audience will find distinct parts of this book of interest. While all readers are likely to benefit from learning about how the CEDAW Committee applies the principles of formal and substantive equality to interests in land or marital property or housing (along with other interests covered in chapter 2), those familiar with a feminist scholarship may wish to skip chapter 3 (which canvasses some of that literature as it applies to CEDAW) to go directly to chapter 4 (which addresses how CEDAW's property jurisprudence answers CEDAW's feminist critics). Those steeped in international investment law may find much in chapter 5 overly familiar but might be more enlightened by chapter 6's illustrations of how the adoption of a human rights frame under the International Covenant on Civil and Political Rights and the International Covenant on Economic, Social and Cultural Rights changes what "property" is and what it means to protect it under international law. Those looking for explanations for why this book treats the relevant CEDAW jurisprudence as involving "property," why the CEDAW Committee's efforts can be described as "progressive," or why what that Committee does can be criticized as "flawed" or "incomplete" may want to turn to chapter 7.

At the outset we should elucidate our sources. Drawing almost entirely from the CEDAW Committee's own words, chapter 2 synthesizes its interpretations of the Convention's property-relating provisions. The background research of this chapter relies on internet-based research using human rights databases, the Office of the UN High Commissioner for Human Rights (OHCHR) website, secondary literature, and background conversations with several CEDAW experts.[3] Other chapters make cross-references to that chapter but also draw on the invaluable two editions of the CEDAW Commentary, other secondary literature, and background interviews conducted with CEDAW experts.

It takes a village, a supportive scholarly community, and an enormous amount of privilege to write books.

Judith Bauder, the author of chapter 2, would like to thank José E. Alvarez, Meghan Campbell, Rebecca Cook, and Patricia Schultz for useful substantive comments on an advanced version of her contribution. She thanks Aniruddha Rajput and Astrid Reisinger Coracini for reading over the introduction from a doctrinal international law viewpoint and Karin Lukas for sharing her social rights expertise. In addition, she thanks Matthias Humer at the University

---

[3] In total, six background conversations were conducted and transcribed and are on file with the authors. In accordance with the informed consent provided by all interviewed CEDAW experts, their statements are anonymized.

of Copenhagen and her former NYU colleagues Meir Yarom, Alec Dawson, and Lauren Stackpoole and her colleagues at the University of Vienna, Céline Braumann, Jane Alice Hofbauer, and Koloman Roiger Simek, who provided useful written feedback, copy editing, and advice on different versions of chapter 2. She also thanks Prof. Erika de Wet, Prof. Jean d'Aspremont, and Lisa Seyfried for providing useful comments at an ESIL abstract writing workshop organized at the University of Graz. Judith would like to give special thanks to Beth Kelley for intelligently and diligently editing and proofreading versions of this chapter twice. She also thanks Kaiqiang Zhang for his excellent blue-booking services and editorial remarks. Beth and Kaiqiang have shown infinite patience and provided reliable support when this book was nearing completion. She also thanks Dune Johnson from the Fulbright Austria Office for his interest in this book and copy edits on the final version of the manuscript.

Judith thanks Lilian Hofmeister—the only CEDAW Committee member from the Republic of Austria who ever served on the Committee—for her mentorship. Lilian generously shared her expertise in all matters related to CEDAW and the development of an Austrian law for the protection against gender-based violence. Judith also thanks her colleagues at the University of Vienna, Astrid Reisinger Coracini from the Public International Law Department and the Austrian Women Society of Public International Lawyers, for her advice and support; also Prof. Elisabeth Holzleithner, head of the Legal Gender Studies department, for her illuminating course on law, power, gender, and beyond; and Prof. Ursula Naue at the Political Sciences Department, who advised Judith on the use of empirical methods, interviewing techniques, and informed consent. A word of thanks also to her supervisor and mentor Prof. August Reinisch, who provided his unconditional support, approval of crucial resources, and his wise advice throughout this project.

Judith also thanks her former colleagues at the NYU Global Justice Clinic, who taught her the craft of human rights research and helped her to improve her writing skills—thank you, Ellie Happel and Meg Satterthwaite. Thanks are due also to S. Priya Morely, Gabriele Wadlig, and Chao-ju Chen for their insightful discussions on feminism, and for offering their advice and support on this project. As always, heartfelt gratitude to Leonie Kapfer for providing her friendship, not to mention her profound insight, and her expertise as a feminist scholar.

Despite a world pandemic and challenging phases of economic precarity in the background of the research and writing process, Judith was privileged to always find a place to write and research. The process of creating this book required a tremendous commitment of time and labor over the course of more than three years. Without the love, care, and patience of her family and friends this book would not exist. Last but not least, Judith would like to thank her mother,

Margarete Bauder, who has taught her not to stop believing in her capabilities. In the week of making the final copy edits on this book, Judith's grandmother passed away. This book is dedicated to her legacy—her generosity, her love for life despite its hardship, and her resilience.

Feminist matters are issues of survival. Judith's contribution to this book is driven by a her motivation to bear testimony to women's experiences facing human rights violations around the world. This task could fill another lifetime. However, to tell women's stories, even if through the language of law, is only a beginning. As effectively as the Committee can teach a lesson through legal language to states, presidents, foreign ministers, corporations, and other public and private actors, this book is a call to investigate why these abuses occur and to seek to mitigate the occurrence of human rights violations happening to women around the world. This book is a call to action for feminists to unite and to create utopian worlds where oppression and inequality might one day be overcome.

Judith would also like to thank Professor Alvarez for giving her this opportunity, first as a research assistant and then for offering to work on a journal article as co-authors, which eventually has led to this book project.

José E. Alvarez, the author of all the other chapters, thanks Fareda Banda, Judith Bauder, Alexander Burdett, Chau-jo Chen, Rebecca Cook, Susan M. Damplo, Rangita de Silva de Alwis, Sophia Moreau, August Reinisch, Stephan Schill, Patricia Schultz, Frank Upham, Gabriele Wadlig, and Katherine Wilhelm for their many valuable substantive and editorial comments. He also thanks the NYU students and guest presenters in the Colloquium on Feminist Jurisprudence, Women's Rights and Gender in Select Asian Countries in the fall of 2022; NYU's international law librarian Alexander Burdett; as well as the many diligent NYU students whose assistance over the past two years has been critical to the project: Vienna Adza, Shirin Asgari, Anja Bassow, Mae Bowen, Anna-Kay Brown, Florencia Garcia, Camilla Isern, Beth Kelley, Sophie Pearlman, Daniel Rosenberg, and Kaiqiang Zhang.

Both authors are also very grateful to Hilary Charlesworth, Christine Chinkin, and Tendayi Achiume for their contributions to this volume. José E. Alvarez is grateful to Catharine A. MacKinnon for her inspiration throughout the years and for suggesting a title for this book. Lastly, both authors thank Robert Cavooris and Lane Berger, as well as project manager Getsy Deva Kirubai and the copy editor Mary Rosewood and indexer Birgitte Necessary from Oxford University Press for their contributions to making this book a reality. Of course, the remaining mistakes in our respective chapters are entirely our own.

José E. Alvarez, New York, USA
Judith Bauder, Vienna, Austria

Foreword

The international community endorsed the empowerment of women and girls as a key objective in 1995 at the Fourth World Conference on Women held in Beijing. Over the past thirty years, this goal has been consistently endorsed, for example, in the UN General Assembly's Sustainable Development Goals, in the UN Security Council's agenda for Women, Peace and Security, and through the creation of machinery for its achievement in the form of UN Women. Despite such regular reiteration, there is no clarity about what empowerment entails nor how it might be achieved, other than general agreement on the importance of women's economic and social independence. Women's access to, ownership of, and use of property are central to such independence and yet there has been little scholarly investigation of what women's property rights entail. José E. Alvarez and Judith Bauder's book takes on this weighty challenge.

The authors begin with the stark fact of the gender gap—indeed a gender chasm—in land and housing ownership, and they examine in detail how one particular body, the UN Committee on the Elimination of Discrimination against Women, has sought to redress it. Their focus on this often overlooked body is valuable. The twenty-three-person, largely female, Committee is the authoritative interpretative body of the 1979 UN Convention on the Elimination of All Forms of Discrimination against Women (CEDAW). Despite the Convention's status as "the most progressive blueprint ever for advancing women's rights," it does not contain an explicit general provision on women's equality with respect to property rights.

The Committee, however, has used the jurisprudential tools at its disposal—Concluding Observations, Inquiries, General Recommendations, and individual communications—to show how property pervades the Convention. It is crafting a detailed understanding of what gendered property rights mean for women and of states' obligations to respect, protect, and fulfill those rights. The Committee does this through its interpretation of specific articles of the Convention, notably Article 13 (social security rights), Article 14 (rights of rural women to an adequate standard of living, to social security, and with respect to agricultural property), Article 15 (legal capacity), and Article 16 (marital property). Perhaps most importantly, the Committee has developed a property jurisprudence in the context of the right of women and girls to be free from gender-based violence, itself another omission from the Convention text.

The authors explain the Committee's stance that a holistic reading of CEDAW requires its states parties "to avoid all forms of de facto or de jure discrimination with respect to credit, to housing, to conclude contracts, to social and economic benefits, and to own, acquire, manage, administer, enjoy, or dispose of marital property." They present a spirited defense of the work of the Committee, pointing to the subtlety of its jurisprudence. The authors describe the Committee's approach to property as progressive in that "it seeks to protect substantive ends related to property (such as rights to shelter, to security, to medical care, to food and other basic needs)" rather than more traditional approaches that seek to protect exclusive ownership and control. The Committee cannot, of course, by itself redress the gendered imbalance in property rights, but it has contributed creatively to reducing the further discriminatory consequences of that inequality.

One significant technique adopted by the Committee in its property jurisprudence is the development of the concept, and categories applicable to, intersectional discrimination. The authors point out that, in this task, the Committee "does not privilege or advance an ideological agenda in favor of the individualization, formalization, and commodification of property" but rather recommends that states ensure that property is used "to advance the dignity, agency, and sometimes the sheer survival of women." This distinguishes the CEDAW Committee—a human rights body mandated to advance women's equality—from the formalist property-protection outlook of the international financial institutions and the international investment regime.

The book is unique in the literature relating to the CEDAW Committee in its detailed account of its jurisprudence on property, analyzing it in light of feminist theories and critiques of human rights law, as well as of wider debates about the human rights agenda. The book also inaugurates a new field of research and inquiry in what the authors term "comparative international property law." The book compares the CEDAW Committee's treatment of property rights with how these are interpreted in different international settings, including by other UN human rights treaty bodies and in investor-state arbitrations. It identifies many differences in approach, outcome, and indeed perceptions of why property rights are to be accorded protection. The authors conclude that there is no "single harmoniously defined 'international right to property.'"

In its pathbreaking juxtaposition of women's rights and foreign investment law, of case analysis and theoretical critiques, *Women's Property Rights Under CEDAW* is a rich and ambitious book. The book will illuminate future scholarship and practice as well as courses on property law, human rights, women's human rights, international institutions, and foreign investment law. We welcome it in particular as an experiment in bringing feminist approaches to international law into the "mainstream" of international legal scholarship.

Hilary Charlesworth
Christine Chinkin
March 2023

1
Introduction

1.1 Realities and Challenges

Women, virtually everywhere, are less likely to have access to property than men. Despite large variations among countries and inadequacies in data collection, the gender gap in land and housing ownership approaches a chasm.[1] According to World Bank statistics that gap is only the tip of the iceberg when it comes to the gender of wealth. Throughout the world women are disproportionately more likely to have low-paying jobs, be engaged in unpaid care work, or be employed in informal sectors. All of this predictably harms their ability to enjoy all forms of property, including social benefits, pensions, other assets generally included within inheritance, and forms of credit needed to run their farms or form a business. Women's relative poverty also imposes constraints on their ability to have recourse to justice to conclude contracts or otherwise protect the property that they have. As Hilary Charlesworth and Christine Chinkin noted long ago, ironically and tragically, many women continue to be treated as "economic commodities" through "modern forms of slavery" such as trafficking and servile marriage.[2] Social attitudes, along with the feminization of poverty, lead to the "the abuse and enslavement of women . . . reinforced by governmental neglect, toleration or even sanction."[3] Catharine MacKinnon puts it more pointedly: "Women are more likely to *be* property than to own any."[4]

International institutions have been directing attention to the gendered property gap for decades. Even in the 1980s, reports by the UN Commission on the Status of Women pointed out that women received only one-tenth of world income and owned less than 1 percent of world property.[5] For organizations like

---

[1] *See, e.g.*, World Bank Group [World Bank], *World Bank Group Gender Strategy (Fy16-23): Gender Equality, Poverty Reduction and Inclusive Growth* (Dec. 16, 2015), https://documents1.worldbank.org/curated/en/820851467992505410/pdf/102114-REVISED-PUBLIC-WBG-Gender-Strategy.pdf [hereinafter *Gender Strategy Report*]. Unless otherwise indicated, all URL cites were last visited on or before May 29, 2023.

[2] HILARY CHARLESWORTH & CHRISTINE CHINKIN, THE BOUNDARIES OF INTERNATIONAL LAW 11 (2000).

[3] *Id.*, at 11 (quoting Kathleen Barry).

[4] CATHARINE A. MACKINNON, ARE WOMEN HUMAN? AND OTHER INTERNATIONAL DIALOGUES? 21 (2006).

[5] *See, e.g.*, Kerry Rittich, *The Properties of Gender Equality, in* HUMAN RIGHTS AND DEVELOPMENT: TOWARDS MUTUAL REINFORCEMENT 87, 87 n.1 (Philip Alston & Mary Robinson eds., 2005).

UN Women, the World Bank, working groups of the United Nations' Economic and Social Council or of the International Law Association, along with NGOs like the Global Initiative for Economic, Social and Cultural Rights, Landesa, and FIAN International, the fact that women constitute half the world's population but control only a small percentage of sources of wealth such as land poses a profound challenge to economic development and to the enjoyment of fundamental human rights.[6] As one report by UN Women put it: "Land is key to a life with dignity and a basis for entitlements which can ensure an adequate standard of living and economic independence and therefore, personal empowerment."[7]

Descriptions of the nature of the problem and prescriptions for addressing it differ starkly, however. Mainstream prescriptions, such as those touted by economists at the World Bank, emphasize the need for women to have title to the property, including land, along with the means to secure such title, particularly access to credit. Needed reforms under this view include increasing the accuracy of immovable property registries for married couples, improved and more accurate information on land titles, and affordable legal assistance to ensure that property titles recognize the rights of women who are particularly vulnerable to discrimination.[8] Others are deeply skeptical of framings that treat land and related natural resources as "globalized economic and financial assets" or "investible" resources grounded in secure and exclusive individual and private property rights that need to be easily transferable, including to large commercial (often foreign) commercial enterprises and agribusinesses.[9] Some of

---

[6] *See, e.g.*, WORLD BANK, WORLD DEVELOPMENT REPORT 2012: GENDER EQUALITY AND DEVELOPMENT (2011); *Gender Strategy Report*, *supra* note 1; Nayda Almodóvar-Retequis et al., *Mapping the Legal Gender Gap in Using Property and Building Credit* (2013), https://thedocs.worldbank.org/en/doc/626611519938668327-0050022011/original/TopicNoteUsingPropertyandBuildingCreditEN.pdf; Glob. Initiative for Econ., Soc. & Cult. Rts., *How to Use Treaty Bodies' Concluding Observations to Advance Women's Land and Property Rights—Kenya Case Study* (Sept. 10, 2020); Minority Rts. Group Int'l, *Moving towards a Right to Land: The Committee on Economic, Social and Cultural Rights' Treatment on Land Rights as Human Rights—Minority Rights* (Oct. 29, 2015); For the Right to Food & Nutrition Int'l, *The Human Right to Land* (Nov. 2017) [hereinafter *FIAN Report*].

[7] UN WOMEN, REALIZING WOMEN'S RIGHTS TO LAND AND OTHER PRODUCTIVE RESOURCES 3 (2013).

[8] The Bank's focus on enabling women to formally own land and giving them title to it is suggested by its rhetoric as well as the data that it collects (such as the percentage of rural land owned by women). *See, e.g.*, Isis Gaddis et al., *Women's Legal Rights and Gender Gaps in Property Ownership in Developing Countries*, 48 POPULATION & DEV. REV. 331 (2022) (discussing Bank initiatives such as its Gender Asset Gaps Report). Such goals are also suggested by the Bank's specific projects. *See, e.g.*, *Albania Gender Equality in Access to Economic Opportunities Development Policy Financing*, https://projects.worldbank.org/en/projects-operations/project-detail/P160594 (last visited Feb. 2, 2023) (indicating that expected actions include an increase in accurate immovable property registries for married couples, improved information on property titles, and affordable legal assistance to ensure that property titles recognize the rights of vulnerable women). For a critical account of the Bank's and other development institutions' continuing emphasis on increasing formal ownership to land as key to advancing "tenure security," *see* Gabriele Wadlig, The (Un) Making of "Tenure Security" (2022) (unpublished dissertation, NYU School of Law) (on file with author).

[9] *See, e.g.*, *FIAN Report*, *supra* note 6, at 13; Wadlig, *supra* note 8.

those critics question whether, in practice, land titling efforts (including as part of land reform) generate greater gender equality.[10] FIAN International, for example, accepts the need for a substantive right to land on behalf of, particularly, Indigenous women, but emphasizes that this ought to be a collective right that would protect local communities from forms of "land grabbing" that enable the privatization or commercialization of natural resources.[11] That organization questions the priority accorded to rights to acquire, dispose, and exclude others from one's personal individual property emphasized by traditional property theorists in much of the West.[12] Comparable debates over the role of property rights in achieving social justice for women divide scholars.[13]

This book addresses how the expert body under the world's most prominent treaty directed at protecting women's equality, the Convention on the Elimination of All Forms of Discrimination against Women (CEDAW),[14] has interpreted and applied CEDAW's protections of various forms of possessions or assets commonly considered forms of property. As enumerated for ease of reference in this book's appendix 1, CEDAW requires its state parties to eliminate discrimination against women with respect to rights to "social security, particularly in cases of retirement, unemployment, sickness, invalidity and old age and other incapacity to work, including paid leave" (Article 11(1)(e)) and "maternity leave with pay or with comparable social benefits" (Article 11(1)(b)). It requires that states take all appropriate measures to eliminate discrimination

---

[10] *See, e.g.*, Stephen W. Makau, *Women and Their Rights to Property at the National and International Levels* (Sept. 2022) (unpublished manuscript), https://papers.ssrn.com/sol3/papers.cfm?abstract_id=4187901 (noting that land titling and registration systems usually have not focused on gender issues and have perpetuated and legalized existing gender-biased practices by, for example, registering ownership only in the name of the (male) head of the family or ignoring cases where women had, under customary rules, rights that are overtaken or undermined by mass formalization of title). *See also* Celestine N. Musembi, *De Soto and Land Relations in Rural Africa: Breathing Life into Dead Theories about Property Rights*, 28 THIRD WORLD Q. 1457 (2007).

[11] *FIAN Report, supra* note 6, at 5–10.

[12] *See, e.g.*, 2 WILLIAM BLACKSTONE, COMMENTARIES *2 (famously defining property as "the sole and despotic dominion which one man claims and exercises over the external things of the world, in total exclusion of the right of any other individual in the universe"); Wadlig, *supra* note 8, at 31–34, 86–90 (citing reliance on the ability to alienate property as critical to scholars and practices in the United States, the United Kingdom, and Australia that have had an impact on others around the world). The ability to exclude others, buy, and sell or otherwise dispose of property are some of the "bundle of sticks" associated with property as traditionally taught in the United States, for example. *See, e.g.*, JERRY L. ANDERSON & DANIEL B. BOGART, PRACTICE, PROBLEMS, AND PERSPECTIVES 4–8 (2014).

[13] Compare the work of those who are skeptical of property rights as a tool to address women's inequality such as MEGHAN CAMPBELL, WOMEN, POVERTY, EQUALITY: THE ROLE OF CEDAW (2018), and MARIA MIES, PATRIARCHY AND ACCUMULATION ON A WORLD SCALE: WOMEN IN THE INTERNATIONAL DIVISION OF LABOUR (Pnina Werbner & Richard Werbner eds., Zed Books 3d ed. 2014), to defenders of property rights such as Rhoda E. Howard-Hassmann, *Reconsidering the Right to Own Property*, 12 J. HUM. RTS. 180 (2013), and, more generally, Carol M. Rose, *Property's Relation to Human Rights*, *in* ECONOMIC LIBERTIES AND HUMAN RIGHTS 69 (Jahel Queralt & Bas van der Vossen eds., 2019).

[14] Convention on the Elimination of All Forms of Discrimination against Women, *open for signature* Dec. 18, 1979, 1249 U.N.T.S. 13 [hereinafter CEDAW].

"in other areas of economic and social life" (Article 13, chapeau), and specifically rights to family benefits (Article 13(a)) and to bank loans, mortgages, and other forms of financial credit (Article 13(b)). It further requires the elimination of discrimination against women in rural areas and, specifically, the need for equal treatment between men and women with respect to agricultural credit and loans, marketing facilities, appropriate technology, and land, and measures taken in pursuit of agrarian reform or land resettlement (Article 14(2)(g)). That Convention's provisions for nondiscrimination as applied to rural women further affirm rights to enjoy "adequate living standards" in relation to "housing" (Article 14(2)(h)). It further requires that men and women have identical legal capacity in civil matters and the same opportunities "to conclude contracts" and "administer property" (Article 15(2)). Finally, the treaty seeks to eliminate discrimination against women "in all matters relating to marriage and family relations," and in particular, by requiring the "same rights for both spouses in respect of the ownership, acquisition, management, administration, enjoyment and disposition of property, whether free of charge or for a valuable consideration" (Article 16(1)(h)).[15]

Chapter 2 puts front and center the Committee's outputs that apply to all the CEDAW's state parties, namely, its General Recommendations and Concluding Observations in response to state reports as these relate to the enumerated provisions above. It also synthesizes the relevant Committee's Views in response to communications and Reports on Inquiries, both of which only apply only with respect to those states that have ratified the CEDAW's Optional Protocol.[16]

As is evident from a close look at chapter 2, which quotes extensively from the CEDAW Committee's own language, the Committee itself rarely invokes the term "property rights" when addressing these treaty obligations. The Committee does not, for example, apply the term "property" to "economic or social benefits" like social security that are nonetheless included in chapter 2. This is, on one level, not surprising as the Convention itself explicitly refers to "property" only in Article 15(2) (referring to the right to "administer" property) and Article 16(2)(h) (referring to rights to property for "both spouses"). The Committee's reticence in invoking "property rights" as such may also reflect uncertainties even among property scholars on what "property" means. As is further addressed in this

---

[15] CEDAW's other provisions relating to employment, such as the right to "equal treatment in respect of work of equal value," contained in Article 11, are outside the scope of this book. But chapter 2's survey of CEDAW's property jurisprudence includes the right to equal remuneration to the extent it overlaps with the right to equal social security benefits.

[16] Optional Protocol to the Convention on the Elimination of All Forms of Discrimination against Women, Oct. 6, 1999, 2131 U.N.T.S. 83 [hereinafter Optional Protocol]. Under that Optional Protocol's Article 8(1), its state parties are only "invited to cooperate" with the CEDAW Committee's requests to investigate "reliable information indicating grave or systematic violations" that can lead to a Report on Inquiry.

book's concluding chapter, it is widely recognized among both national and international lawyers that the concept of property, although fundamental to every form of government, is a socially and legally constructed term subject to varying definitions often loaded with normative implications.[17] As that chapter also addresses, chapter 2's inclusion of social benefits and pensions is consistent with how the European Court of Human Rights (ECtHR) has defined "possessions" and with many states' national laws and practices under which such assets are included in inheritance.[18] Of course, such benefits, including pensions provided by either employers or the state, are monetary assets no less than forms of financial credit under CEDAW's Article 13(b) or agricultural credit or intellectual property protected under Article 14(2)(g), for example. The Committee has, in any case, justified equal rights to all these forms of assets, tangible or intangible, as enabling women's "autonomy in the economic sphere."[19]

The Committee's reticence with respect to referring to property as such does not mean that it has been reluctant to apply the aforementioned provisions broadly. As discussed in chapter 4, the Committee has gone beyond the literal words of these provisions in significant ways. It has, for example, drawn from Article 16(2)(h) (which formally applies only with respect to "both spouses") (perhaps with an assist from the license to demand nondiscrimination with respect to other areas of "economic and social life" in the chapeau to Article 3) equal rights to inheritance broadly in family life and not only connected to traditional heterosexual marriages. The Committee has also broadly interpreted other interests generally understood to constitute property, such as equal rights to all forms of financial credit under Article 13(b), intellectual property as inferred under Article 14(2)(g), other economic rights associated with agricultural land and identified under Article 14(2)(g), rights to housing under Article 14(2)(h), or rights to administer contracts necessary to access property (included, alongside rights to administer property) in Article 14(2)(h).

This book puts the CEDAW Committee interpretations canvassed in chapter 2 in a broader context. Chapter 3 foregrounds criticisms of the CEDAW regime made by many of its feminist critics as well as revisionist critics of international human rights, before turning in chapter 4 to how the Committee has responded to such criticisms in its jurisprudence. Chapter 5 thereafter illustrates

---

[17] *See* chapter 7, section 7.1.
[18] *See, e.g.*, WILLIAM A. SCHABAS, THE EUROPEAN CONVENTION ON HUMAN RIGHTS: A COMMENTARY 969–72 (2015) (describing how the ECtHR has broadly interpreted the concept of "possessions" in Article 1 of Protocol One to include intangible as well as physical assets or property rights, including social benefits).
[19] *See, e.g.*, Beate Rudolf, *Article 13*, *in* THE UN CONVENTION ON THE ELIMINATION OF ALL FORMS OF DISCRIMINATION AGAINST WOMEN AND ITS OPTIONAL PROTOCOL 487, 488–89 (Patricia Schulz et al. eds., 2d ed. 2022) [hereinafter 2022 CEDAW COMMENTARY] (discussing Article 13's "economic and social rights").

how the Committee's protection of equal property rights differs from property protections extended under the international investment regime. Chapter 6 then demonstrates the considerable commonalities between CEDAW's property jurisprudence and that generated by select international human rights regimes.

To be sure, the Committee protects rights to formal equality traditionally associated with property. It criticizes states whose laws, practices, and omissions deprive women equal rights to inheritance, to sign contracts, or to have recourse to the courts or resources (such as credit) that would enable them to enjoy property; the Committee also seeks to protect the substantive ends that relate to property (such as rights to shelter, to security, to medical care, to food and other basic needs).[20] At the same time the CEDAW Committee limits Blackstone's concept of "despotic dominion" over private property[21]—including rights to dispose or purchase individual private property—when these threaten women's lives and well-being. The Committee protects those parts of the formal "bundle of sticks" that some associate with property (such as the right to exclude others from one's own property) only as needed to protect women from *de facto* or *de jure* discrimination.

The CEDAW Committee's property jurisprudence has not received as much scholarly attention as have arbitral rulings generated under investor-state dispute settlement or the property-protecting case law of the European Court of Human Rights or the Inter-American Court of Human Rights.[22] This book seeks

---

[20] All of these concerns are suggested when the Committee affirms in the North Macedonia communications, for example, that the Roma women needed to be supplied with housing adequate to their particular needs. *See* chapter 2, section 2.7.2.1.

[21] *See* BLACKSTONE, *supra* note 12.

[22] For an account of the prominence of the international investment regime, *see* chapter 5, section 5.2. For an illustration of how the "international law of property" is associated with both the international investment regime and the property jurisprudence generated under the European Convention for the Protection of Human Rights, *see, e.g.*, URSULA KRIEBAUM, EIGENTUMSSCHUTZ IM VÖLKERRECHT: EINE VERGLEICHENDE UNTERSUCHUNG ZUM INTERNATIONALEN INVESTITIONSRECHT SOWIE ZUM MENSCHENRECHTSSCHUTZ (2008) (comparing the right to property under European human rights law and international investment law); Ursula Kriebaum, *Property, Right To*, *in* ELGAR ENCYCLOPEDIA OF HUMAN RIGHTS 88 (Christina Binder et al. eds., 2022) (stating that the property case law of the European Court of Human Rights (ECtHR) is "by far the most developed on a regional level"). For additional examples, *see, e.g.*, Suren Gomtsyan & David Gomtsyan, *What Do the Decisions of ECtHR Tell About Property Rights Across Europe?* (Tilburg L. & Econ. Center Discussion Paper, Paper No. 09, 2016), https://ssrn.com/abstract=2762522; Chrisophe Geiger & Elena Izyumenko, *Shaping Intellectual Property Rights through Human Rights Adjudication: The Example of the European Court of Human Rights*, 46 MITCHELL HAMLINE L. REV. 527 (2020); KIRSTEEN SHIELDS, A REVIEW OF EVIDENCE ON LAND ACQUISITION POWERS AND LAND OWNERSHIP RESTRICTIONS IN EUROPEAN COUNTRIES (2022), https://www.gov.scot/publications/review-evidence-land-acquisition-powers-land-owners hip-restrictions-european-countries/documents/; Tom Allen, *Compensation for Property Under the European Convention on Human Rights*, 28 MICH. J. INT'L L. 287 (2007). For a description of the property jurisprudence of the Inter-American Court of Human Rights, *see, e.g.*, José E. Alvarez, *The Human Right of Property*, 72 U. MIAMI L. REV. 580 (2018). To be sure, the two editions of the CEDAW commentaries, published in 2012 and 2022, are exceptions to the absence of scholarly discussion of CEDAW's property jurisprudence. *See generally* 2022 CEDAW Commentary, *supra* note 19; THE

to fill that scholarly gap. It seeks to encourage research on comparative international property law that accords CEDAW due recognition alongside the outputs of other international legal regimes that grapple with property rights and especially the intersection between such rights and nondiscrimination.[23] Such research on comparative international property law would assist adjudicators at the national and international levels,[24] contribute to broader debates about whether human rights are truly universal,[25] help clarify whether or how such rights are implemented into domestic law or otherwise achieve "compliance,"[26] and inform debates about whether international law varies from place to place[27] and not only from one international legal regime to another.[28]

The CEDAW regime's conception of what internationalized property rights mean should be of interest beyond the "Geneva insiders" who follow the activity of UN human rights treaty bodies. The CEDAW Committee's reimagining of property rights merit at least as much scrutiny as has been showered on the World Bank's "gender equality" (and earlier "women's economic empowerment") efforts to date, along with its and others' emphasis on the ostensible connection between economic development and registering titles to property or land.[29] This book contends that the Committee's work merits at least as much attention as the gender "empowerment," "parity," or "equitable" agendas espoused by eminent economists, best-selling authors, and development experts.[30] While a number of

---

UN CONVENTION ON THE ELIMINATION OF ALL FORMS OF DISCRIMINATION AGAINST WOMEN: A COMMENTARY (Marsha A. Freeman et al. eds., 2012) [hereinafter 2012 CEDAW Commentary].

[23] For rare examples of comparative efforts that include CEDAW, see BETH GOLDBLATT, DEVELOPING THE RIGHT TO SOCIAL SECURITY—A GENDER PERSPECTIVE 52–102 (2018) (comparing the development of the human right to social security across the ICCPR, ICESCR, ILO, and CEDAW regimes as well as reports issued by UN Special Rapporteurs on extreme poverty and human rights); Dianne Otto, *Gendering the Right to Social Security in the Era of Crisis Governance: The Need for Transformative Strategies*, in WOMEN'S RIGHTS TO SOCIAL SECURITY AND PROTECTION 215 (Beth Goldblatt & Lucie Lamrche eds., 2014). See also SANDRA FREDMAN, COMPARATIVE HUMAN RIGHTS LAW 303–05 (2018) (briefly discussing CEDAW in comparative study of the right to housing).

[24] See, e.g., FREDMAN, supra note 23, at 3–28 (arguing that judges can usefully be guided by comparativism in human rights law).

[25] See, e.g., Charlesworth & Chinkin, supra note 2, at 222–29 (discussing the challenge posed by cultural relativism).

[26] See generally Robert Howse & Ruti Teitel, *Beyond Compliance: Rethinking Why International Law Really Matters*, 1 GLOBAL POL'Y 127 (2010).

[27] See, e.g., ANTHEA ROBERTS, IS INTERNATIONAL LAW INTERNATIONAL? (2019) (arguing that the content of international law varies from place to place).

[28] Int'l Law Comm'n, Fragmentation of International Law: Difficulties arising from the Diversification and Expansion of International Law, UN Doc. A/CN.4/L.702 (2006).

[29] See generally Rittich, supra note 5; Amrita Kapur, *"Catch-22": The Role of Development Institutions in promoting Gender Equality in Land Law—Lessons Learned in Post-Conflict Pluralist Africa*, 17 BUFF. HUM. RTS. L. REV. 75 (2011); Catherine Powell, *Gender Indicators as Global Governance: Not Your Father's World Bank*, 17 GEO. J. GENDER & L. 777 (2016).

[30] Compare the attention, critical as well as laudatory, paid to NICHOLAS D. KRISTOFF & SHERYL WUDUNN, HALF THE SKY: TURNING OPPRESSION INTO OPPORTUNITY FOR WOMEN WORLDWIDE (2009). See, e.g., Sophie Chong, *Veiled Colonialism: A Feminist Critique of the Half the Sky Movement*,

scholars have suggested that the CEDAW regime "engenders" human rights, the truth is that such rights, including the right to property, have always been gendered: they have historically buttressed a patriarchal order that excludes women and favors men. The CEDAW Committee's efforts to rectify these inequalities should more properly be described as attempts to "re-engender" human rights.

This book makes no claim that the CEDAW Committee's normative outputs are more likely to change the behavior of states than efforts by other UN human rights treaty bodies or regional human rights courts. Nor does it claim that women's property rights are more effectively protected under the CEDAW regime than by national court rulings that upholds a claim of a property rights violation. It does not contend that a human rights framework is necessarily more "effective" than attempts to promote "gender sensitive" development by World Bank economists. The persistence of the gendered property gap between and within nations suggests that none of these mechanisms, including CEDAW's efforts, has achieved anything close to gender parity with respect to interests in property.

The more modest claim here is that the jurisprudence of a unique expert body consisting of twenty-three individuals, mostly women, of diverse nationalities, disciplines, and training is worthy of at least the same attention and scrutiny as that accorded to other developers/interpreters of internationalized property rights. There is no a priori reason to assume that CEDAW's treaty interpreters are less impactful than other UN human rights treaty bodies, UN working groups, or UN Special Rapporteurs. All these attempts to interpret widely ratified human rights treaties contribute to legal discourses that influence how states behave. All are used to "mobilize shame" and/or engage in forms of deliberative discourse against violators of international human rights, sometimes with demonstrable impact.[31] All are critical to the "experimentalist" techniques or other frameworks used to describe how states may be persuaded or "socialized" into "complying" with international human rights.[32]

CEDAW does not purport to include rights to property and compensation independent of discrimination—as is common to nearly all international investment treaties and even some human rights treaties like the European and American human rights conventions. It focuses only on actions or inactions

---

E-International Relations (Apr. 7, 2014), https://www.e-ir.info/2014/04/07/veiled-colonialism-a-feminist-criticism-of-the-half-the-sky-movement/.

[31] *See, e.g.*, Beth Simmons, Mobilizing for Human Rights: International Law in Domestic Politics (2009); Cosette D. Creamer & Beth A. Simmons, *The Proof Is in the Process: Self-Reporting Under International Human Rights Treaties*, 114 Am. J. Int'l L. 1 (2020).

[32] *See, e.g.*, Gráinne de Búrca, *Human Rights Expermimentalism*, 11 Am. J. Int'l L. 277 (2017); Ryan Goodman & Derek Jinks, Socializing States: Promoting Human Rights Through International Law (2013).

by states and non-state parties that, asymmetrically, are "against" the rights of women.[33] This book contends, counterintuitively, that CEDAW's focus on eradicating only *discriminatory* denials of property rights that harm women is potentially more protective of such interests than regimes that are not limited to correcting inequalities. Under CEDAW, unlike treaties that provide guarantees of property protection that extend beyond discrimination, the focus is on protecting the substantive values that *equal* property rights help to ensure—and not the value of "rights to property" or "to possessions" in the abstract. The emphasis is on ensuring that women have equal access to governments' efforts to provide social protection; that they enjoy substantive parity with respect to access to land, along with adequate food, shelter, or medical care. In addition, under CEDAW, other fundamental rights—from access to justice to the rights to an adequate standard of living to the need to respect the rights of others—are considered alongside the equal right to certain property interests and are important means to interpret what genuine equality demands.

The CEDAW Committee treats property rights as a means to an end. It protects both an individual's right to property and the rights of certain collectivities. As the Committee sees it, individual rights to property may need to give way to protecting the rights of groups of women, such as Indigenous or rural women. The Committee adheres to a holistic approach to human rights absent from some property-respecting international instruments. Under international investment treaties, for example, rights other than the property interests of foreign investors—whether civil or political or social, economic, or cultural—become relevant only exceptionally, as when such human rights are invoked as a defense by a state charged with violating a foreign investor's property rights. Investor-state arbitrators address human rights apart from those with respect to property only within an "exceptionalism paradigm."[34]

CEDAW's human rights–integrative property jurisprudence does not elevate the "civil" right to own property over the other civil, political, economic, social, or cultural rights that are specifically embraced by that Convention's

---

[33] *See, e.g.*, Andrew Byrnes & Puja Kapai, *Article 1*, in 2022 CEDAW COMMENTARY, *supra* note 19, at 80 (noting that the treaty filled a need for "an asymmetric guarantee in the form of a sex-specific instrument"). The CEDAW's application to the discriminatory practices of any "person, organization or enterprise" is made clear by its Articles 2(e) and 5.

[34] *See generally* Julian Arato et al., *The Perils of Pandemic Exceptionalism*, 114 AM. J. INT'L L. 627 (2020) (contending that an exceptionalist paradigm tends to expand the underlying right and/or suggest that measures taken in violation of the underlying right are per se illegal). References to human rights (particularly to the case law of the ECtHR) are increasingly made in the course of investor-state dispute settlement. This case law is commonly invoked by foreign investors attempting to use ECtHR case law to advance their claims or, even more commonly, by respondent states attempting to shield themselves from investors' claims. *See, e.g.*, JOSÉ E. ALVAREZ, THE BOUNDARIES OF INVESTMENT ARBITRATION: THE USE OF TRADE AND EUROPEAN HUMAN RIGHTS LAW IN INVESTOR STATE DISPUTES (2018). These uses correspond to what Arato, Clauseen, and Heath call an "exceptionalist paradigm."

Article 1. Because CEDAW incorporates discriminatory denials of all fundamental human rights and because that treaty makes other unique demands on states—such as compelling them to address the underlying structural reasons for women's subordination in the private as well as public spheres and by public and non-state actors—the CEDAW Committee is freer than are many interpreters of international property rights to confront and redress the ways in which traditional conceptions of property—including rights to individual private property—may reify women's inequality. Under the delegation to address substantive equality, that Committee has a broad charge to address the actual impact on women. Accordingly, it does not presume that property rights in favor of market transactions invariably promote efficiency and economic growth. The Committee considers when the individualization, formalization, and commodification of property rights may run counter to the collective interests of women.[35] The Committee's focus on advancing substantive and not only formal equality enables it to consider, case by case as well as more generally, how property rights contribute positively or negatively to the feminization of poverty or intersectional discrimination.

Property rights under CEDAW are not perceived merely as tools of "economic empowerment" for female entrepreneurs. The CEDAW Committee adopts a fulsome view of property rights that, consistent with the CEDAW's preamble, promotes the full development of women's capabilities.[36] The regime's conception of women's property rights overlaps considerably with that produced by the treaty bodies charged with interpreting the International Covenant on Economic, Social and Cultural Rights (ICESCR) and the International Covenant on Civil and Political Rights (ICCPR) but is not merely duplicative of either. The CEDAW Committee's work product has distinctive qualities and frailties. Its unique features, positive and negative, result from its particular composition, interpretative community, procedural rules, institutional context, and the text and object and purpose of the treaty that it is charged with interpreting.

As Sandra Fredman has demonstrated in connection with the right to housing, property rights do not mean the same thing within all international legal regimes that address them.[37] There is no single "international law of property." Distinct international legal regimes produce fragmented versions of the law attentive to different framings of what protected property is and why it is worth protecting in connection with different groups of persons in different contexts. These realities cast doubt on the hopes of those who believe that the international community

---

[35] Compare Rittich, *supra* note 5, at 101–13.
[36] *See generally* AMARTYA SEN, DEVELOPMENT AS FREEDOM (1999).
[37] *See, e.g.*, FREDMAN, *supra* note 23, at 264–304 (comparing national courts' interpretations of the right to housing to interpretations of the right under a number of international human rights regimes).

will eventually agree, despite past failures, on a single comprehensive treaty in defense of property as commodities or possessions.[38] The book entertains the hope that comparisons of how property rights are addressed by international legal regimes may nonetheless inspire efforts to *interpret* the international law of property more holistically to the benefit of both men and women.

1.2 International Property Rights in Context

The adoption of CEDAW in 1979 was not inspired by the ostensible connections between needs to respect women's property rights, enable economic self-empowerment, and grow national economies. That adoption cannot be ascribed to any single event—whether the World Bank's decision to adopt a gender strategy in 2001 or the 1993 Vienna Conference's focus on the connections between gender and economic development. Such an account would be as historically flawed as Sam Moyn's reductionist effort to identify 1977 as the precise year that the international human rights movement began.[39] As discussed in section 1.3 infra, that Convention was the product of a consensus within the UN General Assembly that it was time to enfranchise half of the world's population through a specific human rights treaty to be interpreted by its own expert body.

It is impossible to determine when, if ever, international law *did not elevate* the importance of protecting property. As Martti Koskenniemi notes, "the most important rights struggles from the Magna Carta to American and French revolutions and beyond have been about the recognition of rights to own property."[40] Koskenniemi points out that the giants in Western international law, such as Hersch Lauterpacht, saw strong protection of property as long part of the human rights canon, along with the protection of the rights of foreign investors.[41] The decision to protect property rights at the international level, and in particular to identify the international human right to nondiscriminatory treatment with respect to it was built into the American Declaration of the Rights and Duties of Man (American Declaration) and Universal Declarations of Human Rights (Universal Declaration) back in 1948. The American Declaration's Article XXIII proclaimed that "[e]very person has a right to own such private property as meets

---

[38] *See, e.g.*, JOHN G. SPRANKLING, THE INTERNATIONAL LAW OF PROPERTY (2014).
[39] *See, e.g.*, Philip Alston, *Does the Past Matter? On the Origins of Human Rights*, 126 HARV. L. REV. 2043, 2062–72 (2013).
[40] Martti Koskenniemi, *Rocking the Human Rights Boat: Reflections by a Fellow Passenger, in* THE STRUGGLE FOR HUMAN RIGHTS: ESSAYS IN HONOUR OF PHILIP ALSTON 51, 55 (Nehal Bhuta et al. eds., 2022).
[41] *Id.* (noting that Lauterpacht included John Locke within the human rights canon, that the rights of foreign investors were originally treated as human rights, and that the twentieth century's most visible advocates of liberal economy (Hayek, Röepke, and Friedman) also spoke in human rights terms.)

the essential needs of decent living and helps to maintain the dignity of the individual and the of the home."[42] The Universal Declaration, adopted shortly thereafter, stated in Article 17 that "(1) [e]veryone has the right to own property alone as well as in association with others. (2) [n]o one shall be arbitrarily deprived of his property."[43] Those declarations affirmed that such rights should be extended without discrimination. In the words of the Universal Declarations, "without distinction of any kind, such as race, colour, sex, language, religion, political or other opinion, national or social origin, property, birth or other status."[44]

Subsequent decisions by the drafters of the ICCPR and ICESCR to avoid Cold War divisions by excluding explicit property protections in those texts turned out to be exceptions as international human rights treaties proliferated.[45] Depending on how one defines a "human rights" treaty and how one defines "property rights," there are currently sixteen binding human rights conventions, some adopted as early as 1953, that embrace property rights protections.[46] This

---

[42] The American Declaration on the Rights and Duties of Man was adopted by the Ninth International Conference of American States, held in Bogotá, Colombia from March 30 to May 2, 1948. See *American Declaration on the Rights and Duties of Man*, 41 AM. J. INT'L L. SUPP. 133 (1949) [hereinafter *American Declaration*].

[43] G.A. Res. 217 (III) A, Universal Declaration of Human Rights (Dec. 10, 1948) [hereinafter Universal Declaration].

[44] *Id.* Article 2; *see also American Declaration, supra* note 42, Article II ("without distinction as to race, sex, language, creed or any other factor").

[45] And, in any case, as chapter 6 demonstrates, both Covenants actually protect property interests, at least to the extent such rights are covered by the duty not to discriminate.

[46] While there is no single accepted definition of what a human rights treaty is, one of the coauthors of this book has identified thirty-five international instruments that recognize property rights, including twenty-one that are designated as "human rights" treaties based on their titles. See Alvarez, *supra* note 22, at 580, 647–48 & app. That broader list of thirty-five instruments includes treaties recognizing state duties with respect to intellectual property, protections of possession or property under international humanitarian law, and the ILO's Protection of Wages Convention (No. 95), July 1, 1949, 138 U.N.T.S. 225. It also includes only one treaty, as representative of thousands of bilateral and regional international investment agreements that protect the property rights of foreign investors, as a reminder of the international investment regime. Alvarez addresses the absence of a clear definition of what constitutes a "human rights" treaty. *See id.* at 652–53 (noting that if individuals' rights to property are embraced by the term, thousands of international investment agreements (which generally protect investors as individuals or shareholders, and not merely companies) would be included). If one excludes instruments intended to protect foreign investors as not embracing "human rights" as such, his list of twenty-one instruments includes sixteen human rights treaties with property rights (including those that protect stateless persons, persons with disabilities, migrants, refugees, and ILO conventions that protect the rights of Indigenous people) as well as five well known "soft law" instruments such as the ASEAN Human Rights Declaration and the Standard Minimum Rules for the Treatment of Prisoners. There are, of course, a number of soft law instruments that include property protections. *See, e.g.*, United Nations Declaration on the Rights of Peasants and Other People Working in Rural Areas, Human Rights Council Res. 39/12, UN Doc. A/C.3/73/L.30 (Oct. 28, 2018); G.A. Res. 61/295, United Nations Declaration on the Rights of Indigenous Peoples (Sept. 13, 2007); Food & Agric. Org [FAO], *The Voluntary Guidelines on the Governance of Tenure of Land, Fisheries and Forests in the Context of National Food Security* (May 2022), https://www.fao.org/3/i2801e/i2801e.pdf; OFF. OF HUM. RTS. FOR THE HIGH COMMISSIONER, GUIDING PRINCIPLES ON BUSINESS AND HUMAN RIGHTS: IMPLEMENTING THE UNITED NATIONS "PROTECT, RESPECT AND REMEDY" FRAMEWORK (2011).

includes all UN human rights treaties and regional human rights conventions for the Americas, Africa, Europe, and Arab states concluded after the ICCPR and the ICESCR. While all human rights treaties containing property rights insist that these be applied on a nondiscriminatory basis, some, like regional conventions for human rights, treat the right to own property (or "possessions") as both a "relative" entitlement (dependent on proving discrimination vis-à-vis a relevant comparator) and a comparatively "absolute" entitlement not dependent on discrimination—consistent with the Universal Declaration and American Declaration noted previously.[47]

The American Convention on Human Rights requires state parties to respect and ensure the enumerated rights (including property rights) "without any discrimination for reasons of race, color, sex, language, religion, political or other opinion, national or social origin, economic status, birth, or any other social condition" (Article 1(1)). But that treaty also recognizes a set of "negative" and "positive" obligations on states that do not require proving discrimination.[48] These negative obligations include a duty not to deprive a person or an Indigenous community of their property without respecting the preconditions in Article 21. The positive obligations, also grounded partly on Article 21 (which applies to both individual and collective property), include a duty to ensure collective property rights applicable to ancestral territories. Article 21(1) provides that "[e]veryone has the right to the use and enjoyment of his property. The law may subordinate such use and enjoyment in the interest of society." Article 21(2) adds that "[n]o one shall be deprived of his property except upon payment of just compensation, for reasons of public utility or social interest, and in the cases and according to the forms established by law." Notably, the American Convention on Human Rights requires the payment of "just" compensation if property is taken by the state even for justifiable reasons required by public policy.[49]

The European Convention for the Protection of Human Rights (ECHR), like the American Convention on Human Rights, recognizes a right to property that is not dependent on proof of discrimination. Its Article 1 of Protocol One, proclaims that "[e]very natural or legal person is entitled to the peaceful

---

[47] As noted in chapter 5, in some international legal regimes, such as those on investment, it is common to distinguish "relative" rights premised on discrimination from "absolute" rights, such as rights to transfer capital abroad or to have contracted for property rights respected. Absolute rights under this terminology may be subject to exceptions permitting states to regulate in the public interest. Other terminological distinctions among human rights are, as noted later, also possible: such as between "positive" and "negative" obligations imposed on states.

[48] *See, e.g.*, LUDOVIC HENNEBEL & HELENE TIGROUDJA, THE AMERICAN CONVENTION ON HUMAN RIGHTS: A COMMENTARY 622–32 (2022) (addressing Article 21: right to property).

[49] *Id.*, at 648 (noting that the determination of what constitutes "fair" or "just" compensation applies proportionality standards on a case-by-case basis).

enjoyment of his possessions. No one shall be deprived of his possessions except in the public interest and subject to the conditions provided for by law and by the general principles of international law."[50] Under the case law of the ECtHR, state takings of the property of both aliens and nationals, as well as discriminatory violations of rights to social benefits such as pension rights, have been deemed to be wrongful acts that require just compensation.[51] More significantly for purposes of this book, the ECHR, along with its subsequent Protocol 12, also addresses discriminatory violations of its right to "possessions."[52] Article 14 of the European Convention on Human Rights provides that the enjoyment of rights contained in that treaty shall be secured without discrimination "on any ground such as sex, race, colour, language, religion, political or other opinion, national or social origin, association with a national minority, property, birth or other status."[53] That provision, formally subject to only ancillary application, has nonetheless led to consideration of allegations of discrimination with respect to a number of rights that overlap with those addressed in chapter 2.[54] The ECtHR has addressed discrimination (including directed at women), with respect to pension or survivor's benefits, disability benefits, housing benefits, parental leave allowances, child benefits, other social security payments, respect for home or housing, inheritance, along with rights to access to justice or to effective investigation (as with respect to alleged failures to investigate and to protect in cases of domestic violence).[55] The number of cases in that regime alleging discrimination with respect to the ECHR's right to possessions are expected to rise as more states

---

[50] Protocol 1 to the European Convention for the Protection of Human Rights and Fundamental Freedoms art. 1, Mar. 20, 1952, 213 U.N.T.S. 262.

[51] *See, e.g.*, Kriebaum, *supra* note 22, at 92–93. *See also* Allen, *supra* note 22, at 299–300 (noting that usually the compensation required in cases of takings is determined by the property's fair market value but that the public interest may call for less than that sum). As this suggests, there is considerable overlap between the case law produced by the ECtHR and investor-state arbitral tribunals under international investment agreements with respect to direct takings of property. *See, e.g.*, August Reinisch, *Expropriation*, in THE OXFORD HANDBOOK OF INTERNATIONAL INVESTMENT LAW (Peter Muchlinski et al. eds., 2008)

[52] It should also be noted that to the extent Protocol One, Article 1 of European Convention on Human Rights incorporates, as many assume, customary international law obligations on states that take the property of aliens, that rule requires nondiscriminatory treatment as well as payment of appropriate compensation.

[53] European Convention for the Protection of Human Rights and Fundamental Freedoms art. 14, *opened for signature* Nov. 4, 1950, 213 U.N.T.S. 221.

[54] *See, e.g.*, Eur. Ct. H.R., *Guide on Article 1 of Protocol No. 1 to the European Convention on Human Rights: Protection of Property* (Aug. 31, 2022), https://www.echr.coe.int/Documents/Guide_Art_1_Protocol_1_ENG.pdf. *See also* Allen, *supra* note 22, at 309–10 (describing how the ancillary right under Article 14 has evolved under the ECtHR's jurisprudence to embrace, as protected possessions, the preconditions that states impose on receiving social benefits; as Allen indicates, the ECtHR does not exclude such benefits from protection merely because they have not yet "vested" as the property of an individual).

[55] *See, e.g., id.* ¶¶ 41, 49, 85–86, 94, 100, 183, 222, 226, 238, 246, 252, 253, 256, 258–262 (describing rulings involving the overlap between Articles 14 and Article 1, Protocol One). For a brief discussion of some of these rulings, *see* chapter 6, section 6.4.3.

accede to Protocol 12 which makes nondiscrimination a self-standing substantive right.[56]

The African Charter on Human and Peoples' Rights, insists that individuals within its state parties are entitled to all its rights "without distinction of any kind such as race, ethnic group, colour, sex, language, religion, political or other opinion, national and social origin, fortune, birth or other status." (Article 2). But it also proclaims, in Article 14, that "[t]he right of property shall be guaranteed. It may only be encroached upon in the interest of public need or in the general interest of the community and in accordance with the provisions of appropriate laws."[57] The Protocol to the African Charter on Human and Peoples' Rights on the Rights of Women in Africa, adds considerably to these general rights. Apart from requiring specific measures to eliminate discrimination against women (Article 2), that Protocol protects women's access to a wide number of expressly enumerated economic and social welfare rights (Article 13), to rights to food security including access to drinking water, domestic fuel, land, and "means of producing nutritious food" (Article 15), to adequate housing irrespective of marital status and "acceptable living conditions in a healthy environment"(Article 16), and rights for widows to an "equitable share in the inheritance of the property of her husband" (Article 21).

As the texts of these regional conventions indicate, none of the non-relative property rights accorded under them are "absolute" in the sense of not permitting any exception. In addition to being subject to exceptions for certain forms of government regulation in the public interest,[58] government takings of property may generate financial awards that may deviate from the fair market value of the property taken by the state.[59] Other human rights treaties, such as Convention on the Elimination of Racial Discrimination (CERD), guarantee only nondiscriminatory treatment with respect to property rights.[60]

---

[56] Protocol 12 to the European Convention for the Protection of Human Rights and Fundamental Freedoms, Nov. 4, 2000, E.T.S. No. 177. That protocol had ten state parties as of March 2023.

[57] For an overview of the Charter's possibilities given the realities of women's access to land in Africa, *see* Florence Butegwa, *Using the African Charter on Human and People's Rights to Secure Women's Access to Land in Africa*, in HUMAN RIGHTS OF WOMEN: NATIONAL AND INTERNATIONAL PERSPECTIVES 495 (Rebecca J. Cook ed., 2012).

[58] *See, e.g.*, Protocol No. 1 to The Convention for The Protection of Human Rights and Fundamental Freedoms art. 1(2), Mar. 20, 1952, 213 U.N.T.S. 262 (providing that "[t]he preceding provisions shall not, however, in any way impair the right of a State to enforce such laws as it deems necessary to control the use of property in accordance with the general interest or to secure the payment of taxes or other contributions or penalties.") *See also* Universal Declaration, *supra* note 43, Article 17 (right to own property) versus Article 29 (enabling limitations on all rights determined by law to secure the rights and freedoms of others and meeting the "just requirements of morality, public order, and the general welfare in a democratic society").

[59] *See, e.g.*, Allen, *supra* note 22, at 331–34.

[60] *See, e.g.*, International Convention on the Elimination of All Forms of Racial Discrimination, *opened to signature* Mar. 7, 1966, 660 U.N.T.S. 195 [hereinafter CERD], Article 1(1) (barring racial discrimination but not discrimination on the basis of sex). CERD Article 5(d)(v) includes "the right to own property alone as well as in accordance with others" and (vi) "the right to inherit."

Given the proliferation of human rights treaties containing property protections, it is hardly surprising that such rights are the subject of a considerable number of claims within regional and global human rights jurisprudence. It is estimated that as many as one in six of the thousands of rulings issued by the European Court of Human Rights involve in whole or in part property claims.[61] Significant rulings dealing with property rights have also emerged under the Inter-American human rights system, the Community Court of Justice of Economic Community of West African States (ECOWAS), and the East African Court of Justice.[62] Some of this jurisprudence identifies rights to property as particularly important "gateway" or "strategic" rights essential for the enjoyment of other human rights, including civil and political rights (like the right to vote) as well as economic and social rights (such as rights to housing, food, health, and work).[63] According to the UN Special Rapporteur on the right to food, for example, denials of the right to land open the door to violations of the right to food, to property more generally, and to nondiscriminatory treatment (including as applied to gender).[64] Moreover, the inverse is true as well: states' breaches of civil rights (like rights to access to justice) are a favored tool for violating the property rights of individuals and groups, including the right to land. (This helps to explain the substantial number of communications before the Human Rights Committee under the ICCPR that involve allegations of property deprivations despite that treaty's failure to contain property rights per se.[65]) Indeed, there are notorious cases, even from the twentieth century, in which governments have deployed their powers over their subject's property rights to inflict intentional forms of malnutrition at considerable human cost.[66]

Given these realities, a number of NGOs and civil society coalitions, including Landsea, the Huairou Commission, Habitat for Humanity, the Global Land Tool Network, and the International Land Coalition, back movements such as the "Stand for Her Land Campaign."[67] Such groups see the extension

---

[61] See Eur. Ct. H.R., Overview 1959–2016, at 9 (Mar. 2017), https://www.echr.coe.int/documents/overview_19592016_eng.pdf.

[62] See, e.g., Alvarez, supra note 22 (addressing the Inter-American Court of Human Rights' property jurisprudence).

[63] See, e.g., Glob. Initiative for Econ., Soc. & Cult. Rts., supra note 6, at 9. See also Howard-Hassmann, supra note 13, at 180 (identifying the right to own property as a "strategic" right); JAMES W. ELY, THE GUARDIAN OF EVERY OTHER RIGHT: A CONSTITUTIONAL HISTORY OF PROPERTY Rights (3d ed. 2007) at 26–41 (describing the centrality of the right to property during the revolutionary era leading to the adoption of the United States Constitution).

[64] Olivier D. Shutter, The Emerging Human Right to Land, 12 INT'L COMMUNITY L. REV. 303 (2010).

[65] See chapter 6, section 6.2.

[66] See, e.g., Howard-Hassmann, supra note 13, at 183–86 (describing the consequences of government decisions in Mugabe's Zimbabwe and Chávez's Venezuela).

[67] See generally STAND FOR HER LAND, https://stand4herland.org (last visited Feb. 3, 2023). Such groups are likely to weigh in on the Committee on Economic, Social and Cultural Rights (CESCR)'s current effort to draft a general comment on land. CESCR, General Comment No. 26 (2012) on Land and Economic, Social and Cultural Rights, E/C.12/69/R.2 (May 3, 2021).

of land rights to women as a means to promote "economic empowerment."[68] This is consistent with considerable scholarship, at least in many parts of the West, that relies on ostensibly strong connections between women's access to and ownership of agricultural land and national economic benefits such as increases in agricultural output or reductions in the numbers of persons suffering from hunger. For those engaged in promoting economic development in places like the World Bank and a number of scholars in various disciplines (and not only law), land ownership is also seen as generating wider social, and not merely economic benefits.[69] Many argue that ownership of land enhances women's self-esteem and enables a more equitable distribution of the division of labor within households. Some contend that the right to property reduces marital conflicts, counters the feminization of poverty, and lessens the vulnerability of women to violence. Govind Kelkar argues, in addition, that land distribution is a superior tool over income transfers to women because of its incentive effects; that women's control of land and assets breaks the vicious circle of "poverty-patriarchy-illiteracy-ill health"; that equal inheritance rights enhances women's autonomy within the marital home; and that land transfers in women's names provide comparable benefits, including enabling their increased mobility.[70]

For those situated in and educated in the West, the scholarly provenance of such ideas are obvious, even if the underlying premises and conclusions remain contested.[71] For Western writers in the mainstream, respect for property is a precondition for the enjoyment of all fundamental civil and political rights at both the national and international levels and is essential to "rule of law" governance.[72] Richard Pipes puts it most succinctly: property rights "are a necessary if

---

[68] *See, e.g.*, Int'l L. Ass'n, Committee on Feminism and International Law, *Second Report on Economic Empowerment Of Women: The Contribution of International Law, in* INTERNATIONAL LAW ASSOCIATION, REPORT OF THE SEVENTY-SIXTH CONFERENCE 149 (2014) (discussing gender inequality in land ownership, along with other impediments to women's "entrepreneurial activity" such as denials of credit). *But see FIAN Report, supra* note 6, at 13–15 (criticizing the exclusive framing of land rights as rights to private property only owed respect when protected by individual land titles).

[69] *See, e.g.*, Wadlig, *supra* note 8, at 73–98 (casting doubt on the numerous benefits generally associated with traditional "tenure security").

[70] Govind Kelkar, *The Fog of Entitlement: Women's Inheritance and Land Rights*, 49 ECON. & POL. WKLY. 51, 52–54 (2014).

[71] See chapter 3 for examples of such contestations. Notably, as that chapter illustrates, those defending the general right to property and those refuting them generally do not draw nuanced distinctions between property regimes in distinct countries or under distinctive legal traditions—from civil law systems to those governing Islamic states.

[72] *See, e.g.*, Leonard W. Levy, *Property as a Human Right*, 5 CONST. COMMENTARY 169 (1988) (arguing that free speech is of little value to a propertyless person); Howard-Hassmann, *supra* note 13, at 181 ("the right to own property is an intrinsic human right, valuable in itself as a component of human dignity"); Randy Barnett, *The Right to Liberty in a Good Society*, 69 FORDHAM L. REV. 1603, 1614–15 (2001) (arguing that the role of government is not to engage in resource redistribution through social rights but to protect "each person's liberty rights to acquire, use, and dispose of resources in the world without violating the like rights of others").

insufficient attribute of freedom and the rule of law."[73] In places like the United States, supporters of John Locke's social contract theory argue that the purpose of that contract (and of the rule of law that it justifies) is to enable persons to escape the calamitous state of nature by protecting individuals from one another through norms that further the mutual protection of what each owns.[74] At least in mainstream Western philosophical circles, the divide is between those who maintain, along with Locke, that the social contract and the rule of law necessarily include the protection of property, and those who maintain that the rule of law and property rights are distinct ideals even if both (along with democracy and economic freedom), dominate political morality.

Waldron, a prominent legal philosopher and property scholar, associates himself with the latter view. He argues that only some of the rights contained in the Universal Declaration of Human Rights, namely, Articles 7–11, reflect exactly what the rule of law requires. Waldron pointedly does not include Article 17, containing everyone's right to property, in his list. He distinguishes his own view from those who do not appear to distinguish the right to property from the rule of law itself, such as Friedrich Hayek, Ronald Cass, and Richard Epstein.[75] Of course, Waldron could have named others outside the West who treat property rights as having intrinsic value.[76] Waldron argues that he, along with Lon Fuller, Albert Vann Dicey, Aristotle, Joseph Raz, and Tom Bingham, by contrast, does not consider the right to property to be part of the rule of law while still seeing it as a desirable good whose dimensions are determined by public laws with contents that vary from place to place.[77] But Waldron readily accepts the contention that the *equal application* of property rights satisfies the rule of law requirements that the law be intelligible, clear, and predictable.[78]

Among prominent property theorists in the West, there is broad agreement that *when property rights exist*, these need to be extended to all, irrespective of sex. Even those, like Waldron, Mary Wollstonecraft, and Carol Pateman, who dismiss Locke's arguments for elevating the natural law primacy of property,[79]

---

[73] Richard Pipes, *Private Property, Freedom and the Rule of Law*, HOOVER DIGEST (Apr. 30, 2001), https://www.hoover.org/research/private-property-freedom-and-rule-law.

[74] Compare Howard-Hassmann, *supra* note 13, at 189–90 (supporting Locke's theory of dignity-enhancing property) to JEREMY WALDRON, THE RULE OF LAW AND THE MEASURE OF PROPERTY 1–41 (2012) (critiquing Locke's idea that persons enter into society to preserve their property).

[75] Waldron, *supra* note 74, at 42–75.

[76] *See, e.g.*, Yinka Olomojobi, *Women's Right to Own Property* (Dec. 16, 2015) (unpublished manuscript), https://ssrn.com/abstract=2716902; *see also* TALPADE MOHANTY, FEMINISM WITHOUT BORDERS: DECOLONIZING THEORY, PRACTICING SOLIDARITY (2003) (discussing the global "hegemony" of Western ideas and warning against a singular, monolithic "Third World woman" even while proposing an "anti-capitalist" version of feminism).

[77] WALDRON, *supra* note 74, at 18–19.

[78] *Id.* at 15.

[79] For criticisms of Locke's elevation of property rights as part of the basic social contract and of Locke's premise that one naturally "owns" the property that results from the product of one's labor, *see id.* at 1–41. *See generally* CAROLE PATEMAN, THE SEXUAL CONTRACT (1988). For a discussion of

do not reject the contention that once a state's public law extends property rights to persons, such rights need to be extended to all of a state's nationals without discrimination.[80]

The right not to be discriminated against with respect to property is often justified on the basis of dignity. Waldron, like a number of other commentators in the Western tradition, argue that equal property rights are one way that the law treats humans as dignified agents capable of controlling their actions and advancing their own interests.[81] Waldron, who defines dignity as a status concept wherein persons are "recognized as having the ability to control and regulate her actions in accordance with her own apprehension of norms and reasons that apply to her," argues that this means that "she has the wherewithal to demand that her agency and her presence among us as a human being be taken seriously."[82] In this view, while owning individual property is not a *sine qua non* for having dignity, the right to equal protection with respect to property is one way the law recognizes the dignity of all persons as rights bearers.[83] Perhaps because most people are familiar with the many ways states have "infantilized" women for centuries by denying their capacity to take out a line of credit, apply for a loan, complete a deed without their husbands' signatures, or control marital assets to which they have contributed, today it is common for national laws around the world to affirm, at least as a matter of formal law, that men and women be treated as equals with respect to property.[84]

For those habituated to the West's deep impact on international law, it should come as no surprise that the texts of twentieth-century human rights treaties,

---

Mary Wollstonecraft's descriptions of property as a "poisoned fountain" and a "demon," *see, e.g.*, Lena Halldenius, *Mary Wollstonecraft's Feminist Critique of Property: On Becoming a Thief from Principle*, 29 HYPATIA 942 (2014).

[80] Despite the broad terms of some human rights instruments affirming a general right to property, many states continue to distinguish the rights of their own nationals' property rights from those accorded to foreigners in their territory. The bar on discrimination based on national origin is usually interpreted not to prohibit discrimination based on nationality. This reality helps to account for the existence of the international investment regime discussed in chapter 5.

[81] Jeremy Waldron, *How Law Protects Dignity*, 71 CAMBRIDGE L.J. 200 (2012); *see also* Carol Rose, *Property as the Keystone Right?*, 71 NOTRE DAME L. REV. 329 (1996) (arguing that property ownership enables a person to exercise independent judgment); Sandra L. Rierson, *Race and Gender Discrimination: A Historical Case for Equal Treatment Under the Fourteenth Amendment*, 1 DUKE J. GENDER L. & POL'Y 89 (1994) (drawing historical parallels between the treatment of slaves and married American women, both of whom were denied personal agency in one case because they were considered property and in the second, because they could not own it). As Rierson acknowledges, she is not the first to draw the comparison. *See, e.g.*, John Stuart Mill, *The Subjection of Women*, *in* ESSAYS ON SEX EQUALITY 125 (Alice S. Rossi ed., 1970).

[82] Waldron, *supra* note 81, at 202.

[83] *See, e.g.*, BERNADETTE ATUAHENE, WE WANT WHAT'S OURS: LEARNING FROM SOUTH AFRICA'S LAND RESTITUTION PROGRAM 23–34 (2014) (discussing the concept of "dignity takings" of property).

[84] For a specific example, *see* Janet Walsh, *Women's Property Rights Violations in Kenya*, *in* HUMAN RIGHTS AND DEVELOPMENT: TOWARDS MUTUAL REINFORCEMENT 133 (Philip Alston & Mary Robinson eds., 2005).

despite being the product of international negotiations among diverse nations, share this jurisprudential common ground.[85] With the exception of the two Cold War Covenants which omit express mention of property (but, as shown in chapter 6, protect it nonetheless under other protections, especially the right to non-discrimination), most subsequent human rights treaties have affirmed that if property rights are accorded under national law, these rights need to be extended on a nondiscriminatory basis, at least with respect to a state's nationals. However, as shown in chapter 3, not everyone accepts the primacy of property rights within the human rights canon. For those who see the concept of private property as a form of theft or an invariably tainted product of patriarchy, colonialism, imperialism, and/or capitalism, the widespread acceptance of property rights as human rights is one more reason to reject human rights as a credible tool for promoting the equality of women.[86]

1.3 The Origins of "Property" in CEDAW

When, in 1963, the UN General Assembly requested the Economic and Social Council to invite the Commission on the Status of Women (CSW) to prepare a draft Declaration on the Elimination of Discrimination against Women (DEDAW),[87] a number of prominent human rights instruments had already included property rights protections. By that time, as noted, a state's obligation not to discriminate with respect to property rights generally had been incorporated into the American Declaration of the Rights and Duties of Man (1948), the Universal Declaration of Human Rights (1948), the Convention Relating to the Status of Refugees (1951), the Protocol to the European Convention for the Protection of Human Rights and Fundamental Freedoms (1952), the Convention Relating to the Status of Stateless Persons (1954), at least two ILO Conventions,[88] and some important soft law instruments.[89]

---

[85] *See generally* ANTONY ANGHIE, IMPERIALISM, SOVEREIGNTY AND THE MAKING OF INTERNATIONAL LAW (2005).

[86] *See, e.g.*, MIES, *supra* note 13, at 230 ("The struggle for the human essence, for human dignity, cannot be divided and cannot be won unless all these colonizing divisions, created by patriarchy and capitalism, are rejected and transcended.").

[87] G.A. Res. 1921 (XVIII) (Dec. 5, 1963).

[88] *See, e.g.*, ILO Convention (No. 95) Concerning the Protection of Wages (1949), *supra* note 46; Convention (No. 107) Concerning the Protection and Integration of Indigenous and Other Tribal and Semi-tribal Populations in Independent Countries, June 26, 1957, 328 U.N.T.S. 247. Of course, the basic tenet to respect the equality of men and women is also affirmed in the UN Charter. *See* UN Charter art. 8.

[89] *See, e.g.*, UN Off. on Drugs and Crime, UNITED NATION STANDARD MINIMUM RULES FOR THE TREATMENT OF PRISONERS (1955), https://www.unodc.org/documents/justice-and-prison-reform/Nelson_Mandela_Rules-E-ebook.pdf (recognizing the right to safe custody of money, valuables and other personal effects of those incarcerated).

Given this history, no one could have been surprised when Poland, during the first meeting to draft what became DEDAW, proposed the inclusion of the following text:

> Women shall have equal rights with men to acquire, administer, enjoy, dispose of, and inherit property.
>
> All Limitations of the property rights of women under statutory matrimonial regimes and all discrimination against women in the field of inheritance rights shall be eliminated.[90]

The proposal generated debate over whether DEDAW should be focusing on the obligations of states or should simply be a declaration of fundamental rights which should be enjoyed by women.[91] Poland's proposal clearly contained both. The drafting committee worked off Poland's text to produce, as part of the first draft of DEDAW, the following more simplified text for Article 9:

> Women shall have the same rights as men to acquire, administer, enjoy, dispose of and inherit property.
>
> All States shall abolish all limitations on the property rights of women under statutory matrimonial regimes.[92]

But while those negotiating the text could agree in principle that men and women needed to be accorded equal treatment with respect to property as a fundamental right, deciding what precisely this meant proved difficult. Over the course of several meetings of the CSW, Article 9 (which was ultimately moved to Article 6) became, as the representative from Belgium noted, both "the essential article of the document and the one on which it would be most difficult to reach agreement."[93] A number of countries expressed concern that the provision could deter states from entering into the Declaration to the extent that their national laws (particularly relating to the family) were inconsistent with the demand for equal treatment. Countries expressed different views on how far the Declaration should intrude into family and matrimonial laws and practices. Some sought to give states more flexibility of action. Toward the end

---

[90] Econ. & Soc. Council, *Rep. on the 18th Session of the Commission on the Status of Women*, UN Doc. E/CN.6/442 (Mar. 1965), ¶ 69.
[91] *Id.* ¶ 71.
[92] *Id.* ¶ 77.
[93] UN GAOR, 21st Sess., 1444th 3rd comm. mtg. at 37, UN Doc. A/C-3/SR-1444 (Sept. 1967).

of the negotiations India proposed adding the phrase "as far as possible" to provide that flexibility.[94] While India's effort was defeated, the representative of the Congo was more successful. The Congo argued that the clause be clarified to "safeguard" the "unity and the harmony of the family" and a version of its proposed amendment was narrowly passed by a vote of 40 to 36 with nineteen abstentions.[95] At the end of the day, the Third Committee adopted the following text as part of the DEDAW:

Article 6

1. Without prejudice to the safeguarding of the unity and the harmony of the family, which remains the basic unit of any society, all appropriate measures, particularly legislative measures, shall be taken to ensure to women, married or unmarried, equal rights with men in the field of civil law, and in particular: (a) The right to acquire, administer, enjoy, dispose of and inherit property, including property acquired during marriage; (b) The right to equality in legal capacity and the exercise thereof....
2. All appropriate measures shall be taken to ensure the principle of equality of status of the husband and wife, and in particular ... (b) Women shall have equal rights with men during marriage and at its dissolution...[96]

Article 6 of DEDAW became the fulcrum for the incorporation of property rights when the CSW decided, in 1974, to work toward a single, comprehensive, and international binding instrument to eliminate discrimination against women. The subsequent negotiating history of CEDAW has been undertaken by others and need not be replicated here.[97] As was the case during the negotiations over the DEDAW, the explicit reference to protecting marital or family property in CEDAW proved to be among the most difficult to conclude. Among the fifteen countries represented on the working group charged with drafting the convention, Indonesia, Iran, Pakistan, and Egypt expressed reservations to some of the provisions drawn from the DEDAW, often on the basis of their inconsistency

---

[94] UN Secretary-General, Note by the Secretary-General on DEDAW, Ann. 2, ¶ 1, UN Doc. A/6349 (Aug. 9, 1966).

[95] Rep. of the Third Committee on the Draft Declaration on the Elimination of Discrimination against Women, at 14, UN Doc. A/6880 (Oct. 28, 1967).

[96] G.A. Res. 2263 (XXII) (Nov. 7, 1967). Article 10(1)(b) of the DEDAW also included the "right to equal remuneration with men" and to "equality of treatment in respect of work of equal value." Article 10(1)(c) added the "right to leave with pay, retirement privileges and provision for security in respect of unemployment, sickness, old age or other incapacity to work."

[97] *See especially* LARS A. REHOF, GUIDE TO THE TRAVAUX PRÉPARATOIRES OF THE UNITED NATIONS CONVENTION ON THE ELIMINATION OF ALL FORMS OF DISCRIMINATION AGAINST WOMEN (1993). Aspects of the negotiation history are also addressed in 2012 CEDAW COMMENTARY, *supra* note 22.

with their own national laws.[98] Other countries, including Austria, Belgium, Poland, and Sweden argued that property and relevant rights to it for married couples should be the subject of a separate convention.[99] In the end, however, the texts of these provisions in CEDAW, as modified by a number of amendments, were adopted unanimously although the most contentious proved to be issues at the heart of states' family laws, such as property divisions upon dissolution of a marriage. But even what became the much-amended Article 16(h) (recognizing the "same rights for both spouses" with respect to property) was ultimately adopted unanimously by a vote of 21 in favor and 2 abstentions.[100]

In the end, the text of CEDAW, adopted by the UN General Assembly on December 18, 1979, in force as of September 3, 1981, affirms the general principle, widely accepted since at least the adoption of the Universal Declaration of Human Rights in 1948, that men and women are owed, under international law, equal treatment with respect to property. Notably, the leading instrument to advance women's rights at the global level does not include an explicit guarantee by its state parties to respect property rights irrespective of whether these extend to men, comparable to the rights to property not dependent on a showing of discrimination contained in the American, European, and African conventions on human rights.[101] CEDAW does not contain an affirmation that all persons shall enjoy the right to use and/or enjoy property, a guarantee against deprivation of property without just compensation, or a general entitlement to the peaceful enjoyment of one's possessions—as do some other international instruments. At the same time, it is surprising that, in 1979, at a time when national laws did not uniformly affirm women's equal property rights in accordance with the DEDAW, such protections were nonetheless incorporated among CEDAW's thirty articles.

1.4 CEDAW's Property Provisions

States are required under the relevant subparts of CEDAW's Articles 11, 13, 14, 15, and 16 enumerated above to respect, protect, and fulfill women's rights to equality with respect to access to credit, to housing, to conclude contracts, to social and economic benefits, and to own, acquire, manage, administer, enjoy, or

---

[98] *See, e.g.,* Comm'n on the Status of Women, Communication, dated 13 December 1976, addressed to the Secretary of the Commission on the Status of Women, by the Permanent Rep. of Pakistan to the United Nations Office at Geneva at 3, UN Doc. E/CN.6/606 (Dec. 13, 1976).
[99] UN Secretary-General, Consideration of Proposals Concerning a New Instrument or Instruments of International Law to Eliminate Discrimination Against Women, ¶¶ 92–94, UN Doc. E/CN.6/573 (Nov. 6, 1973).
[100] UN ESCOR, 26th Sess., 652th mtg. ¶ 27, UN Doc. E/CN.6/SR.652 (Sept. 30, 1976).
[101] Compare, for example, the Universal Declaration, *supra* note 43, at art. 17.

dispose of property in family relations.[102] These obligations, whether or not formally designated under the Convention as forms of "property," are contained in a treaty that embraces a very expansive concept of prohibited discrimination and applies to 189 state parties.[103] Article 1 defines "discrimination against women" to mean any distinction, exclusion, or restriction "made on the basis of sex which has the effect or purpose of impairing or nullifying" not only the treaty's enumeration of rights but any "human rights and fundamental freedoms in the political, economic, social, cultural, civil or any other field." Article 2 further requires states to ensure the "effective protection" of women against any act of discrimination (c), and to take "all appropriate measures" to eliminate discrimination by "any person, organization or enterprise" (e). Article 3 demands that states take "all appropriate measures, including legislation" to ensure "the full development and advancement of women, for the purpose of guaranteeing them the exercise and enjoyment of human rights and fundamental freedoms on a basis of equality with men." That obligation to implement the treaty's equality rights extends to "all fields," including political, social, economic, and cultural. Article 5(a) further provides that the duty to take "appropriate measures" includes actions to modify the social and cultural patterns of conduct, prejudices and customary and other practices "based on the idea of the inferiority or the superiority of either of the sexes or on stereotyped roles for men and women."

In accordance with these provisions, CEDAW bars all forms of discriminatory practices, by either state or private parties that adversely impact its enumerated property rights. It requires states to legislate out of existence both formal and substantive forms of inequality, authorizes states to take remedial affirmative measures in pursuit of women's equality, and anticipates that states will pierce public/private divides to eradicate customary practices and stereotypes that get in the way. Moreover, its definition of "discrimination" embraces harms to "fundamental freedoms" with respect to every sphere—whether civil/political or social/economic/cultural.

As CEDAW's preamble's references to the "new international economic order" and the need to eradicate "all forms of racism, racial discrimination, colonialism, neo-colonialism, aggression, foreign occupation and domination and interference in the internal affairs of States," suggest, CEDAW is a product of its time

---

[102] *See supra* text at notes 14–17; see also appendix 1. *See also* Comm. on the Elimination of Discrimination against Women General Recommendation No. 25 on Article 4, Paragraph 1, of the [CEDAW Convention], on Temporary Special Measures, ¶ 4, UN Doc. HRI/GEN1/Rev. 9 (Vol. II) (May 27, 2004). Comm. on the Elimination of Discrimination against Women General Recommendation No. 28 on the Core Obligations of States Parties under Article 2, ¶ 9, UN Doc. CEDAW/C/GC/28 (Dec. 16, 2010).

[103] Subject, of course, to state reservations to relevant reservations even if the legality of these may be contested. *See* apps. 2 & 3.

and of the venue for its negotiation.[104] CEDAW was concluded only shortly after the UN General Assembly produced, with strong support from developing states amid resistance by Western exporters of capital like the United States, the Charter of Economic Rights and Duties of States.[105] Its preamble's sensitivity to concerns associated with the "Group of 77," as filtered later through subsequent influential documents like the Beijing Platform for Action and today's Sustainable Development Goals (SDGs), provides important context to the CEDAW Committee's interpretation of property rights surveyed in chapter 2.[106] At the same time, as debates during the negotiations over its text and subsequent reservations by some states to some of the treaty's property rights provisions reveal, some of CEDAW's state parties continue to resist some of its core property rights provisions, particularly those applicable to marital property.[107] As is evident in appendices 2 and 3 to this book, states' reservations to some of the treaty's property protections, and particularly to Article 16(2)(h), have been subjected to considerable criticism during the state reporting process. (As appendix 3 indicates, however, some of the reservations that have been subject to critical COs have since been removed or modified by the reserving states.) Apart from human rights treaties that protect women from discrimination with respect to property rights, some female entrepreneurs may find additional protections under multilateral, regional, or bilateral international investment agreements, many of which affirm that customary international law and not only treaty law protects the rights of alien property in their host states.[108]

As this suggests, the wealth and property disparities between men and women around the world are not the product of the *absence* of international law. They are the product of gendered law and practices at both the international and national levels. Indeed, for those who draw a close tie between international law's defense of capitalism and the latter's defense of patriarchy, international law disempowers women as much or more than it empowers them.[109]

---

[104] CEDAW, *supra* note 14, Preamble ¶¶ 9–10. *See also* Patricia Schulz et al., *Introduction, in* 2022 CEDAW COMMENTARY, *supra* note 19, sec. G (I).

[105] G.A. Res. 3281 (XXIX) (Dec. 12, 1974).

[106] *See, e.g., Beijing Declaration and Platform for Action, in* 1 REPORT OF THE FOURTH WORLD CONFERENCE ON WOMEN 16, BEIJING, 4–15 SEPTEMBER, 1995, UN Doc. A/CONF.177/20/REV.1, UN Sales No. 96.IV.13 (1996) [hereinafter Beijing Platform] (calling for "people-centered sustainable development"). For an example of the Committee's invocation of the SDGs in its COs, *see, e.g.*, CO on Sweden, CEDAW/C/SWE/CO/10, ¶ 7 (2021).

[107] For a list of relevant state reservations, *see* appendix 2.

[108] *See* chapter 5, particularly section 5.10.

[109] *See generally* MacKinnon, *supra* note 4 (surveying the many ways international law licenses or condones the subordination of women). For a specific example, *see* Silvia Federici, *Precarious Labor: A Feminist Viewpoint*, THE MIDDLE OF A WHIRLWIND (2008), https://inthemiddleofthewhirlwind.wordpress.com/precarious-labor-a-feminist-viewpoint/ (criticizing the turn to "precarious labour" (including remote work from the home) and its connections to capitalism's reliance on unpaid domestic work).

Nor can such inequalities be wholly attributed to the absence of applicable national laws protecting women against discrimination. While it took many years for women to secure equal rights to property related interests under national laws (such as inheritance), national laws formally protecting the equal rights of women to property, typically in the form of gender-neutral application, were common to many states and preceded the conclusion of CEDAW. Further, in the four decades since CEDAW entered into force, many more countries have embraced laws that formally recognize gender equality with respect to land tenure, access to land or other forms of shelter, and other forms of property rights such as access to bank accounts, credit, or rights to conclude and enforce contracts.[110] Parity of rights between men and women is now included in many national constitutions, including many which broadly affirm "everyone's" right to property as proclaimed in the Universal Declaration of Human Rights.[111] As CEDAW's COs reveal, much (but not all) of the problem is that such laws are ignored, often with the backing of political, religious, or cultural groups that share the stereotypical views of women that CEDAW was intended to combat.[112] The gap between formal law and the actual practice of states and private parties remains substantial.

1.5 The Organization of This Book

Chapter 2 looks at how the principal body charged with interpreting the "landmark treaty in the struggle for women's rights,"[113] the CEDAW committee, has interpreted and applied the treaty's provisions previously enumerated in section 1.1 from the date the Convention came into force in 1981 through the present. It surveys the relevant Committee's General Recommendations, its Concluding Observations issued in response to state reports, Committee's Views issued in response to the treaty's communications and inquiry procedures. Following standard practice, this book's reference to the "jurisprudence" of the CEDAW Committee includes all of these outputs as well as the rationales the Committee has given to justify its interpretations.[114]

---

[110] *See, e.g.*, Raquel Rolnik (Special Rapporteur), Rep. on Adequate Housing as a Component of the Right to an Adequate Standard of Living, and on the Right to Non-Discrimination in this Context, UN Doc. A/HRC/19/53 (Dec. 26, 2011) (reporting on legal and policy advancements in the area of women's right to adequate housing).

[111] *See, e.g.*, Hurst Hannum, *The Status of the Universal Declaration of Human Rights in National and International Law*, 25 GA. J. INT'L & COMP. L. 287, 355–76 (1996) (listing constitutional provisions containing references to the Universal Declaration of Human Rights).

[112] In addition, as appendices 2–3 reveal, some CEDAW state parties still purport to reject some of the Convention's property-relating provisions, whether or not these are seen as violating the Convention's object and purpose.

[113] *See* Christine Chinkin & Marsha A. Freeman, *Introduction*, *in* 2012 CEDAW Commentary, *supra* note 22.

[114] *See* chapter 2, particularly section 2.3 and its note 24.

That chapter describes how the CEDAW Committee has used its delegated authority to interpret CEDAW to develop the law relating to proprietary interests in marriage and family relations; in relation to civil and political rights, land, and adequate housing; with respect to seeds and intellectual property, access to financial credit and other forms of economic empowerment, social benefits, and protections from domestic violence. As noted, chapter 2 fills a scholarly gap. Despite women's systematic property disenfranchisement, there have been very few attempts to comprehensively describe (much less assess) how the principal entity charged with protecting women's rights at the multilateral level has sought to advance and elucidate women's property rights over time.

The premises that there should be a global treaty devoted to protecting the rights of women and that it should include property rights in its contents have been controversial. Chapter 3 surveys persistent critiques by feminist scholars, including those who self-identify as "Third World Feminists," of both propositions. As that chapter indicates, some have challenged the elevation of sex or gender—as opposed to race, class, sexual preference, or nationality—as the primary axis for analysis. Critics of "liberal feminism," or of "universal" human rights, have contested the what they consider to be CEDAW's underlying premises—namely, that there is a single category of "women," that women everywhere have always been oppressed, that the measure of women's subordination should be the treatment men receive, or that diverse histories borne of distinct forms of racist or colonial oppression should be overcome by reliance on ideologically tainted conceptions of international law and individualistic but also universal human rights. That chapter also considers contemporary "revisionist" criticisms that internationalized property rights advance a "neo-liberal" agenda in favor of government deregulation, the formalization of property titles, and the commodification of natural resources.[115] It also explores the connection between such views and the broad critique, of older vintage, that all of international law, including human regimes like CEDAW's, are tools seeking to "civilize" states on Western models.[116]

Chapter 4 evaluates CEDAW's property jurisprudence as described in chapter 2 in light of the concerns and criticisms detailed in chapter 3. It compares

---

[115] For a survey of these debates in recent historic accounts of human rights, *see, e.g.*, Joseph R. Slaughter, *Hijacking Human Rights: Neoliberalism, the New Historiography, and the End of the Third World*, 40 HUM. RTS. Q. 735 (2018).

[116] *See generally*, ANGHIE, *supra* note 85; Makau W. Mutua, *Savages, Victims, and Saviors: The Metaphor of Human Rights*, 42 HARV. INT'L L.J. 201 (2001). For contestations of gendered human rights framings, *see, e.g.*, Dianne Otto, *Disconcerting "Masculinities": Reinventing the Gendered Subject(s) of International Human Rights Law, in* INTERNATIONAL LAW: MODERN FEMINIST APPROACHES 105 (Doris Buss & Ambreena Manji eds., 2005); Rana Kapur, *The Tragedy of Victimization Rhetoric: Resurrecting the "Native" Subject in International/Postcolonial Feminist Legal Politics*, 15 HARV. HUM. RTS. L.J. 1 (2002).

the fears some have voiced with respect to the *human right to property* with the CEDAW Committee's interpretations of *equal property rights*. That chapter concludes that CEDAW's property jurisprudence is considerably more nuanced than some of the criticisms of the Convention, of the CEDAW Committee, or of the international human rights movement would suggest. It contends that property rights under CEDAW have not become tools either to fundamentally challenge market capitalism (as some hope) or mechanisms to aid and abet commodification, privatization, and deregulation (as some fear).

Chapters 5 and 6 advance inquiries initiated by others, such as Ursula Kriebaum and Beth Goldblatt, into comparative international property law by bringing CEDAW's jurisprudence into the discussion.[117] Chapter 5 compares CEDAW's property jurisprudence with that generated under investor-state arbitrations in the international investment regime. Chapter 6 compares the property jurisprudence produced under the ICCPR and the ICESCR. These two chapters suggest that while there is no uniformly defined "international right to property," there are sharp differences between international regimes that protect "property rights" under a human rights frame and those that do not.

The concluding chapter undertakes a broader assessment of what the CEDAW Committee has accomplished and where it has fallen short. The Committee has creatively expanded some of CEDAW's original gaps in protecting women's property (such as the original treaty's failure to explicitly include the right of a woman subject to domestic violence to have access to housing irrespective of whether she owns her home). It has been among the leading human rights regimes in developing the concept (and categories applicable to) intersectional discrimination with respect to property (as with respect to other rights included in the Convention), but has not overreached by finding broad, absolute rights to property ownership not contained in the Convention. Chapter 7 contends that CEDAW's asymmetrical focus on women and its delegated authority to launch a frontal attack on the structural underpinnings of women's inequality makes the resulting jurisprudence not only "progressive" but distinctive—and potentially transformative.

At the same time, chapter 7 addresses the many reasons CEDAW's property jurisprudence remains an imperfect work in progress given serious interpretative gaps as well as institutional constraints that are both internal to that Geneva-based body and that stem from the Committee's interlocutors. There are signs that the time and resource restraints on the CEDAW Committee are growing amid a general backlash against human rights regimes.[118] The CEDAW regime's

---

[117] *See* KRIEBAUM, *supra* note 22; *see also* GOLDBLATT, *supra* note 23.
[118] *See, e.g.,* Nick Cummings-Bruce, *Budget Cuts May Undercut the U.N.'s Human Rights Committees*, N.Y. TIMES, May 24, 2019.

prospects for generating genuinely transformational change are under severe challenge.

The CEDAW Committee's discursive efforts on this topic merit attention for the same reasons that the jurisprudence of other global human rights treaty bodies is worth examining: because lawyers and activists use the CEDAW Committee's interpretations to make arguments in many forums, from domestic courts to national legislatures to other international human rights interpreters.[119] The CEDAW Committee's outputs relating to property are worth close scrutiny because they emerge from the only global body specifically charged with assessing, in legal terms, the rights of women. The CEDAW regime's views of property rights are also worthy of study because they have something distinctive to say about what values equal property rights protect.

In responding to the complex realities faced by women and girls around the world, the Committee has begun to carve out a path that is distinct from that advanced by economists at the World Bank or from those who have associated women's self-actualization with materialist needs for bourgeois comforts premised on the right to *own* property.[120] That Committee does not equate states' obligations to enable shelter and security, for example, with individual's rights to *own* their home and exclude others from it.[121] The CEDAW Committee has avoided many of the pitfalls that draw the ire of critics of international law's "civilizing mission" or who allege that all international human rights regimes are complicit in "neo-liberalism." The CEDAW Committee's work on this subject does not merely replicate rules found in Western "rule of law" states or in a number of other international regimes that protect property. Property and discrimination theorists in general, and not only international human rights lawyers, can learn something from it.

---

[119] *See generally* NINA REINERS, TRANSNATIONAL LAWMAKING COALITIONS FOR HUMAN RIGHTS (2021).

[120] *See* chapter 7, particularly section 7.1.

[121] Compare, FREDMAN, *supra* note 23, at 278–93.

2
The CEDAW Committee's Property Jurisprudence

2.1 Introduction

This chapter offers a descriptive account of the Committee on the Elimination of Discrimination against Women's (hereinafter the Committee) engagement with property rights under the Convention on the Elimination of All Forms of Discrimination against Women (CEDAW, or the Convention).[1]

The purpose of chapter 2 is to map a "landscape of the Committee's property jurisprudence," because the Convention allows studying property rights comprehensively from a civil and political as well as economic, social, and cultural rights dimension.[2] The conducted analysis identified Articles 11(1)(e) and (2)(b), chapeau of Article 13, Article 13(b), Article 14(2)(c), (g), and (h), 15, and 16(1)(h) as "property provisions" or at the interface with property rights.[3] However, this chapter does not study the Convention's provisions and other output in a chronological fashion but groups them thematically.

The chapter first briefly explains the Committee's authority as an interpreter of the Convention. It then alludes to the Committee's working methods and provides an overview of the Committee's output on property rights that are contained in its General Recommendations (GRs), Views in response to communications, Inquiry Reports, and Concluding Observations (COs) in response to state reports.

---

[1] Convention on the Elimination of All Forms of Discrimination against Women, *open to signature* Dec. 18, 1979, 1249 U.N.T.S. 13 [hereinafter CEDAW, or the Convention].

[2] Given that neither the notion of property nor property rights are neatly delineated under international human rights law and have different protection scopes in different parts of the world, the European Court of Human Rights jurisprudence under Article 1 of Protocol No. 1 of European Contention of Human Rights served as a guide about what to include under property rights due to its very wide property understanding and its publicity. The author of chapter 2 situated in continental Europe acknowledges that the boundaries of property rights as presented in this chapter are permissible, negotiable, not definite, and vary in different world regions. Thus, this is only one attempt to delineate the scope of property rights in international human rights law. Depending on their situatedness, other scholars might present and interpret the Committee's jurisprudence differently. *See also* chapter 1.

[3] For relevant CEDAW provisions, *see* appendix 1.

Women's Property Rights Under CEDAW. José E. Alvarez and Judith Bauder, Oxford University Press.
© Oxford University Press 2024. DOI: 10.1093/oso/9780197751879.003.0002

The chapter then presents the Committee's substantive engagement with property rights in eight thematic sections: property rights in marriage and family relations; property rights interfacing with different civil and political rights; land rights; housing rights; intellectual property and seed rights; access to financial credit and economic empowerment; rights to social benefits; and the interrelationship between gender-based violence and property rights.

The chapter starts with the backbone property provisions contained in the Convention because they are most commonly referred to as the property provisions under CEDAW. The chapter then presents the Committee's rare engagement with property rights in the civil and political rights context, before it engages with the Committee's rich jurisprudence on property rights in the context of economic, social, and cultural rights. The last section addresses the interrelationship of gender-based violence and property rights.

Each thematic section on the Committee's engagement with property rights addresses the Committee's normative outputs in the following order: the Convention and GRs, communications, Inquiry Reports, and COs in state reports. The Committee's GRs earn pride of place in the analysis because, along with citations to the text of the Convention itself, the Committee accords virtually equal attention to its own GRs throughout its other outputs. Communications and Inquiry Reports are examined next because these two quasi-jurisprudential mechanisms under the Optional Protocol offer detailed interpretations of property rights even if they are few in numbers. Although addressed last, COs provide repeated opportunities for the Committee to apply its property jurisprudence to the particular contexts and facts illuminated in state reports. Since COs arise from the periodic reporting obligations to which all state parties under CEDAW are subject, these provide a more universal picture of the application of that jurisprudence. Of course, dividing the Committee's interpretation in this fashion should not be taken to suggest that the Committee's procedures operate independently of one another. Indeed, the Committee often indicates that conclusions reached in response to a communication or as a CO in response to a state report, inform its GRs or Inquiry Reports, for example.

The detailed account of the Committee's legal output on and engagement with property rights lays the groundwork for analyzing its jurisprudence with human rights and feminist critiques (chapters 3 and 4) and for comparing it with the property regime under international investment law (chapter 5) and the two international human rights Covenants (chapter 6).

2.2 The Committee's Authority as an Interpreter of the Convention

As the "leading United Nations treaty body responsible for the monitoring the implementation of women's human rights,"[4] the CEDAW Committee is empowered to legally interpret a Convention that, with 189 state parties, enjoys a nearly universal reach.[5] The Committee consists of twenty-three human rights experts, primarily women, who come from various disciplines and professional backgrounds, are of high moral character, and were selected based on the geographic diversity required by Article 17 of the Convention and exercise their mandate independently and impartially.[6] The Committee meets three times a year at the UN Office in Geneva.[7] It conducts Working Group sessions, constructive dialogue meetings, and plenary sessions. The administrative staff of the Office of the High Commissioner for Human Rights (OHCHR) supports the Committee's work. The Committee's primary task is "considering the progress made in implementing the present Convention."[8]

While other actors also interpret the Convention, this book spotlights the Committee's interpretation of the Convention as contained in its various outputs. All state parties to the Convention are subject to its periodic state reporting system and have delegated the Committee the power to interpret the Convention through its COs in response to state reports,[9] and GRs issued to all state parties.[10] In addition, 115 states parties have consented to CEDAW's Optional Protocol, which empowers the Committee to exercise a quasi-judicial function.[11] The Optional Protocol entered into force in 2000 and authorized the Committee to hear communications from individuals or groups complaining of

---

[4] Christine Chinkin & Marsha A. Freeman, *Introduction, in* THE UN CONVENTION ON THE ELIMINATION OF ALL FORMS OF DISCRIMINATION AGAINST WOMEN: A COMMENTARY 1 (Marsha A. Freeman et al. eds., 2012) [hereinafter 2012 COMMENTARY].

[5] Consistent with international law, the Committee interprets CEDAW in light of the rules of treaty interpretation contained in the Vienna Convention of the Law of Treaties (VCLT), which are widely regarded as part of customary international law. *See* Vienna Convention on the Law of Treaties Article 31 ex seq., May 23, 1969, 1155 U.N.T.S. 331. *See also* Patricia Schulz et al., *Introduction, in* THE UN CONVENTION ON THE ELIMINATION OF ALL FORMS OF DISCRIMINATION AGAINST WOMEN AND ITS OPTIONAL PROTOCOL 1 (Patricia Schulz et al. eds., 2d ed. 2022) [hereinafter 2022 COMMENTARY].

[6] *See* Ineke Boerefijn & Julie Fraser, *Article 17, in* 2022 COMMENTARY, *supra* note 5, at 685.

[7] *See* Ineke Boerefijn & Julie Fraser, *Article 20, in* 2022 COMMENTARY, *supra* note 5, at 727. Note that the Committee's Rules of Procedure does leave the number of regular sessions to the authorization of states parties. G.A. Res. 56/38 (SUPP), Rules of Procedure of the Committee on the Elimination of Discrimination against Women, at 6, Rule. 2 (2001) [hereinafter Rules of Procedure], https://www2.ohchr.org/english/bodies/cedaw/docs/CEDAW_Rules_en.pdf

[8] *See* Boerefijn & Fraser, *supra* note 6.

[9] *See* Boerefijn & Fraser, *Article 18, in* 2022 COMMENTARY, *supra* note 5, at 701.

[10] *See* Boerefijn & Fraser, *Article 21, in* 2022 COMMENTARY, *supra* note 5, at 733.

[11] As of Mar. 31, 2023. Optional Protocol to the Convention on the Elimination of All Forms of Discrimination against Women, Oct. 6, 1999, 2131 U.N.T.S. 83 [hereinafter Optional Protocol].

violations of the Convention and respond to these by issuing Views that interpret state parties' obligations.[12] The Committee exercises a similar interpretation function through legal findings and recommendations in Inquiry Reports authorized under the Optional Protocol but requires the state party's consent and cooperation.[13]

Despite the far-reaching state consent to monitor states parties' compliance with the Convention and to interpret their obligations, the Committee faces persistent resource and time constraints to fulfill its interpretative functions. These constraints have affected the Committee's working methods and led to a cutback on the speaking time of Committee members in the plenary sessions and a limitation of the page length of its legal documents. For instance, even when the Committee deals with several reporting cycles in one state report, it is limited to providing its COs on a maximum of twenty-one pages.[14] The speaking time for interventions of the CEDAW experts during the constructive dialogue on state reports is limited to a maximum of six minutes with two minutes for follow-up questions all monitored by speech timer.[15] These resource constraints curtail the Committee's capacity to exercise its accountability and monitoring functions.

Nonetheless, the Committee's interpretation of the Convention in its output enjoys highly persuasive and considerable legal authority, even if it is not legally binding.[16] Like those of other human rights bodies, the Committee's Views may be cited by adjudicative bodies as authoritative interpretations of the global human rights treaties under which they operate.[17] Even if the Committee itself regards its recommendations as legally non-binding, some domestic courts have started to treat the Committee's recommendations in communications as binding and implement them as such.[18] Leading international human rights scholars view the Committee's interpretations as "more or less authoritative statements."[19]

---

[12] *Id.* art. 7.

[13] *Id.* arts. 8–10.

[14] *See, e.g.,* CO on Sao Tome, CEDAW/C/STP/CO/1–5 (2023) (the Committee provided its concluding observations on the combined initial and second to fifth reports of Sao Tome and Principe on merely seventeen pages.).

[15] *See* CEDAW COMM., Rules of Procedure and Working Methods, https://www.ohchr.org/en/treaty-bodies/cedaw/rules-procedure-and-working-methods#ftn12 (last visited Mar. 18, 2023).

[16] Chinkin & Freeman, *supra* note 4, at 24. Schulz et al., *supra* note 5.

[17] *See, e.g.,* Ahmadou Sadio Diallo (Guinea v. Dem. Rep. Congo), Judgment, 2010 I.C.J. Rep. 639, ¶ 66 (relying on interpretations of the ICCPR issued by its Human Rights Committee). *But see* Application of the International Convention on the Elimination of All Forms of Racial Discrimination (Qatar v. U.A.E.), Preliminary Objections, Judgment, 2021 I.C.J. Rep. 71, ¶ 101 (disagreeing with an interpretation of the CERD issued by its committee and noting that its judgment in *Diallo* ascribed only "great weight" to interpretations issued by UN human rights treaty).

[18] *See, e.g.,* María de los Ángeles González Carreño v. Ministry of Justice, S.T.S., July 17, 2018 (R.J., No. 1263) (Spain); Machiko Kanetake, *María de los Ángeles González Carreño v. Ministry of Justice*, 113 AM. J. INT'L L. 586 (2019).

[19] INTERNATIONAL HUMAN RIGHTS: THE SUCCESSOR TO INTERNATIONAL HUMAN RIGHTS IN CONTEXT: LAW, POLITICS AND MORALS (Philip Alston & Ryan Goodman eds., 2013).

A number of issues relating to the Committee's property jurisprudence fall outside the scope of this book. This book does not provide a systematic and in-depth empirical study of the interpretative community of CEDAW experts influencing the Committee's approach to property rights.[20] In addition, this chapter is limited to the Committee's interpretation of the Convention, though other actors also interpret the Convention.[21] Moreover, the Committee does not interpret and implement Convention rights in isolation, but formal and informal interactions and processes inform the Committee's work, and through working in symbiosis and entanglement with other actors, including states, civil society, other human rights treaty bodies, international organizations, National Human Rights Institutes, academic institutions, interested individuals, and the administrative staff of the OHCHR secretariat.[22] While subsequent chapters compare the Committee's output with that of other UN human rights treaty bodies to clarify the CEDAW regime's contribution, this chapter focuses on the Committee's understanding of property rights by studying its official, written legal documents in its output. Also outside this work's scope is how property rights are implemented, translated to local contexts, and complied with in different parts of the world.

2.3 The Committee's Procedures and Output on Property Rights

The Committee has interpreted property rights as protected under the Convention in its GRs, Views in response to communications, Inquiry Reports, COs in response to state reports, and in its different follow-up procedures.[23]

---

[20] In other areas of international law, such studies have been undertaken. *See, e.g.,* Melissa Durkee, *Interpretive Entrepreneurs*, 107 VA. L. REV. 431 (2021); Michael Waibel, *Interpretive Communities in International Law, in* INTERPRETATION IN INTERNATIONAL LAW 147 (Andrea Bianchi et al. eds., 2015).

[21] The authors do not address other actors that interpret property rights under CEDAW and create or contribute to property jurisprudence under the Convention, such as states, civil society actors, individuals, other international organizations, treaty bodies, international and domestic courts, etc. *See* for a general account of international lawmaking processes ALAN BOYLE & CHRISTINE CHINKIN, THE MAKING OF INTERNATIONAL LAW (2007). For an overview of international law in domestic courts, *see* INTERNATIONAL LAW IN DOMESTIC COURTS: A CASEBOOK (André Nollkaemper et al. eds., 2018). For an overview of the use of CEDAW in domestic courts, *see* Christopher McCrudden, *Why Do National Court Judges Refer to Human Rights Treaties? A Comparative International Law Analysis of CEDAW*, 109 AM. J. INT'L L. 534 (2015).

[22] Human rights experimentalist scholars have studied these interactions in international human rights lawmaking processes. *See, e.g.,* GRÁINNE DE BÚRCA, REFRAMING HUMAN RIGHTS IN A TURBULENT ERA (2021); NINA REINERS, TRANSNATIONAL LAWMAKING COALITIONS FOR HUMAN RIGHTS (2021); Elisabeth Greif, *Upward Translations—The Role of NGOs in Promoting LGBTI*— Human Rights under the Convention on All Forms of Discrimination Against Women (CEDAW)*, 4 PEACE HUM. RTS. GOVERNANCE. 9 (2020).

[23] The chapter does not survey the Committee's "Statements," in which the Committee clarifies "its position on major international developments and issues that bear upon the implementation of the Convention." *See* CEDAW Comm., Overview of the Current Working Methods of the Committee on the Elimination of Discrimination against Women, Annex X, ¶ 34, UN Doc. A/59/38 (Part I) (2004).

These procedures generate the Committee's so-called "jurisprudence."[24] The following section examines the significance and relevance of each procedure/output and how they influence each other. Of course, diverging views exist about the hierarchy of the Committee's different procedures and the legal authority of the Committee's outputs, but each procedure/output is presented here despite differential assessments of their legal significance. The last section briefly alludes to their interrelationship.

2.3.1 General Recommendations

The Committee issues GRs pursuant to the authority granted under Article 21 of the Convention. Although Article 21 anticipates that such recommendations should be "based on the examination of reports and information received from the State Parties," the Committee also considers input from civil society and scholars in generating GRs. According to the Committee, the GRs enable the Convention to become "a dynamic instrument that accommodates the development of international law" and contribute "to the clarification and understanding of the substantive content of the Convention's articles."[25]

The Committee adopted its first GR in 1986 in its fifth session. Thus far, there does not exist a GR that exclusively dedicates itself to property rights under the Convention. However, of the thirty-nine GRs issued through December 31, 2022, seventeen contain references to property or property rights in various forms and with varying intensity.[26] For this chapter, the relevant GRs were selected when they referred to property rights in a broad sense, including property in general, land, housing, intellectual property and seed rights, access to financial credit and economic empowerment, and social benefits, as well as when they demonstrated a connection between property and gender-based violence. In addition, several GRs alluded to the protection of property rights of women with intersecting

---

[24] With the exception of Reports on Inquiries, the other CEDAW sources are standard among UN human rights treaties, as is the practice of calling the resulting interpretative output "jurisprudence." Some may consider these sources part of the "subsequent practice" of the parties to CEDAW, consistent with the Article 31(3)(b) Vienna Convention on the Law of Treaties. The International Law Commission (ILC) uses the term "pronouncements" for all "relevant factual and normative assessments by expert treaty bodies," but also acknowledges "jurisprudence" and "output" as commonly used terms. For Draft Conclusions on Subsequent Agreements and Subsequent Practice in Relation to The Interpretation of Treaties with Commentaries, see Int'l Law Comm'n, Rep. on the Work of Its Seventy-third Session, UN Doc. A/73/10 (2018). The CEDAW Committee, like other UN human rights treaty bodies, describes its output as "jurisprudence." However, the use of that term to describe all the Committee's four outputs, including its COs, or only those that result from a quasi-judicial process elicits some disagreement. The reference to "jurisprudence" is not intended to suggest that the Committee's outputs are legally binding or are treated as such by CEDAW's state parties.
[25] GR No. 28 on the Core Obligations of States parties, CEDAW/C/GC/28, ¶ 2 (2010).
[26] For a list of the relevant General Recommendations, see appendix 4.

identities, including disabled women, older women, migrant women workers, rural women, and Indigenous women.

The initiative to draft a GR generally comes from individual Committee members with expertise in certain areas or from civil society actors. One Committee member is selected to chair a Working Group to work on the newly proposed GR topic. First a concept note for the new GR must be developed. A Committee member or an OHCHR staff member, under the responsibility of the Working Group chair, prepares a draft concept note that must be approved by the Working Group and then by the Committee in a plenary session. The concept note is then published on the OHCHR website with a call for contributions to the new GR. Different actors can participate in the process of generating a new GR, including UN agencies, National Human Rights Institutes, NGOs, or other human rights mechanisms such as Special Rapporteurs.

A Committee member, external consultant, or an OHCHR staff member, based on the submissions received by contributors, develops the draft for the new GR. In addition, the Working Group chair frequently receives support, such as background research, from one or more academic institutions. Once the Working Group concludes the drafting process of the new GR, the Committee discusses and adopts a draft text in the plenary before it publishes the draft GR on the OHCHR website with a call for comments. These comments then shape the final proposal prepared by the Working Group, which is eventually presented to the plenary for adoption as the new GR.[27]

Committee members can voluntarily join working groups on GRs, depending on their interests and expertise. In addition, there are no requirements on the size or composition of the Working Group regarding the regional group or the professional background of Committee members. Thus, Committee members with both legal and non-legal backgrounds participate in the drafting process for GRs.

However, the background of Committee members influences the content of GRs. For instance, according to background conversations with CEDAW experts, the Committee members who participated in the drafting of GR 34 on rural women did not share a common view of the nature of the property or land rights at issue. Some members have seen the underlying property rights as purely collective, while a few insisted on distinguishing private property from collective notions of property. Given such disagreements, GRs, including GR 34, do not attempt to provide a single definition of "property" applicable to the Convention as a whole.

---

[27] *See* Boerefijn & Fraser, *Article 21, supra* note 10.

While it is generally not publicly known why the Committee chooses to work on a new GR at a certain time, frequently an interpretation gap or lack of consistency in applying certain Convention provisions has given rise to the development of a new GR. For the Committee to discuss an issue that affects the implementation of women's rights in a GR, it relies "on its experience in reviewing States' reports and in the procedures under the Optional Protocol."[28]

Furthermore, the various procedures have a reciprocal influence on each other. The work on a new GR may contribute to increased attention to certain provisions in the Convention when generating outputs. For instance, during the drafting of GR 29 on economic consequences of marriage and family, Committee members appeared more likely to direct attention to marriage/family law matters during the state reporting process and in the resulting COs. Thus, these targeted COs influenced the content of GR 29.[29]

The interpretive value of previously adopted GRs is particularly evident when the underlying principle or concept is not one found explicitly in the Convention but was developed in a GR framework. For instance, in GRs 12, 19, and 35, the Committee established and gave meaning to the prohibition of gender-based violence, though the text of the Convention does not include an explicit prohibition of gender-based violence. Consequently, the Committee references GR 19 or GR 35 when it provides its Views on communications dealing with gender-based violence.

In general, the Committee frequently cites, as the relevant authority, not only the text of the Convention but its own previously issued GRs. Common references to GRs throughout the Committee's jurisprudence indicate that it is one of the most important outputs under the Convention.

2.3.2 Communications

The Optional Protocol that entered into force in 2000 introduced the quasi-judicial mechanism of communications.[30] Communications provide individuals and groups with a right to complain to the Committee about human rights violations upon exhaustion of domestic remedies.[31]

While there exists no conclusive data about the number of communications on which the Committee has adopted Views, the Committee has issued relatively few Views in response to communications. According to the statistics published by the OHCHR secretariat dating back to January 2020, since the entrance into

---

[28] *Id.*
[29] Background conversation on file with the authors.
[30] *See generally*, Optional Protocol, *supra* note 11.
[31] *Id.* arts. 1, 2, & 4.

force of the Optional Protocol in 2000 the Committee had addressed 155 communications, resulting in 72 discontinuances or findings of inadmissibility but only 37 adoptions of Views with 46 pending communications.[32] As of March 15, 2023, the OHCHR jurisprudence database lists 55 communications in which the Committee decided on the merits, 70 inadmissibility decisions, and discontinued 16 communications. As of February 2023, 46 communications are pending.[33] The last adopted decision on the merits in the OHCHR jurisprudence database dates back to October 2022. However, while the systematic analysis of the Committee's annual reports could offer additional insights, there exists no publicly available data on the number of registered communications and their posture.[34]

This chapter presents fourteen communications where the Committee has taken a decision on the merits and touches upon various property issues.[35] The selection was made based on the search results in the OHCHR jurisprudence using the relevant articles[36] and a list of search words.[37] The first decision of the Committee was added manually because it was not contained in the database. Several communications show the complex relationships between gender-based violence and property rights. Almost all selected communications deal with women who experience intersectional discrimination. Notably, the Committee's jurisprudence regarding women's property rights is growing. Based on the chart of pending cases from February 2023, several communications appear to deal with property rights violations and are currently under the Committee's review.[38,39]

---

[32] STATUS OF COMMUNICATIONS REGISTERED BY CEDAW UNDER THE OPTIONAL PROTOCOL, information as of Jan. 28, 2020, https://view.officeapps.live.com/op/view.aspx?src=https%3A%2F%2Fwww.ohchr.org%2Fsites%2Fdefault%2Ffiles%2FDocuments%2FHRBodies%2FCEDAW%2FStatisticalSurvey.xls&wdOrigin=BROWSELINK (last visited Mar. 18, 2023).

[33] OFF. OF HUM. RTS. FOR THE HIGH COMMISSIONER, TABLE OF PENDING CASES BEFORE THE COMMITTEE ON THE ELIMINATION OF ALL FORMS OF DISCRIMINATION AGAINST WOMEN, as of Feb. 2023, https://view.officeapps.live.com/op/view.aspx?src=https%3A%2F%2Fwww.ohchr.org%2Fsites%2Fdefault%2Ffiles%2FDocuments%2FHRBodies%2FCEDAW%2FPendingCases.docx&wdOrigin=BROWSELINK (last visited Mar. 18, 2023) [hereinafter Table of Pending Cases].

[34] Meghan Campbell & Jane Connors, *Optional Protocol*, *in* 2022 COMMENTARY, *supra* note 5.

[35] For Communications mentioning property rights, *see* appendix 5. The chapter does not survey inadmissibility decisions.

[36] Convention on the Elimination of All Forms of Discrimination Against Women art. 11(1)(e) and (2)(b), chapeau of art. 13, arts. 14(2)(c), (g), and (h), 15, and 16(1)(h), *opened for signature* Dec. 18, 1979, 1249 U.N.T.S. 13.

[37] The search words "property," "housing," "land," and "social security" were used.

[38] The subject matters of pending individual communications deal with a lack of adequate protection measures in a domestic violence case regarding Argentina (No. 127/2018), a land rights dispute regarding Cambodia (No. 146/2019), dismissal of a woman from work during her maternity leave regarding Belarus (No. 150/2019), the confiscation of property of a woman co-founder and director of a company regarding Turkmenistan (No. 166/2021), and gender stereotypes about the division of responsibilities in marriage regarding Switzerland (No. 176/2021). *See also* Table of Pending Cases, *supra* note 33.

[39] After the research for this book concluded on March 15, 2023, the Committee adopted Views concerning X. v. Cambodia, CEDAW/C/85/D146/2019 (2023), which is listed as a pending decision

The communications procedure is frequently described as a quasi-judicial function of the Committee. However, the Committee does not operate like a court and its Views are not legally binding. According to Article 3 of the Optional Protocol, the entire procedure is based on written submissions by the author of the communication and the responding state. In rare instances, the Committee may issue its View based only on the communicant's submission, when the respondent state party fails to make its own submission to the Committee.[40]

The CEDAW Working Group on Communications usually consists of five members that serve for two years and are appointed by the regional groups.[41] According to the Working Group's working methods, the members of the Working Group should have a legal background. It appears that most have been, even if there is no formal requirement that they need to be lawyers.[42] It undertakes the drafting of the Committee's Views regarding communications with the assistance of the OHCHR secretariat's Petition Unit. While the written procedure extends over the entire year, the Working Group on Communications

---

in *supra* note 38. This communication constitutes one of the CEDAW Committee's most relevant decisions on property rights. The findings of the Committee will be briefly discussed here. The communication dealt with the land rights of X., a rural woman who was defending her rights in the context of a private land development project. The Committee found a violation of X.'s rights under Articles 2 (c)–(e); 3; 14 (1) and (2) (a), (g), and (h); and 15 (1) of the Convention, interpreted in light of a number of General Recommendations of the Committee (¶ 7). Importantly, the Committee recalled in its Views that "forced eviction is not a gender-neutral phenomenon" (¶ 6.2). It condemned the lack of state protection that X. received despite her many claims and petitions against the private developer that destroyed her land and entitlements, and despite the death threats that she had received (¶ 6.2). The Committee also saw X.'s rights breached due to Cambodia's failure to ensure her effective participation at all levels of the land development project (¶ 6.3). Furthermore, the Committee condemned the lack of equal protection of the law as well as the absence of any legal remedy provided to the victim (¶ 6.4–6.5). The Committee recommended that Cambodia provide reparation and adequate compensation and that the state should ensure that X. could enjoy her rightful access to her land and defend her community's interests safely and freely (¶8 (a)). On a general level, the Committee recommended undertaking legislative and policy measures, with adequate due process to protect rural women's right of access to land and tenure security. The Committee also requested that Cambodia investigates forced evictions and the intimidation of land rights defenders; such that evicted and relocated communities can realize their rights in a safe and enabling environment (¶ 8 (b) (i)–(v)). The Committee recommended judicial training on the Convention, to raise awareness among the judiciary of the human rights of rural women and women human rights defenders (¶ 8 (b) (vi)). Cambodia has thus far failed to submit any observations to the Committee. See the brief preliminary discussion in chapter 5, notes 141–142 and chapter 7, note 19.

[40] *See, e.g.,* Views concerning E.S. and S.C. v. Tanzania, CEDAW/C/60/D/48/2013 (2015). In the usual case, both the author of the communication and the state make submissions.

[41] *See* Rules of Procedure, *supra* note 7, Rule 62. CEDAW Comm., Working Methods of the Committee on the Elimination of Discrimination against Women and Its Working Group on Individual Communications Received Under the Optional Protocol to the CEDAW Convention, Rule 1 & 2 (Nov. 17, 2020), https://www.ohchr.org/en/treaty-bodies/cedaw/individual-communications [hereinafter Working Methods].

[42] At the bottom of the first pages of each Communication, the Committee members who worked on the communication are listed. Working Methods, *supra* note 41.

currently meets for a total of ten days per year before, during and after the three sessions.[43]

The Working Group submits a draft decision to the Committee with its recommendations for discussion and final adoption. The recommendations will indicate whether they have been adopted by consensus or by the majority of the Working Group members.[44]

The recommendations included in the Committee's Views on communications are split into two parts. They first aim to remedy the violation of the individual complainant through individual recommendations. Second, the Committee provides the state party with a set of more general recommendations addressing structural issues with the goal to prevent future violations.

2.3.3 Inquiry Reports

The Committee issues Inquiry Reports based on Articles 8 and 9 of the Optional Protocol, when "the Committee receives reliable information indicating grave or systematic violations by a state Party of rights set forth in the Convention."[45] The Committee has defined those grave and systematic violations in its jurisprudence and has demonstrated that neither criterion must be cumulatively met.[46] Grave violations are determined "by the scale, prevalence, nature of the harm and impact of the violation."[47] Systematic violations are defined as "intentionally discriminatory law or the result of discriminatory laws, with or without an intention to discriminate,"[48] and "a significant and persistent pattern of violations that could not result from a random occurrence, or there is a prevalent pattern of violations that occurred as a result of policies that disproportionately discriminate against women. . . ."[49]

Inquiries occur only on the condition that the state has ratified the Optional Protocol[50] and not opted out of the inquiry procedure.[51] If the state under investigation agrees, "to cooperate in the examination of the information," such states may submit their observations.[52] In addition, the Committee may only conduct a visit within the state territory upon invitation of the state party, and the Committee may designate one or more of its members to conduct an inquiry

---

[43] *See id.* Rule 4. *See also* Boerefijn & Fraser, *Article 20,* in 2022 COMMENTARY, *supra* note 7.
[44] *See* Working Methods, *supra* note 41, Rule 27.
[45] Optional Protocol, *supra* note 11, art. 8(1).
[46] Rep. of the Inquiry concerning Canada, CEDAW/C/OP.8/CAN/1, ¶ 214 (2015).
[47] *Id.* ¶ 213. *See also* Rep. of the Inquiry concerning Philippines, CEDAW/C/OP.8/PHL/1, ¶ 47 (2015).
[48] Rep. of Philippines, *supra* note 47, ¶ 48.
[49] *Id.*
[50] *Id.* art. 8(2).
[51] *Id.* art. 10.
[52] Optional Protocol, *supra* note 11, art. 8(1).

and to report urgently to the Committee. In general, the Committee conducts inquiries confidentially and seeks the states parties' cooperation at all stages.[53] At the end of the procedure, the Committee publishes the full Inquiry Report on its website. The Optional Protocol provides that "the State Party concerned shall, within six months of receiving the findings, comments and recommendations transmitted by the Committee, submit its observations to the Committee."[54] In addition, at the end of the six-month period, the Committee may "invite the State party concerned to inform it of measures taken in response to such an inquiry."[55]

Under the Optional Protocol's inquiry procedure, the Committee has issued Inquiry Reports regarding seven countries (as of March 2023). None of them deals with property rights violations. However, since the Inquiry Reports on Canada and South Africa raised some property rights issues in the gender-based violence context, these are presented in this chapter.[56]

The Inquiry Reports allow for garnering a better understanding of the Committee's interpretation of human rights violations because they constitute in-depth investigations of human rights violations. Though the inquiry procedure is based on civil society input and relies on an extensive exchange between the state party and the Committee with an elaborate follow-up procedure, this chapter focuses only on the output in the Committee's Inquiry Reports.

2.3.4 Concluding Observations

The states parties reporting has been the Committee's leading and oldest procedure for reviewing states parties' implementation of Convention obligations.[57] The Committee has adopted COs in response to states parties' reports since 1994. Because the Committee officially provides COs on state reports on a four-year cycle—even though states parties frequently do not submit their state reports on time or submit one report for several reporting cycles—COs provide insights about what the Committee thinks is necessary to comply with the Convention's requirement of equal treatment with respect to property over time and with respect to all of the state parties of CEDAW. The state reporting cycle is the only procedure of the Committee that enables identification of universal trends regarding property rights violations, given that all state parties must submit state reports.

The COs included in this chapter were selected based on a search of the Universal Human Rights Index using the following terms: property, land,

---

[53] *Id.* art. 8(5).
[54] *Id.* art. 8(4).
[55] *Id.* art. 9(2).
[56] For Inquiry Reports mentioning property rights, *see* appendix 6.
[57] CEDAW, *supra* note 1, art. 18. *See also* Boerefijn & Fraser, *supra* note 9.

land-grabbing, social benefits, housing, shelter, protection and eviction order, access to justice, financial credit, entrepreneur, intellectual property, seed, due diligence, and access to justice. The COs were first surveyed from 2007 through October 2020, and then selectively updated to cover 2021–2022.[58] The results were then organized and analyzed with regard to different subsidiary aspects of property rights.

The COs presented in this chapter result mostly from the standard state reporting procedure. However, as part of broader human rights treaty body reform with the intention of strengthening and enhancing the functioning of the human rights treaty body system,[59] the Committee has switched to a simplified reporting procedure in the past years. The simplified reporting procedure was first made available from January 1, 2015, on a pilot basis, but then suspended the procedure before reinstating it in March 2018. At its eighty-second session in June 2022, the Committee decided to shift from an opt-in model for the simplified reporting procedure to an opt-out model. By September 20, 2022, the Committee had automatically applied the simplified reporting procedure to all state parties as a default procedure unless they have actively opted out and continue reporting under the standard state reporting procedure.[60]

Before the constructive dialogue can take place in either the standard or the simplified reporting procedure, states must report to the Committee in writing and civil society may submit shadow reports on the state report. Other UN specialized agencies may also make submissions and provide information about the state party under review to the Committee.

Under the Standard Reporting Procedure, the reporting procedure starts with the state party's submission of a state report. Based on this state report, civil society may submit a shadow report. Then, the Committee prepares a list of issues prior to reporting in the Pre-Sessional Working Group that the state party must respond to and based on which civil society can make additional submissions before the constructive dialogue takes place. Only then does the constructive dialogue start based on the state report and the reply to the list of issues prior to reporting.

Under the Simplified Reporting Procedure, the procedure no longer starts with a state report, rather the Committee first prepares a list of issues prior to reporting in the Pre-Sessional Working Group. The list of issues prior to reporting consists of maximum twenty-five paragraphs and must not raise more

---

[58] *See* UNIVERSAL HUMAN RIGHTS INDEX, https://uhri.ohchr.org/en/ (last visited Mar. 18, 2023).
[59] G.A. Res. 68/268, Strengthening and Enhancing the Effective Functioning of the Human Rights Treaty Body System (Apr. 21, 2014).
[60] *See* Guidance Note for States Parties for the Preparation of Reports under Article 18 of the Convention on the Elimination of All Forms of Discrimination against Women in the context of the Sustainable Development Goals, CEDAW/C/74/3/Rev.1, ¶ 7 (Sept. 27, 2022).

than seventy-five questions in addition to an introductory paragraph that asks states to provide information on the measures undertaken to implement the Committee's previous COs.[61] Civil society may submit a first shadow report to the Committee to inform the drafting of this list of issues prior to reporting. The state party's reply to the list of issues prior to reporting constitutes their state report under Article 18 of the Convention. Thus, under simplified reporting, the state report consists merely of the state's reply to the list of issues prior to reporting. This simplification makes the state report more focused and should alleviate the labor involved in state reporting leading to excessive delays and low-quality state reports. Civil society may submit a second shadow report to inform the constructive dialogue once this state report has been issued.

The Committee selects a Country Rapporteur for every state party under review. The Country Rapporteur briefs all Committee members about the country, prepares the list of issues prior to reporting in the Pre-Sessional Working Group and leads the constructive dialogue. In addition, the Committee forms a country task force currently consisting of six CEDAW experts (previously nine) that addresses questions to the state delegation in the constructive dialogue.

The constructive dialogue follows the same format and structure under the standard and the simplified reporting procedure. Usually, the Committee members address all articles of the Convention from Articles 1–16. One Committee member is assigned as an expert to each article, though Articles 1 and 2, 7 and 8, and 15 and 16 are clustered as they address similar topics.[62] However, all Committee members may ask questions in the constructive dialogue. Nevertheless, the constructive dialogue is subject to time constraints and asymmetry given that state delegations' speaking time is less restricted than those of Committee members.[63]

The Committee members participating in the state reporting procedure have diverse backgrounds, though the Country Rapporteur typically comes from the same regional group as the state party under review. The diverse background of Committee members who participate in the state reporting procedure is valued as a strength. For instance, Committee members with nonlegal backgrounds often have a better sense of structural issues in societies than lawyers who take a narrow legal approach. CEDAW experts with nonlegal backgrounds also tend to be closer to civil society actors.[64]

---

[61] *See* Rules of Procedure and Working Methods, *supra* note 15.

[62] *See* Rules of Procedure and Working Methods, *supra* note 15.

[63] Several CEDAW experts reported on these limitations. *See* Rules of Procedure and Working Methods, *supra* note 15.

[64] Several CEDAW experts confirmed the advantages of diverse professional backgrounds of Committee members. *See* Ivona Truscan, *Diversity in Membership of the UN Human Rights Treaty Bodies*, Geneva Academy 5, 11, 16, 24, 26, 30 (Feb. 2018), https://www.geneva-academy.ch/joomlatools-files/docman-files/Diversity%20in%20Treaty%20Bodies%20Membership.pdf.

Civil society plays an important role in the constructive dialogue not only thanks to the important background information that they have supplied through shadow reports but also through informal exchanges and meetings before and during the constructive dialogue. Usually, the country task force facilitates public and confidential meetings with civil society actors before the constructive dialogue takes place. This exchange allows the designated Committee members reviewing that country to receive a firsthand impression. Not all meetings between civil society actors and the Committee are accessible to the public to protect civil society actors from reprisal and to ensure an open information exchange.

After the constructive dialogue, the Committee adopts COs in a confidential session as a plenary. They COs follow a twofold structure: the Committee (1) identifies and expresses concerns, and (2) provides recommendations about how to improve the states parties' implementation of the Convention. The Country Rapporteur prepares the first draft of COs with the secretariat's support and other Committee members' input. A second draft is then circulated, and the Committee then adopts the COs by consensus after the constructive dialogue in closed plenary meetings.[65] The scholars Ineke Boerefijn and Julie Fraser view the Committee's recommendations contained in COs as a reflection of "the role of the Committee as a quasi-judicial body not rendering judgments but working as a partner with states parties in the Convention's domestic implementation."[66]

Though COs are not relied upon as legally authoritative, in contrast with Views on communications and legal findings in Inquiry Reports, COs fulfill important legal functions: from a state's perspective, COs are crucial because they provide a periodic legal assessment of their compliance with the Convention. More generally, they serve the progressive development of the Convention over time in specific state contexts and may motivate the formulation of new GRs. The COs are also relied upon in Views on communications, and sometimes the Committee repeats in its Views what it has already recommended to state parties in its COs. Likewise, the Committee in its COs occasionally follows up on the recommendations expressed in its Views.

2.3.5 Follow-Up Procedures

The Optional Protocol foresees follow-up procedures on communications[67] and Inquiry Reports.[68] In addition, in 2008, in its forty-first session, the Committee

---

[65] See also Boerefijn & Fraser, *supra* note 9.
[66] *Id.*
[67] Optional Protocol, art. 7(4)–(5).
[68] *Id.* art. 9.

adopted the follow-up procedure for Concluding Observations.[69] However, it is not explicitly included in the Convention as a procedure.

2.3.5.1 Follow-Up on Communications

The Working Group on Communications conducts the follow-up on communications. The members of the Working Group act as follow-up rapporteurs and facilitate an exchange with the states parties through meetings and in writing, using assessment criteria reaching from satisfactory, partially satisfactory to unsatisfactory.[70] If follow-up efforts fail to produce the desired results, the Committee ceases the dialogue and finds an unsatisfactory implementation of the Committee's recommendations.

2.3.5.2 Follow-Up on Inquiry Reports

The Optional Protocol foresees a follow-up procedure on inquiries. The Committee has the power to request information from the state focused on whether it has implemented the Committee's recommendations. This follow-up procedure is in addition to the requirement under Article 8(4) of the Optional Protocol, where state parties must provide their observations to the Committee within six months after the issuance of the Inquiry Report.

2.3.5.3 Follow-Up on Concluding Observations

The follow-up on COs requires states to provide information to the Committee "on steps taken to implement specific recommendations . . . within a specific time period."[71] Usually, the Committee selects two recommendations on which state parties must submit information within two years regarding their measures for implementation. For these purposes, it is important that COs are "concrete, achievable, but non-prescriptive recommendations" so that a follow-up on implementation is possible for states parties.[72] The Committee's rapporteur, on follow-up of COs and other Committee members, assesses the states parties' compliance based on a spectrum from "satisfactory" to "unsatisfactory." The follow-up procedure for each state party is accessible on the OHCHR's web page.[73]

---

[69] The Committee only adopted the follow-up procedure for Concluding Observations at its forty-first session in 2008). *See also* Boerefijn & Fraser, *supra* note 9.
[70] *See* Rules of Procedure, *supra* note 7, Rule 73. Working methods, *supra* note 41, Rule 30.
[71] Boerefijn & Fraser, *supra* note 9.
[72] *Id.*
[73] *See* FOLLOW-UP TO CONCLUDING OBSERVATIONS, https://www.ohchr.org/en/treaty-bodies/cedaw/follow-concluding-observations (last visited Mar. 18, 2023). For Follow-up Concluding Observations by States, *see* https://tbinternet.ohchr.org/_layouts/15/TreatyBodyExternal/FollowUp.aspx?Treaty=CEDAW&Lang=en (last visited Mar. 19, 2023).

2.4 Property Rights in Marriage and Family Relations

2.4.1 The Convention and General Recommendations

Articles 15 and 16(1)(h) are the core provisions that govern women's property rights under CEDAW. They overlap and frequently are combined to protect women's property rights in family relations. In addition, in GR 21 and 29, the Committee addresses equality in marriage and family relations as well as the economic consequences of these relations. The Committee also addresses intersectional forms of discrimination against women concerning their property rights in family relations, with respect to older women in GR 27, women in conflict prevention in GR 30, and rural women in GR 34.

2.4.1.1 Articles 15 and 16(1)(h)

Article 15(1) presents the core norm on equality between men and women: "State Parties shall accord to women equality with men before the law." Article 15(2) requires states to "accord to women, in civil matters, a legal capacity identical to that of men and the same opportunities to exercise that capacity" and mandates that states "shall give women equal rights . . . to administer property . . ." Based on Article 15, the Committee has also defined women's access to justice.

Article 16 concerns equality between women and men in all aspects of marriage, including dissolution of marriage. Article 16(1)(h) addresses marriage-based restrictions on women's property rights and their economic status and requires

> the same rights for both spouses in respect of the ownership, acquisition, management, administration, enjoyment, and disposition of property, whether free of charge or for a valuable consideration.

Without legal capacity as provided in Article 15, women would not be able to exercise the property rights guaranteed in Article 16(1)(h). The combined articles protect women's status and property rights within the family.[74]

2.4.1.2 GRs 21 and 29 on Women's Property Rights in Family Relations

GR 29 on Economic Consequences of Marriage, Family Relations and Their Dissolution is one of the most important GRs because it deals with the family as

---

[74] For a detailed account of Articles 15 and 16, see chapter 1, section X, at X. See also Aruna D. Nairan, *Article 15*, in 2022 COMMENTARY, *supra* note 5, at 553; Ruth Halperin-Kaddari & Marsha Freeman, *Article 16*, in 2022 COMMENTARY, *supra* note 5, at 577–627.

an "economic construct."[75] When describing the structures impacting women's property rights, the Committee diagnoses that "family structures, gendered labour division within the family and family laws affect women's economic well-being no less than labour market structures and labour laws."[76]

According to the Committee's analysis, "inequality in the family underlies all other aspects of discrimination against women and is often justified in the name of ideology, tradition and culture."[77] It highlights that "in many States, the rights and responsibilities of married partners are governed by the principles of civil or common law, religious or customary laws and practices . . . that discriminate against women and do not comply with . . . the Convention."[78] Moreover, states that govern the rights and responsibilities of married partners by such legal arrangements have entered reservations to all, or parts, of Articles 2 and 16. Opining that these reservations are incompatible with the object and purpose of the treaty, the Committee calls on states to withdraw them.[79]

The Committee expresses concern about the economic condition of women in all stages of family relationships. Separation and divorce mean income loss and dependence on welfare. Poverty is disproportionately common in female-headed households, an issue further exacerbated by the global features of the market economy and its crises. The Committee notes, "[d]espite women's contributions to the economic well-being of the family, their economic inferiority permeates all stages of family relationships, often owing to their responsibility for dependents."[80] The Committee notes that women universally share the experience of being "worse off economically than men in family relationships and following the dissolution of those relationships."[81] Nonetheless, the Committee also highlights that "the entitlement of women to equality within the family is universally acknowledged."[82]

Despite this equality requirement, exemptions from equal protection clauses in constitutions persist regarding personal status laws "relating to marriage, divorce, distribution of marital property, inheritance, guardianship, adoption and other such matters."[83] Some states leave these matters to the self-regulation of ethnic and religious communities within the state party, leading to discriminatory effects.[84] In addition, discriminatory aspects in family law persist

---

[75] GR No. 29 on Economic Consequences of Marriage, Family Relations and Their Dissolution, CEDAW/C/GC/29, ¶ 1 (2013).
[76] *Id.* ¶ 1.
[77] *Id.* ¶ 2.
[78] *Id.* ¶ 2.
[79] *Id.* ¶ 3.
[80] *Id.* ¶ 4
[81] *Id.* ¶ 5
[82] *Id.* ¶ 7.
[83] *Id.*
[84] *Id.*

in some state parties and require revision.[85] All these constitutional and legal arrangements violate "article 2 in conjunction with articles 5, 15 and 16 of the Convention."[86] The Committee recommended that "States parties should guarantee equality between women and men in their constitutions and should eliminate any constitutional exemptions that would serve to preserve discriminatory laws and practices with regard to family relations."[87]

GR 29 addresses various forms of family: marriages (civil, customary, religious), registered partnerships, and *de facto* unions.[88] Moreover, it provides for economic protection of persons living in same-sex relationships when they are recognized in states parties.[89]

The Committee recommends implementing a system of marriage registration, legally requiring it, and raising awareness about marriage registration because it leads to "the protection of property issues upon dissolution of the marriage by death or divorce."[90]

The Committee considers different partnerships and recommends how states should regulate them because of their economic consequences for women, including polygamous relationships, registered partnerships, and *de facto* partnerships. Regarding polygamous marriages, the Committee called for a prohibition because of their serious financial consequences for the wife and her dependents.[91] The Committee asks states parties "to take all legislative and policy measures needed to abolish polygamous marriages."[92] However, it also recognizes that states should protect the economic rights of wives in polygamous marriages.[93] Regarding registered partnerships, the Committee emphasizes the importance of "equal rights, responsibilities and treatment between the partners in economic matters."[94] The Committee notes that when *de facto* partnerships are not legally regulated, "women may be exposed to economic risks when a cohabiting relationship ends, including when they have contributed to maintaining a household and to building other assets."[95] Accordingly, states must eliminate discrimination as part of "State party obligations under article 16(1)" and take "the necessary measures to ensure the protection of economic rights" of women in *de facto* unions.[96]

---

[85] *Id.*
[86] *Id.*
[87] *Id.* ¶ 11.
[88] *Id.* ¶¶ 16–24.
[89] *Id.* ¶ 24
[90] *Id.* ¶ 25.
[91] *Id.* ¶ 27. GR No. 21 on Equality in Marriage and Family Relations, A/49/38, ¶ 14 (1994).
[92] GR No. 29, *supra* note 75, ¶ 28.
[93] *Id.* ¶ 28.
[94] *Id.* ¶ 29.
[95] *Id.* ¶ 30.
[96] *Id.* ¶ 31.

The Committee commented on the economic aspects of different stages and scenarios of a relationship, including at the formation of the relationship and the duration of the relationship, cases of divorce and separation, and cases of widowhood.

During the marriage, the Committee notes that "discriminatory systems of property management" persist. They designate the man as the head of household or the sole economic agent.[97] The legal exclusion of women from managing property, for instance, is a problem in community property regimes.[98] The Committee recommended providing "equal access by both spouses to the marital property and equal legal capacity to manage it. [States parties] should ensure that the right of women to own, acquire, manage, administer, and enjoy separate or non-marital property is equal to that of men."[99]

In case of divorce and dissolution of relationships, the Committee views the financial consequences of fault-based divorce regimes as especially problematic because such regimes frequently disadvantage women and are "abused by husbands to eliminate any financial obligation towards their wives."[100] The Committee recommends a set of measures to state parties, including revising provisions that allow for abuse and free husbands of their financial obligations. For instance, states parties should compensate wives for their "contributions ... to the family's economic well-being during the marriage" in fault-based divorce regimes.[101]

The Committee made several recommendations to avoid discrimination against women in the distribution of property and maintenance after divorce or separation and to protect their economic status. The Committee raised awareness for women's economic vulnerability in the post-dissolution situation:

> Women may be barred from claiming property rights for lack of recognized capacity to own or manage property, or the property regime may not recognize property accumulated during the marriage as subject to division between the parties. Interrupted education and employment histories and childcare responsibilities frequently prevent women from establishing a path to paid employment (opportunity cost) sufficient to support their post-dissolution family. These social and economic factors also prevent women living under a regime of separate property from increasing their individual property during marriage.[102]

---

[97] Id. ¶ 36.
[98] Id. ¶ 37.
[99] Id. ¶ 38.
[100] Id. ¶ 39.
[101] Id. ¶ 40.
[102] Id. ¶ 44.

The Committee issued several guiding principles to avoid property disenfranchisements of women upon the dissolution of marriage: (1) "... [T]he economic advantages and disadvantages ... should be borne equally by both parties"; (2) "The division of roles and functions during the spouses' life together should not result in detrimental economic consequences for either party"; (3) There should be "equality between the parties in the division of all property accumulated during the marriage"; (4) "States parties should recognize the value of indirect, including non-financial, contributions with regard to the acquisition of property acquired during the marriage"; and (5) "States parties should provide for equal formal and de facto legal capacity to own and manage property."[103]

Furthermore, the Committee made specific recommendations about how to achieve both formal and substantive equality with respect to property rights upon the dissolution of marriage. It encouraged states parties to recognize "use rights in property related to livelihood or compensation in order to provide for replacement of property-related livelihood."[104] Furthermore, it asked states to provide "adequate housing to replace the use of the family home."[105] States should provide "equality ... [and] the right to choose property regime, and an understanding of the consequences of each regime," listing community, separate, and hybrid property as different marital property regimes.[106] The marital property subject to division should include "the present-value computation of deferred compensation, pension or other post-dissolution payments resulting from contributions made during the marriage, such as life insurance policies."[107] Importantly, the Committee asks state parties to value

> non-financial contributions to marital property subject to division, including household and family care, lost economic opportunity and tangible or intangible contributions to either spouse's career development and other economic activity and to the development of his or her human capital.[108]

The Committee develops guidelines about property rights after death. It expresses the concern that widows are systematically denied equality with regard to their inheritance and in an economically vulnerable position due to the absence of laws or customs that demand equality or due to a lack of enforcement of existing law that requires formal equality.[109] The Committee calls on states parties "to adopt laws of intestate succession that ... ensure ... [e]qual treatment

---

[103] Id. ¶¶ 45–47.
[104] Id. ¶ 47.
[105] Id.
[106] Id.
[107] Id.
[108] Id.
[109] Id. ¶ 49.

of surviving females and males."[110] The Committee also provides that "States parties are obligated to adopt laws relating to the making of wills that provide equal rights to women and men as testators, heirs and beneficiaries."[111]

The Committee expresses special concerns about customary forms of landholding limiting individual disposal rights upon death of the spouse. Wives may have to "leave the land or may be required to marry a brother of the deceased in order to remain on the land."[112] The existence of children may decide if they can remain on the land. The Committee asks states parties to ensure by law that "customary succession to use rights or title to land cannot be conditioned on forced marriage to a deceased spouse's brother (levirate marriage) or any other person, or on the existence or absence of minor children of the marriage."[113]

The Committee also expresses its concern that widows are subjected to "property dispossession" or "property grabbing" where "the relatives of a deceased husband, claiming customary rights, dispossess the widow and her children from property accumulated during the marriage, including property that is not held according to custom."[114] They remove, ignore, and sometimes even banish widows from the community.[115] The Committee requires states to ensure that "disinheritance of the surviving spouse is prohibited" and that "property dispossession/grabbing" is criminalized, and that "offenders are duly prosecuted."[116]

2.4.1.3 GRs on Intersectional Discrimination on Women's Property Rights in Family Relations

Several GRs have addressed the impact of intersecting identities and of the circumstances of women when they seek to claim property rights in family relations, for instance of older women, women in conflict situations, and rural women.

According to GR 27, older women are particularly vulnerable to property disenfranchisement in family relations:

> Under some statutory and customary laws, women do not have the right to inherit and administer marital property on the death of their spouse. Some legal systems justify this by providing widows with other means of economic security, such as support payments from the deceased's estate. However, in reality, such provisions are seldom enforced, and widows are often left destitute. Some

---

[110] *Id.* ¶ 53.
[111] *Id.* ¶ 52.
[112] *Id.* ¶ 50.
[113] *Id.* ¶ 53.
[114] *Id.* ¶ 50.
[115] *Id.*
[116] *Id.* ¶ 53.

laws particularly discriminate against older widows, and some widows are victims of "property grabbing."[117]

GR 27 also raises awareness of the negative impact when older women do not have legal capacity.[118] The Committee urged state parties to GR 27 to "enable older women to seek redress for and resolve infringements of their rights, including the right to administer property...."[119]

GR 27 also recommends repealing discriminatory legislation against older women "in the area of marriage and in the event of its dissolution, including with regard to property and inheritance."[120] Older women should be protected from land-grabbing.[121] The Committee also encourages adoption of "laws of intestate succession that comply with their obligations under the Convention."[122] Older women in polygamous unions are especially precarious. The Committee recommends ensuring "that upon the death of a polygamous husband, his estate is shared equally among his wives and their respective children."[123]

According to GR 30, women in conflict situations face increased vulnerability in their equal access to property as guaranteed by Article 16(1)(h). The number of female-headed households increases in post-conflict situations because of family separation, widowhood, and displacement. Women's lack of legal title to land and property may jeopardize their livelihood.[124]

GR 34 on Rural Women stipulates rural women's equality before the law and their equal rights in marriage based on Articles 15 and 16, GR 21, and GR 29.[125] Pointing to Article 15's assertion of rural women's equality before the law, GR 34 notes that rural women enjoy the same legal capacity as men, including administering property independent of their husbands or male guardians.[126] GR 34 also emphasizes rural women's equal rights in marriage based on Article 16, GR 21, and GR 29. This includes their right "to marital property upon divorce or death of their spouse and to maintenance or alimony."[127] The Committee asks state parties to "ensure that legislation guarantees rural women's rights to land, water and other natural resources on an equal basis with men, irrespective of

---

[117] GR No. 27 on Older Women and Protection of Their Human Rights, CEDAW/C/GC/27, ¶ 26 (2010).
[118] Id. ¶ 27.
[119] Id. ¶ 34.
[120] Id. ¶ 51.
[121] Id. ¶ 52.
[122] Id.
[123] Id. ¶ 53.
[124] Id. ¶ 63.
[125] GR No. 34 on the Rights of Rural Women, CEDAW/C/GC/34, ¶¶ 30–33, 59 (2016).
[126] Id. ¶¶ 30–31.
[127] Id. ¶¶ 33.

their civil and marital status or of a male guardian or guarantor, and that they have full legal capacity."[128]

2.4.2 Communications

The Committee decided two communications based on Article 16(1)(h), finding a violation in both.[129] *Cecilia Kell v. Canada* deals with a violation under Article 16(1)(h) because Kell had been denied her right to administer her property. *E.S. and S.C. v. United Republic of Tanzania* concerns the surviving wives' property rights in inheritance.

2.4.2.1 *Cecilia Kell v. Canada*

In *Cecilia Kell v. Canada*, the Committee addressed property rights violations experienced by an Indigenous Canadian woman. Cecilia Kell's husband arbitrarily evicted her from their jointly owned house, and the Canadian Courts denied her any legal relief. Cecilia Kell claimed violations of Articles 1, 2(d)–(e), 14(2)(h), 15(1)–(4), and 16(1)(h).[130] The Committee affirmed a violation regarding Articles 2(d)–(e) and 16(1)(h), in conjunction with Article 1, but not regarding Article 14(2)(h).[131]

Cecilia Kell and her husband applied as a family for a house on leasehold land when a local housing scheme became available for the Indigenous population in Rae-Edzo, a community in the Northwest Territories.[132] Though only Cecilia Kell was Indigenous and had access to this housing scheme, they had purchased the house together. The Northwest Territories Housing Corporation (hereinafter the Housing Corporation), a Canadian public authority, issued an Agreement for Purchase and Sale to Cecilia Kell and her partner as purchasers (co-owners) of the house.[133] After years of domestic violence,[134] Cecilia Kell's husband evicted her from the jointly owned house. Without her knowledge or consent, he asked the Housing Corporation to remove her name from the Assignment of Lease.[135]

---

[128] *Id.* ¶¶ 59.
[129] Views concerning Cecilia Kell v. Canada, CEDAW/C/51/D/19/2008 (2012); Views concerning E.S & S.C. v. United Republic of Tanzania, CEDAW/C/60/D/48/2013 (2015).
[130] Cecilia Kell v. Canada, *supra* note 129, ¶ 1.
[131] *Id.* ¶ 11.
[132] Since the time of the events described, Rae-Edzo has been formally renamed Behchokǫ̀ to reflect the name used by the local Tłı̨chǫ community. *See* Land Claims and Self Government Agreement Among the Tłı̨chǫ and the Government of the Northwest Territories, Aug. 25, 2003, S.C. 2005, c. 1, https://laws-lois.justice.gc.ca/eng/annualstatutes/2005_1/page-1.html.
[133] Cecilia Kell v. Canada, *supra* note 129, ¶¶ 2.1–2.3.
[134] *Id.* ¶ 2.4.
[135] *Id.* ¶ 2.5.

He then denied her physical access to the house and demanded that she vacate the house in a letter from his lawyer.[136]

The Canadian courts denied Cecilia Kell access to justice in three court actions. First, she sought compensation for the loss of her home and consequential payment of rent and attendant expenses, but her legal aid lawyer advised her to comply with the eviction.[137] Her second court action to reclaim her property against the estate of her then deceased husband and the new tenant was unsuccessful.[138] In a third court action, Cecilia Kell again sought her interest in and right to the leasehold title and possession of the property; the Canadian court dismissed her action because she could not pay the court fees.[139]

In its consideration of the merits, the Committee considered three sets of facts relevant to find that Canada discriminated against Cecilia Kell based on Article 1.[140]

First, the Committee considered the removal of her name from the Assignment of Lease, which made her partner the sole owner of the property. This enabled her partner to deprive her of her share in the house through a fraudulent transaction. Cecilia Kell's property rights were thus prejudiced by an act of a Canadian public authority in combination with her ex-husband.[141] The Committee determined that changing the Assignment of Lease

> was impossible without action or inaction of the Housing Corporation; that the Housing Corporation was an agent of the State party; that her partner was serving as a director of the Housing Authority Board and therefore occupied a position of authority; that she was not informed by the Housing Corporation of the annulment of her property rights, despite the fact that she was an eligible right holder as a member of the Rae-Edzo community.[142]

Second, the Committee found that Cecilia Kell's experience of domestic violence at the hands of her ex-partner was relevant. The denial of access to their family home, the changing of the locks, and the eviction during her attempt to seek protection in a battered women's shelter to escape the violent relationship all contributed to this abuse.[143]

Third, the Committee addressed Cecilia Kell's lack of access to justice. In particular, the fact that the lawyer she was assigned by the Legal Services Board

---

[136] *Id.* ¶ 2.6.
[137] *Id.* ¶ 2.7.
[138] *Id.* ¶ 2.10.
[139] *Id.* ¶¶ 2.11–2.12.
[140] *Id.* ¶ 10.2.
[141] *Id.*
[142] *Id.*
[143] *Id.*

"advised her to follow the eviction request made by her partner and did not challenge the validity of such request" prejudiced Cecilia Kell's rights.[144]

Based on all these circumstances, the Committee found that Cecilia Kell experienced intersectional discrimination under Article 1:

> The Committee considers that the author has established a distinction based on the fact that she was an aboriginal woman victim of domestic violence, which she clearly submitted in her first lawsuit against her partner, and that such violence had the effect of impairing the exercise of her property rights. [Citation to GR 28 para. 18 omitted] Accordingly, the Committee finds that an act of intersectional discrimination has taken place against the author.[145]

Next, the Committee addressed Canada's human rights commitments under Article 2(d) and (e) of the Convention. It made clear that "as the author is an aboriginal woman who is in a vulnerable position, the state party is obliged to ensure the effective elimination of intersectional discrimination."[146] The Committee found a violation of Article 2(e) and (d) in the light of GR 28. It recalled that states parties must adopt measures that ensure women's equality with men, including measures that ensure that women have access to effective remedies.[147]

Regarding remedies, the Committee took note of the state party's submission that several efforts were made by the Housing Corporation upon the removal of Cecilia Kell's name from the Assignment of Lease, including offering her other homes in the community or monetary compensation.[148] However, Cecilia Kell rejected these offers. The Committee found that the state party's efforts to rectify the situation were not sufficient to offset the violation of Cecilia Kell's right to administer her property. During the settlement negotiations, the Housing Corporation was no longer the registered owner of the property and could not offer one-half of the property. However, when Cecilia Kell's name was removed from the Assignment of the Lease, the Housing Corporation was managing the property. The Committee noted that her partner was reassigned her share even though he was not eligible for such accommodation. Moreover, the alternative accommodations and monetary compensation were both inadequate and offered only three years after the eviction that they were ineffective.[149] In addition, the legal representation that Cecilia Kell was provided was inadequate: her attorney pressured her to settle for monetary compensation instead of

---

[144] Id.
[145] Id.
[146] Id. ¶ 10.3.
[147] Id. ¶ 10.5.
[148] Id. ¶ 10.3.
[149] Id. ¶ 10.4.

pursuing her preferred remedy of property restitution. The lawyers that advised her demonstrated bias regarding both the domestic violence complaint and her property-related lawsuits.[150]

The Committee did not find violations of Articles 14(2)(h) because the Committee assessed that the discrimination Cecilia Kell experienced did not relate "to her originating from a rural area or that she was prevented from residing in another property in the community of Rae-Edzo, in the Northwest Territories of Canada."[151]

Several factors contributed to the Committee's determination that Canada violated Article 16(1)(h). Drawing from the state party's submission, the Committee did not find that property laws, customs, or practices "interfered with her ownership, acquisition, management, administration or enjoyment of the Rae-Edzo property in particular" or "any discriminatory conduct on the part of the authorities in respect of the removal of her name from the Assignment of the Lease for said property."[152] However, the Committee took issue with the state party's oversight, because the Housing Authority should not have advised Cecilia Kell to add her husband's name to the housing application. This was not an eligibility criterion to get access to housing targeted at Indigenous communities—in fact, only Cecilia Kell was eligible as an Indigenous person. In addition, it was important that Cecilia Kell was a victim of domestic violence seeking protection in a battered women's shelter when the eviction took place. Moreover, when the Northwest Territories Housing Corporation removed her name from the Assignment of Lease without her knowledge and without informing her, it failed to consider that Cecilia Kell's and her husband's combined income were used to assess her eligibility for the housing scheme.[153]

The Committee recommended rectifying Cecilia Kell's housing and property rights violations by providing her with "housing commensurate in quality, location, and size to the one that she was deprived of" and "appropriate monetary compensation for material and moral damages commensurate with the gravity of the violations of her rights."[154]

Moreover, the Committee made the General Recommendations to improve Aboriginal women's access to justice when asserting their property rights. To that end, it suggested that Canada "recruit and train more aboriginal women to provide legal aid to women from their communities, including . . . property rights."[155] It also recommended that Canada review its "legal aid system to

---

[150] Id. ¶ 10.5.
[151] Id. ¶ 10.6.
[152] Id. ¶ 10.7.
[153] Id.
[154] Id. ¶ 11.
[155] Id.

ensure that aboriginal women who are victims of domestic violence have effective access to justice."[156]

In a four-page dissenting opinion, Patricia Schulz argued strongly against finding a violation of Cecilia Kell's property rights by the state party. While she agreed with the Committee's view that there was no violation of Cecilia Kell's rights under Article 14(2)(h), she disagreed with the finding of a violation under Article 2(d) and (e) or under Article 16(1)(h). On the one hand, she did not believe that Cecilia Kell was a victim of domestic violence when her name was removed from the Assignment of Lease, or at least she believed that the Canadian authority was not informed about that situation. On the other hand, she also found it exaggerated that the consideration of incomes of both partners would already constitute a violation of Article 16, Paragraph 1(h), because the consideration of the combined income allowed for the purchase of the house in the first place. She also found it relevant that Kell was not forced to add her former partner's name to the application but that this was simply suggested to improve the chances of her application. Last, she viewed the Northwest Territories Housing Corporation's failure to inform Kell about the removal of her name from the contract not as an act of discrimination on the basis of sex in violation of Article 16(1)(h), but simply as a "fraudulent act or an error which had what were certainly dramatic consequences for the author."[157]

No detailed follow-up procedure on the individual communication *Cecilia Kell v. Canada* is publicly available. However, had Canada followed the Committee's previous recommendations in COs and complied with its obligations toward Indigenous women's property rights, the violations which Cecilia Kell experienced probably could have been avoided.

In its COs on Canada in 2016, the Committee noted with concern that its Views had not been fully implemented nor had Canada provided information about the actions it has taken.[158] The Committee urged Canada to

(a) To fully implement the Committee's views concerning communication No. 19/2008 regarding reparation and compensation for the author of the communication and inform the Committee without delay of all measures taken and planned as a consequence of its recommendations;
(b) To recruit and train more indigenous women to provide legal aid to women from their communities, including in domestic violence cases and on property rights, and to review its legal aid scheme to ensure that indigenous women who are victims of domestic violence have effective access to justice.[159]

---

[156] *Id.*
[157] *See* Cecilia Kell v. Canada, *supra* note 129, Patricia Schulz, dissenting, ¶ 3.9.
[158] CO on Canada, CEDAW/C/CAN/CO/8–9, ¶¶ 16–17 (2016).
[159] *Id.*

In the Committee's annual report from 2019, the Committee found the implementation of the Cecilia Kell decision partially satisfactory.[160]

However, it is noteworthy that in its Inquiry Report on Canada,[161] the Committee referred to important findings in the *Cecilia Kell v. Canada* decision to frame Canada's obligations regarding intersectional discrimination and Indigenous women's housing and property rights. In this way, *Cecilia Kell v. Canada* has provided a yardstick for interpreting obligations under the Convention.[162] Moreover, regarding property and housing rights in situations of gender-based violence, the Committee also referred to *Cecilia Kell v. Canada*, "in which the Committee found a close connection between being able to escape violence and having adequate legal aid to assist with property and housing issues."[163]

2.4.2.2 *E.S. and S.C. v. United Republic of Tanzania*

In *E.S. and S.C. v. United Republic of Tanzania*, two widowed Tanzanian women were disenfranchised of their family property because their customary inheritance laws did not respect the Convention. The Committee found a violation of Articles 2(c) and (f), 5(a), 1(b), 15(1) and (2), and 16(1)(c) and (h) of the Convention, read in the light of GRs 21, 28, and 29.[164]

E.S. and S.C. were both married to their husbands under customary law. When their husbands passed away, their brothers-in-law administered their deceased husbands' estates and disenfranchised them of the ownership, administration, and use of their family homes. Both were forced to vacate their houses and to give up their jointly owned property. Neither received any financial support for themselves or their children from their deceased husbands' families.[165] E.S. and S.C. petitioned Tanzania's High Court to strike down these customary inheritance provisions discriminating against widows, daughters, and other female relatives because they violated "the constitutional guarantees of equal protection and non-discrimination."[166] However, while the Tanzanian High Court affirmed that the customary inheritance laws were discriminatory, making women legally inferior to men and providing preferential protection to men, the court refused to grant relief because the majority of customs were discriminatory.[167] E.S. and S.C. appealed the decision without success.[168]

---

[160] Comm. on the CEDAW, Rep. of the Seventieth Session, Chapter V. Activities carried out under the Optional Protocol, ¶ 21, UN Doc. A/74/38 (2019).
[161] *See* discussion in *infra* section 2.11, "Gender-Based Violence and Property Rights."
[162] Cecilia Kell v. Canada, *supra* note 129, ¶¶ 10.2–10.3.
[163] Rep. of the Inquiry concerning Canada, CEDAW/C/OP.8/CAN/1, ¶ 36, n. 19 (2015).
[164] E.S. and S.C. v. Tanzania, *supra* note 40, ¶ 8.
[165] *Id.* ¶¶ 2.5–2.6
[166] *Id.* ¶ 2.7.
[167] *Id.* ¶ 2.8.
[168] *Id.* ¶¶ 2.9, 2.10.

In its consideration of the merits, the Committee recalled several articles and GRs of relevance to this communication. First, it recalled states parties' obligation according to Articles 2(f) and 5(a)

> to adopt appropriate measures to amend or abolish not only existing laws and regulations but also customs and practices that constitute discrimination against women, including when States parties have multiple legal systems in which different personal status laws apply to individuals on the basis of identity factors such as ethnicity or religion.[169]

The Committee also emphasized that the acts or omissions of the judiciary of a state party lead to state responsibility under Article 2.[170] Regarding Article 16(1) and GR 29, the Committee emphasized the obligation of states parties "to adopt laws of intestate succession that comply with the principles of the Convention and that ensure equal treatment of surviving females and males ... [and] to ensure that disinheritance of the surviving spouse is prohibited."[171] The Committee also referred to GR 21, Article 16(1)(h), and Article 15(2) when highlighting the states parties' obligation "to give women equal rights to administer property" as a critical feature of their "financial independence" and "their ability to earn a livelihood and to provide adequate housing and nutrition for themselves and for their children, especially in the event of the death of their spouse."[172] It also restated the states parties' obligation under Article 13 to eliminate discrimination against women "with regard to their right to bank loans, mortgages and other forms of financial credit."[173] It further disapproved of discriminatory customs that perpetuate "gender stereotypes and discriminatory attitudes about the roles and responsibilities of women and prevents women from enjoying equality of status in the family and in society at large."[174]

The Committee then presented its case-specific findings. Notably, the Committee received no state submission and so deliberated exclusively based on the author's submission, which was prepared by two US-based nonprofit organizations—the Women's Legal Aid Centre and the International Women's Human Rights Clinic.

The Committee presented the following facts as relevant for its holding that Tanzania violated Article 2(f) in conjunction with Articles 5, 15, and 16 of the Convention and considering GR 29. Inheritance matters are governed by multiple

---

[169] Id. ¶ 7.2.
[170] Id..
[171] Id.
[172] Id. ¶ 7.3.
[173] Id. ¶ 7.4.
[174] Id. ¶ 7.5

legal systems, and E.S. and S.C. were governed by customary law based on their ethnicity. In addition, despite existing equal protection and nondiscrimination clauses, Tanzania failed "to revise or adopt legislation to eliminate the remaining discriminatory aspects of its codified customary law provisions with regard to widows."[175] The Committee found that Tanzania violated E.S. and S.C.'s property rights, as they "were deprived of the right to administer their husbands' estates and excluded from inheriting any property upon the death of their spouses."[176] It further determined that Tanzania's legal framework was discriminatory because it "treats widows and widowers differently in terms of their access to ownership, acquisition, management, administration, enjoyment and disposition of property."[177]

The Committee also found several judicial shortcomings that led to a denial of justice and a violation of Article 2(c) because, despite a judgment that acknowledged that the application of customary law had discriminatory effect, "the High Court refused to impugn the relevant provisions on the ground that it was impossible to effect customary change by judicial pronouncement and that doing so would be opening a Pandora's Box."[178] The efforts to appeal the decision were fruitless for four years because the appeal was not heard and was then dismissed on procedural grounds.[179] The Committee was of the view that such shortcomings on the part of the judiciary constituted a denial of access to justice and thereby amounted to a failure to provide an effective remedy to the authors, in violation of Article 2(c).[180]

The Committee found that Tanzania violated Article 13. Influential in this decision was the view that "widows in the State party are forced to perpetually depend on their male relatives and their children and therefore do not enjoy economic opportunities."[181] Moreover, the Committee noted that E.S. and S.C. were evicted when their husbands died. The Committee stated that they were left "economically vulnerable, with no property, no home to live in with their children and no form of financial support."[182] This restricted their economic autonomy and prevented them from enjoying equal economic opportunities.[183]

In summary, the Committee considered that Tanzania has denied E.S. and S.C. equality in respect of inheritance and property rights:

[175] Id. ¶ 7.6.
[176] Id.
[177] Id.
[178] Id. ¶ 7.7.
[179] Id.
[180] Id.
[181] Id. ¶ 7.8.
[182] Id.
[183] Id.

... [T]he State party, by condoning such legal restraints on inheritance and property rights, has denied the authors equality in respect of inheritance and failed to provide them with any other means of economic security or any form of adequate redress, thereby failing to discharge its obligations under articles 2(c), 2(f), 5(a), 13(b), 15(1), 15(2), 16(1)(c) and 16(1)(h) of the Convention.[184]

The Committee recommended granting E.S. and S.C. "appropriate reparation and adequate compensation commensurate with the seriousness of the violation of the rights."[185] As a General Recommendation, Tanzania should "expedite the constitutional review process and address the status of customary laws to ensure that rights guaranteed under the Convention have precedence over inconsistent and discriminatory customary provisions."[186] The Committee, in particular, recommended ensuring

> that all discriminatory customary laws applicable in the State party ... are repealed or amended and brought into full compliance with the Convention and the Committee's general recommendations ... providing women and girls with equal administration and inheritance rights upon the dissolution of marriage by death, irrespective of their ethnicity or religion.[187]

Further, the Committee recommended that Tanzania review, repeal, and amend customary laws, ensure that the Convention's rights take precedence, and facilitate dialogue among different stakeholders to remove discriminatory customary law provisions.[188] The Committee similarly encouraged Tanzania to promote dialogue between civil society, women's organizations, and customary leaders to facilitate the removal of discriminatory customary law provisions.[189] Stressing the need for access to effective remedies, and the Committee recommended improving the judiciary's capacity to hear cases regarding CEDAW.[190] To encourage women to take advantage of these judicial remedies, the Committee recommended that Tanzania undertake educational and awareness-raising measures to enhance women's knowledge of their rights under the Convention in rural and remote areas.[191]

According to the Committee's annual reports, the follow-up procedure with Tanzania in the Working Group on Communications is still ongoing. While the

[184] *Id.* ¶ 7.9.
[185] *Id.* ¶ 9.
[186] *Id.*
[187] *Id.*
[188] *Id.*
[189] *Id.*
[190] *Id.*
[191] *Id.*

Committee does not publish information in detail on the states parties' implementation of its Views, it promotes state parties' compliance in its COs on state reports. In its COs to the United Republic of Tanzania, the Committee expressed concern "that discriminatory customary laws and practices persist with regard to marriage and family relations, including concerning inheritance by widows and daughters and property ownership."[192] The Committee expressed concern that its View on *E.S. and S.C. v. United Republic of Tanzania* have not been implemented.[193] Consequently, the Committee urged the Tanzania to implement the recommended reparation and compensation.[194] Moreover, it repeated the states party's obligation to "take all measures necessary to repeal or amend discriminatory customary law provisions and harmonize competing legal systems governing succession or inheritance in the State party...."[195]

2.4.3 Concluding Observations

The Committee's COs tackle property rights regarding marriage, inheritance, family relations, and personal status laws. The Committee provided recommendations on the distribution, governance, administration, and control of marital property to state parties in all world regions. In addition, the Committee applied its recommendations to women living in various types of relationships and who experience the impacts of intersectional discrimination. Furthermore, it frequently recommended amending all discriminatory provisions relating to family, marriage, and divorce to ensure that legislation recognizes women's right to inheritance and women's access to property on an equal basis with men around the world.

2.4.3.1 Equal Legal Capacity to Administer and Manage Property

The Committee has expressed concern when legal provisions designate the husband as the administrator of the marital property or grant the husband decision-making supremacy.[196] Similarly, the Committee has taken issue with laws providing that the husband is the head of the household and providing for paternal powers.[197] The Committee has also criticized states when husbands manage joint property and the wives' property, and when women require their husband's

---

[192] CO on United Republic of Tanzania, CEDAW/C/TZA/CO/7-8, ¶¶ 48–51 (2016).
[193] *Id.*
[194] *Id.*
[195] *Id.*
[196] *See, e.g.*, CO on Ecuador, CEDAW/C/ECU/CO/8-9, ¶ 42 (2015); Philippines, CEDAW/C/PHL/CO/7-8, ¶ 49 (2016).
[197] *See, e.g.*, CO on Niger CEDAW/C/NER/CO/3-4, ¶ 12 (2017); Democratic Republic of the Congo, CEDAW/C/COD/CO/8, ¶ 52 (2019).

authorization or consent to participate in legal procedures regarding their property rights.[198] The Committee has also taken issue with states that rely on the concept of male guardianship and require women to obtain permission from men in matters of personal status, including inheritance and property ownership.[199] The Committee requires states to establish that spouses have the same rights and the same responsibilities in administration of marital property.[200] Moreover, states should repeal discriminatory provisions in civil codes and family laws relating to the administration of family property solely by the husband.[201] In order to safeguard these rights, the Committee has recommended ensuring equal legal capacity between women and men in inheritance and ownership rights.[202]

2.4.3.2 Control over Marital Property

The Committee has expressed concern over states lacking a legal regime recognizing, defining, or setting out rules for control over marital property during marriage.[203] The Committee has also highlighted as problematic situations in which "women are [. . .] unable to exercise their rights to an equal share in marital property owing to the transfer of such property to the families of the husband or other third parties."[204] The Committee requires states to provide for equal access to property, not equitable access because the latter is not compliant with the Committee's standard of equality.[205]

2.4.3.3 Joint Ownership of Marital Property

The Committee has recommended joint ownership of martial property as a default legal regime.[206] Joint ownership should ensure that upon dissolution of marriage, women have equal rights to property acquired during marriage.[207] To protect these rights effectively, the Committee has recommended registering the jointly owned property of women and men in both partners' names.[208]

---

[198] See, e.g., CO on Chile, CEDAW/C/CHL/CO/7, ¶ 50 (2018); Eswatini, CEDAW/C/SWZ/CO/1-2, ¶ 40 (2014).
[199] See, e.g., CO on Saudi Arabia, CEDAW/C/SAU/CO/2, ¶ 15 (2008); Brunei Darussalam, CEDAW/C/BRN/CO/1-2, ¶ 38 (2014).
[200] See, e.g., CO on Madagascar, CEDAW/C/MDG/CO/5, ¶36 (2008); Malta, CEDAW/C/MLT/CO/4, ¶ 37 (2010).
[201] See, e.g., CO on Gabon, CEDAW/C/GAB/CO/6, ¶ 45 (2015); Chile, CEDAW/C/CHL/CO/7, ¶ 51 (2018).
[202] See, e.g., CO on Timor-Leste, CEDAW/C/TLS/CO/1, ¶ 46 (2009).
[203] See, e.g., CO on Bangladesh, CEDAW/C/BGD/CO/8, ¶ 42 (2016).
[204] See, e.g., CO on Uzbekistan, CEDAW/C/UZB/CO/5, ¶ 33 (2015).
[205] CO on Gambia, CEDAW/C/GMB/CO/4-5, ¶¶ 48-49 (2015).
[206] See, e.g., CO on Albania, CEDAW/C/ALB/CO/4, ¶¶ 41-42 (2016).
[207] See, e.g., CO on Tunisia, CEDAW/C/TUN/CO/6, ¶ 61 (2010); Uzbekistan, CEDAW/C/UZB/CO/5, ¶ 34 (2015).
[208] COs on Cabo Verde (CEDAW/C/CPV/CO/9, ¶ 47), Eritrea (CEDAW/C/ERI/CO/6, ¶ 52), Serbia (CEDAW/C/SRB/CO/4, ¶ 48).

2.4.3.4 Equal Division of Marital Property

The Committee has criticized inequality in property distribution during divorce. States should follow the equal division and distribution of marital property as a matter of principle in case of divorce.[209] Moreover, the Committee has recommended the equal division of joint property, including of intangible property, upon divorce.[210]

The Committee has demonstrated great concern when states lack clear legislation for the division of marital property on an equal basis between spouses upon divorce because it might lead to economic vulnerability of the wife.[211] The Committee has recommended incorporating the principle of equal distribution of marital property upon dissolution of the marriage and amending discriminatory provisions in law or enacting legal provisions that distribute property equally.[212] As an additional layer of security, the Committee has recommended adopting legislative measures that redress possible economic disparities and shortfalls upon divorce.[213]

The Committee has recommended that legislation provides for equal distribution of joint property.[214] It has recommended presuming that each spouse contributed half.[215] This presumption entails abolishing any requirement for women to prove their share in and contribution to such joint property.[216]

More generally, the Committee has recommended enhancing women's economic rights upon divorce. The Committee has called on state parties to conduct research on economic consequences of divorce for both spouses.[217] The Committee has also expressed concerns about women's lack of access to justice upon divorce, owing to their limited resources, competing jurisdictions, and lack of uniform law governing divorce.[218]

---

[209] *See, e.g.*, CO on Egypt, CEDAW/C/EGY/CO/7, ¶ 50 (2010), Ethiopia, CEDAW/C/ETH/CO/6-7, ¶ 51 (2011).
[210] CO on Armenia (CEDAW/C/ARM/CO/4, ¶ 39), Croatia (CEDAW/C/HRV/CO/4-5, ¶¶ 42-43), Azerbaijan (CEDAW/C/AZE/CO/5, ¶¶ 38-39).
[211] *See, e.g.*, CO on Bangladesh, CEDAW/C/BGD/CO/8, ¶ 42 (2016); CO on Singapore, CEDAW/C/SGP/CO/4/Rev.1, ¶¶ 33-34 (2011).
[212] CO on Nepal, CEDAW/C/NPL/CO/4-5, ¶ 44 (2011); Morocco, CEDAW/C/MAR/CO/4, ¶ 39 (2008); Maldives, CEDAW/C/MDV/CO/4-5, ¶ 45 (2015).
[213] *See, e.g.*, CO on Bahrain, CEDAW/C/BHR/CO/2, ¶ 41 (2008); Luxembourg, CEDAW/C/LUX/CO/6-7, ¶ 51 (2018).
[214] *See, e.g.*, CO on Korea, CEDAW/C/KOR/CO/8, ¶ 47 (2018).
[215] *See, e.g.*, CO on Cyprus, CEDAW/C/CYP/CO/8, ¶¶ 50-51 (2018).
[216] *See, e.g.*, CO on North Macedonia, CEDAW/C/MKD/CO/6, ¶ 48 (2018); Montenegro, CEDAW/C/MNE/CO/2, ¶ 53 (2017).
[217] *See, e.g.*, CO on Peru, CEDAW/C/PER/CO/7-8, ¶ 42 (2014).
[218] *See, e.g.*, CO on Kenya, CEDAW/C/KEN/CO/8, ¶ 50 (2017); CO on Cyprus, CEDAW/C/CYP/CO/6-7, ¶ 35 (2013).

2.4.3.5 Recognition and Distribution of Joint Marital Property

The Committee has noted states' failure to define joint marital property.[219] Similarly, the Committee has expressed concern about the lack of recognition of nonmonetary contribution of women in marital property.[220] The Committee has recommended that state parties not only consider nonfinancial contributions to joint property but also accord equal value to such contributions.[221]

Another trend with which the Committee has taken issue is legislation on distribution of assets that do not recognize intangible assets, which further contributes to economic disparities.[222] Joint marital property must include tangible and intangible property, including work-related benefits, pensions, insurance benefits, and savings funds, as well as other work-related benefits, career assets, and future earning capacity. Failure to recognize such contributions could disadvantage women economically in the event of separation or divorce.[223] The Committee recommended legislative measures to recognize tangible and intangible property as part of the joint property to be divided equally upon divorce.[224] Moreover, it recommended dividing such joint property equally regardless of each spouse's individual contribution and compensating women for their unequal share in unpaid work.[225]

In legislation regarding property distribution in the event of separation, the Committee has noted a widespread failure to consider gender-based economic disparities between spouses resulting from the existing sex segregation of the labor market, persistent gender pay gaps, traditional work and family life patterns, women's greater share in unpaid work such as child care, and potential career interruptions due to family responsibilities.[226] The Committee has emphasized that these economic disparities often lead to enhanced or increased human capital and earning potential for men, while women may experience the opposite, so that spouses currently do not equitably share in the economic consequences of the marriage and its dissolution.[227] Owing to their unpaid care

---

[219] *See, e.g.*, CO on Slovenia, CEDAW/C/SVN/CO/4, ¶ 33 (2008).

[220] *See, e.g.*, CO on Montenegro, CEDAW/C/MNE/CO/2, ¶ 53 (2017).

[221] *See, e.g.*, CO on Poland (CEDAW/C/POL/CO/7-8, ¶ 42), Antigua and Barbuda (CEDAW/C/ATG/CO/4-7, ¶ 49), Singapore (CEDAW/C/SGP/CO/4/Rev.1, ¶ 34).

[222] *See, e.g.*, CO on Sweden, CEDAW/C/SWE/CO/8-9, ¶ 38 (2016); CO on Lithuania, CEDAW/C/LTU/CO/4, ¶ 30 (2008).

[223] CO on Venezuela, CEDAW/C/VEN/CO/7-8, ¶ 40-41 (2014); CO on Croatia, CEDAW/C/HRV/CO/4-5, ¶¶ 42-43 (2015); CO on Russian Federation, CEDAW/C/RUS/CO/8, ¶¶ 45-46 (2015).

[224] *See, e.g.*, CO on Azerbaijan, CEDAW/C/AZE/CO/5, ¶¶ 38-39 (2015); CO on Mexico, CEDAW/C/MEX/CO/7-8, ¶¶ 36-37 (2012).

[225] *See, e.g.*, CO on Paraguay (CEDAW/C/PRY/CO/7, ¶ 47), Finland (CEDAW/C/FIN/CO/7, ¶ 38), North Macedonia (CEDAW/C/MKD/CO/6, ¶ 48).

[226] *See, e.g.*, CO on Sweden, CEDAW/C/SWE/CO/8-9, ¶ 38 (2016); CO on Germany, CEDAW/C/DEU/CO/7-8, ¶ 49 (2017).

[227] *See, e.g.*, CO on Slovakia, CEDAW/C/SVK/CO/5-6, ¶ 41 (2015); CO on Norway, CEDAW/C/NOR/CO/8, ¶ 37 (2012); CO on Montenegro, CEDAW/C/MNE/CO/2, ¶ 52 (2017); CO on Denmark, CEDAW/C/DNK/CO/8, ¶ 41 (2015).

responsibilities, women may be exposed to poverty.[228] The Committee noted that many states failed to present information on these economic disparities and failed to enact legal mechanisms to compensate for economic disparities.[229]

The Committee has recommended adopting legal measures to redress economic disparities. States should recognize all career-related assets, such as earning potential, personal goodwill, and enhanced human capital as part of the marital assets. Those assets should be distributed between the spouses upon divorce or taken into account in the award of post-divorce periodic payments.[230] Moreover, states should guarantee women's financial equality upon divorce because of women's contributions to the family's economic well-being during the marriage.[231] For instance, this entails consideration of unremunerated domestic work as part of the joint marital property to be distributed upon divorce and for which the economically disadvantaged spouse should be compensated.[232] States should consider the enhanced human capital and earning potential of male spouses, based on their full-time and uninterrupted career pattern, the gender disparity regarding future earning capacity, the length of the marriage, and the number of children, as well as pension rights and work-related benefits.[233] Looking toward the future, the Committee has recommended the establishment of adequate mechanisms redressing economic disparity between spouses.[234] The Committee has recommended awarding periodic payments to compensate women for the loss of earning potential during marriage.[235]

2.4.3.6 Separate Property

The Committee has noted concern regarding marital regimes of separate property that often discriminate against women in marriage and family relations.[236] For instance, the Committee expressed concern regarding Italy: "While the default matrimonial property regime is that of community property, many couples opt to contract separate property, which often results in detrimental outcomes for women."[237] Where the joint property regime is not the default legal regime,

---

[228] CO on Germany, CEDAW/C/DEU/CO/7-8, ¶ 49 (2017).
[229] *See, e.g.*, CO on Liechtenstein, CEDAW/C/LIE/CO/4, ¶ 42 (2011); CO on Paraguay, CEDAW/C/PRY/CO/6, ¶ 36 (2011); *See also* CO on Paraguay, CEDAW/C/PRY/CO/7, ¶ 46 (2017).
[230] *See, e.g.*, CO on Denmark, CEDAW/C/DNK/CO/8, ¶ 42 (2015); CO on North Macedonia, CEDAW/C/MKD/CO/6, ¶ 48 (2018).
[231] CO on Nepal, CEDAW/C/NPL/CO/6, ¶ 43 (2018).
[232] CO on Bolivia, CEDAW/C/BOL/CO/5-6, ¶ 39 (2015); CO on Costa Rica, CEDAW/C/CRI/CO/7, ¶ 43 (2017).
[233] *See, e.g.*, CO on Finland, CEDAW/C/FIN/CO/7, ¶ 39 (2014); CO on Ecuador, CEDAW/C/ECU/CO/8-9, ¶ 43 (2015).
[234] *See, e.g.*, CO on Italy, CEDAW/C/ITA/CO/7, ¶ 52 (2017); CO on Mexico, CEDAW/C/MEX/CO/7-8, ¶ 37 (2012).
[235] CO on Slovakia, CEDAW/C/SVK/CO/5-6, ¶ 42 (2015).
[236] COs on Morocco (CEDAW/C/MAR/CO/4, ¶ 38), Pakistan (CEDAW/C/PAK/CO/4, ¶ 37), Jordan (CEDAW/C/JOR/CO/5, ¶ 49), India (CEDAW/C/IND/CO/4-5, ¶ 40).
[237] CO on Italy, CEDAW/C/ITA/CO/7, ¶ 51 (2017).

wives face economic vulnerability.[238] Moreover, in separate marital property regimes, the property acquired by both spouses during marriage is not equally distributed between them following the divorce, unless the spouses have entered into a specific agreement to the contrary. The Committee recommended making necessary legal amendments to ensure that in separate property regimes, the jointly acquired property during marriage or property over which neither of the spouses can establish their exclusive right of ownership is regarded as owned by both spouses in undivided co-ownership and is hence divided equally between them upon dissolution of their marriage.[239]

2.4.3.7 Intestate Succession and Inheritance

The Committee has expressed concern about the inadequate protection of a woman's marital property in the event of the intestate death of her husband.[240] Distribution of property in intestate succession and inheritance frequently discriminates against women.[241] Moreover, sons are frequently prioritized over daughters in inheritance matters, including regarding the inheritance of family land.[242] Women farmers are also frequently disenfranchised from inheriting farms in the event of their husbands' deaths.[243] For instance, with regard to China, the Committee expressed the concern that in case of "divorce or inheritance title to property reverts back to the original investor, a decision which has the effect of indirectly discriminating against women and depriving them of titles to property."[244]

The Committee has recommended taking measures to ensure that men and women inherit property, including land, equally and that women's property rights are protected when their husbands die.[245] It urged countries with discriminatory inheritance laws to consider the experience of countries with similar cultural backgrounds and legal systems that have revised their laws to provide women with equal property rights in inheritance.[246]

Widows enjoy fewer legal protections regarding their inheritance than widowers due to persistent discriminatory family laws and customary laws and practices.[247] The Committee has called on states to implement laws and adopt measures "to modify social and cultural patterns that perpetuate women's

---

[238] CO on Comoros, CEDAW/C/COM/CO/1–4, ¶ 39 (2012).
[239] CO on Monaco, CEDAW/C/MCO/CO/1–3, ¶¶ 47–48 (2017).
[240] CO on New Zealand, CEDAW/C/COK/CO/1, ¶¶ 40–41 (2007).
[241] CO on Sierra Leone, CEDAW/C/SLE/CO/5, ¶ 38 (2007).
[242] CO on Serbia, CEDAW/C/SRB/CO/4, ¶ 47 (2019).
[243] CO on Switzerland, CEDAW/C/CHE/CO/4–5, ¶ 44 (2016).
[244] CO on China, CEDAW/C/CHN/CO/7–8, ¶ 44 (2014).
[245] CO on New Zealand, *supra* note 240, ¶¶ 40–41 (2007).
[246] CO on Algeria, CEDAW/C/DZA/CO/3–4, ¶ 47 (2012).
[247] *See, e.g.*, CO on Jordan, CEDAW/C/JOR/CO/6, ¶ 56 (2012); CO on United Republic of Tanzania, CEDAW/C/TZA/CO/7–8, ¶ 48 (2016).

inferiority and impede their access to property and inheritance" and to ensure widows' rights without restrictions.[248]

2.4.3.8 Property Rights in Different Types of Family Relations

The Committee addressed property rights in different types of family relations, including women in polygamous unions, customary marriages, *de facto* unions, and same-sex relationships.

Women in polygamous unions require economic protection of their rights to land and property accumulated during such unions.[249] For instance, the Committee has expressed concern that second or subsequent wives do not have any rights concerning property, inheritance, or maintenance in polygamous unions.[250] Moreover, it was concerned that the surviving widows of the deceased polygamous husband would only obtain property in proportion to the length of their marriage.[251]

In customary marriages, gender inequalities regarding property rights persist. Regarding several states, the Committee has recommended recognizing customary marriages and women's associated property rights.[252] It has urged states to bring women's property rights in customary marriages into line with those in civil marriages.[253] Moreover, the Committee has also recommended adopting all legislative means necessary to protect the rights of women upon dissolution of customary marriages, regardless of their registration status, in particular with respect to their inheritance rights.[254] In some states, the Committee noted the problem that civil laws providing equality to spouses do not apply to customary and religious marriages.[255] The Committee has generally recommended legal reform of discriminatory provisions in customary law.[256]

De facto unions frequently lack legal recognition, resulting in a lack of protection for women's property and economic rights.[257] Without adequate prior contractual agreements, women find themselves in precarious situations when their relationships break down, and they frequently face economic hardship.[258]

---

[248] CO on Sierra Leone, CEDAW/C/SLE/CO/6, ¶ 10 (2014).
[249] CO on Rwanda, CEDAW/C/RWA/CO/7-9, ¶ 50 (2017); CO on Turkmenistan, CEDAW/C/TKM/CO/5, ¶¶ 50-51 (2018).
[250] CO on Tajikistan, CEDAW/C/TJK/CO/3, ¶ 35 (2007).
[251] CO on Cameroon, CEDAW/C/CMR/CO/4-5, ¶ 40 (2014).
[252] CO on Namibia, CEDAW/C/NAM/CO/3, ¶ 28-29 (2007); CO on Mauritius, CEDAW/C/MUS/CO/8, ¶ 37 (2018).
[253] *Id.* ¶¶ 28-29 (2007).
[254] CO on Gabon, CEDAW/C/GAB/CO/6, ¶ 44 (2015).
[255] CO on Botswana, CEDAW/C/BOT/CO/3, ¶ 41-42 (2010).
[256] CO on Cameroon, *supra* note 251, ¶ 39 (2014).
[257] COs on Czechia (CEDAW/C/CZE/CO/5, ¶ 40), Antigua and Barbuda (CEDAW/C/ATG/CO/4-7, ¶ 48), Denmark (CEDAW/C/DNK/CO/8, ¶ 42), Turkmenistan (CEDAW/C/TKM/CO/5, ¶ 50), Korea (CEDAW/C/KOR/CO/8, ¶ 46).
[258] COs on Russian Federation (CEDAW/C/USR/CO/7, ¶ 48), Norway (CEDAW/C/NOR/CO/7, ¶ 31; CEDAW/C/NOR/CO/9, ¶ 48), Costa Rica (CEDAW/C/CRI/CO/7, ¶ 42).

The Committee has expressed concern that women do not enjoy the right to property acquired during the union or financial support from their partners.[259] The Committee also expressed concern that women lack redress in the case of separation from a partner.[260] Lack of registration also means that women in *de facto* unions cannot inherit property from a deceased partner or claim pension benefits.[261] The Committee has noted a lack of information about property distribution upon dissolution of *de facto* relationships, in particular with respect to future earning capacity.[262] Moreover, in some states, women lack awareness about the economic implications of *de facto* unions.[263]

The Committee recommended to states parties to amend their legislation to recognize *de facto* unions to ensure that partners have the same rights and responsibilities within and upon dissolution of such unions.[264] The Committee recommended that states undertake effective measures to ensure equal rights to property and assets accumulated during *de facto* unions when the relationship breaks down.[265] By adopting legal measures, states can enhance the economic protection of women living in *de facto* relationships.[266] States should also undertake reforms giving women the right to financial support, if necessary, upon the termination of *de facto* unions.[267] Furthermore, the Committee has recommended extending the current legal system governing inheritance and property rights of married women to couples living in *de facto* unions.[268] The Committee has also recommended measures to raise awareness about the economic implications of *de facto* unions.[269]

The Committee has noted with concern that same-sex couples are placed at a disadvantage regarding the distribution of property upon dissolution of their union in states where they cannot register their partnership or marry. Accordingly, the Committee has recommended harmonizing "the treatment of all women, including those in de facto unions and same-sex relationships, with regard to the distribution of property upon dissolution of their union or relationship."[270]

---

[259] CO on St. Vincent and the Grenadines, CEDAW/C/VCT/CO/4-8, ¶¶ 42–43 (2015).
[260] CO on Togo, CEDAW/C/TGO/CO/6-7, ¶ 40 (2012); CO on Slovakia, CEDAW/C/SVK/CO/5-6, ¶ 41 (2015).
[261] CO on Suriname, CEDAW/C/SUR/CO/4-6, ¶ 52 (2018).
[262] CO on Canada, CEDAW/C/CAN/CO/7, ¶ 47 (2008).
[263] CO on Uruguay, CEDAW/C/URY/CO/8-9, ¶ 45 (2016).
[264] CO on Czechia, CEDAW/C/CZE/CO/5, ¶ 41 (2010).
[265] COs on Norway (CEDAW/C/NOR/CO/7, ¶ 32), Russian Federation (CEDAW/C/USR/CO/7, ¶ 49), Costa Rica, CEDAW/C/CRI/CO/7, ¶ 43), Austria (CEDAW/C/AUT/CO/7-8, ¶¶ 50–51).
[266] COs on Switzerland (CEDAW/C/CHE/CO/3, ¶¶ 41–42), Korea (CEDAW/C/KOR/CO/8, ¶ 46), North Macedonia (CEDAW/C/MKD/CO/6, ¶ 48), Uruguay (CEDAW/C/URY/CO/8-9, ¶ 46).
[267] CO on St. Vincent and the Grenadines, *supra* note 259, ¶¶ 42–43 (2015).
[268] CO on Singapore (CEDAW/C/SGP/CO/4/Rev.1, ¶ 34), Greece (CEDAW/C/GRC/CO/7, ¶ 37), Malta (CEDAW/C/MLT/CO/4, ¶ 36), Czechia (CEDAW/C/CZE/CO/5, ¶ 41).
[269] CO on Uruguay, CEDAW/C/URY/CO/8-9, ¶¶ 45–46 (2016).
[270] CO on Luxembourg, CEDAW/C/LUX/CO/6-7, ¶ 52 (2018).

The Committee has expressed concern regarding unmarried women and women who do not own property, because they often face barriers to accessing and acquiring financial resources. This may have a negative impact on women in the agricultural sector.[271]

2.4.3.9 The Impact of Intersectional Discrimination on Women's Property

The Committee has addressed the different ways in which women who experience intersectional forms of discrimination are impacted. Intersectional discrimination toward Aboriginal and rural women has been a particular concern for the Committee. In Canada's 2008 state report, the Committee expressed concern that "the division of matrimonial property in case of divorce does not apply to aboriginal women living on reserves, owing to the application of the Indian Act, which does not address the issue of matrimonial property."[272] While Canada followed the Committee's recommendation to adopt legislation addressing the matrimonial property rights of Aboriginal women living on reserves, the Committee expressed concern in its COs on Canada's subsequent state report that the enacted legislation did not apply to the First Nations reserves. It recommended adopting "guidelines or minimum standards that should be incorporated by First Nations to ensure women's matrimonial property rights."[273] Similarly, women in rural and remote areas in *de facto* marriages often lack legal protection of their property rights.[274]

2.4.3.10 Elimination of Discriminatory Legal Provisions

The Committee has recommended amending all discriminatory provisions relating to family, marriage, and divorce to ensure that legislation recognizes women's right to inheritance and women's access to property on an equal basis with men.[275]

The Committee has expressed particular concern about constitutional exemptions from nondiscrimination requirements regarding matters of personal law concerning marriage, divorce, burial, and devolution of property.[276] The Committee recommended reviewing and repealing discriminatory constitutional provisions against women on all grounds, including devolution of property in personal law and customary law and distribution of marital property upon divorce.[277]

---

[271] CO on Antigua and Barbuda, CEDAW/C/ATG/CO/4-7, ¶ 40 (2019).
[272] CO on Canada, CEDAW/C/CAN/CO/7, ¶ 19 (2008).
[273] CO on Canada, CEDAW/C/CAN/CO/8-9, ¶ 51 (2016).
[274] CO on Kyrgyzstan, CEDAW/C/KGZ/CO/3, ¶¶ 39-40 (2008).
[275] COs on India (CEDAW/C/IND/CO/4-5, ¶ 41), Samoa (CEDAW/C/WSM/CO/4-5, ¶ 39), Lesotho (CEDAW/C/LSO/CO/1-4, ¶ 38), Bolivia (CEDAW/C/BOL/CO/5-6, ¶¶ 38-39).
[276] COs on Mauritius (CEDAW/C/MUS/CO/6-7, ¶ 14), Solomon Island (CEDAW/C/SLB/CO/1-3, ¶ 9), Sierra Leone (CEDAW/C/SLE/CO/6, ¶ 10), Gambia (CEDAW/C/GMB/CO/4-5, ¶ 8).
[277] CO on Nepal, CEDAW/C/NPL/CO/6, ¶ 8 (2018).

The Committee has supported revision of family laws that discriminate against women concerning their matrimonial property.[278] States parties should prepare unified family codes based on the principles of equality and nondiscrimination, which address and abolish polygamy and unequal inheritance, property, and land rights, while making civil provisions available for all women.[279] Moreover, the Committee recommended studying the effects and impacts of family laws on the economic situation of women upon divorce and to assess the effectiveness of current regulations in protecting the property rights of women upon the break-up of marriage or of *de facto* unions.[280] Finally, the Committee has recommended eliminating fault-based exceptions to the equal division of matrimonial property.[281]

Personal status codes are another area where the Committee has noted discriminatory provisions regarding property rights in family relations. Such codes concern marriage and its dissolution; the ownership, inheritance, transfer, and disposal of land; and property relations, legal capacity, and inheritance.[282] The Committee has recommended amending personal status codes to several states parties.[283] The Committee also has recommended offering a civil alternative to the personal status act based on the principles of equality and nondiscrimination: this should alleviate women's legal, economic, and social marginalization.[284] In undertaking legislative review of personal status law to provide women with equal rights regarding property, the Committee has reiterated the value of considering the experience of other countries with similar cultural backgrounds and legal norms.[285]

The Committee has called on state parties to ensure that provisions in civil codes address all discrimination against women in all areas covered by Articles 15 and 16, with respect to property in case of inheritance, divorce, and legal capacity.[286]

Customary law governing marriage and family relations may conflict with the Convention due to their discriminatory effect on women's access to property, land, and inheritance.[287] The Committee has criticized that in several states,

---

[278] CO on Samoa, CEDAW/C/WSM/CO/6, ¶ 43 (2018).
[279] COs on South Africa (CEDAW/C/ZAF/CO/4, ¶ 42), Sri Lanka (CEDAW/C/LKA/CO/8, ¶¶ 13, 45), Saudi Arabia (CEDAW/C/SAU/CO/3-4, ¶ 64), Afghanistan (CEDAW/C/AFG/CO/1-2, ¶ 43).
[280] *See, e.g.*, CO on UK, CEDAW/C/GBR/CO/7, ¶ 65 (2013).
[281] *See, e.g.*, CO on Lao People's Democratic Republic, CEDAW/C/LAO/CO/7, ¶¶ 48–49 (2009).
[282] COs on Kuwait (CEDAW/C/KWT/CO/3-4, ¶ 50), Sri Lanka (CEDAW/C/LKA/CO/7, ¶ 45), Gambia (CEDAW/C/GMB/CO/4-5, ¶ 48).
[283] COs on Mauritania (CEDAW/C/MRT/CO/1, ¶ 44), Yemen (CEDAW/C/YEM/CO/6, ¶¶ 38–39), Tunisia (CEDAW/C/TUN/CO/6, ¶¶ 60–61).
[284] *See, e.g.*, CO on Saudi Arabia, CEDAW/C/SAU/CO/3-4, ¶ 64 (2018).
[285] CO on United Arab Emirates, CEDAW/C/ARE/CO/2-3, ¶ 46 (2015).
[286] COs on Timor-Leste (CEDAW/C/TLS/CO/1, ¶ 46), Gabon (CEDAW/C/GAB/CO/6, ¶ 45), Chile (CEDAW/C/CHL/CO/7, ¶ 51).
[287] COs on Vanuatu (CEDAW/C/VUT/CO/3, ¶¶ 38–39), Solomon Islands (CEDAW/C/SLB/CO/1-3, ¶¶ 44–45), Burundi (CEDAW/C/BDI/CO/5-6, ¶ 50), Sri Lanka (CEDAW/C/LKA/CO/8, ¶ 45).

customary law remains in force and even takes precedence by law or by practice over civil law in personal status matters.[288] Thus, even when civil laws would provide for equality, they do not apply.[289] The same problem remained in states where multiple legal systems regulating marriage and family relations coexist, resulting in persistent discrimination against women regarding their property rights.[290] The Committee noted states' reluctance to review their policy of noninterference in the personal affairs of communities.[291] Even within the customary law regime, the Committee expressed concern about women's lack of knowledge about their property, marriage, and inheritance rights and their varied economic implications.[292] Furthermore, the Committee has recalled that women married under customary rules do not have access to civil courts to defend their rights.[293] Discriminatory customary laws and practices persist, especially in rural areas and remote communities, preventing rural women from inheriting or acquiring ownership of land and other property.[294]

2.5 Property Rights in the Context of Civil and Political Rights

2.5.1 The Convention and General Recommendations

The status of women as property owners affects their enjoyment of civil and political rights, including with regard to women's voting rights, their right to a nationality, and their access to justice more broadly. The text of the Convention does not make this connection visible at the outset, but the Committee's interpretations in three GRs are particularly relevant in this regard: GR 23 on Women in Political and Public Life, GR 32 on the Gender-Related Dimensions of Refugee Status, Asylum, Nationality and Statelessness of Women, and GR 33 on Women's Access to Justice.

2.5.1.1 Article 7 and GR 23 on Women in Political and Public Life
Women's property ownership or lack thereof may impact if they can realize their right to vote under Article 7. The Committee has specified in GR 23 that under

---

[288] *See, e.g.*, COs on Sierra Leone (CEDAW/C/SLE/CO/6, ¶ 10) and Zambia (CEDAW/C/ZMB/CO/5-6, ¶ 41).
[289] *See, e.g.*, CO on Botswana, CEDAW/C/BOT/CO/3, ¶¶ 41–42 (2010).
[290] *See, e.g.*, CO on Equatorial Guinea, CEDAW/C/GNQ/CO/6, ¶ 43 (2012).
[291] *See, e.g.*, CO on India, CEDAW/C/IND/CO/4-5, ¶ 41 (2014).
[292] *See, e.g.*, CO on Paraguay, CEDAW/C/PRY/CO/6, ¶¶ 36–37 (2011); CO on Eswatini, CEDAW/C/SWZ/CO/1-2, ¶¶ 41–42 (2014).
[293] *See, e.g.*, CO on Equatorial Guinea, CEDAW/C/GNQ/CO/6, ¶ 43 (2012).
[294] COs on Samoa (CEDAW/C/WSM/CO/4-5, ¶¶ 38–39), Jordan (CEDAW/C/JOR/CO/5, ¶¶ 41–42) (2012), Cameroon (CEDAW/C/CMR/CO/4-5, ¶¶ 11, 35, 38–39).

Article 7(a) of the Convention, women's voting rights cannot be limited based on property qualifications. The Committee states:

> ... [L]imiting the right to vote to persons ... who possess a minimum property qualification ... is not only unreasonable, it may violate the universal guarantee of human rights. It is also likely to have a disproportionate impact on women, thereby contravening the provisions of the Convention.[295]

2.5.1.2 Article 9 and GR 32 on Refugee Status, Asylum, Nationality, and Statelessness of Women

Women's right to a nationality under Article 9 is linked to property rights. In GR 32, the Committee emphasizes that stateless women may be deprived from their access to rights flowing from status as national such as the right to property.[296] Moreover, GR 32 points to the indirect discrimination caused by naturalizations requirements that are more difficult to meet for women, for instance, requirements such as property ownership.[297]

2.5.1.3 Article 15 and GR 33 on Women's Access to Justice

Article 15 regarding the equality of women and men before the law and equal protection by the law is also particularly relevant for their access to justice (see also section 2.3.1.1 *ex seq.*). GR 33 emphasizes that women must have equal access to justice regarding their property rights.[298]

GR 33 stresses that access to justice empowers women as "individuals and as rights holders."[299] The Committee views "effective access to justice" as a way to realize the "emancipatory and transformative potential" of the Convention.[300] However, the Committee also notes that the widespread failure to ensure that economic accessibility of judicial mechanisms for women compromises their access to justice.[301] Intersecting forms of discrimination make it difficult for women to gain access to justice, and socioeconomic status and property ownership are factors that impact women's access to justice.[302]

GR 33 lists six interrelated components as essential for women's access to justice: "justiciability, availability, accessibility, good quality, provision of remedies

---

[295] GR No. 23 on Political and Public Life, A/52/38, ¶ 23.
[296] GR No. 32 on the Gender-Related Dimensions of Refugee Status, Asylum, Nationality and Statelessness of Women, CEDAW/C/GC/32, ¶ 53 (2014).
[297] *Id.* ¶ 55.
[298] GR No. 33 on Women's Access to Justice, CEDAW/C/GC/33, ¶ 43 (2015).
[299] GR No. 33, *supra* note 298, ¶ 2.
[300] *Id.* ¶ 2.
[301] *Id.* ¶ 3.
[302] GR No. 33, *supra* note 298, ¶ 8 (citing GR No. 28, *supra* note 25, ¶ 18).

for victims and accountability of justice systems."[303] With regard to accessibility, it recommends that states

> [r]emove economic barriers to justice by providing legal aid and ensure that fees for issuing and filing documents, as well as court costs, are reduced for women with low incomes and waived for women living in poverty.[304]

The Committee also calls for a gender-sensitive lens for reparations for human rights violations. States parties should ensure that "remedies are adequate, effective, promptly attributed, holistic and proportional to the gravity of the harm suffered."[305] When assessing damages, states parties should "take full account of the unremunerated domestic and caregiving activities of women in assessments of damages for the purposes of determining appropriate compensation for harm in all civil, criminal, administrative or other proceedings."[306]

The Committee affirms that, in accordance with Article 15, women and men are equal before the law in civil law disputes. This means that "States parties must accord to women a legal capacity in civil matters identical to that of men and the same opportunities to exercise that capacity."[307] It specifically requires that women must have access to civil law procedures and remedies in the field of "inheritance, land and property rights."[308] The Committee recommends that states parties

> [e]liminate all gender-based barriers to access to civil law procedures, such as requiring that women obtain permission from judicial or administrative authorities or family members before beginning legal action, or that they furnish documents relating to identity or title to property.[309]

The Committee called on states parties to withdraw reservations from Article 15 to ensure women's access to justice. In particular, states, shall "accord to women a legal capacity in civil matters identical to that of men and the same opportunities to exercise that capacity, and give women equal rights to conclude contracts and to administer property and . . . treat them equally in all stages of procedure in courts and tribunals."[310]

---

[303] Id. ¶ 14
[304] Id. ¶ 17.
[305] Id. ¶ 19.
[306] Id. ¶ 19.
[307] Id. ¶ 43.
[308] Id. ¶ 43.
[309] Id. ¶ 44.
[310] GR No. 33, *supra* note 298, ¶ 65.

In accordance with Article 15 and 16, state parties should "adopt written family codes or personal status laws that provide for equal access to justice between spouses or partners."[311] States should also consider creating "gender-sensitive family judicial or quasi-judicial mechanisms to deal with issues such as property settlement, land rights, inheritance, dissolution of marriage."[312] The Committee requires states not only to change their laws but also to change real-world practices and to create institutions to guarantee women's property rights in a gender-sensitive manner. Moreover, the Committee stresses that states should withdraw reservations to Articles 15 and 16 to improve access to justice.[313]

2.5.2 Concluding Observations

In the civil and political rights context, the Committee engaged with the connection between women's right to a nationality and the role of property rights to access this status. In addition, it highlighted the importance of women's access to justice in relation to land and property matters.

2.5.2.1 Property Rights, Identity Documents, and Citizenship

The Committee has criticized states parties that denied women identity documents, which impeded them from accessing property, as well as states which required property ownership to obtain nationality or identity documents. For instance, the Committee expressed the concern to Kazakhstan that women and girls face a high risk of statelessness because legislation requires property ownership to acquire or reacquire nationality and recommended lifting this legislation.[314] Meanwhile, in Angola, the Committee took issue with barriers to obtaining identity documents which restricted rural women's access to property.[315] Similarly, the Committee expressed concern that women and in particular single mothers in Nepal were "denied citizenship certificates and registration of their children, which prevents those women and their children from . . . managing their property."[316] Regarding Afghanistan, the Committee noted that a high proportion of women lack personal identity documentation, not only increasing their risk of statelessness but restricting their enjoyment of other rights, "such as to secure land and property."[317]

---

[311] *Id.* ¶ 46.
[312] *Id.*
[313] *Id.* ¶ 66.
[314] CO on Kazakhstan, CEDAW/C/KAZ/CO/5, ¶¶ 33–34 (2019).
[315] CO on Angola, CEDAW/C/AGO/CO/7, ¶ 33 (2019).
[316] CO on Nepal, CEDAW/C/NPL/CO/6, ¶ 30 (2018).
[317] CO on Afghanistan, CEDAW/C/AFG/CO/1–2, ¶ 30 (2013).

2.5.2.2 Access to Justice and Property Rights

The Committee has emphasized the importance of ensuring women's access to justice in relation to land and property matters. Regarding Panama, it recommended in line with GR 33 to "adopt a comprehensive plan of action to modernize, expedite and ensure access to justice for women in all areas of law, including in relation to land and property matters."[318] The Committee recommended to South Sudan to "ensure access to justice and effective remedies for women who have been disposed of housing, land and property in divorce, inheritance and widowhood disputes, and to provide legal aid and support programs to the women concerned."[319] In other cases, the Committee has highlighted that lack of access to functioning family courts and delays in the settlement of property disputes deprive women of adequate access to justice.[320]

Several COs highlight that lack of legal aid negatively affects women's access to justice in property matters.[321] For instance, the Committee recommended free legal aid regardless of income,[322] and especially for women without sufficient economic means.[323]

Women experiencing intersecting forms of discrimination are particularly injured by economic barriers that impede them from realizing their access to justice.[324] For instance, regarding Senegal the Committee recommended to "expedite the adoption of the law on legal aid to ensure that legal aid is available, affordable and accessible to all women in all settings, especially marginalized groups of women."[325]

2.6 Land Rights

2.6.1 Convention and General Recommendations

Article 14(2)(g) and Article 13's chapeau of the Convention protect women's rights to land. In addition, several GRs deal with women's land rights, but GRs 34, 37, and 39 are crucial. GR 34 on rural women serves as both a comprehensive consideration of land rights and a basis for later GRs which address narrower

---

[318] CO on Panama, CEDAW/C/PAN/CO/8, ¶ 24 (2022).
[319] CO on South Sudan, CEDAW/C/SSD/CO/1, ¶ 51 (2021).
[320] CO on Fiji, CEDAW/C/FJI/CO/5, ¶ 59 (2018).
[321] CO on Costa Rica, CEDAW/C/CRI/CO/7, ¶ 42 (2017); CO on United Arab Emirates, CEDAW/C/ARE/CO/4, ¶¶ 16–17 (2022).
[322] CO on Azerbaijan, CEDAW/C/AZE/CO/6, ¶ 12 (2022).
[323] CO on Turkey, CEDAW/C/TUR/CO/8, ¶ 21 (2022).
[324] CO on UK, CEDAW/C/GBR/CO/8, ¶ 24 (2013).
[325] CO on Senegal, CEDAW/C/SEN/CO/8, ¶¶ 13–14 (2022).

issues. The Committee addresses women's land rights in the context of climate change through GR 37. GR 39 deals with Indigenous women's land rights.

2.6.1.1 Article 14(2)(g) and Article 13's Chapeau

Article 14(2)(g) contains an explicit provision that protect rural women's right to land. According to Article 14(2)(g), states shall ensure that women in rural areas enjoy access to "equal treatment in land" as compared to men.

In addition, the chapeau of Article 13 could also be read to entail women's right to land more broadly, reading that "States Parties shall take all appropriate measures to eliminate discrimination against women in other areas of economic and social life in order to ensure, on a basis of equality of men and women, the same rights...."[326,327]

2.6.1.2 GR 34 on Rural Women

GR 34 addresses systemic discrimination against women in rural areas regarding their access to land. GR 34 observes that rural women "face systematic discrimination in access to land and natural resources."[328] GR 34 prohibits the intersectional discrimination that rural women experience in all areas of lives. GR 34 mentions several disadvantaged and marginalized groups of rural women which states parties should protect from intersecting forms of discrimination, "including those belonging to indigenous, Afro-descendent, ethnic and religious minorities, heads of household, peasants, pastoralists, fisherfolk, landless women, migrants and conflict-affected rural women," "rural women with disabilities," and "older rural women."[329] GR 34 recognizes rural landless women as a vulnerable group that is subject to intersectional and disproportionate discrimination.[330]

GR 34 acknowledges that the disenfranchisements rural women experience regarding their land rights stem from broader economic policies:

> Discrimination against rural women cannot be fully understood without taking into account the macroeconomic roots of gender inequality.... Bilateral and multilateral agreements on trade, tax and other economic and fiscal policies can have a significant negative impact on the lives of rural women.... States parties should ... address the negative and differential impacts of economic

---

[326] See GR No. 34, supra note 125, ¶ 55 ex. seq. (referring to "art. 14, para. 2(g), read alongside art. 13" in the section that deals with land and natural resources).
[327] See Fareda Banda, Article 14, in 2022 COMMENTARY, supra note 5. Beate Rudolf, Article 13, in 2022 COMMENTARY, supra note 5.
[328] GR No. 34, supra note 125, ¶ 5.
[329] Id. ¶ 15.
[330] Id. ¶¶ 14–15.

policies, including agricultural and general trade liberalization, privatization and the commodification of land, water and natural resources, on the lives of rural women and the fulfilment of their rights....[331]

GR 34 also connects land and soil degradation to the larger phenomena of climate change and disasters that are induced by human activities such as the use of pesticides, agrochemicals, and extractive industries.[332] The Committee calls on states parties to "alleviate and mitigate those threats and ensure that rural women enjoy a safe, clean and healthy environment."[333]

Given the involvement of private actors in land administration and the frequent negative interference of private corporations with rural women's land rights, GR 34 emphasizes the state responsibility to regulate private as well as public activities on its territory and extraterritorially.[334]

GR 34 elaborates on discriminatory stereotypes and harmful practices such as property grabbing that affect rural women in their enjoyment of "rights over land, water and natural resources."[335] GR 34 calls on states parties to eliminate discriminatory stereotypes in line with Article 5(a), "including those that compromise the equal rights of rural women to land, water and other natural resources."[336]

Rural women who defend human rights often experience violence when they seek to secure natural resource rights and land rights.[337] GR 34 urges state parties to prevent violence against rural women human rights defenders.[338]

GR 34 links rural women's land rights to their right to development. The Committee notes that states should integrate and maintain a gender perspective in all agricultural and rural development policies.[339]

GR 34 asserts land as a fundamental human right:

> The Committee considers rural women's rights to land, natural resources, including water, seeds and forests, and fisheries as fundamental human rights.[340]

Acknowledging that the mere existence of a right does not guarantee its enjoyment, GR 34 lists several barriers to women exercising land rights, including

---

[331] *Id.* ¶¶ 10–11.
[332] *Id.* ¶ 12.
[333] *Id.*
[334] *Id.* ¶ 13.
[335] *Id.* ¶ 22.
[336] *Id.* ¶ 23.
[337] *Id.*
[338] *Id.* ¶ 25 (connecting this with GR 19 on violence against women and GR 33 on women's access to justice).
[339] *Id.* ¶ 36.
[340] *Id.* ¶ 56.

"discriminatory laws, the lack of harmonization of laws and their ineffective implementation... and discriminatory cultural attitudes and practices."[341]

The Committee requires states to eliminate harmful practices that compromise rural women's equal rights to land.[342] This may involve necessary temporary special measures to achieve substantive equality of rural women in relation to land and natural resources.[343] Moreover, states parties should "design and implement a comprehensive strategy to address discriminatory stereotypes, attitudes and practices that impede their rights to land and natural resources."[344] States are also responsible for ensuring that customary systems that govern land management, administration, and transfer do not discriminate against rural women.[345] Legislation should ensure rural women a right to land on an equal basis with men and irrespective of their personal status; women should also be granted full legal capacity to exercise their land rights without a male guardian.[346]

Indigenous women are particularly vulnerable to land dispossession, which the Committee emphasizes states must take action to prevent:

> They should ensure that indigenous women in rural areas have equal access with indigenous men to ownership and possession of and control over land, water, forests, fisheries, aquaculture and other resources that they have traditionally owned, occupied or otherwise used or acquired, including by protecting them against discrimination and dispossession.[347]

GR 34 addresses certain agricultural and land policies that create or exacerbate inequality in access to land. One particular concern is the sale and leasing of land due to crisis:

> Global food, energy, financial and environmental crises have led to the increased sale and leasing of land owned by the State or other actors to local, national and foreign investors. Such agreements, often accompanied by expropriations, have put rural women at risk of forced eviction and increased poverty and have further diminished their access to and control over land, territories and natural resources, ... Displacement negatively affects rural women in multiple ways, and they often suffer gender-based violence in that context.[348]

---

[341] Id.
[342] Id. ¶ 23.
[343] Id. ¶ 57.
[344] Id.
[345] Id. ¶ 58.
[346] Id. ¶ 59.
[347] Id. ¶ 59.
[348] Id. ¶ 61.

Acknowledging the risk of land dispossession through the sale and lease of land, GR 34 notes that states parties should

> [e]nsure that land acquisitions, including land lease contracts, do not violate the rights of rural women or result in forced eviction, and protect rural women from the negative impacts of the acquisition of land by national and transnational companies, development projects, extractive industries and megaprojects.

The Committee recommended obtaining rural women's free and informed consent for land acquisition projects or any lease and sale of land that might result in their expropriation or resettlement. In addition, rural women should be adequately compensated if land acquisitions occur.[349] The Committee also recommended to "adopt and effectively implement laws and policies that limit the quantity and quality of rural land offered for sale or lease to third States or companies."[350]

In addition, land acquisition and resettlement is frequently impacted by gender inequality, putting rural women at a disadvantage:

> Land and agrarian reform often exclude rural women and are not implemented in a gender-responsive manner. Land reform policies sometimes have a male bias, such as registering land only in men's names, making compensation payments mostly in their name or compensating for land use restrictions (resulting in the loss of land, the loss of use and the loss of land value) based only on men's activities.[351]

In response, the Committee advises states to prioritize "rural women's equal rights to land when undertaking land and agrarian reforms."[352] GR 34 makes the following detailed recommendations. The Committee recommends to state parties to integrate "gender-specific goals, targets and measures, and advance both formal and substantive equality" in land and agrarian reform programs.[353] The Committee mentions joint titling and requiring "the wife's consent for the sale or mortgage of jointly owned land or for engaging in financial transactions linked to the land" as gender-specific measures.[354] It also recommends recognizing and including "rural women's equal rights to land in any land

---

[349] *Id.* ¶ 62 c–e.
[350] *Id.* ¶ 62 c–e.
[351] *Id.* ¶ 77.
[352] *Id.* ¶¶ 77–78.
[353] *Id.* ¶ 78.
[354] *Id.* ¶ 78.

distribution, registration and titling or certification schemes."[355] Furthermore, the Committee recommends the formal recognition of Indigenous women's land rights and reviewing any laws, traditions, customs, and land tenure systems with the goal of eliminating discriminatory provisions.[356] The Committee also recommends implementing temporary special measures to enable rural women to benefit from the public distribution, lease, or use of land. Moreover, states parties should prioritize landless rural women when allocating public lands.[357]

2.6.1.3 GR 37 on Climate Change

GR 37 addresses the effects of climate change on rural women's land rights under the right to an adequate standard of living and groups it together with the right to "Food, land, housing, water and sanitation."[358] The impacts of climate change are connected to land degradation. The Committee analyzes that "the effects of food, land and water insecurity are not gender-neutral and that women are more likely to suffer from undernourishment and malnutrition in times of food scarcity."[359]

The Committee acknowledges the impact of climate change on rural and Indigenous women as food producers, agricultural workers, and subsistence farmers. GR 37 expresses concern that discriminatory laws and social norms result in women lacking secure land tenure and being allotted farmland of inferior quality, more prone to adverse climatic events. Moreover, women are increasingly left with the sole responsibility for farming when men move away from areas affected by climate change, yet women often do not possess the legal and socially recognized land ownership necessary to effectively adapt to changing climatic conditions.[360]

In response, GR 37 provides that states parties should "promote and protect women's equal rights to ... land and natural resources ... and take positive measures to guarantee the availability and accessibility of those rights, even during times of scarcity."[361]

2.6.1.4 GR 39 on the Rights of Indigenous Women and Girls

In GR 39, the Committee has significantly expanded its understanding of land rights and dedicates an entire section to "Rights to land, territories and natural resources" according to Articles 13 and 14 of the Convention. Already in the introduction, when setting the terms for the intersectional discrimination that

---

[355] *Id.* ¶ 78.
[356] *Id.* ¶ 78.
[357] *Id.* ¶ 78.
[358] GR No. 37 on Gender-Related Dimensions of Disaster Risk Reduction in a Changing Climate, CEDAW/C/GC/37, ¶ 70 (2018).
[359] *Id.*
[360] *Id.*
[361] *Id.*

Indigenous women and girls experience, GR 39 emphasizes that "Indigenous women and girls often have an inextricable link and relation to their peoples, lands, territories, natural resources and culture."[362]

The protection of Indigenous women's land rights must be guaranteed as such under Articles 13 and 14. GR 39 also points to GR 34 on the rights of rural women.[363] In addition, Indigenous women's land rights are connected to a full spectrum of other rights under the Convention: the general prohibition of discrimination,[364] the right to effective participation in political and public life,[365] the right to culture,[366] the rights to food, water, and seeds,[367] and the right to a clean, healthy, and sustainable environment.[368]

Under the general prohibition of discrimination, states parties must ensure the rights of Indigenous women "to access to and the integrity of their lands, territories and resources, culture and environment."[369] The Committee asks states parties to address the deep-rooted causes of injustices that Indigenous women experience and to address intersectional discrimination in its individual and collective dimension, including those Indigenous women's land rights. The dispossession of their lands and the loss of territories and natural resources through forced displacement constitutes one of those deep-rooted injustice experienced by Indigenous women.[370] Regarding the collective dimension of intersectional discrimination, the Committee states that Indigenous women's land rights are curtailed because states parties fail to protect their "rights to self-determination, collective security of tenure over ancestral lands and resources."[371]

Moreover, GR 39 stresses that gender stereotypes and racism are underlying causes of discrimination that affect Indigenous women's land rights directly and indirectly:

> [They] impede the access of Indigenous women and girls to land use and ownership, the exercise of their rights over their territories, natural and economic resources, and their access to credit, financial services and income-generating opportunities. The underlying causes also impede the recognition and protection of and support for collective and cooperative forms of land ownership and use."[372]

---

[362] GR No. 39 on the Rights of Indigenous Women and Girls, CEDAW/C/GC/39, ¶ 3 (2022).
[363] *Id.* ¶¶ 22, 56–57.
[364] *Id.* ¶¶ 6, 28; *see also* CEDAW, *supra* note 1, arts. 1–2.
[365] *See* CEDAW, *supra* note 1, arts. 7–9; *see* GR No. 39, *supra* note 362, ¶¶ 43–46.
[366] *See* CEDAW, *supra* note 1, arts. 3, 5, 14, & 15.7–9; *see* GR No. 39, *supra* note 362, ¶¶ 53–55.
[367] *See* CEDAW, *supra* note 1, arts. 12 & 14; *see* GR No. 39, *supra* note 362, ¶ 56.
[368] *See* CEDAW, *supra* note 1, arts. 12 & 14; *see* GR No. 39, *supra* note 362, ¶ 60.
[369] GR No. 39, *supra* note 362, ¶ 6.
[370] *Id.* ¶ 11.
[371] *Id.* ¶ 18.
[372] *Id.* ¶ 20.

The Committee also expressed concern that the weak legal protections of Indigenous women's land rights puts them at risk of "dispossession, displacement, confinement, expropriation and exploitation."[373] Especially, the lack of legal title increases their vulnerability in the context of economic development projects.[374] The barriers that Indigenous women and girls face regarding their access to land might result in a loss of their livelihoods and jeopardizes a full spectrum of rights that is tied to their land rights.[375]

GR 39 refers to GR 34 which underscored Indigenous women's "rights to land and collective ownership, natural resources, water, seeds, forests and fisheries under Article 14 of the Convention."[376] GR 39 explains that one of the many barriers is "the commercialization, commodification and financialization of land and natural resources."[377] The Committee urges states to

> adopt legislation to fully ensure the rights of Indigenous women and girls to land, water and other natural resources . . . [and ensure] equal access to ownership, title, possession and control of land, water, forests, fisheries, aquaculture and other resources that they have owned, occupied or otherwise used or acquired, including by protecting them against discrimination and dispossession.[378]

The Committee also recommends adopting "effective measures to legally recognize and protect the lands, territories, and natural resources."[379]

GR 39 sets out the states obligations with regard to the protection of Indigenous women's rights to land, territories, and natural resources under Articles 13 and 14. It highlights the all-encompassing significance of Indigenous women's right to land, territories, and resources.

> Land and territories are an integral part of the identity, views, livelihood, culture and spirit of Indigenous women and girls. Their lives, well-being, culture and survival are intrinsically linked to the use and enjoyment of their lands, territories and natural resources. The limited recognition of ownership of their ancestral territories; the absence of titles to their lands and legal protection of their traditions and heritage; and the lack of recognition of Indigenous Peoples' land and native title rights at the treaty, constitutional and legislative levels in many countries undermine and fuel disrespect for their rights by State and private actors, specifically the rights to collective ownership, possession use and enjoyment of land and

[373] Id. ¶ 20.
[374] Id. ¶ 20.
[375] Id. ¶ 20.
[376] Id. ¶ 22.
[377] Id.
[378] Id.
[379] Id.

resources. Lack of recognition of Indigenous land rights can lead to poverty; food and water insecurity; and barriers to access to natural resources needed for survival, and can create unsafe conditions, which give rise to gender-based violence against Indigenous women and girls. States are required under international law to delimit, demarcate, title and ensure security of title to Indigenous Peoples' territories to prevent discrimination against Indigenous women and girls.[380]

The Committee issues a broad list of recommendations to states parties. First, it recommends recognizing the "individual and collective ownership and control over lands encompassed by their customary land tenure systems, and develop policies and laws that adequately reflect this recognition in the local and national economies."[381] Second, it also recommends recognizing the right to self-determination and the mere "existence and rights of Indigenous Peoples to their lands, territories and natural resources in treaties, constitutions and laws at the national level."[382] Third, it stipulates that free, prior, and informed consent is required before authorizing any "economic, development, extractive and climate mitigation and adaptation projects on their lands and territories."[383] Fourth, the Committee recommended implementing due diligence measures with regard to private actors that impact Indigenous women's rights to land. State parties must

> [p]revent and regulate activities by businesses, corporations and other private actors that may undermine the rights of Indigenous women and girls to their lands, territories and environment, including measures to punish, ensure the availability of remedies, grant reparations and prevent the repetition of these human rights violations.[384]

Last, the Committee recommended adopting a "comprehensive strategy to address discriminatory stereotypes, attitudes and practices that undermine Indigenous women's rights to land, territories and natural resources."[385]

The Committee highlights the negative impact of businesses activities and particularly extractive industries in the context of climate change. The Committee observes:

> Extractive activities carried out by business enterprises and other industrial, financial, public and private actors often have a devastating impact on

---

[380] *Id.* ¶ 56.
[381] *Id.* ¶ 57.
[382] *Id.* ¶ 57.
[383] *Id.* ¶ 57.
[384] *Id.* ¶ 57.
[385] *Id.* ¶ 57.

the ... land, ..., territories and natural resources of Indigenous Peoples and may infringe the rights of Indigenous women and girls.... States parties have an obligation to ensure that State actors and business enterprises take measures without delay to guarantee a clean, healthy and sustainable environment..., including the prevention of ... socioeconomic and environmental violence....[386]

The Committee calls on states parties to "guarantee that Indigenous women and girls are protected from discrimination by both State and non-State actors, including businesses and companies, inside and outside their territories...."[387]

In the context of economic development projects, Indigenous women's land rights are especially jeopardized because Indigenous women's effective participation is not guaranteed and their consent is not obtained.[388] Moreover, Indigenous women defending human rights are especially vulnerable when exercising their effective participation rights, "advancing their land and territorial rights, and ... opposing the implementation of development projects without the free, prior and informed consent of the Indigenous Peoples concerned."[389] Indigenous women's right to effective participation regarding "economic activities carried out by State and private actors in Indigenous territories," as the Committee emphasizes, requires Indigenous women's consent and consultation.[390] The Committee recommends that states parties .

[e]nsure that economic activities, including those related to logging, development, investment, tourism, extraction, mining, climate mitigation and adaptation programmes, and conservation projects are only implemented in Indigenous territories and protected areas with the effective participation of Indigenous women, including full respect for their right to free, prior and informed consent and the adequate consultation processes. It is key that these economic activities do not adversely impact human rights, including those of Indigenous women and girls.[391]

The Committee addresses Indigenous women's land rights regarding the right to culture.[392] The Committee expresses concern that

the dispossession, lack of legal recognition and unauthorized use of Indigenous territories, lands and natural resources, as well as environmental

---

[386] *Id.* ¶ 7.
[387] *Id.* ¶ 23 g).
[388] *Id.* ¶ 11.
[389] *Id.* ¶ 45.
[390] *Id.* ¶ 43.
[391] *Id.* ¶ 46 f).
[392] *Id.* ¶ 53. In particular, CEDAW, *supra* note 1, arts. 3, 5, 13, & 14; 12 & 14.

degradation ... are direct threats to the self-determination, cultural integrity and survival of Indigenous women and girls...."[393]

In response, the Committee recommends that states "[r]espect, protect and expand the rights of Indigenous Peoples to land, territories, resources ... as a precondition for preserving the culture of Indigenous women and girls"; and "act with due diligence to respect and protect the sacred places of Indigenous Peoples and their territories, and hold those who violate them accountable."[394]

In the context of the rights to food, water, and seeds, the Committee stresses that "[t]he dispossession of their territories, forced displacement and lack of recognition of Indigenous land rights limits their opportunities to achieve food and water security and to manage these needed natural resources."[395] Ensuring adequate access to sufficient food, nutrition, and water, implicitly requires states to protect Indigenous women's land.[396]

Finally, the right to a healthy environment cannot be ensured without respecting Indigenous women's vital link between their lands, territories, and natural resources and a healthy environment.[397] However, the Committee stresses that Indigenous women should not be the ones to bear the cost for climate mitigation measures. The Committee recommends that state parties

> [e]nsure the free, prior and informed consent of Indigenous women and girls in matters affecting their ... lands, ... and natural resources, including any proposal to designate their lands as a protected area for conservation or climate change mitigation purposes or carbon sequestration and trading or to implement a green energy project on their lands, ...[398]

2.6.2 Concluding Observations

The Committee has engaged with women's disenfranchisement from their right to land around the world. It depicts lack of land registries and land registration and the lack of access to agricultural land as parts of the problem. In the business context where land-grabbing through development projects occurs, the Committee pointed to a heightened vulnerability of Indigenous women. The Committee made several recommendations about how to address land

---

[393] *Id.* ¶ 54.
[394] *Id.* ¶ 55 b)–c).
[395] *Id.* ¶ 58.
[396] *Id.* ¶ 59.
[397] *Id.* ¶ 60.
[398] *Id.* ¶ 61.

rights violations. It recommended that women participate in decision-making processes on land policies, to eliminate discriminatory legislation, policies, and practices, to raise awareness about land rights, and to undertake temporary special measures in cases of intersectional discrimination to mitigate the impact on women. Women's land rights are especially precarious in conflict situations.

2.6.2.1 Rural Women's Disenfranchisement of Land and Property Rights

The Committee has expressed concern about women's disenfranchisement from their right to land. Only a low percentage of women living in rural areas own and inherit land because of their disadvantaged position.[399] Many rural women only enjoy limited access to land ownership and use, and property rights.[400]

Customs and traditional and discriminatory practices are prevalent in rural areas and prevent women from inheriting or acquiring ownership of land and other property.[401] For instance, regarding South Africa, the Committee noted the concern that "discriminatory customary practices . . . continue to restrict rural women's access to land ownership, property and inheritance . . ." In response, the Committee recommended ensuring "that legislation and policies on land reform and land use fully recognize and protect the right of rural women to owning and using the land."[402]

In some countries, legislation fails to recognize women farmers as land and property owners.[403] The Committee noted with concern that widows were prevented by law from inheriting farms upon the death of their husbands.[404] Some states parties simply fail to repeal legal provisions that are discriminatory against women in the area of access to and control and ownership of land.[405] Moreover, the Committee criticized countries that fail to accord land access to women despite formal laws that recognize women's ownership.[406]

Indigenous women are frequently not recognized as landowners or eligible land users and discriminated against by customs and law.[407] There frequently

---

[399] *See, e.g.*, CO on United Republic of Tanzania, CEDAW/C/TZA/CO/6, ¶ 43 (2009); Republic of Korea, CEDAW/C/KOR/CO/7, ¶ 36 (2011).

[400] *See, e.g.*, CO on Mongolia, CEDAW/C/MNG/CO/10, ¶ 36 (2022); Azerbaijan, CEDAW/C/AZE/CO/6, ¶ 37 (2022).

[401] *See, e.g.*, COs on Bangladesh (CEDAW/C/BGD/CO/7, ¶ 35), Jordan (CEDAW/C/JOR/CO/5, ¶ 41), Zimbabwe (CEDAW/C/ZWE/CO/2-5, ¶ 35), Iraq (CEDAW/C/IRQ/CO/4-6, ¶ 44), India (CEDAW/C/IND/CO/4-5, ¶ 32).

[402] CO on South Africa, CEDAW/C/ZAF/CO/5, ¶ 56 (2021).

[403] CO on Pakistan, CEDAW/C/PAK/CO/4, ¶¶ 33-34 (2013).

[404] CO on Switzerland, CEDAW/C/CHE/CO/4-5, ¶ 44 (2016).

[405] CO on Uganda, CEDAW/C/UGA/CO/8-9, ¶ 13 (2022).

[406] CO on United Republic of Tanzania, CEDAW/C/TZA/CO/6, ¶ 43 (2009).

[407] CO on Indonesia, CEDAW/C/IDN/CO/8, ¶¶ 45-46 (2021).

existed a lack of legislation protecting the rights of Indigenous women to their traditional lands.[408]

2.6.2.2 Land Registration

The Committee sees the lack of land registries and irregularities in the registration of land as root causes that prevent rural women from accessing land, property, credit, and capital.[409] Generally, the Committee recommended that state parties "facilitate access of women and girls to land certificates."[410] The Committee pointed out two areas where the lack of land title registration were a problem: in family relations and in public land programs.

The lack of land title registration is an issue in family relations because it affects women's ownership rights of land. The Committee notes with regard to Azerbaijan that "[t]he practice of not officially registering property, including plots of land, which results in women being deprived of any real estate or land . . ."[411] For instance, regarding Albania, the Committee noted that "only 8 percent of women own property, even though title registration under only the husband's name is unlawful."[412] Regarding China, the Committee expressed concern that due to "certain traditions and practices in rural areas, women are still unable to hold or register land in their names and risk losing land ownership upon changes in their marital status."[413] The Committee recommended states to

> review all laws, customs and traditions that impede women's access and title to land in both rural and urban settings and take effective measures to ensure that women fully enjoy their property rights regardless of their marital status....[414]

However, the lack of land registration is also a problem in public land programs: without title, land ownership cannot be regularized. For instance, the Committee recommended that Ecuador implement a land program "in order to register the land tenure and property of rural women and adopt a national programme aimed at regularizing land tenure."[415]

---

[408] COs on Ecuador (CEDAW/C/ECU/CO/10, ¶ 46) and Sweden (CEDAW/C/SWE/CO/10, ¶¶ 43–44).
[409] *See, e.g.*, CO Comoros, CEDAW/C/COM/CO/1–4, ¶ 37 (2012); CO on Cabo Verde, CEDAW/C/CPV/CO/7–8, ¶ 31 (2013).
[410] CO on Côte d'Ivoire, CEDAW/C/CIV/CO/4, ¶ 48 (2019).
[411] CO on Azerbaijan, CEDAW/C/AZE/CO/6, ¶ 37 (2022).
[412] CO on Albania, CEDAW/C/ALB/CO/3, ¶ 36 (2010).
[413] CO on China, CEDAW/C/CHN/CO/7–8, ¶ 44 (2014).
[414] CO on China, CEDAW/C/CHN/CO/7–8, ¶ 45 (2014).
[415] CO on Ecuador, CEDAW/C/ECU/CO/8–9, ¶ 37 (2015).

2.6.2.3 Access to Agricultural Land as a Source of Livelihood

The Committee expressed concern about the wide gap between the number of women working in agriculture compared to the number of women who own agricultural land in all world regions. For instance, regarding Albania, the Committee noted its concern that "in rural areas, where only 6 per cent of farms are owned or managed by women, . . . 70 per cent of women work in agriculture."[416] In Cabo Verde, "only 8.5 per cent of women in agriculture have access to land ownership and use for agricultural purposes."[417] Similarly, the Committee expressed concern that in Denmark, "only 5 per cent of farmland is owned by women."[418] Regarding Kazakhstan, it noted the "the low percentage of female ownership of land, with only one in five peasant and farm households headed by women."[419] In Egypt, the Committee expressed concern about rural women's "limited access . . . to land ownership, formal credit and loans, despite being the main workforce in the agriculture sector."[420]

The Committee emphasized the vital importance for rural women of agricultural and fertile land as a source of their livelihood and that they must have access to income-generating projects.[421] For instance, regarding Austria, the Committee recommended that ". . . rural women working in agriculture . . . have access to . . . land . . . on an equal basis with rural men."[422]

2.6.2.4 Combating Poverty Through Providing for Land Ownership and Land Use

Poverty is a crucial obstacle to gaining access to land.[423] At the same time, the "feminization of poverty" is connected to "rural women's limited access to and control over agricultural resources, including land . . ."[424] In response, the Committee recommended combating poverty among rural women by ensuring access to ownership and use of land.[425] For instance, regarding Kyrgyzstan, the Committee noted that the majority of women lived in rural areas and that they experienced disproportionately high poverty rates, because of their "very limited access to land ownership and agricultural assets. . . ."[426]

---

[416] CO on Albania, CEDAW/C/ALB/CO/3, ¶ 36 (2010).
[417] CO on Cabo Verde, CEDAW/C/CPV/CO/9, ¶ 40 (2019).
[418] CO on Denmark, CEDAW/C/DNK/CO/9, ¶ 36 (2021).
[419] CO on Kazakhstan, CEDAW/C/KAZ/CO/5, ¶ 41 (2019).
[420] CO on Egypt, CEDAW/C/EGY/CO/8-10, ¶ 43 (2021).
[421] *See, e.g.,* COs on Jordan (CEDAW/C/JOR/CO/6, ¶ 49), Zambia (CEDAW/C/ZMB/CO/5-6, ¶¶ 37-38), Pakistan (CEDAW/C/PAK/CO/4, ¶¶ 33-34), Timor-Leste (CEDAW/C/TLS/CO/2-3, ¶ 34).
[422] CO on Austria, CEDAW/C/AUT/CO/9, ¶ 39 (2019).
[423] *See, e.g.,* CO on Zambia, CEDAW/C/ZMB/CO/5-6, ¶ 37 (2011); CO on Saudi Arabia, CEDAW/C/SAU/CO/3-4, ¶ 51 (2018).
[424] CO on Bolivia, CEDAW/C/BOL/CO/7, ¶ 31 (2022).
[425] COs on Azerbaijan (CEDAW/C/AZE/CO/6, ¶ 38), Bolivia (CEDAW/C/BOL/CO/7, ¶ 32), Turkey (CEDAW/C/TUR/CO/8, ¶ 52), Uzbekistan (CEDAW/C/UZB/CO/6, ¶ 38) (2022).
[426] CO on Kyrgyzstan, CEDAW/C/KGZ/CO/5, ¶ 39 (2021).

2.6.2.5 Land-Grabbing, Development Projects, and Indigenous Women's Land Rights

The Committee has addressed land-grabbing by foreign investors as a phenomenon that negatively impacts rural and Indigenous women's land rights and frequently increases their poverty.[427] For instance, the Committee expressed its concern with regard to Senegal that "land grabbing by huge agricultural companies from local farmers who are the traditional users ... contributes to the increase in poverty of rural women."[428] Regarding Cameroon, the Committee noted that land-grabbing negatively affected "indigenous people and small-scale farmers, which denies them the means to earn a livelihood, and obstacles to obtaining land titles, including prohibitive land transaction fees, which disproportionately affect women."[429]

Mega-projects, extractive industries, land acquisition, and development projects negatively impact women's land rights,[430] especially those of Indigenous women. For instance, the Committee noted that in Ecuador, "numerous foreign and national mining, oil, logging and agribusiness multinationals are threatening the territorial, cultural and socioeconomic integrity of indigenous women and girls ... causing socio-environmental damages that violate their collective rights."[431] Similarly, in Indonesia, "rural and indigenous women are disproportionately affected by development projects, including the exploitation of natural resources, deforestation and agricultural expansion, and land conflicts caused thereby."[432] The Committee recommended that Indigenous women participate in the decision-making process regarding development projects and provide their free, prior, and informed consent when their collective rights to land ownership are affected and share the benefits of these development projects.[433]

One issue of particular concern is states' failure to provide fair compensation or reallocate land if rural or Indigenous women's property is expropriated or dispossessed to facilitate development or extraction projects. For instance, the Committee expressed concern that Timor-Leste's "large-scale rural infrastructure projects that involve forced eviction, acquisition and relocation violate the rights of rural women to fair compensation and reallocation of land."[434] Similarly, the Committee urged India to "study the impact of megaprojects on tribal and rural women and institute safeguards against their displacement

---

[427] CO on Fiji, CEDAW/C/FJI/CO/5, ¶ 49 (2018).
[428] CO on Senegal, CEDAW/C/SEN/CO/3–7, ¶ 32 (2015).
[429] CO on Cameroon, CEDAW/C/CMR/CO/4–5, ¶ 34 (2014).
[430] CO on Niger, CEDAW/C/NER/CO/3–4, ¶ 37 (2017).
[431] CO on Ecuador, CEDAW/C/ECU/CO/10, ¶ 45 (2021).
[432] CO on Indonesia, CEDAW/C/IDN/CO/8, ¶ 45 (2021).
[433] CO on Ecuador, CEDAW/C/ECU/CO/10, ¶ 46 (2021); CO on Panama, CEDAW/C/PAN/CO/8, ¶ 44 (2022).
[434] CO on Timor-Leste, CEDAW/C/TLS/CO/2–3, ¶ 34 (2015).

and violation of their human rights," to "ensure that surplus land given to displaced rural and tribal women is cultivable."[435] In its detailed CO to Uganda pointing out "the dispossession of land owned by women and forced evictions of women ... to facilitate land transfers to a coffee plantation company,"[436] the Committee recommended that "evictions are court-ordered and subject to strict procedural safeguards, in line with international standards, and expedite court proceedings for prompt and adequate compensation and rehabilitation in the case concerning the land evictions...."[437] Also with regard to Panama, the Committee recommended protecting "indigenous women's access to and ownership of collective titles of their lands ... from eviction due to the business activities of large corporations in extractive industries."[438] Moreover, it recommended adopting "policies that provide for compensation and reparations to indigenous and Afro-descendant women in regions negatively affected by investment projects."[439]

2.6.2.6 Participation in Decision-Making Process on Land Policies

The Committee recommended not only that women's access to land increase but that women be represented in the decision-making processes concerning their land.[440] For instance, regarding Gabon, the Committee criticized that "rural women ... face patriarchal attitudes which prevent them from owning land and participating in decision making on matters of rural development and policy."[441]

The effective participation of rural women in decision-making is especially relevant with regard to agricultural policies and the associated land use.[442] The Committee recommended with regard to Senegal, the "equal participation of rural women and girls ... concerning land allocation and public investment management in rural areas."[443] In its COs to Panama, the Committee recommended that Panama ensure that women can "meaningfully participate in the development and implementation of agricultural and development policies, including with regard to decision on land use."[444]

The Committee stressed that states parties must especially ensure the participation of Indigenous women in land-reform processes.[445] Women human rights

---

[435] CO on India, CEDAW/C/IND/CO/3, ¶¶ 46–47 (2007).
[436] CO on Uganda, CEDAW/C/UGA/CO/8-9, ¶ 45 (2022).
[437] Id. ¶ 46.
[438] CO on Panama, CEDAW/C/PAN/CO/8, ¶ 44 (2022).
[439] Id.
[440] CO on Namibia, CEDAW/C/NAM/CO/6, ¶ 46 (2022).
[441] CO on Gabon, CEDAW/C/GAB/CO/7, ¶ 34 (2022).
[442] CO on Bolivia, CEDAW/C/BOL/CO/7, ¶ 32 (2022); Gabon, CEDAW/C/GAB/CO/7, ¶ 35 (2022).
[443] CO on Senegal, CEDAW/C/SEN/CO/8, ¶ 38 (2022).
[444] CO on Panama, CEDAW/C//PAN/CO/8, ¶ 42 (2022).
[445] CO on the Democratic Republic of Congo, CEDAW/C/COD/CO/8, ¶ 45 (2019).

defenders, who actively use their participation rights and advocate for land rights, should not be intimidated, harassed, or threatened.[446]

2.6.2.7 Elimination of Discriminatory Legislation, Policies, and Practices

The Committee has recommended the elimination of discriminatory legislation and the establishment of a legislative framework that protects women's rights in access to and ownership of land and inheritance.[447] For instance, regarding Denmark, it recommended to "review practices that may impede land ownership by rural women and adopt legislation to protect their right to own land."[448] Simultaneously, the Committee has encouraged modification or elimination of discriminatory customary and traditional practices.[449] In adopting policy and undertaking practical measures, states should aim to ensure that gender equality reaches rural areas and facilitates women's ownership of land and property.[450]

2.6.2.8 Visibility and Awareness Raising About Land Rights

With the ultimate goal of increasing the percentage of women owning land, the Committee has supported data collection to make women's disadvantages more visible.[451] For instance, regarding South Africa, the Committee recommended to "collect data on rural women's access to land and inheritance and develop policies and programmes to ensure their economic empowerment."[452]

Public awareness about women's equal access to land is an important factor for development and for achieving substantive equality between women and men.[453] To that end, the Committee suggests awareness-raising efforts concerning women's property rights.[454] For instance, regarding Mongolia, the Committee recommended to "increase awareness among rural women of the importance of land ownership and property rights and challenge traditional attitudes related to gender and property."[455]

---

[446] CO on Indonesia, CEDAW/C/IDN/CO/8, ¶ 33 (2021).
[447] CO on Bangladesh, CEDAW/C/BGD/CO/7, ¶ 35 (2011); Zambia, CEDAW/C/ZMB/CO/5–6, ¶ 38 (2011).
[448] CO on Denmark, CEDAW/C/DNK/CO/9, ¶ 37 (2021).
[449] COs on Bangladesh (CEDAW/C/BGD/CO/7, ¶ 35), Samoa (CEDAW/C/WSM/CO/4–5, ¶ 35), Equatorial Guinea (CEDAW/C/GNQ/CO/6, ¶ 40), Serbia (CEDAW/C/SRB/CO/2–3, ¶ 35).
[450] CO on the Republic of Korea, CEDAW/C/KOR/CO/7, ¶ 37 (2011).
[451] *See, e.g.*, CO on Kenya, CEDAW/C/KEN/CO/6, ¶ 42 (2007); CO on United Republic of Tanzania, CEDAW/C/TZA/CO/6, ¶ 44 (2009).
[452] CO on South Africa, CEDAW/C/ZAF/CO/5, ¶ 56 (2021).
[453] CO on Senegal, CEDAW/C/SEN/CO/3–7, ¶ 33 (2015).
[454] CO on Jordan, CEDAW/C/JOR/CO/6, ¶ 50 (2017); Côte d'Ivoire, CEDAW/C/CIV/CO/4, ¶ 48 (2019).
[455] CO on Mongolia, CEDAW/C/MNG/CO/10, ¶ 37 (2022).

2.6.2.9 Temporary Special Measures

In cases of intersectional discrimination, the Committee has recommended temporary special measures to mitigate the impact on women. For instance, concerning Mexico, the Committee recommended temporary special measures to correct the disparities that Indigenous rural women face regarding access to land and property.[456] Regarding Cambodia, temporary measures should lead to the "substantive equality of women and men," and they should target women in disadvantaged situations by reallocating and distributing land to them so that they have equal ownership of land.[457]

2.6.2.10 Land Rights in Conflict Situations

The Committee raised disenfranchisements of women's land rights in conflict situations, including in Yemen and Myanmar. Regarding Yemen, the Committee expressed concern about "the precarious situation of rural women and girls in Yemen ... [because] the conflict has further deprived them of their rights to ... access to land owing to unlawful seizures and forced displacement...."[458]

Regarding Myanmar, the Committee recommended protecting Rohingya land from confiscation by any government entity or private actor. The Committee expressed its deep concern about the consequences of the

> displacement endured by Rohingya women and girls, in particular the impact on the enjoyment of their human rights to ... property, ... and access to economic opportunities, and about the lack of information on measures taken to assist with their rehabilitation, including adequate compensation.[459]

The Committee urged Myanmar to ensure "that affected Rohingya women and girls may return and resettle, on a voluntary basis, to their previously inhabited lands and refrain from further implementing the Natural Disaster Management Law in a way that dispossesses Rohingya women and girls of their property."[460] Moreover, the Committee urged Myanmar to "assist Rohingya women and girls in recovering, to the extent possible, their property and possessions left behind or that they were dispossessed of and, when such recovery is not possible, to provide appropriate compensation or other forms of just reparation, including

---

[456] CO on Mexico, CEDAW/C/MEX/CO/7-8, ¶ 35 (2012).
[457] CO on Cambodia, CEDAW/C/KHM/CO/6, ¶ 21 (2019). See also the Views concerning X. v. Cambodia, CEDAW/C/85/D146/2019 (2023) under *supra* note 39.
[458] CO on Yemen, CEDAW/C/YEM/CO/7-8, ¶ 41 (2021).
[459] CO on Myanmar, CEDAW/C/MMR/CO/EP/1, ¶ 55 (2019).
[460] CO on Myanmar, CEDAW/C/MMR/CO/EP/1, ¶ 52 (2019).

access to compensation schemes, such as crop and land compensation, and provide free legal aid in that regard."[461]

2.7 Housing Rights

2.7.1 Convention and General Recommendations

The Convention protects the right to adequate housing in Article 14(2)(h) and Article 13's chapeau provision. Moreover, the Committee addressed the right to housing in several GRs, including GR 27 on Older Women, GR 34 on Rural Women, and GR 37 on the Gender-Related Dimensions of Disaster Risk Reduction in the Context of Climate Change. The Committee refers to women's housing rights as part of women's right to adequate living conditions and sometimes mentions them together with land rights. However, the Committee does not refer to housing rights as "property rights" in any explicit fashion. Furthermore, it frequently limits private property rights that negatively impact women's housing rights in its jurisprudence.

2.7.1.1 Article 14(2)(h) and Article 13's Chapeau

Article 14(2)(h) protects housing rights regarding rural women. Article 14(2)(h) provides that states shall ensure that rural women "enjoy adequate living conditions, particularly in relation to housing..." In addition, a right to adequate housing could also derive from Article 13's chapeau provision stating that "States parties shall take all appropriate measures to eliminate discrimination against women in other areas of economic and social life in order to ensure on a basis of equality of men and women, the same rights..."[462] The Committee appears to have extended the housing rights provision contained in Article 14 from rural women to all women; it does not explicitly refer to Article 13's chapeau provision in its jurisprudence.[463]

2.7.1.2 GR 27 on Older Women, GR 34 on Rural Women, and GR 37 on Climate Change

In GR 27 on Older Women, the Committee recommended that states parties provide adequate housing to older women and protect their land and property

---

[461] CO on Myanmar, CEDAW/C/MMR/CO/EP/1, ¶ 57 (2019).

[462] *See* for an overview of both provisions in Fareda Banda, *Article 14*, *supra* note 5; *see also* Beate Rudolf, *Article 13*, *in* 2022 COMMENTARY, *supra* note 5, at 487–519.

[463] In its COs on housing rights, the Committee does not state if it protects housing rights based on Article 14(2)(h) or Article 13's chapeau provision. However, Beate Rudolf presents the recommendations of the Committee with regard to housing rights in its COs under Article 13. *See* Beate Rudolf, *Article 13*, *in* 2022 COMMENTARY, *supra* note 5.

rights but does not cite a particular Convention provision for states parties to do so. It also does not elaborate on whether the Committee views housing rights as property rights or as part of an adequate standard of living. It merely provides that states should

> take necessary measures to ensure older women have access to adequate housing that meet their specific needs, . . . Laws and practices that negatively affect older women's right to housing, land and property should be abolished. States parties should also protect older women against forced evictions and homelessness.[464]

Furthermore, GR 34 provides rural women with the right to adequate housing in accordance with Article 14(2)(h) as part of "women's adequate living conditions." GR 34 affirms:

> The right to adequate housing is of particular concern in rural areas . . . Many of the measures that protect rural women's rights to land (for example, the recognition of women's legal capacity, the recognition of the security of tenure and the elimination of discrimination against women in registration and titling) can be applied to protect their right to adequate housing. . . . However, additional measures can also be taken to improve the conditions of rural housing from a gender-responsive perspective.[465]

In GR 34, the Committee also calls on states parties to "protect rural women effectively from forced eviction by State and non-State actors."[466]

GR 37 highlights the importance of protecting women's right to adequate housing in times of disaster and climate change. The Committee analyzed that

> gender inequalities limit the control that women and girls have over decisions governing their lives, as well as their access to . . . adequate housing . . . .[467]

The Committee also viewed "women heads of household . . . [as] more likely to live in inadequate housing in urban and rural areas of low land value that are vulnerable to such impacts of climate-related events . . . ."[468]

To provide for an adequate standard of living, the Committee calls on states parties to "promote and protect women's equal rights to . . . housing . . . [and] take

---

[464] GR No. 27, *supra* note 117, ¶ 48 (2010).
[465] GR No. 34, *supra* note 125, ¶¶ 79–80.
[466] GR No. 34, *supra* note 125, ¶¶ 79–80.
[467] GR No. 37, *supra* note 358, ¶ 3.
[468] *Id.* ¶ 4.

positive measures to guarantee the availability and accessibility of those rights, even during times of scarcity."[469] The Committee recommended that "particular attention should be paid to ensuring that women living in poverty, in particular those in informal settlements in both urban and rural areas, have access to adequate housing... especially in the context of disasters and climate change."[470]

Moreover, the Committee recommended that states adopt "legislation, programmes and policies and allocate budgets to eliminate homelessness and to ensure that adequate and disaster resilient housing is available and accessible to all women, including those with disabilities."[471] The Committee also recommended that states parties take measures to "protect women against forced eviction and to ensure that public housing and rental assistance schemes accord priority and respond to the specific needs of groups of women."[472]

2.7.2 Communications

The Committee addressed violations of women's housing rights based on Article 14(2)(h) in three communications. In *L.A. et al. v. North Macedonia*[473] and *S.N. and E.R. v. North Macedonia*,[474] the Committee found a violation of Roma women's housing rights when the land they resided on was privatized and when state authorities evicted them because of a building project. In *Cecilia Kell v. Canada*,[475] it did not find a violation under Article 14 because the Committee did not deem Cecilia Kell, an Indigenous Canadian woman, to fall within the category of rural woman. However, Kell successfully claimed rights violations under Article 15 and 16 (see section 2.4.2.1).

2.7.2.1 *L.A. et al. v. North Macedonia* and *S.N. and E.R. v. North Macedonia*

In 2020, in two joint communications, *L.A. et al. v. North Macedonia* and *S.N. and E.R. v. North Macedonia*, the Committee found Article 14 violations when several pregnant women of Roma ethnicity were evicted from their informal settlement and deprived of adequate housing.

The joint communications were brought on behalf of several women of Roma ethnicity who were nationals of North Macedonia. All were pregnant and/or mothers with infant children. They resided in an informal settlement in the old town part of Skopje, the capital of North Macedonia, without tenure to the land. The

---

[469] Id. ¶ 72.
[470] Id.
[471] Id.
[472] Id.
[473] Views concerning L.A. et al. v. North Macedonia, CEDAW/C/75/D/110/2016 (2020).
[474] Views concerning S.N. and E.R. v. North Macedonia, CEDAW/C/75/D/107/2016 (2020).
[475] Cecilia Kell v. Canada, *supra* note 129.

state had repeatedly destroyed their dwellings and property prior to their final eviction in 2016, which triggered the underlying claims. Living conditions were poor in the settlement, but the Roma women did not have another place to live. The state privatized the land on which the settlement was located. When the city proceeded with a plan to construct a road, state authorities of North Macedonia evicted the Roma women and 130 people of Roma descent living in the settlement. They did not receive a prior formal notice before the police destroyed the settlement's main water source and bulldozed their dwellings. The authors were not offered adequate alternative housing or shelter. The informal offers they received for shelter or alternative housing were of such poor quality that some of the women chose to live in the open area or return to the destroyed settlement. The women alleged, *inter alia*, that North Macedonia had violated Article 14(2)(h) "when evicting them without offering timely and appropriate alternative housing."[476]

In *S.N. and E.R. v. North Macedonia*, the Committee acknowledged the authors' claim that "they have suffered intersectional discrimination on the basis of gender, ethnicity, age and health status in violation of article 2(d) and (f) of the Convention."[477] The Committee further took note

> that the State party, by evicting them without taking measures to ensure appropriate alternative housing, health and maternal care, did not consider their extremely vulnerable situation and the particularly disproportionate and discriminatory effect on Roma pregnant adolescents.[478]

Regarding the evictions, the Committee remarked that "forced evictions are relatively rare in the State party and tend to disproportionately target Roma communities."[479] The Committee also highlighted "the authors' claim that, in addition to not refraining from forced evictions, which amounts to indirect discrimination against Roma communities, the state party failed to undertake appropriate positive measures for the elimination of the discriminatory practice of the eviction of Roma communities, including Roma pregnant women, and failed to provide any adequate remedy to the authors."[480]

The Committee recalled that states must undertake temporary special measures "to eliminate multiple forms of discrimination against women who may suffer from discrimination based on, . . . race, ethnic, or religious identity."[481]

---

[476] L.A. et al. v. North Macedonia, *supra* note 474, ¶ 3.7; S.N. and E.R. v. North Macedonia, *supra* note 475, ¶ 3.7.
[477] S.N. and E.R. v. North Macedonia, *supra* note 475, ¶ 9.2.
[478] *Id.* ¶ 9.2.
[479] *Id.* ¶ 9.3.
[480] *Id.*
[481] *Id. See also* citation to GR No. 25 on Temporary Special Measures, CEDAW/C/GC/25, ¶12 (2004).

And it recalled that it had recommended to North Macedonia to adopt "special measures ... in situations in which women from ethnic minorities are disadvantaged."[482] The Committee observed:

> Despite being minors and pregnant, the authors were treated no differently than other evicted persons and were left homeless and in a condition of extreme destitution. The Committee also observes that the right to be free from discrimination entails not only treating people equally when they are in similar situations, but also treating them differently when they are in different situations.[483]

The Committee held that North Macedonia did not "respect, protect or fulfil the right of the authors to non-discrimination and did not undertake temporary special measures aimed at addressing the specific urgent needs of minor Roma pregnant women in the particular case of eviction."[484] Thus, North Macedonia breached Article 2(d) and (f) of the Convention.

Regarding North Macedonia's failure to provide adequate accommodation after the eviction, the Committee made several observations, including that they lived in the open during their pregnancies, lacked drinking water, were offered neither social housing nor social support due to their undocumented status, and received only brief housing in a shelter which was inadequate.[485]

In *L.A. et al. v. North Macedonia*, the Committee addressed the same issues raised in *S.N. and E.R. v. North Macedonia*, namely, if North Macedonia "took the measures necessary to address the discrimination faced by the authors as members of a marginalized ethnic minority group in the context of their eviction ...."[486]

As important factors, the Committee considered that at the time of eviction the "authors were in a particularly vulnerable situation [as] ... single, young women and/or minors of Roma ethnicity who were pregnant or had recently given birth, and some of them had minor children."[487] The fact that North Macedonia failed to take the authors' particularly vulnerable situation into consideration when demolishing their homes and only water source without warning was considered particularly relevant. The Committee also noted that the accommodation offered in the aftermath of the eviction failed to meet acceptable security standards and

---

[482] S.N. and E.R. v. North Macedonia, *supra* note 475, ¶ 9.3; *see* citation to CO on North Macedonia, CEDAW/C/MKD/CO/4–5, ¶ 19 (2013).
[483] S.N. and E.R. v. North Macedonia, *supra* note 475, ¶ 9.3.
[484] *Id.* ¶ 9.4.
[485] *Id.* ¶¶ 9.7–9.9.
[486] L.A. et al. v. North Macedonia, *supra* note 474, ¶ 9.2.
[487] *Id.* ¶ 9.3.

living conditions, such that some of the affected women chose to live in the open instead.[488] The Committee concluded in weighing these factors that

> ... the State party has not given due consideration to the pre-existing conditions of the authors so as to refrain from engaging in discrimination against them in the context of the eviction. ... The State party instead implemented a decision to evict the entire community without due notice, resulting in the authors' giving birth while on the street or residing in a social centre, where their particular needs as young pregnant Roma women were not adequately addressed.[489]

In both individual communications, *S.N. and E.R. v. North Macedonia* and *L.A. et al. v. North Macedonia*, the Committee held that North Macedonia violated Articles 2(d) and (f), 4(1), 12(1) and (2), and 14(2)(b) and (h).[490]

What is remarkable about the Committee's Views in the case is that it saw Article 14(2)(h) violated because the Rome women and girls lived in the center of Skopje, the capital of North Macedonia, and this would not qualify them as "rural women" strictly speaking. The recommended remedy for the Article 14(2)(h) violation was that North Macedonia should "provide adequate reparation, including recognition of the material and moral damages that they suffered owing to inadequate access to housing ... aggravated by their eviction."[491] Additionally, North Macedonia should "provide suitable accommodation."[492]

To combat "intersecting forms of discrimination against Roma women and girls," the Committee recommended adopting, pursuing, and reinforcing effective policies, programs, and temporary special measures in accordance with Article 4(1) and GR 25.[493] Another key recommendation was ensuring "effective access to adequate housing for Roma women and girls" and "that no forced eviction of Roma women and girls is carried out if no alternative housing has been provided to those affected."[494] To address the greater problem of poverty within the Roma community, the Committee advised North Macedonia to "develop specific poverty alleviation and social inclusion programmes for Roma women and girls."[495]

Lastly, the Committee turned its attention to Roma women's access to justice. To improve the deficit of access for such groups, the Committee recommended

---

[488] *Id.* ¶¶ 9.3–9.4.
[489] *Id.* ¶ 9.4.
[490] L.A. et al. v. North Macedonia, *supra* note 474, ¶ 9.7; S.N. and E.R. v. North Macedonia, *supra* note 475, ¶ 10.
[491] L.A. et al. v. North Macedonia, *supra* note 474, ¶ 9.8; S.N. and E.R. v. North Macedonia, *supra* note 475, ¶ 11.
[492] *Id.*
[493] S.N. and E.R. v. North Macedonia, *supra* note 475, ¶ 11 b).
[494] L.A. et al. v. North Macedonia, *supra* note 474, ¶ 9.8 b); S.N. and E.R. v. North Macedonia, *supra* note 475, ¶ 11 b).
[495] *Id.*

that North Macedonia "engage actively, including through the provision of financial support, with civil society and human rights and women's organizations representing Roma women and girls in order to strengthen advocacy against intersectional forms of discrimination based on sex, gender and ethnicity, and promote tolerance and the equal participation of Roma women in all areas of life."[496] Also highlighted as important was ensuring that Roma women have access to information about their rights and how to effectively claim them.[497] Moreover, North Macedonia was urged to ensure "Roma women and girls have recourse to effective, affordable, accessible and timely remedies with legal aid and assistance as necessary, to be settled in a fair hearing by a competent and independent court or tribunal, where appropriate, or by other public institutions."[498] The Committee has yet to report on the follow-up procedure with Macedonia regarding both communications.

2.7.3 Concluding Observations

The Committee has made recommendations to states parties regarding the protection of women's housing rights in all world regions. Especially, women who experience intersectional discrimination are affected negatively by discrimination against their housing rights. Notably, the Committee extends the protection of housing rights contained in Article 14(2)(h) to all women and not only rural women, mentioning Roma women, Indigenous women, women with disabilities, and older women. Furthermore, feminized poverty and economic precarity and housing rights disenfranchisements are closely connected. The lack of property ownership is not explicitly mentioned as a contributing factor to housing rights disenfranchisements. The Committee frequently links housing with land rights and with economic and social rights. The Committee points out that disasters and conflict may jeopardize housing rights as well as development projects that dispossess women. The Committee recommended temporary special measures to protect women's housing rights.

2.7.3.1 Intersectional Discrimination Affecting Women's Housing Rights

Several COs tackle discrimination with respect to rural women's right to housing.[499] For instance, regarding Mongolia, the Committee noted with concern "rural women's limited access to land ownership and use, and property

---

[496] *Id.*
[497] *Id.*
[498] *Id.*
[499] COs on Equatorial Guinea (CEDAW/C/GNQ/CO/6, ¶ 39), Cabo Verde (CEDAW/C/CPV/CO/7-8, ¶ 31.

rights, as well as to ... housing ...."⁵⁰⁰ The Committee has recommended that states parties intensify their efforts to ensure rural women's effective access to housing.⁵⁰¹

Roma women experience systematic discrimination regarding their access to housing rights.⁵⁰² Regarding North Macedonia, the Committee noted with concern that public policies and strategies had failed to improve Roma women's access to housing, and stateless Roma people were especially affected from lack of access to housing.⁵⁰³ The Committee recommended adopting targeted measures to ensure their access to housing.⁵⁰⁴

Indigenous women are frequently disenfranchised regarding their housing rights.⁵⁰⁵ For instance, in Australia, Indigenous women "face a disproportionately high risk of homelessness and of living in overcrowded and poor housing conditions."⁵⁰⁶ In response, the Committee urged Australia to "ensure long-term funding for safe, secure and affordable housing for indigenous women ..."⁵⁰⁷

The Committee highlighted that woman with disabilities face difficulties in obtaining access to housing.⁵⁰⁸ The Committee has recommended policies to protect the housing rights of women with disabilities and increase their affordable housing options.⁵⁰⁹ More broadly, the Committee has underscored that women with disabilities should enjoy decent, equal, and accessible housing.⁵¹⁰ The Committee also recommended enhancing older women's access to affordable and adequate housing.⁵¹¹

The Committee has expressed concern that in many states parties housing rights are not guaranteed for migrants, refugees, and asylum seekers, and so that it has recommended eliminating this gap.⁵¹² Moreover, the Committee took

---

⁵⁰⁰ CO on Mongolia, CEDAW/C/MNG/CO/10, ¶ 36 (2022).
⁵⁰¹ COs on Gabon (CEDAW/C/GAB/CO/7, ¶ 35), Uzbekistan (CEDAW/C/UZB/CO/6, ¶ 36), Egypt (CEDAW/C/EGY/CO/8-10, ¶ 44), Ecuador (CEDAW/C/ECU/CO/10, ¶ 42), Angola (CEDAW/C/AGO/CO/7, ¶ 42).
⁵⁰² CO on Hungary, CEDAW/C/HUN/CO/6, ¶¶ 30-31 (2007); CO on Portugal, CEDAW/C/PRT/CO/10, ¶ 38 (2022).
⁵⁰³ CO on North Macedonia, CEDAW/C/MKD/CO/6, ¶¶ 32, 43 (2018).
⁵⁰⁴ *See, e.g.*, CO on Bulgaria, CEDAW/C/BGR/CO/8, ¶ 42 (2021).
⁵⁰⁵ *See, e.g.*, CO Guatemala, CEDAW/C/GTM/CO/8-9, ¶¶ 40-41 (2017).
⁵⁰⁶ CO on Australia, CEDAW/C/AUS/CO/8, ¶ 51 (2018).
⁵⁰⁷ *Id.* ¶ 52 (2018).
⁵⁰⁸ COs on Mongolia (CEDAW/C/MNG/CO/8-9, ¶ 34), Namibia (CEDAW/C/NAM/CO/6, ¶ 47), Barbados (CEDAW/C/BRB/CO/5-8, ¶ 41), Kenya (CEDAW/C/KEN/CO/8, ¶ 47).
⁵⁰⁹ CO on Namibia, CEDAW/C/NAM/CO/6, ¶ 48 (2022); CO on Barbados, CEDAW/C/BRB/CO/5-8, ¶ 42 (2017).
⁵¹⁰ COs on Portugal (CEDAW/C/PRT/CO/10, ¶ 41), Angola (CEDAW/C/AGO/CO/7, ¶ 44), Kenya (CEDAW/C/KEN/CO/8, ¶ 47).
⁵¹¹ COs on Australia (CEDAW/C/AUS/CO/8, ¶ 46), Singapore (CEDAW/C/SGP/CO/5, ¶ 39), Ukraine (CEDAW/C/UKR/CO/8, ¶ 44).
⁵¹² COs on Mexico (CEDAW/C/MKD/CO/6, ¶¶ 47-48), North Macedonia (CEDAW/C/MKD/CO/6, ¶ 46).

issue with administrative barriers to obtaining identification documents, as they are essential for women's access to housing.[513]

The Committee has expressed concern when women's socioeconomic status and poverty limit their housing rights.[514] Accordingly, women would benefit from housing schemes for low-income people.[515] For instance, the Committee advised Kazakhstan to "review its social protection and housing scheme with a view to reducing feminized poverty, consider developing a housing or home ownership scheme for large families living in poverty and ensure the availability of pathways for poor women wishing to graduate out of State welfare."[516]

Women who experience intersectional discrimination of various forms are more frequently exposed to homelessness.[517]

2.7.3.2 Economic Precarity and Housing Rights

Women doing unpaid care work are often discriminated against regarding their housing rights. state parties should provide affordable public housing services for women who provide care work.[518] It also advised states to "take steps to recognize, reduce and redistribute the unpaid care and domestic work of rural women through investment in infrastructure and social services such as . . . affordable housing…"[519]

The Committee has identified women who have experienced trafficking as in particular need of support to obtain adequate access to housing and shelter.[520] Regarding women in vulnerable situations more generally, the Committee has stressed the need for effective access to housing. For instance, effective housing access was highlighted as crucial in the United Kingdom to avoid resort to "sex for rent."[521]

Women working in the informal sector, such as domestic workers, frequently find themselves at risk of losing their housing. This is a trend which intensified during the COVID-19 pandemic.[522] In some states, the Committee observed a complete absence of legislation protecting the housing rights of women domestic workers.[523]

---

[513] COs on Panama (CEDAW/C/PAN/CO/8, ¶ 46), Cambodia (CEDAW/C/KHM/CO/6, ¶¶ 32–33).
[514] CO on Botswana, CEDAW/C/BWA/CO/4, ¶ 39 (2019); CO on Barbados, CEDAW/C/BRB/CO/5–8, ¶ 40 (2017).
[515] Id. ¶ 40.
[516] CO on Kazakhstan, CEDAW/C/KAZ/CO/5, ¶ 42 (2019).
[517] CO on Bangladesh, CEDAW/C/BGD/CO/7, ¶ 37 (2011).
[518] CO on Azerbaijan (CEDAW/C/AZE/CO/6, ¶ 36), Ecuador (CEDAW/C/ECU/CO/10, ¶ 38), Kyrgyzstan (CEDAW/C/KGZ/CO/5, ¶ 38).
[519] CO on Cabo Verde, CEDAW/C/CPV/CO/9, ¶ 41 (2019).
[520] CO on Guyana, CEDAW/C/GUY/CO/9, ¶ 28 (2019).
[521] CO on UK, CEDAW/C/GBR/CO/8, ¶ 36 (2019).
[522] CO on Panama, CEDAW/C/PAN/CO/8, ¶ 35 (2022).
[523] CO on South Africa, CEDAW/C/ZAF/CO/5, ¶ 49 (2021); CO on Kuwait, CEDAW/C/KWT/CO/5, ¶ 36 (2017).

2.7.3.3 Development Projects and Housing Rights

Women's housing rights are also affected when economic and development projects are implemented. For instance, it recommended to Mozambique in the context of mining operations that led to the displacement and resettlement of rural women to "ensure that women and their families who are evicted from their lands are provided with adequate alternative housing and receive compensation."[524]

In countries where women were deprived of their homes with short notice and inadequate or no compensation due to housing renewal and reconstruction programs in urban areas, the Committee recommended to "ensure fair and non-discriminatory compensation."[525] The Committee also recommended to review housing and construction laws when they negatively impact the housing rights of women who are experiencing intersectional discrimination.[526]

2.7.3.4 Impact of Disasters and Conflict Situations on Housing

The Committee noted with concern the negative impact of natural disasters on the availability of housing.[527] For instance, after the tsunami in Indonesia in 2005, the Committee expressed concern that women's needs for housing had not been met and that women heads of households had suffered discriminatory treatment regarding their access to housing.[528] The Committee expressed concern that an earthquake in Nepal in 2015 had exacerbated the lack of access to housing particularly for women of "oppressed classes."[529] The Committee recommended adopting temporary special measures in case of disaster to enhance women's access to housing.[530]

The COVID-19 pandemic has exacerbated existing structural barriers of inequality, including regarding housing.[531] The Committee has advocated "all necessary measures through the recovery and resilience funds and all legislation and public policies to overcome the structural barriers of inequality faced by women, regarding their access to housing."[532]

Especially in conflict and post-conflict situations, the Committee has observed risks to women regarding the protection of their housing rights. The Committee has expressed its concern regarding internally displaced women in conflict situations and their access to housing.[533] For instance, regarding

---

[524] CO on Mozambique, CEDAW/C/MOZ/CO/3-5, ¶¶ 39–40 (2019).
[525] CO on Turkmenistan, CEDAW/C/TKM/CO/5, ¶¶ 42–43 (2018).
[526] CO on Slovakia, CEDAW/C/SVK/CO/5-6, ¶ 37 (2015).
[527] CO on Mozambique, CEDAW/C/MOZ/CO/3-5, ¶ 39 (2019).
[528] CO on Indonesia, CEDAW/C/IDN/CO/5, ¶¶ 38–39 (2007).
[529] CO on Nepal, CEDAW/C/NPL/CO/6, ¶ 40 (2018).
[530] *Id.* ¶ 41.
[531] CO on Portugal, CEDAW/C/PRT/CO/10, ¶ 34 (2022).
[532] *Id.* ¶ 35 (2022).
[533] CO on Azerbaijan, CEDAW/C/AZE/CO/6, ¶ 13 (2022); CO on Turkey CEDAW/C/TUR/CO/8, ¶¶ 32–33 (2022).

the Nagorno-Karabakh conflict, the Committee expressed its concern that internally displaced women in Azerbaijan have limited access to housing.[534] Furthermore, in its COs on Turkey, the Committee expressed its concern regarding Kurdish women who had "been evicted from their homes, . . . often subjected to intersecting forms of discrimination and who are exposed to additional risks of sexual and other forms of gender-based violence when compelled to sleep on the street."[535] The Committee recommended ensuring "access for internally displaced women and girls to . . . housing and swiftly ensure that they can return to their homes and that their homes are rehabilitated to decent housing conditions."[536]

2.7.3.5 Temporary Special Measures

On a broader scale, the Committee has recommended adopting temporary special measures to support disadvantaged women and women experiencing intersectional discrimination in accessing secure housing.[537] The Committee also recommended adopting temporary special measures to address situations in which women lack substantive equality with regard to their access to adequate housing.[538] For instance, it recommended that Cambodia adopt temporary special measures to "increase tenure security for women living in informal settlements and to improve access by women, especially indigenous women, women belonging to ethnic minority groups and rural women, to adequate housing including through the mechanisms established under the national housing policy."[539] Sanctions for noncompliance should accompany those temporary special measures.[540]

2.8 Intellectual Property and Seed Rights

2.8.1 The Convention and General Recommendations

Article 14(2)(g) protects women's seed rights and their intellectual property rights. Moreover, women's intellectual property rights are addressed in two

---

[534] CO on Azerbaijan, CEDAW/C/AZE/CO/6, ¶ 13 (2022).
[535] CO on Turkey, CEDAW/C/TUR/CO/8 ¶ 32 (2022).
[536] CO on Turkey, CEDAW/C/TUR/CO/8 ¶ 33 (2022).
[537] COs on Uzbekistan (CEDAW/C/UZB/CO/6, ¶ 18), Serbia (CEDAW/C/SRB/CO/4, ¶ 42), Tajikistan (CEDAW/C/TJK/CO/6, ¶ 42).
[538] CO on Cambodia, CEDAW/C/KHM/CO/6, ¶ 20 (2019); CO on Botswana (CEDAW/C/BWA/CO/4, ¶21).
[539] Id. ¶ 21.
[540] CO on Botswana, CEDAW/C/BWA/CO/4, ¶ 22 (2019).

GRs: GR 34 on Rural Women in the context of farming and seeds and GR 39 regarding Indigenous women's right to culture and seed rights.

2.8.1.1 Article 14(2)(g)

Article 14(2)(g) provides rural women with "access to ... appropriate technology and equal treatment in land and agrarian reform as well as in land resettlement schemes." It protects women's seed rights as well as their intellectual property rights.[541]

2.8.1.2 GR 34 on Rural Women and GR 39 on Indigenous Women

GR 34 protects women's rights to seeds against land and property grabs in the context of industrial farming:

> The consequences of industrial agriculture have often been detrimental to rural women farmers.... The controversial use of genetically modified organisms and the patenting of genetically altered crops are also linked to increased agricultural industrialization. Rural women, however, are more often engaged in organic and sustainable farming practices.
>
> States parties should implement agricultural policies that support rural women farmers, recognize and protect the natural commons, promote organic farming and protect rural women from harmful pesticides and fertilizers. They should ensure that rural women have effective access to agricultural resources, including high-quality seeds, tools, knowledge and information, as well as equipment and resources for organic farming.[542]

GR 34 also strengthens rural women's intellectual property rights by protecting their native seeds while limiting patenting practices by transnational corporations that harm rural women. The Committee recommends that states parties

(a) Respect and protect rural women's traditional and eco-friendly agricultural knowledge, in particular the right of women to preserve, use and exchange traditional and native seeds;

(b) Protect and conserve native and endemic plant species and varieties that are a source of food and medicine, and prevent patenting by national and transnational companies to the extent that it threatens the rights of rural women. States parties should prohibit contractual requirements on the mandatory

---

[541] *See* Fareda Banda, *Article 14*, *in* 2022 COMMENTARY, *supra* note 5.
[542] GR No. 34, *supra* note 125, ¶¶ 60–62.

purchase of seeds producing plants whose seeds are sterile ("terminator seeds"), which prevent rural women from saving fertile seeds.[543]

In GR 39, the Committee frames Indigenous women's intellectual property rights as part of their right to culture, providing protection under the Convention. It recommends that states parties act with due diligence when "cultural knowledge and heritage of Indigenous women and girls" is used without their prior consent and without sharing the benefits with them.[544]

The Committee formulates a very broad protection requirement for states regarding Indigenous women's intellectual property rights. It recommends that states

> [r]ecognize and protect Indigenous women's intellectual property; cultural heritage; scientific and medical knowledge; forms of literary, artistic, musical and dance expressions; and natural resources.[545]

The Committee provides a long list of measures that it would like states to adopt to protect Indigenous women's various intellectual property rights, including "the recognition, registration and protection of the individual or collective authorship of Indigenous women and girls under national intellectual property rights regime."[546] The goal of all those measures should be to prevent the unauthorized use of their intellectual property rights. The Committee also calls on state parties to ensure that Indigenous women's preferences are considered and that their free, prior ,and informed consent is respected. The Committee calls on states to

> respect the principle of free, prior and informed consent of Indigenous women authors and artists and the oral or other customary forms of transmission of their traditional knowledge, cultural heritage and scientific, literary or artistic expressions.[547]

In particular, the Committee emphasizes Indigenous women's intellectual property rights regarding their right to seeds. Specifically, the Committee observes "increasing commercialization of seeds, which are an essential part of the ancestral knowledge and cultural heritage of Indigenous Peoples."[548] As

---

[543] Id.
[544] GR No. 39, *supra* note 362, ¶ 55.
[545] Id. ¶ 23 h).
[546] Id.
[547] Id.
[548] Id. ¶ 58.

with other forms of intellectual property, the Committee notes that the benefits that stem from this commercialization are not shared with Indigenous women. Moreover, Indigenous women and girls feel the negative consequences of the proliferation of transgenic or genetically modified crops without being able to participate.[549] The Committee recommends ensuring access to sufficient seeds, meaningful participation in the management and control of natural resources, and access to the benefits of scientific progress and technological innovation to be able to achieve food and water security.[550] The Committee also recommends that state parties recognize and compensate Indigenous women for their technical and scientific contributions.[551]

2.8.2 Concluding Observations

The Committee linked the protection of women's intellectual property rights with their economic empowerment. Moreover, it reflected upon the relationship between women's rights to seeds and intellectual property rights.

2.8.2.1 Intellectual Property Rights and Economic Empowerment

To enhance the economic empowerment of women, the Committee recommended "protecting the ancestral intellectual property of women especially in the area of artisanal and craft production."[552] Regarding the Maldives, it recommended that states "establish the legal and operational framework to increase women's participation in entrepreneurship and assist women in finding a suitable market for their products domestically, in protecting their intellectual property and in navigating the export procedure for their products."[553] With respect to Kyrgyzstan, it also advised the state to "economically protect women's intergenerational intellectual property in their textile, artisanal and craft production."[554]

2.8.2.2 Rights to Seeds

The Committee also portrayed the critical juncture between women's rights to seeds and intellectual property rights—frequently, the latter curtail women's access to seeds even if the Committee did not make this explicit in its jurisprudence. It recommended Lebanon to "facilitate rural women's access to technical support and training for agricultural innovation and new technologies,

---

[549] Id.
[550] Id. ¶ 59.
[551] Id.
[552] CO on Ecuador, CEDAW/C/ECU/CO/10, ¶ 36 (2021).
[553] CO on Maldives, CEDAW/C/MDV/CO/6, ¶ 42 (2021).
[554] CO on Kyrgyzstan, CEDAW/C/KGZ/CO/5, ¶ 38 a) (2021).

agricultural assets such as ... seeds ...."⁵⁵⁵ With regard to Gambia and Eritrea, the Committee recommended to ensure rural women's access to seeds, and other resources.⁵⁵⁶

2.9 Access to Financial Credit and Economic Empowerment

2.9.1 Convention and General Recommendations

Articles 13(b) and 14(2)(g) protect women's access to financial credit and economic empowerment more broadly. Women's right to economic empowerment, entrepreneurship, and access to credit is protected in a several GRs.⁵⁵⁷

2.9.1.1 Article 13(b) and Article 14(2)(g)

Article 13(b) provides women with "the right to bank loans, mortgages and other forms of financial credit ... ." It is the backbone provision of women's economic autonomy because it provides women with an equal right to financial resources, which empowers women and serves as a gateway right to economic independence.

Article 14(2)(g) provides that states shall ensure that rural women "have access to agricultural credit and loans, marketing facilities, appropriate technology and equal treatment in land and agrarian reform as well as in land resettlement schemes."⁵⁵⁸

2.9.1.2 GR 21 on Family Relations

GR 21 on Equality in Marriage and Family Relations addresses the overlap between Articles 13 and 15. Women's autonomy and equality to contract mean that their right to financial credit without male permission must be protected:

> When a woman cannot enter into a contract at all, or have access to financial credit, or can do so only with her husband's or a male relative's concurrence or

---

⁵⁵⁵ Co on Lebanon, CEDAW/C/LBN/CO/6, ¶ 52 (2022).
⁵⁵⁶ CO on Gambia, CEDAW/C/GMB/CO/4-5 ¶ 41 (2015); CO on Eritrea, CEDAW/C/ERI/CO/5, ¶ 37 (2015).
⁵⁵⁷ *See* GR No. 21, *supra* note 91 (concerning equality in marriage and family relations), GR No. 27, *supra* note 117 (concerning older women and protection of their human rights), GR No. 34, *supra* note 125 (concerning the rights of rural women), GR No. 37, *supra* note 358 (concerning the gender-related dimensions of disaster risk reduction in the context of climate change), GR No. 38 on Trafficking in Women and Girls in The Context of Global Migration, CEDAW/C/GC/38 (2020) (concerning trafficking in women and girls in the context of global migration), and GR No. 39, *supra* note 362 (concerning on the rights of Indigenous women and girls).
⁵⁵⁸ *See* for a detailed overview of both provisions in Beate Rudolf, *Article 13*, *supra* note 5; *see also* Fareda Banda, *Article 14*, *supra* note 5.

guarantee, she is denied legal autonomy. Any such restriction ... precludes her from the legal management of her own business ... Such restrictions seriously limit the woman's ability to provide for herself and her dependents.[559]

2.9.1.3 GR 27 on Older Women

GR 27 on Older Women protects older women's rights to financial credit and their participation in economic and social life. Regarding older women's right to access financial credit, the Committee expresses concern about age restrictions negatively affecting older women: "Microcredit and finance schemes usually have age restrictions or other criteria that prevent older women from accessing them."[560] States parties have a duty to provide access to financial credit to older women. It recommends that states parties remove all barriers based on age and gender to access credits and loans. Moreover, they should provide "special support systems and collateral-free microcredit, as well as encourage microentrepreneurship for older women...."[561]

2.9.1.4 GR 34 on Rural Women

GR 34 on Rural Women contains several provisions on rural women's economic empowerment, exploring the link between Articles 13 and 14. The GR highlights that rural women in both developing and developed countries suffer discrimination and challenges regarding economic empowerment.[562] The Committee stresses that providing access to economic resources and financial services to older rural women should empower them "to live life with dignity."[563] Moreover, states parties should expand "opportunities for rural women to run businesses and other enterprises, including through microcredit facilities."[564]

Regarding the connection between Article 14(2)(g) and Article 13, the Committee makes some explicit recommendations regarding financial services, including agricultural credit, loans, and insurance. The Committee highlights that "access to financial services on fair terms is crucial for the development of rural women's enterprises and for their income-generating and livelihood strategies as producers and entrepreneurs."[565] The Committee lists legal and policy barriers as a hurdle for "women to apply for credit in their own right."[566] Moreover, discriminatory attitudes or discriminatory requirements such as having collateral prevent "women from holding bank accounts or entering into contracts without

---

[559] GR No. 21, *supra* note 91, ¶ 7.
[560] GR No. 27, *supra* note 117, ¶ 23.
[561] *Id.* ¶ 47.
[562] GR No. 34, *supra* note 125, ¶ 2.
[563] *Id.* ¶ 15.
[564] *Id.* ¶¶ 48–52.
[565] *Id.* ¶ 67.
[566] *Id.*

the consent of a male relative."[567] In response, the Committee recommends that states parties promote "rural women's access to credit, loans, . . . on the basis of equality with rural men, and promote their economic, financial and business skills."[568] The Committee makes detailed recommendations regarding rural women's equal access to financial services such as "community-managed and mobile financial services, which should address rural women's needs, for example by lending to women who may lack collaterals, employ simplified, low-cost banking practices and facilitate rural women's access to formal financial service providers."[569] In addition, states parties should provide information and financial skills-building.[570] The Committee also foresees concrete steps for how to ensure that financial services represent gender-responsive mechanisms, such as that no male guarantor is needed to access credit and loans or that registration procedures are adapted to rural women's needs.[571] In addition, states parties should ensure agricultural credit and loans "for the untenured nature of the smallholdings held by many women farmers, so that rural women who may lack formal tenure rights are still able to gain access to them."[572] Furthermore, GR 34 also recommends that rural women's activities as entrepreneurs and that their market access be promoted.[573]

2.9.1.5 GR 37 on Climate Change

GR 37 on the Gender-Related Dimensions of Disaster Risk Reduction in the context of Climate diagnoses that "gender inequalities limit the control that women and girls have over decisions governing their lives, as well as their access to resources such as . . . credit."[574] The Committee treats women's lack of access to financial credit as a restricting factor on women's mobility which limited their capacity to respond to disasters and to adapt to changes in climatic conditions.[575] In response, the Committee recommends that "States parties should . . . facilitate equal access for women to markets, financial services, credit and insurance schemes . . . ."[576]

2.9.1.6 GR 38 on Trafficking in Women and Girls

GR 38 on Trafficking in Women and Girls in the context of Global Migration places trafficking in the context of global economic policies. Lack of access to

---

[567] Id.
[568] Id. ¶ 68.
[569] Id. ¶ 68 a).
[570] Id. ¶ 68 b)–c).
[571] Id. ¶ 68 d).
[572] Id. ¶ 69.
[573] Id. ¶¶ 70–72.
[574] GR No. 37, *supra* note 358, ¶ 3.
[575] Id. ¶¶ 3, 63.
[576] Id. ¶ 64.

credit can increase the risk of women and girls being lured into human trafficking networks. The Committee recommends to "eliminate social structures which limit women's autonomy and access to key resources."[577]

2.9.1.7 GR 39 on Indigenous Women

GR 39 on Indigenous Women emphasizes that discrimination against Indigenous women impedes their access to "credit, financial services and income-generating opportunities."[578] As part of states parties' obligation to protect Indigenous women's right to work encompassed in Articles 11 and 14, the Committee recommends

> expanding opportunities for Indigenous women to run businesses and become entrepreneurs. States should support Indigenous-women-led businesses and help Indigenous communities to generate wealth by improving access to capital and business opportunities.[579]

The Committee also recommends promoting Indigenous women's "equal access to loans and other forms of financial credit, without collateral, to enable them to create their own businesses and advance their economic autonomy."[580]

2.9.2 Concluding Observations

The COs on state reports address state obligations to eliminate barriers to accessing financial services. However, the Committee also presents the opportunities that financial credit represents for women, namely, female entrepreneurship, income-generating activities, and women's economic empowerment. The Committee has addressed the significance of access to microcredit for poverty reduction in developing countries. Acknowledging the importance of financial credit, the Committee highlights the impacts of intersectional discrimination on accessing such credit.

2.9.2.1 Access to Financial Services

The Committee highlights property ownership as a barrier for women in accessing financial services, including women's access to credit and loans.[581]

---

[577] GR No. 38, *supra* note 558, ¶ 51 (2020).
[578] GR No. 39, *supra* note 362, ¶ 20.
[579] *Id.* ¶ 50 a).
[580] *Id.*
[581] *See, e.g.*, COs on Bosnia and Herzegovina (CEDAW/C/BIH/CO/6, ¶ 39), Guatemala (CEDAW/C/GTM/CO/8–9, ¶ 38), Madagascar (CEDAW/C/MDG/CO/5, ¶¶ 32–33).

The Committee also expressed concern that lack of collateral in the form of real estate and lack of a steady income or employment pose challenges to accessing credit.[582] For instance, with regard to the Lao People's Democratic Republic, the Committee expressed concern that "women often face barriers to financial resources and acquisitions, despite legislation that guarantees the equal rights of women and men to the use of banking and credit system."[583] Consequently, the Committee recommended taking "steps to eliminate obstacles to equal access to land and other property by women, including through awareness-raising campaigns on their equal rights to property and inheritance, so as to enhance their access to financial credit and loans."[584]

One area of concern is barriers for married women seeking bank loans in their own names. Regarding Kuwait, the Committee recommended the adoption of a law to protect this right.[585] Similarly, female heads of households are sometimes disadvantaged in accessing bank loans. For instance, the Committee recommended that Sri Lanka "ensure equal eligibility criteria for women and men for obtaining bank loans, mortgages and other forms of financial credit from public and private institutions by removing any additional requirements for women" and "introduce low-interest or interest-free credit schemes for women heads of households and families living in poverty, with recovery plans adapted to their income generation patterns."[586]

2.9.2.2 Access to Financial Credit to Promote Women's Economic Empowerment

The Committee links the access to financial credit to women's economic empowerment, including women's entrepreneurship, opportunity to start their own (small) businesses, and ability to create income-generating activities. The Committee has made recommendations to strengthen access to financial credit to countries in Latin America,[587] Africa,[588] the Asian-Pacific Region,[589] and a few European countries.[590] Regarding Luxembourg, the Committee addressed that there existed "insufficient funding opportunities for enterprises

---

[582] CO on Bosnia and Herzegovina, CEDAW/C/BIH/CO/6, ¶¶ 39–40 (2019).
[583] CO on Lao People's Democratic Republic, CEDAW/C/LAO/CO/8-9, ¶¶ 43–44 (2018).
[584] Id.
[585] CO on Kuwait, CEDAW/C/KWT/CO/5, ¶ 40 (2017).
[586] CO on Sri Lanka, CEDAW/C/LKA/CO/8, ¶ 37 (2017).
[587] CO on Colombia (CEDAW/C/COL/CO/9, ¶ 40 c) (2019); Mexico, CEDAW/C/MEX/CO/9, ¶¶ 43–44 (2018).
[588] See, e.g., COs on Democratic Republic of Congo (CEDAW/C/COD/CO/6-7, ¶¶ 29–30), Togo (2012) ¶¶ 32–33; Côte d'Ivoire (2011) ¶ 39; Djibouti (2011) ¶ 29.
[589] CO on Lao People's Democratic, CEDAW/C/LAO/CO/8-9, ¶¶ 43–44 (2018); Turkmenistan, CEDAW/C/TKM/CO/5, ¶ 43 (2018).
[590] CO on Luxembourg, CEDAW/C/LUX/CO/6-7, ¶¶ 47–48 (2018); Republic of Moldova, CEDAW/C/MDA/CO/6, ¶ 37 b) (2020).

led by women" to enhance female-led enterprises. In response, the Committee recommended to analyze the situation of women entrepreneurs and to develop a strategy to support their initiation and continuation of their economic initiatives covering micro- and macro-enterprises. For instance, the Committee advised Mozambique to "provide adequate support for women's entrepreneurship by facilitating their access to financial services, including low-interest credit, seed capital and other economic opportunities."[591] The Committee further recommended adopting targeted measures for the economic empowerment of women, including by "facilitating their access to income-generating opportunities and financial credit, including low-interest loans without collateral."[592]

2.9.2.3 Access to Microcredit for Poverty Reduction

The Committee framed access to microcredit and loans as a strategy for poverty reduction. For instance, regarding Myanmar, the Committee recommended that it intensify poverty reduction and sustainable development "by facilitating the participation of women in the formulation of economic development plans and their access to credit and loan facilities." Moreover, it recommended intensifying "efforts to eliminate all customs and traditions that negatively affect women's access to economic resources."[593]

2.9.2.4 Intersectionality and Economic Empowerment

The Committee emphasized that states parties should take measures to improve the economic empowerment of women who experience intersecting forms of discrimination. For instance, it recommended that Colombia and Mexico promote entrepreneurship among women and empower them economically, with particular attention to Indigenous women, Colombian and Mexican women of African descent, and women with disabilities.[594]

Rural women and rural women farmers are frequently disenfranchised in accessing bank loans and financial credit.[595] For instance, the Committee expressed concern regarding Bangladesh and "limited access by rural women to financial credit and loans from public loans, given that laws and policies do not recognize them as farmers."[596] The Committee similarly recommended that the Solomon Islands "strengthen its programmes to provide income-generating

---

[591] CO on Mozambique, CEDAW/C/MOZ/CO/3–5, ¶ 38 c) (2019).
[592] CO on Mongolia, CEDAW/C/MNG/CO/10, ¶ 35 (2022).
[593] CO on Myanmar, CEDAW/C/MMR/CO/EP/1, ¶ 41 (2016).
[594] CO on Colombia, CEDAW/C/COL/CO/9, ¶ 40 c) (2019); CO on Mexico, CEDAW/C/MEX/CO/9, ¶ 44 (2018).
[595] CO on Namibia, CEDAW/C/NAM/CO/6, ¶ 43 (2022).
[596] CO on Bangladesh, CEDAW/C/BGD/CO/8, ¶ 36 (2016).

opportunities for rural women, including through credit and loans with long-term and low-interest reimbursement schemes and by developing rural women's entrepreneurial skills."[597] Providing financial credit for agribusinesses is another recommended method for state parties to combat poverty among rural women.[598]

2.10 Rights to Social Benefits

2.10.1 The Convention and General Recommendations

Access to social benefits is protected by several articles in the Convention as part of women's right to social security. The Convention addresses employment-related benefits in Article 11, benefits from self-employment, benefits unrelated to employment, and family benefits in Article 13, and benefits for rural women in Article 14(2).[599]

In addition, the Committee addresses the protection of social benefits in several GRs. In its early GRs, the Committee tackled women's unpaid work and required it to be assessed for social security payments.[600] Later on, it dealt particularly with social security payments in family relations as part of the economic consequences.[601] A number of GRs tied the assessment of social benefits to the various intersecting multiple identities of women[602] or to other particular experience.[603]

The Committee bases its jurisprudence regarding social benefits on the right to social security as it exists at the universal level, referring to the Convention's right to social security provisions. In addition, it sometimes refers to Conventions of the International Labor Organization (ILO) that mirror those arrangements. The Committee deals with different types of social benefits as part of the right

---

[597] CO on Solomon Island, CEDAW/C/SLB/CO/1–3, ¶ 39 (2014).
[598] CO on Azerbaijan, CEDAW/C/AZE/CO/6, ¶ 38 (2022).
[599] *See* 2022 COMMENTARY, *supra* note 5 on Article 11 (Frances Raday & Shai Oksenberg, 414–415), Article 13 (Beate Rudolf, 487), and Article 14 (Fareda Banda, 519).
[600] *See generally*, GR No. 16 on Unpaid Women Workers in Rural and Urban Family Enterprises, A/46/38 (1991); GR No. 17 on Measurement and Quantification of The Unremunerated Domestic Activities of Women and Their Recognition in the Gross National Product, A/46/38 (1991).
[601] GR No. 29, *supra* note 75 (on the economic consequences of marriage, family relations and their dissolution).
[602] *See* GR No. 18 on Disabled Women, A/46/38 (1991). GR No. 26 on Women Migrant Workers, CEDAW/C/2009/WP.1/R (2008); GR No. 27, *supra* note 117 (on older women and protection of their human rights); GR No. 34, *supra* note 125 (on the rights of rural women); GR No. 39, *supra* note 362 (on the rights of Indigenous women and girls).
[603] *See* GR No. 37, *supra* note 358 (on the gender-related dimensions of disaster risk reduction in the context of climate change); GR No. 38, *supra* note 558 (on trafficking in women and girls in the context of global migration).

to social security but never refers to them as property rights. Neither in its GRs, Views, or COs does the Committee refer to contributory or noncontributory social benefits as property rights. It also never references the jurisprudence of the European Court of Human Rights that would deal with those under the right to property according to Article 1 Protocol 1 to the European Convention on Human Rights (ECHR) given that no separate right to social security exits in this regional human rights system. It also never references the Inter-American Court of Human Rights, which has also dealt with pension benefits under property rights.[604]

2.10.1.1 Articles 11, 13, and 14

Article 11 protects women's access to social security, social benefits in employment relationships, and maternity benefits. Article 11(1)(e) requires that women enjoy the same rights as men regarding "the right to social security, particularly in cases of retirement, unemployment, sickness, invalidity and old age and other incapacity to work, as well as the right to paid leave." Article 11(2)(b) protects women against discrimination on the grounds of marriage or maternity in employment relationships, including women's rights to maternity benefits. States should take appropriate measures "to introduce maternity leave with pay or with comparable social benefits without loss of former employment, seniority or social allowances." Article 13(a) guarantees women's equality regarding family benefits covering non-work-related family benefits. In addition, the chapeau of Article 13 entails several economic and social rights protections, potentially including the right to social security as a catch-all provision. Article 14(2)(c) protects rural women's "right to benefit directly from social security programmes."

2.10.1.2 GRs on Social Benefits in the Context of Unpaid Care Work in Families and Informal Work in Family Enterprises

GR 16 addresses the lack of social security and social benefits afforded to women who work in family-owned enterprises, usually owned by male members of the family. The Committee recommends that states collect and include data on "women who work without payment, social security and social benefits in enterprises owned by a family member" and "take the necessary steps to guarantee payment, social security and social benefits for women who work without such benefits in enterprises owned by a family member."[605]

---

[604] *See* Eur. Ct. H.R., *Guide on Article 1 of Protocol No. 1 to the European Convention on Human Rights: Protection of Property* (Aug. 31, 2022), https://www.echr.coe.int/Documents/Guide_Art_1_Protocol_1_ENG.pdf. *See* a more detailed explanation of the Inter-American Court of Human Rights jurisprudence in chapter 1.

[605] GR No. 16, *supra* note 601.

GR 17 concerns the measurement, quantification, and recognition of women's unremunerated domestic activities.[606] Making these activities visible impacts the amount of social security benefits available to women.

GR 29 on the Economic Consequences of Marriage, Family Relations and their Dissolution criticizes social security systems that, while "nominally designed to improve economic status," may effectively discriminate against female heads of household who cannot access social security benefits due to persistent poverty and the underlying structural factors that prompt persistent income inequality.[607]

GR 27 on Older Women highlights that many older women are caregivers for others but face impediments to qualifying for family benefits.[608] The Committee recommends that they should "have access to appropriate social and economic benefits, such as childcare benefits, as well as access to all necessary support when caring for elderly parents or relatives."[609]

GR 34 emphasizes the contribution of rural women to the economic survival of families and society and calls on states parties to consider the economic value of their paid and unpaid work on family farms.[610] State parties should ensure that rural women are able to benefit from social security.[611]

2.10.1.3 GRs on Social Benefits in the Context of Informal Employment

GR 26 on Women Migrant Workers frequently employed in informal employment situations stipulates that states must undertake their obligations "in recognition of the social and economic contribution of women migrant workers to their own countries and countries of destination, including through caregiving and domestic work."[612] The Committee does not explicitly refer to social security obligations toward migrant women based on their contributions, but they can be implied as part of states' obligations.

GR 34 on the Rights of Rural Women points out that rural women are frequently not covered by social protection.[613] It contains several provisions on rural women's social protection based on Article 14(2)(c), read alongside Articles 11(1)(e) and (2)(b) and 13(a).[614] The Committee points out that rural women face increased risks of not being protected by social security legislation because of their limited access to formal employment and their frequent engagement in

---

[606] GR No. 17, *supra* note 601.
[607] GR No. 29, *supra* note 75, ¶¶ 4–5.
[608] GR No. 27, *supra* note 117, ¶¶ 20 & 22.
[609] *Id.* ¶ 43.
[610] GR No. 34, *supra* note 125, ¶ 16.
[611] *Id.* ¶ 17.
[612] GR No. 26, *supra* note 603, ¶ 3.
[613] GR No. 34, *supra* note 125, ¶ 5.
[614] *Id.* ¶¶ 40–41.

unrelated activities. The Committee recommended eliminating discrimination through ensuring

> ... that rural women engaged in unpaid work or in the informal sector have access to non-contributory social protection ..., and that those employed in the formal sector have access to contributory social security benefits in their own right....[615]

Regarding the connection between the rights contained in Articles 14(2)(e) and 11 in the context of employment, the Committee recommends providing "paid maternity leave" and "social security to rural women, including in cases of sickness or invalidity."[616]

GR 38 highlights that women without social protection and benefits are more vulnerable to being trafficked.[617] The Committee recommends strengthening and enforcing the implementation of the labor rights framework in informal employment relationships and improving social protection to combat risk factors for trafficking.[618]

GR 39 on Indigenous Women and Girls highlights that their "overrepresentation in informal employment translates into weak income, benefits and social protection."[619] The Committee recommends that states parties ensure income security and social protection coverage for Indigenous women in employment relations and when self-employed.[620]

2.10.1.4 GRs on Pension Benefits and Survivorship Benefits

GR 27 on Older Women deals with older women's pension benefits. It noted that women's pensions are lower due to gender-based discrimination in employment, including wage discrimination, throughout their life. In addition, the different mandatory retirement age for women also implies the accumulation of lower pension benefits.[621] In response, the Committee calls on states to monitor the impact of gender-related pay gaps impacting older women's pension benefits in contribution-based systems.[622]

The Committee provides that contributory and noncontributory pension schemes must not discriminate against women pensioners. The Committee points out states' obligations in this regard: states parties should ensure that

---

[615] *Id.* ¶ 40.
[616] *Id.* ¶¶ 48–52.
[617] GR No. 38, *supra* note 558, ¶ 20.
[618] *Id.* ¶ 53.
[619] GR No. 39, *supra* note 362, ¶ 49.
[620] *Id.* ¶ 50.
[621] GR No. 27, *supra* note 117, ¶ 20.
[622] *Id.* ¶ 41.

the retirement age is not discriminatory in the public and private sectors; they should ensure that pension policies are not discriminatory also when women opt to retire early. Older women should have access to adequate pensions, and states should undertake appropriate or even temporary measures where necessary to guarantee such adequate pensions.[623] The Committee calls on states parties to provide "adequate non-contributory pensions, on an equal basis with men, to all women who have no other pension or insufficient income security."[624]

In GR 29, the Committee indicates that spousal and survivorship benefits from social security and pension systems are relevant for the distribution of property upon the death of one spouse. It states that

> [s]urvivorship rights to social security payments (pensions and disability payments) and in contributory pension systems play a large role in States parties in which couples pay significant sums into those systems during the relationship. States parties are obligated to provide for equality between men and women in terms of spousal and survivorship benefits from social security and pension systems.[625]

According to GR 37 addressing women's rights in the context of climate change and disasters, the Committee calls on states parties to prioritize women's equal access to insurance schemes. States should regulate "the informal economy to ensure that women are able to claim pensions and other employment-related social security entitlements."[626]

2.10.2 Communications

The Committee has issued four communications regarding the protection of social benefits based on Article 11:[627] *Ms. Dung Thi Thuy Nguyen v. The Netherlands*, *Elisabeth de Blok et al. v. The Netherlands*, *Natalia Ciobanu v. Republic of Moldova*, and *V.P. v. Belarus*. *Ms. Dung Thi Thuy Nguyen v. The Netherlands* was the Committee's first decision on maternity benefits of self-employed women. Even

---

[623] *Id.* ¶ 42.
[624] *Id.* ¶ 44.
[625] GR No. 29, *supra* note 75, ¶ 51.
[626] *Id.* ¶ 64.
[627] *Ms. Dung Thi Thuy Nguyen v. The Netherlands*, Communication No. 3/2004, CEDAW/C/36/D/3/2004 (Aug. 29, 2006); *Elisabeth de Blok et al. v. The Netherlands*, Communication No. 36/2012, CEDAW/C/57/D/36/2012 (Mar. 24, 2014); *Natalia Ciobanu v. Republic of Moldova*, Communication No. 104/2016, CEDAW/C/74/D/104/2016 (Dec. 17, 2019); *V.P. v. Belarus*, Communication No. 131/2018, CEDAW/C/79/D/131/2018 (Aug. 10, 2021).

though the Committee found no violation of Article 11(2)(b), the dissenting opinion on the communication led to a shift in the Committee's jurisprudence a few years later in *Elisabeth de Blok et al. v. The Netherlands*, where self-employed women in the Netherlands were also disenfranchised regarding their maternity benefits. *Natalia Ciobanu v. Republic of Moldova* concerns a pension benefits case highlighting the discrimination that women experience when states parties fail to consider unpaid care work in contributory pension schemes. *V.P. v. Belarus* deals with a pension case where a woman was refused her contributory pension due to a lack of pensionable service after a legal change but could also not qualify for the old-age pension based on a noncontributory pension scheme.

2.10.2.1 Ms. Dung Thi Thuy Nguyen v. The Netherlands

In *Ms. Dung Thi Thuy Nguyen v. The Netherlands*, the Committee dealt with the alleged violation by the Netherlands of Article 11(2)(b). While the Committee did not find the claim justified, several individual members expressed in their dissenting opinion that indirect discrimination occurred and provided recommendations.

Ms. Dung Thi Thuy Nguyen worked as a part-time salaried employee in addition to working with her husband in his enterprise. Because of this, she was insured under two different schemes. One stemmed from her salaried employment (Sickness Benefit Act, or ZW) and the other from her employment in her husband's enterprise (Invalidity Insurance (Self-Employed Persons) Act, or WAZ).[628]

During her first maternity leave in 1999, due to the non-accumulation clause of the insurance scheme from her activity in her husband's enterprise (WAZ), she received no compensation from that scheme. Accordingly, she was compensated for her lost income only by the insurance scheme attached to her salaried employment (ZW). The non-accumulation clause allowed her to receive benefits under the ZW but not WAZ. The Dutch Court of Appeal did not find that the anti-accumulation clause led to an unfavorable treatment of women compared to men. Moreover, it held that Article 11 of the Convention would lack direct effect.[629] In 2002, when the author began a second maternity leave and again applied for benefits, the benefits agency decided that the author's entitlement under ZW would be supplemented by the difference between her claim under WAZ and her entitlement under ZW, but she did not receive full benefits under both schemes.[630]

The author complained that she was a victim of a violation by the state party of Article 11(2)(b), which entitles women to maternity leave with full compensation

---

[628] *Ms. Dung Thi Thuy Nguyen v. The Netherlands*, ¶¶ 2.1–2.3.
[629] *Id.* ¶ 2.5.
[630] *Id.* ¶ 2.6.

for loss of income from their work. According to her complaint, partial compensation for lost income does not fulfill the requirements and amounts to direct discrimination against women because of their pregnancy.[631]

The Committee had to determine if the application of the non-accumulation clause of the WAZ scheme violated Article 11(2)(b) of the Convention. Ms. Dung Thi Thuy Nguyen received lower payments than she would have received had the provision not been in operation. Moreover, had she been able to claim benefits as an employee and as a co-working spouse independently of each other she would have received the full amount of benefits.[632] Weighing these factors, the Committee found no violation.

The Committee stated that the aim of Article 11(2) was to "address discrimination against women working in gainful employment outside the home on grounds of pregnancy and childbirth."[633] It also stated that the "author has not shown that the application of the . . . [non-accumulation clause] was discriminatory towards her as a woman on the grounds laid down in Article 11(2) of the Convention, namely of marriage or maternity."[634] Article 11(2)(b) obliges states parties in such cases to "introduce maternity leave with pay or comparable social benefits without loss of former employment, seniority or social allowances."[635] The Committee noted that Article 11(2)(b) does not use the term "full" pay, nor does it use "full compensation for loss of income" resulting from pregnancy and childbirth. The Convention leaves to states parties "a certain margin of discretion to devise a system of maternity leave benefits to fulfil Convention requirements."[636]

The Committee found that "self-employed women and co-working spouses as well as salaried women are entitled to maternity leave-albeit under different insurance schemes."[637] The only restriction to receiving benefits under different insurance schemes is a maximum payable amount, but entitlements can be sought simultaneously and awarded under different schemes. Contributions to the scheme covering self-employed women and co-working spouses are adjusted with income from their salaried employment.[638]

Moreover, the Committee held:

It is within the State party's margin of discretion to determine the appropriate maternity benefits within the meaning of article 11(2)(b) of the Convention for

---

[631] *Id.* ¶ 3.1.
[632] *Id.* ¶ 10.2.
[633] *Id.*
[634] *Id.*
[635] *Id.*
[636] *Id.*
[637] *Id.*
[638] *Id.*

all employed women, with separate rules for self-employed women that take into account fluctuating income and related contributions. It is also within the state party's margin of discretion to apply those rules in combination to women who are partly self-employed and partly salaried workers.[639]

The Committee concluded that the application of the non-accumulation clause did not result in any discriminatory treatment of the author. It found no violation of Article 11(2)(b).[640]

The dissenting Committee members[641] assessed the situation differently and found a violation of Article 11(2)(b), determining that the non-accumulation clause in the Dutch legislation leads to indirect discrimination.

According to the dissenters, Article 11(2)(b) places an obligation on states parties to provide "maternity leave with pay or with comparable social benefits without loss of former employment, seniority or social allowance."[642] Even if Article 11(2)(b) provides states parties with a margin of discretion and does not use the term "full" pay, states parties are obliged to provide maternity benefits for self-employed women just as they would for salaried employees.[643]

While the dissenters did not find that the Dutch legislation directly discriminates, they found that the non-accumulation clause leads to indirect discrimination:[644]

> ... [W]e are concerned at the fact that the so-called "equivalence" principle does not seem to take into account the potential situation of a women working in a situation of both salaried part-time and self-employment, in which the number of her working hours in both categories of work equal or even may go beyond the hours of a full-time salaried female employee, who, in the Netherlands, to our knowledge, receives a maternity benefit which equals full pay for a certain period of time. In addition, the 1996 Equal Treatment (Full-time and Part-time Workers) (WOA) requires full-time and part-time employees to be treated equally. Therefore, we are of the view that the so-called anti-accumulation clause ... may constitute a form of indirect discrimination based on sex. This view is based on the assumption that an employment situation in which salaried part-time work and self-employment is combined, as described by the complainant, is one which mainly women experience in the Netherlands, since, in general, it is mainly women who work part-time as

---

[639] *Id.*
[640] *Id.*
[641] *Id.* Naela Mohamed Gabr, Hanna Beate Schöpp-Schilling, Ms. Heisoo Shin.
[642] *Id.* Dissenting, ¶ 10.3.
[643] *Id.* ¶ 10.3.
[644] *Id.* ¶¶ 10.4–10.5.

salaried workers in addition to working as family helpers in their husbands' enterprises....[645]

The dissenters recommended to the Netherlands to "collect data on the number of women working in the combination of part-time salaried employment and as self-employed persons as compared to men in order to assess the percentage of women versus men in this situation."[646] It also recommended reviewing and amending Dutch legislation on the anti-accumulation clause to make sure that any principle of equivalence takes into account the overall number of hours of work in combined employment situations to avoid indirect discrimination for women in such employment situations when pregnant or giving birth.[647] The Committee recommended bringing Dutch law on maternity leave benefits in line with the Convention for all women working in various forms of employment, including women who combine self-employment with part-time salaried employment.[648]

2.10.2.2 Elisabeth de Blok et al. v. The Netherlands

In *Elisabeth de Blok et al. v. The Netherlands*, the Committee considered an Article 11(2)(b) violation when the Netherlands removed an existing maternity leave scheme for self-employed women in 2004 without offering any alternatives. This left the six self-employed authors of the communication without maternity leave benefits after giving birth in 2005 and 2006.[649] The women sought compensation equal to the benefits that they would have received under the Incapacity Insurance (Self-Employed Persons) Act, which the Dutch legislature repealed without transitory provisions or a replacing legislation.[650] The Committee found that the Netherlands violated Article 11(2)(b).[651]

Regarding the Netherlands argument, the Committee made it clear that Article 11(2)(b) applies to self-employed women and female employees.[652] It rejected the Netherlands argument that "article 11(2)(b) applies only to women in paid employment and cannot be interpreted as meaning protection for self-employed persons."[653] The Committee saw this interpretation as being too narrow. The Committee stated that "nothing in the wording of article 11, generally, or article 11(2)(b), specifically, supports such a narrow

---

[645] *Id.* ¶ 10.5.
[646] *Id.*
[647] *Id.*
[648] *Id.*
[649] Elisabeth de Blok et al. v. The Netherlands, *supra* note 628, ¶ 8.3.
[650] *Id.* ¶ 8.2.
[651] *Id.* ¶ 8.4.
[652] *Id.*
[653] *Id.* ¶ 8.2.

interpretation"[654] that it would only apply to self-employed women. The Committee referenced its Views in *Nguyen* and in COs to support its legal reasoning that Article 11(2)(b) covers "all employed women" not only women in employment relationships, but also those self-employed.[655]

The Committee emphasized that Article 11(2)(b) was directly applicable to state parties, expressing its concern about the status of the Convention in the legal system of the Netherlands.[656] The Committee recalled its prior COs to the Netherlands in which it had emphasized the direct applicability of the Convention within the Netherlands. It called upon the Netherlands to reconsider its position that not all the substantive provisions of the Convention were directly applicable within the domestic legal order. Moreover, the Netherlands should ensure that all the provisions of the Convention were fully executed. The Committee disagreed with the Dutch Court's decision that "article 11(2)(b) of the Convention was not directly applicable because it contained a mere 'instruction' for State parties to introduce maternity leave, leaving State parties the freedom to determine how specifically to achieve that in practice."[657] The Committee also dismissed the Netherlands' understanding that it considered its "obligation to take 'appropriate measures' to prevent discrimination against women on the grounds of maternity" as a "best-efforts obligation" only.[658]

The Committee reminded the Netherlands that it had committed to providing remedies to individuals who were victims of violations of their rights under the Convention. It recalled that repealing the Invalidity Insurance (Self-Employed Persons) Act in 2004 had resulted in the termination of maternity allowances for self-employed women.[659] It repeated that "the Committee had specifically called upon the State party to reinstate maternity benefits for all women, to include self-employed persons, in line with article 11(2)(b) of the Convention."[660]

The Committee also dismissed the relevance of a margin of appreciation argument regarding its obligations under Article 11(2)(b) of the Convention. It did not agree with the Netherlands' argument that it was within the margin of appreciation of the "national authorities to decide on the exact manner in which a maternity leave scheme was to be applied; that the payments for such insurance were tax-deductible; and that in any event private insurers were free to determine the exact financial parameters regarding risk coverage."[661] The

---

[654] *Id.* ¶ 8.4.
[655] *Id.*
[656] *Id.* ¶ 8.6 (citing CO on the Netherlands, CEDAW/C/NLD/CO/4, ¶¶ 11, 12, 29, & 30 (2007)).
[657] *Id.* ¶ 8.5.
[658] *Id.*
[659] *Id.* ¶ 8.6.
[660] *Id.* (citing CO on the Netherlands, *supra* note 657, ¶¶ 29–30).
[661] *Id.* ¶ 8.7.

2004 reform negatively affected self-employed women's maternity leave benefits in comparison with the previous scheme and without offering women any alternative.[662]

The Committee then said that the authors, except for Ms. de Blok, had received no benefits for loss of income after having given birth in 2005 and 2006.[663] Thus, the failure to provide maternity benefits adversely affected pregnant women and constituted direct sex- and gender-based discrimination against women, in violation of the Netherlands' Article 11(2)(b) obligation to take all appropriate measures to eliminate discrimination.[664]

The Committee recommended that the Netherlands "provide reparation, including appropriate monetary compensation, for the loss of maternity benefits."[665] In general, the Committee noted that the Netherlands amended its legislation in June 2008 (with the entry into force of the Work and Care Act) and ensured that a maternity leave scheme would be available to self-employed women, thus preventing reoccurrence of similar violations.[666] However, the Committee noted that "no compensation is possible for self-employed women, such as the authors, who gave birth between 1 August 2004 and 4 June 2008."[667] In this regard, the Committee invited the Netherlands to address and redress the harm to mothers who had been abandoned by the state through nonpayment of their due maternity benefits.[668]

The Committee published the result of its follow-up procedure in its 2019 annual report but provided few details. It closed the follow-up dialogue with a finding of partially satisfactory resolution of the recommendations.[669]

2.10.2.3 *Natalia Ciobanu v. Republic of Moldova*

In *Natalia Ciobanu v. Republic of Moldova*, Ms. Natalia Ciobanu claimed that her rights were violated under Article 3 and Article 11(2)(c) of the Convention. The Committee added to its analysis consideration under Article 11(1)(e).[670] The Committee found that Moldova violated Ms. Ciobanu's rights under all three provisions.[671]

---

[662] *Id.* ¶ 8.8.
[663] Ms. de Blok had taken out private insurance and received a one-time lump-sum payment from her insurer, but only after notifying the insurance company that she intended to pursue the matter in court.
[664] *Id.* ¶ 8.9.
[665] *Id.* ¶ 9.
[666] *Id.*
[667] *Id.*
[668] *Id.*
[669] *See generally* CEDAW Comm., Rep. on Its Seventieth Session, Seventy-first Session and Seventy-second Session, UN Doc. A/74/38 (2019).
[670] Natalia Ciobanu v. Republic of Moldova, *supra* note 628, ¶ 1.
[671] *Id.* ¶ 8.

Ms. Ciobanu provided permanent personal care to her disabled daughter from 1993 until her daughter's death in 2012.[672] Ms. Ciobanu left her paid job to provide such care as a matter of preference but also because the state provided no care institutions for children with disabilities.[673] Only after her daughter's death did Moldova introduce a social service of "personal assistant" through new legislation.[674] When Ms. Ciobanu applied for retirement, she received very little pension due to the 1999 Act on Public Social Insurance Pensions, which excluded from Ms. Ciobanu's compensation period the time between the act's entry into force and the death of Ms. Ciobanu's daughter in 2012, during which she performed unpaid care work. Ms. Ciobanu and other women who provided care for their children with severe disabilities complained to Moldova's Equality Council. The Equality Council indeed found that the women had been discriminated against with regard to their social insurance pension and recommended recalculating the social insurance pension contribution period to include the time after the Act on Public Social Insurance Pensions entered into force on January 1, 1999.[675] However, the Ministry of Health, Labour and Social Protection did not implement this recommendation.[676] Ms. Ciobanu then brought a lawsuit seeking "recognition of discrimination in access to social insurance and social protection services, as compared with parents who had decided to place their children with disabilities in residential institutions and who could therefore work and secure their contribution periods."[677] Her case was dismissed in all instances.

The Committee considered whether Moldova had violated her rights under Article 3, Article 11(1)(e), and Article(2)(c) by excluding the contribution period during which Ms. Ciobanu cared for her daughter and by failing to provide appropriate care facilities for children with disabilities, which would allow women to combine child care with other work responsibilities.[678]

The Committee stated that "the right to social security, including in cases of the social insurance (old-age) pension, is of central importance in guaranteeing human dignity."[679] It then went on to calibrate the right to social security, writing that "the right to social security carries significant financial implications for States, but the latter should ensure the satisfaction of, at the very least, minimum essential levels of that right."[680]

---

[672] Id. ¶¶ 2.1–2.2.
[673] Id. ¶ 2.1.
[674] Id. ¶ 2.2.
[675] Id. ¶ 2.4.
[676] Id.
[677] Id. ¶ 2.5.
[678] Id. ¶ 7.3.
[679] Id. ¶ 7.6.
[680] Id.

The Committee explained that states must ensure access to a social security scheme: a minimum essential level of benefits, without discrimination of any kind. Furthermore, states should provide noncontributory old-age benefits, social services, and other assistance for all older persons when they have not completed a qualifying period of contributions, are not otherwise entitled to an old-age insurance-based pension or other social security assistance, and have no other source of income.[681] The Committee said that the effects of noncontributory schemes were gendered: women are more likely to live in poverty than men, they often have the sole responsibility for the care of their children, and they often have no contributory pensions.[682]

The Committee noted that state parties enjoyed a large margin of appreciation regarding "the measures that they consider necessary to ensure that everyone enjoys the right to social security, with a view to, inter alia, ensuring that retirement pension systems are efficient, sustainable and accessible for everyone."[683] Eligibility requirements or conditions for social security, retirement pension, or other benefits from social security schemes should be "reasonable, proportionate and transparent" and publicly communicated in a "timely and sufficient manner"[684] to ensure predictability. This is especially important regarding regressive measures and when transitional arrangements are lacking.[685]

The Committee addressed the intersectional dimension Ms. Ciobanu experienced as an older woman in a critical economic situation as well as the associational discrimination that her disabled daughter experienced.[686] Moreover, the Committee took note of the author's allegations that "the lack of social security policies for parents of children with disabilities disproportionately affects women."[687] While the legal provisions might have been formulated neutrally on their face, their impact led to indirect discrimination on the grounds of gender. The Committee confirmed this discriminatory impact in light of publicly available information that "those engaged exclusively in unpaid domestic care work, including care for children with and without disabilities, are almost entirely female."[688] On a more general level, the Committee noted that states should take steps to eliminate the factors that prevent women from making equal contributions to social security schemes that link benefits with contributions, or ensure that schemes take account of such factors in the design of benefit formulas,

---

[681] *Id.*
[682] *Id.*
[683] *Id.* ¶ 7.7.
[684] *Id.* ¶ 7.7.
[685] *Id.*
[686] *Id.* ¶ 7.11.
[687] *Id.* ¶ 7.12.
[688] *Id.* ¶ 7.13. The Committee also called on states more generally to address stereotypes and other persistent causes of structural discrimination, such as those seen in this case.

for example, by considering periods spent, especially by women, taking care of children and adult dependents, both with and without disabilities.[689]

The state party indirectly refers in its observations to the gender neutrality of the Act on Public Social Insurance Pensions by enumerating a list of noncontributing periods that are counted toward the social insurance calculation, which appear neutral on their face.[690] However, the Committee took issue with the fact that the "State party has not provided any explanation or justification as to why... periods of providing care for persons with disabilities including children up to 16 years of age, were included in the social insurance calculation only until 31 December 1998."[691] The Committee then drew attention to the fact that mandatory military service for men is counted toward social insurance calculation even after January 1, 1999, highlighting how men's social responsibilities are treated compared to those performed largely by women.[692] One can read disapproval of Moldova's implicit value judgment that men protecting the nation through military service are valued more highly than women protecting the life of a disabled child.[693]

As a result, the Committee considered that Moldova committed indirect discrimination against women through these social security exclusions, leaving them in a state of destitution, vulnerability, and economic insecurity in old age, depriving them of economic autonomy. Thus, Moldova violated Ms. Ciobanu's rights under Article 3 and Article 11(1)(e) of the Convention, both in the denial of social security and in the failure to provide "any other means of economic security or any form of adequate redress."[694] The Committee further found that Moldova had failed "to take all appropriate measures, including through legislation, to ensure the full development and advancement of women providing care for their children with disabilities in a society that traditionally attributes caregiving responsibilities to women, affected the author adversely and therefore constitutes indirect gender-based discrimination against her and a violation of her obligation by the State party, under article 11(2)(c) of the Convention, to guarantee women the exercise and enjoyment of human rights and fundamental freedoms on a basis of equality with men."[695]

The Committee issued specific recommendations regarding Ms. Ciobanu and General Recommendations to Moldova on how to prevent future violations.

The Committee recommended that Moldova recalculate Ms. Ciobanu's social insurance pension. In addition, the Committee recommended awarding her

---

[689] *Id.* ¶ 7.10.
[690] *Id.* ¶ 7.14.
[691] *Id.*
[692] *Id.*
[693] *Id.*
[694] *Id.* ¶ 7.15.
[695] *Id.* ¶ 7.16.

"adequate compensation for the violations suffered during the period in which she was denied her right to her social insurance pension, commensurate with the non-contributing periods that should have been counted towards the social insurance period,"[696] and "adequate compensation for the moral damages suffered owing to the lack of support services provided for her as a parent caring for her disabled child who had to end her employment activities."[697] Lastly, the Committee recommended reimbursing her for "the legal costs reasonably incurred in the processing of the present communication."[698]

At the general level, the Committee noted a change in legislation had already been effected, preventing similar violations from reoccurring in the future. Moldova's Act on Public Social Insurance Pensions was reformed so that it ensures that from January 1, 2017, periods of providing care for children with severe disabilities are counted toward the social insurance pension of their parents.[699] However, the Committee recommended remedying the situation of women who have received no compensation for the time they provided care for their children with severe disabilities between January 1, 1999, and December 31, 2016, including through legislative measures in reasonable time.[700] Moreover, the Committee recommended providing "adequate support services to allow mothers of severely disabled children to remain employed."[701]

The Committee has not published information about the follow-up procedure regarding the *Ciobanu* case, but the follow-up procedure is ongoing.

2.10.2.4 V.P. v. Belarus

In V.P. v. Belarus,[702] V.P. claimed that Belarus violated her rights when she was denied her old-age pension due to a lack of pensionable services because of the periods in her life during which she provided unpaid care work.[703] However, the Committee did not see V.P.'s rights violated under Article 2(b)–(d) and (f) and Article 11(1)(e) read in conjunction with Article 1. The changes to the domestic legal framework and to the requirements for the old-age pension influenced V.P. in her personal life but did not amount to a breach of her rights.[704]

The local pension commission denied V.P.'s application for an old-age pension on the basis that her contribution to the pension service did not suffice.[705] Under the pension law, she was eligible for the contributory old-age pension: she

---

[696] *Id.* ¶ 8.
[697] *Id.*
[698] *Id.*
[699] *Id.*
[700] *Id.* ¶ 8.
[701] *Id.*
[702] V.P. v. Belarus, *supra* note 628.
[703] *Id.* ¶ 1.
[704] *Id.* ¶ 7.14.
[705] *Id.* ¶¶ 2.1–2.2.

fulfilled the preconditions regarding the years of general labor and of pensionable service of those years, and she had reached the retirement age of fifty-five years. However, one month before V.P. applied for the pension, a presidential order came into force that increased the number of years that one must have contributed to the pension insurance fund to be entitled to old-age pension. The presidential order superseded the pension law.[706] V.P. unsuccessfully appealed the local pension commission's decision in all instances. In her first appeal, she criticized that the period during which she took care of her children and looked after an individual with a disability only counted toward her years of general labor but not toward the pensionable services. Moreover, she complained because she was not eligible for the noncontributory pension schemes because they were only available at the age of sixty. However, the court of first instance dismissed her claim on the grounds that V.P. did not contribute to the pension insurance fund during those unpaid care work times. In her second appeal, she emphasized that the domestic pension law was indirectly discriminatory against women who carried out unpaid care work that did not count toward their pensionable services in the contributory pension scheme. However, the second instance court also dismissed her appeal, as did all subsequent ordinary and extraordinary appeal mechanisms.[707]

V.P. complained that Belarus had violated her rights under Article 11(1)(e), read in conjunction with Article 1, when "refusing her application for an old-age pension." According to her, Belarus had indirectly discriminated against her on the grounds of gender because women would be unable to accumulate the amount of pensionable service due to unpaid family care obligations.[708] Moreover, V.P. claimed that Belarus had violated Article 2(b)-(f) when failing to abolish discriminatory laws and regulations and failing to establish a domestic legal framework capable of providing sufficient legal protection against gender-based discrimination.[709]

When the Committee considered if Belarus failed to comply with its obligations when "changing the legal framework and the requirements for the old-age pension,"[710] it started its legal analysis by recalling states obligations to prohibit direct and indirect discrimination and their obligations under the right to social security. It repeated that states parties engaged in indirect discrimination when "laws, policies or practices that appear neutral . . . have a disproportionate impact on the exercise of Convention rights as distinguished by prohibited grounds of discrimination."[711]

---

[706] *Id.*
[707] *Id.* ¶¶ 2.5–2.8.
[708] *Id.* ¶ 7.2.
[709] *Id.*
[710] *Id.* ¶ 7.3.
[711] *Id.* ¶ 7.4.

Moreover, the Committee highlighted that "the right to social security is of central importance in guaranteeing human dignity."[712] The Committee recalled that states parties should "ensure access to a social security scheme that provides a minimum essential level of benefits, without discrimination of any kind."[713] It lists states obligations that they should provide for

> [n]on-contributory old-age benefits, social services and other assistance for all older persons who, when reaching the retirement age prescribed in national legislation, have not completed a qualifying period of contributions or are not otherwise entitled to an old-age insurance-based pension or other social security benefit or assistance and who have no other source of income.[714]

Based on its prior jurisprudence in *Ciobanu v. Republic of Moldova*, the Committee also emphasized that women relied more frequently on noncontributory pension schemes as caretakers of their children.[715] The Committee recalled states parties' "large margin of appreciation" when implementing a right to social security. However, it also emphasized that states parties must ensure that "retirement pension systems are efficient, sustainable and accessible for everyone."[716] Eligibility requirements for social security schemes must be "reasonable, proportionate and transparent."[717] Moreover, the Committee stressed that eligibility requirements and conditions must be "communicated to the public in a timely and sufficient manner so as to ensure that access to retirement pensions is predictable."[718] The bar for publicity is higher when states adopt regressive measures without any transitional arrangements potentially negatively impacting women.[719] Furthermore, the Committee highlighted states obligation to review any "restrictions on access to social security schemes to ensure that they do not discriminate against women in law or in practice."[720] It mentions women's unpaid care work for children with and without disabilities and for adult dependents as one factor that states must take into account because it leads to the circumstance that women can make fewer contributions to contributory pension schemes.[721]

When engaging with the present case, the Committee did not find a violation even though the issue was precisely that V.P. could not qualify for the contributory old-age pension. Under the requirements of new law, she lacked enough

[712] *Id.* ¶ 7.5.
[713] *Id.*
[714] *Id.*
[715] *Id.* (citing Ciobanu v. Republic of Moldova, *supra* note 628, ¶¶ 7.6–7.7).
[716] *Id.* ¶ 7.6.
[717] *Id.*
[718] *Id.*
[719] *Id.*
[720] *Id.* ¶ 7.7.
[721] *Id.*

pensionable service due to her unpaid care work despite having reached the eligible retirement age under that scheme.[722] However, the Committee noted that there existed contributory and noncontributory pension schemes in Belarus. While it noted that periods of time of unpaid caretaking did not count toward the pensionable service period potentially having a discriminatory effect on women, the Committee found the argument that in practice this would not have a discriminatory effect convincing. The statistical statement by Belarus was sufficient, showing that "[t]he proportion of women of retirement age denied old-age pension benefits was very low in general and just marginally higher than that of men."[723] The Committee also considered different remedial measures that introduced "less strict pensionable service requirements, inter alia, for mothers with several children or children with disabilities"[724] as sufficient. The Committee held that "it could not be said that the legal framework in itself creates a discriminatory environment that is more burdensome for women."[725]

Last, the Committee noted that the changes to the pension law did affect V.P. in her personal situation, but it did not find that the "failure to meet the requirements for any of the existing contributory pension schemes could be fully attributed to the State party."[726] The Committee viewed it as relevant that V.P. did not sufficiently specify her son's illness that made her extend her maternity leave and prevented her from seeking gainful employment for a lengthy period of time.[727] The Committee also stated that she had not explained why she had not applied for employment assistance and then had withdrawn after a couple of months once she did. Moreover, V.P. did not provide information if she had challenged private employers' hiring decisions in court.[728] This all led to her not having not sufficient pensionable services but this was not solely attributable to Belarus. Consequently, the Committee did not find V.P.'s claim to be sufficiently substantiated and did not find a breach.[729]

2.10.3 Concluding Observations

The COs address issues on social benefits from various angles. The Committee frequently expressed concerns about the systemic informality of women's employment relationships and the consequent lack of social security protection

---

[722] Id. ¶ 7.8.
[723] Id. ¶ 7.11.
[724] Id.
[725] Id.
[726] Id. ¶ 7.13.
[727] Id. ¶ 7.12.
[728] Id. ¶¶ 7.12–7.13.
[729] Id. ¶ 7.14.

and payment of social benefits through those employment relationships. The COs address different types of social benefits that states parties must provide, including social security benefits, paid maternity leave, and pension benefits, among others. The Committee also deals with women who are marginalized and excluded from access to any social security benefits.

2.10.3.1 Social Security in the Informal Sector

The Committee has addressed the lack of social protection in informal employment relationships as a salient issue in Latin American, Caribbean, African, and Asian-Pacific countries.[730] For instance, regarding Mexico, the Committee expressed concern that "56,6 per cent of the female working population is engaged in the informal labour sector and hence lacks access to social security benefits."[731] The Committee similarly expressed concern regarding the Congo because "70 per cent of women work in the informal sector, leaving them in most cases outside of the social protection scheme."[732] Regarding Timor-Leste, the Committee expressed disapproval that "most women do not participate at all in the labour force: 78 percent of those who do participate are engaged in the informal sector without appropriate social security coverage."[733] The activities women perform in the informal sector range from unpaid family work to agriculture, domestic work and services, home-based work, care work, food processing, work in the *maquiladora* industry, or sewing.[734] The Committee also noted the negative impact on social security protection when countries shift from regular to irregular employment relationships, for instance, through "conversion of women's contracts from regular workers to non-regular, part-time or short-term workers."[735]

According to the COs, in Europe, the systematic informality of employment and the resulting lack of social protection primarily concerns groups at the margins of society due to their socioeconomic status or with irregular immigration status, like sex workers,[736] migrant women working in the domestic sphere,[737] domestic workers in private households, and home-care workers[738] or women working low-paid jobs.[739]

---

[730] *See, e.g.*, CO on Costa Rica, CEDAW/C/CRI/CO/7, ¶ 28 (2017); on Congo, CEDAW/C/COG/CO/6, ¶ 33 (2012); Tajikistan, CEDAW/C/TJK/CO/6, ¶ 41 (2018); Iraq, CEDAW/C/IRQ/CO/7, ¶ 31 a) (2019); the Philippines, CEDAW/C/PHL/CO/7-8, ¶ 41 (2016).
[731] CO on Mexico, CEDAW/C/MEX/CO/7-8, ¶ 28 (2012); CO on Mexico, CEDAW/C/MEX/CO/9, ¶¶ 39, 43 (2018).
[732] CO on Congo, CEDAW/C/COG/CO/7, ¶ 42 (2018).
[733] CO on Timor-Leste, CEDAW/C/TLS/CO/2-3, ¶ 28 (2015).
[734] *See, e.g.*, CO on Guyana, CEDAW/C/GUY/CO/9, ¶¶ 37–38 (2019); on Colombia, CEDAW/C/COL/CO/9, ¶ 39 (2019); Eritrea, CEDAW/C/ERI/CO/6, ¶ 38 a) (2020).
[735] CO on Republic of Korea, CEDAW/C/KOR/CO/7, ¶ 32 (2011).
[736] CO on Norway, CEDAW/C/NOR/CO/9, ¶ 29 (2017).
[737] CO on United Kingdom of Great Britain and Northern Ireland, CEDAW/C/GBR/CO/8, ¶ 36 a) (2019).
[738] CO on Netherlands, CEDAW/C/NLD/CO/5, ¶ 38 (2010).
[739] CO on Turkey, CEDAW/C/TUR/CO/7, ¶ 45 (2016).

Even when informal workers have the right to social security benefits, they frequently lack the awareness necessary to access them, and states allocate insufficient funds to their social protection funds.[740] For instance, regarding Nepal, the Committee recommended raising awareness among women employed in the formal and informal sectors of their right to social protection and gathering sufficient resources to implement a contributions-based social security legislation.[741]

The Committee suggested different measures to reconcile the lack of access to social security in the informal employment sector. In response to several state reports, the Committee recommended the establishment of a regulatory framework for the coverage of women in the informal sector by unemployment, pension, and other social security benefits.[742] Collecting sex-disaggregated data about women in the private and informal sectors is essential to know how many women are left out of social security protection due to their informal employment relationships.[743]

The Committee also highlighted the need to increase women's access to the national social security system and develop coordinated social protection and compensation programs for women.[744] For instance, regarding Samoa, the Committee recommended increasing "access for women to the social security system and develop coordinated social protection and compensation programmes, including unemployment benefits, for women, in line with ILO Recommendation No. 202 concerning national floors of social protection."[745] If states choose not to extend the national social security fund to informal sector workers, then the Committee recommends developing a separate national social protection scheme for those workers.[746] The Committee also advised ensuring women's access to social services and social security in the informal sector.[747] The Committee also noted the importance of working closely with the private sector to create beneficial policies for women in the informal sector.[748]

---

[740] CO on Nepal, CEDAW/C/NPL/CO/6, ¶ 34 b) (2018).
[741] Id. ¶ 35.
[742] See, e.g., CO on Guyana, CEDAW/C/GUY/CO/9, ¶ 38 (2019); Lesotho, CEDAW/C/LSO/CO/1–4, ¶ 31 (2011); Tunisia, CEDAW/C/TUN/CO/6, ¶ 49 (2010); Pakistan, CEDAW/C/PAK/CO/4, ¶ 29 (2013).
[743] CO on Côte d'Ivoire, CEDAW/C/CIV/CO/1–3, ¶ 39 (2011); CO on Djibouti, CEDAW/C/DJI/CO/1–3, ¶ 29 (2011).
[744] See, e.g., CO on Colombia, CEDAW/C/COL/CO/9, ¶ 40 a) (2019); on Mexico, CEDAW/C/MEX/CO/9, ¶ 44 (2018); on Guatemala, CEDAW/C/GTM/CO/8–9, ¶ 39 (2017); on Djibouti, CEDAW/C/DJI/CO/1–3, ¶ 29 (2011).
[745] CO on Samoa, CEDAW/C/WSM/CO/6, ¶ 36 (2018).
[746] CO on Congo, CEDAW/C/COG/CO/6, ¶ 34 (2012); CO on Djibouti, CEDAW/C/DJI/CO/1–3, ¶ 29 (2011).
[747] See, e.g., Bosnia and Herzegovina, CEDAW/C/BIH/CO/4–5, ¶ 34 (2013); Timor-Leste, CEDAW/C/TLS/CO/2–3, ¶ 29 (2015); Chad, CEDAW/C/TCD/CO/1–4, ¶ 33 (2011); Pakistan, CEDAW/C/PAK/CO/4 ¶ 30 (2013).
[748] CO on Zambia, CEDAW/C/ZMB/CO/5–6, ¶ 32 (2011).

2.10.3.2 Women Domestic Workers

The Committee expressed several concerns about women domestic workers who frequently work in the informal employment sector and are excluded from social security.[749] A key problem is the "limited number of domestic workers formally registered so as to access social security."[750] The low income of domestic workers leads to low contribution and subsequent lack of coverage.[751] The Committee expressed its concern regarding "lesser accumulation of social security contributions by women employed in the domestic and care sector."[752] Migrant women who are domestic workers are especially disenfranchised regarding social security coverage because they do not even enjoy the same legal guarantees as other migrant workers.[753]

To alleviate the human rights violations women domestic workers experience, the Committee recommended introducing or amending legislation to improve access to social security benefits.[754] For instance, regarding Uruguay, the Committee advised "strengthening public awareness of the rights of women domestic workers, ensuring national coverage of and accessible information about complaint mechanisms" and encouraged the state to "develop a national campaign to promote enrolment in and periodic contributions to the social security system by employers of domestic and care workers and raise awareness among women of social security."[755] In addition, disability benefits should be available to domestic workers and home-care workers, as well as for women working in the informal sector, who frequently lack access to such benefits.[756]

2.10.3.3 Self-Employed Women

Regarding several countries, the Committee expressed concern that self-employed women did not adequately enjoy social security and maternity benefits,[757] especially when they fall within the informal sector.[758] For instance, the Committee recommended that Luxembourg ensure "self-employed mothers and fathers are covered by social security and maternity benefits and delink the

---

[749] See, e.g., CO on Cambodia, CEDAW/C/KHM/CO/6, ¶ 37 (2019); on Dominican Republic, CEDAW/C/DOM/CO/6-7, ¶ 34 (2013); on Indonesia, CEDAW/C/IDN/CO/6-7, ¶ 37 (2012).
[750] CO on El Salvador, CEDAW/C/SLV/CO/8-9, ¶ 34 (2017).
[751] CO on Micronesia, CEDAW/C/FSM/CO/1-3, ¶ 34 (2017).
[752] CO on Uruguay, CEDAW/C/URY/CO/8-9, ¶ 33 (2016).
[753] CO Malaysia, CEDAW/C/MYS/CO/3-5, ¶ 43 (2018); CO on Kuwait, CEDAW/C/KWT/CO/3-4, ¶ 40 (2011).
[754] CO on Paraguay, CEDAW/C/PRY/CO/6, ¶ 29 (2011); CO on Indonesia, CEDAW/C/IDN/CO/6-7, ¶ 38 (2012).
[755] CO on Uruguay, CEDAW/C/URY/CO/8-9, ¶ 34 (2016).
[756] CO on the Netherlands, CEDAW/C/NLD/CO/5, ¶¶ 38-39 (2010); CO on Lao, CEDAW/C/LAO/CO/8-9, ¶ 44 (2018).
[757] CO on Luxembourg, CEDAW/C/LUX/CO/6-7, ¶¶ 47-48 (2018).
[758] CO on Vanuatu, CEDAW/C/VUT/CO/4-5, ¶¶ 28-29 (2016).

calculation of maternity benefits from income fluctuations, which are typical in self-employment."[759]

2.10.3.4 Pension Benefits and Survivorship Benefits

In general, states should have pension legislation in places that ensures "a decent standard of living for retired women."[760] The Committee recommended that states sanction employers when they failed to contribute to the pension fund and social security system for their female employees.[761] The Committee criticized that women working in the informal sector were excluded from receiving pension benefits with particular frequency.[762] The Committee urged states to measure and credit women's unpaid care work toward pension entitlements and social benefits.[763] It also expressed concern about the persistent gender wage gap, in addition to career breaks and part-time employment due to childbearing, adversely affects pension benefits.[764] The Committee noted the negative long-term negative impact of austerity measures on social benefits and pension schemes.[765] The Committee recommended to ensure "adequate pensions, social security, and other benefits" for widows.[766] Regarding survivorship benefits, the Committee emphasized that women were entitled "to equal social security benefits as men upon the death of a spouse."[767]

2.10.3.5 Unemployment Benefits

The Committee expressed concern that women faced discrimination in unemployment benefits and called on states to remedy it.[768] Some groups of women like "domestic workers working in private households and home-care workers financed by public schemes . . . have . . . limited access to social security, notably unemployment and disability benefits and pensions."[769] The Committee recommended taking measures "to ensure that women domestic workers are duly provided with full social rights and that they are not deprived of social security and labour benefits."[770] The Committee also urged states to increase "access for women to the

---

[759] CO on Luxembourg, CEDAW/C/LUX/CO/6–7, ¶ 48 (2018).
[760] CO on Germany, CEDAW/C/DEU/CO/7–8, ¶ 36 (2017).
[761] CO on Bosnia and Herzegovina, CEDAW/C/BIH/CO/6, ¶ 36 (2019).
[762] CO on Botswana, CEDAW/C/BWA/CO/4, ¶ 35 (2019).
[763] CO on Lithuania (CEDAW/C/LTU/CO/6, ¶ 41 a)), Mexico (CEDAW/C/MEX/CO/9, ¶ 43), Turkmenistan (CEDAW/C/TKM/CO/5, ¶ 43).
[764] CO on Italy (CEDAW/C/ITA/CO/7, ¶ 37), Belgium (CEDAW/C/BEL/CO/7, ¶ 32), Azerbaijan (CEDAW/C/AZE/CO/5, ¶ 31 d)).
[765] *See, e.g.*, CO on Suriname, CEDAW/C/SUR/CO/4–6, ¶ 40 (2018); on Italy, CEDAW/C/ITA/CO/7, ¶ 37 (2017); on Congo, CEDAW/C/COG/CO/7, ¶ 42 (2018).
[766] CO Iraq, CEDAW/C/IRQ/CO/4–6, ¶ 47 (2014); CO on Kuwait, CEDAW/C/KWT/CO/5, ¶ 40 (2017).
[767] *Id.* ¶ 41 (2017).
[768] CO on Belgium, CEDAW/C/BEL/CO/6, ¶ 25 (2008).
[769] CO on Netherlands, CEDAW/C/NLD/CO/5, ¶ 38 (2010).
[770] *Id.* ¶ 39 (2010).

social security system and develop coordinated social protection and compensation programmes, including unemployment benefits, for women, in line with ILO Recommendation No. 202 concerning national floors of social protection."[771]

2.10.3.6 Maternity Benefits and Paid Maternity Leave

The Committee noted the importance of ensuring paid maternity leave, as well as paternity and parental leave.[772] The Committee criticized states when they failed to regulate private sector employers' provision of paid maternity leave.[773] Women working in the informal sector, women in low-wage and unskilled jobs, and women working in fixed-duration contracts in particular lack paid maternity leave.[774]

2.10.3.7 Discriminatory Social Security Legislation and Temporary Special Measures

The Committee expressed concern regarding persistent discriminatory provisions in the social security laws of several countries and recommended amendment.[775] The Committee took issue with gender-neutral approaches to social security legislation, which may result in indirect discrimination,[776] but also criticized outright discrimination in social security legislation.[777] When intersectional discrimination was at stake, the Committee also recommended temporary special measures regarding social security.[778] Overall, the Committee recommended economic empowerment of women through the provision of social security benefits.[779]

2.10.3.8 Intersectional Discrimination and Access to Social Security Benefits

Women experiencing intersectional discrimination experience structural barriers to accessing social benefits, including women experiencing poverty, women as heads of households, rural women, migrant women, Roma women, ethnic minorities, women with disabilities, and older women. They frequently

---

[771] CO on Samoa, CEDAW/C/WSM/CO/6, ¶ 36 (2018).

[772] *See, e.g.,* CO on Eritrea, CEDAW/C/ERI/CO/6, ¶ 38 e) (2020); on Bosnia and Herzegovina, CEDAW/C/BIH/CO/6, ¶ 36 (2019); on Lesotho, CEDAW/C/LSO/CO/1-4, ¶ 31 (2011).

[773] CO on Tanzania, CEDAW/C/TZA/CO/6, ¶ 131 (2009); CO on Uganda, CEDAW/C/UGA/CO/7, ¶¶ 33-34 (2010).

[774] CO on Cambodia, CEDAW/C/KHM/CO/6, ¶¶ 36-37 (2019); CO on Cabo Verde, CEDAW/C/CPV/CO/7-8, ¶ 5 (2013).

[775] CO on Oman (CEDAW/C/OMN/CO/2-3, ¶ 11), Jordan (CEDAW/C/JOR/CO/6, ¶ 19), Lebanon (CEDAW/C/LBN/CO/4-5, ¶ 19).

[776] CO on New Zealand, CEDAW/C/NZL/CO/8, ¶¶ 36-37 (2018).

[777] CO on the Democratic Republic of the Congo, CEDAW/C/COD/CO/8, ¶ 34 c) (2019).

[778] *See, e.g.,* CO on Armenia, CEDAW/C/ARM/CO/5-6, ¶ 41 (2016); on Costa Rica, CEDAW/C/CRI/CO/7, ¶ 13 (2017); on Bolivia, CEDAW/C/BOL/CO/5-6, ¶ 26 (2015).

[779] CO on Turkmenistan, CEDAW/C/TKM/CO/5, ¶ 43 (2018).

experience disenfranchisements regarding noncontributory social benefits and find themselves outside of employment related social benefit schemes.

The Committee addressed the connection between the feminization of poverty and the denial of social benefits, especially affecting women who experience intersectional forms of discrimination.[780] The Committee expressed concern about the lack of a robust social security and protection system failing to prevent women from living in poverty. For instance, regarding Mozambique, the Committee recommended allocating "sufficient human, technical and financial resources to non-contributory social protection schemes to provide social security and protection benefits to women living in poverty, unemployed women and women engaging in unpaid work."[781]

The Committee recommended creating a social security system for women heads of households.[782] States parties should take into consideration the role of women as heads of households when revising the social security benefits system.[783]

Rural women are prone to experiencing disenfranchisement with respect to the rights and benefits of social protection.[784] The Committee recommended providing access to social security according to the needs of rural women.[785] In addition, the Committee recommended adopting temporary special measures to ensure rural women's access to social security and retirement schemes.[786]

The Committee expressed concern that migrant women do not have access to social protection or social security.[787] The Committee recommended expanding social security coverage for migrant women and girls.[788]

The Committee expressed concern that Roma women lack coverage under existing social protection schemes. It recommended extending the coverage of social protection schemes to Roma women.[789]

The Committee made several observations regarding women with disabilities who frequently have limited access to social security schemes.[790] In addition, the

---

[780] *See, e.g.,* CO on CO Guatemala, CEDAW/C/GTM/CO/8-9, ¶ 39 (2017); on Botswana, CEDAW/C/BWA/CO/4, ¶ 41 (2019); on Bangladesh CEDAW/C/BGD/CO/8, ¶ 36 (2016).
[781] CO on Mozambique, CEDAW/C/MOZ/CO/35, ¶ 38 a) (2019).
[782] CO on Sri Lanka, CEDAW/C/LKA/CO/8, ¶ 37 (2017).
[783] CO on Kuwait, CEDAW/C/KWT/CO/5, ¶ 41 (2017).
[784] *See, e.g.* CO on Mauritania, CEDAW/C/MRT/CO/1 (2007); Lebanon, CEDAW/C/LBN/CO/3 (2008); on Turkey, CEDAW/C/TUR/CO/7, ¶ 49 (2016); on Tajikistan, CEDAW/C/TJK/CO/6, ¶ 42 (2018).
[785] CO on Togo, CEDAW/C/TGO/CO/6-7, ¶ 37 (2012); CO on Burundi, CEDAW/C/BDI/CO/5-6, ¶ 43 (2016).
[786] CO on Serbia, CEDAW/C/SRB/CO/4, ¶ 42 (2019); CO on Tajikistan, CEDAW/C/TJK/CO/6, ¶ 42 (2018).
[787] CO on Laos, CEDAW/C/LAO/CO/8-9, ¶ 43 (2018); CO on Kazakhstan, CEDAW/C/KAZ/CO/5, ¶¶ 37-38 (2019).
[788] *See, e.g.,* CO on the Republic of Moldova, CEDAW/C/MDA/CO/6, ¶ 37 a) (2020); on Lao People's Democratic Republic, CEDAW/C/LAO/CO/8-9, ¶ 44 (2018).
[789] CO on Moldova, CEDAW/C/MDA/CO/6, ¶ 37 (2020).
[790] CO on Kazakhstan, CEDAW/C/KAZ/CO/5, ¶¶ 37-38 (2019).

Committee criticized states where women with disabilities were afforded less social security protection than women experiencing other forms of discrimination.[791] Older women represent another group vulnerable to discrimination in their access to social security.[792]

2.10.3.9 Importing Standards from ILO Conventions

The Committee called on states parties to ratify various ILO Conventions linking them with CEDAW's standards: the ILO Social Security (Minimum Standards) Convention, 1952 (No. 102),[793] the ILO Domestic Workers Convention, 2011 (No. 189),[794] the ILO Maternity Protection Convention, 2000 (No. 183),[795] the ILO Recommendation No. 202 concerning national floors of social protection,[796] and ILO Convention No. 156 on workers with family responsibilities.[797]

2.11 Gender-Based Violence and Property Rights

The Committee considers violence against women and gender-based violence forms of discrimination. The Committee has addressed property rights violations as both a specific form of gender-based violence and as a contributing factor to women's oppression due their economic subordination. Economic dependence frequently traps women in violent relationships. Accordingly, the Committee has held that states must intervene to protect women's physical and psychological safety and well-being inside their own homes by placing at least temporal restrictions on the perpetrator's exercise of certain private property rights (e.g., the use of the family home). Over time, the Committee has created due diligence obligations for states to protect women's and children's right to life and to physical, sexual, and psychological integrity in the private sphere by limiting the perpetrators' rights to exercise their housing and private property rights to protect women. The Committee has emphasized states parties' obligations to ensure women's access to shelter, housing, and/or land protecting women against gender-based violence. The Committee has also imposed due

---

[791] CO on Finland, CEDAW/C/FIN/CO/7, ¶ 32 (2014).
[792] CO on Cambodia, CEDAW/C/KHM/CO/4–5, ¶ 44 (2013).
[793] CO on Moldova, CEDAW/C/MDA/CO/6, ¶ 37 c) (2020).
[794] *See, e.g.*, CO on Eritrea, CEDAW/C/ERI/CO/6, ¶ 38 (2020); on Mexico, CEDAW/C/MEX/CO/7–8, ¶ 28 (2012); on Spain, CEDAW/C/ESP/CO/7–8, ¶ 28 (2015); on Thailand, CEDAW/C/THA/CO/6–7, ¶ 37 (2017).
[795] CO on Cambodia, CEDAW/C/KHM/CO/6, ¶ 37 (2019).
[796] CO on Colombia (CEDAW/C/COL/CO/9, ¶ 40 b)), Cambodia (CEDAW/C/KHM/CO/6, ¶ 37), Philippines (CEDAW/C/PHL/CO/7–8, ¶ 42).
[797] CO on Mexico, CEDAW/C/MEX/CO/7–8, ¶ 29 (2012).

diligence obligations to regulate economic actors that commit gender-based economic violence such as trafficking and systemic abuse of women migrant workers. Generally, the Committee notes that women who experience intersectional forms of discrimination are at greater risk of experiencing gender-based violence.[798]

2.11.1 The Convention and General Recommendations

The Convention does not include an explicit prohibition of gender-based violence but developed this prohibition based on Article 1 in three GRs: GR 12 on violence against women, GR 19 on violence against women, and GR 35 on gender-based violence against women. In addition, the Committee has highlighted the prohibition of gender-based violence regarding women experiencing various forms of intersectional discrimination, including women migrant workers, rural women, and Indigenous women.[799] Importantly, the Committee also engages with the relationship between property rights and gender-based violence in its GRs.

2.11.1.1 The Prohibition of Gender-Based Violence and the Link to Property

Neither the Convention nor its predecessor, the Declaration on the Elimination of Discrimination against Women,[800] explicitly protected against violence against women or gender-based violence.[801] However, when developing the concept of gender-based violence, the Committee demonstrated an awareness of the link between violence and property: it took issue with the fact that husbands treated their wives as their possessions and as objects:[802]

> Violence against wives is a function of the belief, fostered in all cultures, that men are superior and that the women they live with are their possessions or chattels that they can treat as they wish and as they consider appropriate.[803]

Only in 1989, when the Committee adopted GR 12, did the Committee conceive of a prohibition of gender-based violence. In GR 12, the Committee

---

[798] For an overview of the Committee's approach on gender-based violence, *see* Christine Chinkin, *Violence against Women*, *in* 2022 COMMENTARY, *supra* note 5, at 627.

[799] GR No. 26, *supra* note 603 (on women migrant workers); GR No. 34, *supra* note 125 (on the rights of rural women), and GR No. 39, *supra* note 362 (on the rights of Indigenous women and girls).

[800] G.A. Res. 2263 (XXII), Declaration on the Elimination of Discrimination against Women (Dec. 18, 1979).

[801] Christine Chinkin, *Violence against Women*, *in* 2012 COMMENTARY, *supra* note 4, at 443.

[802] *Id.* at 447. This link was shown in a critical study in 1989 on "Violence against Women in the Family." UN, VIOLENCE AGAINST WOMEN IN THE FAMILY, UN Sales No. E.8.IV.5 (1989).

[803] Chinkin, *supra* note, at 447.

considers that "articles 2, 5, 11, 12 and 16 of the Convention require the states parties to act to protect women against violence of any kind occurring within the family, at the workplace or in any other area of social life."[804] It recommended to states parties to include information about their "legislation in force to protect women against the incidence of all kinds of violence in everyday life," "other measures adopted to eradicate this violence," "the existence of support services for women who are the victims of aggression or abuses," and "statistical data on the incidence of violence of all kinds against women and on women who are the victims of violence."[805] GR 12 was a first important step on the way to developing the Committee's rich jurisprudence on the prohibition of gender-based violence.

GR 19 states that the Article 1 definition of discrimination includes gender-based violence, defined as "violence that is directed against a woman because she is a woman or that affects women disproportionately [including] acts that inflict physical, mental or sexual harm or suffering, threats of such acts, coercion and other deprivations of liberty."[806] GR 19 also clarifies that "gender-based violence may breach specific provisions of the Convention, regardless of whether those provisions expressly mention violence."[807] The Committee refers to GR 19 as "a key catalyst" for the recognition of gender-based violence.[808]

GR 35 categorizes the prohibition of gender-based violence as a principle of customary international law.[809] It added to the definition of gender-based violence set forth in GR 19, elaborating on the individual and structural dimension: gender-based violence is a "social rather than an individual problem" and "one of the fundamental social, political and economic means by which the subordinate position of women with respect to men and their stereotyped roles are perpetuated."[810] In addition, the Committee recognized that acts of gender-based violence can "result from acts or omissions of State or non-State actors, acting territorially or extraterritorially, including ... extraterritorial operations of private corporations."[811] (Footnotes omitted.)

The Committee does not explicitly list a right to property as part of women's rights to a life free from gender-based violence:

> [W]omen's right to a life free from gender-based violence is indivisible from and interdependent on other human rights, including the rights to ... liberty

---

[804] GR No. 12 on Violence against Women, A/44/38 (1989), at Preamble.
[805] *Id.* ¶¶ 1–4.
[806] GR No. 19 on Violence against Women, A/47/38, ¶ 6 (1992).
[807] *Id.*
[808] GR No. 35 Gender-Based Violence against Women updating No. 19, CEDAW/C/GC/35, ¶ 2 (2017).
[809] *Id.*
[810] *Id.* ¶ 10.
[811] *Id.* ¶ 20.

and security of the person, equality and equal protection within the family ....[812]

However, with reference to GR 28 on states obligations and GR 33 on access to justice, GR 35 repeats that discrimination against women is inextricably linked to other factors that affect women's lives, such as women's socioeconomic status, caste, and position as property owners (or lack thereof).[813]

2.11.1.2 Gender-Based Violence in Family Relations

The Committee recognizes that women's lack of economic independence contributes to gender-based violence at the individual level in family relations. According to GR 19, family violence is "one of the most insidious forms of violence against women."[814] Lack of economic independence forces women to stay in violent family relationships.

The Committee recognizes property grabbing as a particular form of gender-based violence in family relations that violently dispossesses widows. Property-grabbing is defined as a situation in which

> relatives of a deceased husband, claiming customary rights, dispossess the widow and her children from property accumulated during the marriage, including property that is not held according to custom. They remove the widow from the family home and claim all the chattels, then ignore their concomitant customary responsibility to support the widow and children. In some States parties, widows are marginalized or banished to a different community.[815]

Older women, widows,[816] and rural women[817] are the main victims of property-grabbing. GR 29 demands that state parties criminalize "property dispossession/grabbing" and prosecute offenders.[818]

2.11.1.3 Harmful Economic Activities and Human Trafficking as Forms of Gender-Based Violence

In GR 35, the Committee addressed economic harms as a form of gender-based violence:

---

[812] *Id.* ¶ 15.
[813] GR No. 28, *supra* note 25, ¶ 8. GR No. 35, *supra* note 809, ¶ 12.
[814] GR No. 19, *supra* note 807, ¶ 23.
[815] GR No. 29, *supra* note 75, ¶ 50.
[816] GR No. 27, *supra* note 117, ¶¶ 26, 52.
[817] GR No. 34, *supra* note 125, ¶ 22.
[818] GR No. 29, *supra* note 75, ¶ 53.

Gender based violence against women is affected and often exacerbated by ... economic ... factors, as evidenced, among other things, in the contexts of ... the increased globalization of economic activities, including global supply chains, the extractive and offshoring industry.... Gender-based violence against women is also affected by political, economic, and social crises ... and the destruction or degradation of natural resources.[819]

Human trafficking constitutes gender-based violence prohibited under Article 6 of the Convention. GR 19 is first to define trafficking of women as a form of gender-based violence, establishing poverty as a root cause.[820] GR 38 emphasizes "sex-based and gender-based structural inequality and the feminization of poverty"[821] as root causes of trafficking. The Committee calls on states to address these economic root causes of trafficking through

> ... eradicating the pervasive and persistent gender inequality that results in an economic, social, and legal status of women and girls that is lower in comparison with that which is enjoyed by men and boys, [and] by adopting economic and public policies that prevent a lack of sustainable livelihood options and basic living standards for women and girls.[822]

The Committee notes that women experiencing intersectional discrimination face a heightened risk of human trafficking.[823] Rural women[824] and Indigenous women are especially vulnerable.[825]

2.11.1.4 The Regulation of Private Actors and Limitation of Their Property Rights in the Face of Gender-Based Violence as Part of State Parties' Due Diligence Obligations

According to GR 35, "gender-based violence against women constitutes discrimination against women under article 1 and therefore engages all obligations under the Convention."[826] Because acts of domestic and gender-based violence are frequently committed by private actors and in the private sphere, the Committee has extensively developed state's due diligence obligations in GR 19 and GR 35, creating state responsibility for private acts.

---

[819] GR No. 35, *supra* note 809, ¶ 14.
[820] GR No. 19, *supra* note 807, ¶ 13.
[821] GR No. 38, *supra* note 558, ¶ 20.
[822] *Id.* ¶¶ 49–53.
[823] GR No. 38, *supra* note 558, ¶¶ 20–21.
[824] GR No. 34, *supra* note 125, ¶¶ 26–27.
[825] GR No. 39, *supra* note 362, ¶ 37.
[826] GR No. 35, *supra* note 809, ¶ 21.

GR 19 is the first to state that in accordance with Article 2(e), states are responsible for private acts if they fail to act with due diligence to prevent violations of rights or to investigate and punish acts of violence, and for providing compensation.[827]

GR 35 further develops state's due diligence obligation according to Article 2(e):

> States parties will be held responsible should they fail to take all appropriate measures to prevent, as well as to investigate, prosecute, punish and provide reparations for, acts or omissions by non-State actors that result in gender-based violence against women, including actions taken by corporations operating extraterritorially. In particular, States parties are required to take the steps necessary to prevent human rights violations perpetrated abroad by corporations over which they may exercise influence, whether through regulatory means or the use of incentives, including economic incentives. Under the obligation of due diligence, States parties must adopt and implement diverse measures to tackle gender-based violence against women committed by non-State actors, including having laws, institutions, and a system in place to address such violence and ensuring that they function effectively in practice and are supported by all State agents and bodies who diligently enforce the laws. The failure of a State party to take all appropriate measures to prevent acts of gender based violence against women in cases in which its authorities are aware or should be aware of the risk of such violence, or the failure to investigate, to prosecute and punish perpetrators and to provide reparations to victims/survivors of such acts, provides tacit permission or encouragement to perpetrate acts of gender based violence against women. Such failures or omissions constitute human rights violations.[828] (Footnotes omitted.)

Despite the wide formulation applying to a range of private actors in GR 19 and GR 35, the Committee's most explicit references to states' due diligence obligations regarding domestic violence appear in its communications and COs. In those, the link between states' due diligence obligations and the limitation of perpetrators' rights to private property is made explicit as a regulation of private conduct to prevent harm from women. In addition, GR 38 also applies states' due diligence obligations in the context of human trafficking through regulating also economic actors who engage in such practices.[829]

---

[827] GR No. 19, *supra* note 807, ¶ 9.
[828] GR No. 35, *supra* note 809, ¶ 24.
[829] GR No. 38, *supra* note 558, ¶¶ 17, 62.

2.11.1.5 Intervention in Private Property Rights as a Protective Measure in Domestic Violence Situations

In GR 35, the Committee recommends intervention in the private property rights of perpetrators of domestic violence to protect women's safety:

> [P]roviding appropriate and accessible protective mechanisms to prevent further or potential violence, . . . should include immediate risk assessment and protection comprising a wide range of effective measures and, where appropriate, the issuance and monitoring of eviction, protection, restraining or emergency barring orders against alleged perpetrators, including adequate sanctions for non-compliance. . . . The rights or claims of perpetrators or alleged perpetrators during and after judicial proceedings, including with respect to property, . . . should be determined in the light of women's and children's human rights to life and physical, sexual and psychological integrity and guided by the principle of the best interests of the child.[830]

In GR 33 on women's access to justice, the Committee recommends state intervention into the private sphere in domestic violence situations, through criminal justice measures and the timely issuance of protection orders.[831]

2.11.1.6 Access to Housing, Land, and Shelter in Gender-Based Violence Situations

In domestic violence situations, the Committee recommends to implement protective measures such as ensuring access "to affordable housing and land . . . for women victims/survivors and their family members,"[832] in addition to adequate emergency shelters.[833] Especially with regard to rural women, the Committee recommends that states "ensure that integrated services for victims, including emergency shelters . . . are accessible to women and girls in rural areas."[834] With regard to Indigenous women, the Committee emphasizes that shelters must be "available, accessible and culturally appropriate."[835]

2.11.1.7 Gender-Based Violence as a Form of Intersectional Discrimination

The Committee recognizes that gender-based violence disproportionately affects vulnerable groups of women as well as those who experience intersectional

---

[830] GR No. 35, *supra* note 809, ¶ 31(a)(ii).
[831] *Id.* ¶ 51.
[832] *Id.* ¶ 31(a)(iii).
[833] *Id.*
[834] GR No. 34, *supra* note 125, ¶ 25 (d).
[835] GR No. 39, *supra* note 362, ¶ 42 d).

discrimination.[836] In several GRs, the Committee showed the disproportionate effect of different forms of gender-based violence on migrant,[837] rural,[838] and Indigenous women.[839]

Regarding migrant women, the Committee identified a link between "the universal prevalence of gender-based violence and the worldwide feminization of poverty and labor migration."[840]

With regard to rural and Indigenous women, the Committee recognized that rural women frequently experienced violence when defending their land rights. The Committee recommended that states "implement measures to prevent and address threats and attacks against rural women human rights defenders... on issues relating to land and natural resources...."[841]

The Committee demonstrates awareness for the specific forms of violence that Indigenous women experience regarding their land and natural resources. For instance, the Committee presents spiritual violence as a form of gender-based violence against Indigenous women and girls "harming the collective identity of their communities and their connection to their spiritual life, culture, territories, environment and natural resources."[842] Moreover, "forced displacement is a major form of violence that affects Indigenous women and girls, severing their connection to their lands, territories and natural resources and permanently harming their life plans and communities."[843] It emphasizes states' due diligence obligations.[844] The Committee especially recommends addressing "violence attributable to extractive industries,"[845] placing gender-based violence against Indigenous women in the context of the global economy.

2.11.2 Communications

The Committee has addressed the interplay between women's right to be free from domestic violence and property rights in several communications. The perpetrator's private property rights had to be limited to protect women's

---

[836] GR No. 35, *supra* note 809, ¶ 12 (pointing to GR 28 on the core obligations of states parties under Article 2 of the Convention and GR 33 on women's access to justice).
[837] GR No. 26, *supra* note 603, ¶ 5.
[838] GR No. 34, *supra* note 125, ¶ 6. *See also id.* ¶¶ 24–25 (a detailed description of the negative impact of gender-based violence on rural women referring to GR 19).
[839] GR No. 39, *supra* note 362, ¶¶ 34–42.
[840] GR No. 26, *supra* note 603, ¶ 5.
[841] GR No. 34, *supra* note 125, ¶ 25 e).
[842] GR No. 39, *supra* note 362, ¶ 36.
[843] *Id.* ¶ 37.
[844] *Id.* ¶ 39.
[845] *Id.* ¶ 42 b).

well-being and safety in the following communications:[846] *Ms. A.T. v. Hungary, Şahide Goekce v. Austria, Yildirim v. Austria, V.K. v. Bulgaria, J.I. v. Finland,* and *S.T. v. Russian Federation.*

2.11.2.1 Ms. A.T. v. Hungary

Ms. A.T. v. Hungary, received in 2003, is the first communication that the Committee heard, setting an important precedent for states' due diligence obligations regarding private acts of violence against women.

Ms. A.T., a Hungarian national, and her two children experienced severe domestic violence and serious threats of continued violence by her husband in their jointly owned family residence.[847] Ms. A.T. tried to obtain "sole possession of the apartment to avoid a continuation of the violence."[848] However, under Hungary's established law and jurisprudence, "battered individuals have no right to the exclusive use of the jointly owned/leased apartments on grounds of domestic violence."[849] Ms. A.T. could not go to a shelter to protect herself because none was available for mothers with "fully disabled [sic]" children.[850] Neither protection orders nor restraining orders were available under Hungarian law.[851]

In its views, the Committee addressed whether Ms. A.T. was "the victim of a violation of articles 2(a), (b) and (e), 5(a) and 16 of the Convention because Hungary had failed to provide her with effective protection against her former common law husband who jeopardized her physical integrity, physical and mental health, and her life."[852] In making its determination, the Committee referred to GR 19 and recalled the state's responsibility for private acts and due diligence obligations.[853]

The Committee found that Hungary had failed to provide Ms. A.T. with effective protection from serious risk to her physical integrity, physical and mental health, and life,[854] in particular, that Hungary had violated her right to security of person under Article 2(a), (b), and (e). Hungary did not have remedies in place that were "capable of providing immediate protection to her against ill-treatment by her former partner and, furthermore, that legal and institutional

---

[846] *See* Views concerning A.T. v. Hungary, CEDAW/C/32/D/2/2003 (2005). Views concerning Şahide Goekce v. Austria, CEDAW/C/39/D/5/2005 (2007); Views concerning Yildirim v. Austria, CEDAW/C/39/D/6/2005 (2007); Views concerning V.K. v. Bulgaria, CEDAW/C/49/D/20/2008 (2011); Views concerning J.I. v. Finland, CEDAW/C/69/D/103/2016 (2018); Views concerning S.T. v. Russian Federation, CEDAW/C/72/D/65/2014 (2019).
[847] A.T. v. Hungary, *supra* note 847, ¶ 2.4.
[848] *Id.* ¶ 6.8.
[849] *Id.*
[850] *Id.* ¶ 2.1.
[851] *Id.*
[852] *Id.* ¶ 9.2.
[853] GR No. 19 as cited in *Ms. A.T. v. Hungary,* ¶ 9.2.
[854] *Id.* ¶¶ 9.2, 9.6.

arrangements in the State party are not yet ready to ensure the internationally expected, coordinated, comprehensive and effective protection and support for the victims of domestic violence."[855] The Committee emphasized that "[w]omen's human rights to life and to physical and mental integrity cannot be superseded by other rights, including the right to property...."[856] In this regard, the Committee also recalled its concluding comments on Hungary's state reports,[857] in which it had expressed concerns that "no specific legislation has been enacted to combat domestic violence and sexual harassment and that no protection or exclusion orders or shelters exist for the immediate protection of women victims of domestic violence."[858]

The Committee also found that Hungary had violated Articles 5(a) and 16 of the Convention, as interpreted by GR 19 and GR 21.[859] To make this legal determination, the Committee found it decisive that "she has been unsuccessful, either through civil or criminal proceedings, to temporarily or permanently bar" her abuser from the family apartment and that there existed no restraining or protection orders or shelters that would accept her and her disabled child.[860]

In its recommendations to Hungary, the Committee demanded alleviation of the violation against Ms. A.T. through "immediate and effective measures to guarantee the physical and mental integrity of A. T. and her family" and to ensure that Ms. A.T. "is given a safe home in which to live with her children ... as well as reparation proportionate to the physical and mental harm undergone and the gravity of the violations of her rights."[861] On a more general level, the Committee demanded that Hungary "assure victims of domestic violence the maximum protection of the law by acting with due diligence to prevent and respond to such violence against women."[862] Hungary should implement a "a specific law... prohibiting domestic violence against women, which would provide for protection and exclusion orders as well as support services, including shelters."[863]

The Committee pursued a follow-up procedure with Hungary as of 2006.[864] Hungary communicated upon request that it complied with the Committee's recommendations: it offered housing to Ms. A.T., introduced new criminal

---

[855] *Id.* ¶ 9.3.
[856] *Id.* ¶ 9.3.
[857] Concluding Comments preceded COs. This is a mere change of terminology.
[858] A.T. v. Hungary, *supra* note 847, ¶ 9.3.
[859] *Id.* ¶ 9.4.
[860] *Id.*
[861] *Id.* ¶ 9.6.
[862] *Id.*
[863] *Id.*
[864] Comm. on the CEDAW, Annual Rep. of Thirty-fourth Session, Thirty-fifth Session and Thirty-sixth Session, Chapter V, Activities carried out under the Optional Protocol to the CEDAW, ¶ 348, UN Doc. A/61/38(SUPP) (2006).

legislation including restraining orders as a new coercive measure, and began providing crisis shelters for victims of domestic violence.[865] However, Ms. A.T. was not satisfied with how Hungary claimed to have implemented the Committee's recommendations: she stated the flat she was offered was no adequate alternative, requests for restraining orders were not linked with domestic violence and no law defined domestic violence, and the establishment of one crisis center for ten million inhabitants was inadequate.[866] Thereafter, the Committee sent another follow-up inquiring about the measures employed to guarantee the safety of the author and her children and the implementation of restraining orders in domestic violence cases more generally. However, the Committee ended the follow-up without providing information on Hungary's response to the request in its thirty-sixth session.[867]

The Committee pursued additional and complementary follow-up in the State Reporting Procedure. In its Concluding Comments in 2007, the Committee reiterated the recommendations that it had already provided in *Ms. A.T. v. Hungary*:

> The Committee calls upon the State party to ensure that all women who are victims of domestic violence, including rural women, have access to immediate means of redress and protection, including protection orders, and access to a sufficient number of safe shelters and legal aid. The Committee reiterates its recommendation that the State party elaborate a specific law on domestic violence against women which provides for such redress and protection....[868]

In its Concluding Observations in 2013, the Committee repeated the necessity to introduce further protective measures to eliminate domestic and gender-based violence, including with regard to unmarried partners, Roma women, and older women, and expressed renewed concern about the insufficient number of shelters.[869] It urged Hungary to

> amend its legislation concerning restraining orders with a view to providing adequate protection to victims in all types of cohabitation and extend the duration of restraining orders"; and "[p]rovide adequate assistance and protection to women victims of violence and their children, by increasing the number and capacity of State-supported shelters...[870]

---

[865] Comm. on the CEDAW, Annual Rep. of Forty-fourth Session, Annex XII: Rep. of the Committee under the Optional Protocol on follow-up to views of the Committee on individual communications, at 116, UN Doc. A/65/38(SUPP) (2009).
[866] *Id.* at 117.
[867] *Id.* at 118.
[868] CO on Hungary, CEDAW/C/HUN/CO/6, ¶¶ 18–19 (2007).
[869] CO on Hungary, CEDAW/C/HUN/CO/7-8, ¶ 20 (2013).
[870] *Id.* ¶ 21.

2.11.2.2 Şahide Goekce v. Austria

Two separate Austrian communications, *Şahide Goekce v. Austria* and *Yildirim v. Austria*, brought to the Committee's attention at the same time, referred to property rights when addressing states' due diligence obligations.

Şahide Goekce, an Austrian national of Turkish descent, was murdered by her husband in their family apartment. The Committee found that Austria had failed to protect her and to exercise due diligence.[871]

While protective measures, including a three-month interim injunction, had formally prohibited the perpetrator from returning to the family apartment, Ms. Goekce's husband did not respect them, and the Austrian courts failed to detain her husband despite the risk of violence against Ms. Goekce. The Committee found that the state's failure to enforce the protective mechanisms led to continued gender-based violence and ultimately to the killing of Ms. Goekce. These conclusions led the Committee to find violations of the rights to life and physical and mental integrity under Article 2(a), (c)–(f), and Article 3 of the Convention, in conjunction with Article 1 of the Convention and GR 19.[872] The Committee emphasized that "the perpetrator's rights cannot supersede women's human rights to life and to physical and mental integrity."[873]

While the Committee balanced Ms. Goekce's right to life with the perpetrator's right to freedom of movement and a fair trial, its recommendation to Austria was sufficiently general to encompass property rights as well: it recommended that Austria "ensure that in all action taken to protect women from violence, due consideration is given to the safety of women, emphasizing that the perpetrator's rights cannot supersede women's human rights to life and to physical and mental integrity."[874] The follow-up procedures did not address this any further.[875]

2.11.2.3 Yildirim v. Austria

Fatma Yildirim, an Austrian national of Turkish origin, was killed by her husband on her way home. The Committee found that Austria had failed to protect her rights to "life and to physical and mental integrity under article 2(a), (c)–(f) and article 3 of the Convention read in conjunction with article 1 and GR 19."[876]

As in *Şahide Goekce v. Austria*, the Committee found that the state had a due diligence obligation to eliminate violence against Fatma Yildirim under

---

[871] Şahide Goekce v. Austria, *supra* note 847, ¶¶ 12.1.3–12.1.4.
[872] *Id.* ¶ 12.3.
[873] *Id.* ¶ 12.1.5 (citing ¶ 9.3 of the A.T. v. Hungary).
[874] *Id.* ¶ 12.3.b.
[875] CEDAW Comm., Rep. of Forty-fourth Session, *supra* note 866.
[876] Yildirim v. Austria, *supra* note 847, ¶ 12.3.

Article 2(a), (c)–(f), and Article 3 of the Convention and under GR 19. In the face of death threats and physical assaults by the husband, the Austrian police and Austrian courts had issued expulsion and prohibition to return orders prohibiting the perpetrator's return to the family apartment. The Committee found that the state party had breached its due diligence obligation because it had failed to detain the violent husband as a last resort to protect Fatma Yildirim's life and physical integrity.

The Committee recommended that Austria

> ... ensure that in all action taken to protect women from violence, due consideration is given to the safety of women, emphasizing that the perpetrator's rights cannot supersede women's human rights to life and to physical and mental integrity.[877]

In this case as well, the Committee implicitly indicated that limiting property rights of others is vindicated when a woman's right to life and physical integrity requires this. The follow-up procedure did not add anything on this point.[878]

2.11.2.4 V.K. v. Bulgaria

In *V.K. v. Bulgaria*, the Committee found that economic abuse and lack of economic independence contributed to the domestic violence which V.K. experienced at the hands of her husband. In this case, the Committee focused on the question of whether Bulgaria had violated V.K.'s right to be protected against domestic violence through the failure of the responsible Court to issue a permanent protection order and the unavailability of suitable shelters.[879] The Committee held that Bulgaria had violated the complainant's rights under Article 2(c) through (f), in conjunction with Articles 1, 5(a), and 16(1) of the Convention, considered in light of GR 19.[880]

On the merits, the Committee considered whether (1) Bulgaria's failure to issue a permanent protection order against V.K.'s husband, or (2) the unavailability of shelters had violated Bulgaria's obligation to protect the author against domestic violence effectively.[881]

The Committee concluded that the Bulgarian court had refused to issue a permanent protection order based on "stereotyped, preconceived and thus discriminatory notions of what constitutes domestic violence."[882] It found Bulgaria

---

[877] Id.
[878] CEDAW Comm., Rep. of Forty-fourth Session, *supra* note 866.
[879] V.K. v. Bulgaria, *supra* note 847, ¶ 9.4.
[880] Id. ¶ 9.15.
[881] Id. ¶ 9.4.
[882] Id. ¶ 9.12.

to be responsible for failing to protect V.K. against domestic and gender-based violence under Articles 5 and 16 and GR 19.[883] It further deemed the unavailability of shelters a violation of the state's obligations under Article 2(c) and (e). Recalling its GR 19, the Committee concluded that Bulgaria had failed "to provide for the immediate protection of women from violence, including domestic violence."[884] The Committee recommended amending Bulgaria's law on protection against domestic violence to ensure that "protection orders are available without placing undue administrative and legal burdens on applicants" and to "ensure that a sufficient number of State-funded shelters are available to victims of domestic violence and their children . . . ."[885] In its follow-up procedure, the Committee found a "satisfactory resolution of its recommendations" but did not report any details.[886]

2.11.2.5 J.I. v. Finland

In *J.I. v. Finland*, the Committee addressed whether Finish authorities had fulfilled their due diligence obligations to take reasonable steps to ensure, without discrimination based on sex, the protection of the author and her son from continuing domestic violence.[887] To make this determination, it phrased states' due diligence obligations so that they must limit a perpetrator's property rights to protect the life and physical integrity of women victims/survivors of domestic violence:

> Under the obligation of due diligence, States parties must adopt and implement diverse measures to tackle gender-based violence against women committed by non-State actors . . . . The rights or claims of perpetrators or alleged perpetrators during and after judicial proceedings, including with respect to property, . . . should be determined in the light of the human rights of women and children to life and physical, sexual, and psychological integrity, and guided by the principle of the best interests of the child.[888]

The Committee recommended that Finland strengthen "the application of the legal framework to ensure that the competent authorities may respond with due diligence to situations of domestic violence."[889] No follow-up procedure is publicly available on this case.

---

[883] *Id.* ¶ 9.11.
[884] *Id.* ¶ 9.13.
[885] *Id.* ¶ 9.16.
[886] CEDAW Comm., Annual Rep. on Its Sixty-third Session, UN Doc A/71/38 (2016).
[887] J.I. v. Finland, *supra* note 847, ¶ 8.2.
[888] *Id.* ¶ 8.8.
[889] *Id.* ¶ 10.

2.11.2.6 S.T. v. Russian Federation

In *S.T. v. Russian Federation*, the Committee found that the Russian Federation had failed to protect S.T., a Chechen woman, against her husband's acts of gender-based violence, including an attempt to kill her. S.T.'s lack of economic independence and inability to exclude her husband from their shared family residency, where the violent acts occurred, contributed to her lack of physical safety and integrity. The Committee found that the Russian Federation "violated the author's rights under article 2 (c) and (d), read in conjunction with article 1, and article 5(a) of the Convention, and taking into consideration general recommendations No. 19 and No. 35."[890]

The Committee concluded that the Russian Federation's authorities had failed to protect her against domestic violence or punish the perpetrator adequately for the attempted murder.[891] Some of the failings the Committee highlighted in this regard concerned the lack of access to shelters and the lack of a "restraining or protection order as the law does not provide for such options."[892] It recommended that the Russian Federation make legal instruments such as restraining orders and orders of protection legally available to victims.[893] In addition, the Committee recommended in line with GR 33 on access to justice that the Russian Federation "ensure that victims of domestic violence and their children are provided with prompt and adequate support, including shelter..."[894]

As a follow-up, the Committee recommended in COs to Russia to "accelerate the implementation of the recommendations made by the Committee in its Views in *X and Y v. Russian Federation*... and *S.T. v. Russian Federation*..."[895]

2.11.3 Inquiry Reports

In the Inquiry Report on Canada and on South Africa, the Committee addressed property related aspects regarding gender-based violence.[896]

2.11.3.1 Inquiry Concerning Canada

The Committee's Inquiry Report on Canada concerned the systemic issue of missing and murdered Aboriginal women. The Committee started the inquiry in 2011 because of the high levels of violence, disappearances, and murder that

---

[890] S.T. v. Russian Federation, *supra* note 847, ¶ 10.
[891] *Id.* ¶ 9.9.
[892] *Id.* ¶ 9.8.
[893] *Id.* ¶ 11.b.ii.
[894] *Id.* ¶ 11.b.iv.
[895] CO on Russian Federation, CEDAW/C/RUS/CO/9, ¶ 25 (2021).
[896] Rep. of the Inquiry concerning Canada, CEDAW/C/OP.8/CAN/1 (2015); Rep. of the Inquiry concerning South Africa, CEDAW/C/ZAF/IR/1 (2021).

Aboriginal women and girls experience, in part because of their vulnerability due to unfavorable social and economic conditions.[897]

2.11.3.1.1 Context and Facts

In the context of the report, the Committee tied the violence that Aboriginal women experience today to the continuing legacies of colonial violence. The Committee found that forcible displacement had caused intergenerational trauma and violence to the Aboriginal population.[898] The Committee considered that

> the legacy of colonization ... such as the ... persistent tensions resulting from land claims and treaty rights are all factors that cannot be separated from the current violence against aboriginal women and the continued and increased vulnerability of aboriginal women to such violence.[899]

It viewed systematic disenfranchisements of Indigenous land rights, housing rights, and other economic and social rights, paired with the persistent high levels of poverty, as historical legacies and harms affecting the Aboriginal population.[900] The Committee noted that "the socioeconomic marginalization of aboriginal women is reflected in the high incidence of poverty among them," and this was linked "to inadequate housing and homelessness ..."[901] Furthermore, the Committee maintained that "unless urgent attention is given to addressing the root cause of the vulnerability of aboriginal women to violence, the problem will persist unabated."[902]

2.11.3.1.2 Legal Assessment of Human Rights Violations

The Committee clarified in its report that the yardstick for Canada's due diligence obligations to prevent violence was influenced by the identified vulnerabilities which Aboriginal women face.[903] Given that socioeconomic disenfranchisements have contributed to Aboriginal women's vulnerability, the Committee suggested that Canada needed to address those conditions to prevent violence.

The Committee found that Canada had committed grave violations of the Convention given "the magnitude and severity of the issues of murdered and missing aboriginal women and the gender-based violence against aboriginal

---

[897] Rep. of Canada, *supra* note 897, ¶ 3.
[898] *Id.* ¶¶ 22–23.
[899] *Id.* ¶ 129.
[900] *Id.* ¶¶ 25–26.
[901] *Id.* ¶ 112.
[902] *Id.* ¶ 119.
[903] *Id.* ¶ 202.

women."[904] It found that Canada was in violation of "the rights of aboriginal women victims of violence, in particular those victims of murder and disappearance and their family members, under articles 1, 2(c), 2(d), 2(e), 3 and 5(a), read in conjunction with articles 14(1) and 15(1), of the Convention," and that it had failed to fulfill the Committee's specific recommendations in its COs or its General Recommendations in GR 19 and GR 28.[905]

One of the Committee's main recommendations to Canada was to "improve the socioeconomic situation of aboriginal women . . ." through comprehensive measures.[906] The Committee also recommended overcoming the legacy of the colonial period by addressing the history of dispossession and marginalization of the Aboriginal community in Canada in public education and information campaigns.[907]

2.11.3.2 Inquiry Concerning South Africa

The Committee decided to conduct an inquiry in South Africa because of the information it received on grave and systematic domestic violence against women and girls.[908] The Committee issued a report in May 2021, with follow-up procedures conducted in 2022. The following will focus on domestic violence and its relationship to women's socioeconomic status.

2.11.3.2.1 Legal Framework and Facts

The Committee's presentation of South Africa's legal framework affirmed that there exist legal procedures to obtain protection orders and that women under threat of violence were entitled to assistance in finding suitable shelter.[909] At the same time, the Committee noted the country had not established a specific offense targeting gender-based violence.[910]

However, the Committee determined that the implementation and enforcement of the legal framework on protection orders were flawed. As few as 15 percent of applications for protection orders were granted.[911] The legal proceeding to obtain an interim protection order put victims at risk of revictimization: victims choose not to appear at protection order proceedings out of the fear of confronting the perpetrator at the hearing and potential retaliation.[912] In addition, the lack of economic and human resources was

---

[904] *Id.* ¶ 214.
[905] *Id.* ¶ 215.
[906] *Id.* ¶¶ 216, 218.
[907] *Id.* ¶ 219.
[908] Rep. of South Africa, *supra* note 897, ¶ 4.
[909] *Id.* ¶ 16.
[910] *Id.* ¶ 17.
[911] The Committee cites a Department of Justice report that states that "22,211 out of 143,824 applications for protection orders were granted in 2018/19." *Id.* ¶ 27.
[912] *Id.* ¶ 60.

found to negatively affect women's application for protection orders: they received insufficient assistance in the application process for protective orders and experienced delays and lack of engagement with their cases through the magistrates. Moreover, magistrates could refer their cases to alternative mediation mechanisms due to scarce resources and heavy caseload.[913] Even in cases where a protective order was issued, the content of a protection order could put a victim at risk or lead to revictimization.[914] Furthermore, police enforcement of protection orders was deficient.[915]

The Committee viewed South Africa's legacies of poverty and women's economic dependence as underlying causes of domestic violence.[916] Economic dependence was one of many reasons why women did not report gender-based violence.[917] Women in shelters frequently returned to perpetrators because they were economically depended on their partners.[918] The Committee relied on NGOs' reports when analyzing economic violence as a form of gender-based violence.

> Several victims experienced economic violence, as their partners deprived them of food, money, access to education or employment, or did not pay alimony or child maintenance following divorce. NGOs stressed that women's limited access to resources exposed them to domestic violence.[919]

The Committee viewed women's lack of autonomy as a contributing factor for them to stay in abusive relationships. Furthermore, women's lack of access to affordable housing forced them to stay in abusive relationships.[920]

The Committee noted that property arrangement in the marital property regime was decisive for women's exit options from abusive relationships:

> Joint marital property is often not shared equally upon divorce. Although customary law allows for the division of marital property, many women are unaware that they must claim it or are precluded from doing so by cultural norms.[921]

2.11.3.2.2 Legal Findings and Recommendations
The Committee assessed states parties' obligations under the Convention. Gender-based violence constitutes discrimination and involves all obligations

---

[913] Id. ¶ 61.
[914] Id. ¶ 63.
[915] Id. ¶¶ 63–64.
[916] Id. ¶ 19.
[917] Id. ¶ 69.
[918] Id. ¶ 28.
[919] Id. ¶ 32.
[920] Id. ¶ 80.
[921] Id. ¶¶ 81–82.

under the Convention.[922] Moreover, South Africa has due diligence obligations under Article 2(e) to "take all appropriate measures to prevent, investigate, prosecute, punish and provide reparations for acts or omissions by non-State actors that result in gender-based violence against women, including domestic violence."[923] Under Articles 2(c) and 15, states parties must ensure that victims of domestic violence have access to affordable, accessible, and timely remedies, with legal aid, if necessary, free of charge, and access to effective reparations.[924] Additionally, under Article 2(c), states parties should protect and assist women complainants of domestic violence by ensuring, among other things, sufficient numbers of safe and adequately equipped shelters and affordable housing.[925]

Regarding the right to live free from domestic violence, the Committee found several violations of South Africa's state obligations. First, it held that South Africa had violated Articles 1, 2(f), 3, 5(a), 10(c) and (h), and 16, considered in light of GR 35, by failing to take sustained measures to prevent domestic violence and eliminate harmful practices by eradicating the discriminatory stereotypes and practices that are the root causes of domestic violence.[926]

Second, it held that South Africa had violated Articles "2(b), (c) and (e), read in conjunction with 5(a) and 15, by failing to effectively enforce and monitor protection orders against alleged perpetrators and impose adequate sanctions for non-compliance," also citing GR 19 on domestic violence. This conclusion suggests that protection orders that might limit domestic abusers' access to their property are a legitimate tool to protect women.

The Committee affirmed that women's lack of access to justice made the country's protection and eviction orders ineffective in practice. It noted that women victimized by gender-based violence often lacked information about either their rights or applicable judicial procedures, and even if they overcame that hurdle, they frequently faced court procedures that were not gender-sensitive.[927] Accordingly, the Committee found that South Africa had failed to remove "economic barriers to access to justice faced by victims of domestic violence"[928] and was therefore in violation of Articles 2(c), 5(a), and 15.[929]

The Committee acknowledged that victims' limited access to support services undermined the victim's right to an effective remedy.[930] In South Africa specifically, the state's legal and social services centers lack funding and are inaccessible

---

[922] *Id.* ¶ 87.
[923] *Id.* ¶ 88.
[924] *Id.* ¶ 90.
[925] *Id.* ¶ 91.
[926] *Id.* ¶ 102 a).
[927] *Id.* ¶ 104.
[928] *Id.* ¶ 105.
[929] *Id.* ¶ 110 a).
[930] *Id.* ¶ 107.

for many women in rural areas. In this regard, the Committee pointed to South Africa's failure "to ensure the budgetary allocations necessary for victim support services ... such as affordable housing."⁹³¹ It cited the recommendation it had already made in South Africa's combined second, third, and fourth periodic report in 2011.⁹³²

In connection with protection and support services, the Committee noted "the absence of state-run shelters for women and their children."⁹³³ It further observed "the limited capacity of NGO-run shelters and safe houses that provide medical, psychological and legal services to victims ... are direct consequences of the limited financial support they receive...."⁹³⁴

In addition, the Committee considered that "women's insufficient economic protection upon divorce ... perpetuate[s] women's dependence on abusive partners."⁹³⁵ The Committee found violations of Articles 2(c) and (e), 10, 13, and 16, as failing to ensure women's adequate protection in divorce discourages victims of domestic violence from leaving abusive relationships.⁹³⁶

The Committee poignantly summed up the untenable options faced by those subjected to gender-based violence:

> The situation gives women and girls who are victims of domestic violence two options: to remain in the abusive domestic relationship; or to leave the relationship at the risk of retaliation, separation from their children, poverty and stigmatization, and with limited access to justice, protection and support services. In either case, victims often find themselves without effective protection from further violence....⁹³⁷

The Committee found that South Africa was responsible for grave and systematic violations. The violations were grave because South Africa had "failed to protect a significant number of women and girls from domestic violence and ... enable women to leave abusive domestic relationships, thereby exposing them to or unnecessarily prolonging their severe physical and mental suffering." The violations were systematic because it had "knowingly omitted to take effective measures," including "to remove the economic and social barriers faced by victims of domestic violence ...."⁹³⁸ The Committee considered that South

---

⁹³¹ *Id.*
⁹³² CO on South Africa, CEDAW/C/ZAF/CO/4, ¶ 25 (d). The Committee calls upon the state party to: "d) Ensure the necessary budgetary allocations for the implementation of the various projects and programmes, including social support services for victims."
⁹³³ Rep. of South Africa, *supra* note 897, ¶ 108.
⁹³⁴ *Id.* ¶¶ 108, 110 (b).
⁹³⁵ *Id.* ¶ 109.
⁹³⁶ *Id.* ¶ 110 c).
⁹³⁷ *Id.* ¶ 115.
⁹³⁸ *Id.* ¶ 116.

Africa simply had accepted "these omissions, which are not a random occurrence, as evidenced by the extremely high levels of domestic violence in the state party. They constitute elements of systematic violations of rights under the Convention."[939]

The Committee recommended improving the South African legal and institutional framework, including women's access to justice through protection orders.[940] Regarding access to shelters and adequate housing, the Committee called on South Africa to ensure "that shelters and safe houses have sufficient capacity to receive victims of domestic violence" and "that survivors of domestic violence and their children have access to affordable housing . . . , and are economically empowered to gain economic autonomy to leave and recover from abusive relationships."[941]

2.11.4 Concluding Observations

The surveyed COs on gender-based violence addressed states parties' several facets of preventing and addressing different forms of gender-based violence. The Committee addressed specific forms of gender-based violence, such as property-grabbing and economic violence. Moreover, it referred to states parties' due diligence obligations in the context of gender-based violence, even if those only implicitly impose limitations on private property rights holders who harm women and whom the state must therefore regulate to prevent this harm. It called on states to implement and enforce protection and eviction orders to limit the perpetrator's private property or housing rights to protect women and to provide access to shelter.

2.11.4.1 Property-Grabbing and Economic Violence

The Committee alluded to property-grabbing as a specific form of gender-based violence in several COs on African countries.[942] For instance, regarding Zambia, the Committee criticized harmful practices such as "property grabbing" contributing to the "persistence of violence against women." The Committee recommended "measures to address negative customs and harmful practices such as property-grabbing, especially in rural areas, which affect the full enjoyment of the right to property by women."[943] It recommended to criminalize and

---

[939] *Id.* ¶ 117.
[940] *Id.* ¶ 119.
[941] *Id.* ¶ 121.
[942] COs on Malawi (CEDAW/C/MWI/CO/6, ¶¶ 42–43); Ethiopia (CEDAW/C/ETH/CO/6-7, ¶¶ 41–42); Zambia (CEDAW/C/ZMB/CO/5-6, ¶¶ 13, 19, 37–38).
[943] CO on Zambia, CEDAW/C/ZMB/CO/5-6, ¶¶ 37–38 (2011).

prohibit the practice of property-grabbing and to enforce the legislation.[944] The Committee urged several countries to define economic violence as a form of gender-based violence.[945]

2.11.4.2 State's Due Diligence Obligations Entail a Limitation on Perpetrator's Private Property Rights

The Committee emphasized that states parties' due diligence obligations exist for all crimes that state and non-state actors commit against women and girls. It recommended states to investigate, prosecute, and punish state and non-state perpetrators and provide redress to women who have been victims of violence regardless of the context and of the alleged perpetrators.[946] The Committee expressed concern that around the world, the levels of domestic and gender-based violence are increasing, while the exercise of due diligence obligations is decreasing.[947] It criticized when states failed to exercise due diligence to prevent gender-based violence and provide redress.[948]

The Committee also takes up due diligence obligations regarding non-state actors in the form of businesses and corporations when they perform acts of economic violence that count as gender-based violence. For instance, the Committee reminded Luxembourg that "under the obligation of due diligence, it may be held responsible should it fail to take all appropriate measures to prevent, as well as to investigate, prosecute and punish perpetrators of and provide reparations for, acts or omissions by non-State actors, including actions taken by corporations operating extraterritorially."[949] Regarding Sweden, the Committee recommended to "uphold its due diligence obligations to ensure that companies under its jurisdiction or control respect, protect and fulfil women's human rights when operating abroad."[950]

2.11.4.3 Protection and Eviction Orders

The Committee expressed concern about the limited access for women to protection orders.[951] Generally, the Committee recommended that states parties

---

[944] CO on Malawi, CEDAW/C/MWI/CO/6, ¶¶ 43 (2010).
[945] COs on Portugal (CEDAW/C/PRT/CO/10, ¶ 23), Bulgaria (CEDAW/C/BGR/CO/8, ¶ 23); Senegal (CEDAW/C/SEN/CO/8, ¶ 24).
[946] COs on Mexico (CEDAW/C/MEX/CO/7–8, ¶ 12), Afghanistan (CEDAW/C/AFG/CO/1–2, ¶ 23).
[947] See, e.g., Turkey's withdrawal from the Istanbul Convention is mentioned as one example. CO on Turkey, CEDAW/C/TUR/CO/8, ¶ 28 (2022).
[948] See, e.g., CO on Bolivia (CEDAW/C/BOL/CO/7, ¶ 17); Timor-Leste (CEDAW/C/TLS/CO/2–3, ¶ 16).
[949] CO on Luxembourg, CEDAW/C/LUX/CO/6–7, ¶ 10 (2018).
[950] CO on Sweden, CEDAW/C/SWE/CO/8–9, ¶ 35 (2016).
[951] COs on Namibia (CEDAW/C/NAM/CO/6, ¶ 28) and Mauritius (CEDAW/C/MUS/CO/8, ¶ 17).

provide protection orders to victims of gender-based violence.[952] In countries, where there are no or insufficient laws on gender-based violence against women that provide for risk assessments and exercise of due diligence, the Committee urged states parties to adopt such laws.[953]

Moreover, the Committee expressed its concern that protection and eviction orders were not adequately enforced even if legal provisions mandate them. For instance, the Committee noted that "eviction orders for perpetrators to leave the family home are executed only if that person has no other residence."[954] The Committee recommended to several states parties that they ensure the timely and effective issuance, implementation, and monitoring of eviction orders.[955] This is especially salient in situations where emergency protection orders are required.[956]

2.11.4.4 Shelter

Around the world, there is a lack of access and capacity regarding shelters to house battered women, a persistent lack of funding, and a general shortage of shelters despite the increase of gender-based and domestic violence.[957] The Committee recommended providing shelters for victims, especially in rural areas.[958] It recommended that states parties provide sufficient resources, including human, technical, and financial resources to shelters for women victims of violence to enable them to provide adequate services to victims.[959]

---

[952] COs on Senegal (CEDAW/C/SEN/CO/8, ¶ 24), South Africa (CEDAW/C/ZAF/CO/5, ¶ 14), and Mauritius (CEDAW/C/MUS/CO/8, ¶18).
[953] COs on Dominican Republic (CEDAW/C/DOM/CO/6-7, ¶ 22) and Cambodia (CEDAW/C/KHM/CO/6, ¶ 25).
[954] CO on Kazakhstan, CEDAW/C/KAZ/CO/5, ¶ 25 (2019).
[955] COs on Kazakhstan (CEDAW/C/KAZ/CO/5, ¶ 25), Bolivia (CEDAW/C/BOL/CO/7, ¶ 18).
[956] CO on Serbia, CEDAW/C/SRB/CO/4, ¶ 24 (2019).
[957] COs on Lithuania (CEDAW/C/LTU/CO/6, ¶ 38), Kazakhstan (CEDAW/C/KAZ/CO/5, ¶¶ 25-26), Bolivia (CEDAW/C/BOL/CO/7, ¶ 17); Lebanon (CEDAW/C/LBN/CO/6, ¶¶ 25-26); Uganda (CEDAW/C/UGA/CO/8-9, ¶ 25); Morocco (CEDAW/C/MAR/CO/5-6, ¶ 23); Colombia (CEDAW/C/COL/CO/9, ¶ 25).
[958] COs on Russian Federation (CEDAW/C/RUS/CO/9, ¶ 43) and Bulgaria (CEDAW/C/BGR/CO/8, ¶ 25).
[959] COs on Afghanistan (CEDAW/C/AFG/CO/1-2, ¶ 23), Gabon (CEDAW/C/GAB/CO/7, ¶ 19), and Indonesia (CEDAW/C/IDN/CO/8, ¶ 26).

3
Critiques of the CEDAW Regime, International Law, and International Human Rights

Before proceeding to a consideration of the implications of CEDAW's property jurisprudence as described in chapter 2, it is useful to put the CEDAW Committee's outputs in a broader context. The CEDAW Committee has been in implicit dialogue with a number of critiques that have been directed at it or the Convention by external scholars. Its property jurisprudence responds, in part, to such critiques. Section 3.1 of this chapter synthesizes a number of the most prominent criticisms made by those who have been and may remain skeptical of a regime to protect women's equality devised, negotiated, and established by the same governments that have been complicit in undermining that equality. Section 3.2 turns to more expansive critiques of international law and international human rights that also appear relevant to assessing CEDAW's property jurisprudence. This includes contemporary "revisionist" critiques of the human rights movement, particularly its inclusion of property rights as "human rights." The next chapter addresses what the CEDAW Committee's property jurisprudence tells us about these critiques. But first we need to understand what they are.

3.1 Feminist Critiques: Then and Now

3.1.1 Early Critiques of CEDAW

Despite its prominence as the leading treaty addressing the rights of women, the CEDAW Convention has drawn mixed feelings from the start, including from feminist scholars. Hilary Charlesworth, Christine Chinkin, and Shelly Wright, in their pathbreaking early work, characterized the treaty as an "ambiguous offering."[1] Those authors expressed qualms about the treaty's reliance on an "ethic

---

[1] Hilary Charlesworth et al., *Feminist Approaches to International Law*, 85 AM. J. INT'L L. 613, 634 (1991).

of rights," which they associated with abstract notions of "right and wrong, fairness, logic, rationality, winners and losers" that was less responsive to those who spoke in a "different voice" of care, context, and relationships.[2] They questioned whether a focus on according formal legal rights genuinely advances women's equality, pointing out that an emphasis on individual rights ignores demands for collective rights made by many in the developing world, serves to deflect attention from the realities of power, presumes that respect for civil and political rights will address forms of economic, social, and cultural oppression, and overlooks the problem that some individual rights (e.g., to freedom of religion) may be detrimental to women or that the need to "balance" competing rights among individuals may do the same.[3]

Charlesworth and her co-authors argued that, worse still, the CEDAW Convention emphasized a particular type of right—the right to be treated as men—as if that standard, demanded by liberal feminists in the privileged West, had the same attraction for those outside the West. Women in some developing countries, they argued, faced "intensely patriarchal" forms of "masculinist" discourse no less oppressive for being less reliant on positivist laws—and possibly less subject to remedy through resort to the "western rationalist language of the law."[4]

Keenly aware of the many ways international law has shown itself to be "impervious to the voices of women" for centuries, Charlesworth, Chinkin, and Wright questioned whether "the most prominent international normative instrument recognizing the special concerns of women" offered "real or chimerical possibility of change."[5] The latter seems more likely given those authors' thoroughgoing analysis of international law's gendered shortcomings. These include, most prominently, international law's deep-seated reliance on public/private distinctions prevalent within liberal theory. International human rights law privileging of rights in the public sphere, it is argued, has made it more difficult to prohibit practices in the private sphere where a great deal of subordination of women occurs. It has made it harder for international law to banish violence against women or trafficking in women and imposed blinkers on what the rights to development or self-determination mean.[6] While Charlesworth, Chinkin, and Wright praised the Convention for going beyond formal equality, they argued that its emphasis on equality of opportunity and result applied, in

---

[2] *Id.* at 615 (citing Carol Gilligan's suggestions that women speak in a "different voice" based on an "ethic of care.")

[3] *Id.* at 634–38. *See also id.* at 618–19 (noting, for example, that right of women to be free from violence in the home may be balanced against the "property rights of men in the home").

[4] *Id.* at 619.

[5] *Id.* at 631.

[6] *Id.* at 625–31, 638–43.

all but special circumstances, a male standard.[7] They took treaty drafters to task for presuming that equality meant "freedom to be treated without regard to sex" when the real challenge was to secure "freedom from systematic subordination because of sex."[8] They argued further that CEDAW's absence of limitations on states' reservations and weak enforcement provisions—which relied on "good will, education and changing attitudes" as the agent of change—seemed to presume that women could achieve equality within existing social and legal structures.[9]

Nine years later, Charlesworth and Chinkin leaned into a number of their previously expressed concerns with CEDAW. In 2000, when CEDAW had been in force for over twenty years, the two authors expressed at greater depth their fears that CEDAW was marginalizing this "specialized branch of human rights law."[10] Their qualms that CEDAW would become a silo or "ghetto" for women's concerns had a history. Such fears had been expressed even while the Convention was being negotiated given its unusual trajectory as compared to other UN human rights treaties. Unlike the International Covenant on Civil and Political Rights (ICCPR) or the International Covenant on Economic, Social and Cultural Rights (ICESCR), the idea for CEDAW had originated in the specialized domain of the Commission on the Status of Women (CSW) within the Economic and Social Council (ECOSOC). Unlike those other mainstream human rights conventions, the proposed treaty was thereafter vetted by the Third (Social) Committee of the General Assembly rather than the Sixth (Legal) Committee. The decision that the new treaty and its expert committee would be assisted by UN Secretariat staff located in New York rather than in Geneva—unlike other human rights bodies—was seen as a further step to marginalize women's rights, as was the decision not to include within the Convention a provision (as under the ICCPR) enabling states to complain about each other's compliance.[11]

Charlesworth and Chinkin argued that the prospect for successful implementation of CEDAW's protection was undermined by the treaty's "weak" language, the reservations states had been permitted to take to its terms (which permitted

---

[7] *Id.* 631-32. *See also* Hilary Charlesworth & Christine Chinkin, *Between the Margins and the Mainstream: The Case of Women's Rights*, *in* THE LIMITS OF HUMAN RIGHTS 205, 210 (Bardo Fassbender & Knut Traisbach eds., 2019).

[8] *Id.* at 632.

[9] *Id.* at 632-34. These complaints persist. *See, e.g.*, Loveday Hodson, *Women's Rights and the Periphery: CEDAW's Optional Protocol*, 25 EUR. J. INT'L L. 561, 566 (2014).

[10] HILARY CHARLESWORTH & CHRISTINE CHINKIN, THE BOUNDARIES OF INTERNATIONAL LAW 218 (2000). *See also* Charlesworth & Chinkin, *supra* note 7.

[11] *See, e.g.*, Patricia Schulz et al., *Introduction*, *in* THE UN CONVENTION ON THE ELIMINATION OF ALL FORMS OF DISCRIMINATION AGAINST WOMEN AND ITS OPTIONAL PROTOCOL 1 (Patricia Schulz et al. eds., 2d ed. 2022) [hereinafter 2022 COMMENTARY], at Sec. F (I). Compare, for example, International Covenant on Civil and Political Rights art. 41, *opened for signature* Dec 16, 1966, 999 U.N.T.S. 171 (enabling ratifying states to indicate whether they accept the possibility of interstate communications).

wide-open "claw back" exceptions to protect "cultural" practices), and the limited monitoring methods accorded to its Committee.[12] They pointed out that by borrowing the standard for discrimination contained in the ICCPR and the ICESCR, CEDAW had adopted a limited understanding of "equality" which sought to "place women in the same position as men in the public sphere."[13] They argued that this standard failed to consider whether existing male standards were appropriate, seemed to presume that women's inequality would be achieved once women were allowed to participate equally in decision-making fora, and ignored "the underlying structures and power relations that contribute to the oppression of women."[14]

Charlesworth and Chinkin's pathbreaking and influential book described CEDAW as reinforcing rather than directly challenging gendered public/private distinctions. The authors argued that the Convention's limited recognition that women were oppressed in the private sphere did not displace its focus "on public life, the economy, the legal system and education."[15] They feared that the treaty would only reify familiar public/private distinctions within international human rights law (and between ostensibly "first" and "second" generations of human rights) that fail to respond to the reality that women are in an inferior position not simply because they face discrimination relative to men but "because they lack economic, social or political power in both the public and private worlds."[16] The two authors worried that even the "comparatively broad definition of discrimination" contained in CEDAW would be insufficient to address women's insubordination in the real world since the treaty appeared to rely, with one exception, on the familiar list of gendered fundamental rights and freedoms taken from other human rights instruments.[17]

---

[12] CHARLESWORTH & CHINKIN, *supra* note 10, at 220–21 (noting that unlike the International Convention on the Elimination of All Forms of Racial Discrimination (CERD) states were accorded considerable discretion since most of the treaty's obligations anticipated "all appropriate methods;" that unlike other treaties (like CERD, the ICCPR, and Convention Against Torture), CEDAW only anticipated requirements for state reporting rather than interstate and individual complaints mechanisms; and that the CEDAW Committee was hampered by more limited resources and more limited time to examine state reports than other UN human rights bodies). *See also id.* at 222–29 (discussing the undermining of "universal" rights under the guise of "cultural relativism"). The adoption in October of 1999 of an Optional Protocol to CEDAW partially addressed only one of these concerns. States that adhered to the Protocol (which came into force on Dec. 22, 2000) agreed to permit individuals and groups to file communications to the CEDAW Committee. *See* G.A. Res. A/RES/54/4, Optional Protocol to the Convention on the Elimination of All Forms of Discrimination against Women, Articles 1–7 (Oct. 6, 1999) [hereinafter Optional Protocol]. In addition, states that adhered to that Protocol which did not object also accepted the right of the Committee to request their cooperation to conduct an inquiry in response to reliable information indicating "grave or systematic" violations. *Id.* Articles 8–10.

[13] CHARLESWORTH & CHINKIN, *supra* note 10, at 229.
[14] *Id.* at 231.
[15] *Id.* at 231.
[16] *Id.* at 229.
[17] *Id.* at 230 (noting that the one exception was Article 6's prohibition on all forms of trafficking in women).

They suggested that these inherent limitations explained the Convention's failure to prohibit violence against women. Such violence, typically characterized as "private" when committed inside the home, was, they argued, difficult to embrace given "the public frame of the Convention" and ill-suited to a framing that equality meant equal status vis-à-vis men.[18] For all these reasons, Charlesworth and Chinkin argued that the treaty's reliance on "accepted human rights and fundamental freedoms" made it an unlikely tool to promote "any real form of equality" or transformational change.[19]

3.1.2 Continuing Critiques of CEDAW

It is striking how many of the early critiques of CEDAW have continued to appear in feminist scholarship. Charlesworth's and Chinkin's fears that CEDAW and its Committee would be set apart from "mainstream" human rights bodies and that the very existence of a "woman's rights" regime would create a silo outside the mainstream have resonated over time.[20] Substantive complaints about what the Convention includes and leaves out have also been persistent over time. A number of feminist critics, then as now, continue to argue that the CEDAW Convention equates equality with formal equality (namely, the right to be treated the same as men), affirms a gender "binary" that forecloses broader inquiries into gendered power relations and creating blind spots for protecting LGBTQ+ rights, and continues to slot women into "favored tropes" such as wives/mothers needing protection, women who operate only in the public realm, or victims of colonialism or sexual violence.

In the first (2012) edition of the leading commentary on CEDAW, Chinkin and Freeman renewed concerns over CEDAW's blinkered focus. They argued that the CEDAW's reliance on an undifferentiated, binary category of woman reflected a homogeneity that did not exist in the real world. "The Convention itself," they wrote, "does not stress the importance of social signifiers in addition to those of sex and gender and apart from Article 14 on rural women relies on the single signifier—women. This fails to capture the diversity of women and thus the range of their experiences. Nor does it recognize the complexity of

---

[18] *Id.* at 231.
[19] *Id.* at 230.
[20] *Id. See e.g.*, Fleur Van Leeuwen, *"Women's Rights Are Human Rights!": The Practice of the United Nations Human Rights Committee and the Committee on Economic, Social and Cultural Rights, in* WOMEN'S HUMAN RIGHTS: CEDAW IN INTERNATIONAL, REGIONAL AND NATIONAL LAW 242, 249 (Anne Hellum et al. eds., 2013) (citing concerns over "ghettoization" by, among others, Byrnes, Gallagher, Johnstone, and Reanda); Hodson, *supra* note 9 (contending that the CEDAW Committee's work continues to be overlooked despite its potential for transforming human rights norms).

discriminatory practices which may be directed at a multiplicity of intersecting identities."[21]

Chinkin has, over time, become more specific in her criticisms of the failures of CEDAW's text to address the intersectional identities of its singular category of "women." In a 2016 publication, she explained that, with the exception of its provisions for rural women, CEDAW did not acknowledge that women may not work in the paid economy, may not have access to educational institutions, may not be seeking to participate in the public worlds of politics or financial transactions, may not be married to men, and may not be of child-bearing age.[22] She also argued that the Convention fails to account for the fact that women often fulfill multiple roles simultaneously, and that such intersectionality often results in overlapping forms of discrimination that need to be recognized.

To this day, some scholars continue to argue that CEDAW's insistence on formally identical treatment with men undermines its efforts to secure genuine equality.[23] Others make related critiques by arguing that CEDAW's reliance on sex rather than gender disqualifies it from engaging with the many cultural and social forms of discrimination at play.[24] Darren Rosenblum, for example, echoing and developing critiques made by Janet Halley and Dianne Otto, among others, argues that CEDAW's focus on women "reifies an oppositional binary"[25]

---

[21] Christine Chinkin and Marsha A. Freeman, *Introduction, in* THE UN CONVENTION ON THE ELIMINATION OF ALL FORMS OF DISCRIMINATION AGAINST WOMEN: A COMMENTARY 19 (Marsha A. Freeman et. al. eds., 2012) [hereinafter 2012 Commentary].

[22] *See, e.g.*, Christine Chinkin, *The Convention on the Elimination of All Forms of Discrimination against Women, in* HANDBOOK ON GENDER IN WORLD POLITICS 318, 320 (Jill Steans & Daniela Tepe-Belfrage eds., 2006). *See also* Dianne Otto, *Lost in Translation: Re-scripting in the Sexed Subjects of International Human Rights Law, in* INTERNATIONAL LAW AND ITS OTHERS 318, 320 (Anne Orford ed., 2006) (discussing the favored "tropes" of wife/mother needing protection, women who are formally equal in the public realm, and victims of colonialism and sexual vulnerability).

[23] *See, e.g.*, Rosa Ehrenreich Brooks, *Feminist Justice, at Home and Abroad: Feminism and International Law: An Opportunity for Transformation*, 14 YALE J.L. & FEMINISM 345, 351 (2002) (criticizing CEDAW's presumption that gender equality would be achieved if women were treated the same way as men). According to Dianne Otto, the very existence of CEDAW "strengthen[s] the props that produce protecting, defending, civilizing and rescuing forms of masculinity as the universal." Dianne Otto, *Disconcerting "Masculinities": Reinventing the Gendered Subject(s) of International Human Rights Law, in* INTERNATIONAL LAW: MODERN FEMINIST APPROACHES 105, 124 (Doris E Buss & Ambreena Manji eds., 2005).

[24] While Charlesworth and Chinkin had suggested this critique, *see* CHARLESWORTH & CHINKIN, *supra* note 10, at 3–4, it continues to drive debates between those who would "unsex" CEDAW by avoiding the men/women "binary," *see* Darren Rosenblum, *Unsex CEDAW, or What's Wrong with Women's Rights*, 20 COLUM. J. GENDER & L. 98 (2011), and those who argue that the CEDAW regime should retain its focus on the categories of "women," "sex," and "gender," *see* Berta E. Hernández-Truyol, *Unsex CEDAW? No! Super-Sex It!*, 20 COLUM. J. GENDER & L. 195 (2011). For general discussions on this topic, *see* Rovina Gallaher, *Redefining CEDAW to Include LGBT Rights*, 29 S. CAL. INTERDISC. L.J. 637 (2020); Gabrielle Simm, *Queering CEDAW? Sexual Orientation, Gender Identity and Expression and Sex Characteristics (SOGIESC) in International Human Rights Law*, 29 GRIFFITH L. REV. 374 (2021). For a stirring rebuttal of the "postmodern" critique that a focus on women necessarily incorporates a homogeneous or essentialist concept of women, *see* Catharine A. Mackinnon, Are Women Human? And Other International Dialogues, at 50–54 (2006).

[25] Rosenblum, *supra* note 24, at 151.

that implicitly refers to "white women" and reinforces imperialist responses to "saving" Third World women.[26] Rosenblum argues that CEDAW's binary further affirms the "masculinity of the universal subject," ignores the fluidity of gender identification, generally depicts women as victims, men as perpetrators and not themselves possible victims of sex discrimination, marginalizes a "woman's rights" regime from human rights regimes not focused on identity, and leaves transgender persons and others outside CEDAW's protection.[27]

For other feminist critics, CEDAW's ostensible "single" basis for discrimination means that "intersecting discrimination is often approached from an additive or cumulative perspective," requiring claimants wishing to plead more than one ground of discrimination to prove each ground separately, thereby missing "the complex interactions between identity characteristics."[28] Like Charlesworth and Chinkin years earlier, Nicola Lacey criticizes the CEDAW's apparent reliance on values associated with liberal feminism, namely, individual autonomy, ostensibly "universal" rights, formal equality, equal citizenship, and democracy or democratic participation.[29] She agrees that a focus on women's rights perpetuates a stereotypical, overly harmonious view of "women" that treats them as "victims" in need of special protection.[30] CEDAW's reliance on ostensibly "universal" individual liberties further obscures differently situated subjects; ignores many systematic patterns of exclusion and disadvantage; underplays the significance or role of social and political institutions; underestimates the need for positive government action (and not only the government's role in protecting negative freedoms from interference); and plays into the misleading public/private dichotomy.[31] Like Charlesworth and Chinkin four years earlier, Lacey appears more sympathetic to "radical," "Marxist," or "socialist" feminists, more likely to be skeptical of reliance on individual rights and the reliance on a male standard and more likely to emphasize the "class" or "economic" bases for women's subordination.[32]

Others have advanced more pragmatic "internal" critiques of the CEDAW Committee's actions and inactions. Disappointment with the numbers of individual communications filed under CEDAW's Optional Protocol and with the Committee's failures to proceed with discussing the merits of many of those

---

[26] *Id.* at 169.
[27] *Id.* at 134–77.
[28] Meghan Campbell, *CEDAW and Women's Intersecting Identities: A Pioneering New Approach to Intersectional Discrimination*, 11 DIREITO GV L. REV. 479, 483 (2015) (surveying criticisms made by others that CEDAW is based "on a monolithic woman").
[29] Nicola Lacey, *Feminist Legal Theory and the Rights of Women*, in GENDER AND HUMAN RIGHTS 13, 19–22 (Karen Knop ed., 2004).
[30] *Id.* at 29.
[31] *Id.* at 19–22.
[32] *See, e.g.*, CHARLESWORTH & CHINKIN, *supra* note 10, at 28–48. Jim Murdoch, *Unfulfilled Expectations: The Optional Protocol to the Convention on the Elimination of All Forms of Discrimination against Women*, 1 EUR. HUM. RTS. L. REV. 26 (2010).

communications it manages to receive are a common theme. Jim Murdoch concludes, after reviewing the first eight years of communications, that these have "yet to yield any real practical benefits."[33] He disparages the communications procedure for focusing on relatively few complaints from inside Europe, failing to generate consistent rationales on admissibility, and failing to fully explain the Committee's findings on the merits. Murdoch also criticizes the CEDAW Committee's published views in response to communications for failing to make cross-references to the jurisprudence of other human rights adjudicators. He argues that such references would be desirable not necessarily to enable harmonious human rights law to develop but to suggest to potential claimants that face a choice among forums why there may be an advantage in going to CEDAW rather than elsewhere. Murdoch suggests that CEDAW Committee's relatively parsimonious rulings fail to take advantage of opportunities to demonstrate to the public whether CEDAW has "add-on value" compared to other possible venues to vindicate women's rights.[34]

A number of other recent assessments of the CEDAW Committee's work echo these complaints. Catherine Briddick describes the Committee's attempts to describe state practices that generate gender disadvantage as "frequently partial, elliptical, or even absent" in their reasoning.[35] She also castigates the Committee for articulating standards for states in its general recommendations that it fails to adhere to when responding to individual communications. She contends that there is a "striking disparity" between the Committee's official interpretations of the Convention's rights in its recommendations and its applications of those interpretations to states.[36] She contends that the Committee speaks in a "distinctively less protective voice" in its Views in response to communications, as compared with its more "robust" defense of women's equality in its General Recommendations (GRs).[37] The same theme has been picked up by others who also contend that the Committee is more likely to uphold communications complaining of discriminatory practices relating to reproductive health or violence than it has in response to complaints of violations of other civil, political, or economic rights.[38]

In light of the literature, it is easy to read Andrew Byrnes's description of "transformative equality" in the first edition of the Commentary on the CEDAW

---

[33] Murdock, *supra* note 32, at 45.
[34] *Id.* at 46.
[35] Catherine Briddick, *When Does Migration Law Discriminate Against Women?*, 115 AM. J. INT'L L. UNBOUND 356, 359 (2021).
[36] *Id.* at 360. *See also* Catherine Briddick, *Unprincipled and Unrealised: CEDAW and Discrimination Experienced in the Context of Migration Control*, 22 INT'L J. DISCRIMINATION & L. 224 (2022).
[37] Briddick, *supra* note 35, at 360.
[38] *See, e.g.*, Simone Cusack & Lisa Pusey, *CEDAW and the Rights to Non-Discrimination and Equality*, 14 MELB. J. INT'L L. 54 (2013). *See also* Hodson, *supra* note 9, at 571–74.

Convention as an implicit criticism of the more delimited standard for equality contained in that treaty.[39] Byrnes describes a more radical conception of equality:

> Equality as transformation does not aim at a gender-neutral future ... The future is not simply one of allowing women into a male-defined world. Instead, equality for women entails a re-structuring [of] society so that it is no longer male-defined. Transformation requires a redistribution of power and resources and a change in the institutional structures which perpetuate women's oppression. It requires a dismantling of the public-private divide and a reconstruction of the public world. ... [E]quality as transformation requires not just the removal of barriers, but also positive measures to bring about change.[40]

For their part, Lolita Buckener Inniss, Jessie Hohmann, and Enzamaria Tramontana illustrate the many ways that, in their view, the CEDAW Committee fails to demand transformational equality by rewriting one of the communications discussed in chapter 2, *Cecilia Kell v. Canada*.[41] The three authors argue that while Kell prevailed on her claim under Articles 2(d) and (e) and 16(1)(h), the Committee failed to take the opportunity to address Kell's other claims under Articles 14(2)(h), 15 (1), (2), (3), and (4). In their view, the Committee bypassed the opportunity to "fully expose" the "multiple ways in which the law marginalized and silenced Cecilia Kell" and also failed to elaborate on the meaning of rights to housing, to conclude a contract, and to own property.[42] The authors' rewritten version of *Kell v. Canada* seeks to correct the Committee's overly limited conception of the right to housing for rural women, give "full expression" to Kell's independent right to property as an adult independent rights holder and economic actor, flesh out the intersectional discriminations to which Kell was subjected (particularly as an Indigenous woman), and highlight the procedural failings of the Canadian legal system that the real Committee managed to obfuscate.[43] Their more enlightened version of Kell also highlights the contributing roles played by Kell's abusive partner and the Canadian legal system in preventing Kell from exercising her legal rights.[44] Their revised admissibility portion replaces procedural details with a punchier account that ends not with the original's bare

---

[39] *Cf.* Andrew Byrnes, *Article 1*, *in* 2012 COMMENTARY, *supra* note 21, at 51, 53–56 (describing "transformative equality") to Hodson, *supra* note 9, at 565 (noting that CEDAW's creators were not terribly ambitious and adopted "a minimalist liberal agenda, focusing, [as the treaty's name suggests] primarily on the equality of men and women.").

[40] Byrnes, *supra* note 39, at 55 (quoting S. Fredman).

[41] Lolita Buckner Inniss et al., *Cecilia Kell v. Canada*, *in* FEMINIST JUDGMENTS IN INTERNATIONAL LAW 333 (Loveday Hodson & Troy Lavers eds., 2019)

[42] *Id.* at 334.

[43] *Id.* at 338–39.

[44] *Id.* at 344–45 (¶¶ 3.1 & 3.2).

conclusion that the communication is admissible but with an explicitly normative conclusion: the Canadian justice system "diminished" Kell's claims.[45]

With respect to the merits, while the original View had omitted discussion of Kell's claims to being denied the right to contract under Article 15 (2), the rewritten version states plainly that Kell's status as an "Aboriginal parent" made her especially vulnerable to being denial her housing rights. It replaces the original's one-sentence dismissal of Kell's Article 14 claims with a fulsome description of what states are expected to do to satisfy the right to housing.[46] It also deploys the ICESCR Committee's finding that the right to an adequate standard of living under the ICESCR includes a right to housing to reach the conclusion that the housing right in Article 14(2)(h) extends beyond rural women.[47] It also specifically adopts the ICESCR Committee's jurisprudence that the right to housing includes seven guarantees: security of tenure, availability of certain services and facilities, affordability, habitability, accessibility, locational concerns, and cultural adequacy.[48] As rewritten, *Kell v. Canada* treats domestic violence as a form of forced eviction,[49] and specifically finds that Kell's denial of housing, deeply connected to her cultural identity, was violated by Canada's failure of due diligence to protect her from eviction.[50] It also finds additional violations of due diligence in Canada's failure to protect Kell's housing rights from the actions of private parties[51] and for failing to ensure accessibility to her home.[52] Finally, it provides a far more fulsome account of how Canada violated Article 16(1)(h).[53]

Others have argued the Committee's failures to recognize the full dimensions of intersectional discrimination have not been limited to *Kell v. Canada*. A number of scholars have suggested that the Convention's lack of specific provisions recognizing women's intersectional identities is to blame. Megan Campbell, by contrast, has defended what she calls the Committee's "expansive and fluid" approach to intersectional discrimination in its General Recommendations, but argues that the Committee nonetheless has been inconsistent in applying this approach in its Concluding Observations and Views.[54]

---

[45] *Id.* at 349 (¶¶ 5.4 & 5.5).
[46] Compare Views concerning Cecilia Kell v. Canada, CEDAW/C/51/D/19/2008, ¶ 10.6 (2012) to Inniss et al., *supra* note 41, at 353–55 (¶¶ 7.1 to 7.8).
[47] *Inniss et al., supra* note 41, at 355 (¶ 7.5).
[48] *Id.* at 355 (¶ 7.6). Paragraph 7.8 concludes that while the ICESCR imposes only a standard of progressive realization in its Article 2(1), Article 14(2)(h) has no such limits and has immediate effect. *Id.* at 356.
[49] *Id.* at 356 (¶¶ 7.9 to 7.11).
[50] *Id.* at 353–58 (¶¶ 7.14 to 7.19) (concluding that Canada failed in its duty to protect Kell from domestic violence and its consequences and failed to remedy the illegal removal of her name from the property lease).
[51] *Id.* at 358 (¶ 7.20).
[52] *Id.* at 358–59 (¶¶ 7.21 to 7.23).
[53] *Id.* at 359–60 (¶¶ 8.2 to 8.4), 360 (¶ 9.2), and 361 (¶ 9.7).
[54] Campbell, *supra* note 28, *id.* at 480–86, 494–99.

Campbell also criticizes the Committee for failing to fully embrace transformative equality's four goals: breaking the cycle of disadvantage, promoting respect for dignity and worth, accommodating difference through structural change, and promoting political and social inclusion and participation.[55]

3.2 Criticisms of International Law and International Human Rights

A number of critics of what they see as the Eurocentricism inherent "liberal feminism," such as Chandra Talpade Mohanty, who self-identifies as a "Third World Feminist," draw transnational connections.[56] Like others who question the elevation of gender—as opposed to race, class, sexual preference, or nationality—as the primary axis for analysis, Mohanty sees the focus on the single category of "women" as essentializing women in both the so-called "First" or "Third" Worlds.[57] She contests the monolithic image of "Third World women" as always and everywhere victimized, unrelentingly oppressed by 'their' uniformly patriarchal cultures.[58]

Mohanty criticizes those who would ignore the diverse histories of oppression women have faced or the distinct underlying root causes of their subordination. She argues that ignoring context and nuance is not just descriptively inaccurate. Presuming the universality of female oppression across the Third World while ignoring its forms in the so-called First World underestimates the prospects for agency that may exist for both—as well as the potential for cross-cultural or interstate forms of resistance and alliances.[59] For her, the root causes for women's subordination differ among nations but include, most prominently, histories and experiences borne out of racist and colonial domination (and the present-day legacies of both).

For Mohanty and other contemporary critics of globalized capitalism, the path to women's equality requires "decolonializing" feminism by "demystifying" capitalism and challenging the "international division of labor" that the latter

---

[55] Id. at 493, 498–99 (applying Fredman's transformative equality framework).
[56] CHANDRA TALPADE MOHANTY, FEMINISM WITHOUT BORDERS: DECOLONIZING THEORY, PRACTICING SOLIDARITY (2003).
[57] Id. at 21–24.
[58] Id. at 38–39. See also Sunera Thobani, Reviewing Feminism without Borders: Decolonizing Theory, Practicing Solidarity, 20(3) HYPATIA 222 (2005) (summarizing Mohanty's critiques); RATNA KAPUR, EROTIC JUSTICE: LAW AND THE NEW POLITICS OF POSTCOLONIALISM 96 (2005) (describing the "hegemonic victim subject").
[59] See also KAPUR, supra note 58, at 5 (critiquing the "partiality" of the universal truth claims and cultural assumptions of Western feminists who speak for the "global," including through the "hegemonic" use of the word "gender").

produces.[60] On this view, those who want to understand and dismantle the notion of "women's work" in the North or South need to understand how it is constructed by economic, cultural, and political forces in both. Mohanty urges feminists to stop promoting "financial equality" between men and women grounded in "U.S. capitalist values" of individualism and "profit, competition, and accumulation."[61] She urges feminists around the world to engage in an "anticapitalist critique" that demonstrates that capitalism is "seriously incompatible with feminist visions of social and economic justice" and promotes an alternative form of "socialist feminism."[62] Like Anne Orford, she directs attention to the risk of producing a monolithic "Third World woman" that suppresses difference and privileges "ethnocentric universality."[63] Mohanty is critical of "economic reductionism" that presumes all Third World women have similar interests and goals. This ignores differences between urban and rural, paid labor and unpaid,[64] and presumes uniformity in the harms caused by public/private distinctions, when in reality, these operate differently even as between White women and persons of color in the United States.[65] Arguing that "systems of racial, class, and gender domination do not have identical effects on women in Third World contexts," she also criticizes what she sees as the uniform development policies and assumptions of international financial institutions.[66]

Those, like Mohanty, who are hostile to the "consumerist and corporatist values" inherent to the "neo-liberal" free market, are deeply skeptical of the prescriptions to "economically empower" women made by the World Bank or publicists like Nicholas D. Kristoff and Sheryl WuDunn.[67] Mohanty's views connect to Inniss and her co-authors' criticisms of Kell and their call on the CEDAW Committee to "go well beyond the liberal legal subject" and the premise that they are assisting an "atomized, self-interested, competitive being."[68] They also dovetail with those who voice general concerns about the "Western-centric" and liberal premises embodied in international law, its perpetual mission to "civilize"

---

[60] Mohanty, *supra* note 56, at 139–68. *See generally* SUNDHYA PAHUJA, DECOLONISING INTERNATIONAL LAW: DEVELOPMENT, ECONOMIC GROWTH AND THE POLITICS OF UNIVERSALITY (2011).
[61] Mohanty, *supra* note 56, at 6.
[62] *Id.* at 9.
[63] *Id.* at 17–22.
[64] *Id.* at 29–42.
[65] *Id.* at 51.
[66] *Id.* at 55. Mohanty also argues that many harmful property practices—including limiting property rights to men and the "freezing" of patriarchal practices with respect their exercise on marriage or succession—can be attributed to the continued impact of colonialism. *Id.* at 61–62. There are clear continuities between Mohanty's views and that of another socialist feminist based in the United States, ANGELA Y. DAVIS, WOMEN, RACE & CLASS (1981) (drawing lines between the institution of slavery, which viewed women, no less than men, as "profitable labor-units" and contemporary battles for women's emancipation).
[67] *See, e.g.*, Thobani, *supra* note 58, at 221.
[68] Inniss et al., *supra* note 41, at 367.

other states by exporting (along with capitalism) delimited conceptions of "the rule of law," and its use of international legal institutions to demand, on pain of market sanctions, specific "neo-liberal" recipes for "good governance."[69]

Individual writers on the left have focused on distinct ways that the West (at first Europe and then the United States) has used international law since the nineteenth century to impose its will on others, whether by legalizing violent colonization, authorizing capitalist expansion, or imposing ideological harmony.[70] For purposes of this book, the most relevant common element in this scholarship is the premise that international law, its institutions, and its subregimes—from that protecting trade in goods to capital to regimes ostensibly protecting "human" rights—are fundamentally directed at protecting capitalism and specifically private property. To Ntina Tzouvala, for example, the "unequal treaties" once imposed on "uncivilized states" to protect the property and interests of the West's foreign investors in the Global South have simply taken on new forms in the twentieth and twenty-first centuries.[71] On this view, modern international property rights regimes for foreigners or others are only more subtle versions of the discredited "civilizing mission."[72] These critical, sometimes avowedly Marxist, histories of international law also charge that international lawyers fetishize the significance of the individual—particularly the individual's claim to property—over those of groups of persons, whether defined by class, race, ethnicity, or gender, or those seeking collective rights (e.g., rural women or urban workers).

This is the scholarly backdrop that gives certain critiques of UN human rights treaty bodies and Western liberals' concerns with the rights of individuals their particular sting. Consider the criticism of human rights committees made by

---

[69] There is a growing literature on international law's debt to the "civilizing mission," along with the West's efforts to export capitalism and ideologically defined recipes for "good governance." It includes histories told for a purpose, such as ANTONY ANGHIE, IMPERIALISM, SOVEREIGNTY, AND THE MAKING OF INTERNATIONAL LAW (2005); BALAKRISHNAN RAJAGOPAL, INTERNATIONAL LAW FROM BELOW: DEVELOPMENT, SOCIAL MOVEMENTS AND THIRD WORLD RESISTANCE (2003); GERRY SIMPSON, GREAT POWERS AND OUTLAW STATES: UNEQUAL SOVEREIGNS IN THE INTERNATIONAL LEGAL ORDER (2004); CHINA MIÉVILLE, BETWEEN EQUAL RIGHTS: A Marxist THEORY OF INTERNATIONAL LAW (2006). It also includes critical re-examinations of the histories of specific international legal doctrines or regimes, such as ANNE ORFORD, READING HUMANITARIAN INTERVENTION: HUMAN RIGHTS AND THE USE OF FORCE IN INTERNATIONAL LAW (2003).

[70] See, e.g., SYLVIA TAMALE, DECOLONIZATION AND AFRO-FEMINISM (2020); NTINA TZOUVALA, CAPITALISM AS CIVILISATION: A HISTORY OF INTERNATIONAL LAW 18 (2020). Tzouvala argues that international law's "civilizing mission" has never truly faded but continues beneath surface even if it is no longer cited as a rationale.

[71] TZOUVALA, supra note 70, at 59. See also id. at 73–84 (discussing the use of extraterritorial law to protect Western capitalists in the Global South).

[72] See generally id. For specific examples of the centrality of the protection of property to the "civilizing mission," see, e.g., Bhupinder S. Chimni, An Outline of a Marxist Course on Public International Law, 17 LEIDEN J. INT'L L. 1 (2004); Bhupinder S. Chimni, Customary International Law: A Third World Perspective, 112 AM. J. INT'L L. 1 (2018); MUTHUCUMARASWAMY SORNARAJAH, THE INTERNATIONAL LAW ON FOREIGN INVESTMENT (2d ed. 2004).

Susan Marks, a self-described Marxist. Marks contends that in an effort to avoid political engagement (and therefore controversy), UN human rights committees condemn state repressions of civil protests, for example, but say nothing about why repression occurs or what prompted large groups of people to protest to begin with. She argues that when such bodies address the "causes" of the rights violations that are their bread and butter, such as trafficking in women or the feminization of poverty, they identify the victims and the perpetrators but not the *beneficiaries* of the underlying acts.[73] Their "investigation of causes is halted too soon."[74]

Marks argues that human rights appliers fall short when it comes to addressing how women come to be so vulnerable or what it would truly take to bring about real change. To the extent "root causes" for abuses are mentioned, the emphasis is on "technical" fixes in lieu of remedies that might address the conditions—often economic—that systematically reproduce them. Human rights interpreters blame generalized "racism" or "sexism" instead, as if pointing this out will prompt states to make the needed changes. Marks, among others, contends that no one (at least within the United Nations' human rights committees) raises the question of whether racist or sexist policies are deployed by the state (and/or market actors that governments enable) as tools of class or economic exploitation.[75]

The contention that the CEDAW Committee does not challenge social/economic class or existing hierarchies of power and wealth evokes the broader critique that such entities were not designed to challenge the discomforting structural realities imposed by the pursuit of capitalism and its reliance on protecting property.[76] As Gina Heathcote puts it in the context of evaluating CEDAW, the "necessity of working within the pre-existing, largely liberal, structures of international institutions mutes alternative feminist strategies and, potentially, lends gender equality strategies as amenable to neoliberal co-optation."[77] Heathcote draws attention to how the gender expertise within the CEDAW Committee is "filtered through the political and ethical frameworks that institutions are structured around."[78] She fears that universalizing gender "quickly collapses into a failure to regard local gender knowledge as relevant."[79] Others suggest that this is

---

[73] Susan Marks, *Human Rights and Root Causes*, 74 MOD. L. REV. 57, 76 (2011).
[74] *Id.* at 70.
[75] *Id.* at 72–73. *See also* Leeuwen, *supra* note 20, at 262 (noting that the general approach of the Human Rights and ICESCR Committees is not to address the root causes of physical violence against women but rather to call on states to criminal prosecute offenders). Van Leeuwen, like Marks, argues that these committees fight the "symptoms" rather than the "actual disease." *Id.* at 262 & 264. *See also* Christine Chinkin & Lisa Gromley, *Violence Against Women, in* 2022 COMMENTARY, *supra* note 11, at 683.
[76] *See generally* Marks, *supra* note 73.
[77] GINA HEATHCOTE, FEMINIST DIALOGUES ON INTERNATIONAL LAW: SUCCESS, TENSIONS, FUTURES 93–94 (2019).
[78] *Id.* at 59.
[79] *Id.*

not an incidental by-product: all international human rights regimes, including CEDAW, are intentionally circumscribed from the start; they were meant to uphold the de facto "standard of civilization" that presumes the correctness of capitalism and its reliance on rights to property.[80]

The most explicit argument that the emancipatory potential that may have once been contained in the idea of international human rights has long since given way to a "hegemonic conception of human rights" is made by Jessica Whyte.[81] As she tells the story, international human rights regimes promote and seek to enforce only those rights that are compatible with market economies. This, she argues, has occurred in stages. First, human rights, derived from the colonialist "civilizing mission" required "beating" the newly decolonized "into submission" to force them to develop along the lines dictated by their "morally superior" former colonial masters.[82] Second, there was an all too brief period in the 1960s when the struggle for human rights promised to address the need for structural changes in places like Algeria, British Malaya, and Palestine but which was quickly crushed under the "pejorative umbrella of Third Worldism."[83] In the third stage, "neoliberal" rights reached their peak in Pinochet's Chile, where Amnesty International's exclusive focus on civil and political rights enabled economic "shock" treatment to be applied without human rights complaint.[84] A final stage is set by using the posture of Liberté sans Frontieres (LSF) as the basis for the contention that human rights are deployed to advance a specific set of priorities aimed at protecting the individual against specific individualized harms and not structurally imposed ones, disfavoring economic and social rights, and discouraging redistributive projects in order to entrench "the institutional and moral foundations of a competitive market economy."[85] In Whyte's retelling, human rights end up being, not Samuel Moyn's "powerless companion" to neoliberalism but affirmative contributors to its expansion, that is, its "fellow traveler."[86]

Sylvia Tamale's turn to "afro-feminism" encapsulates many of the same critiques from the perspective of those at the receiving end of the West's efforts to promote human rights in developing countries.[87] Tamale defines afro-feminism as sharing some values with Western feminism but departing from liberal feminists' reliance on individual dignity or agency and individual human rights.

---

[80] *See generally* TZOUVALA, *supra* note 70; Anne Orford, *Feminism, Imperialism and the Mission of International Law*, 71 NORDIC J. INT'L L. 275 (2002).

[81] Jessica Whyte, *Powerless Companions or Fellow Travelers? Human Rights and the Neoliberal Assault on Post-colonial Economic Justice*, 2(2) RADICAL PHILOSOPHY 13–29 (June 2018).

[82] *Id.* at 40–45.

[83] *Id.* at 199–200.

[84] *Id.* at 158–59, 179–80.

[85] *Id.* at 227.

[86] *Id.* at 198–233. *See* discussion *infra* of Moyn's views.

[87] *See generally* Tamale, *supra* note 70.

Afro-feminism seeks to respond to diverse African realities by "reclaim[ing] the rich histories of Black women in challenging all forms of domination, in particular as they related to patriarchy, race, class, sexuality and global imperialism."[88] Building on the work of Mohanty, among others, Tamale mounts a fundamental challenge to the set of "universalizing" ideas exported to the continent under politico-economic colonization.[89] Among her targets are international human rights regimes, including CEDAW. She asserts that the juridical principle of equality, mentioned twenty-two times in CEDAW's text, is "foreign" to Africa.[90] "[M]ost African women know that 'gender equality' is a mirage, a 'pipe dream,' that needs to be unpacked," she writes, an "abstract alien concept" deployed selectively without yielding "any significant results for women" in either the Global North or South.[91] Apart from attacking its "western origins," Tamale argues that the equality principle elevates atomistic individualist values over collective ones, ignores group-based systematic oppression, essentializes the idea of men and women, presumes that the measure of equal treatment is the standard male, and principally benefits privileged women that are most similar to the standard male and who have the resources to access the underlying legal rights.[92]

Tamale challenges other key principles in CEDAW. She argues that the turn to "substantive equality" as translated into CEDAW's insistence on "equality of results," does not and cannot achieve transformative change because it does not constitute the "epistemic shift from the liberal human rights paradigm" that is truly needed.[93] She agrees with Ratna Kapur's "blunt" conclusion that "on some level, our rights-related liberal projects are on life support and further palliation is pointless."[94]

At the same time, Tamale is careful to distinguish her afro-feminist critique from older complaints by cultural or religious relativists opposed to human rights. She condemns relativists who abuse the idea of "legal pluralism" to defend, for example, "traditional family" values.[95] While afro-feminism opposes Western universalizing ideologies as do relativists, it parts ways with them when they use the defense of culture or religion to secure or enhance the control of women or to "construct moral codes based on hegemonic systems of power and control that work to reinforce hetero-patriarchy and capitalism."[96] She argues that the "decolonization" of African legal systems requires rejecting the

[88] Id. at xiii.
[89] Id. at 19–22, 118–22.
[90] Id. at 131.
[91] Id. at 131–32.
[92] Id. at 133–34 & 137.
[93] Id. at 138.
[94] Id. at 130.
[95] Id. at 114.
[96] Id. at 114–15.

universalizing rhetoric of the West while also replacing "colonial customary law" with "living" customary law shorn of those practices that subordinate women.[97] She endorses the development of "hybrid" gender justice that does not simply dismiss African values but embraces Ubuntu, that is, "the African traditional ideology of fairness and justice based on the philosophies of humanness, communitarianism, solidarity and interdependence."[98]

In a similar vein, Celestine Myamu Musembi deploys examples from eastern and southern African states to question whether CEDAW needs to be interpreted as requiring the wholesale displacement of "moral codes" contained in local community customs and religious norms.[99] Musembi argues that when the CEDAW Committee is confronted with practices that appear to evince wrongful stereotypes governed by Article 5(a) (such as polygamy), it tends to adopt an "abolitionist" approach seeking to immediately terminate the practice by prohibitory legislation.[100] She contrasts that absolutist approach to the 'legal pluralism' promoted under the Protocol to the African Charter on Human and Peoples' Rights on the Rights of Women in Africa (the Maputo Protocol), particularly its provisions that call on states to take measures against cultural practices that go against the rights of women but also provides for women's rights to live in a "positive cultural context."[101] Unlike CEDAW, which only considers culture as a negative force that oppresses women, the Maputo Protocol, she contends, takes a more gradualist approach to practices like polygamy.[102] Musembi canvasses legal reforms in the African countries she examines and concludes that none follow the abolitionist approach recommended by the CEDAW Committee.[103] She ends by examining a number of real-world examples in which local African cultural norms protect women's property rights and urges the CEDAW Committee to heed the lesson that "there is potential for expansion of the spaces for women's agency" by working with and not inflexibly opposing the cultural context in which women live.[104]

David Kennedy's well-known critiques of international human rights presaged some of these criticisms for a Western audience. In a pathbreaking book that has

[97] *Id.* at 106.
[98] *Id.* at xiv, 106–09.
[99] Celestine Nyamu Musembi, *Pulling Apart? Treatment of Pluralism in the CEDAW and the Maputo Protocol*, in WOMEN'S HUMAN RIGHTS: CEDAW IN INTERNATIONAL, REGIONAL AND NATIONAL LAW 183 (Anne Hellum & Henriette Sinding Aasen eds., 2013).
[100] *Id.* at 186.
[101] Afr. Union, Protocol to the African Charter on Human and Peoples' Rights on the Rights of Women in Africa art. 17, *adopted* July 11, 2003, https://www.refworld.org/docid/3f4b139d4.html.
[102] Musembi, *supra* note 99, at 197 (contending the Maputo Protocol simply calls on states to signal that monogamy is the preferred form of marriage but also pass laws that ensure the rights of women in marital and family rights are respected in polygamous relationships).
[103] *Id.* at 203–04.
[104] *Id.* at 204–13.

been influential among adherents to "Third World Approaches to International Law" (TWAIL), David Kennedy found considerable "dark sides" to the supposedly virtuous agendas of human rights advocates.[105] Like Marks and later Whyte and Tamale, Kennedy contends that international human rights interpreters in global institutions are unlikely to challenge economic institutions or income inequalities but he goes further. He argues that human rights institutions legitimize those inequalities by emphasizing civil and political rights (like rights to participation) and by channeling emancipatory energy into narrow and ideologically defined efforts to promote or defend economic "liberty."[106]

Kennedy contends that human rights treaty bodies' failure to address "root causes" is not an accidental byproduct but an intentional feature.[107] To convince people that what is at stake is the even-handed pursuit of *universal* and individualistic rights, one needs to render countries' differing background social and political conditions less visible. It requires, in his view, "backgrounding the background."[108] A side effect of this is, he argues, that rights talk elicits 'civilized' demands to change the law rather than politically charged efforts to force structural, transformational change.[109] From this perspective, the focus on public law is intentionally built into modern rights discourse. Global human rights are directed at state action in the traditional "public" sphere to deflect attention from the actions or inactions of private entrepreneurs. Avoiding the imposition of treaty obligations on private actors is a structural feature rationalized on the basis that market actors should be left largely alone to allow them to follow the price signals of market economies conducive to economic development.[110]

To Kennedy and other critics of international law's defense of capitalism, the elevation of individual property rights is central to the human rights enterprise.[111] The insistence on stable property rights discourages challenges to those who already have them and avoids threats to the existing social/economic order. Moreover, insistence on the value of property and legalizing that value provides a vital strut to globalization and its global supply chains. It enables economic development to be pursued along lines most acceptable to Western democracies while narrowing the socioeconomic choices of, and impoverishing local political discourses in, the developing world.[112] Kennedy contends that under prevailing

---

[105] DAVID KENNEDY, THE DARK SIDES OF VIRTUE: REASSESSING INTERNATIONAL HUMANITARIANISM (2004).
[106] *Id.* at 11–12.
[107] *Id.* at 11.
[108] *Id.* at 12–13.
[109] *Id.* at 19.
[110] *Id.* at 11–12.
[111] *See also* Tamale, *supra* note 70, at 125 (criticizing the "social contract" and the reliance on private property).
[112] KENNEDY, *supra* note 105, at 18–21. *See generally* The IGLP Law and Global Production Working Group, *The Role of Law in Global Value Chains: A Research Manifesto*, 4 LONDON REV. INT'L L. 57 (2016).

Western ideology, property rights are best protected by formalizing them—in deeds and leases, contracts and titles—as these are deemed necessary for transparency, for the security of title, and for the generation of economic returns. This, he argues, demonstrates that international law and specifically the human rights movement is a "neo-liberal" project.[113]

While there are many definitions of "neo-liberalism," the most common is that it is a "specific institutional and regulatory programme to promote economic growth through greater market integration, the facilitation of market transactions, and the easing of regulatory burdens for investors."[114] Kennedy's invocation of De Soto, winner of the 2004 Milton Friedman Prize, founder of the Institute for Liberty and Democracy (an NGO devoted to promoting property rights around the world), and widely seen as one of the progenitors of the so-called "Washington Consensus" is significant.[115] Musembi also uses De Soto as a foil to demonstrate the shortcomings of efforts to link formal land title to productivity in sub-Saharan Africa.[116] Musembi argues that formalization of land titles equates legal pluralism (and alternative ways to enable men and women to have access to property) with harmful extralegality, presumes that individual ownership is evolutionarily inevitable in all social contexts, relies on an unproven link between accessing credit and formal title, reflects an overly narrow conception of markets in land, and fails to acknowledge that formalization can sometimes lead to insecurity.[117]

Kennedy, Mohanty, Tamale, Whyte, Marks, and others invite readers to draw connections between general criticisms that international law, including human rights regimes, are embedded in or affirmatively contribute to neo-liberal prescriptions for good governance and specific criticisms of the inclusion of property rights in CEDAW. Readers are urged to see the latter as one of the tools of the former. The suggestion is that both emphasize, albeit in different ways, the need for states to stabilize and prioritize private property rights, privatize public services or formerly state-owned enterprises, and pursue business deregulation—and that all of this harms both men and women.

Definitions of "neo-liberalism" are about as abundant as criticisms of it among left-lending critics. Those who see it as indistinguishable from monetarism,

---

[113] KENNEDY, *supra* note 105, at 158–62.
[114] Kerry Rittich, *Social Rights and Social Policy: Transformations on the International Landscape*, in EXPLORING SOCIAL RIGHTS: BETWEEN THEORY AND PRACTICE 107, 111 (Daphne Barak-Erez & Aeyal M. Gross eds., 2007).
[115] KENNEDY, *supra* note 105, at 161–62.
[116] Celestine Nyamu Musembi, *De Soto and Land Relations in Rural Africa: Breathing Life into Dead Theories about Property Rights*, 28 THIRD WORLD Q. 1457 (2007).
[117] *Id. See also* Tamale, *supra* note 70, at 135 (criticizing strategies to advance women's rights by focusing on individual land ownership at the risk of undermining the customary entitlements to land that many women enjoy that are invisible to the formal legal system).

rational expectations theory, supply-side economics, crowding out theory, or real business cycle theory, contrast neo-liberalism with "traditional economic orthodox Keynesian theory."[118] Whereas Keynesians defend an active form of state capitalism—where the government undertakes fiscal policy, supplies an ever-expanding range of public goods such as education and infrastructure, and corrects for "market failures" such as environmental destruction—the neo-liberal is said to resist state intervention in the "free market" except to prop up that market. On this view, neo-liberals rely on individual liberty and individual freedom of choice, unobstructed by the government, to drive an economy defined by private property and their price signals. With legitimate government action restricted to intrusions to defend property rights and provide for military security and basic public order, this version of neo-liberal theory presumes that the market will assure "optimal economic outcomes in every respect—efficiency, income distribution, economic growth, and technological progress—as well as secur[e] individual liberty."[119] The specific neo-liberal formulas for "smaller government" to "liberate" the "animal spirits" of the private sector are familiar: deregulate the financial sector; weaken environmental, consumer product, and work safety regulations; lessen the enforcement of antitrust laws; privatize public functions; cut back social welfare programs; and reduce taxes for generators of GDP such as owners of the business and the wealthy.[120] For many, neo-liberalism can be defined by the aphorism: economic freedom is individual freedom (and vice versa).

Others deny the contention that neo-liberalism needs to be associated with the rollback of the state and the return of laissez-faire—as it may have been in places that led its export to others, namely, Thatcher's United Kingdom or Reagan's United States. They argue that neo-liberalism has enjoyed many lives and has adapted to different settings over time, experiencing "kaleidoscope refraction" and splintering and recombining over the decades.[121] Like those who see the "civilizing mission" in many (often hidden) guises, some critics of neo-liberalism apply it to encompass the form of state capitalism now seen in China. They also see neo-liberalism's expansion through the embrace of new forms of property—including protecting data generated by artificial intelligence. The essence of neo-liberalism, some argue, is less about the suitable amount of state action and more about ensuring that everything has a price ("commodification") and that those prices control their exchange in the market. A far-right strain of so-called lifeboat neo-liberals believe that every human should, as "homo economicus," be ranked by their economic utility as human capital. Some go as

---

[118] See, e.g., DAVID M. KOTZ, THE RISE AND FALL OF NEOLIBERAL CAPITALISM 8–12 (2015).
[119] Id. at 12.
[120] Id. at 14. See also Rittich, supra note 114.
[121] See, e.g., NINE LIVES OF NEOLIBERALISM 2–3 (Dieter Plehwe et al. eds., 2020).

far as to use this premise to justify racist border closures that keep out "less economically productive" foreigners.[122] This version of neo-liberalism may also be fundamentally opposed to government policies that would redistribute income or otherwise promote government-dictated equality among "inherently unequal" persons. Notwithstanding the elasticity of neo-liberalism's many "lives," in most of its guises it shares a core premise: the role of government and law is to protect individual private property rights.[123]

Debates over the economic wisdom of one characteristic neo-liberalist prescription—the need for the formalization of titles to property—need not overly concern us here.[124] But that debate should not be seen as parochial, involving only academics, or unimportant to evaluating CEDAW's jurisprudence. Much of the World Bank's current efforts to promote "gender equality" continues to rely on the formalization of property titles by way of promoting greater "security of tenure" for example.[125] Awareness of these efforts to "economically empower" women as well as the neo-liberal critiques of international human rights helps us to understand the larger stakes involved in feminist critiques of CEDAW and responses to them by stakeholders such as human rights NGOs.

Some supporters of women's rights, like Heathcote, worry that reliance on CEDAW's protection of property will implicate them in Western prescriptions to "civilize" those who are perceived as "victims needing rescue" in the Third World.[126] Writing at the same time as Kennedy, Anne Orford warns against "feminist internationalization" that "homogenizes" the poor by opting for individual rights.[127] Echoing the neo-liberalism critique of human rights, she argues that a rights focus ignores the impact of class or race, sees the world purely as a "battleground of male and female individualism" that neglects the role of economic structures in producing a gendered division of labor, and treats

---

[122] *Id.* at 10.

[123] Kotz, *supra* note 118, at 39–40.

[124] *Cf.* Frank Upham, *Mythmaking in the Rule of Law Orthodoxy* (Carnegie Endowment for Int'l Peace, Working Paper No. 30, 2020), https://carnegieendowment.org/2002/09/10/mythmaking-in-rule-of-law-orthodoxy-pub-1063 (criticizing the "Western orthodoxy" that promises a virtuous circle between respect for property, respect for other civil and political rights, and economic development); FRANK UPHAM, THE GREAT PROPERTY FALLACY: THEORY, REALITY AND GROWTH IN DEVELOPING COUNTRIES (2018) (arguing against the "myth" that economic development is dependent on formal property rights through case studies of property laws as developed in England, the United States, Japan, China, and Cambodia). As Upham's work suggests, that Western orthodoxy, common to a certain breed of economists' dominant in places like the World Bank, may continue to prevail within international financial institutions. *See also* Musembi, *supra* note 99.

[125] *See* Gabriele Wadlig, *The International (un)Making of "Tenure Security"* (2022) (J.S.D. Dissertation, New York University) (on file with author).

[126] *See* HEATHCOTE, *supra* note 77, text and accompanying notes 78–80. *See also* Rosenblum, *supra* note 24, at 102–03 (noting that his critique of CEDAW seeks to achieve a middle ground between the criticisms of Charlesworth and Chinkin and those of Kennedy in *The Dark Sides of Virtue*).

[127] Orford, *supra* note 80, at 280–81.

"Foreign Capital as the agent of wealth and prosperity" as do international financial institutions.[128] Others have argued more specifically that it is wrong to treat rights to land as human rights precisely because this will end up supporting the wrong kind of land rights, such as the right to sell the small plots of land on which many women rely to large-scale agri-businesses.[129] From this perspective, one essential problem with protecting property as a right is that this necessarily emphasizes the right to freely *dispose* as well as to *acquire* property; the essence of traditional property's bundle of sticks, after all, is that it is a commodity that is free for anyone to purchase or sell for any purpose.[130]

As Philip Alston and others have addressed at length, neo-liberalism critiques of international law have inspired a new wave of "revisionist" critics of the "international human rights movement."[131] Consistent with earlier warnings by Kennedy, Orford, and critics of "liberal feminist" theory, revisionists argue that international human rights, and not only those that include protection for property rights, are "neo-liberal" tools for maintaining the economic status quo long favored by many Western governments. Different reasons have been suggested for why the "human rights movement" should be seen as an important aider and abettor to neo-liberalism.[132] Some, like Whyte, link the rise of the human rights movement (or at least its most recent affirmation in the 1970s) to neo-liberal "shock" treatments carried out in places like post-Allende Chile.[133] Some connect the human rights movement to a turn to "trade-related, market-friendly human rights."[134] Some, like Mohanty, Kennedy, and Tamale, focus on the parity of ideas, drawing ideological connections between basic tenets of neo-liberalism and the human rights movement's alleged emphasis on civil/political rights or defense of the "atomistic individual" over group or collective rights.[135] Others extend the critique to social/economic rights, arguing that when the enforcement

---

[128] *Id.* at 289.

[129] *See, e.g.,* Poul Wisborg, *Human Rights Against Land Grabbing: A Reflection on Norms, Policies, and Power,* 16 J. AGRIC. ENVTL. ETHICS 1199, 1202–03 (2013).

[130] *See, e.g.,* Wadlig, *supra* note 125, at 31–32.

[131] *See, e.g.,* Philip Alston, *Does the Past Matter?,* 126 HARV. L. REV. 2071 (2013); Joseph R. Slaughter, *Hijacking Human Rights: Neoliberalism, the New Historiography, and the End of the Third World,* 40 HUM. RTS. Q. 735 (2018).

[132] Slaughter, *supra* note 131, at 765–69.

[133] *See* Whyte, *supra* note 81, text and accompany note 85. *See also* NAOMI KLEIN, THE SHOCK DOCTRINE: THE RISE OF DISASTER CAPITALISM 147 (2007) (connecting the restricted focus on individual political prisoners by human rights groups to the spread of "the Chicago School ideology").

[134] UPENDRA BAXI, THE FUTURE OF HUMAN RIGHTS 6 (2002) (3d ed. 2012). Some see this trend as happening with respect to constitutionally backed fundamental rights as well. *See, e.g.,* Paul O'Connell, *The Death of Socio-Economic Rights,* 74 MOD. L. REV. 532 (2011) (discussing how constitutional courts are transforming fundamental rights into "atomistic," "market friendly," and "neo-liberal" concepts).

[135] Slaughter, *supra* note 131, at 767 (citing to his own prior work); Antony Anghie, *Legal Aspects of the New International Economic Order,* 6 HUMAN. J. 154 (2015) (arguing that the Euro-American focus on civil and political rights lends itself "perfectly to the task of negating the NIEO").

of such rights is closely examined, they benefit middle-class and upper-class groups rather than the poor.[136]

Others are less direct in associating neo-liberalism with international human rights. Samuel Moyn, who has contributed significantly to the revisionist, modern critique of international human rights,[137] purports to see no "direct connection" between the rise of neo-liberalist recipes for development and the international human rights movement but does see "troubling" coincidences in the twin "births" of the two, along with positive interactions.[138] Moyn argues that the "minimalist" agendas of human rights institutions make them powerless to resist the evils of neo-liberalism. In this view, this leaves neo-liberalism's advocates free to pursue their agenda on a parallel track.[139] Martti Koskenniemi takes a comparable view. He points to the assertion of the human right to property—which he considers not to be a genuine fundamental right inherent to persons like the right not to be tortured—as an indication that human rights "can be made to stand for almost whatever claims or policies."[140] The author of *From Apology to Utopia* argues, not surprisingly, that human rights can be either apology for neo-liberalism or its opponent, depending on who is using them and for what purpose.

In other work, Koskenniemi has expressed deep skepticism about the usefulness of relying on rights generally. He argues that "once rights become institutionalized . . . they lose their transformative effect and are petrified into a legalistic paradigm."[141] The "technological language" of rights colonizes political culture and "constrains politics."[142] Rights language restates the interests of the group as "characteristics of all people" and is made to appear "ahistorical and universal."[143] These characteristics make rights ill-suited, in his view, to deal with

---

[136] *See, e.g.*, David Landau, *The Reality of Social Rights Enforcement*, 53 HARV. INT'L L.J. 190 (2012) (surveying evidence from attempts at judicial enforcement in a number of countries). *See also* Tamale, *supra* note 70, at 134 (arguing that the liberal principle of equality tends to benefit already privileged women).

[137] SAMUEL MOYN, THE LAST UTOPIA: HUMAN RIGHTS IN HISTORY (2010). For a powerful critique of Moyn's historical account of the rise of the human rights movement, *see* Alston, *supra* note 131, at 2066–77.

[138] Samuel Moyn, *A Powerless Companion: Human Rights in the Age of Neoliberalism*, 77 LAW & CONTEMP. PROB. 147 (2014). Moyn argues that neo-liberals have not needed to rely on human rights but accepts that neo-liberalism and human rights share "ideological building blocks" such as elevating the individual over collectivist endeavors and a shared antipathy to the state. *Id.* at 156.

[139] Moyn, *supra* note 138, at 159–63 (citing Susan Marks, among others, citing a disjuncture between the agenda of promoters of economic/social rights and those seeking a more "ambitious egalitarian agenda").

[140] Martti Koskenniemi, *Rocking the Human Rights Boat Reflections by a Fellow Passenger*, *in* THE STRUGGLE FOR HUMAN RIGHTS: ESSAYS IN HONOUR OF PHILIP ALSTON 51, 52–55 (Nehal Bhuta et al. eds, 2021) (noting how "neoliberals" like Hayek spoke in rights terms while seeking "to liberate the creative energies of individuals from oppressive economic planning").

[141] Martti Koskenniemi, *The Effect of Rights on Political Culture*, *in* THE EU AND HUMAN RIGHTS 99, 100 (Philip Alston ed., 2000).

[142] *Id.* at 100–01.

[143] *Id.* at 101.

Indigenous groups, the sexual relations between men and women (including in the family), economic, social, and cultural rights that are not merely "programmatic" and lack enforcement, or the needs of oppressed minorities.[144]

Although revisionist critics of human rights come in as many flavors as do the different strands of neo-liberalism, Joseph Slaughter captures the sweeping nature of the underlying critique in the following passage:

> Insofar as the neoliberalization of human rights turned them into a discourse of individual suffering, and depended on the defeat of the NIEO, it also entailed (among things) the end of Third-Worldism as a radical alternative to neoliberal globalization and the end of the Third World itself as the custodian of an expansive commitment to human self-determination. That is, the reduction of the moral compass of human rights to the civil and political rights of suffering individuals, the increasing neoliberalization of the world economy (as well as that of human rights and terrorism), the "resubordination" of the Global South to the old and new Western imperial powers, the recapture of international law from the post-colonial majority, as well as the efforts by newly independent states to reserve for themselves exclusive rights to self-determination, all combined with the inversion in the discourse on terrorism and the discrediting of collective national liberation struggles to effect the "decomposition of the Third World" as a site of solidarity and an "autonomous source of alternative global visions."[145]

---

[144] *Id.* at 103–04.
[145] Slaughter, *supra* note 131, at 769 (citations omitted).

4
Re-engendering Property

Introduction

As is evident by the many state actions and omissions that have drawn the ire of the CEDAW Committee as synthesized in chapter 2, laws relevant to property have been historically gendered. For centuries, in countries large and small, rich or poor, property rights have largely benefited men. The CEDAW Committee's property jurisprudence is designed to re-engender property rights—to affirm that men and women are entitled to enjoy property rights equally in law and in fact.

In doing so, the CEDAW Committee has sought to advance distinct forms of equality. A number of the CEDAW outputs surveyed deploy the principle of formal equality. General Recommendation (GR) 21, for example, emphasizes the need for states to accord women the same legal power as men to conclude contracts as well as eliminate any requirement of a co-signature by male family members.[1] The need for equal treatment with men is also reflected in that GR's insistence that men and women be assured the same access to seek redress in courts; that they have equal access to ownership of land irrespective of marital status; and that they have the same right to distribution of property, including marital assets, after a divorce or death of a spouse.[2] Many of the Committee's Concluding Observations, as reflected in chapter 2, echo this insistence on equal treatment with men, as in response to state laws in the Congo that explicitly discriminate against women with respect to social benefits for public officials or cases where the state's enforcement of certain customary norms interfere with women's equal access to credit.[3] A number of the Views in chapter 2 evince the same concern. This includes *E.S. and S.C. v. Tanzania*, where the Committee found the two communicants, two widows disenfranchised from their deceased husbands' estates by Tanzania's enforcement of customary inheritance rules, to have suffered discrimination in violation of Articles 2, 5, 13, 15, and 16.[4]

---

[1] GR No. 21 on Equality in Marriage and Family Relations, A/49/38, 7 (1994).
[2] *Id.* 1–2, 8, 26, 28, & 31.
[3] *See, e.g.*, chapter 2, sections 2.9.2 and 2.10.3.
[4] Chapter 2, section 2.4.2.2. Chapter 2 also enumerates many other cases where widows face direct or indirect discrimination under states' marital or family laws, inheritance rules, or rules or practices with respect to social benefits, including rights to pensions. *Id.* section 2.4.

Chapter 2 also includes multiple findings of indirect discrimination in violation of Articles 13(b) or 14(2)(g), arising from legal impediments to access credit or financial services (such as, ironically, a requirement that those seeking credit own property).[5]

A considerable portion of CEDAW's relevant jurisprudence, however, addresses failures of substantive equality where states' failures to take into account structural, cultural, or other barriers faced by women generally or by particular groups of women produce unequal results. This includes the Committee's multiple efforts—through GRs, Views, Concluding Observations (COs), and two Reports on Inquiries—to redress the vulnerabilities of women subjected to domestic violence who fail to secure protective orders barring abusive partners from returning to the family home or are unable to attain adequate shelters.[6] In these cases, the states' failures to act were found to violate rights to life, physical, and mental integrity, as well as rights to adequate living conditions (including housing) contained in the Convention.[7] A number of the Committee's outputs surveyed in chapter 2 found violations of substantive equality, for example, arising from social security programs that failed to consider the special circumstances of women, including rural women and women caregivers, engaged in unpaid work.[8] This included Elisabeth de Blok, whose communication was upheld because her government had denied her maternity leave benefits as a self-employed person, and Natalia Ciobanu, who was improperly denied a significant portion of her social security benefits because she worked unpaid to care for a disabled daughter.[9] Violations of substantive equality were also at the heart of chapter 2's description of the Canadian Inquiry—which drew connections between the "socioeconomic marginalization of aboriginal women" to persistent violations of that country's duties to provide adequate housing and address homelessness.[10] This was the case as well with respect to the Inquiry into South

---

[5] See, e.g., id. section 2.9.2.1.

[6] See, e.g., id. sections 2.11.1.1 and 2.11.2–2.11.4. A number of these Committee outputs also reflect the goal of advancing *de facto* equality under Article 4(1) of CEDAW. See Convention on the Elimination of All Forms of Discrimination against Women art. 4(1), *opened for signature* Dec. 18, 1979, 1249 U.N.T.S. 13 [hereinafter CEDAW] (providing that "temporary special measures aimed at accelerating de facto equality" shall be not considered discrimination). See, e.g., GR No. 25 on Temporary Special Measures, CEDAW/C/GC/25 (2004) (noting that Article 3 of the Convention (authorizing "all appropriate measures") lays the ground for these special measures which apply to all the substantive Articles 6–16).

[7] See chapter 2, section 2.11.2 (describing Views in A.T. v. Hungary, Sahide Goekce v. Austria, Yildirim v. Austria, V.K. v. Bulgaria, J.I. v. Finland, S.T. v. Russian Federation). A number of these Views found violations based on states' failures of due diligence in limiting alleged abuser's property rights to protect the life and physical integrity of women.

[8] See, e.g., id. sections 2.10.1.2 (describing GRs on social benefits in the context of unpaid or informal family care work); 2.10.1.3 (discussing GRs addressing social benefits in informal employment); and 2.10.2.3 (discussing Views adopted in Natalia Ciobanu v. Republic of Moldova).

[9] Id. section 2.10.2.2 (addressing Elisabeth de Blok v. The Netherlands).

[10] Id. section 2.11.3.1 (describing the Canada Inquiry).

Africa, which addressed that state's serious deficiencies in responding to systemic patterns of domestic violence and their underlying causes.[11]

Much of the jurisprudence covered in chapter 2 stems from the CEDAW Committee's findings of unremedied forms of intersectional discrimination. The Committee's COs have, for example, addressed women in poverty in connection with social benefits, those in the informal sector denied unemployment or pension benefits, women farmers denied bank loans, and disabled women denied access to housing. Its GRs recommend that states take measures to avoid forced evictions of and homelessness among older women and rural women (as in the course of rural development programs), as well as in the wake of disasters or in response to climate change.[12] Intersectional discrimination was particularly pertinent to the Committee's treatment of the communications in *L.A. v. North Macedonia*, *S.N. and E.R. v. Macedonia*, and *Cecilia Kell v. Canada*. In the Macedonia cases, the Committee upheld violations of Articles 2 and 14(2)(b) in cases where several pregnant women of Roma ethnicity were evicted from their informal settlement and left without adequate housing.[13] In *Kell*, the Committee found violations of Articles 2 and 16(1)(h) when an Indigenous women was arbitrarily evicted from her jointly owned home by her husband and the Canadian courts failed to provide her with legal relief.[14]

As chapter 2 makes clear, the Committee sometimes protects the economic interests of women by applying states' general duties to bar all forms of discrimination against women under Article 2 of the Convention. It also protects these interests by treating certain rights identified in the Convention, such as rights to land, social benefits, adequate living conditions, and marital or family property, as rights in themselves—as when it affirms that states need to adopt gender-sensitive social protection floors for all rural women.[15] The Committee frequently draws connections between women's property rights and other rights in the Convention. It argues that access to such rights without discrimination enables women to enjoy other Convention rights, including rights to effective participation in political and public life, to culture, to food, to water and seeds, and to a clean, healthy, and sustainable environment.[16]

---

[11] *Id.* section 2.11.3.2 (describing the South Africa Inquiry).
[12] *Id.* sections 2.6.1.2 (discussing GR 34 on rural women); 2.6.1.3 and 2.9.1.5 (discussing GR 37 on the gendered impacts of climate change); 2.9.1.3 (discussing GR 27 on older women). See also *id.* section 2.4.1.3 (discussing GRs that address the impact of intersectional discrimination on women's property rights in family relations).
[13] *Id.* section 2.7.2.1 (discussing the North Macedonia communications).
[14] *Id.* section 2.4.2.1 (discussing Cecilia Kell v. Canada).
[15] *Id.* section 2.10.1.3 (quoting from GR 34, ¶¶ 40–41).
[16] *See, e.g.*, GR No. 34 on the rights of rural women). Compare CESCR Committee, GC No. 26, E/C.12/GC/26, ¶¶ 5–11 (2022) (identifying the connections between access to land and other rights in the ICESCR).

This chapter addresses how this jurisprudence compares to the often sharp critiques directed at the CEDAW, its Committee, international human rights regimes in general, and international law as a whole as surveyed in chapter 3. It draws five general lessons from this comparison.

4.1 Lesson One: The CEDAW's Interpretation Evolves over Time

A number of the feminist critiques in section 3.1 of chapter 3 are based on the literal text of CEDAW. The contention that the Convention equates the principle of equality with being treated the same as men reflects a text that affirms, more than once, that women need to be treated "on equal terms with men" (in Preamble, Paragraph 7, and Articles 7 and 8), "on an equal basis with men" (in Article 2(c)), and "on a basis of equality with men" (in Article 3). Other parts of the treaty's text also suggest that equality should be measured by the male standard. This includes references to "equal rights with men" (in Article 9), "the same rights" between men and women (in Article 11), "on the basis of equality of men and women, the same rights" (in Article 13), "on a basis of equality of men and women" (in Article 14(2)), "equality with men before the law" (in Article 15(1)), and the "same rights for both spouses" (in Article 16(1)(h)). The Convention also confirms that the violations of this male-centered principle of equality are only those distinctions, restrictions or exclusions "made on the basis of sex" (in Article 1).

It is but a short step from this language to persistent criticisms that the Convention reifies a "binary" between men and women, reduces the principle of equality to what men typically receive (especially in the public sphere) without regard to the biological or socially constructed characteristics of women, essentializes certain tropes of women, addresses an inflexible ostensibly universal concept of equality without regard to geography or other context, and focuses exclusively on discrimination on the basis of biological sex to the exclusion of everything else—thereby erasing from view fluid conceptions of gender, race, language, religion, social origin or caste, ethnicity, class, or any other status. Contentions that the Convention envisions rights only for individuals and that it therefore embraces only rights to individual private property, could also be implied from the preamble's elevation of "dignity and worth of the human person" (Preamble, Paragraph 1), as well as the Convention's many lost opportunities to mention collective rights as such.

And yet, as chapter 2 makes clear, the Committee's property jurisprudence has not been limited to considering violations of formal equality. The Committee has gone beyond the "same treatment" provisions of the Convention and used other language in its text to demand that states advance substantive equality attentive to intersectional discrimination that has "the effect or purpose of impairing or nullifying the recognition, enjoyment or exercise" of the Convention's rights.[17] The Committee's reach beyond equal treatment vis-à-vis men can also be justified on the basis that the treaty's object and purpose, as determined by the entirety of its preamble as well as Article 3, is to ensure the "full development and advancement of women" by barring "all forms of discrimination" in order to achieve "full equality."[18] The Committee's evolving interpretations of CEDAW over time as described in chapter 2 resist the homogenization of women, do not insist that equality be measured by whether a (male) comparator gets the same right, and make a serious effort to consider, along with sex, other characteristics that have an impact on whether women enjoy equal rights in fact.

The Committee's interpretations as reflected in chapter 2 do not focus solely on vindicating the rights of individuals. Most of the Committee's recommendations to states in its GRs and COs are actually directed at correcting inequalities imposed on collective groups of women, including the elderly, widows, rural women, single women, unpaid workers, and those who identify with racial, ethnic, or Indigenous groups that have long been subject to structural or other forms of discrimination. And even when the Committee has responded to communications filed on behalf of individuals, its recommendations for remedial relief have not been limited to those individuals.[19] Nor has the ostensible "binary" of sex discrimination precluded the Committee from including as prohibited discrimination, some state actions or inactions that result in the unequal treatment *de facto* or *de jure* of individuals and groups who identify as "LGBTQ+".[20]

Broader criticisms of international human rights, including CEDAW, that are surveyed in section 3.2 of chapter 3, might also be based on language in the Convention. The text of that treaty, as well as its silences, might be read to suggest that the CEDAW regime is a mere continuation of international law's "civilizing mission" and is, like other international human rights regimes, either a "powerless companion" to, a "fellow traveler" of, or an intentional ally of those who support "neo-liberal" government policies. The Convention's preamble signals, after all, that its embrace of rights is designed in part to advance the "participation" of women in the economic life of their countries in order to encourage "growth"

---

[17] CEDAW, *supra* note 6, art. 1. The Committee's embrace of substantive equality is also supported by Article 5's demand that states address social and cultural patterns of conduct, prejudices, and customary and all other practices and Article 4's recognition of the need for "temporary special measures" to accelerate *de facto* equality.

[18] CEDAW, *supra* note 6, preamble, ¶ 15. *Id.* art. 3.

[19] *See, e.g.*, chapter 2, section 2.10.2.2 (discussing the Committee's recommendations in Elisabeth de Blok v. The Netherlands).

[20] *See, e.g., id* section 2.4.1.2 (discussing GR 29's inclusion of same-sex relationships within the type of relationships covered by Article 16(1)(h)).

and "prosperity" (Preamble, Paragraph 7).[21] One might assume that is the purpose behind the inclusion of Articles 11(1)(b) and (e) and (2)(b), 13(b), 14(2)(g) and (h), 15(2), and 16(1)(h) in the Convention. The inclusion of these rights refutes the suggestion by Sam Moyn that "human rights orders... have lost their associations to the defense of freedom of contract and private property."[22] These provisions make it difficult to argue that the Convention recognizes a rigid separation between economic liberties, justified on instrumentalist grounds, and what some would consider to be genuine human rights that protect persons' inherent dignity.[23] There is nothing in the CEDAW Convention that demarcates these economic protections from its other protections. There is nothing to suggest that a breach of property rights would be any less a form of "discrimination against women" demanded by "the principles of equality of rights and respect for human dignity" that the treaty affirms.[24] Accordingly, no one should be surprised that in applying these provisions, the CEDAW Committee does not shy away from claiming that it is seeking, in a number of cases, to "economically empower" women to operate in the market.[25]

It is also not plausible to argue, as Philip Alston once did in response to Ernst Petersmann's contentions that the WTO includes the right to property among other rights, that CEDAW does not include such rights as *individual* rights.[26] The text of the treaty says as much. The Convention articles just enumerated that underlie chapter 2's survey of jurisprudence are not some kind of subsidiary or lesser rights that apply only when these are otherwise consistent with other goals, whether to promote economic development or to enable a more equitable distribution of income. There is nothing in the text of CEDAW that indicates that the obligations imposed on states under the above-mentioned Articles 11, 13, 14, 15, and 16 are not part of a set of intertwined and equally binding rights on behalf of individual women. The rights relating to property in CEDAW are no less legally cognizable as others in the Convention and, as chapter 2 indicates, they are treated as such by the CEDAW Committee—as they were in the cases affirming

---

[21] *See, e.g.*, chapter 3, section 3.2 (surveying contentions that "hegemonic human rights" are designed to promote blinkered neo-liberalist recipes for economic development and that international lawyers' emphasis on civil and political rights elevates "participation" within established government structures over more radical social action that might better achieve genuinely redistributive change).

[22] Samuel Moyn, *A Powerless Companion: Human Rights in the Age of Neoliberalism*, 77 LAW & CONTEMP. PROBS. 147 (2014).

[23] This separation is implied by Martti Koskenniemi's distinction between property rights and rights to be free from torture. *See* chapter 3, section 3.2, at text and note 140.

[24] CEDAW, *supra* note 6, preamble.

[25] *See, e.g.*, chapter 2, section 2.9.

[26] Philip Alston, *Resisting the Merger and Acquisition of Human Rights by Trade Law: A Reply to Petersmann*, 4 EUR. J. INT'L L. 815 (2002). Even Alston had to acknowledge that the WTO protected at least one form of property right—that of authors and inventors to their interests—that was a recognized right under the Article 15 of ICESCR. *See id.* at 826.

the individual rights of, for example, Elisabeth de Blok, Natalia Ciobanu, or Cecilia Kell.

As chapter 2 makes clear, the CEDAW Committee sees itself as protecting women's rights to "economic security" (such as equal rights to pensions) and "economic empowerment" (such as equal access to credit or to use the law to conclude contracts or administer property (from rights to a home to those related to a business)). These rights do not, on their face, pose threats to capitalist or free market states. And while it is true that the Committee's relevant jurisprudence also sometimes addresses what some may see as the negative externalities of capitalism, such as the feminization of poverty, it often promotes such goals in ways that can be seen as advancing the goals of market capitalism and not challenging it head-on—as when the Committee recommends that states enable all heads of households (including women) to secure marital property or agricultural land. Such recommendations, like Hernando de Soto's for more land titles, could be seen as increasing the number of people with a stake in maintaining status quo capitalism. The same can be said of the Committee's recommendations that states ensure that rural women, migrant workers, or others in the informal economy have equal access to social security or other benefits. These too can be seen as making sure that everyone has a stake in capitalism's success.[27]

And yet close scrutiny of the CEDAW Committee's actual property jurisprudence suggests the need for considerable more nuance by its critics. Those criticisms would be far more convincing if they were to acknowledge what the Convention has become, thanks to the Committee's evolving interpretations over time.

Acknowledging that the meaning of CEDAW has evolved thanks to the efforts of its Committee should not be equated with a general conclusion that the CEDAW Committee engages in more "dynamic" or "judicially activist" treaty interpretation than other human rights treaty bodies. That conclusion would require a broader comparative law effort than we undertake in chapter 6. Nor can it be said that any of the Committee's interpretations in chapter 2 clearly violate the traditional rules for treaty interpretation under international law. As is well known, those rules—particularly the broad license to consider the "the object and purpose" and not only the plain text of a treaty and to consider the "relevant rules of international law among the parties"—are highly malleable. Some of those Committee interpretations are predictable applications of the Convention, while others are more innovative or creative.[28]

---

[27] *See* chapter 3, section 3.2 (discussing criticisms leveled at international human rights regimes generally by Mohanty, Tamale, Whyte, and others).

[28] Vienna Convention on the Law of Treaties arts. 31–32, May 23, 1969, 1155 U.N.T.S. 331 [hereinafter VCLT].

Consider the many cases in chapter 2 where the Committee elevates the significance of economic and social rights over civil and political rights—a move that might surprise those who assume that the CEDAW regime enforces only "traditional" civil and political rights. The Committee's serious effort to implement the economic and social rights of women is a routine interpretation of the Convention. In doing so, the Committee is merely respecting a treaty that includes civil and political rights like the right to security or bodily integrity of the person, to equality before the law, and to vote or otherwise participate in governance, alongside economic/social rights like the right to an adequate standard of living (including housing), to access to health care, and to social security benefits. That interpretation faithfully adheres to a text that also requires states to eliminate distinctions that have the purpose or effect of impairing or nullifying the recognition, enjoyment or exercise of not only the rights expressly contained in CEDAW but of other "human rights and fundamental freedoms in the political, economic, social, cultural, civil or any other field."[29] Reflecting the need for treaty interpreters to read treaties in light of both their text and "context,"[30] CEDAW's property jurisprudence, like the Convention itself, accordingly resists the separate spheres of "generational" rights (sometimes framed as "negative," "positive," or individual/collective) reflected in the adoption of the separate Covenants (the International Covenant on Civil and Political Rights (ICCPR) and the International Covenant on Economic, Social and Cultural Rights (ICESCR)) and the Cold War ideological divisions that spurred those divisions.[31] In accordance with CEDAW's text, which unlike most of the rights under the ICESR, requires CEDAW's obligations on states to respect, protect, promote, and fulfill to take effect "without delay,"[32] the Committee also does not denigrate economic or social rights by suggesting that these are only subject to "programmatic" implementation premised on best efforts over time. The Committee's relevant recommendations to states with respect to rights associated with the ICESCR do not generally contemplate anything other than immediate compliance.[33]

---

[29] CEDAW, *supra* note 6, art. 1.

[30] *See* VCLT, *supra* note 28, art. 31(1).

[31] *See generally* CHARLESWORTH & CHINKIN, *supra* note 31, at 216–44 (2000). To be sure, the CEDAW Committee indicates that the communal rights of Indigenous women need to be "balanced" against individual rights to property. *See, e.g.*, GR No. 39 on the Rights of Indigenous Women and Girls, CEDAW/C/GC/39 (2022).

[32] Compare Article 2 of CEDAW ("by all appropriate means and without delay") to Article 2(1) of the ICESCR (993 UNTS 53, adopted Dec. 16, 1966) (requiring states "to take steps . . . to the maximum of its available resources, with a view to achieving progressively the full realization of rights . . ."). CEDAW's duties on states not to discriminate are much more comparable to the specific obligation on states under the IESCR not to discriminate. *See* ICESCR, *id*, art. 3 (directing states to "ensure the equal right of men and women" without the qualifications imposed under Article 2(1) of ICESCR).

[33] *See, e.g.*, chapter 2, section 2.11.1.6 (discussing access to housing, land, and shelter). *See also* the comparisons of the CEDAW and ICESCR regimes in chapter 6, section 6.4.

The Committee's inclusion of women's inheritance rights is, despite the lack of explicit mention of "inheritance" in the treaty, another example of an unexceptional reading of what is presumptively included under the chapeau clause of Article 13 (calling for the elimination of discrimination against women in "other areas of economic and social life"), Article 15's right to "administer property," and/or Article 16(1)(h)'s protections for marital or family property. More audacious is the Committee's continuing efforts to expand the applicability of that last provision, namely, Article 16(1)(h)'s protections to "both spouses," to require nondiscrimination with respect to various forms of relationships, including same-sex unions.[34] The Committee's resort to Article 14 to address the rights of Roma women residing in an urban environment in the communications involving Macedonia is another example of a creative, perhaps teleological, interpretation of the Convention's object and purpose.[35] The same can be said for the Committee's implicit resort to Article 14 in that instance and other occasions as a license to consider the many different and overlapping identities of women for purposes of addressing intersectional discrimination—a concept that is not mentioned in CEDAW's text but may also be encompassed by its broad object and purpose.[36] A similarly dynamic form of interpretation of the treaty occurred when the Committee, in GRs 19 and 35, "clarified" that discrimination against women, as defined in Article 1, included gender-based violence—thereby leading to the jurisprudence protecting the right to adequate housing in that context surveyed in chapter 2.[37]

The Committee's interpretations of the Convention are subject to contestation. This may occur in the course of the Committee's internal procedures, including follow-up procedures with respect to its Views, as well as dialogues with states during the reporting process. The Committee's interpretations also may be contested in other forums, such as the International Court of Justice (ICJ).[38] The Convention's interpretation may also evolve through other human rights bodies' efforts to apply it, through national laws or practices attempting to give effect to it, or through national judges' efforts to interpret women's rights in light

---

[34] GR No. 29 on Economic Consequences of Marriage, Family Relations and Their Dissolution, CEDAW/C/GC/29, ¶ 24 (2013) (embracing same-sex relationships as within the protections of Article 16(1)(h) if these are "recognized" by the state as a *de facto* union, registered partnership or marriage). It is therefore no surprise that, according to background interviews conducted for this book, ¶ 24 of GR 29 proved particularly contentious within the Committee.
[35] Chapter 2, section 2.7.2.1 (discussing the North Macedonia communications).
[36] *See, e.g.*, chapter 2, sections 2.4.1.3, 2.7.3.1, 2.9.2.4, and 2.11.1.7.
[37] GR No. 19 on Violence against Women, CEDAW/C/GC/19 (1992); GR No. 35 updating GR No. 19, CEDAW/C/GC/35 (2017); *see also* chapter 2, section 2.11.
[38] Compare *Ahmadou Sadio Daillo* (Guinea v. Dem. Rep. Congo), Judgment, 2010 I.C.J. Rep. 639, ¶ 66 (refusing to accept an interpretation issued by the Committee under the Convention on the Elimination of All Forms of Racial Discrimination (CERD)).

of the Convention. The meaning of CEDAW may also change stemming from bottom-up efforts to apply it in particularized local contexts including, but not only, in legal fora.[39] While the CEDAW Committee is the principal agent of the Convention's evolving interpretation, it is not the only venue in which the treaty is continuously re-interpreted—and avoids stasis.

4.2 Lesson Two: CEDAW's Property Jurisprudence Does Not Reflect a "Neo-Liberal" Agenda as That Term Is Most Commonly Defined

As is discussed in chapter 3, the most commonly accepted definition of "neo-liberalism" is a "specific institutional and regulatory program" defined by a number of prescriptions for states, namely, (1) legal protections for individual private property along with its formalization through individual titles (including with respect to land); (2) the commodification of all forms of property by legal support for the full bundle of sticks traditionally associated with property (including the ability to freely purchase and dispose of it); and (3) government policies that support the "free market" by privatizing formerly state-owned businesses, deregulating market actors, and opening up state economies to better enable economic globalization. This is the definition of "neo-liberalism" that seems to motivate core critiques surveyed in chapter 3 articulated by Kerry Rittich, Jessica Whyte, Sam Moyn, David Kennedy, and Martti Koskenniemi, as well as those who defend international human rights from such criticisms (e.g., Philip Alston) or describe the respective antagonists in neo-liberal debates (e.g., Joseph Slaughter).[40] Aspects of this trifold "neo-liberal" agenda also make their way into a number of the avowedly Marxist critiques surveyed in chapter 3 by Susan Marks, Anne Orford, Talpade Mohanty, and Ntina Tzouvala—even as those authors appear to identify "neo-liberalism" with capitalism writ large.[41] A close examination of CEDAW's property jurisprudence reveals that it is a caricature to describe that jurisprudence as neo-liberalism's close companion, fellow traveler, or enabler—at least as neo-liberalism is most often defined.[42]

---

[39] *See, e.g.*, Sally Merry & Peggy Levitt, *The Vernacularization of Women's Human Rights, in* HUMAN RIGHTS FUTURES (Stephen Hopgood et al. eds., 2017).

[40] *See* chapter 3, section 3.2. The trifold description of neo-liberalism's characteristics also seems to be the foil for other scholarly works cited in that section, including work by David Kotz.

[41] *Id.*

[42] *See also* chapter 7, section 7.1.

4.2.1 Private Property and Titling

The CEDAW does not insist as a matter of principle, as would Hernando de Soto, that all individuals have the right to own, manage, or dispose of all forms of property and that this bundle of entitlements must be formalized by contract, deed, lease, or title.[43] Neither the CEDAW nor its Committee adopts private property ownership or the right to title to it as freestanding goals distinct from protecting women from being discriminated with respect to either. The Committee condemns property qualifications generally, given their discriminatory impact on women, including preventing women from exercising their civil or political rights like the right to vote.[44] The Committee has not recommended that states need to accord individual title to property in all contexts. The CEDAW Committee has been careful not to confuse the specific rights relating to property in the Convention with an individual's *exclusive* rights to *own* property or to exclude others from their property. To be sure, it has criticized requirements for identity documents or citizenship certificates when these prevent women from accessing or managing their property, but has steered clear of suggesting that such access rights need to rely on formal legal title.[45] As these examples suggest, the CEDAW Committee emphasizes the need for states to respect women's enjoyment of *certain* of property's sticks—such as access—over the importance of ownership or title.

To be sure, the Committee's property jurisprudence recognizes, as Article 16(1)(h) explicitly does, that rights to property may consist of a bundle of entitlements, namely, ownership, acquisition, management, administration, enjoyment, and disposition. But the CEDAW Committee has not suggested that either national or international law requires states to protect all these entitlements, as would be the case if the Convention contained a right to property irrespective of evidence of discrimination. The Committee's jurisprudence relies on a state

---

[43] *See, e.g.*, HERNANDO DE SOTO, THE MYSTERY OF CAPITAL: WHY CAPITALISM TRIUMPHS IN THE WEST AND FAILS EVERYWHERE ELSE (2000); HERNANDO DE SOTO, THE OTHER PATH: THE INVISIBLE REVOLUTION IN THE THIRD WORLD (1989). De Soto's impact has been felt in many places other than the World Bank. *See, e.g.*, Int'l Labor Org. [ILO], World Comm'n on the Soc. Dimension of Globalization, *A Fair Globalization: Creating Opportunities for All* (2004) (identifying the formalization of property rights as critical for reducing poverty and achieving social progress throughout the developing world).

[44] *See, e.g.*, GR No. 32 on the Gender-related Dimensions of Refugee Status, Asylum, Nationality and Statelessness of Women, CEDAW/C/GC/32, ¶ 23 (2014). *See* also CO on Kazakhstan, CEDAW/C/KAZ/CO/5, 33–34 (2019) (condemning the requirement of property ownership to acquire or reacquire nationality; COs on Bosnia and Herzegovina (CEDAW/C/BIH/CO/6, 39–40), Guatemala (CEDAW/C/GTM/CO/8-9, 38–39), Rwanda (CEDAW/C/RWA/CO/7-9, ¶¶ 40–41), Albania (CEDAW/C/ALB/CO/4, ¶¶ 34–35), Madagascar (CEDAW/C/MDG/CO/6-7, ¶¶ 40–41), and Nigeria (CEDAW/C/NGA/CO/7-8, ¶¶ 39–40) (all expressing concern about barriers to accessing financial services imposed by requiring property ownership).

[45] *See* COs on Angola (CEDAW/C/AGO/CO/7, ¶¶ 33–34) and Nepal (CEDAW/C/NPL/CO/6, ¶ 30).

deciding for itself, consistent with its rights to self-determination but subject to the constraint on non-discrimination, the type of property regime it will adopt. CEDAW's property jurisprudence does not distinguish "market" states from socialist or communist ones, and its Concluding Observations on state reports do not try to convert the latter two systems by requiring them all to protect private property as neo-liberals would wish.

The North Macedonia individual communications discussed in chapter 2 suggest the distance between the Committee's approach to property rights and that endorsed by neo-liberalism.

The Committee's determinations that North Macedonia violated the right to housing in Article 14(2)(h) and its insistence that North Macedonia provide adequate reparation for the denial of that right are based on the government's destroying dwellings and property that the complainants did not own. The Roma women in these cases were not owed restitution of property because the state took their property. They were owed damages—which significantly included moral damages due to their suffering and not compensation for the material worth of property as valued on the open market—because the state had privatized the informal settlements on which they lived and did not provide suitable and adequate housing as a state-provided alternative. The rights of the private parties that benefited from the state's privatization of the informal settlements—whose rights would be critical in a regime that focused solely on protecting private property—were not relevant to the case. Nor did those rights to private property need to be "balanced" against the Roma women's rights to safe shelter.

In these communications, the "right to housing" is framed as unrelated to the traditional bundle of sticks or entitlements associated with neo-liberal private property. The right to housing affirmed in these cases is derived from the welfare state's duty of care to provide shelter and medical care to pregnant women or mothers of infants with few other recourses. It emerges from, among other things, the Convention's affirmation of rights to "adequate living conditions, particularly in relation to housing" under Article 14(2)(h). The housing right in these instances is not premised on the need to protect individuals' exclusive possession, to incentivize entrepreneurs, to signal the correct market price, or to promote economic development through global supplies in support of globalization. It is a means to a social end that responds to the income inequalities and other forms of intersectional discrimination inflicted on a particular group of people. Moreover, while the CEDAW Committee's communications involving North Macedonia are superficially about the rights of certain individuals, the Committee responds by calling out the harms imposed on a collective, namely, Roma women needing shelter. This is reflected in the fact that some of its recommendations for remedy respond to those collective concerns. Those recommendations signal to states generally what they need to do to satisfy such collective rights in similar contexts. The same can be said about the CEDAW Committee's insistence in its other outputs that states need to protect access to independent housing or shelters for women trying to escape domestic violence or violent relationships.[46]

Some of the wording in GR 34 and the Committee's Concluding Observations in a number of instances seem to imply that states need to accord rural women certain absolute guarantees, including to file land titles, register land in their own names, or have priority with respect to land allocations.[47] One could read the views of the Committee in *Kell v. Canada* as suggesting that women in general have a right to own the family home or read the Committee's conclusions in the North Macedonia cases as implying that government-supplied shelters are a general entitlement irrespective of circumstance. But caution is warranted in reading into CEDAW property jurisprudence such apparently absolute entitlements—as if formal title or registration is always essential or women in general have a "right" to own a home or have shelter irrespective of context. The Committee in *Kell* and the North Macedonia communications recommends remedies in response to particular instances of demonstrated intersectional discrimination. Nor should the Committee's Concluding Observations in response to one of China's state reports, for instance, be interpreted as a requirement that women should in all cases be entitled to register land in their names. As the Committee indicates, its recommendations to China are in a context where certain traditions and practices in rural areas impede women's enjoyment of property otherwise.[48]

The Committee's actions in these instances are consistent with a Convention that only targets "discrimination against women." Even with respect to rural women where the Convention's list of specific entitlements is extensive, absolute entitlements related to property, akin to those recommended by de Soto, are not required. The protections owed to rural women under Article 14(2)(a)(h) are preceded by a chapeau that directs states to take all appropriate measures to "eliminate discrimination ... in order to ensure, on a basis of equality of men and women." Read in context, the right to enjoy adequate living conditions, including rights to housing in Article 14(h), just like the right to access to agricultural credit and loans in Article 14(g), are, like other rights under the chapeau in Article 14(2), directed at eliminating discrimination and ensuring equal treatment. As indicated in GR 34, what states need to avoid are laws or practices that reflect a male

---

[46] *See, e.g.*, chapter 2, sections 2.7.1 (describing General Recommendations on housing rights), 2.11.1 (describing General Recommendations on the intersection between gender-based violence and property rights), and 2.11.2 (discussing Communications involving gender-based violence).

[47] *See, e.g.*, chapter 2, section 2.6.2 (describing Concluding Observations on rural women's access to land). In these instances, the Committee treats the absence of land registries or other irregularities in the registration of land as root causes which prevent rural women from accessing land, property, and credit and capital. *Id.* sections 2.6.2.1 and 2.6.2.2.

[48] Chapter 2, section 2.6.2.2, at text and notes 413 and 414.

bias, such as those that, by default, permit only men to enjoy access to property in the absence of formal registration or because only one sex registers in fact.[49] Similarly, when the Committee discusses desirable public practices in the course of land reform, resettlement policies, rules regarding expropriation or resulting compensation, or registration or certification schemes, the context is always about ensuring equal rights to men and women. The remedies recommended by the Committee in these cases are corrective measures *rendered necessary by preexisting discriminatory practices* that generally fail to protect women's rights.

The relationship between formal law and customary practices—and between the state and private parties—that emerges in CEDAW's property jurisprudence is generally different from the relationships envisioned by neo-liberals. Although CEDAW's property jurisprudence often demands changes in customary, Indigenous, and religious practices, its recommendations for reform are not usually about formalizing in law rights to property or possessions that are already recognized in informal law or customary practice.[50] In the instances canvassed in chapter 2 involving challenges to customary practices, the Committee recommends, whether in Views in response to individual communications, Concluding Observations to state reports, or in General Recommendations, changes to customs that *prevent* women from enjoying property rights. To be sure, the CEDAW Committee often treats customary or Indigenous practices as the problem, not the solution, but the Committee's focus is not on whether those practices prevent titling as such but on whether those practices constitute *de jure* or *de facto* discrimination.[51] The informal norms that the CEDAW Committee targets under Article 5 are not those that frustrate entrepreneurs who are hostile to state "mercantilism" and that neo-liberals want to redress by requiring formal legal titles.[52] The targets of the CEDAW jurisprudence are *both* formal law and informal practices that undermine equality between the sexes.[53] In some cases, the problem that the Committee identifies is the gap between *formal* laws that respect equality and customary or cultural practices or stereotypes that do not.[54]

---

[49] GR No. 34 on the Rights of Rural Women, CEDAW/C/GC/34, ¶ 69 (2016).

[50] Compare de Soto's argument that legal reformers should seek to protect rights to land through formal legal title since less formal methods are inefficient and inadequate. DE SOTO, THE OTHER PATH, *supra* note 43, at 55–57, 159–63.

[51] *See, e.g.*, GR No. 39, *supra* note 31, at ¶ 23.

[52] *Id.* at ¶ 56.

[53] *See, e.g.*, chapter 2, sections 2.4.3 (canvassing Concluding Observations that challenge not only formal laws but also customary, religious, or cultural practices involving family relations); 2.4.1.2 (discussing General Recommendations 21 and 29 and their focus on the gap between formal law and customary practices, the absence of formal law, or inadequate formal law that do not ensure equal property rights for married women in general, those married under aboriginal law, those in polygamous, de facto, or customary unions, including with respect to inheritance or after a separation or divorce); and 2.4.1.3 (addressing GR 27's emphasis on the many reasons older women are vulnerable to property disenfranchisement).

[54] *See, e.g., id.*, section 2.4.3.10, particularly text and notes 287–294.

The Committee's GR 34, to cite another example, is at a considerable philosophical remove from the elevation of rights to private property that is so critical to neo-liberalism's defenders.[55] That GR demonstrates that even when it is applying the property-respecting rights in the Convention, the Committee applies all the rights contained in that treaty—including the economic and social obligations (as under the ICESCR) that require more from the state than mere abstention from interference with market actors. This serves as a reminder that CEDAW is something of a throwback among contemporary human rights treaties. Its diverse collection of rights harkens back to the Universal Declaration of Human Rights. Like the Universal Declaration, CEDAW contains civil and political as well as economic and social rights. This accords with the feminist insight that since women are economically, socially, politically, culturally, and legally disadvantaged as compared to men, a treaty that seeks to equalize the scales must include the full range of rights.[56] The CEDAW Committee's embrace of this comprehensive set of rights, evident throughout chapter 2, undermines the claim that the Committee—or specifically its property jurisprudence—prioritizes the traditional civil and political right to private property enshrined in the West while disparaging other rights that may undermine it.

To be sure, CEDAW's property rights jurisprudence recognizes, as noted, that rights to property, housing, certain proprietary assets (as conveyed in a contract), or certain possessions (such as the family home as inheritance) may be prerequisites to the enjoyment of both civil/political and economic/social rights.[57] We should beware of any suggestion, however, that this recognition serves to elevate property rights over others in the Convention. Recognition that property rights may be what others call a "keystone right," works differently in the context of this treaty. As the CEDAW Committee sees it, the connection between property and other rights recognized in the treaty is a reminder that property rights intersect with other CEDAW enumerated rights, as well as with human rights recognized by general international law, need to be interpreted as consistent with those other rights, and that attaining women's equality rights may be contingent on enjoying those other rights (like the right to equal access to courts, to participate equally in land reform efforts, or to benefit from customary norms that ensure access to land even without title).[58]

[55] GR No. 34, *supra* note 49.
[56] *See, e.g.*, CHARLESWORTH & CHINKIN, *supra* note 31, at 249.
[57] *See also* chapter 6, section 6.4.1 (discussing commonalities between the CEDAW and ICESCR regimes).
[58] *See, e.g.*, chapter 2, sections 2.5.2.2 (discussing access to justice and property rights), 2.6.2.6 (discussing Concluding Observations on the need for equal participation in decision-making), and 2.6.2.3 (discussing Concluding Observations on the need for access to agricultural land). CEDAW's embrace of other rights beyond those specifically included in the treaty itself is suggested by the reference to "human rights and fundamental freedoms" in both Articles 1 and 3. *See* Christine Chinkin & Beate Rudolf, *Introduction, in* THE UN CONVENTION ON THE ELIMINATION OF ALL FORMS OF

4.2.2 Commodification

As the outputs in chapter 2 demonstrate, the CEDAW Committee is more likely to address the right to "housing" or "personal security" than the abstract right to property or, with the exception of affirming battered spouses' to exclude the abuser, the right to exclude all others. The Committee's property jurisprudence is less about tangible things that persons need to own exclusively than about the human capabilities that certain possessions enable.[59] Even when the Committee addresses tangible forms of property specifically mentioned in the treaty, such as bank loans, mortgages, and other forms of financial credit indicated under Article 13(h) or agricultural credit and loans or other assets mentioned in Article 14(2)(g), the Committee treats these as tools to advance economic security for battered spouses, to enable economic self-determination for Indigenous or rural women, or to secure financial independence for married women and widows.[60] The Committee's proffered rationales for these property protections suggest that it is more concerned with property as a means to achieving certain substantive ends—both civil liberties traditionally associated with traditional Western democracies and rights to human security associated with more socialist regimes—than property as a commodity or possession with a set price and as an end in and of itself.[61]

The CEDAW's emphasis on eliminating all impediments to women's substantive equality means that its Committee is as vigilant in protecting women from the abuse of property rights (as by businesses) as it is in making sure that women enjoy these rights. This, along with the CEDAW preamble's emphasis on the need to eradicate the vestiges of, among other things, colonialism and

DISCRIMINATION AGAINST WOMEN: A COMMENTARY 51, sec. III (Marsha A. Freeman et al. eds., 2012). This broad incorporation is also suggested by the cross references to the ICCPR and ICESCR and other "international conventions concluded under the auspices of the United Nations and the specialized agencies promoting the equality of rights of men and women" in the Convention's preamble. It is true, however, that cross-references to non-CEDAW sources of authority, including other treaties or soft law, are relatively rare in the Committee's outputs. They tend to appear in the Committee's General Recommendations rather than in its responses to individual communication or Concluding Observations. For a particular example, *see generally* GR No. 39, *supra* note 31 (containing citations to outputs of the ILO, other human rights treaty bodies, and other UN reports).

[59] Compare AMARTYA SEN, DEVELOPMENT AS FREEDOM (1999).
[60] *See, e.g.,* chapter 2, section 2.9.2.4 (describing Concluding Observations addressing intersectionality and economic empowerment).
[61] The Committee's rationales for protecting property in the course of responding to threats of domestic violence provide abundant examples. *See, e.g.,* Rep. of the Inquiry concerning South Africa, CEDAW/C/ZAF/IR/1, ¶¶ 76–79, 108, 110 (2021) (explaining the inadequacies of the state's shelters in light of the victim's needs for services and protection); *id.* at ¶ 121 (explaining its recommendations for shelters, safe houses, and affordable housing in terms of needs for economic protection upon divorce or to gain economic autonomy to escape from abusive relationships); *id.* ¶¶ 81–82 (explaining the need to share joint marital property in terms of "economic empowerment" crucial to "strengthening victims' resilience").

neo-colonialism, are reflected in the Committee's resistance to, for example, the commodification of agricultural land as a tool to enhance exports or the Committee's criticisms of other state policies that purport to advance "economic development" at the expense of women's interests.[62]

4.2.3 Privatization, Business Deregulation, and Support for Economic Globalization

CEDAW's property jurisprudence leaves the method by which these equality rights are given effect generally to governments to decide. This jurisprudence does not demand that governments "minimize" government regulation on the private sphere. On the contrary, it demands, as the treaty itself anticipates, a considerable degree of government interference into the private sphere precisely because that is where women, all too often, have faced direct and indirect discrimination. That jurisprudence often encourages states to regulate property, including for purposes of redistributing it, rendering land ownership more equal, or avoiding forced eviction or displacements. Moreover, the conditions the Committee imposes on rural development, land resettlement, or land and agrarian reforms seek, under the general chapeau of Article 14(2), "equal treatment"—not the protection of entrepreneurs as such nor the general right to own property of all persons irrespective of whether gender discrimination exists.

The CEDAW Committee's property-related recommendations are not directed at limiting the options of states to intrude in the free market. The Committee's focus is on promoting the *de facto* equality of women, not on promoting one form of economic governance on the presumption that this is the best way to further economic development. Contrary to Orford's fears, CEDAW's property jurisprudence does not treat "Foreign Capital as the agent of wealth or prosperity."[63]

As is addressed in depth in chapter 5, the deprivations of property attributed to the state that arise under CEDAW's property jurisprudence are quite different from the ones that tend to arise under international investment agreements (IIAs) and the investor-state arbitral jurisprudence generated under them. The international investment regime's key rationales for imposing obligations on states are consistent with neo-liberals' assertions that governments need

---

[62] *See, e.g.*, CO on Timor-Liste, CEDAW/C/TLS/CO/2–3, ¶¶ 34 & 35 (2015) (expressing concern with rural infrastructure projects that involve forced eviction and threaten rural women's fair compensation); CO on India, CEDAW/C/IDN/CO/8, ¶¶ 45–46 (2021) (concern over megaprojects' displacement of tribal and rural women). *See also* JOHN G. SPRANKLING, THE INTERNATIONAL LAW OF PROPERTY 208–09 (2014) (arguing that these features of CEDAW indicate that it is not designed to advance the right to property as such).

[63] Chapter 3, section 3.2, at text and note 128 (quoting Orford).

to protect entrepreneurial expectations and promote national and foreign investment.[64] Unlike that regime, the CEDAW regime steers clear of protecting foreign investments or businesses as such; this is not the purpose of the Convention. Accordingly, under the CEDAW Committee's jurisprudence, a state that expropriates property from a private party is not obligated to pay for that privilege—unless there is evidence that the absence of payment reflects direct or indirect discrimination against women (as would be the case if the state only makes such payments to men or imposes conditions that only make men eligible for payment).[65] By contrast with the international investment regime, the deprivations of property with which the CEDAW Committee are concerned—such as failures by states to prevent "property-grabbing" by private parties or "forced evictions" (whether taken by government authorities or private parties)—are not designed to prevent the "unjust enrichment" of states, rectify financial injuries suffered by foreign investors, or preclude allegedly "protectionist" measures that hinder the free flow of capital critical to economic globalization.

The CEDAW Committee has not suggested that all states should adopt any one model for protecting private property.[66] It does not urge that states privatize property that is now public. While CEDAW's property jurisprudence promotes rules that harmoniously enable equal treatment for men and women, it does not seek to produce harmonious or stable property rules for their own sake. The default mode of CEDAW's property rights jurisprudence is not to defer to the market—as libertarians desire—but to use, proactively, government regulation to defend women's equal rights even when such regulation intrudes upon the preferences of free market agents in the "private sphere"—whether such agents are employers or male relatives of a deceased spouse.

While the target of neo-liberals' ire is the state when it interferes with "private" markets, the CEDAW regime's relationship with the state is more complex. Feminist critics are correct to point out that CEDAW, like most human rights treaties, generally directs its concerns to violations by the state. Nonetheless, as demonstrated in chapter 2, a significant part of CEDAW's property jurisprudence seeks to use the state to regulate private parties when they act in either the private or public spheres. Many of the Committee's recommendations— to adopt specific regulations to safeguard the property of women in *de facto* unions, provide adequate shelters for those suffering from domestic abuse,

---

[64] *See* chapter 5, section 5.2.

[65] Compare chapter 5, section 5.9 (describing the distinct arbitral remedies accorded to foreign investors).

[66] Even when the Committee has urged states to adopt models from the civil law, it has recommended that states consider the experience of other countries with similar cultural backgrounds and legal norms. *See, e.g.*, CO on UAE, CEDAW/C/ARE/CO/4, ¶ 55 (2022).

combat forced marriages, add additional protections under Personal Status Laws or Civil Codes, or enable the collection of additional data—would interfere with the actions of private parties or add to their regulatory burdens.[67] Moreover, the Committee often requires that the states ensure and protect women in the "private sphere."[68] These demands run counter to neo-liberals' insistence that the state generally refrain from interfering in "sacrosanct" private domains.

Claims that international human rights law, and particularly human rights relating to property, undermine the goals of the Third World or specifically the New International Economic Order (NIEO) are not a good fit with CEDAW's property jurisprudence. GR 34, discussed in chapter 2, reflects the influence of NIEO-influenced documents like the Beijing Platform for Action.[69] According to that General Recommendation, states should

> ensure that macroeconomic policies, including trade, fiscal and investment policies, as well bilateral and multilateral agreements, are responsive to the needs of rural women and strengthen the productive and investing capacities of small-scale women producers. They should address the negative and differential impacts of economic policies, including agricultural and general *trade liberalization, privatization, and the commodification of land,* water and natural resources, on the lives of rural women and the fulfillment of their rights.[70]

These Committee warnings, and Concluding Observations consistent with them, run counter to the goals of neo-libertarians. They are also contrary to many of the prescriptions for "rule of law" reform favored by international financial institutions that remain in thrall to the Washington Consensus or any of its "post" iterations.[71] CEDAW's property-related recommendations to states, as indicated in its responses to governments like China, are meant to apply to states that consider themselves communist no less than Western-styled democracies.

The CEDAW Committee warns states against exacerbating rural women's unequal access to land or contributing to the feminization of poverty, even at

---

[67] *See, e.g.,* chapter 2, section 2.4.3 (describing Concluding Observations relating to obligations to respect women's equality with respect to marriage).

[68] *See, e.g.,* GR No. 29, *supra* note 34, ¶¶ 10–15 (directing states to eliminate all forms of *de facto* or *de jure* discrimination in their personal status laws relating to marriage, divorce, distribution of marital property, inheritance, guardianship, adoption, and related matters).

[69] *Beijing Declaration and Platform for Action, in* 1 REPORT OF THE FOURTH WORLD CONFERENCE ON WOMEN, BEIJING, 4–15 SEPTEMBER, 1995, UN Doc. A/CONF.177/20/REV.1, UN Sales No. 96.IV.13 (1996).

[70] GR No. 34, *supra* note 49, ¶ 11 (emphasis added).

[71] *See, e.g.,* chapter 2, section 2.6.2.5 (describing CEDAW's Concluding Observations on land-grabbing and development projects).

the expense of economic globalization.[72] It warns states against reifying colonist practices and urges states to remove barriers to access to land for Indigenous peoples to enable them to exercise self-determination.[73] In GR 39, it recommends that states "prevent and regulate activities by businesses, corporations and other private actors that may undermine the rights of Indigenous women and girls to their lands, territories and environment, including measures to punish, ensure the availability of remedies, grant reparations and prevent the repetition of these human rights violations."[74] In GR 34, the Committee criticizes land agreements that displace rural women or result in forced evictions, demands that states protect rural women from acquisitions of land by national or transnational companies, development projects, extractive industries or megaprojects, condemns forms of "property grabbing" by such entities (no less than when widows' possessions are seized by male relatives of her husband), and prioritizes redistributive goals over the rights of entrepreneurs to freely acquire property.[75] None of these actions are consistent with neo-liberal prescriptions.

The Committee's jurisprudence also implies that the need to protect women's equality may demand, in accord with Article 14, that governments pick some winners and losers—at least with respect to rural areas and relevant commercial sectors—rather than leave some things for private parties (or the "free market") to decide.[76] This too is inconsistent with neo-liberalism's demands. While, consistent with Article 14(2)(g), GR 34 makes a number of recommendations to protect the rights of women as entrepreneurs or economic agents, these reflect concerns about equity and fairness in contexts where male economic agents face no comparable constraints.[77] It would be a gross distortion to suggest that these recommendations are motivated by an ideologically tinged agenda in favor of securing property rights backed by legal title among individuals competing in a capitalist market.

While some of the CEDAW Committee's outputs seek to reform the internal structures of states, the nature of and motivation for such prescriptions are very different from reforms sought by those who want to change states to make them better agents of economic globalization. When, for example, GR 29 addresses the causes of the feminization of poverty, the Committee does not suggest that the

---

[72] This is hardly consistent with using property rights to obscure "the continued impact of colonialism" on development recipes favored by international financial institutions. See chapter 3, section 3.2, text and note 66 (discussing the views of Mohanty).

[73] See, e.g., Rep. of the Inquiry concerning South Africa, supra note 61, ¶ 19; GR No. 39, supra note 31, ¶ 57.

[74] GR No. 39, supra note 31, ¶ 57(d).

[75] See chapter 2, section 2.9.1.4 (discussing GR 34).

[76] See, e.g., GR No. 34, supra note 49, ¶¶ 59–62 (e.g., recommending the promotion of women's participation in agricultural cooperatives and organic farming, and the setting of limits on the quantity and quality of land offered for sale or lease to third states or companies).

[77] Id. ¶¶ 52(g), 67–72 (directed at remedying discriminatory practices applied to rural women).

underlying causes are states' failures to promote economic globalization. Among the structural causes the Committee highlights instead are "global developments such as the market economy and its crises" and persistent income inequality within and between states.[78]

Under the Committee's jurisprudence, it is up to states to determine which property entitlement its law will protect and in what context—so long as when the state decides to recognize these in a particular context, that entitlement is equally extended to women not just in law but in fact. GR 29 is, for example, careful when addressing how states need to "provide equal access by both spouses to the marital property and equal legal capacity to manage it."[79] Access denotes enjoyment, not necessarily ownership, acquisition, or other entitlements. Absent proof of direct or indirect discrimination against women, the Committee does not prejudge whether women need to "own" marital property after divorce or get to "own" the family home after the death of a spouse. The kind of property right enjoyed in either case depends on what men get in similar circumstances under the particular states' legal system or whether structural or other impediments otherwise demonstrate a breach of women's rights to substantive equality. All that the Committee demands in that GR—consistent with the text of Article 16(1)(h)—is that women's rights to "own, acquire, manage, administer and enjoy separate or non-marital property is equal to that of men."[80] For the same reasons, despite the treaty's intrusion into family law, the CEDAW Committee carefully avoids statements that imply that states must adopt a particular property regime under its marriage or family laws—whether community property, separate property, joint, or hybrid.[81] In its Concluding Observations, the Committee typically insists that women have the right to title to land or to register the family home only to the extent those rights are accorded to men in similar circumstances.

As noted in chapter 1, CEDAW does not contain the general property entitlements found in the American, African, or European human rights treaties; it does not anticipate that all government takings of property, irrespective of discrimination, require compensation.[82] The absence of such provisions

---

[78] *See, e.g.,* GR No. 29, *supra* note 34, ¶ 4.
[79] *Id.* ¶ 38.
[80] *Id.*
[81] Concluding Observations that criticize particular states' regimes for marital property, such as separate or joint property regimes, focus their criticism on aspects of such regimes that discriminate against women, not the regimes themselves. *See, e.g.,* COs on Armenia (CEDAW/C/ARM/CO/4, ¶ 39) and on Cabo Verde (CEDAW/C/CPV/CO/9, ¶ 43). The Committee recommends that in those states that adhere to joint property, property should be registered in both partners' names from the outset to protect women's rights most effectively. *Id.* ¶ 44. *See also* CO on Eritrea, CEDAW/C/ERI/CO/6, ¶ 52 (2020).
[82] Compare a number of human rights regimes that protect a general right to property as discussed in chapter 1, section 1.2. *See also* Tom Allen, *Compensation for Property Under the European Convention on Human Rights,* 28 MICH. J. INT'L L. 287 (2007); LUDOVIC HENNEBEL & HELENE TIGROUDJA, THE AMERICAN CONVENTION ON HUMAN RIGHTS: A COMMENTARY 650 (2022).

denies the CEDAW Committee the capacity to second-guess how states structure their property rights entitlements except when these are discriminatory against women. It also means that the CEDAW Committee does not purport to decide what portion of property is in private or state hands or should belong to individuals as opposed to collectivities.

One way to counter Lesson Two is to redefine neo-liberalism. Some of the critics surveyed in chapter 3 adopt a far broader definition of "neo-liberalism." This is certainly tenable since the term "neo-liberalism" is hardly a term of legal art and has had "many lives" and formulations.[83] If, as is suggested by the scholarship of Tzouvala and Marks, neo-liberalism is simply a model of capitalist accumulation and consumption reliant on markets, including state capitalism as practiced in China, it is not hard to portray CEDAW as consistent with such a broad conception. This should not surprise anyone. CEDAW is, after all, a treaty negotiated largely by capitalist states and intended, at least in part, for their use. It would be quite surprising if the Committee refused to apply economic and property rights expressly included in the Convention because they were applied in capitalist states.

If the target of criticism is capitalism more generally and not a particular kind (neo-liberalism), it is easy to portray much of what the Committee does as described in chapter 2—from attempting to increase women's access to credit, to land, to adequate housing, and to more equal social welfare benefits—as propping up capitalist governance. For self-defined Marxist critics of international law or of international human rights, it is by definition problematic when human rights treaty bodies endorse, as the CEDAW Committee explicitly does, women's rights to certain forms of intellectual property, female entrepreneurship and income-generating activities, and women's economic empowerment.[84]

An assessment of criticisms that the CEDAW Committee's efforts to equalize women's enjoyment of property rights are harmful simply because capitalism is harmful lies outside the scope of this book. The relative merits of capitalism and its alternatives is not our subject. This book addresses the more limited argument that the CEDAW Committee's "ameliorative" steps to promote equality postpones the necessary revolution that would topple the capitalist modes of production. That contention rests on a contestable theory of social change addressed in Lesson Three that follows. A version of that proposition—the argument that the CEDAW Committee's efforts are incapable of generating the kind

---

[83] *See, e.g.*, NINE LIVES OF NEOLIBERALISM (Dieter Plehwe et al. eds., 2020).

[84] Compare chapter 2, sections 2.8 (describing the Committee's GRs to protect certain forms of intellectual property) and 2.9 (describing the Committee's GRs to address inequality with respect to access to credit and "economic empowerment") to Vasuku Nesiah, *Indebted: The Cruel Optimism of Leaning in to Empowerment*, *in* GOVERNANCE FEMINISM: AN INTRODUCTION 509 (2018) (arguing that CEDAW addresses equality and does not mention "economic empowerment").

of "transformational change" needed to achieve the goals of the Convention—is addressed in chapter 7.

4.3 Lesson Three: Beware Universalizing Concepts and Binary Arguments—Whether Expressed by CEDAW's Defenders or Its Critics

The contention that the CEDAW regime privileges "universal" human rights over culture, long propounded by "cultural relativist" opponents of international human rights has a long history.[85] The same can be said of criticisms of CEDAW's binary divisions—whether explicit (dividing women from men) or implicit (elevating the interests of liberal Western women over "victimized" women elsewhere).[86] Celestine Musembi's sophisticated and more contemporary critique, discussed in chapter 3, raises anew the familiar dilemma posed by ostensibly universal rights such as those in CEDAW: When do such rights need contextualization or, in the words of anthropologist Sally Merry, "vernaculization" to respond to local contexts?[87]

Some of CEDAW's property jurisprudence supports Musembi's contention that the CEDAW Committee is predisposed against customary norms. She is correct that CEDAW GRs and COs do not always target the specific ways such norms run counter to the property rights in the Convention but appear to criticize states' reliance on or deference to such norms in general.[88] The Committee does seem to presume that since such norms often run counter to the rights of women, particularly with respect to equal access to land for rural women or to marital or family property in rural or urban areas, states should resist enforcing them altogether.[89] At the same time, the Committee's views on this subject appear to be evolving. The Committee's latest word on the rights of Indigenous women, GR 39, is careful to echo Musembi's core insight: namely, that the Convention itself affirms the "right to culture" and that therefore "indigenous women have a right not only to enjoy their culture but also to challenge aspects of their culture that they consider discriminatory."[90] In that GR, the Committee affirms that Indigenous norms, including rights to land collectively that do not rely on land titles, merit protection and that lack of recognition of such informal rights can

---

[85] See, e.g., chapter 3, section 3.2 (discussing the views of Tamale and the cultural relativists with whom she engages).
[86] See, e.g., id. section 3.1.
[87] Id. section 3.2, text and notes 99–104. See also Merry & Levitt, supra note 39.
[88] Chapter 3, section 3.2 at text and note 100 (citing Musembi).
[89] See, e.g., chapter 2, section 2.4.3.9, particularly the Concluding Observations discussed at text and notes 287–294.
[90] GR No. 39, supra note 31, ¶ 53.

lead to grievous harms to women, including gender-based violence.[91] This goes some way toward revisiting what Musembi calls CEDAW's "abolitionist" approach to local "moral codes." It may be that the Committee has come to understand that a failure to embrace both the principle of equality and what Musembi calls "legal pluralism" may undermine its equality goals as well as generate backlash from governments, collectivities of women, and even individual women for whom customary or religious practices are part of their lived experiences that are an indispensable part of their identities.[92]

Musembi's insights are valuable precisely because she resists binary thinking—namely, the assumption that internationalizing human rights is necessarily inconsistent with respecting local norms. The same cannot be said with many of the other critics surveyed in chapter 3. Many of those criticizing international human rights regimes' tendency to universalize and draw artificial binaries need to address the same flaws in their own work.

Koskenniemi, Tzouvala, and Marks all argue that reliance on "rights talk" depoliticizes what ought to be political.[93] For all three, the resort to human rights postpones more radical or revolutionary change by channeling energy, resources, and time into legal avenues for redress that, intentionally or not, substitute mere palliatives for genuine changes that can only be achieved through political action. They posit, in short, a binary between the use of law to advance human rights and resort to political action, as if there is no prospect that the first can promote the other.

For Sam Moyn, international human rights rhetoric leaves "neo-liberal" government polities unchecked; the first is "powerless" against the second, and there is no in-between.[94] For Sylvia Tamale, the Western origins and individualistic biases of CEDAW's principle of gender equality turns it into an alien concept that is "inappropriate" to the African continent and can yield no significant results for African women.[95] In her view, gender equality and African culture are binaries that cannot (and should not) be overcome.

For Whyte, international human rights have been transformed in the modern era into "hegemonic rights" closely associated with the economic "shock treatment" imposed on Chile by Pinochet and pursued ever since by international financial institutions and other powerful promoters of "economic development."[96]

---

[91] Id. ¶ 56.
[92] See Celestine Nyamu Musembi, *Pulling Apart? Treatment of Pluralism in the CEDAW and the Maputo Protocol*, in WOMEN'S HUMAN RIGHTS: CEDAW IN INTERNATIONAL, REGIONAL AND NATIONAL LAW 183–213 (Anne Hellum & Henriette Sinding Aasen eds., 2013).
[93] See chapter 3, section 3.2.
[94] Id. at text and notes 137–139 (discussing Moyn's views).
[95] Id. at text and notes 87–92 (discussing Tamale's views).
[96] JESSICA WHYTE, THE MORALS OF THE MARKET: HUMAN RIGHTS AND THE RISE OF THE MARKET (2019). See also chapter 3, section 3.2, at text and notes 81–86 (summarizing Whyte's views).

Once that Rubicon was crossed, she suggests, there is no going back. International human rights have become "a central component of the neoliberal attempt to inculcate the morals of the market."[97] Whyte is quite explicit in adopting the definition of neo-liberalism associated with protecting private property, deregulation of business, protecting foreign investments, and economic globalization. She argues that reliance on international human rights necessarily promotes all the elements of neo-liberalism defined by the economists of the "Chicago School" who advised Pinochet. Such rights enforce only a select few individualized civil and political rights and dismiss others, individual or collective, in the Universal Declaration of Human Rights and now the ICESCR, to the political realm;[98] use individual property rights to keep foreign investments safe, to move capital freely across borders, and impose "good governance" across the globe;[99] restrict the meaning of equality to narrow formal equality that prevents state interventions in the market or redistributive measures;[100] and cabin dignity to a quality that only the self-reliant and responsible can enjoy.[101]

For all of these critics of contemporary human rights efforts, the universal truths they posit and binaries they construct mean that there is no need to look closely at what the human rights treaty bodies most closely involved actually say. For Whyte, for example, it is sufficient to look at the activity of prominent human rights organizations like Amnesty International to conclude that "human rights" as a whole is closely associated with the stark formulation of neo-liberalism favored by scholars like Friedrich Hayek.[102] If Amnesty evinces a minimalist agenda hostile to redistributionist agendas such as those of the NIEO, she implies that the CEDAW Committee does as well—particularly if what the CEDAW regime is doing is attempting to enforce property rights.

The universalizing premises and binary conclusions of these critiques practically leap from the page. Closer scrutiny of these premises and conclusions are surely warranted given the CEDAW Committee's efforts to avoid these premises and conclusions. As noted, that Committee uses the property-relating articles in CEDAW to advance traditional civil and political and but also socioeconomic rights and advance both substantive and formal equality. It deploys property rights to protect the land and other rights of the Indigenous, to ensure equality among men and women in the family and outside of it, and to protect equal access to justice (including courts).[103] It seeks to advance both individual autonomy and the rights of distinct groups of women subjected to intersectional

---

[97] Whyte, *supra* note 96, at 21.
[98] *Id.* at 29–30, 75–115.
[99] *Id.* at 25.
[100] *Id.* at 24.
[101] *Id.* at 27.
[102] *Id.* at 156–57, 179–84, 195–96.
[103] *See generally* GR No. 39, *supra* note 31.

forms of discrimination.[104] It uses the property-related provisions in the Convention to resolve conflicts between rights—as between a woman's rights to personal integrity and both spouses' right of access to the family home or between an Indigenous woman and her tribe.[105] It protects women's rights to equal access to property but not in all cases the right to sell it to the highest bidder to advance free capital flows.

As even Whyte acknowledges in passing, rights "can open up a democratic space for "perspectival claims" that seek to persuade rather than to shut down political contestation."[106] It would be good if she, and Koskenniemi, Tzouvala, and Marks, would explore whether the jurisprudence surveyed in this book actually shuts down political change as they predict or emboldens it—and whether that might differ from place to place and is not subject to universally applicable generalizations.[107] It would be good if instead of presuming that rights talk by the CEDAW Committee or other human rights treaty bodies is "powerless," they seriously consider the evidence that it is not, particularly when rights talk is deployed, as it often is, by political activists.[108]

Moreover, for those who define "neo-liberalism" as any form of capitalist state, it would be wise to reexamine the premise that reformist measures to alleviate some of the horrors associated with capitalism (including income inequalities and the feminization of poverty) actually run counter to or undermine meaningful structural change. Even those with a prior normative commitment to a Marxist state need to explain why efforts like those of the CEDAW Committee are harmful "palliatives" that forestall the desirable Marxist revolution. Such contentions appear to be based on a highly contestable (and overly generalized) theory of social change. Even if these critics are correct that revolutionary action is needed to fundamentally transform women's lives, might it be possible that in particular contexts ameliorative steps to promote women's equality that actually improve the lives of many women help to foment fundamental structural

---

[104] *See, e.g.*, chapter 2, sections 2.4.3.9, 2.9.2.4, 2.10.3.8, and 2.11.1.7.
[105] Compare chapter 2, section 2.11.1.5 and 2.11.1.6 (examples from the CEDAW jurisprudence on women's access to shelter in cases of gender-based violence) to Martti Koskenniemi, *The Effect of Rights on Political Culture*, in THE EU AND HUMAN RIGHTS 99, 107 (Philip Alston ed., 2000) (arguing that rights conflict and that such conflicts cannot be resolved by rights talk).
[106] WHYTE, *supra* note 96, at 33.
[107] Much of the evidence on the impact of human rights on local communities suggests that such generalizations ought to be avoided since the local context matters. *See, e.g.*, Carmen Diana Deere, *Women's Land Rights, Rural Social Movements, and the State in the 21st-century Latin American Agrarian Reforms*, 17 J. AGRARIAN CHANGE 258 (2016) (discussing how "progressive" reforms in formal land rights undertaken in four Latin American countries—including joint titling of land to couples, prioritization to female heads of households, and mandatory joint allocation of land to couples—differed considerably in impact depending on the existence of strong local rural women's movements who served as advocates for women's land rights).
[108] *See, e.g.*, Deere, *supra* note 107.

changes?[109] Tocqueville, applying lessons from the French Revolution, certainly thought so.[110]

4.4 Lesson Four: Many Other Criticisms of the CEDAW Regime Need Nuance

Some of the more general criticisms canvassed in sections 3.1 and 3.2 of chapter 3 are reflected in CEDAW's property jurisprudence. As chapter 2 makes clear, the CEDAW Committee is charged with and deploys the language and ethic of rights. The Committee's recommendations to states accordingly suggest, as rights talk dictates, that some of their practices or omissions are internationally wrongful acts inconsistent with their duties under the Convention. It is also the case, as previously noted, that some of the Committee's General Recommendations are premised on protecting women as "economic agents." It is inescapably the case that the Committee protects the "liberal legal subject" insofar as it endorses at times the values of individual autonomy, universal rights, formal equality, and equal citizenship (including equal participation rights) that Nicola Lacey, among others, sees as problematic.[111] It is also true that in protecting the liberal female subject, some Committee recommendations protect women in the delimited roles or categories that Chinkin and others criticize.[112] It is also the case that the ethic and language of rights that drives the Convention—and the Committee—poses the risk that women's rights will sometimes be "balanced" with opposing concerns. The Committee indicates, for example, the communal Indigenous rights and the cultural traditions that arise alongside them may need to give way to a woman's individual rights.[113] And yet one specific risk that some

---

[109] As is further addressed in chapter 7, there is a tendency for revisionists critics of international human rights to either presume that the CEDAW regime has no effect in practice or to be indifferent to the substantial number of women who may benefit from the CEDAW regime's "palliative" outputs. For only one example of the kinds of tangible benefits inspired by the CEDAW regime, see, e.g., Carmen Diana Deere & Magdalena León, Consensual Unions, Property Rights, and Patrimonial Violence against Women in Latin America, 29 SOC. POL. 608 (2022) (discussing the substantial number of countries in Latin America that recognized consensual unions in the wake of CEDAW and the attention it drew to the need to improve the economic status of women raising families outside of marriage).

[110] This well-known theory of social change, known as the "Tocqueville effect" posits that increasing immiseration is not the only route to revolutionary change. See, e.g., RICHARD SWEBERG, TOCQUEVILLE'S POLITICAL ECONOMY 259–60 (2009) (discussing Tocqueville's analysis of economic improvements and other events in France, spanning decades, that, in his view, led to the French Revolution).

[111] Chapter 3, section 3.1.2, at text and notes 29–31 (summarizing Lacey's views).

[112] See, e.g., chapter 2, section 2.9.1.6 (discussing General Recommendation 38 on trafficking in women and girls).

[113] See, e.g., chapter 2, section 2.9.1.7 (discussing General Recommendation 39's support for individual economic autonomy for Indigenous women).

have articulated, namely, that women's rights to be free from domestic violence would be countermanded by the husband's rights to access the family home, is not borne out by CEDAW's relevant jurisprudence.[114]

As this last example suggests, general broadsides against CEDAW or its expert committee's interpretations need to be approached with caution. Five other broad feminist critiques of the CEDAW regime—that it remains constrained by the public/private divide, that it falls short with respect to recognizing intersectional discrimination, that it marginalizes women's rights, that it fails to address "root causes," or that it fails to push for structural changes needed to achieve transformational equality—need nuance if the intended target is CEDAW's property jurisprudence.

4.4.1 The Public/Private Divide

The criticism that the CEDAW Convention's limited intrusions into the "private" sphere of marriage and family in Article 16 fail to dismantle, root and branch, mythical public/private dichotomies prevalent in national and international law is true[115]—but only to a point. CEDAW's property jurisprudence's intrusion into the ostensible "private" sphere of family law is no small thing. That jurisprudence has taken Article 16's clear demand that states "eliminate discrimination against women in all matters relating to marriage and family relations" quite seriously. GR 21 and 29 have deployed that authority to condemn other seemingly "private" realms apart from the family, such as norms arising from religion, ethnic custom, or other practices to the extent these interfere with Article 16's equality demands.[116] It is of no consequence to the Committee whether the private beliefs of persons would prefer, as would the personal status laws of some states, that widows be disinherited along with female children, for instance.[117] Those recommendations' ample reach into the "private" sphere shows how Article 16's insistence on gender equality is amplified by Article 5's demand that states modify "social and cultural patterns," eliminate "prejudices and customary and all other practices," change family education, undermine or disrupt traditional understandings of "maternity" and caretaking responsibilities.

Moreover, in accordance with the multiple set of state obligations imposed under the ICESCR, the CEDAW Committee has indicated, consistent with

---

[114] Chapter 2, section 2.11.2 (describing the Communications alleging gender-based violence where the Committee has refused to "balance" the rights of women under threat of domestic violence with the husband's property interests).
[115] Compare CHARLESWORTH & CHINKIN, *supra* note 31, at 218–44.
[116] GR No. 21, *supra* note 1, ¶ 13; GR No. 29, *supra* note 34, ¶¶ 10–15.
[117] GR No. 29, *supra* note 34, ¶ 50.

Article 3 of the Convention, that states are also under obligations "to respect, protect, promote and fulfill" the right of nondiscrimination "to ensure the development and advancement of women in order to improve their position to one of de jure as well as de facto equality with men."[118] This comprehensive obligation has also served to puncture the "public/private" divide insofar as the Committee insists that states ensure that women's equal property rights be protected from the discriminatory actions of private parties—from national employers to foreign agri-businesses.[119] A particular example is GR 34's recommended measures to ensure that national and transnational companies that acquire agricultural land do so in accord with the property protections accorded to rural women under Article 14.[120]

4.4.2 Intersectionality

A close look at chapter 2 suggest that concerns that the Convention's preoccupation with "women" as such would preclude its resulting jurisprudence from recognizing the full diversity of women, north and south, or the fluidity of gender discrimination seem overstated. The GRs, COs, and other outputs surveyed in that chapter provide multiple examples where the Committee adapts property protections to the distinct but overlapping identities or roles of women living in acute poverty or rural areas—as well as to those who are refugees or internal migrants, married, single, or women living in formally unrecognized relationships, older women, women under threat of domestic abuse, or who are targeted for other forms of socioeconomic discrimination based on "LGBTQ+" status or caste.[121] That jurisprudence provides no evidence that rural women—singled out in Article 14—are the only exception from the Convention's

---

[118] GR No. 25, *supra* note 6, ¶ 4. *See also* Christine Chinkin & Lisa Gormley, Article 3, section E, *in* THE UN CONVENTION ON THE ELIMINATION OF ALL FORMS OF DISCRIMINATION AGAINST WOMEN AND ITS OPTIONAL PROTOCOL: A COMMENTARY (Patricia Schulz et al. eds., 2022).

[119] *See generally*, GR No. 28 on the Core Obligations of States Parties, CEDAW/C/GC/28, ¶ 9 (2010) (grounding this duty in states' general obligation to "protect") and ¶ 13 (interpreting Article 2 of the Convention as imposing a "due diligence" obligation on states to prevent discrimination by private actors). *See also* chapter 2, section 2.6.2.5 (discussing Concluding Observations criticizing land grabbing by private investors).

[120] GR No. 34, *supra* note 49, ¶ 62(c).

[121] *See, e.g.*, chapter 2, sections 2.9.1.3 (focusing on older women), 2.9.1.4 (focusing on rural women), 2.9.1.7 (focusing on Indigenous women), and 2.9.2.4 (discussing intersectional discrimination that impinges on economic empowerment). As these examples suggest, the Committee's jurisprudence does not suggest that it has been hampered by the Convention's lack of specific provisions recognizing women's intersectional identities (with the exception of art. 14 that addresses rural women). The treaty's expert interpreters have not elevated the status of a "homogenous" category of "woman." The CEDAW Committee's evolving recognition of different categories of women who face intersectional discrimination also demonstrates that the treaty's categories of women subject to intersectional discrimination are not closed.

supposedly homogenous category of "women" or that the Committee considers only the biological trait of being female as relevant.[122]

As this suggests, some of the early criticisms of CEDAW by feminists underestimated the creativity of the CEDAW Committee. The category of "rural women" in Article 14 (as well as other language in the Convention) has, in the hands of that Committee, licensed a broad capacity to recognize intersectional forms of discrimination. In the joint individual communications brought against North Macedonia, for example, the Committee found the claims of the destitute Roma women admissible. On the merits it upheld claims of breach of adequate living conditions including housing under Article 14(2)(h) precisely because of the combined forms of discrimination to which the complainants were subject. The fact that the women were destitute (and presumptively unable to access more timely legal assistance), were not offered adequate alternatives to the destroyed Roma settlement in which they originally lived, and suffered consequential harms (such as lack of adequate health care) due to their forced evictions and denials of temporary special measures to which they were entitled led the Committee to its conclusions. In those cases the Committee creatively stretched the guarantees formally accorded under CEDAW only to "rural" women under Article 14 to a group of Roma women living in urban areas that were subjected to intersectional discrimination. As is made clear by GR 39, the Committee has done the same with respect to Indigenous women, whether or not, these would qualify as living in "rural" areas.[123] GR 39 provides another clear example of the Committee's efforts to expand the categories of intersectional discrimination and find new ways to puncture the public/private divide.[124]

---

[122] For analysis of the CEDAW Committee's use of "gender" and "intersectionality" to address to some extent the rights of LGBTQ+ individuals, including those who identify as "intersex," see, e.g., Elisabeth Greif, *Upward Translations—The Role of NGOs in Promoting LGBTI—Human Rights under the Convention on All Forms of Discrimination Against Women (CEDAW)*, 4 Peace Hum. Rts. Governance 9 (2020). But note that the CEDAW Committee has not suggested that CEDAW's protections extend, for example, to cis-males who face gender discrimination.

[123] GR 39 adapts the protections from denials of legal capacity to conclude property, administer, or inherit property to Indigenous women, including under marriage and family laws. GR No. 39, *supra* note 31, ¶¶ 23–33. It recognizes property protections to individual Indigenous women threatened by gender-based violence. See id. ¶¶ 34–42, while accepting that such violence also "undermines the collective spiritual, cultural, and social fabric of Indigenous peoples and their communities." Id. ¶ 40. GR 39 adopts the Committee's jurisprudence with respect to access to loans and credits—essential to protect the right to work—to Indigenous women. Id. ¶ 50(a)(vii). But the Committee recognizes the unique importance that rights to land, other natural resources, along with food, water, and seeds have in the context of Indigenous women for whom land and territories "are an integral part the identify, worldview livelihood, culture, and spirit." Id. ¶ 53.

[124] See, e.g., id. ¶ 23(a) (expanding on GR 34 (which addressed rural women) to threats faced by Indigenous women with disabilities or who are lesbian, gay, bisexual, transgender, and intersex); Id. ¶ 22 (targeting discrimination "in both the private and public spheres" including "in the digital space"), and ¶¶ 58–59 (recognizing the key role Indigenous women play in securing food and livelihood and indicating concerns for the commercialization of seeds without benefit sharing and the proliferation of transgenics or modified crops without the participation of Indigenous women and girls).

The recognition of the cumulative and often devastating effects triggered by intersectional discriminatory practices, especially under traditional or customary norms, underlie many of the Committee's demands that states take temporary special measures.[125] Apart from the expansive GR 34 detailing the systemic forms of discrimination imposed on rural women, other General Recommendations, such as GR 27 addressing rights to administer property and to conclude contracts under Article 15(2), focus on other forms of intersectional discrimination imposed upon, for example, older women.[126]

The Committee's approach to intersectional discrimination does not consist of merely adding layers or discrete identities over one another and if enough emerge, using this to conclude that discrimination has occurred. While it is true that the Committee sometimes points to the fact that a communicant fits multiple categories to suggest discrimination is more likely, it does not seem to apply one formula for determining the existence of intersectional discrimination. It simply indicates that it applies a "gender perspective," an "intersectional approach," an "Indigenous women and girls' perspective," an "intercultural perspective," and a "multidisciplinary approach" all for the sake of achieving a single goal: eradicating discrimination to fulfill social justice.[127] Many praise this pragmatic approach for its adaptability to context. The Committee, it is said, is "pioneering a new and fluid approach to intersectional discrimination that ... integrates theory and practice."[128]

At the same time, as discussed in chapter 7, the Committee's engagement with intersectional discrimination leaves many interpretative questions unresolved and subject to contestation.[129] It may be the case that these uncertainties will be addressed given another aspect of the Committee's jurisprudence evident in chapter 2: namely, its efforts to compel states to generate more specific data relevant to evaluating the existence (and persistence) of intersectional discrimination. The Committee has repeatedly invoked Article 14's explicit recognition of the particular posture of rural women, for example, as a reason for demanding distinct remedies from states under its COs in response to state reports that fail to include the gender desegregated data needed to identify whether states are respecting land rights.[130] In these and other cases, it has demanded greater state

---

[125] *See, e.g.,* chapter 2, section 2.6.2.9 (addressing Concluding Observations that recommend that states take temporary special measures).

[126] GR No. 27 on Older Women and Protection of Their Human Rights, CEDAW/C/GC/27, ¶ 34 (2010). *See also* chapter 2, section 2.9.1.3 (discussing General Recommendation 27).

[127] GR No. 39, *supra* note 31, ¶ 4.

[128] *See, e.g.,* Meghan Campbell, *CEDAW and Women's Intersecting Identities: A Pioneering New Approach to Intersectional Discrimination,* 11 DIREITO GV L. REV. 479, 483 (2015). Notably, even Tamale sees the "theory of intersectionality" as "key to Africa's decolonial and transformational agenda." SYLVIA TAMALE, DECOLONIZATION AND AFRO-FEMINISM 46 (2020).

[129] Chapter 7, section 7.2.2.

[130] Chapter 2, section 2.6.2.8 (describing Concluding Observations demanding relevant data on women's access to land rights).

accountability through the collection of more transparent disaggregated data to make more visible the discriminatory access to land imposed on rural women, women farmers, widows, and members of Indigenous groups.[131]

4.4.3 Marginalization

Fears that the CEDAW regime would marginalize women's rights into a distinct "silo" separate and apart from "mainstream" human rights bodies also need some nuance. As noted in chapter 1, CEDAW's property jurisprudence is part of a web of treaties protecting forms of property rights, including over twenty human rights instruments. As addressed in depth in chapter 6, there is considerable overlap between that jurisprudence and the work of treaty bodies under the ICCPR and ICESCR. The CESCR's GC 26 from 2022 provides one example. Like the CEDAW Committee, the CESCR Committee argues that access to land is a means for guaranteeing security, expresses concerns with "land grabs," and connects the lack of protection for land tenure to increasing vulnerability, poverty, and socioeconomic inequality.[132] That General Comment overlaps substantially with CEDAW's jurisprudence on the same issues as reflected in chapter 2. The CESCR Committee, like the CEDAW Committee, identifies various ways to secure women's equal access to resources, including land, housing, and other forms of property and sees these as essential to women's well-being, economic independence, and autonomy.

The CEDAW Committee's recommendations and underlying rationales surveyed in this book also intersect with the CESCR's interpretations of rights to an adequate standard of living, health, and food;[133] treaty regimes on Indigenous peoples;[134] UN Special Rapporteurs concerned with the right to adequate housing;[135] and other UN bodies charged with responding to forced

---

[131] *Id.*

[132] ICESCR GC No. 26, *supra* note 16, ¶¶ 1–3.

[133] *See generally id. See also* Olivier D. Shutter, *The Emerging Human Right to Land*, 12 INT'L COMMUNITY L. REV. 303 (2010) (discussing the interconnections with the rights of Indigenous peoples and the right to food).

[134] *See, e.g.*, Shutter, *supra* note 133.

[135] *See, e.g.*, Balakrishnan Rajagopal (Special Rapporteur on the Right to Adequate Housing), *Rep. on Covid-19 and the Right to Adequate Housing: Impacts and the Way Forward*, UN Doc. A/75/148 (July 27, 2020) (discussing ICESCR rights in the context of COVID); Balakrishnan Rajagopal (Special Rapporteur on the Right to Adequate Housing), *Rep. on Twenty years of Promoting and Protecting the Right to Adequate Housing: Taking Stock and Moving*, A/HRC/47/43 (June 14, 2021) (discussing, *inter alia*, the problems of discriminatory evictions, displacement, access to land, and standard of living). Indeed, UN Habitant's Fact Sheet on The Right to Adequate Housing relies on the CEDAW Committee's relevant jurisprudence as well as that of other human rights bodies. UN Habitat & Off. of the UN High Comm'r for Hum. Rts., *The Right to Adequate Housing: Fact Sheet No. 21/Rev. 1.*

evictions.[136] The CEDAW Committee's suggestions that some aspects of its work, such as dealing with the consequences of violence against women, involve applications of customary international law also might be seen as a bid to resist marginalization.[137]

At the same time, the CEDAW Committee usually does not refer to how other human rights exports or entities have addressed property rights. The Committee usually refers only to its own inputs.[138] Further, when other bodies or expert groups explicitly cite to the CEDAW regimes' outputs, these are frequently relegated to a section devoted only to women's equality—as if the CEDAW Committee's general insights on the meaning of discrimination, for example, were of no relevance.[139] Moreover, apart from a handful of feminist scholars who focus on specific issues such as the right to housing, there is a general lack of awareness of the jurisprudence that is the subject of this book.[140]

4.4.4 Root Causes

And what of the charge, made generally by Susan Marks and more specifically by the authors of the rewritten *Kell* opinion discussed in chapter 3, that UN human rights committees like CEDAW's fail to address the root causes for the subordination of women?[141] Are critics correct that, particularly in its Views, the CEDAW Committee fails to fully address and denounce the economic institutions and practices and ideologies that underlie the communications that come before it?

It is true that none of the Committee's responses to individual communications canvassed in chapter 2 comes close to the elaborately reasoned rewritten version of *Kell v. Canada* by Lolita Buckner Inniss and her colleagues. If that revised version of *Kell* is what it takes to "personify feminist justice" through fully fleshed explanations of intersectional discrimination more widely applied to cover all the Convention's state parties, that is not now occurring. Nor is such

---

[136] *See, e.g.*, UN Comm'n on Human Rights Res. 1993/77, UN Doc. E/CN.4/RES/1993/77 (Mar. 10, 1993).

[137] *See, e.g.*, chapter 2, section 2.11.1.4 (discussing General Recommendation 35's efforts to link CEDAW's obligations with respect to gender-based violence with states' due diligence obligations).

[138] But this may be changing. *See, e.g.*, GR No. 39, *supra* note 31, ¶¶ 19, 22, 34, which cites to a number of other UN treaty bodies, along with other UN reports.

[139] *See, e.g.*, ICESCR, GC No. 26, *supra* note 16, ¶¶ 16–17 (citing to CEDAW outputs but only in the section on women's discrimination with respect to land).

[140] As we wrote this book, it was striking how often even human rights scholars seemed unaware that CEDAW even contained rights relevant to property protections.

[141] *See* chapter 3, section 3.1.2 (discussing criticisms that the human rights committees generally fail to probe deeply into the "root causes" of states' violations of human rights). *See also* Inniss et al., *Cecilia Kell v. Canada*, in FEMINIST JUDGMENTS IN INTERNATIONAL LAW 333 (Loveday Hodson & Troy Lavers eds., 2019).

an outcome likely to happen absent structural changes to the CEDAW regime, including the termination of existing state reservations to many of the relevant articles of the Convention,[142] greatly expanding the resources available to the CEDAW Committee, demanding that all state parties to the treaty adhere to the Optional Protocol, and amending that Protocol to make Committee's Views legally binding. The kind of "judgment" anticipated by Inniss and her colleagues is not likely to emerge from the present twenty-three-person committee operating under its current institutional constraints. That Committee consists of many non-lawyers, receives only a diminished number of communications brought by a limited number of women within mostly European states where individual access to the Committee is more encouraged and supported by civil society, and is empowered to issue, in response to the small number of communications that it has time to consider, only nonbinding "Views" premised on the need to persuade, not coerce, states to comply.[143]

Fortunately, for those sympathetic to the concerns expressed by Inniss and her colleagues, CEDAW's property jurisprudence extends beyond the relatively meager number of Views it has issued in response to individual communications. If one examines with care CEDAW's other outputs, namely the Committee's more fulsome General Recommendations, the cumulative impact of its COs which apply to all state parties, and its Reports on Inquiries with respect to Canada and South Africa, the charge that the Committee does not address "root causes" is harder to maintain.

It is revealing that the rewritten version of *Kell v. Canada* relies on, for example, the Committee's own GR 21. As this suggests, a number of the GRs canvassed in chapter 2 go a considerable way toward addressing the underlying reasons for failures of substantive equality. CEDAW's property jurisprudence as a whole does identify the inadequacies of national laws and procedures in the face of intersectional discrimination. It highlights, as Inniss and her colleagues would urge in the case of *Kell*, the diverse ways the absence of the right to housing and shelter disadvantages women. It provides abundant examples of how domestic violence—and states' inadequate responses to it—undermine the security of tenure essential to the right to housing.[144] The Committee's General Recommendations and Concluding Observations provide considerable examples, as the rewritten Kell does, demonstrating how access to property results from the many underlying impediments women face.[145]

---

[142] For a list of these, *see* appendix 3.

[143] *See* chapter 2, section 2.3.5 (discussing the CEDAW Committee's follow-up procedures). *See also* discussion in chapter 7, section 7.2.3 (enumerating the Committee's institutional constraints and challenges).

[144] Chapter 2, sections 2.11.1 and 2.11.2.

[145] *See, e.g.*, GR No. 39 *supra* note 31, ¶¶ 7, 11–12.

Defenders of CEDAW's property jurisprudence would contend, with some justice, that the CEDAW Committee's efforts to address failures in achieving substantive equality do not *as a whole* ignore "root causes."[146] Addressing the causes of discrimination is, after all, inherent to the Convention's demand that states correct the stereotypical or other structural biases that underlie the subordination of women. The Committee's Inquiry Report concerning Canada, discussed in chapter 2, for example, canvasses "the historical context of the root causes of the disproportionate vulnerability of aboriginal women and girls to violence."[147] That report accepts, as acknowledged by the Canadian government itself, that the violence directed at such women and girls is associated with intergenerational trauma caused by poverty, language minority issues and cultural loss, and the legacy of a residential school system which separated more than 150,000 Aboriginal children from their families.[148] That report points out that the separate school system subjected the children to abuses and barred them from speaking their traditional languages or practicing their culture.[149] Moreover, it acknowledges that this resulted in the loss of parenting skills with far-reaching and intergenerational impacts.[150] In recognition of these facts, the Committee imposes on Canada a number of specific obligations to "overcome the legacy of the colonial period" intended to strike at the root causes of discrimination against Aboriginal women.[151]

This example would probably not satisfy critics like Susan Marks, however. Like the critics of *Kell v. Canada* noted earlier who critique the Committee's failures to address and redress Kell's identity as an Aboriginal woman, Marks would probably respond that the Committee (and the Canadian government's) consideration of root causes in that Inquiry Report was "halted too soon." That report does not ask who benefited from the intergenerational impoverishment of Aboriginal peoples or how the economic substructure of Canadian society contributed to the government's underlying goals. The CEDAW Committee did not go into what may have prompted the Canadian government to believe that it needed to intentionally "assimilate" Aboriginal children in the first place or what led that government (or the general public in Canada) to ignore the dire consequences or to believe that such costs were outweighed by the supposed benefits of building a more "harmonious" Canada.

---

[146] *See, e.g.,* Loveday Hodson, *Gender Equality Untethered? CEDAW's Contribution to Intersectionality, in* FRONTIERS OF GENDER EQUALITY: TRANSNATIONAL LEGAL PERSPECTIVES 175 (Rebecca J. Cook ed., 2023) (praising the Committee's appreciation of the root causes or factors that underlie intersectional discrimination).
[147] Rep. of the Inquiry concerning Canada, CEDAW/C/OP.8/CAN/1, ¶ 36 (2015).
[148] *Id.* ¶ 37.
[149] *Id.*
[150] *Id.*
[151] *Id.* ¶ 219.

As feminist scholars have pointed out, the exploration of "root causes" is a layered and nuanced enterprise. Description of underlying causes and prescriptions for addressing them vary greatly, corresponding to the depth of analysis.[152] In cases where the Committee alludes to or blames "cultural" stereotypes and calls upon states to address them, for example, it often does not plumb these further—to consider, for example, whether these arise from the state's commitment to the "free market" and/or capitalism or because the state has chosen to follow prescriptions for "development" touted by institutions like the World Bank or the IMF.[153] It is also not difficult to challenge the seriousness or consistency of the CEDAW Committee's consideration of "root causes" across its outputs—from Inquiry Reports to Views to GRs or COs. The problem, some might say, is not just that the Committee is not consistent in challenging the existing (male) hierarchies of power and wealth and may, as arguably occurred with some aspects of Kell's claims, be content with ruling in favor of the communicant on the basis that her right to formal equality was denied. It may be that, as the Canadian report suggests, the Committee is sometimes content to address only those "root causes" that are acknowledged and addressed by the governments under scrutiny.[154]

Whether it really is a good idea for the Committee's Views to address "root causes" and claims not made by the communicants or respondent states in the case before it remains to be seen. A Committee that, as Inniss and her colleagues would urge, would reach out to adopt explicitly the "seven guarantees" embraced by the CESCR Committee with respect to the ICESCR's right to adequate housing would certainly be responsive to the probable "deep roots" of Kell's complaint but at the cost of being perceived as a judicially activist body. Whether including those seven guarantees in the Committee's demands for action from Canada would have enhanced or undermined Canada's compliance with those recommendations may prompt disagreement.

Some may believe that the goals of transformational equality are better served by a combination of far-reaching General Recommendations by the Committee and more "judicially minimalist" responses to individual communications that address only that which is necessary to resolve the immediate case at hand.[155]

---

[152] *See, e.g.*, Rebecca J. Cook, *Introduction*, in FRONTIERS OF GENDER EQUALITY: TRANSNATIONAL LEGAL PERSPECTIVES 1 (Rebecca J. Cook ed., 2023) (discussing how different authors in her edited book present distinct accounts of the underlying causes of gender discrimination).

[153] But the Committee has, on occasion, and not consistently, urged states to consider the "macro-economic roots of gender equality," including its policies on trade liberalization and the commodification of land and other natural resources. *See* GR No. 39, *supra* note 31, ¶¶ 11–12.

[154] Indeed, the Committee's exploration of deep causes in the course of the Canadian Inquiry discussed at text and notes 147–151 earlier relied heavily on the Canadian government's own account of the underlying causes.

[155] Differing degrees of adjudicative activism might also be expected simply because of certain realities. The CEDAW Committee, which relies on a minimal staff, has some twenty-four hours to draft Concluding Observations in response to a state's report. By contrast, it has a few weeks to

General Recommendations provide opportunities to expand the law and explain it—in a context where no particular state is charged with a violation and may resist. Views provide opportunities to provide effective remedies to individuals, but only if the states charged with violations are persuaded to comply which might be assisted by interactions between the Committee and the state through follow-up procedures. Concluding Observations and Reports on Inquiries have their own characteristics: both enable multiple interactions between the Committee and states in the form of "constructive dialogues" with particular states in the first case and perhaps a more confrontational "mobilization of shame" approach in the second. The state reporting process (and possibly Inquiry Reports that are the product of multiple interactions) might be more akin to that followed by "managerial courts" engaged in experimentalist forms of compliance.[156]

Even assuming all agree that fundamental structural change should be the CEDAW Committee's goal, reasonable people can differ on how best to instrumentalize that goal given the existing institutional constraints of the CEDAW regime. Even if the CEDAW Committee's examinations of "root causes" in its Views are relatively shallow in the ways that some suggest,[157] not all would agree that it is the Committee's role in responding to individual communications to go beyond the pleadings of the litigants before it. This may be particularly true if the underlying "root" reasons that some critics would like to see addressed (and redressed) point the finger of blame at global capitalism. What some critics like Whyte would have human rights treaty bodies do—namely, blame "the morals of the market"—would put the CEDAW Committee on one side of divisive ideological debates.[158] Even assuming that the diverse members of the Committee were to agree that capitalism was the single greatest impediment to women's equality, expanding the Committee's remedial ambit to demand that states fundamentally reform their systems of economic governance would seriously threaten the regime's legitimacy within a significant part of its global constituency. That may be precisely what some critics of international human rights regimes intend, but whether that would actually redound to benefit women's equality in the short or long run remains to be seen.

For perhaps similar reasons, the CEDAW Committee has, to date, not provided a full-throated philosophical or other defense of the right to property akin to those provided by Leonard Levy, Rhonda Howard-Hassmann, Randy Barnett,

---

draft its views in response to an individual communication, and from two to four years to draft a General Recommendation. *See* generally chapter 2, section 2.3 for an account of the Committee's procedures.

[156] *See, e.g.*, Gráinne de Búrca, *Human Rights Experimentalism*, 111 AM. J. INT'L L. 277 (2017).
[157] Compare Inniss et al., *supra* note 141.
[158] *See generally* WHYTE, *supra* note 96.

or Richard Pipes.[159] Some Committee members might silently believe, consistent with the strongest defenders of property and even human rights bodies like the ICESCR, that access to credit and land economically empowers, enhances status, promotes respect among spouses, reduces domestic violence, improves health outcomes, and enables access to culture.[160] Some may believe that property rights safeguard a zone of autonomy for individuals, protect their dignity and signal respect for others', create a basis for undertaking useful projects in the world that promote sustainable development, diffuse political authority among actors thereby deflecting concentrations of power, maintain individuals' independence and shield them from subservience to others, incentivize the creation of wealth, and enable the efficient management of resources.[161] Some might think that the institution of property, because it requires deference to others' claim to exclusive access or ownership, acts as a "practical education in what it means to have and to respect rights."[162] Neither has the Committee given voice to some contrary views on the left and surveyed in chapter 3: namely, those who see property as a neo-colonist remnant that undermines the dignity and equal worth of all human beings, including women. We can only speculate about Committee members' actual normative commitments precisely because the Committee as a whole generally refrains from giving full voice to such sociopolitical rationales, from the right or left, within its outputs.

The Committee is more minimalist in its Views than, for example, the rewriters of *Kell* would like.[163] Critics of this reticence would be more persuasive if they addressed the many possible reasons for such reticence. It may be that the Committee cannot achieve consensus on expressing any such general opinions in any of its outputs and, in the case, of Views, seeks to achieve consensus as much as possible rather than have its internal disagreements be aired through dissenting opinions. It may believe that certain justifications or forms of philosophizing are ill-suited to its role or are counterproductive. It may believe that some form of adjudicative minimalism in response to communications under the Optional Protocol may be what states parties to the Protocol expect,

---

[159] *See, e.g.*, Leonard W. Levy, *Property as a Human Right*, 5 CONST. COMMENTARY 169 (1988); Rhoda E. Howard-Hassmann, *Reconsidering the Right to Own Property*, 12 J. HUM. RTS. 180 (2013); Randy Barnett, *The Right to Liberty in a Good Society*, 69 FORDHAM L. REV. 1603 (2001); Richard Pipes, *Private Property, Freedom and the Rule of Law*, HOOVER DIGEST (Apr. 30, 2001), https://www.hoover.org/research/private-property-freedom-and-rule-law.

[160] *See, e.g.*, ICESCR, GC No. 26, *supra* note 16, ¶¶ 16–17.

[161] *See, e.g.*, Carol M. Rose, *Property's Relation to Human Rights*, in ECONOMIC LIBERTIES AND HUMAN RIGHTS 69–70 (Jahel Queralt & Bas van der Vossen eds., 2019) (citing the rationales offered by, among others, Bentham and Blackstone); *see also* Karen O. Mason & Helen M. Carlsson, *The Development Impact of Gender Equality in Land Rights*, in HUMAN RIGHTS AND DEVELOPMENT: TOWARDS MUTUAL REINFORCEMENT (Philip Alston & Mary Robinson eds., 2015).

[162] Rose, *supra* note 161, at 70.

[163] *See* Inniss et al., *supra* note 141.

what may best compel eventual compliance, what may encourage more parties to the Convention to join the Protocol, or what may encourage other state actions (such as the termination or modification of states' treaty reservations). It may also refuse to engage in such rhetoric out of deference to future members of the Committee and the capacity of the Committee to change its mind in response to evolving conditions (including with respect to how best to adapt property rights to an existential crisis such as climate change).

If one assumes, as Koskenniemi does, that what is wrong with international human rights is precisely that it deflects the politics that might inspire real change, the CEDAW Committee's evasions with respect to certain kinds of "root causes" are a mistake.[164] If one takes the view that CEDAW's property jurisprudence is silent when it needs to be vocal, it is easy to treat such silences as demonstrating the Committee's complicity in the neo-liberal enterprise (as Marks and Koskenniemi imply).[165] From the opposite vantage point, the Committee's less than robust defense of property rights makes it a less than vital partner in global efforts to reduce the gender gap with respect to access and enjoyment of all forms of property.

4.4.5 Structural Change

CEDAW's property jurisprudence, as described in chapter 2, suggests that feminist critics are correct that some of the Committee's efforts are directed, consistent with the Convention itself, at making sure that women receive, with respect to property, identical treatment to that accorded to men as a matter of formal black-letter law and actual practice. At the same time, the Committee's focus on ensuring substantive or *de facto* equality and not only *de jure* identical treatment is a key element in most of the Committee's General Recommendations listed in appendix 1 and explains much of their contents.

The Committee's insistence that states seek to achieve substantive equality between men and women underpins its recommendations that states make major changes to their national laws and practices. As chapter 2 indicates, the Committee has repeatedly urged states to change what is included as "marital property." GR 29 and the Committee's responses to state reports accordingly insist that equal treatment of marital assets after a divorce requires giving

---

[164] *See, e.g.*, Martti Koskenniemi, *Rocking the Human Rights Boat: Reflections by a Fellow Passenger*, in THE STRUGGLE FOR HUMAN RIGHTS: ESSAYS IN HONOUR OF PHILIP ALSTON 51, 115–17 (Nehal Bhuta et al. eds., 2022). Of course, this presumes that the CEDAW regime successfully depoliticizes issues. Some would argue that the impact of, for example, the CEDAW reporting process is precisely to uncover issues that will lead to political confrontations both inside states and externally as other states and international civil society reacts.

[165] Chapter 3, section 3.2.

equal weight to a spouse's nonfinancial contributions to the marriage, that presumptions based on there being a "head of the household" (usually a male) be eliminated, that in community property states women need be consulted when marital property is sold or disposed of, and that unmarried women in *de facto* relationships receive the same treatment as married men and women.[166]

In ways large and small, these recommendations and many others (such as those expected of states in response to the vulnerabilities of Indigenous women or the need to respond to gender-based violence) are responsive to those demanding transformational equality.[167] Consistent with Megan Campbell's and Sandra Fredman's description of the goals of transformational equality, these recommendations for reform seem designed to break the cycle of disadvantage, promote respect for dignity and worth, accommodate different treatment for women, and encourage political and social inclusion and participation.[168]

It is important to recall that the Convention also authorizes temporary special measures "to accelerate de facto equality."[169] Other provisions in the Convention can be interpreted to permit distinct remedies responsive to women's distinctive identities or qualities.[170] These underpin efforts by the Committee directing states to make accommodations for women in response to special handicaps imposed on women—such as illiteracy, expectations to be the unpaid caregiver, and relative lack of employment opportunities outside the home. A number of GRs surveyed in chapter 2 provide relevant examples. GR 29, for example, suggests that states need to take special steps to protect women's ability to claim equal property rights upon dissolution of a marriage because of "interrupted education and employment histories and childcare responsibilities."[171] Those steps include a demand that states include women's unpaid contributions as part of marital assets.[172] That recommendation also recognizes the need for some state measures needed to protect women because of special circumstances that apply

---

[166] *See* chapter 2, sections 2.4.1.2 (discussing General Recommendations 21 and 29) and 2.4.3 (describing Concluding Observations addressing property rights during marriage and with respect to family relations).

[167] For discussion of how the goal of substantive equality can achieve transformational change, *see* Sandra Fredman, *Engendering Socio-Economic Rights, in* WOMEN'S HUMAN RIGHTS: CEDAW IN INTERNATIONAL, REGIONAL AND NATIONAL LAW 217 (Anne Hellum & Henriette Sinding eds., 2013).

[168] *See also* chapter 7, section 7.1.

[169] CEDAW, *supra* note 6, art. 4.

[170] In addressing the rights of women to nutrition in the course of disasters, for example, GR 37 relies on both Articles 12 and 14. GR No. 37 on Gender-related Dimensions of Disaster Risk Reduction in a Changing Climate, CEDAW/C/GC/37, ¶ 71 (2018). Article 12(2) of the Convention, which directs states to ensure pregnancy services, including free services when necessary, is a clear example of recommendations based on women's unique reproductive needs and capacities. The role pregnancy played in the Committee's consideration of intersectional discrimination in response to the communications directed at North Macedonia provides another example. *See* chapter 2, section 2.7.2.1 (discussing those Communications).

[171] GR No. 29, *supra* note 34, ¶ 44.

[172] *Id.* at ¶¶ 49–53.

only to them. These include demands that states criminalize property dispossession or "land grabbing" by male relatives of deceased husbands; that states redress disparities between men and women imposed by structural or cultural barriers by taking proactive steps to prevent the concealment of matrimonial property; and that states ban the practice of levirate marriage or the conditioning of nationality on the holding of property.[173]

Other CEDAW recommendations are designed to enable better protection of equal property rights by responding to the unique procedural impediments imposed on particular categories of women under local laws and practices. The Committee has responded by requiring more transparent procedures in cases of divorce, distribution of marital property, or the award of custody and the provision of financial and other assistance to women in such cases.[174] Some recommendations attempt to redress the gap between the law's formal promises to implement equality and the realities of practices on the ground. These include Committee recommendations directed at proactive steps to ensure that government officials follow the law on the books, as well as groups whose cultural practices would suggest otherwise.[175] The Committee also recognizes that seemingly neutral laws or practices—for example, general government decisions against providing safe and adequate shelters for those rendered homeless, denying capacity building for judges, prosecutors, or police, or denying legal aid or forms of victim support services—need change because, as applied, women are disproportionately impacted and proactive steps are necessary to achieve equal treatment in fact.[176]

Article 14 is grounded in the "particular problems" faced by rural women and their role in the "economic survival" of their families.[177] Significantly, GR 34 addresses these measures and extends them to women's rights to communal, and not just individual, land.[178] That recommendation also imposes a number of conditions on land reform and land resettlement schemes to ensure that rural women's equal rights to land are respected. It also recognizes the need for "temporary special measures" in the course of land reform that would "enable rural

---

[173] *See, e.g.*, chapter 2, sections 2.4.3.1, 2.4.3.5, and 2.4.3.8 (discussing a number of Concluding Observations relating to equal rights during marriage).

[174] *See, e.g., id.*, sections 2.4.3.4–2.4.3.6 (discussing a number of Concluding Observations relating to equal rights on the dissolution of marriage).

[175] *See generally* GR No. 35, *supra* note 37, ¶ 31 (recommending specific measures to protect property rights in cases involving gender-based violence); GR No. 33 on Women's Access to Justice, CEDAW/C/GC/33, ¶¶ 54–64 (2015) (recommending specific measures to improve women's access to justice). Note that the latter includes recommendations that states improve their criminal law responses to domestic violence by, for example, expediting application for orders of protection, recording emergency calls, and taking photographic evidence of property destruction. *Id.* ¶ 51.

[176] *See, e.g.*, Rep. of the Inquiry concerning South Africa, *supra* note 61, ¶¶ 76–79, 100–01, 103–09, 119–21.

[177] CEDAW, *supra* note 6, art. 14(1).

[178] GR No. 34, *supra* note 49, ¶¶ 55–59; *see also* GR No. 39, *supra* note 31, ¶ 57.

women to benefit from the public distribution, lease or use of land, water bodies, fisheries and forests."[179] In these instances, the Committee seems to go beyond an insistence that women be treated without regard to sex. It appears to be responding to the realities of power by requiring structural changes that address forms of female subordination that occur *because of their sex*.

4.5 Lesson Five: CEDAW's Supranational Security Is Necessary

"Historically, women have had to leave home to get justice within it."
–Catherine A. MacKinnon, *Are Women Human?*

Catherine MacKinnon is, as is well known, one of the foremost critics of international law's gendered inequalities.[180] She has, as her words here suggest, also argued that no one can trust mostly male-dominated states to provide justice for women and that, therefore, women need the help of international law and its institutions to call out their actions. The need for ongoing supranational scrutiny over states' actions or inactions or the omissions or acts committed by private parties subject to their jurisdiction seems vindicated by chapter 2. No state party to CEDAW appears to be immune from charges that they are violating one or more of its property-respecting provisions. All state parties stand accused by name with violating women's equal property rights through the Committee's COs, Views, or Reports on Inquiries, or all three. Many state and non-state actor practices are further critiqued in the Committee's relevant GRs—which identify the objectionable practices and not the states or other parties as such. The Concluding Observations cited throughout chapter 2—only a sample of many others that make comparable criticisms of state actions and inactions—are an especially potent demonstration of the universal need for continuous Committee scrutiny to patrol the intersection of the principle of equality and property rights.

As chapter 2 indicates by manifold example, the principle of equality is violated by democracies, autocracies, and all regimes in between; by rich and poor countries; by those with a proud tradition of passing "gender neutral"

---

[179] GR No. 34, *supra* note 49, ¶ 78. With that exception, the Committee does not specify in GR 34 which of its corrective measures with respect to rural women are intended to be only "temporary" as anticipated by Article 4(1).

[180] MacKinnon's essays on international law reinforce criticisms made by Hilary Charlesworth and Christine Chinkin. *See generally* CHARLESWORTH & CHINKIN, *supra* note 31; CATHARINE A. MACKINNON, ARE WOMEN HUMAN? AND OTHER INTERNATIONAL DIALOGUES? (2006). At the same time, MacKinnon's essays on international law see promise in discrete pockets of international law, such as international criminal law. *See*, e.g., *id.* at 237–46.

laws that require formal equality between men and women;[181] as well as by those whose CEDAW reservations to relevant provisions like Article 16(2)(h) suggest their own doubts about the applying the principle (much less the reality) of gender equality.[182] The CEDAW Committee has criticized in its Views or Inquires countries like The Netherlands or Canada—despite those nations' long-standing public pronouncements and laws in favor of women's rights, including the principle of gender equality.[183] Intersectional discrimination relating to the property-respecting provisions in CEDAW seems rampant—irrespective of whether a state acknowledges that its population includes Indigenous women or other racially or ethnically discriminated groups. The broad reach and need for supranational scrutiny over forms of intersectional discrimination is particularly evident as the Committee has made clear that the Convention covers both sex and gender-based discrimination against women, thereby reaching discrimination based on "socially constructed identities, attributes and roles" and enabling close scrutiny over "any distinction, exclusion, or restriction which has the effect or purpose of impairing or nullifying the recognition, enjoyment or exercise by women of human rights and fundamental freedoms."[184] Over time, the Committee has vastly expanded the concept of intersectional discrimination as it has gone far beyond the categories commonly included in nondiscrimination provisions in human rights treaties. In GR 35, it indicated that the Committee's will examine direct or indirect forms of discrimination arising from

> women's ethnicity/race, indigenous or minority status, colour, socioeconomic status and/or caste, language, religion or belief, political opinion, national origin, marital status, maternity, parental status age, urban or rural location, health status, disability, property ownership, being lesbian, bisexual, transgender or intersex, illiteracy, seeking asylum, being a refugee, internally displace or stateless, widowhood, migration status, heading households, living with HIV/AIDS, being deprived of liberty, and being in prostitution, as well as trafficking in women, situations of armed conflict, geographical remoteness and the stigmatization of women who fight for their rights, including human rights defenders.[185]

---

[181] *See, e.g.*, Ruth Halperin-Kaddari & Marsha A. Freeman, *Backlash Goes Global: Men's Groups, Patriarchal Family Policy and the False Promise of Gender-Neutral Laws*, 28 CANADIAN J. WOMEN & L. 165 (2016).
[182] *See* appendices 2 & 3.
[183] *See, e.g.*, chapter 2, sections 2.10.2.2 (criticizing the actions of The Netherlands in response to the communication by Blok) and 2.11.3.1 (criticizing Canada in the course of an Inquiry).
[184] GR No. 28, *supra* note 119, ¶ 5
[185] GR No. 35, *supra* note 37, ¶ 12. *See also* GR No. 34, *supra* note 49, ¶ 15 (identifying other candidates for intersectional discrimination within "rural women," namely, those belonging to Indigenous, Afro-descendent, ethnic, religious communities or minorities, women who are heads of household, peasants, pastoralists, fisherfolk, landless, migrants, or affected by conflicts).

Given the sweep of these identities, attributes, or roles, no country can escape the Committee's "second look" at their actions or omissions.

The universality of the targets of Committee's outputs undermines claims that a treaty focused on "homogenized" women would focus its criticisms on "exotic" human rights violations found mostly in the developing world and leave largely undisturbed actions or omissions accepted as "natural" in the West. That most of the Committee's Views address problems in European states further undermines the latter claim. The Committee is as likely to criticize gendered stereotypes applied to Indigenous women in Canada[186] and stereotypes applied to women in Sweden,[187] as customary biases applied to widows in Tanzania.[188]

To be sure, supranational scrutiny remains contentious, particularly for those who see such an examination as providing a "needless" second look over actions that have previously been examined and approved by independent national courts that operate consistently with the rule of law.[189] Unless one believes that the Committee got it wrong in cases like *Kell v. Canada* or its the Report on Inquiry regarding that same country, however, it would appear that even "independent" courts in democratic states can violate, sometimes gravely, women's equal rights. As chapter 2 demonstrates, one virtue of the Committee is precisely its broad mandate to examine and call out for redress substantive inequalities—a delegation of supervisory authority rare among national courts or administrative proceedings. Unless one disagrees with that broad mandate, supranational scrutiny seems both necessary and vital to achieving the goals that CEDAW's ratifying states have endorsed—while perhaps failing to anticipate its consequences.[190]

Meghan Campbell's criticisms of what she calls the "devastating impact" of the United Kingdom's austerity-motivated "caps" on the social benefits claimants can receive provides a concrete example of the potential value of CEDAW's substantive equality "second look."[191] Campbell engages in a close look at efforts by women, particularly those solely responsible for the care of children, to challenge in UK courts and using the European Convention on Human Rights (ECHR)

---

[186] Chapter 2, section 2.11.3.1 (describing the Inquiry Report Concerning Canada).
[187] CO on Sweden, CEDAW/C/SWE/CO/8–9, ¶ 24 (2016).
[188] Views concerning E.S. and S.C. v. United Republic of Tanzania, CEDAW/C/60/D/48/2013 (2015), discussed in chapter 2, section 2.4.2.2.
[189] For an insightful account of the hostility among many in Britain to the idea that an external institution should be empowered to pass judgment on British legal arrangements when the European Convention on Human Rights was first proposed and for many years thereafter, *see* A.W. BRIAN SIMPSON, HUMAN RIGHTS AND THE END OF EMPIRE BRITAIN AND THE GENESIS OF THE EUROPEAN CONVENTION (2001).
[190] As Simpson argues in his in-depth historical account, British lawmakers were repeatedly surprised when UK actions became the subject of repeated early attention before the ECtHR. *See id.*
[191] Megan Campbell, *The Austerity of Lone Motherhood: Discrimination Law and Benefit Reform*, 41 OXFORD J. LEGAL STUD. 1197 (2021).

government restrictions placed on the value of "Universal Credit" social benefits. Under recent UK reforms, claimants can escape caps placed on such benefits if they engage in a certain amount of paid work; in addition, such benefits are subject to certain work conditionalities and are no longer available for a woman's third or subsequent child ("the two-child limit.")[192] Campbell criticizes the UK judgments for rejecting the women's claims that the restrictions interfered with their peaceful enjoyment of their possessions under Article 1 of Protocol One of the ECHR insofar as discriminated against them contrary to Article 14 of the ECHR. She notes that while the UK court in the underlying ruling *SC and others v. Secretary of State for Work and Pensions* acknowledged that the cap on benefits was discriminatory under the ECHR, it found the government's action justified under the minimal scrutiny it found applicable.[193]

Campbell points out how this UK ruling failed to recognize the intersectional vulnerabilities (gender, reproductive care responsibilities, and poverty) at play. She argues that the female challengers would and should have prevailed had that court applied a substantive equality lens.[194] She notes that the UK courts only considered the economic impact of the UK reforms and wrongly dismissed the women's claims on the premise that courts need to defer to the way policymakers evaluate how many persons in poverty the state can afford to pay. UK judges tend to see complaints premised on economic inequality or poverty as best suited for redress by politicians and not judges who are better suited to redress "status inequalities."[195] This, she argues, explains the United Kingdom's "light-touch" review and the court's failure to engage with the antecedent disadvantages in unpaid work or the stigma imposed on lone mothers.[196]

Whether or not the claimants in those cases ought to have prevailed under ECHR law, it seems clear, based on the Committee's Views issued in response to the communications by Elisabeth de Blok and Natalia Ciobanu, that their claims would have received much closer scrutiny before the CEDAW Committee.[197] As is evident throughout chapter 2, the Committee does not shy away from recommending to states measures to address comparable issues of poverty, particularly when these intersect with intersectional discrimination targeting women as mothers and sole caretakers. Moreover, the Committee's property jurisprudence frequently intersects with the feminization of poverty; the Committee does not retreat from such issues or relegate them, along

---

[192] *Id.* at 1197–98.
[193] *Id.* at 1203–04.
[194] *Id.* at 1198–1200.
[195] *Id.* at 1202.
[196] *Id.* at 1198–99.
[197] Compare chapter 2, sections 2.10.2.2 and 2.10.2.3 (discussing the Blok and Ciobanu communications). To be clear, Campbell does not address CEDAW in her article; she only addresses UK and ECHR law.

with other "economic" concerns, to the unexamined discretion of national legislatures.

This is not to suggest that the UK claimants would have clearly prevailed before the CEDAW Committee. As the divided Views issued by the Committee in *Ms. Dung Thi Thuy Nguyen v. The Netherlands*, also addressed in chapter 2, suggest, the Committee has not spoken with one clear voice when it comes to the level of deference, or, as it put it in that case, "margin of discretion," owed to governments when it comes to social benefits paid to those who are self-employed or only partly salaried.[198] But as the view of the dissenters in the *Nguyen* case and the successes of *Blok* and *Ciobanu* demonstrate, the CEDAW Committee is more likely to grapple with the structural impediments faced by distinct women and the need for social benefits policies to respond to these UK courts. Campbell's case study illustrates the potential benefits of CEDAW's second look, even when it comes to policies pursued by a country that is, rightly or not, proud of its adherence to the rule of law and subject to a regional human rights system that has produced the most extensive property-respecting human rights jurisprudence in the world.[199]

Campbell's case study illustrates another potential benefit of CEDAW's supranational "second look": the CEDAW Committee is not the functional equivalent of a national court or any other international venue for formal adjudication. While this difference is often viewed as a flaw, there is a potential benefit. While the Committee's Views and Reports on Inquiries suggest its role as a "quasi-judicial" body, its COs and GRs are not as easy to characterize. The ways GRs respond to facts that the Committee has uncovered in the course of state reports (and NGO shadow reports issued in response) resemble the kinds of evidence-gathering that generally precedes acts by parliaments, legislatures, or executive agencies charged with rulemaking. As others have recognized, the Committee functions as whistle-blower and standard-settler and not merely as dispute-settler.[200] The Committee does not just settle disputes through its communications procedure. Its role as quasi-law maker and "authoritative" treaty interpreter enables it to avoid traps like those described by Campbell. It is less likely to act like national judges who use separation of powers excuses to dismiss claims for injustice, leaving these to be remedied by the political process. CEDAW's legal process—flawed as it is—leads to "political" recommendations for legal change.

---

[198] Chapter 2, section 2.10.2.1 (discussing Nguyen v. The Netherlands).
[199] *See, e.g.*, THE POLITICAL ECONOMY OF THE INVESTMENT TREATY REGIME 84–85 (Jonathan Bonnitcha et al. eds., 2016) (indicating that between 1990 and 2015, over 8,800 property disputes were brought before the ECtHR).
[200] *See, e.g.*, Ruth Halperin-Kaddari, *Human Rights Treaty Bodies as Standard-Setting Mechanisms: The Case of Family Law in CEDAW*, *in* STRENGTHENING HUMAN RIGHTS PROTECTIONS IN GENEVA, ISRAEL, THE WEST BANK AND BEYOND 82, 82–102 (Joseph E. David et al. eds., 2021).

Criticisms that the Committee intentionally or unconsciously privileges some countries or legal traditions over others while engaging in nearly universal supranational scrutiny require more attention. As noted in this chapter's Lesson Four, some criticize the Committee with being less tolerant of Indigenous or religious practices with which its members, however cosmopolitan, are less familiar.[201] It is possible that the Committee has unduly deferred to government policies with which it is more familiar. As the previously discussed *Nguyen v. The Netherlands* case illustrates, the Committee has not clarified what degree of deference is owed to states generally or whether the level of deference it will extend differs depending on what provision of the Convention is alleged to be infringed or other factors. Articulating such standards would allow observers to better assess such criticisms.

---

[201] Compare, *e.g.*, CO on Sweden, CEDAW/C/SWE/CO/10, ¶ 22 (b) (2021) (urging Sweden to enforce its laws against polygamy by "prosecuting and punishing perpetrators") to chapter 3, section 3.2 (criticisms by Musembi).

5
Two Separate Worlds: Foreign Investors' Property vs. Women's Property Rights Under CEDAW

5.1 Introduction

This chapter compares the different goals and relevant jurisprudence of the international investment and the Convention on the Elimination of All Forms of Discrimination against Women (CEDAW) regimes. This comparison is relevant to skepticism, canvassed in chapter 3, about whether property rights should be treated as "human rights" and related concerns, rebutted in chapter 4, that to the extent the CEDAW regime protects such rights, it is an aider and abettor to neo-liberalism.

As evident from prior chapters, CEDAW adopts a human rights frame of analysis when protecting property rights.[1] Under the terms of that Convention, states cannot discriminate against women individually or as a group because they owe all persons, including their own nationals, respect for their human dignity—and not because or, to the extent that, equal property rights between men and women would further the state's economic development.[2] Accordingly, CEDAW's Article 1 defines discrimination as impairments on women's "human rights and fundamental freedoms in the political, economic, social, cultural, civil or any other field." By contrast, the typical international investment agreement (IIA) (which includes bilateral investment treaties (BITs), as well as investment chapters within Free Trade Agreements) protects companies of the state parties or shareholders of such a company that engage in doing business in the other state party, as well as the activities associated with doing business such as the

---

[1] *See, e.g.,* Patricia Schulz et al., *Introduction, in* THE UN CONVENTION ON THE ELIMINATION OF ALL FORMS OF DISCRIMINATION AGAINST WOMEN AND ITS OPTIONAL PROTOCOL 1 (Patricia Schulz et al. eds., 2d ed. 2022) [hereinafter 2022 CEDAW COMMENTARY], sec. F(I) (discussing the human rights origins of the Convention, its connections to UN human rights conferences, and its debts to and continued interactions with other UN human rights treaties); *see also id.* sec. D(V) (discussing the CEDAW Committee's adoption of the respect, protect, fulfill typology for analysis and interpretation originating in the International Covenant on Economic, Social and Cultural Rights (ICESCR)).

[2] *See, e.g.,* Convention on the Elimination of All Forms of Discrimination against Women, Preamble, *opened for signature* Dec. 18, 1979, 1249 U.N.T.S. 13 [hereinafter CEDAW].

organization, operation, maintenance, and disposition of facilities or the making, performing, or enforcing of contracts.[3] IIAs do not suggest that protected foreign investors are owed respect for their property in order to respect their "dignity" or because of their "human rights." As is suggested by the typical preambles of such treaties, IIAs protect the property interests of foreign investors on the assumption that freer trade and capital flows will promote economic development.[4]

The comparison attempted here faces one challenge from the outset: it is difficult to compare the property jurisprudence produced under a single treaty interpreter, namely, the CEDAW Committee, under a single treaty, with that generated under roughly three thousand IIAs now in existence—as interpreted by hundreds of distinct three-person arbitral tribunals, each established to hear one investor-state dispute under one of those treaties, one at a time. Although IIAs generally share common objectives—namely, to protect the private enterprises and, in most cases, the state enterprises of their state parties—they do not adhere to a single harmonious text and they lack (at least for now) a single standing interpretative body.[5] Even when IIAs follow certain model texts drafted by leading IIA signatories, their contents vary depending on the outcome of the particular (often bilateral) treaty negotiation. Although nearly all such treaties require the contracting states to provide both national treatment (NT) and most-favored-nation (MFN) treatment on their intended beneficiaries, namely, foreign investors from each of the state parties, the precise ways such rights to nondiscrimination have been defined differ. Such textual variations may matter a great deal to adjudicators urged, under international law, to accord pride of place to the ordinary meaning of treaty texts.[6]

Moreover, IIAs remain subject to formal amendment, termination, or, where such treaties so provide, subsequent joint interpretations issued by their state parties.[7] Such treaties are also subject to the potentially evolving interpretations

---

[3] *See id. See also* Treaty between United States of America and the Argentine republic Concerning the reciprocal encouragement and protection of investment, U.S.-Arg., Nov. 14, 1991, S. Treaty Doc No. 103-2 (1991) [hereinafter US-Argentina BIT]. Article 1(1)(b) of US-Argentina BIT defines protected companies, and Article 1(e) defines protected "associated activities."

[4] Thus, the preamble to the US-Argentina BIT, *id.*, suggests that its object and purpose is to enable the "fair and equitable treatment of investment . . . in order to maintain a stable framework for investment and maximum effective use of economic resources."

[5] As discussed *infra* at section 5.9, most IIAs permit resort to investor-state dispute settlement (ISDS). The European Union's proposal to replace this arbitral remedy with a single International Investment Court is far from reality, even though such a Tribunal and Appellate Body has now replaced investor-state arbitration in a few IIAs such as the Investment Protection Agreement between the European Union and the Socialist Republic of Viet Nam arts. 3.38–3.39, E.U.-Viet., June 30, 2019, https://investmentpolicy.unctad.org/international-investment-agreements/treaty-files/5868/download.

[6] *See, e.g.*, Vienna Convention on the Law of Treaties art. 31(1), May 23, 1969, 1155 U.N.T.S. 331.

[7] *See, e.g.*, 2012 US Model Bilateral Investment Treaty art. 30.3, https://ustr.gov/sites/default/files/BIT%20text%20for%20ACIEP%20Meeting.pdf [hereinafter US Model BIT of 2012] (indicating that a joint decision of its state parties declaring their interpretation of a provision of the treaty shall be binding on arbitral tribunals established to consider investment disputes under the treaty).

INTRODUCTION 237

of their terms by investor-state arbitrators delegated with that authority. In addition, there is evidence that some IIAs concluded over the past two decades differ in their contents from earlier generations of mostly BITs concluded in the 1990s. The resulting web of IIAs has become denser over time and their contents less harmonious. This complex web of treaties with overlapping or distinct treaty parties now includes both "first generation" compacts with exceptionally strong protections accorded to foreign investors as well as "second" or "third" generation IIAs that generally provide the host states of foreign investors with greater room to exercise their regulatory authority.[8]

For its part, while CEDAW has the benefit of a single text and a single treaty-authorized interpreter, that regime poses its own set of challenges to those attempting to compare its jurisprudence with other regimes. Members of the CEDAW Committee change over time and cannot be expected to share common views on relative priorities—including with respect to the importance of generating harmonious, consistent jurisprudence over time throughout all the Committee's distinct outputs. Given these realities as well as the other distinctions between the two regimes that are surveyed in this chapter, readers may indeed be skeptical that comparisons can be drawn between these "apples" and "oranges."

This chapter attempts to overcome these challenges by generalizing from a few US BITs and the US Model BIT of 2012, and arbitral interpretations based on them and drawing comparisons to the CEDAW jurisprudence set out in chapter 2.[9] While this simplifies the complex web of IIAs in existence, precedents set by the US BIT program have been exceptionally influential on the web of today's IIAs.[10] Indeed, the wording of what is possibly the most significant IIA in existence, the Comprehensive and Progressive Trans-Pacific Partnership (CPTPP)'s investment chapter, seems strikingly similar to texts initiated by the United States.[11] This chapter's comparison of the two regimes is also facilitated

---

[8] *See, e.g.,* UN Conference on Trade and Development, IIA Issues Note: Taking Stock of IIA Reform, UNCTAD/WEB/DIAE/PCB/2016/3 (Mar. 2016).

[9] A more precise picture of how the two regimes compare would require comparing CEDAW's jurisprudence with a particular arbitral ruling issued in the course of interpreting the text of the IIA involved in that case (of the roughly 3,000 now existing) in light of relevant arbitral "caselaw" cited in the course of that ruling.

[10] *See generally* José E. Alvarez, *Introduction: The United States Contribution to International Investment Law, in* INTERNATIONAL INVESTMENT LAW 1 (José E. Alvarez ed., 2017).

[11] This is ironic because the United States under the Trump administration withdrew from further negotiations under that treaty which subsequently came into force for eleven countries, not including the United States. *See* Wolfgang Alschner & Dmitriy Skougarevskiy, *The New Gold Standard: Empirically Situating the Trans-Pacific Partnership in the Investment Treaty Universe,* 17 J. WORLD INV. & TRADE 339 (2016) (textual comparison finding that 82 percent of the text of the original TPP's investment chapter, replicated in the CPTPP, was taken from the US-Columbia FTA's Investment Chapter). *See also* José E. Alvarez, *Is the Trans-Pacific Partnership's Investment Chapter the New "Gold Standard"?,* 47 VICTORIA UNIV. OF WELLINGTON L. REV. 503 (2016).

by standard treatises in investment law that elucidate trends in the underlying investor-state arbitral case law despite the absence of a single harmonious text comparable to, for example, the General Agreement on Tariffs and Trade (GATT) covered agreements. That comparison is also facilitated by this book's selective focus: what we seek to compare here is how the two regimes address the protection of property interests at the international level.

This chapter begins by explaining why the international investment regime has tended to dominate discussions of international law's protection of property. Subsequent sections address the distinct types of "property" accorded protection under each regime, the different obligations imposed on states to enable such protection, and the two regime's approaches to discrimination, territorial scope, sources of authority, permissible derogations, and remedies and enforcement tools. While these sections highlight the differences between the two regimes, there remains potential for overlapping coverage in particular instances. The final section explores how the two regimes might respond to a discrimination claim made by a hypothetical female entrepreneur. As this chapter makes clear, CEDAW's protection of equality is at a considerable remove from efforts under IIAs to protect the transnational flows of capital deemed essential to economic globalization.

5.2 Explaining the Relative Prominence of International Investment Law

Most international lawyers associate the "international law of property" with the international investment regime, consisting of some three thousand international investment agreements, including bilateral investment treaties, and interpretations of these in the course of investor-state dispute settlement (ISDS).[12] That regime, or, more precisely, the "case law" generated under ISDS, tends to dominate the discussion of how international law protects property because of two characteristics: vintage and geographic ambit.

International law has always been engaged in protecting property, particularly the property of aliens from powerful states.[13] Although the German BIT of 1959 is often considered the first investment protection treaty, it was a successor to considerably older treaties that sought to protect distinct forms of property stemming from either trade in goods or capital intended for business investment or

---

[12] *See, e.g.*, José E. Alvarez, *The International Law of Property*, 112 AM. J. INT'L L. 771 (2018).
[13] *See, e.g.*, Martti Koskenniemi, *Rocking the Human Rights Boat: Reflections by a Fellow Passenger*, in THE STRUGGLE FOR HUMAN RIGHTS: ESSAYS IN HONOUR OF PHILIP ALSTON 51, 55 (Nehal Bhuta et al. eds., 2022)).

both.[14] Moreover, today's IIAs were designed to provide a treaty basis (and usually specific treaty remedies such as investor-state arbitration) for guarantees made to foreign investors that, particularly from the perspective of Western international lawyers, had been affirmed under customary international law at least since the early twentieth century. Those customary rights included, most prominently, assurances that foreign investors, once permitted unto a state's territory, were entitled to the "international minimum standard" of treatment. That minimum standard includes assurances that aliens (including individuals or their business enterprises) would not encounter "denials of justice" while residing in other states.[15] As evident in the course of a dispute with Mexico in 1938, the United States has also argued, and many states have since agreed, that alien or foreign investors abroad were also entitled under international customary law to prompt, adequate, and effective compensation should their property be expropriated by their host states.[16] Throughout the twentieth century, leading capital-exporting states have repeatedly claimed that long-standing customary international law, and not merely bilateral arrangements among distinct states, guaranteed foreign investors fair treatment and the right to the full value of their property.[17] This is why many international lawyers have insisted, even before the proliferation of treaties designed to protect alien investors, that there was a distinct subfield within international law, namely, state responsibility to aliens.[18]

International law's centuries-old solicitude for foreign investors' property rights was not predicated on treating such property rights as "international human rights" since that regime did not exist as such before World War II.[19] Property rights

---

[14] *See, e.g.*, Alvarez, *supra* note 10, at 1–14 (discussing the antecedents of IIAs, including the US "Jay" Treaty of 1794 and much later Treaties of Friendship, Commerce and Navigation).

[15] *See, e.g.*, Edwin Borchard, *The Minimum Standard of the Treatment of Aliens*, 33 AM. SOC'Y INT'L L. PROC. 51 (1939).

[16] *See* Exchange of Letters between Cordell Hull and the Mexican Government, Department of State Press Release, No. 354, July 21, 1938, *reprinted in* INTERNATIONAL INVESTMENT LAW, *supra* note 10, at 235. For discussion of the subsequent impact of the "Hull standard" on customary international law, *see, e.g.*, SURYA P. SUBEDI, INTERNATIONAL INVESTMENT LAW RECONCILING POLICY AND PRINCIPLE 16–18 (2008).

[17] For examples of US public reports and speeches by US officials upholding international law principles of state responsibility to uphold the rights of aliens, *see, e.g.*, Alvarez, *supra* note 10, at 150–296; for examples of US treaty practice to the same effect, see *id.* at 299–537. *See also* Ole Thomas Johnson, Jr. & Jonathan Gimblett, *From Gunboats to BITs: The Evolution of Modern International Investment Law*, 2010–2011 Y.B. INT'L INV. L. & POL'Y 649 (2012) (discussing the impact of the United States, the leading capital exporter throughout the twentieth century, on the practice of other capital exporting states).

[18] *But see* Loewen Group, Inc. v. U.S.A., ICSID Case No. ARB(AF)/98/3, Opinion of Sir Robert Jennings (Oct. 26, 1998), 7 ICSID Rep. 421 (2005) (arguing that despite US government claims to the contrary, there has never been any such subbranch of state responsibility).

[19] While there is a rich history of international law being used to protect the rights of some persons, including those subjected to the slave trade and inhuman acts during war, the contemporary field of international human rights is a post-UN Charter phenomenon. *See, e.g.*, Louis Henkin, *The Universality of the Concept of Human Rights*, 506 ANNALS AM. ACAD. POL. & SOC. SCI. 10 (1989) (emphasizing the debt owed to the Universal Declaration of Human Rights of 1948).

became associated with human rights and not only investor rights thanks to the rise of international human rights law after the establishment of the United Nations. Precedents set with respect to the "international minimum standard" and "denial of justice" in venues like the US-Mexican Claims Tribunal were nonetheless important precursors to human rights subsequently incorporated into the Universal Declaration of Human Rights, such as its Articles 2 and 7 (nondiscrimination and equal protection), Article 8 (right to an effective remedy), and Article 17 (right to own property and not be arbitrarily deprived of property).[20]

Another factor that explains the prominence of the international investment regime is its universal scope. As noted, at least some of the regime's protections for alien property purport to arise under generally applicable rules of custom and are merely affirmed by IIAs.[21] Moreover, even those who contest that proposition acknowledge that the regime's treaty-based protections have a wide geographical scope since most states are parties to at least one IIA.[22] The investment regime's prominence is also enhanced by the relative abundance of public investor-state arbitral awards issued under many of those IIAs.

Once states entered into multilateral agreements to support resort to arbitral enforcement of international investment agreements, such as the Convention on the Settlement of Investment Disputes between States and Nationals of Other States (ICSID), investment law came to be characterized by both "judicialization" and "treatification."[23] Starting in the mid-1990s, in the wake of the end of the Cold War, investor-state arbitrations in venues such as ICSID gained in popularity. What began as a slow trickle of mostly nontransparent private awards and discrete investor-state settlements turned into a flood of publicly available arbitral rulings. At present, the number of such awards as well as rulings issued by the European Court of Human Rights (ECtHR) (many of which deal with

---

[20] Universal Declaration of Human Rights, GA Res. 217A (III), Dec. 10, 1948. For antecedents in US practice, see Alvarez, supra note 10, at 60–62; Edwin Brochard, The "Minimum Standard" of the Treatment of Aliens, reprinted in INTERNATIONAL INVESTMENT LAW, supra note 10, at 545.

[21] But see, e.g., MUTHUCUMARASWAMY SORNARAJAH, THE INTERNATIONAL LAW ON FOREIGN INVESTMENT 89 (2d ed. 2021) (contending that there is little genuine customary international law requiring the protection of alien foreign investment and no consensus among states that they must pay compensation when they take alien property in the exercise of their regulatory powers).

[22] JOSÉ E. ALVAREZ, THE PUBLIC INTERNATIONAL LAW REGIME GOVERNING INTERNATIONAL INVESTMENT 29 (2011) (noting that as of 2008, 180 states were parties to at least one BIT).

[23] Convention on the Settlement of Investment Disputes Between States and Nationals of Other States, Mar. 18, 1965, 575 U.N.T.S. 159, reproduced in 4 INT'L LEGAL MATERIALS 532 (1965) [hereinafter ICSID Convention]. For descriptions of the "treatification" and "judicialization" of the investment regime, see ALVAREZ, supra note 22, at 407 & 429–36. For early appraisals of the role of investor-state tribunals in developing international law jurisprudence, see Jeffery P. Commission, An Analysis of a Developing Jurisprudence in International Investment Law—What Investment Treaty Tribunals Are Saying and Doing, 6 TRANSNAT'L DISP. MGMT. 1 (2009). On the "legitimacy crisis" generated by the turn to "privatized" dispute settlement, see, e.g., Susan D. Franck, The Legitimacy Crisis in Investment Treaty Arbitration: Privatizing Public International Law through Inconsistent Decisions, 73 FORDHAM L. REV. 1521 (2005).

property) vastly eclipse the number of binding international rulings issued by any other treaty regime with a global scope, including the numbers of the CEDAW Committee's Views or its Reports on Inquiries.[24]

The rules governing the protection of foreign investors' property have evolved in depth and scope thanks to investor-state arbitrators' treaty interpretations over time. The publication of arbitral rulings has had significant consequences on the development of international investment law. It has become a species of case law. Many of these rulings attempt to provide more predictable guidance to states and investors through the production of "jurisprudence constante."[25] Although ISDS rulings do not formally set precedents, previously issued ISDS arbitral rulings are the most frequently cited source of authority before such tribunals.[26] Innumerable treatises, practitioner manuals, and casebooks intended for law school and law firm use around the world treat that jurisprudence as international investment law.[27] The demanders for all this output include, most prominently, lawyers in private practice highly motivated by the prospect of sharing in the potentially large monetary awards generated under investor-state arbitrations. Such lawyers and their investor-state claimants serve as the investment regime's enforcers or "attorney generals." Practitioners engaged in the niche but lucrative practice of international investment law constitute a significant part of the regime's stakeholders but other stakeholders include those who need to defend themselves from such claims, namely, respondent states and their lawyers—whether in private practice or government ministries. The latter also

---

[24] *See, e.g.*, PLURICOURTS INVESTMENT TREATY ARBITRATION DATABASE (PITAD), https://pitad.org/index#welcome (identifying over 300 public investor-state arbitral awards issued from 1990 through June 2016). The creators of that database estimated that such public awards reflected only 69 percent of all known investor-state rulings at that time. JOSÉ E. ALVAREZ, THE BOUNDARIES OF INVESTMENT ARBITRATION: THE USE OF TRADE AND EUROPEAN HUMAN RIGHTS LAW IN INVESTOR-STATE DISPUTES 2–3 (2018). Binding rulings issued by ECtHR vastly exceed these numbers. According to the International Justice Resource Center, since 1959 the ECtHR has issued more than 10,000 rulings, *see* INTERNATIONAL JUSTICE RESOURCE CENTER, https://ijrcenter.org/european-court-of-human-rights/#:~:text=The%20European%20Court%20of%20Human,European%20Convention%20on%20Human%20Rights (last visited Feb. 8, 2023). By comparison, as of the end of 2021, the CEDAW Committee had completed seven inquiries under the Optional Protocol, Article 8. *See* Schulz et al., *supra* note 1, sec. E(III). The number of adopted Views by the CEDAW Committee is, as noted in chapter 2, somewhat uncertain but according to publicly available data, the Committee had addressed 155 communications as of January 2020 and adopted Views in only 37. *See* chapter 2, section 2.3.2.

[25] For early recognition of a system of *de facto* precedent under ISDS, *see* STEPHAN W. SCHILL, THE MULTILATERALIZATION OF INTERNATIONAL INVESTMENT LAW 321–39 (2009).

[26] *See, e.g.*, Ole K. Fauchald, *The Legal Reasoning of ICSID Tribunals—An Empirical Analysis*, 19 EUR. J. INT'L L. 301 (2008) (documenting that prior ICSID rulings were the most widely used source of authority within ICSID tribunals).

[27] Arbitral case law dominates such materials. *See, e.g.*, DOAK R. BISHOP ET AL., FOREIGN INVESTMENT DISPUTES CASES, MATERIALS AND COMMENTARY (2D ED. 2014); KRISTA N. SCHEFER, INTERNATIONAL INVESTMENT LAW: TEXT, CASES AND MATERIALS (2D ED. 2016). AUGUST REINSICH & CHRISTOPH SCHREUER, INTERNATIONAL PROTECTION OF INVESTMENTS: THE SUBSTANTIVE STANDARDS (2020).

have to keep track of ISDS case law, even when they were not directly involved as litigants in prior cases, given its impact as *de facto* precedent.

Given these developments, with international investment law now one of the leading topics in eminent peer-reviewed publications, no one should be surprised if elite international lawyers in the West see the international investment regime's treatment of property as the principal way international law conceptualizes, protects, and enforces the "international law of property" at the global level. At the regional level, there are considerably more cases dealing with property rights brought under the Article 1 of the First Protocol of the European Convention on Human Rights than under the international investment regime.[28] The sheer number of property rights rulings brought under the two regimes explains why both draw attention as well as comparisons.[29] By contrast, only a subset of human rights scholars and activists pay close attention to how UN human rights treaty bodies protect property interests—with an even smaller group even aware that CEDAW includes property protections.

The combination of treatification and judicialization has given international investment law—and its treatment of property rights—a thick texture rare among international legal regimes. The investment and CEDAW regimes' respective turn to "case law" in response to claims by private parties have not evolved equally. Investor-state arbitrators have had far greater opportunities to opine on IIAs than the CEDAW Committee has had to interpret CEDAW under the communications procedure to which 141 states have consented by ratifying CEDAW's Optional Protocol.[30]

Scholarly comparisons between investment law's treatment of property and CEDAW's are relatively rare because those interested in each regime tend to remain in their respective silos. While in recent years, there has been an increased interest in the potential for overlap between ISDS claims and human rights regimes, much of that literature is a direct response to the complaint that ISDS and/or the underlying IIAs are insufficiently sensitive to states' human rights obligations.[31] Scholarly explorations of the investment/human rights law interface have tended to share a specific normative agenda: to "harmonize" or "defragment" the two regimes either by proposing changes to the content of IIAs or

---

[28] *See, e.g.,* THE POLITICAL ECONOMY OF THE INVESTMENT TREATY REGIME 84–85 (Jonathan Bonnitcha et al. eds., 2016) (indicating that between 1990 and 2015 over 8,800 property disputes were brought before the ECtHR).

[29] *See, e.g.,* URSULA KRIEBAUM, EIGENTUMSSCHUTZ IM VÖLKERRECHT: EINE VERGLEICHENDE UNTERSUCHUNG ZUM INTERNATIONALEN INVESTITIONSRECHT SOWIE ZUM MENSCHENRECHTSSCHUTZ (2008) (Ger.) (comparing the right to property under European human rights law and international investment law).

[30] *See supra* note 24 (number of Communications/Views issued by the Committee).

[31] *See, e.g.,* HUMAN RIGHTS IN INTERNATIONAL INVESTMENT LAW AND ARBITRATION (Pierre-Marie Dupuy et al. eds., 2009) (particularly chapters by Moshe Hirsch, Clara Reiner, and Christoph Schreuer).

proposing new ways to incorporate human rights into ongoing interpretations of such treaties under ISDS.[32] At the same time, even efforts to develop a more "human rights friendly" investment law case law have tended to ignore the potential relevance of the CEDAW Committee's property jurisprudence.[33]

The estrangement between the CEDAW and international investment regimes exists not only among scholars but also as matter of adjudicative practice. The two regimes' respective adjudicators—the CEDAW Committee and investor-state arbitral tribunals—ignore each other. While a number of ISDS rulings cite to the rulings of the regional court with the highest number of publicly available rulings, the ECtHR, these arbitral awards ignore CEDAW.[34] That estrangement is mutual: the CEDAW Committee's property case law surveyed in chapter 2 does not mention ISDS rulings even when these purport to apply principles of customary law presumptively applicable to all states. Further, even when the two regimes appear to be at odds—as when the CEDAW Committee criticizes economic development projects' adverse effects and their impact on Indigenous women's land rights (as under GR 39)—the Committee does not directly address the conflict between states' duties under CEDAW and under IIAs.[35] Although

---

[32] See, e.g., Bruno Simma, Foreign Investment Arbitration: A Place for Human Rights?, 60 INT'L & COMP. L.Q. 573 (2011); Pierre-Marie Dupuy, Unification Rather than Fragmentation of International Law? The Case of International Investment Law and Human Rights Law, in HUMAN RIGHTS IN INTERNATIONAL INVESTMENT LAW AND ARBITRATION, supra note 31, at 45. Such proposals are often part of broader reform agendas for the investment regime. See, e.g., SECOND THOUGHTS INVESTOR-STATE ARBITRATION BETWEEN DEVELOPED DEMOCRACIES (Armand de Mestral ed., 2017); THE BACKLASH AGAINST INVESTMENT ARBITRATION: PERCEPTIONS AND REALITY (Michael Waibel et al. eds., 2010); José E. Alvarez, ISDS Reform: The Long View, 36 ICSID REV. FOREIGN INV. L.J. 1 (2021).

[33] See, e.g., Rep. of the Independent Expert on the effects of Foreign Debt and other Related International Financial Obligations of States on the Full Enjoyment of All Human Rights, Particularly Economic, Social and Cultural Rights, ¶¶ 20–55, UN Doc. A/72/153 (July 17, 2017). For a proposal to bridge the interpretative divide between IIAs and states' obligations under the ICESCR, see Bruno Simma & Diane A. Desierto, Bridging the Public Interest Divide: Committee Assistance for Investor-Host State Compliance with the ICESCR, 10 TRANSNAT'L DISP. MGMT. 1 (2013). For an exceptional (if cursory) mention of CEDAW's property jurisprudence in the course of discussing the general international law of property, see JOHN G. SPRANKLING, THE INTERNATIONAL LAW OF PROPERTY 207–09 (2014). Sparkling comments that the CEDAW regime does not "expressly recognize[s] the right to property" and categorizes it, along with CERD, as designed "to protect vulnerable groups against discrimination in the exercise of rights that already exist within a particular state, not to impose new rights that the state does not recognize." Id. at 208.

[34] See, e.g., ALVAREZ, supra note 24, at 2, 48, app. I & tbl. I (identifying 65 cases within the PluriCourt Investment Treaty Database with a reference to European human rights law, of which 53 have more than a passing reference). This study reveals that some 20 percent of public ISDS rulings issued between 1990 and June 2016 contained references to the European Convention of Human Rights or to the case law of the European Court of Human Rights. References to the considerably less abundant "caselaw" generated under other human rights regimes were minimal.

[35] The Inter-American Court of Human Rights, by contrast, has suggested that the American Convention of Human Rights "stands in a class of its own," "generates rights for individual human beings and does not depend entirely on reciprocity among States," and therefore needs to prevail over bilateral investment treaties. Sawhoyamaxa Indigenous Cmty. v. Paraguay, Reparations and Costs, Judgment, Inter-Am. Ct. H.R. (ser. C) No. 146, ¶ 140 (Mar. 29, 2006).

both regimes address international law's treatment of property and the challenge of discrimination, the two operate as if they existed in separate universes.[36]

5.3 Two Approaches to Defining Protected Property

Both the CEDAW and the investment regimes are reticent about embracing the term "property" or "property rights."

IIAs typically address the protection of "investors," "investments," and sometimes activities "associated" with an investment.[37] The term "property" tends to be explicitly identified as only one form of protected interest under these terms, but alien investors' right to acquire or dispose of property is certainly included.[38] There are also considerable disputes about whether the property interests protected under IIAs need to satisfy distinct requirements colloquially associated with undertaking an "investment"—such as committing capital or other resources, doing either with the expectation of gain or profit, or by assuming some risk.[39] Some arbitral decisions have suggested that either particular IIAs' reference to "investment" or the term "investment" under the ICSID Convention implicitly requires proof of all or some of these characteristics, while others have suggested that no such requirements need to be shown for an activity to qualify as an investment.[40] Some second- or third-generation IIAs have resolved such questions by expressly defining protected investment to require the satisfaction of some or all of those characteristics.[41]

---

[36] While the two regimes ignore each other, this is not because each regime is 'self-contained'. Both regimes, after all, apply international law. Further, as illustrated by chapter 6, the CEDAW Committee's property jurisprudence overlaps with the work of other UN human rights treaty bodies. Similarly, litigants before investor-state tribunals, investor-state arbitrators, and investment law commentators often refer to the law under the WTO and, as noted at the prior note, to the case law of the ECtHR. This is consistent with the observation that no genuinely "self-contained" regimes exist under international law. See Bruno Simma, Self-Contained Regimes, 16 NETHERLANDS Y.B. INT'L L.111 (1985).

[37] See, e.g., US-Argentina BIT, supra note 3, art. I (extending its protections to "investment," companies incorporated in or natural persons of the state parties, and "associated activities"); US Model BIT of 2012, supra note 7, art. 1 (protecting "investment" and "investors of a Party").

[38] See, e.g., US-Argentina BIT, supra note 3, art. I (1)(a) (defining "investment" as including "tangible and intangible property, including rights, such as mortgages, liens and pledges"); id. art. I (1) (e) (defining "associated activities" as including "the acquisition, use, protection and disposition of property of all kinds including intellectual and industrial property rights").

[39] As this indicates, not every proprietary interest may be deemed "protected investment" or "associated activities," but the inverse seems to be true. All investments and associated activities are protected forms of property or in the terms of many IIAs' "assets."

[40] See, e.g., SCHEFER, supra note 27, at 69–112.

[41] See, e.g., US Model BIT of 2012, supra note 7, art. 1 (defining "investment" as "every asset that an investor owns or controls, directly or indirectly, that has the characteristics of investment, including such characteristics as the commitment of capital or other resources, the expectation of gain or profit, or the assumption of risk").

CEDAW explicitly mentions the term "property" only twice in its text. Its Article 15(2) indicates that states must accord equal rights to women to administer property, while Article 16(1)(h) requires states to extend equal rights to "both spouses in respect of the ownership, acquisition, management, administration, enjoyment and disposition of property." Like IIAs, CEDAW does not contain a general definition of what "property" interests are included in states' obligations. In lieu of that or additional references to property, this book includes in its chapter 2 distinct forms of economic interests that many (but not all) would consider to be proprietary interests. This includes rights to social security (Article 11(1)(e)); social benefits (Article 11(2)(b)); family benefits (Article 13(a)); bank loans, mortgages, and other forms of financial credit (Article 13(b)); agricultural credit or loans (Article 14(2)(g)); intellectual property (as under Article 14(2)(g) ("appropriate technology"); adequate housing (Article 14(2)(h)); and the right to conclude contracts involving property (Article 15(2)). Unlike the typical IIA, CEDAW does not explicitly indicate that states must enable women to own tangible assets such as a family home, buildings associated with running a business, or land or less tangible assets or financial interests, including intellectual property. *By its terms*, CEDAW only protects women's nondiscriminatory access to or enjoyment of its enumerated property interests.[42]

And yet both regimes are, in reality, quite expansive in terms of the kind of property or financial interests they protect. Protected investment under early US BITs defined it in the broadest possible terms. The US-Argentina BIT, for example, defines investment in a circular fashion, to extend to "any kind of investment," including tangible and intangible property (including liens and mortgages), shares of stock, any claim to money or for performance having economic value, all forms of intellectual property, and any "right conferred by law or contract, and any licenses and permits pursuant to law."[43] Although, as noted previously, the US Model BIT of 2012 expressly includes some specific characteristics of what protected investment means, and indicates that this involves an "asset," its definition of protected investment is also circular. Investment in that treaty is defined as every asset that has the characteristic of an investment. That US Model BIT goes on to include the same broad list of tangible and intangible forms of financial interest contained in early US BITs but is more cautious about extending protection to short-term debts resulting from the sale of goods or services or based on interests, such as licenses or permits, that do not create rights under domestic law.[44]

---

[42] *See, e.g.*, CEDAW, *supra* note 2, art. 13(a) (affirming rights to family benefits "on the basis of equality of men and women"); *id.* art. 14(2)(h) (affirming women's rights to "enjoy" adequate living conditions "particularly in relation to housing").
[43] US-Argentina BIT, *supra* note 3, art. I (1).
[44] US Model BIT of 2012, *supra* note 7, art. 1 and accompanying notes 1 and 2.

The expansive nature of CEDAW's protection of property is demonstrated, as discussed later, by its capacious embrace of the right to equality and definition of nondiscrimination. It is also illustrated by that treaty's embrace of women's "equality with men before the law" under Article 15.[45] That right to "legal capacity identical to that of men" and to the "same opportunities to exercise that capacity" specifically includes a duty on states to provide equal rights "to conclude contracts and administer property."[46] These obligations coincide to some extent with assurances in IIAs that protect activities "associated" with investments (including the making and enforcing of contracts), as well as guarantees that foreign investors are entitled to the "minimum standard of treatment" under customary international law.[47] But CEDAW's equal treatment obligation on states applies to all rights included under that Convention, and not only the commercial or financial interests of aliens. CEDAW's Article 15 does not limit states' equal access to justice obligation to property owned by investors or to the handling of interests "associated" with doing business as under IIAs.

The two regimes recognize that respect for property ordinarily includes protecting a bundle of "sticks," that is, particular entitlements. That bundle of rights is expressly incorporated into IIAs by, for example, including them in the definition of protected associated activities. Protected "associated activities" under the US-Argentina BIT include the "organization, control, operation, maintenance and disposition of companies, the conduct of business, the making, performance and enforcement of contracts; the acquisition, use, protection and disposition of property of all kinds, including intellectual and industrial property rights; and the borrowing of funds, the purchase, issuance, and sale of equity shares and other securities, and the purchase of foreign exchange for imports."[48] While this is a more fulsome list of property's "sticks" than anything that can be found in the text of CEDAW, that treaty's Article 16(1(h)), requiring equal treatment with respect to property in marriage and family relations, extends to "the ownership, acquisition, management, administration, enjoyment and disposition of property . . . ." While that is the only mention of this bundle of property entitlements in CEDAW, the CEDAW Committee has given no indication that those identified entitlements apply in principle only with respect to property relating to marriage and family relations.[49]

---

[45] *See generally* GR No. 33 on Women's Access to Justice, CEDAW/C/GC/33 (2015).
[46] *Id.* ¶ 44. *See also* CEDAW, *supra* note 2, art. 15(3).
[47] *See supra* notes 43 and 47.
[48] US-Argentina BIT, *supra* note 3, art. I (1)(e).
[49] Notably, Article 15(2) of CEDAW also mentions the right to "administer" property. Further, the Committee has suggested that the enjoyment of property rights in general are crucial to women's financial independence. GR No. 21 on Equality in Marriage and Family Relations, A/49/38, ¶ 26 (1994).

5.4 Distinct State Obligations Other Than the Duty Not to Discriminate

Unlike CEDAW's core focus on eliminating all forms of discrimination against women, IIAs protect property owners—namely, foreign investors—by according them many rights, such as a guarantee of "fair and equitable treatment" (FET), that do not require proof of discrimination.[50] IIAs typically include a number of property protections that are not based on a relative comparison with how someone else has been treated. International investment lawyers and scholars use the term "absolute" to describe such rights in contradistinction from "relative" rights grounded in discrimination. Apart from FET, the absolute guarantees typically found in IIAs include state obligations to accord "full protection and security" (FPS), assurances to permit alien investors to transfer funds in and out of the host state associated with doing business, and promises to fully compensate alien investors for takings of their property.[51] The precise content of such rights varies depending on the text of the particular IIA and subsequent arbitral interpretations of such texts. A prominent investor-state ruling finding that a common FET clause accords investors protection against any form of interference or harassment, and not merely rights derived from customary international law, for example, has had a considerable impact on later interpretations of the meaning of such clauses—despite considerable scholarly criticism that such an interpretation imposes a highly idealized demand for "good governance" that few governments can satisfy.[52]

Broad readings of the FET right—such as those that entail the protection of the "legitimate expectations" of foreign investors—have been criticized for not according sufficient deference to the sovereign prerogatives of FDI host states to regulate in the public interest.[53] The FET guarantee, which has proven to be the most successful on behalf of investor claimants, is not the only such clause that has been so criticized as undermining the right of states to regulate in the public interest. The US-Argentina BIT, like many BITs of the 1990s, requires

---

[50] *See, e.g.*, RUDOLF DOLZER ET AL., PRINCIPLES OF INTERNATIONAL INVESTMENT LAW 186–230 (3d ed. 2022) (addressing FET).

[51] *See, e.g.*, DOLZER ET AL., *supra* note 50, at 230–38 (FPS), 146–85 (expropriation), 290–95 (transfer of funds).

[52] A tribunal under the NAFTA asserted that FET requires "the host state to act in a consistent manner, free from ambiguity and totally transparently...." *See* Técnicas Medioambientales Tecmed, S.A. v. The United Mexican States, ICSID Case No. ARB (AF)/00/2, Award, ¶ 154 (May 29, 2003), 10 ICSID Rep. 130 (2006). While that ruling has been widely relied upon in other ISDS awards, other tribunals have interpreted some FET clauses to extend only the "minimum standard of treatment" due aliens under customary international law, suggesting that foreign investors are only protected from denials of justice within host states' courts. *See, e.g.*, DOLZER ET AL., *supra* note 50, 195–205.

[53] *See, e.g.*, JONATHAN BONNITCHA ET AL., THE POLITICAL ECONOMY OF THE INVESTMENT TREATY REGIME 238–44 (2017) (discussing the problem of "regulatory chill.")

states to avoid "arbitrary," and not only "discriminatory," measures that may impair the ample bundle of entitlements "associated" with investments.[54] That treaty, like many IIAs, also requires states to respect any obligations it may have entered into with regard to investments; provide effective means of asserting claims and enforcing rights; and make public all laws, regulations, administrative practices and procedures, and adjudicatory decisions that pertain to or affect investments.[55] These obligations can also be premised on oral assurances provided by a state's representative and need not be based on express undertakings made by a host state under a written contract.

These cumulative obligations on states can transform breaches of contract, failure to provide access to domestic remedies, or shortcomings in transparency into breaches of an investment treaty—and not merely breaches of national law. When so transformed, such actions by a host state can trigger investment treaties' formidable remedies: including investor-state arbitration. Such treaty rights combined with automatic access to arbitral remedies, critics say, result in unrealistic demands for "perfect justice" and are one reason why the investment regime has generated "sovereign backlash."[56]

IIAs' typical guarantee that investments shall not be subject to expropriation or nationalization by the host state absent payment of prompt, adequate, and effective compensation is singularly expansive, at least in the first-generation of BITs, which do not limit the concept of indirect expropriation.[57] That guarantee usually applies to both indirect and direct forms of expropriation, including to a series of government actions or inactions that culminate in *de facto* takings of property or, in the language of the US-Argentina BIT, are "tantamount" to an expropriation.[58] The assurance of compensation in cases of expropriation, like the other "absolute" guarantees noted earlier, does not require a showing of discrimination and is not dependent on a state actually taking title to the expropriated property.[59] In most IIAs, the duty to provide compensation (which may be explicitly required to be "prompt, adequate and effective") is subject to no explicit treaty exception.[60]

---

[54] US-Argentina BIT, *supra* note 3, art. II (2)(b).
[55] *Id.* arts. II (2)(c), II (6), & II (7).
[56] *See generally* THE BACKLASH AGAINST INVESTMENT ARBITRATION: PERCEPTIONS AND REALITY (Michael Waibel et al. eds., 2010).
[57] *See, e.g.*, US-Argentina BIT, *supra* note 3, art. IV; US Model BIT of 2012, *supra* note 7, art. 6.
[58] *See, e.g.*, DOLZER ET AL., *supra note* 50, at 146–85; US-Argentina BIT, *supra* note 3, art. IV (1).
[59] *See, e.g.*, SCHEFER, *supra* note 27, at 190–317.
[60] In the early 2000s, when some 2,000 IIAs were in force, only nine out of ten such treaties contained treaty exceptions (otherwise known as "measures not precluded" clauses). William Burke-White & Andreas von Staden, *Investment Protection in Extraordinary Times: The Interpretation and Application of Non-Precluded Measures provision in Bilateral Investment Treaties*, 48 VA. J. INT'L L. 307, 313 (2008). Whether investment treaties with or without "measures not precluded" exceptions permit host states to invoke the residual exceptions to state responsibility under customary international law (such as those arising from distress or necessity) remains a contentious issue that may turn

5.5 Distinct Approaches to Discrimination

Both CEDAW and IIAs require state parties to prohibit discriminatory treatment. Both impose asymmetrical obligations in this respect. As previously noted, the asymmetry in CEDAW arises because it targets discrimination "against women"—and not, for example, any discrimination on the basis of sex (which would license scrutiny of any state actions that discriminate against men). The asymmetry in IIAs arises because they only require their state parties not to discriminate against foreign investors from other treaty parties. The BIT between the United States and Argentina only requires, for example, that the US government not discriminate against Argentine investors in the United States and that Argentina do the same with respect to US investors in its territory. That treaty does not purport to control, for example, whether Argentina discriminates against other countries' investors or whether Argentina discriminates against all or some of its own national entrepreneurs in favor of US investors. Indeed, since the typical IIA grants only foreign investors the right to proceed directly to international arbitration without exhausting local remedies, at least in that respect such treaties accord foreign investors better treatment than a state's own citizens.

International investment law's insistence that foreign investors get the benefit of national and MFN treatment is otherwise limited in scope. These particular obligations on states only police state laws and practices that inflict differential treatment on the basis of nationality and not other characteristics (such as sex).[61] While some IIAs include, in addition to requirements for national and MFN treatment, additional assurances that foreign investors will also be protected from "discriminatory" or "arbitrary" treatment, the claims that have arisen under such clauses usually involve assertions that a host state has harmed protected aliens of the other state party without providing a rational reason for doing so.[62]

In the typical case involving an allegation of denial of national or MFN treatment, the state actor need not be shown to have acted on the basis of a clear intent to discriminate; discriminatory effect or impact is sufficient.[63] But such

---

on the express wording of the investment treaty at issue. *See, e.g.,* ALVAREZ, *supra* note 22, at 272–78 (discussing arbitral rulings on both sides of that question).

[61] DOLZER ET AL., *supra* note 50, at 252–70 (discussing national and MFN treatment).

[62] *See id.* at 249–61. *See, e.g.,* US-Argentina BIT, *supra* note 3, art. II (1). But note that a BIT that ensures, beyond national or most-favored-nation treatment, that host states not "discriminate" or avoid "arbitrary" treatment could enable a foreign investor to claim that they have been discriminated on some other basis, including on the basis of sex or race. For an example, see *infra* at note 138.

[63] While many IIAs fail to indicate whether a showing of discriminatory effect suffices, the trend among ISDS tribunals is not to require a showing of express intent. *See, e.g.,* DOLZER ET AL., *supra* note 50, at 261. While under first generation BITs, it was also not clear that a foreign investor needed to prove that it suffered real financial harm in filing a claim under ISDS, at least some later IIAs require such proof. *See, e.g.,* US Model BIT of 2012, *supra* note 7, art. 24(1)(a)(ii). This clarification

violations usually require comparing the treatment received by the investor claimant to another investor from either the host state or another third-party nation that secures "more favorable treatment in like circumstances." What constitutes "in like circumstances" varies with the facts and permits a considerable amount of arbitral discretion. ISDS rulings differ on whether, for example, like circumstances require that the foreign investor and the comparator engage in the same kind of business activity or economic sector or whether it is sufficient that both engage in commercial activity.[64] Respondent states charged with violating national or MFN can defend themselves by showing that the two businesses being compared are not, in fact, "in like circumstances,"[65] or that any differential treatment was justified.[66]

By comparison, CEDAW anticipates far more comprehensive protection against discrimination, including in the context of property rights, for both individual women and groups of women. CEDAW's Article 1 empowers the Committee to redress "any distinction, exclusion or restriction made on the basis of sex" *with the effect* or purpose of impairing the recognition, enjoyment or exercise of the property rights contained in Articles 11 and 13–16. Under this broad delegation of authority, the Committee has no need to find evidence of discriminatory intent, concrete financial injury, or a direct relevant male comparator who receives "better" treatment in like circumstances.[67] This broad inquiry means, as is demonstrated by numerous examples in chapter 2, that the CEDAW Committee can redress any form of intersectional discrimination. The focus on discriminatory effect (whether or not financial in nature), in conjunction with Article 1's recognition that discrimination against women can result from violations of other "human rights and fundamental freedoms in the political, economic, social, cultural, civil or any other field," enables the CEDAW Committee to ground violations of the right to be free from direct or indirect forms of discrimination in any number of human rights violations. Most of those rights and fundamental freedoms are not encompassed by IIAs' specific enumeration of "relative" or "absolute" investor rights. For example, a state's failure to

---

underscores a critical goal of ISDS: it seeks to restore any foreign investor harmed by actions in violation of the IIA to its financial posture *ex ante*.

[64] *See, e.g.*, DOLZER ET AL., *supra* note 50, at 254–55.
[65] *Id.* at 254–56.
[66] Such a justification may also be justified if permitted under the IIA's derogation clauses. *See* discussion *infra* at section 5.8.
[67] *See* Andrew Byrnes & Puja Kopai, *Article 1, in* 2022 COMMENTARY, *supra* note 1, at 83–84 (discussing how the CEDAW Committee's interpretation of "substantive equality" goes beyond formal equality and "is not constrained to the same extent to find comparators in order to demonstrate unequal treatment"). The pregnant or nursing Roma women in the Macedonia cases, *see* chapter 2, section 2.7.2.1, for example, did not need to find a male comparator to demonstrate a violation of substantive equality.

respect women's rights to participate in political processes can violate CEDAW Articles 1, 3, or 7, and, depending on the impact of that failure, can expose the state to a violation of the chapeau clause to Article 14 and therefore to an alleged breach of the state's duty to accord women equal treatment with respect to agricultural credit and loans under Article 14(2)(g). IIAs, by comparison, do not extend rights to political participation or most of the rights included in the international bill of rights to foreign investors.

While formally both CEDAW and IIAs typically require states to refrain from both direct and indirect forms of discriminatory action and both cover *de jure* as well as *de facto* acts or omissions that discriminate, CEDAW's Articles 1–3, 5, and 24 license broad inquiries into state policies in both the public and private spheres. CEDAW is also charged with looking into shortcomings in substantive equality for women generally and not only for individual communicants under its Optional Protocol. While ISDS cases involving allegations of discrimination typically focus on whether a single alien investor (or, in rare cases, a class of foreign investors with identical claims) has been denied national or MFN treatment, the CEDAW Committee's General Recommendations (GRs), Views, Concluding Observations (COs), and Reports on Inquiries may demand that states address the underlying structural bases ("root causes") for discrimination for women as a group. Consistent with Article 5, the Committee may demand that states modify the underlying patriarchal assumptions and economic, social, and cultural patterns of conduct that underlie women's subordinate status, even if this occurs within the family.[68] The Committee may require the state to intrude on discriminatory actions by private parties, including (controversially) Indigenous or religious group practices that discriminate against women's property rights.[69]

The "full development and advancement of women," anticipated by Article 3, is a "freestanding legal objective" that also considerably broadens, relative to IIAs, the range of state practices that can amount to discrimination whether with respect to individual women or women as part of certain groups (such as rural women). This overarching goal enables the CEDAW Committee to criticize, for example, gender-neutral "head of household" laws that, given economic and cultural realities, do not treat permit women to have equal access to the family property in fact.

CEDAW's embrace of equality in substantive terms has also entailed a shift "from the negative concept of non-discrimination to the positive obligation of

---

[68] *See* Alexandra Timmer & Rikki Holtmaat, *Article 5*, *in* 2022 COMMENTARY, *supra* note 1, at 242–44.

[69] CEDAW, *supra* note 2, art. 2(e). As the 2022 COMMENTARY indicates, this enables scrutiny of not only the vertical relationship between the state and individual investors (as under IIAs), but the horizontal relationships among individuals as developed through the Committee's application of the concept of due diligence. *See* Schulz et al., *supra* note 1, at 15.

equality."[70] Under, for example, CEDAW Article 3, states are obligated to take proactive measures to advance women's equality and not merely abstain from taking discriminatory actions. Such proactive actions include, under Article 5, measures to modify "social and cultural patterns of conduct" that impair women's property rights even if this occurs within the family, such as stereotypes that lead to denying women rights to marital property after the death of the spouse. A state's failure to take appropriate measures to rectify these stereotypes would also fall within the concept of discrimination under CEDAW. IIAs, by comparison, do not demand that hosts of foreign investors change their views of certain foreign businesses, however stereotypical.

5.6 Distinct Territorial and Jurisdictional Scope

IIAs typically only apply to the respective territories of its treaty parties.[71] They impose duties only on those state parties and only with respect to their own actions or inactions that have adverse effects on foreign investors from the other treaty party located in their territory.[72] They generally do not impose extraterritorial obligations on their state parties, and they do not require state parties to change the behavior of private parties even when these are within their territory. They do not, for example, compel corporations headquartered in the territory of state parties not to discriminate against anyone, and they certainly do not tell states that they must ban such practices when their national companies do business in third states.

By comparison, CEDAW's obligation to ensure nondiscrimination is not subject to clear territorial limits and extends to private parties acting extraterritorially.[73] This includes the duty imposed on CEDAW state parties

---

[70] Christine Chinkin & Beate Rudolf, *Preamble, in* 2022 COMMENTARY, *supra* note 1, at 69 n. 38 (drawing from the wording of the preamble's Paragraph 3 which reflects the language of Article 3 of the International Covenant on Civil and Political Rights and the ICESCR). The preamble, along with other CEDAW provisions, invites the use of those human rights instruments to interpret the Convention. *See id.* n. 39 (noting that GR No. 19 on Violence against women, CEDAW/C/GC/35, ¶ 7 (1992), identifies rights that not included directly in CEDAW but are included in those two Covenants).

[71] *See, e.g.*, US-Argentina BIT, *supra* note 3, art. I (1)(f) (definition of territory).

[72] But note that the US-Argentina BIT, like many contemporary treaties concluded by the United States in the 1990s, also includes rights to equal treatment to *prospective* investors from the other treaty party. *See id.* art. II (1) (right to establish an investment). Most investment treaties extend their protections only to foreign investors once these have been admitted into the host state.

[73] *See, e.g.*, GR No. 35 on Gender-based Violence Against Women, Updating GR No. 19, CEDAW/C/GC/35, ¶ 20 (2017) (recognizing that states need to prevent gender-based violence including through the "extraterritorial operations of private corporations"); CEDAW/C/NOR/CO/9, Nov. 22, 2017, ¶ 14 (expressing concern over Norway's extraterritorial oil extractive activities in the Arctic given the impact of climate change and its disproportionate impact on women, especially those in poverty).

under Paragraph 9 of CEDAW's GR No. 28, namely, to "take steps directly aimed at eliminating customary and all other practices that prejudice and perpetuate the notion of inferiority or superiority of either of the sexes."[74] CEDAW's extraterritorial effects are also the product of the treaty's incorporation, by reference, of states' duties not to discriminate with respect to the rights contained in the IESCR—a treaty which is presumed to impose extraterritorial obligations on states.[75] CEDAW's definition of barred discrimination clearly extends beyond state actors to include "any person, organization or enterprise."[76] The Committee has accordingly interpreted the Convention to impose a duty on state parties to bar the discriminatory conduct of private actors that are within their jurisdiction, even when these act outside that state's territory. A state violates its due diligence obligations under the Convention if it does not ensure that its companies abroad are no less compliant with the Convention as those inside its territory.[77]

5.7 Distinct Sources of Authority

To date, the two regimes rely on distinct sources of legal authority to justify their respective outputs. A lawyer engaged in investor-state dispute settlement needs to become expert in hundreds of ISDS rulings which, as noted, are the leading source of authority cited by investor-state arbitrators. Those filing communications before the CEDAW Committee and those interacting with the CEDAW Committee as part of the state reporting process or in the hopes of influencing the drafting of a GR have, on the contrary, fewer direct CEDAW outputs on which to draw.

Lawyers interacting with each regime face distinct challenges. International investment lawyers face the challenge of uncovering a consistent line of authority among disparate treaties and a welter of arbitral awards, even if their clients were not involved in those prior cases. Those engaged with the CEDAW regime may need to overcome the absence of a directly relevant CEDAW output—given the relatively few GRs or other Committee work products available on point. They may need to resort to other lines of authority—including that established by the output of other UN human rights treaty bodies, regional human rights courts,

---

[74] GR No. 28 on the Core Obligations of States Parties under Article 2 of CEDAW, CEDAW/C/GC/28, ¶ 9 (2010).

[75] For the far-reaching implications of this, *see, e.g.*, Olivier de Schutter et. al., *Commentary to the Maastricht Principles on Extraterritorial Obligations of States in the Area of Economic, Social and Cultural Rights*, 34 Hum. Rts. Q. 1084 (2012).

[76] CEDAW, *supra* note 2, art. 2(a)–(e).

[77] *See, e.g.*, chapter 2, section 2.11.4.2, at text and notes 950 and 951 (describing Concluding Observations affirming that CEDAW imposes extraterritorial duties on states—namely to ensure that states' corporations act in accordance with CEDAW even when acting abroad).

UN Special Rapporteurs, as well as UN reports arising from UN conferences. In the future, as more national courts incorporate or make reference to CEDAW's jurisprudence, this may include citations to national judicial decisions or local laws relating to women's rights. While none of these are authoritative, they may be cited as persuasive authority.

There are significant substantive gaps in the CEDAW Committee's property jurisprudence addressed in this book. The CEDAW Committee has, as noted, adopted relatively few Views in general as compared to the wealth of publicly available investor-state arbitral awards and, as appendix 5 indicates, even fewer Views responding to Communications raising property rights. In theory, the Committee's GRs and COs could fill those gaps. But it is not clear how much the CEDAW Committee has prioritized the need to generate the kind of harmonious jurisprudence across all its outputs that would compare to the "jurisprudence constante" that motivates a number of investor-state arbitrators. While some investor-state arbiters have opined that they are under a duty not to depart, without sufficient reason, from prior well-reasoned awards issued by their predecessors, no comparable statement has emerged from the CEDAW Committee.[78]

While GRs—a tool not available to investor-state arbitrators—are the perfect mechanism for harmonizing the expectations of those who interact with the CEDAW Committee, the Committee's use of GRs for the purpose of generating reliable harmonious jurisprudence has been uneven and varies among the rights that the Committee addresses. The Committee has not indicated, in its GRs, one way or the other whether there ought to be a normative hierarchy among the Convention's articles. Such hierarchies exist in other human rights treaties, and some have been developed in the course of interpretation by their adjudicators.[79] Nor has the Committee used GRs to articulate a set of

---

[78] *See, e.g.*, Bayindir Insaat Turizm Ticaret Ve Sanayi A.S. v. Islamic Republic of Pak., ICSID Case No. ARB/03/29, Award, ¶ 145 (Aug. 27, 2009), 20 ICSID Rep. 99 (2020) (noting that ICSID tribunals should pay "due regard" to earlier ICSID decisions and stating further that "unless there are compelling reasons to the contrary, it ought to follow solutions established in a series of consistent cases ... By doing so, it will meet its duty to seek to contribute to the harmonious development of investment law and thereby to meet the legitimate expectations of the community of States and investors towards certainty of the rule of law."); Saba Fakes v. Republic of Turk., ICSID Case No. ARB/07/20, Award, ¶ 96 (July 14, 2010), 19 ICSID Rep. 279 (2021). The Committee's failure to endorse a comparable approach may be due in part to the absence of consensus among international lawyers as to whether all international adjudicator-interpreters, including those serving on human rights committees, have a duty to produce harmonious "*jurisprudence constante*." Compare Institut De Droit International, 2nd Commission, Precedents and Case Law (Jurisprudence) in Interstate Litigation and Advisory Proceedings, Resolution, Sept. 1, 2023, https://www.idi-iil.org/app/uploads/2023/09/2023_angers_02_en.pdf (indicating that the generation of *jurisprudence constante* in the course of interstate adjudication promotes consistency and predictability but indicating (at ¶ 7) that this may have "possible application" to other forms of international proceedings).

[79] The most well-known examples of a treaty whose text elevates the importance of some rights over others is, of course, the non-derogable rights in the ICCPR's Article 4. For an example of an

harmonizing interpretations or even processes for addressing them that would resolve gaps, ambiguities, or inconsistencies among the Committee's Views, Reports on Inquiries, or COs over time. The Committee has not issued a timetable for issuing GRs on particular topics, explained how the topics on which GRs have been issued were sequenced, or attempted to assign relative values to GRs that it has issued in the past. Outsiders have been left to speculate why particular topics have been selected for the kind of deep analysis that can only be undertaken by the Committee through the issuance of a GR. Some CEDAW insiders consulted in the course of writing this book suggest that GRs respond to injustices that have appeared in state reports or individual communications or emerge because the topic is of particular interest to an influential NGO active before the Committee, or because an individual Committee member has taken an interest and is willing to undertake the formidable task of being the lead rapporteur for a new GR. Some of these CEDAW insiders suggest that the Committee's relative lack of interest in generating harmonious law may be partly due to the Committee's mixed composition: as has long been evident from its composition over time the Committee—unlike other human rights treaty bodies like the Human Rights Committee—has not been composed largely of lawyers.

There may be other reasons for the relative lack of "jurisprudence constante" within the CEDAW regime. The breadth and depth of CEDAW's mandate to consider, case by case, all forms of formal and substantive discrimination, including forms of intersectional discrimination against particular groups of women, encourages Views and COs that are situated in and respond to particular factual contexts.[80] This renders extrapolations from one case with distinct facts to another more difficult than for regimes like investment (or trade) which demand, more simply, formally identical treatment for businesses "in like

---

adjudicative innovation along the same lines, see the line of rulings by the Inter-American Court of Human Rights dealing with cases of "special gravity." José E. Alvarez, *The Human Right of Property*, 72 U. MIAMI L. REV. 580, 630–33 (2018). Establishing priorities among rights within the CEDAW may be relevant to Committee determinations of what constitutes a wrongful reservation that violates the treaty's "object and purpose." They may also be relevant to determining whether a "grave or systematic" violation has occurred for purposes of initiating an inquiry under the Optional Protocol's Article 8. At a more pragmatic level, the Committee may also wish to assign priorities in responding to state reports given its time constraints. A system where the Committee proceeds in order through the Convention's articles and has less time to address, for example, serious violations of Article 16 rights, may not appeal to everyone.

[80] *See, e.g.*, CO on Canada, CEDAW/C/CAN/CO/7, ¶¶ 19–20 (2008) (dealing with discrimination on the matrimonial property rights of aboriginal women living on reserves); CO on Antigua and Barbuda, ¶ 40 (denials of access to financial resources for unmarried women without property); CO on Switzerland, CEDAW/C/CHE/CO/4–5, ¶ 44 (2016) (discriminatory customary laws and practices and family law provisions that discriminate against the inheritance rights of widows); CO on Luxembourg, CEDAW/C/LUX/CO/6–7, ¶¶ 51–52 (2018) (disadvantages faced by same-sex couples on the distribution of property upon dissolution of their unions); CO on Kenya, CEDAW/C/KEN/CO/8, ¶¶ 50–51 (2017) (law that renders a widow's inheritance rights void if she remarries).

circumstances."[81] There is nothing really comparable to intersectionality analysis in investment arbitration.

5.8 Distinct Approaches to Derogation

The regimes also differ in how they approach limits on property rights relative to the rights (or duties) of states as regulators. CEDAW has no single "derogation" clause. Its clause reserving the rights of states to accord greater equality rights between men and women (Article 23), is not such a provision. While it permits states to deviate from the precise terms of CEDAW it only does so to the extent the states' actions are designed to further the treaty's goal of substantive equality, not undermine it. The same can be said with respect to Article 4, permitting states to enact temporary measures that favor women over men for the sake of achieving the Convention's goal of ensuring, consistent with Article 3, the "full development and advancement of women." That Convention has no savings clause, comparable to that in many contemporary IIAs indicating, as further discussed later, that states are not precluded from taking certain measures under certain circumstances.

This difference may be due to a basic difference between the two regimes. IIAs presume an adversarial relationship between states and foreign investors that requires on the one hand imposing strict state duties bounded by delimited defenses that are absolutely necessary to secure states' consent to IIAs. The investment regime focuses chiefly on the perceived threats to alien property interests posed by their state hosts and only secondarily on what those hosts need to protect their general population and regulate in the public interest. The CEDAW regime treats states not only as potential threats to women's equality but as potential collaborators in a common endeavor to advance women's equality by all means necessary and by both state and non-state actors.[82] That regime is deeply invested in how a state regulates domestically in order to respect, protect, and fulfill Convention rights.

The absence of one or more derogation clauses does not mean that CEDAW rejects the legitimate rights/duties of states to regulate in other contexts, however. Rather, that Convention permits deference to sovereigns' regulatory concerns through chapeau or other clauses throughout the treaty that anticipate states need to take "appropriate" legislation, means or action. Such requirements,

---

[81] The precise results and rationales on offer in Views concerning Communication No. 19/2008, Cecilia Kell v. Canada, CEDAW/C/51/D/19/2008 (2008), for example, which relies on intersectional discrimination directed at an Aboriginal women and victim of sexual violence, may be difficult to extrapolate to another communicant with neither of those characteristics.

[82] As noted in chapter 3, CEDAW's reliance on managerial compliance by the very states that it criticizes for discriminating against women may be seen as one of the regime's flaws.

found in Article 2(a), (b), (e), (f), Articles 5, 6, 7, 8, 10, 11(1) and (2), 12(1), 13, 14(1) and (2), and Article 16(1), are two-faced. On the one hand, insisting on only "appropriate" action by states acknowledges (as suggested by many GRs and COs surveyed in chapter 2) that states have some (relatively undefined) discretion to achieve equality in different ways and by using different means, including legislation, regulation or adjudicative decision.[83] But, on the other hand, insisting that states take appropriate action has become a formula for the Committee to insist, as under its COs and in accord with CEDAW's Article 3, that states take "all" measures consistent with their duty to exercise due diligence, to ensure, protect, and fulfill, for example, women's equal access to bank loans, mortgages, and other forms of financial credit (Article 13(b)). As is clear from chapter 2, the Committee retains the power to ultimately decide—as through COs—whether the state's determination that it has taken "appropriate action" actually achieves the equality demanded by the Convention. CEDAW's deference to how states fulfill their obligations has limits, even if these are ill or inconsistently defined.[84] CEDAW's Article 2, after all, requires states to pursue by "all appropriate means" but also "without delay" a policy of eliminating discrimination against women, thereby narrowing the permissible range of state (in)action in meeting this goal.

IIAs, on the other hand, provide more absolute property protections that are subject to immediate application with potentially huge financial consequences for states found to be in violation of such investor guarantees under ISDS. Given the possible consequences for states, one would expect such treaties, negotiated by states, to include explicit safe harbors precluding liability. But, as noted previously, a surprising high number of IIAs, particularly from the wave of such treaties concluded in the 1990s, do not include such derogation clauses, perhaps reflecting states' confidence that the ordinary excuses from state responsibility found under customary law, now codified in the Articles on the Responsibility of States for Internationally Wrongful Acts, would be applicable in investor-state cases and would be sufficient to provide a defense.[85] US BITs filled this gap early on by including a "measure not precluded" clause. The US-Argentina BIT provides, as do many subsequent BITs, that its terms "do not preclude the application by either Party of measures necessary for the maintenance of public order, the fulfillment of its obligations with respect to the maintenance or restoration of international peace and security, or the protection of its own essential security interests."[86] The potential narrowness of such a derogation clause became

---

[83] Notably, the margin to apply only "appropriate" measures is not accorded under some CEDAW articles, such as Article 15 on access to justice.

[84] Compare chapter 2, sections 2.10.2.1 and 2.10.2.2 (enumerating the different views adopted by the CEDAW Committee on the extent states are owed a "margin of discretion" or "margin of appreciation" as shown by the Views adopted in Nguyen v. The Netherlands and Blok v. The Netherlands).

[85] *See* Burke-White & von Staden, *supra* note 60.

[86] *See, e.g.,* US-Argentina BIT, *supra* note 3, art. XI.

evident (and controversial) over the course of several arbitral rulings, particularly involving investment disputes in the wake of Argentina's "economic" crisis in 2001–2002.[87] As those cases suggest, one counterintuitive result of adopting a specific clause permitting certain exceptions from these treaty's guarantees to foreign investors is that those specific derogation clauses may be interpreted as the exclusive means for respondent states to escape their duties to investors. This may make it harder for a host state to argue, more generally, that the rights extended to alien property needs to give way to general sovereign powers to regulate in the public interest. This may mean that in practice, host states' obligations to alien investors are the default rule and that enabling states to exercise a general right to regulate not spelled out in an IIA is the exception.[88]

Because some ISDS awards have taken narrow views of derogation clauses, some recent IIAs have expanded the content of their derogation clauses or have otherwise sought to limit the scope of their investor-property protections. For example, the US Model BIT of 2012 and treaties based on it permit regulatory action that serves interests other than the host state's "essential security." It accomplishes this by eliminating or narrowing all the investor guarantees found in earlier US BITs, adding additional derogation clauses, and precluding some investor rights from being enforced through binding arbitration. Notably, the US Model BIT of 2012 also expands the "essential security" exception quoted previously by vesting the host state (as opposed to a tribunal) with the right to determine for itself that a measure is needed to protect its essential security.[89]

5.9 Distinct Remedies Subject to Distinct Enforcement

The investment and CEDAW regimes differ with respect to likely remedies, even if we compare investor-state claims only with CEDAW's individual communications to which they most resemble. On rare occasions, investor-state tribunals have issued legally binding interim measures of protection or injunctive relief, pending resolution of an investment dispute.[90] When investor

---

[87] *See, e.g.*, ALVAREZ, *supra* note 22, at 247–99.

[88] This "exceptionalist paradigm" is not limited to the investment regime. *See, e.g.*, Julian Arato et al., *The Perils of Pandemic Exceptionalism*, 114 AM. J. INT'L L. 627 (2020).

[89] José E. Alvarez, *The Once and Future Foreign Investment Regime*, *in* LOOKING TO THE FUTURE: ESSAYS ON INTERNATIONAL LAW IN HONOR OF W. MICHAEL REISMAN 628–32, tbl. at 641–48 (Mahnoush H. Arsanjani et al. eds., 2011) (comparing the US Model BIT of 1984 (comparable to the US-Argentina BIT) to the US Model BIT of 2004, which is (comparable to the US Model BIT of 2012)). A "self-judging" essential security clause may effectively eviscerate the treaty's investor protections even if a tribunal demands that it be exercised in "good faith."

[90] *See, e.g.*, Enron Corporation and Ponderosa Assets, L.P. v. The Arg. Republic, ICSID Case No. ARB/01/3, Decision on Jurisdiction (Jan. 14, 2004), 11 ICSID Rep. 268 (2007).

claimants win before such tribunals, their remedy is usually an award of financial damages premised on the need to accord "full restitution" for any property lost or harmed.[91] Awards other than such damages for the harm done to an investor's property interests—including restitution—are rare.[92]

As would be expected given their reliance on damages, investor-state arbitrators devote substantial attention to distilling legal principles on how best to value property as a commodity, asset, or business.[93] ISDS rulings are now the leading source of authority on how to interpret, under contemporary conditions, the vague injunction in the Permanent Court of International Justice (PCIJ)'s award in *Chorzow Factory* that foreign investors harmed by state action in violation of international law need to be put in the same financial position they enjoyed prior to any breach of their property rights.[94]

IIAs generally indicate that states need to pay "prompt, adequate and effective" compensation when they take alien property. The treaties do not always specify precisely what those terms mean,[95] and even when they do, there remains considerable room for debate on what formulas need to be used to assign numbers to these terms.[96] The resort to the use of expert testimony and differing assessments of the credibility of particular experts further obscures the nature of ISDS law on the evaluation of property for such purposes, even if general principles have emerged on what should be included in assessing the value of a business that was never allowed to operate versus one that was ongoing at the time of the state action alleged to be in violation of an IIA.[97] Arbitrators enjoy even more discretion in awarding damages in cases not involving expropriations since IIAs frequently lack guidance on what investors are owed if other investor treaty rights, such as FET or FSP or guarantees to accord national or MFN treatment are violated.[98] ISDS cases have generated a welter of precedents relating to other compensation questions, such as whether the investor has done enough to mitigate its damages or whether or to what extent counterclaims by the respondent state related to the

---

[91] *See, e.g.*, BONNITCHA ET AL., *supra* note 53, at 75–76.

[92] *See, e.g.*, CAMPBELL MCLACHLAN ET AL., INTERNATIONAL INVESTMENT ARBITRATION: SUBSTANTIVE PRINCIPLES 341 (2d ed. 2007).

[93] *See, e.g.*, DOLZER ET AL., *supra* note 50, at 425–33 (enumerating the standard remedies of restitution, satisfaction, damages, compensation for expropriations, interest, and costs of the proceedings).

[94] *See, e.g.*, MCLACHLAN ET AL., *supra* note 92, at 315–49 (outlining principles of compensation applicable under ISDS).

[95] *See generally* BISHOP ET AL., *supra* note 27, at 1305–31.

[96] *Id.* at 1331–71.

[97] MCLACHLAN ET AL., *supra* note 92, at 319–33 (outlining various means of evaluation, including liquidation value, replacement value, book value, discounted cash flow value, and other valuation methods).

[98] *Id.* at 334–41 (outlining arbitral approaches to provide compensation for non-expropriatory breaches of IIAs even when the treaty does not address the point). *See also* MARK KANTOR, VALUATION FOR ARBITRATION COMPENSATION STANDARDS, VALUATION METHODS AND EXPERT EVIDENCE (2008).

underlying claim should be used to reduce the sums that may otherwise be owed by the respondent state.[99]

The CEDAW Committee appears to agree in principle that, consistent with customary rules of state responsibility, a state's violation of CEDAW that harms property interests should result in reparation. It has sometimes recommended remedies based on tort-like determinations of prior bad conduct, urging parties to provide "appropriate compensation that is commensurate with the gravity of the violations of the victim's rights."[100] But even in such cases, the Committee generally leaves it up to states to decide on "appropriate reparations," even though it is doubtlessly aware that under the applicable rules of state responsibility that term encompasses a wide range of measures—from promises to cease the illegal act to apologies to restitution of property or forms of financial recompense.[101] The Committee rarely attempts to go further. It does not itself assess the precise value of property harms for purposes of remedy except when this has been preset by governments (such as when the Committee determines that social benefits or portions of such benefits have been denied to women and requires states to compensate women for such losses).[102] Nor does it attempt to assign an economic value to opportunities that may have been denied to the authors of individual communicants or women generally because of long-standing discriminatory actions owing to, for example, cultural or other stereotypes.

In the majority of Views discussed in chapter 2 and also in COs or GRs on point, the Committee seems content with recommendations that the states remove the offending measure. In a few cases, as in *Kell*, the Committee may recommend that the successful claimant be provided with housing, but even in such cases the Committee does not, in addition, attempt to calculate the financial damages that the communicant might have suffered and require the state to award such sums.[103] No one would recommend the CEDAW Committee's outputs, including its Views, as a place to look for guidance on the law regarding the evaluation of property for purposes of redressing international wrongful

---

[99] *Id.* at 327–28 & 341 (discussing the investor claimants' duty to mitigate its damages); Andrea K. Bjorklund, *Emergency Exceptions: State of Necessity and Force Majeure*, in THE OXFORD HANDBOOK OF INTERNATIONAL INVESTMENT LAW 459 (Peter Muchlinski et al. eds., 2008).

[100] Meghan Campbell & Jane Connors, *Optional Protocol*, in 2022 COMMENTARY, *supra* note 1, at 872. *See, e.g.*, CO on India, CEDAW/C/IND/CO/SP.1, ¶ 35 (2010) (urging in a post-conflict situation that women victims be allowed to return to their original homes but where that was not possible that the state "provide or assist these persons in obtaining appropriate compensation or another form of just reparation").

[101] For the Articles on Responsibility of States for Internationally Wrongful Acts and the ILC commentary to the articles, *see* Int'l Law Comm'n, Rep. on the Work of Its Fifty-third Session, UN Doc. A/56/10, arts. 34–37 (2001).

[102] The CEDAW Committee's usual deference to states with respect to how they calculate adequate social security benefits but insistence that any such compensation not discriminate against women is well illustrated in its Views in Natalia Ciobanu v. Moldova, discussed in chapter 2, section 2.10.2.3.

[103] *See* chapter 2, section 2.4.2.1 (discussion of Cecilia Kell v. Canada).

acts.[104] By contrast, ISDS tribunals are a favored place for finding what "international law" (or more accurately, the rules of state responsibility) requires by way of property compensation after proof of breach of a treaty (or underlying customary law).[105]

It is possible that, as has occurred within the ECtHR and the Inter-American Court, the CEDAW Committee may come, over time, to become more comfortable with recommendations that communicants be awarded financial compensation commensurate with the value of the property interests that have been violated.[106] But such a change in direction may not happen for a number of reasons. Financial recompense reflecting the "fair market value" of lost property may seem less germane to a regime that is less interested in the loss of property per se than, for example, the absence of shelter resulting from a state's wrongful actions.[107] In addition, such a change may be difficult if Committee members are more concerned with encouraging proactive state action to prevent future harm to women and fear the consequences of attempting to divert scarce state resources for corrective recompense that benefits only certain individuals. Finally, to the extent the CEDAW Committee is concerned with providing a remedy to potentially large groups of women who have been subject to discrimination for substantial periods of time, the Committee may be more favorable to remedies akin to those adopted for transitional justice that are not dependent on financial recompense—including specific promises of nonrepetition of certain practices, commemorations of those harmed by prior wrongful acts accompanied by formal state apologies, or processes to preserve collective memory or accountability such as truth commissions.[108]

The CEDAW Committee's apparent reluctance to assess the worth of property may also result from that body's refusal to treat interest in property as a commodity. Even in cases dealing with denials of women's access or enjoyment of tangible assets like the family home, the Committee is more likely to look to what the home protects in devising a suitable remedy than what a willing buyer

---

[104] *See, e.g.*, UN Secretary-General, *Responsibility of States For Internationally Wrongful Acts: Compilation of Decisions of International Courts, Tribunals and Other Bodies*, UN Doc. A/77/74 (Apr. 29, 2022) (citing repeatedly to ICSID and other arbitral rulings, the ICJ, and a handful of human rights forums (especially the ECtHR) but not CEDAW sources).

[105] *See, e.g.*, BONNITCHA ET AL., *supra* note 53, at 121–25.

[106] Citations about the growing number of financial awards in human rights cases by both courts.

[107] *See generally* DINAH SHELTON, REMEDIES IN INTERNATIONAL HUMAN RIGHTS LAW 315–42 (3d ed. 2015) (discussing the applicability and evolution of the use of compensation in international human rights law for purposes of corrective justice).

[108] *See generally* Pablo de Grieff, *The Vernacularization of Transitional Justice: Is Transitional Justice Useful in Pre-Conflict Settings?*, in THE COMPLEXITY OF HUMAN RIGHTS: FROM VERNACULARIZATION TO QUANTIFICATION (Philip Alston ed., Quantification (forthcoming 2023) (on file with author). For comparable discussions within a human rights regime, *see, e.g.*, Ruth Rubio-Marín & Clara Sandoval, *Engendering the Reparations Jurisprudence of the Inter-American Court of Human Rights: The Promise of the Cotton Field Judgment*, 33 HUM. RTS. Q. 1062 (2011).

would pay for it. Thus, when a woman's human right to adequate housing is lost or threatened, the CEDAW Committee tries to remedy the underlying harm to physical and psychological security in the particular context.[109] In doing so, the Committee evinces a solicitude for protecting the quality of life of injured complainants not usually found in the investment regime. As Thomas Merrills has argued, neither the US takings jurisprudence nor that under IIAs recognizes that property taken by a state may have special emotional or moral value that exceeds its fair market value.[110] He argues that in such cases, the traditional compensation accorded is "incomplete."[111] By comparison, the CEDAW Committee does not treat the distinct harms, including those that are not usually commodified, felt by particular women as outside its cognizance. It also takes a broader view of what constitutes "economic harm." It identifies women's lack of economic independence as forcing women to stay in violent relationships and therefore identifies that "economic harm" as a form of gender-based violence, for example.[112] That sensitivity to victims' physical and mental integrity is particularly on display, for example, in the Committee's suggested remedies in cases of domestic violence involving denials of shelter or housing.[113] But that solicitude for the actual harm done to women as a result of denials of property is not likely to generate, within the foreseeable future, damage amounts that are anywhere near the sums awarded under IIAs even if the CEDAW Committee were to follow the lead of regional human rights courts that have increasingly turned to financial remedies.

The differences between the two regimes' respective approaches to remedial enforcement are substantial. As is well known, most IIAs include exceptionally effective, mandatory international dispute settlement. In most cases, investment protection treaties provide that foreign investors who believe that they have been harmed by a breach of one or more of the rights accorded under such treaties can, subject to conditions imposed under the specific treaty, resort to binding arbitration.[114] Once the treaty's preconditions are satisfied, investor claimants

---

[109] *See, e.g.*, chapter 2, section 2.11.2.6 (discussing S.T. v. the Russian Federation where the state's failure to exclude husband from shared family residence was found to threaten Chechen woman's physical safety and integrity); *see also* Views concerning Communication No. 2/2003, Ms. A.T. v. Hungary, CEDAW/C/36/D/2/2003 (2005) (failure to grant woman sole possession of apartment and absence of shelters violated Convention), discussed in chapter 2, section 2.11.2.1.

[110] *See, e.g.*, Thomas A. Merrills, *Incomplete Compensation for Takings*, 11 N.Y.U. ENVTL. L.J. 110 (2002).

[111] *Id.*

[112] *See* GR No. 19, *supra* note 81, ¶¶ 14 & 16; and GR No. 35, *supra* note 73, ¶ 10 (2017).

[113] *See, e.g.*, Campbell & Connors, *supra* note 100, at 873 (citing A.T. v. Hungary, L.R. v. Moldova, R.B.P. v. Philippines, S.L. v. Bulgaria)—cases where the Committee recommended, alongside safe housing, free psychological counseling. *See also* Views concerning Communication No. 20/2008, V.K. v. Bulgaria, CEDAW/C/49/D/20/2008 (2011) (deeming the unavailability of state-funded shelters for women subject to domestic violence).

[114] *See, e.g.*, US-Argentina BIT, *supra* note 3, art. VII (2) (requiring parties to the dispute to seek a resolution initially through consultation and negotiation but, thereafter, requiring investor claimants

typically have access to a number of arbitration options—to which the host state has usually consented in advance or as part of the IIA.

Typical options under IIAs include arbitrating investor claims against the host state under ICSID or under rules issued by the United Nations Commission on International Trade Law (UNCITRAL). Under both the terms of IIAs and multilateral conventions concerning arbitration, investor-state awards arising under these treaties are legally binding.[115] Under the typical IIA, respondent states usually do not have the option of initiating counterclaims against investor claimants that go beyond the subject matter covered by the investor's original claim.[116] ISDS is accurately described as a largely one-sided remedial scheme designed to benefit foreign investors—and overcome the presumed prejudice of the host state's courts.[117] Respondent states are generally precluded under ISDS from initiating their own claims against investors—as for failure to pay taxes, abide by their contracts, or abide by other domestic laws—and their counterclaims (as to secure recompense for such harms) are limited to those that arise "directly out of the subject-matter" of the underlying investor claim at least under ISCID.

Further, investor-state arbitral awards can usually be enforced by domestic courts pursuant to multilateral conventions such as the ISCID or New York Conventions and are subject to very limited grounds permitting either annulments (under ISCID) or refusals to enforce (under the New York Convention).[118] There is considerable evidence that investor-state awards directed at states, are, despite the sovereign immunity that continues to protect direct enforcement actions, subject to a high level of usually voluntary state compliance even when the sums involve in excess of tens of millions of dollars.[119] Market forces are presumed to account for a level of compliance that is perceived as rare among international legal regimes. States that fail to comply with ISDS awards may experience over

---

to choose whether to submit its dispute to the host state's courts or administrative tribunals, adhere to any previously agreed dispute settlement procedures between the parties, or opt for arbitration as provided under Article VII (3)). Some IIAs may require, instead, an investor to exhaust local remedies or wait for a period of time before engaging in arbitration. A few contemporary IIAs involving the European Union, now provide, in lieu of access to arbitration, access to permanent international investment court established under the IIA. *See, e.g.,* Investment Protection Agreement between the European Union and Singapore, E.U.-Sing., Oct. 15, 2018, https://eur-lex.europa.eu/EN/legal-content/summary/investment-protection-agreement-between-the-eu-and-singapore.html.

[115] *See, e.g.,* US-Argentina BIT, *supra* note 3, art. VII (6); ICSID Convention, *supra* note 23, art. 54.
[116] *See, e.g.,* ICSID Convention, *supra* note 23, art. 46.
[117] *See generally* BONNITCHA ET AL., *supra* note 53, at 59–76 & 127–54 (describing IIAs' dispute settlement mechanisms but also casting doubt on the underlying premises, including the assumption that host state courts are biased against foreign investors).
[118] ICSID Convention, *supra* note 23, art. 52(1); United Nations Convention on the Recognition and Enforcement of Foreign Arbitral Awards art. V(1), *opened for signature* June 10, 1958, 21 U.S.T. 2517 [hereinafter New York Convention]; *see also* BONNITCHA ET AL., *supra* note 53, at 77–78.
[119] BONNITCHA ET AL., *supra* note 53, at 78–81.

the long term adverse market consequences leading to decreased capital investment, unilateral economic threats by the home states of aggrieved investors, or downgrades in credit ratings.[120]

The CEDAW Committee, on the other hand, lacks any comparable, legally binding enforcement scheme *of its own*. It relies on "managerial" or what some call "mobilization of shame" techniques familiar to other UN human rights regimes to achieve compliance.[121] While many see CEDAW's COs, GRs, Views, and Inquiry Reports as interpretations of the Convention that are rendered "authoritative" since they are issued by the only treaty body authorized to provide them,[122] these outputs are not legally binding under the terms of the Convention.[123] While the Convention permits state parties to refer inter-state disputes regarding the interpretation and application of the Convention to arbitration or the ICJ, such resorts to formal adjudication have not yet occurred.[124]

CEDAW's Optional Protocol permitting the Committee to receive communications from individuals and groups or engage in inquiries of states does not, however, insist that this is the exclusive remedy for adjudicating claims that a state is violating the Convention. Many national courts have considered such claims or have used CEDAW to interpret domestic law.[125] Some national courts have even treated CEDAW as directly enforceable without need for separate implementing legislation, while other courts have found that they authorized to apply CEDAW pursuant to national law or even national constitutions.[126] The CEDAW Committee's Views have also been cited or relied up in other human rights venues, including by regional courts of human rights, other UN human rights treaty bodies, and UN Special Rapporteurs.[127] Particularly grave

---

[120] *Id.*

[121] CEDAW insiders that we have consulted appear divided on whether or how much the Committee relies on managerial persuasion as opposed to more adversarial mobilization of shame techniques. Some argue that the latter is precisely what occurs in connection with Reports on Inquires. Others point out that whatever the Committee thinks it is doing, activists who are motivated to follow up on the hard work of "enforcement" apply a variety of tactics that they deem suited to local circumstances, including responding to a recalcitrant government.

[122] *See* chapter 2, section 2.2.

[123] *But see* María de los Ángeles González Carreño v. Ministry of Justice, S.T.S., July 17, 2018 (R.J., No. 1263) (Spain) [hereinafter Carreño v. Ministry of Justice] (drawing on Article 7(4) of the Optional Protocol which obliges states to give due consideration to the CEDAW Committee's View for its conclusion that the CEDAW Committee's findings of violation "engages the legal obligation" of Spain).

[124] CEDAW, *supra* note 2, art. 29.

[125] *See, e.g.*, Christopher McCrudden, *Why Do National Court Judges Refer to Human Rights Courts*, 109 AM. J. INT'L L. 534 (2015).

[126] *See, e.g.*, Carreño v. Ministry of Justice, *supra* note 123; Marta Rodriquez de Assis Machado & Mariana Mota Prado, *Institutional Dimensions of Gender Equality: The Maria da Pehna Case*, *in* FRONTIERS OF GENDER EQUALITY: TRANSNATIONAL LEGAL PERSPECTIVES 384 (Rebecca J. Cook ed., 2023).

[127] For examples, *see* chapter 6. As far as we are aware, there are no empirical surveys examining the numbers of national court rulings relying on CEDAW compared to national court rulings applying the provisions of an IIA.

or egregious violations of women's rights (including to property)—as by the Taliban—have also led to unilateral responses by objecting states. If one considers all these alternative venues of "enforcement" or "compliance," it is not true that the rights that the CEDAW protects lack any legal binding forms of enforcement.

The differences between the two regimes on the level of enforcement should not be overstated for yet another reason. Ultimately, both the international investment and CEDAW regimes rely, as do all regimes under international law, on voluntary state compliance.[128] Whether a state complies with either ISDS awards or the CEDAW Committee's recommendations depends on the state's assessment of whether the reputational or other costs resulting from continued defiance or the perceived benefits of compliance matter more to them. If ISDS rulings elicit greater compliance by states than the CEDAW Committee's recommendations do, that is likely the product of circumstances that may have less to do with the formally binding nature of the former. As a matter of fact, most ISDS awards are the subject of voluntary state compliance and not the result of enforcement actions in national courts as authorized by arbitration conventions.[129] Such enforcement actions would, in many cases, encounter other obstacles to actual payment, such as sovereign immunity.[130] Compliance with most ISDS awards results from voluntary payments made by states albeit in the shadow of possible enforcement actions. This suggests that the investment regime's impressive compliance record may be due largely to the powerful market forces that persuade states that compliance is in their self-interest and not the formally binding nature of ISDS.

5.10 Comparing the Two Regimes: A Hypothetical

The comparison between the CEDAW and international investment regimes can be made less abstract by considering a hypothetical female entrepreneur, Viola, from State X who faces discriminatory restrictions in concluding business contracts to establish a business or to expand her existing business in State Y. If both State X and State Y are parties to a BIT comparable to that between the United States and Argentina and those states are also parties to CEDAW and its Optional Protocol, in principle, our entrepreneur could possibly rely on, depending on the circumstances, relevant provisions of the CEDAW or on certain investor guarantees in the X-Y BIT to file either an individual communication to the CEDAW Committee or an investor-state claim under the BIT. As this

---

[128] As noted earlier, even investor-state arbitral awards are subject to sovereign immunity. *See, e.g.*, ICSID Convention, *supra* note 23, art. 55.
[129] *See, e.g.*, BONNITCHA ET AL., *supra* note 53, at 77–81.
[130] *See, e.g.*, BISHOP ET AL., *supra* note 27, at 1613–53.

hypothetical suggests, notwithstanding the substantial differences between the two regimes outlined in the preceding sections of this chapter, it is possible that the protections accorded under the two may overlap. But even in that scenario, as we will see, the two treaty regimes are likely to generate different legal arguments and produce different outcomes. Much of these differences stem from the two regimes' markedly different approach to the concept of and actionable forms of discrimination—as well as distinct conceptions of equality or equal treatment, the proper basis for a claim, and the defenses available to State Y. Underlying these differences are the fundamentally different purposes of the two regimes. The principal goal of IIAs is to facilitate capital flows between their state parties consistent with demands of economic globalization and on the assumption that protecting the property interests of foreign investors generates economic development for the states that host such investors. The overriding goal of the CEDAW regime is to secure equal rights for women.

In our hypothetical, should Viola face discrimination in investing in State Y (because, for example, she was denied the right to conclude necessary contracts to form or expand her business or was denied entry under Y's process for permitting business entrants), she would have a plausible claim under the BIT's right to NT and MFN on entry and/or post-entry treatment.[131] Viola could also have a legitimate complaint under CEDAW, but the result is less clear. CEDAW does not explicitly cover nondiscrimination with respect to establishing a business and does not explicitly protect the rights of foreigners or aliens. It does protect women's rights to conclude contracts, however, and to equal treatment under the law and this would presumably extend to any discrimination against Viola in concluding contracts in order to enter Y or to expand her existing business in Y. CEDAW also does not distinguish citizens from noncitizens and Viola, as a foreign female entrepreneur, can plausibly assert that State Y is "responsible for all their actions affecting human rights, regardless of whether the affected persons are in their territories."[132] Where denials of entry into Y result from unequal treatment under Y's laws governing entry or unequal treatment with respect to her ability to conclude contracts, such claims could be actionable under CEDAW's Article 15. Such claims might also be viable under CEDAW's Article 1

---

[131] *See supra* texts and accompanying notes 63–64. Note that while only a small number of IIAs extend the right to national and MFN treatment to the right to enter, most extend that right to postentry treatment, including to operate and extend one's established business in the host state. Should the IIA applicable to Viola's case include a provision extending protection against "discrimination" more generally, it is possible that Viola might be able to file a claim if she can show that she was discriminated against on the basis of sex. *See, e.g., infra* note 138.

[132] GR No. 28, *supra* note 74, ¶ 12. But, as the CEDAW Commentary explains, the extent the CEDAW Committee embraces the "extraterritorial" application of the Convention remains a work in progress and is unclear. *See* Andrew Byrnes & Meghan Campbell, *Article 2, in* 2022 COMMENTARY, *supra* note 1, at 136–41.

if Viola faced discrimination in ways that violate other human rights treaties or fundamental freedoms.[133]

As the foregoing suggests, the bases for Viola's rights would be different under the two regimes. A claim under CEDAW requires proving discrimination as defined in the Convention. This includes demonstrating that State Y has violated one of the state obligations imposed under that treaty, such as Article 15, or, consistent with Article 1 of the CEDAW, evidence that Y has violated Viola's right to equality in a way that impairs or nullifies other human rights or fundamental freedoms. Her claim under an IIA would be based on an explicit clause that extends the treaty's rights to national and MFN treatment to aliens seeking either to enter the country to establish a business or that extends that guarantee (or a distinct right not to face "discrimination") for post-entry activities "associated" with an investment.[134]

The nature of Viola's proposed new or expanded business may matter under both regimes but for very different reasons. If, for example, Viola was being prohibited from establishing or expanding her business to provide reproductive services, it would probably not undermine her CEDAW claim if Y had in place generally applicable laws—applicable to both men and women, foreigners, or nationals—barring any form of reproductive services that could lead to an abortion under any circumstances. Facially neutral laws would not necessarily bar an actionable claim under CEDAW for *de facto* substantive discrimination if, for example, Viola could demonstrate that because of underlying cultural stereotypes men in State Y could secure such contracts notwithstanding Y's formal ban on such businesses.[135] If, for example, there was evidence that State Y's courts regularly assumed that men but not women could perform medical procedures and the law banning health services leading to abortion was rarely enforced, Viola's claim to a violation of CEDAW's Article 15 would be on solid ground. Viola would have a second argument to support her CEDAW communication: she could also argue that, based on CEDAW's incorporation of other fundamental rights, a discriminatory denial of her ability to conclude contracts to establish or expand such a business would impede all women's access to basic health services. In these circumstances, Viola's CEDAW complaint would not only be based on an alleged violation of her own personal right to administer contracts but on the ground that denying her right to establish her proposed business would violate

---

[133] A female refugee who claims that her claim for asylum was being treated differently than those of males would appear to have a claim under Article 1 or possibly Article 15. If Viola were not only a prospective entrepreneur but a refugee escaping persecution, for example, she would potentially have a claim if discriminatory denial of entry were in violation of her rights to asylum.

[134] *See, e.g.*, US-Argentina BIT, *supra* note 3, art. I (1)(c) (definition of associated activities), art. II (1) (NT and MFN treatment for both entry and post-entry), art. II (2)(b) (protection against "arbitrary" or "discriminatory" measures).

[135] *See, e.g.*, Alexandra Timmer & Rikki Holtmaat, *supra* note 68, sec. (II)(1)(c).

the fundamental rights of women in State Y, namely, access to rights to reproductive services that the CEDAW Committee has previously affirmed.[136]

The nature of Viola's business could also matter under the BIT. If State Y had included reproductive health services as a sector exempted from national and MFN treatment or if Y bars all persons irrespective of nationality from establishing such a business, that would probably be fatal to Viola's investor-state claim.[137] Under the BIT, even when national and MFN guarantees apply, what matters is whether either another Y national or any other foreigner can establish or expand such a business. If everyone, irrespective of nationality, is barred from such a business, there is no BIT violation—even if the consequences for women's access to vital health services are dire. As this suggests, under IIAs, formal equality—as shown by facially neutral laws that do not differ on the basis of nationality—usually ends the inquiry. Under a BIT, it is also of no consequence whether Y's law is the product of cultural prejudices that subordinate women's rights to control their own reproductive choices. Nor would it be relevant if, at least with respect to national and MFN treatment, Y's neutral law is actually applied to preclude women from concluding such contracts or operating the resulting business.[138]

Other possible facts could influence the viability of Viola's complaint under CEDAW. Assume that Viola was not only a female medical service provider but also a member of a racial or ethnic minority commonly subject to discrimination in host State Y. In such a case, the CEDAW Committee would care even less about finding a male comparator to determine whether Viola was the subject of direct or indirect discrimination. The Committee's inquiry would likely shift to determining whether Viola was denied her right to substantive equality—in the form of establishing or expanding her business by concluding contracts—because of any or all of her identities.[139] Under

---

[136] *See, e.g.*, Verónica Undurraga & Rebecca J. Cook, *Article 12, in* 2022 COMMENTARY, *supra* note 1, at 469–475 (nondiscrimination in health care).

[137] *See, e.g.*, US-Argentina BIT, *supra* note 3, art. II (1) (permitting state parties to include sectoral exemptions from national and MFN treatment, including on entry).

[138] There is, however, a possibility that discriminating against Viola on the basis of her sex might be an actionable claim under an IIA that includes a clause, apart from NT and MFN, that bans states from "arbitrary" or "discriminatory" measures. *See, e.g.*, Bernhard von Pezold and Others v. Republic of Zim., ICSID Case No. ARB/10/15, Award, ¶ 501 (July 28, 2015), 18 ICSID Rep. 360 (2020) (upholding a claim under a treaty obligation not to discriminate with respect to expropriation based on skin color). Recent IIAs, however, including those concluded by the United States, generally omit the broad protection against arbitrary/discriminatory measures but retain the ban on "discriminatory" expropriations. *See, e.g.*, US Model BIT of 2012, *supra* note 7, art. 6 (insisting that expropriations be made "in a non-discriminatory manner").

[139] The CEDAW Committee frequently criticizes states for practices that disproportionately impact women based on their particular identities. *See, e.g.*, CO on UK and Northern Ireland, CEDAW/C/GBR/CO/7, ¶ 22 (2013) (limits on legal aid that push ethnic minorities into informal community arbitration systems (including faith-based tribunals) that do not act in conformity with the Convention); CO on Myanmar, CEDAW/C/MMR/CO/EP/1 (2019) (focusing on dispossessions

the BIT, by contrast, Viola's intersectional identity would generally have no bearing on any claim to a violation of national or MFN treatment; the only relevant question would be whether Viola was discriminated against because of her nationality.

At the same time, our female entrepreneur's claim of discrimination may trigger defenses from State Y under CEDAW that generally would not arise under the limited derogation ("measure not precluded") clause under the X-Y BIT.[140] It would matter, for example, if Viola was not engaged in a medical practice but was instead attempting to conclude contracts to purchase land to run an agri-business that would vastly increase the capacity of State Y to export soybeans, one of Y's leading exports. Should Y affirm that Viola was denied this right because such a foreign agri-businesses would threaten the livelihood of many women in Y who run family farms for this purpose, even though they do not hold formal title to such lands, such a defense could prove fatal to the success of Viola's CEDAW communication. As a number of the Committee's outputs in chapter 2 illustrate, that Committee is sensitive to the negative externalities posed by economic globalization.[141] In such a case, the CEDAW Committee would likely take into account the broader economic and social rights of women affected by the investment decision, and not only the individual entrepreneur's rights; it could very well decide that, on balance, Y had taken "appropriate"

---

of Rohingya women and girls); CO on Israel, CEDAW/C/ISR/CO/5, ¶ 28 (2011) (demolitions of property, homes, and schools and forced eviction with serious effects on Palestinian women); GR No. 27 on Older Women and Protection of Their Human Rights, CEDAW/C/GC/27, ¶ 26 (2010) (addressing older women's vulnerability to property disenfranchisements involving family relations, including through the practice of "property grabbing"). *See generally* 2022 COMMENTARY, *supra* note 1, on Article 4 (Ulrike Lembke, sec. (B)(II)), Article 5 (Alexandra Timmer & Rikki Holtmaat, sec. (B)(4)), Article 6 (Janie Chuang/Sulini Sarugaser-Hug, sec. (D)(4)), Article 11 (Frances Raday & Shai Oksenberg, sec. (C)(III)), Article 14 (Fareda Banda, sec. (C)(VII)), and Article 15 (Aruna D. Nairan, sec. (C)(IV)).

[140] As noted *infra*, the CEDAW Committee is likely to consider relevant the type of business that the hypothetical entrepreneur seeks to engage and the impact of that business on women, and not only the economic impact of the state's action on the entrepreneur herself, for example.

[141] *See, e.g.*, chapter 2, section 2.6.2.5 (describing Concluding Observations on land-grabbing and development projects). Views concerning X. v. Cambodia, CDAW/C/85/D/146/2019, issued on May 19, 2023, after the closing date for research undertaken to produce chapter 2 of this book (and therefore not included in the relevant Communications in Appendix 5) illustrate the differences between the investment and CEDAW regimes. In that case, the Committee upheld the claims by a Cambodian rural woman who had been evicted from her family farm by the actions of KDC International, a development company owned by the wife of then Minister of Mines and Energy in Cambodia. The Committee found that this "land grab" by a private company who pressured residents of a commune to sell their land and, with apparent government complicity, threatened with violence and arrest those who resisted, including the applicant, had engaged in a discriminatory forced eviction and subsequent denials of equal justice to a human rights defender in violations of CEDAW arts. 2(c-e), 3, and 14 (1) and (2)(a), (g), and (h) as well as art. 15(1). The Committee upheld these claims even though the applicant, like many others in the commune, did not have documented legal title to the land.

action consistent with its rights to regulate in order to protect the substantive equality of women.[142]

Under CEDAW, the collective rights of women, as well as the underlying reasons for the absence of substantive equality, matter. Under the BIT, on the other hand, the fact that Viola was attempting to increase State Y's exports would likely be seen as perfectly consistent with the fundamental purpose of that investment promotion treaty. A treaty like the X-Y BIT (modeled after the US-Argentina BIT under our facts) presumes that an increase in foreign capital is desirable precisely because this would "increase the competitiveness" of inefficient domestic businesses.[143] Under such a treaty, State Y's defense to the allegation that it was denying Viola's rights would most likely be treated as an illegitimate "protectionist" reaction at odds with its object and purpose.[144] As this suggests, the CEDAW Committee's solicitude to structural and other forms of discrimination against *groups* of women, such as rural women or members of Indigenous groups who rely on the land, and not only to individuals alleging discrimination, is another reason that outcomes may differ between the two regimes in cases that pit an individual's discrimination claim against the rights of women more generally.

The considerable differences between the two regimes' remedial approaches surveyed in section 5.9 would also pose quandaries for our hypothetical female entrepreneur. Her choice of the legal regime may depend on the kind of remedy she seeks to obtain and/or the likelihood of securing it. If Viola is seeking financial compensation for economic harms that she experienced as a result of being discriminated against, she has much higher prospects for securing that remedy and securing such funds under the investment regime. If, however, she seeks redress for discrimination that was indirect, systemic, structural, or intersectional and is motivated not just by acknowledgment of individual injustice but also by the prevention of future harm to women in a similar position, CEDAW's much broader set of remedial options would be preferable.

If Viola, the reproductive services entrepreneur, were to succeed with her communication before the CEDAW Committee, the CEDAW Committee would

---

[142] *See supra* text and accompanying notes 135–136. Thus, in X v. Cambodia, discussed *supra* note 141, the Committee made extensive recommendations to ensure: that rural women in general, and not only the applicant, enjoy access to land and tenure security; that land acquisitions follow due process (including free, prior, and informed consent); that claims of forced evictions and intimidation are addressed and investigated; and that evicted communities are relocated to sites that enable adequate housing. *Id.* ¶ 8 (i–iv).

[143] *See, e.g.*, BONNITCHA ET AL., *supra* note 53, at 137–47 (critiquing the premise that IIAs are needed to induce economically efficient state actions).

[144] As a prominent international investment scholar once put it, the aim of investment treaties is "to restrain host country action against the interests of investors—in other words, to enable the form of legal commitments made to investor[s] to resist the forces of change often demanded b the political and economic life in host countries." Jeswald Salacuse, *The Treatification of International Investment Law: A Victory of Form over Life? A Crossroad Crossed?*, 3 TRANSNAT'L DISP. MGMT. 3 (2006).

likely recommend that State Y simply let her conclude her contracts and open her reproductive services clinics. Success before an investor-state tribunal, on the other hand, could lead to a financial award that would enable Viola to recover her legal costs and any other demonstrable financial harms. But an ISDS tribunal would be decidedly less likely to force Y to let Viola establish her business since investor-state arbitrators are reluctant to compel specific performance.[145] At the same time, any ISDS award for financial recompense would be legally binding and potentially enforceable.[146] Y would likely pay the awarded amount or at least agree to a negotiated amount, even without an attempt by Viola to enforce the arbitral award via court action.[147] While this might suggest that Viola would therefore prefer to file an ISDS claim to vindicate her rights, Viola's choices in the real world are likely to be far more constrained.

Bringing an investor-state arbitral claim is a very expensive proposition.[148] The anticipated legally binding and relatively enforceable remedy under ISDS is simply not a real prospect for most women (or indeed for most men) in the world, including for most persons in the Global North. For those most likely to be subjected to discrimination, ISDS is simply out of reach. While there are considerable hurdles to filing a communication under CEDAW—including lack of access to lawyers who could assist—it is financially cost-free. Moreover, the ability to draw on a wider range of (admittedly soft) remedies under the CEDAW regime might, in some cases, provide a distinct reason to opt for CEDAW's remedies. The CEDAW Committee's remedial process generates recommendations, frequently backed by elements of civil society, urging states to remove offending measures, clarify existing laws, or adopt new laws to prevent future or continuing breaches of the Convention.[149] Viola's communication could result in recommendations by the CEDAW Committee that State Y adopt

---

[145] But note that proving damages for the denial of rights to establish an investment is likely to be difficult and that this may explain why such claims are rarely encountered in practice. Although investors denied such rights could seek financial recompense for the lost opportunity costs or for their anticipated stream of profits, proving either would be difficult.

[146] *See supra* at section 5.9.

[147] *Id.*

[148] *See, e.g.*, BONNITCHA ET AL., *supra* note 53, at 87 (noting that the *average* cost of an investor-state arbitral claim was $10 million in 2012).

[149] *See, e.g.*, COs recommending the adoption of unified family codes with more equal provisions with respect to inheritance, property, and land rights with respect to Samoa (CEDAW/C/WSM/CO/6, ¶¶ 43–44), Lesotho (CEDAW/C/LSO/CO/1–4, ¶¶ 38–39), South Africa (CEDAW/C/ZAF/CO/5, ¶¶ 55–56), Sri Lanka (CEDAW/C/LKA/CO/8, ¶¶ 12, 13, 40, & 45), Saudi Arabia (CEDAW/C/SAU/CO/3-4, ¶¶ 63–64), Solomon Islands (CEDAW/C/SLB/CO/1–3, ¶¶ 44 & 46). *See also* CO on Greece, CEDAW/C/GRC/CO/7, ¶ 37 (2013) (demanding law to ensure women's equal access to all property accumulated during a relationship). In other cases it has recommended that states engage in further study of existing family laws to determine their impact on the property rights of women in cases where marriages or *de facto* unions break up. *See, e.g.*, CO on UK and Northern Ireland, A/63/38, ¶ 291 (2008), CO on Estonia, CEDAW/C/EST/CO/4, ¶ 30 (2007). *See generally* Ineke Boerefijn & Julie Fraser, *Article 18*, *in* 2022 COMMENTARY, *supra* note 1, at 711–15.

relevant temporary special measures aimed at "accelerating" *de facto* equality (as authorized under Article 4) or adopt government measures to modify social and cultural patterns of conduct (as anticipated by Article 5). The Committee's View in Viola's case could influence the Committee, in later COs or GRs, to urge other states to adopt expedited procedures for establishing reproductive health clinics either by national or foreigners because this would make health care more freely available, less expensive, or both. The Committee would be all more likely to do so in the face of evidence that cultural or religious prejudices now discourage or prevent the establishment of such clinics. If enhancing access to reproductive health care was Viola's principal goal—and not personal financial recompense—the CEDAW regime's anticipated remedies might be more desirable.[150]

There is one further reason why Viola, even in a world in which she had the resources to file an investor-state claim, might opt for CEDAW. It is possible that the CEDAW Committee might respond to Viola's case by recommending that State Y not only permit her to conclude the needed contracts to open her clinics but also provide financial compensation for any costs she incurred as a result of Y's actions or inactions. To be sure, it is unlikely that even in a hypothetical case involving harm to individual financial business interests, the CEDAW Committee would engage in the kind of detailed assessments of the value of lost business opportunities that is the bread and butter of investor-state tribunals. Nonetheless, the Committee has often recommended that financial recompense be awarded in cases resulting in harm to property interests.[151] Interestingly, when the Committee has done so, it has sometimes suggested that such financial recompense may not only include loss of income, social benefits, or legal costs but also compensation for emotional anguish and the need for physical and psychological rehabilitation.[152] As this suggests, the Committee has sometimes taken into account the need to compensate for harms, such as emotional harm, that would not be cognizable under ISDS and its focus on the fair market value of the property as a mere commodity.[153] It is possible that the CEDAW Committee

---

[150] While actions on behalf of a class of foreign investors have been accepted under ISDS, these have been rare and limited to a class of specifically enumerated investors which can demonstrate cognizable (and measurable) adverse financial impact. *See, e.g.*, Georges Chalfoun, *Mass Proceedings before ICSID: Life after Abaclat and Ambiente Ufficio* (Sept. 23, 2013), https://us.practicallaw.thomson reuters.com/4-538-2308. Even in such cases, when investor claimants win in the course of ISDS, the result is usually specific remedial compensation in response to past harms suffered as a result of the respondent state's breach of treaty—but not arbitral demands that states change their laws to avoid comparable harms to other investors in the future. As noted, the CEDAW Committee's remedial recommendations in its outputs often address the need for states to change laws or practices to avoid future harms to women in general.

[151] *See, e.g.*, chapter 2, section 2.4.3.5 (discussing Concluding Observations recommending recognition and distribution of joint marital property).

[152] Campbell & Connors, *supra* note 100, at 872 n. 323. This may also be included in national court awards that enforce CEDAW. *Id.* n. 324 (discussing Gonzalez Carreno v. Spain).

[153] *See* Merrill, *supra* note 110.

might recommend financial recompense from State Y that would exceed the fair market value of the underlying property interests.

There is yet another consideration that may affect Viola's remedial choices. ISDS tribunals, as noted, focus on remedying the harm inflicted on an individual investor or a business enterprise. Investor-state arbitrators are likely to show little or no regard to the surrounding context, including the impact of an award on an impoverished state. The CEDAW Committee's recommendations in response to communications filed by individuals, by contrast, are likely to consider how any remedy accorded to an individual interacts with the rights of others. As noted, were Viola to be engaged in reproductive health care services, the Committee's recommended remedies would like include consideration of the impact on the availability of such services for women generally—and not solely the impact on Viola. As suggested by the agri-business example, the CEDAW Committee would consider in that case the negative externalities imposed by such a business on the rights of women. It could be relevant to the Committee's consideration of Viola's communication whether, for example, a win for Viola would contribute to social unrest in Y[154] or undermine Y's land reform or other efforts to benefit rural women.[155] The CEDAW Committee's more holistic approach to remedies may make predicting the outcome of its processes less predictable for prospective communicants.

5.11 Conclusions

Legal comparisons between regimes, national or international, are justified on various grounds. Comparativists argue that one can learn much about one's own legal system from the study of another's. Comparing the CEDAW and investment regimes can illuminate the qualities of CEDAW even for those most familiar with it. This chapter's distinctions between the two regimes at sections 5.2–5.9 and how these may affect real world claims as illustrated in section 5.10 reveals much about the CEDAW Committee's radically different approach to individual rights to private property protected under the international investment regime.

The CEDAW Committee has addressed proprietary interests comparable to those identified as "assets" under IIAs but addresses those that are enjoyed

---

[154] Compare the majority award to the dissent by Philip Sands in Bear Creek Mining Corporation v. Republic of Peru. *See* Bear Creek Mining Corporation v. Republic of Peru, ICSID Case No. ARB/14/21, Award and Partial Dissenting Opinion of Professor Philippe Sands (Nov. 30, 2017), https://www.italaw.com/cases/2848.

[155] *See, e.g.*, Martins Paparinskis, *A Case Against Crippling Compensation in International Law of State Responsibility*, 83 MOD. L. REV. 1246 (2020) (acknowledging but criticizing the obligation of "full compensation" irrespective of consequence in the investment regime).

collectively and not merely individually—from rights to graze and fish on Indigenous lands, to rights to adequate shelter for women made vulnerable from various forms of intersectional discrimination, to equal social security or pension benefits denied to women with unpaid care responsibilities. It has pursued substantive equality and not merely formal equality, thereby closely examining whether underlying structural conditions or cultural or other stereotypes undermine laws that appear to be, but are actually not, gender neutral. It has sought to protect the principle of equality with respect to publically supplied proprietary interests—from social security benefits to state-supplied rural development programs. It has further punctured the public/private divide left intact by IIAs by intruding into "private" spaces such as the home. Unlike IIAs, which accord benefits to (foreign) businesses without imposing additional burdens, the CEDAW regime has sought to impose duties on privately owned as well as state-owned businesses and extended those obligations beyond its own territory. With respect to such businesses, it has refused to accord them nonrelative rights such as open-ended guarantees of fair and equitable treatment or rights to prompt, adequate, and effective compensation in cases involving direct or indirect expropriation. It has greatly increased the regulatory burdens on both states and private parties within them by requiring both to eliminate all forms of discrimination, direct or indirect, and does not delimit states' efforts to achieve that goal through narrow derogation clauses. Moreover, as illustrated by the hypothetical at section 5.10, the CEDAW regimes "soft" approaches to applicable remedies and their enforcement enable more gender-sensitive remedies. These include "moral" and not just "compensatory" damages to both individual and groups, as well as a greater spectrum of forms of reparation than is the case under investor-state arbitration. When these distinctions are considered as a whole, it becomes even more evident how the CEDAW Committee has responded to claims that it is yet another international tool to support colonial-era conceptions of property rights as defined by capital exporters from the West. Viewed from the perspective of the international investment regime, CEDAW's property jurisprudence suggests an effort to de-colonize, and not merely re-engender, the concept of property.

The comparisons of CEDAW and IIAs in this chapter are relevant to the contentions made by a number of critics of CEDAW and international human rights regimes canvassed in chapters 3 and 4. The comparison demonstrates that international law has more than one way of protecting economic interests that are common to market states, however these are defined under national law. It shows that it matters whether property rights are being protected in order to protect equal rights for women or whether they are protected to promote global free markets. It demonstrates that it matters how property is protected— whether through guarantees of compensatory payment should commodified property interests be harmed by state action or through remedies designed to rectify violations of substantive equality to protect both individual women and groups of women. It matters whether these rights are protected to protect the intersectional identities of persons or the profits of foreign investors facing discrimination on the single basis of nationality. And, as section 5.10 illustrates, the comparison reveals that these abstract distinctions will matter should someone seek a remedy under one regime versus the other.

CEDAW focuses only on discrimination against women, whether or not the affected person is a foreign investor or an entrepreneur. It applies an exceedingly capacious concept of discrimination that requires states to correct direct and indirect forms of it by either the state or private parties both within and outside its territory and incorporates other human rights and fundamental freedoms. As interpreted, CEDAW imposes on states a freestanding goal to promote equality. CEDAW's exceedingly broad embrace of all forms of systemic and structural discrimination enables the contestation of state practices that are immune from supranational scrutiny under the more formalistic "like treatment" test applicable under IIAs. On the other hand, the Committee's recommendations are not legally binding under the Convention and the level of state compliance with such recommendations is probably no greater than that achieved by other global human rights regimes.

At a high level of generality, it is debatable whether both regimes and not only the investment regime should be seen as embodying international law's "civilizing mission." Although CEDAW treats property as a "human" and not a corporate or commercial right, a number of its property protections reflect assumptions about how market states operate—and how women in such states need to be "economically empowered" to protect many of their underlying rights. That Committee sometimes emphasizes, as would proponents of "gender equality/equity" within the World Bank, the need for women to have formal title to land when such titles are available to men, particularly with respect to rural land.[156] In response to

---

[156] *See, e.g.*, CO on Korea, CEDAW/C/KOR/CO/7, ¶ 36 (2011) (expressing concern that over 70 percent of family farms are owned by men) as well as COs on Comoros (CEDAW/C/COM/CO/1–4, ¶ 38), Cabo Verde (CEDAW/C/CPV/CO/7–8, ¶¶ 30–31), Albania (CEDAW/C/ALB/CO/3, ¶ 36), and China (CEDAW/C/CHN/CO/7–8, ¶ 44) (addressing difficulties with respect to land registration). The CEDAW Committee also regularly urges states to adopt joint titling in the context of marriage to protect women's rights under Article 16(1)(h). *See, e.g.*, COs on Armenia (CEDAW/C/ARM/CO/4, ¶ 39), Bulgaria (CEDAW/C/BGR/CO/4–7, ¶ 48), Croatia (CEDAW/C/HRV/CO/4–5, ¶ 43), Tunisia (CEDAW/C/TUN/CO/6, ¶ 61), Azerbaijan (CEDAW/C/AZE/CO/5, ¶ 39), and Togo (CEDAW/C/TGO/CO/6–7, ¶ 41). Moreover, its oft-repeated recommendations to states to "harmonize" statutory and customary law regarding women's right to property (*e.g.*, CO on Liberia, CEDAW/C/LBR/CO/7–8, ¶¶ 43–44) or ensure that property rights are governed by "civil contractual and property law rather than religious law" (*e.g.*, CO on Sri Lanka, CEDAW/C/LKA/CO/8, ¶ 45) may also encourage titling. See also GR No. 34 on the Rights of Rural Women, CEDAW/C/GC/34, ¶ 77 (2016) (expressing concern that in the course of land reform land is registered only in men's names) and GR No. 37 on Gender-Related Dimensions of Disaster Risk Reduction in the Context of Climate

evidence of discrimination against women, the Committee has sometimes made recommendations that state-issued legal titles should supersede the traditional practices of certain Indigenous, cultural, or religious groups.[157] These aspects of the Committee's jurisprudence might be read to suggest that the Committee, like the strong investor-protective US-Argentina BIT, values only one model of "good governance."[158] For those who define "neo-liberalism" so broadly as to embrace any reliance on market capitalism, the CEDAW Committee's failure to condemn capitalism or denounce individual private property would make the CEDAW regime as complicit in neo-liberalism as all other human rights regimes.[159]

But context matters. When the CEDAW Committee makes recommendations that sound like some that would be made by Hernando de Soto, it is in response to evidence that the absence of legal title in a particular state is having a discriminatory impact on women. Fundamentally, the CEDAW and investment regimes take very different attitudes toward economic globalization and the value of free capital and trade flows. This difference, reflected in this chapter, flows from their different origins. When the United States launched its highly influential program to convince developing states to conclude treaties to protect foreign investors in the 1980s and inspired the enormous wave of BIT ratifications in the 1990s, its negotiators sought to convince prospective treaty partners that the exceptionally strong property protections in the US Model BIT of 1987 only codified basic rules for running a modern capitalist economy.[160] The United States argued that the investor rights in these treaties were those expected of states anxious to turn the page away from former state-run models to market capitalism.[161] Concluding an investment treaty with the United States in the waning days of the Cold War was widely seen as a way of joining the Capitalist Side of the Cold War divide. As time passed, however, critics of IIAs came to see those agreements

Change, CEDAW/C/GC/37, ¶¶ 69–70 (2018) (expressing concern with the disparity between the large numbers of female subsistence farmers and the percentage that own land).

[157] *See, e.g.*, COs on Vanuato (CEDAW/C/VUT/CO/4–5, ¶¶ 32–33), Sierra Leone (CEDAW/C/SLE/CO/6, ¶¶ 34–37), Botswana (CEDAW/C/BOT/CO/3, ¶¶ 39–40), Solomon Islands (CEDAW/C/SLB/CO/1–3, ¶ 45), Burundi (CEDAW/C/BDI/1, ¶¶ 39–42), Equatorial Guinea (A/59/38, ¶ 190) (all expressing concern about discriminatory provisions in customary law governing marriage and family relations or traditional practices regarding access to property, land, and inheritance). *See also* Views concerning Communication No. 48/2013, E.S & S.C. v. United Republic of Tanzania, CEDAW/C/60/D/48/2013 (2015) (finding Tanzania in violation because it enforced customary laws that denied two widows their family property). Compare chapter 3, section 3.2 (discussing Hernando de Soto's views and his critics).

[158] *See generally* Kerry Rittich, *The Properties of Gender Equality*, in HUMAN RIGHTS AND DEVELOPMENT: TOWARDS MUTUAL REINFORCEMENT 87 (Philip Alston & Mary Robinson eds., 2005).

[159] *See* chapter 3, section 3.2 (discussing de Soto's disparagement of customary practices, including "informal" land ownership).

[160] *See, e.g.*, Kenneth Vandevelde, *Investment Liberalization and Economic Development: The Role of Bilateral Investment Treaties*, 36 COLUM. J. TRANSNAT'L L. 501 (1998).

[161] *Id.*

as the modern-day equivalent of promises that were once extracted (sometimes literally at gunpoint) from developing states during the age of imperialism.[162] By contrast, CEDAW's near-universal ratification was achieved without comparable ideological baggage. Contrary to those who suggest that international human rights regimes were intended to be accessories to capitalism, it is important to point out the obvious: states did not ratify CEDAW in order to signal their approval of market capitalism over alternatives.

By contrast, the investment regime's approach to protecting property is the embodiment of neo-liberalism however that term is defined.[163] International investment protection treaties have been and, on the whole remain, instruments on behalf of "homo economicus."[164] Their principal object continues to be to advance the economic development of states by opening the door to greater capital flows. Those treaties and ISDS jurisprudence seek to protect the individual property rights of investors. Indeed, that regime retains its prominence over rival human rights conceptions of property rights because the world's most powerful states continue, as leading capital exporters, to endorse that goal. That regime favors the formalization, individualization, and commodification of property— precisely the tripartite conventional wisdom used to promote globalization-cum-development that elicits the ire of critics of international law's neo-colonialist "civilizing mission."[165]

Comparative law is also commonly justified as a tool to enable lessons to be drawn from one regime to the other. For those now engaged in reforming IIAs and ISDS in response to the "sovereign backlash" that has engulfed both, CEDAW's property jurisprudence presents a rich set of alternative conceptions of what it means to protect property rights. The CEDAW regime could suggest the need to reform IIAs to enable a much wider scope to permit states to regulate property to protect equality for women without incurring the threat of possible investor-state claims. It could inspire derogation clauses in IIAs that would enable states not only to protect the environment or labor rights but explicitly authorize good faith efforts by states to comply with their obligations under CEDAW and other human rights treaties, including with respect to land

---

[162] *See, e.g.*, Andrew Guzman, *Why LDCs Sign Treaties That Hurt Them: Explaining the Popularity of Bilateral Investment Treaties*, 38 VA. J. INT'L L. 639 (1998) (arguing that BITs may harm LDCs but that these countries faced great constraints in acting on behalf of their common interests).

[163] For discussion of definitions of "neo-liberalism," see chapter 3, section 3.2.

[164] *See generally* THE NINE LIVES OF NEOLIBERALISM 4 (Quinn Slobodian et al. eds., 2020). The gender specificity of the term, given the domination of men in the corporate world writ large, seems apt.

[165] *See generally* Rittich, *supra* note 158; Muthucumaraswamy Sornarajah, *The Neo-Liberal Agenda in Investment*, *in* REDEFINING SOVEREIGNTY IN INTERNATIONAL ECONOMIC LAW (Wenhua Shan et al. eds., 2005); ANTONY ANGHIE, IMPERIALISM, SOVEREIGNTY AND THE MAKING OF INTERNATIONAL LAW (2005). *See also* discussion of critics of international law's "civilizing mission" in chapter 3, section 3.2.

reforms and urban renewal designed to protect women's rights. Consideration of CEDAW's jurisprudence could inspire limits on the guarantees offered to foreign investors in future IIAs, including limits on their abilities to expand their business, irrespective of the consequences on women's inequality. These need not require formal amendments to existing treaties but could include CEDAW-friendly interpretations by state parties where such joint party interpretations, binding on investor-state arbitrators, are authorized by an IIA. CEDAW's progressive property jurisprudence might inspire reforms to the relatively strict rules that now constrain the capacity of states to file successful counterclaims against investor-claimants.[166] More radically, the next generation of IIAs could impose arbitral, enforceable obligations on foreign investors consistent with states' obligations under CEDAW to ensure that private parties do not discriminate against women, enable states to file counterclaims against businesses that violate CEDAW, or impose compliance with CEDAW's jurisprudence as a precondition for investors to resort to ISDS.[167] That would change the very nature of the international investment regime.

There are also possible lessons for human rights activists who argue that human rights regimes like CEDAW need to be reformed to permit legally binding and enforceable remedies in response to individual claims. Some who dismiss CEDAW as powerless rhetoric have penance-envy. They would like the regime to have more sticks in the form of binding arbitration or adjudication, like the investment (and WTO) regimes. The investment regime is a reminder that such remedies, depending on how they are structured and financed, may be financially costly and may require lengthy proceedings. Enforceable adjudicative justice is not free and is not necessarily timely. Arbitral enforcement generates resentment—as the sovereign backlash against both the investment and trade regimes' dispute settlement systems suggest.

It is harder to imagine potential lessens for the CEDAW Committee from the investment regime but some possibilities exist. As discussed more specifically in chapter 6, the law of remedies under universally applicable human rights treaties, including CEDAW, is still under development. It is neither harmonious nor coherent. It is possible that the CEDAW Committee could learn something from investor-state tribunals' more rigorous consideration of what are

---

[166] These may enable respondent states in investor-state arbitrators to file counterclaims that would enable women to be compensated for certain environmental harms resulting from private parties' abuse of property rights to the detriment of women among others. *See generally* Maxi Scherer et al., *Environmental Counterclaims in Investment Treaty Arbitration*, 36 ICSID Rev. Foreign Inv. L.J. 413 (2021).

[167] *See, e.g.*, UN Conference on Trade and Development, UNCTAD's Reform Package for the International Investment Regime (2018 ed. 2018); Int'l Inst. for Sustainable Dev., Model International Agreement on Investment for Sustainable Investment: Negotiators' Handbook (2d ed. 2006).

appropriate financial remedies when certain property interests are undermined. The Committee's understandable resistance to the commodification of property need not prevent the Committee from being more specific (and less differential to states) when it comes to making recommendations that would provide suitable recompense to women who have been financially harmed by the violation of their equal property rights. There remains room, even with respect to transitional justice styled remedies for groups of women, to design financial recompense or forms of reparations that do not simply return the women harmed by discriminatory practices to the status-quo ante but "subvert, even if in a modest way, those pre-existing conditions" by, for example, requiring states by way of providing guarantees of nonrepetition to undertake changes to structures and practices that led to the underlying harms.[168] Greater attention to providing CEDAW's stakeholders with more predictable guidance on likely remedies may also enhance the legitimacy (and appeal) of its communications procedure. More generally, future CEDAW Committee members may want to borrow a page from investor-state arbitrators' general concern for generating "jurisprudence constant" with respect to the substantive law and not merely remedies. CEDAW's property jurisprudence might have a greater impact—and elicit more use by activists—if it was both more accessible and more consistent.

No one can predict with certainty whether the international investment and CEDAW regimes will continue to occupy separate silos. It is possible that the two regimes' respective property jurisprudence will converge over time. As suggested previously in section 5.10, overlapping claims in the two regimes could generate common jurisprudence at least with respect to some issues. Some may hope that a combination of reforms to the contents of IIAs and more enlightened or progressive interpretations of such treaties by investor-state arbitrators (or by a future global investment court) will expand the regulatory space for states, shrink the investment guarantees offered exclusively to foreign investors, or both. There is, to be sure, some evidence of such "progressive" trends.[169] Second- and third-generation IIAs have made more space for the consideration of human rights, and some recent ISDS rulings, such as *Urbaser v. Argentina*, have shown a greater solicitude for human rights, at least *in dicta* if not outcomes.[170]

---

[168] Rubio-Marín & Sandoval, *supra* note 108, at 1070–71.

[169] *See, e.g.*, UN Conference on Trade and Development, IIA Issues Note, The Changing Landscape: New Treaties and Recent Policy Developments, UNCTAD/DIAE/PCB/INF/2020/4 (July 2020).

[170] Urbaser S.A. and Consorcio de Aguas Bilbao Bizkaia, Bilbao Biskaia Ur Partzuergoa v. The Arg. Republic, ICSID Case No. ARB/07/26, Award (Dec. 8, 2016), 18 ICSID Rep. 554 (2020) (addressing the merits of Argentina's counterclaim against the foreign investor in which that state alleged that the investors' actions had undermined Argentina's duty under international law to supply clean water to its population). The award in *Urbaser* affirmed, *in dicta*, the right to clean water under international law and, while it ultimately dismissed Argentina's counterclaim and upheld the investor's claim, also did not award monetary damages to the "winning" investor.

There are many reasons why the worlds of property jurisprudence depicted in this chapter may remain in separate silos, however. Most of the older, strongly investor-protective BITs remain in place, continue to generate most of today's ISDS claims and ISDS jurisprudence, and are likely to continue to generate disparate results between the two regimes.[171] The business stakeholders that support IIAs have not shown any inclination to transform these treaties into tools to enforce international human rights and they are not as likely to rely on IIAs that greatly dim the prospects of winning an investor-state claim. To the extent possible, powerful multinational corporations will find ways to secure access to arbitration and favorable rights through alternatives, including direct contracts with their host states. Most investor-state arbitrators are very likely to continue to rely principally on rulings issued by prior ISDS tribunals, with a frequent second source being WTO case law (particularly with respect to the trade's regime similar emphasis on national and MFN treatment)—albeit with a glancing look at ECtHR case law under an exceptionalist paradigm.[172] It is unlikely that ISDS will be wholly displaced by the establishment of a single international investment court and very likely that most investor-state arbitrators will continue to have backgrounds in commercial or public international law but not human rights.[173]

Absent radical structural changes to the international investment regime, the past of ISDS, including the path dependencies under which its adjudicators operate, portends its future. The international investment regime is unlikely to become the progressive developer of property rights that CEDAW now is. Moreover, as the next chapter will suggest, the CEDAW Committee's own path dependencies—its reliance not only on own internal sources of authority but on commonalities with other human rights regimes—are likely to perpetuate the distinctions between the two regimes described in this chapter.

---

[171] *See, e.g.*, discussion *supra* section 5.1. *See also* Alvarez, *supra* note 32.

[172] *See, e.g.*, ALVAREZ, *supra* note 24, at 204–06 (discussing ISDS rulings that either draw from or distinguish WTO case law on national or MFN treatment but also a number of rulings that address ECtHR jurisprudence).

[173] For a description of the professional backgrounds of investor-state arbitrators, *see* Joost Pauwelyn, *The Rule of Law without the Rule of Lawyers? Why Investment Arbitrators Are from Mars, Trade Adjudicators from Venus*, 109 AM. J. INT'L L. 761 (2015).

6
Unity Within Diversity: Comparisons with the ICCPR and the ICESCR

6.1 Introduction

Given CEDAW's origins, text, and object and purpose, it is not surprising that the CEDAW Committee's output has been influenced by and has itself influenced the jurisprudence generated by other UN human rights treaty bodies. This chapter describes the jurisprudence relating to property produced by the Human Rights Committee (HRC) under the International Covenant on Civil and Political Rights (ICCPR)[1] and the Committee on Economic, Social and Cultural Rights (CESCR) under the International Covenant on Economic, Social and Cultural Rights (ICESCR), with a view toward drawing comparisons with CEDAW's property jurisprudence.[2] Although the two Covenants, as is well known, omit explicit mention of the right to property contained in the Universal Declaration of Human Rights, the jurisprudence under all three regimes address many of the same issues that are the subject of this book. Despite a number of differences in the texts of the three human rights treaties, the underlying property jurisprudence shares considerable unity under a shared human rights framework.

6.2 Property and Equality in the ICCPR Framework

6.2.1 The ICCPR's Equality Framework

The ICCPR's nondiscrimination framework centers on the guarantees found in Article 2(1) (the obligation to "respect and to ensure" Covenant rights "without distinction of any kind, such as race, colour, sex, language, religion, political or other opinion, national or social origin, property, birth or other status"), Article

---

[1] International Covenant on Civil and Political Rights, opened for signature Dec. 19, 1966, 999 U.N.T.S. 171.
[2] International Covenant on Economic, Social and Cultural Rights, opened for signature Dec. 16, 1966, 993 U.N.T.S. 3; Convention on the Elimination of All Forms of Discrimination Against Women, opened for signature Dec. 18, 1979, 1249 U.N.T.S. 13.

3 (the undertaking to ensure the equal right of men and women to the enjoyment of Covenant rights), and Article 26 (the right to equality before the law and equal protection of the law). These basic provisions are supplemented by Article 4(1) (permitting derogations for public emergency but barring any discrimination on the ground of race, color, sex, language, religion, or social origin), Article 14(1) (equality before courts and tribunals), and Article 23(4) (equality of rights and responsibilities of spouses).

Both Article 2(1) and Article 3 are "accessory" prohibitions or "subordinate norms,"[3] guaranteeing nondiscriminatory enjoyment of the rights otherwise in the Covenant. Article 26's guarantee, by contrast, is an autonomous right, extending its protection for equality under the law to bar any discrimination on the same listed grounds as under Article (2)(1) to rights that may not be explicitly included in the Covenant.[4] Under one of the HRC's landmark decisions, *S.W.M. Broeks v. Netherlands*, Article 26's scope of application was interpreted as extending to socioeconomic rights otherwise beyond the scope of the ICCPR.[5] In combination, these three provisions should achieve, in principle, the same goal as under CEDAW: namely, a bar on discrimination on the basis of sex with regard to all civil, political, economic, social, and cultural rights.

Given its scope, Article 26 has been one of the most significant Covenant rights, with the Committee having decided over 120 individual communications on the merits under it alone, far more than the number of Views issued to date under the CEDAW.[6] The ICCPR discrimination jurisprudence has been called "rich and dynamic,"[7] particularly since it extends not only to economic, social, and cultural rights but also to discrimination on the basis of homosexuality[8] and nationality.[9]

As indicated by Article 4(1), the HRC has affirmed in several of its General Comments (GCs) that states' nondiscrimination obligations have a special status.[10] It has indicated that "the equal enjoyment of human rights by women must be protected during a state of emergency"[11] and that there may be "no restriction upon or derogation from equal enjoyment by women of all

---

[3] Paul M. Taylor, A Commentary on the International Covenant on Civil and Political Rights: The UN Human Rights Committee's Monitoring of ICCPR Rights 60 (2020) [hereinafter ICCPR Commentary].

[4] *See* HRC GC No. 18 on Non-discrimination, CCPR/C/21/Rev.1/Add.1, ¶ 12 (1989).

[5] HRC Views concerning S.W.M. Broeks v. Netherlands, CCPR/C/29/D/172/1987 (1990). *See also* HRC Views Concerning Zwaan-de-Vries v. Netherlands, CCPR/C/OP/2/209/1984 (1987).

[6] Shreya Atrey, *Fifty Years On: The Curious Case of Intersectional Discrimination in the ICCPR*, 35 Nordic J. Hum. Rts. 220 (2017).

[7] *Id.*

[8] HRC Views concerning Toonen v. Australia, CCPR/C/50/D/488/1992 (1994).

[9] HRC Views concerning Gueye v. France, CCPR/C/35/D/196/1985 (1989).

[10] *See* HRC GC No. 18, *supra* note 4, ¶ 2.

[11] *Id.* ¶ 7.

fundamental human rights recognized or existing pursuant to law, conventions, regulations or customs, on the pretext that Covenant does not recognize such rights or that it recognizes them to a lesser extent."[12] The HRC has confirmed that Article 2(1) requires states parties to "respect" and to "ensure" with immediate effect, all Covenant rights to all persons who may be within their territory and to all persons subject to their jurisdiction.[13] The obligation to "respect" in Article 2(1) imposes restraints on the state itself, which cannot restrict the enjoyment of rights beyond the permissible limits circumscribed for each right.[14] The obligation to "ensure" "requires States parties to take all necessary steps to enable every person to enjoy those rights,"[15] which "includes the removal of obstacles to the equal enjoyment of rights, the education of the population and state officials in human rights, and the adjustment of domestic legislation so as to give effect to the Covenant rights."[16] According to the HRC, Article 2(1) obligations are both negative and positive in nature.[17] States' positive obligations can only be fully discharged if individuals are also protected against violations committed by private persons or entities.[18] This includes a duty to exercise due diligence to prevent, punish, investigate, or redress harm caused by non-state actors.[19] State parties must therefore end discriminatory actions, both in the public and private sectors.[20] The Committee has also used Article 26 to justify states' duties to prohibit private acts of discrimination[21] and to uphold affirmative action as a legitimate tool to combat discrimination.[22] States' duties to take all necessary measures to achieve these ends are also deemed to have immediate effect and be subject to no qualification.[23] Reservations to Article 2 are considered incompatible with

---

[12] HRC GC No. 28: Article 3 (The Equality of Rights Between Men and Women), CCPR/C/21/Rev.1/Add.10, ¶ 9 (2000).
[13] HRC GC No. 31[80], The Nature of the General Legal Obligation Imposed on States Parties to the Covenant, CCPR/C/21/Rev.1/Add.13, ¶ 10 (2004).
[14] *Id.* ¶ 6.
[15] HRC GC No. 28, *supra* note 12, ¶ 3.
[16] *Id.*
[17] HRC GC No. 31[80], *supra* note 13, ¶ 6.
[18] *Id.* ¶ 8; *See also* HRC GC No. 28, *supra* note 12, ¶ 4.
[19] HRC GC No. 31[80], *supra* note 13, ¶ 8.
[20] HRC GC No. 28, *supra* note 12, ¶ 3.
[21] HRC Views concerning Love et al. v. Australia, CCPR/C/77/D/983/2001 (2003).
[22] HRC Views concerning Ballantyne v. Canada, CCPR/C/47/D/359/1989 (1993).
[23] HRC GC No. 31[80], *supra* note 13, ¶ 14. Nowak, in the ICCPR Commentary, argues that all provisions of the Covenant are directly applicable and, with the entry into force of the Covenant for any state party, place that state under an immediate international obligation to respect and ensure these rights, the only exception in his view being Article 23(4) that obligates states merely to "implement the equality of [rights and responsibilities of spouses as to marriage] progressively." MANFRED NOWAK, U.N. COVENANT ON CIVIL AND POLITICAL RIGHTS: CCPR COMMENTARY 61 (3d ed. 2019) (noting that art. 23(4) requires states to "take appropriate steps to ensure equality.") As many have noted, the ICESCR's reliance on progressive implementation was deemed inappropriate for the ICCPR since the strongest supporters of civil and political rights (namely Western states) were accustomed to the direct and immediate enforcement of such rights.

the object and purpose of the ICCPR.[24] A state cannot attempt to justify a failure to adopt the necessary measures, as required under Article 2(2), by reference to political, social, cultural, or economic considerations.[25]

6.2.2 Women's Equality

The HRC's affirmation that the "right to equality before the law and freedom from discrimination requires action against discrimination by public and private agencies in all fields,"[26] including "in fields affecting basic aspects of ordinary life such as work or housing," has a special significance for women.[27] Since the Covenant also imposes positive duties on state parties to take measures to guarantee the equality of rights of the persons concerned,[28] state parties must not only adopt protective measures but also take "positive measures in all areas" to achieve the effective and equal empowerment of women.[29] The Committee has also stated that the principle of equality requires states parties to take affirmative action in order to diminish or eliminate conditions which cause or help to perpetuate discrimination prohibited by the Covenant. Affirmative action may address historic, national, or cultural prejudice, and may involve granting preferential treatment for a time in specific matters. Such legitimate differentiations, comparable to those authorized under CEDAW's Article 4, can remain in place so long as needed to correct discrimination.[30]

The Committee has repeatedly acknowledged in both its GC and Concluding Observations (COs) that inequality in the enjoyment of rights suffered by women and their subordinate role is "embedded in tradition, history and culture, including religious attitudes."[31] It has called out these barriers to achieving gender equality,[32] noting that gender discrimination is deeply rooted in social structures such as presumptively male heads of family,[33] patriarchal attitudes and prejudices,[34] and customary law[35] that lead, in some cases, to women being treated as minors.[36] Accordingly, the HRC has repeatedly rejected appeals to

---

[24] HRC GC No. 31[80], *supra* note 13, ¶ 5.
[25] *Id.*
[26] HRC GC No. 28, *supra* note 12, ¶ 31.
[27] *Id.* ¶ 8.
[28] HRC GC No. 18, *supra* note 4, ¶ 5.
[29] HRC GC No. 28, *supra* note 12, ¶ 3.
[30] HRC GC No. 18, *supra* note 4, ¶ 10.
[31] HRC GC No. 28, *supra* note 12, ¶ 5.
[32] *See, e.g.*, HRC CO on Georgia, CCPR/C/GEO/CO/5, ¶¶ 16(a) & 24(a) (2022).
[33] *See, e.g.*, HRC CO on Korea CCPR/C/79/Add.114, ¶ 10 (1999).
[34] *See, e.g.*, HRC CO on Jordan CCPR/C/79/Add.35, ¶ 15 (1994).
[35] *See, e.g.*, HRC CO on Gambia, CCPR/CO/75/GMB, ¶ 16 (2002).
[36] *See, e.g.*, HRC CO on Lesotho CCPR/C/79/Add.106, ¶ 10 (1999).

long-standing tradition as a justification for differential treatment based on gender[37] and declared legislation based on gender stereotypes discriminatory.[38]

The HRC has also noted the particular socioeconomic vulnerability of women in both its GCs and COs, including a higher propensity to suffer from poverty,[39] be unemployed,[40] work in the informal sector,[41] and earn only the minimum wage.[42] In some of its COs, the Committee has begun to criticize gendered barriers to social security benefits.[43]

6.2.3 The Meaning of Discrimination

While the ICCPR itself does not define "discrimination," the HRC has explicitly drawn on jurisprudence under both the Convention on the Elimination of All Forms of Racial Discrimination (CERD) and CEDAW to shape its own interpretation.[44] The HRC has defined discrimination in GC 18 as

> any distinction, exclusion, restriction or preferences which is based on any ground such as race, colour, sex, language, religions, political or other opinion, national or social origin, property, birth or other status, and which has the purpose or effect of impairing or nullifying or impairing the recognition, enjoyment or exercise by all persons, on an equal footing, of all rights and freedoms.[45]

That General Comment 8 further affirms that the enjoyment of rights and freedoms on an equal footing "does not mean identical treatment in every instance."[46] At the same time, the Committee has required those claiming discrimination to prove that they have been treated differently from others in similar situations that must not be relevantly distinguishable.[47]

---

[37] *See, e.g.*, HRC Views concerning Müller and Engelhard v. Namibia, CCPR/C/74/D/919/2000 (2002).
[38] *See, e.g.*, S.W.M. Broeks v. the Netherlands, *supra* note 5; F.H. Zwaan-de-Vries v. the Netherlands, *supra* note 5.
[39] *See, e.g.*, HRC CO on Russia, CCPR/CO/79/RUS, ¶ 9 (2003).
[40] HRC CO on France, CCPR/C/FRA/CO/4, ¶ 13 (2008).
[41] *See, e.g.*, HRC CO on Cambodia, CCPR/C/KHM/CO/3, ¶ 16 (2022).
[42] *See, e.g.*, HRC CO on New Zealand, CCPR/C/NZL/CO/6, ¶ 17 (2016). The Committee has also repeatedly problematized discriminatory labor practices such as pregnancy tests prior to hiring and dismissals on the grounds of pregnancy or childbirth. *See, e.g.*, HRC CO on Japan, CCPR/C/JPN/CO/6, ¶ 9 (2014).
[43] HRC CO on Mexico, CCPR/C/MEX/CO/6, ¶ 11 (2019).
[44] *See, e.g.*, HRC GC No. 18, *supra* note 4, ¶ 6 (citing to the relevant provisions of CERD and CEDAW)
[45] *Id.* ¶ 7.
[46] *Id.* ¶ 8.
[47] ICCPR COMMENTARY, *supra* note 3, at 729–86 (discussing Article 26, namely equality before the law or equal protection).

The reference to "purpose or effect" in the HRC's preceding definition demonstrates that both direct and indirect discrimination are covered in principle by the Covenant. Critics argue that in practice, however, the Committee has consistently fallen short in recognizing forms of indirect discrimination under its communications procedure.[48] Central to this failure is the Committee's view that rules or decisions with detrimental impact for persons of a protected category do not amount to discrimination if they are based on "objective or reasonable grounds."[49] Despite the centrality of this test, the HRC has never specified the meaning of those underlying terms. Even in its GC 18, the Committee merely repeats that the criteria for a differentiation have to be "reasonable and objective" and that the distinction has to achieve a legitimate purpose in order to be justified.[50] Critics have argued that these terms are too vague to provide reliable guidance. Niels Petersen argues that the result is that the Committee appears to pay "lip-service to the concept [of indirect discrimination] without actually engaging with its substance and implications."[51] The Committee has also at times summarily rejected a claim of discrimination on the basis that the law in question "affects all individuals equally," without even contemplating the possibility of indirect discrimination.[52]

Commentators have also complained that the ICCPR's discrimination jurisprudence, while vast, has historically turned a blind eye to inequalities which occur not only on the basis of a single ground but on two or more intersecting grounds.[53] The HRC's "pathological" aversion to intersectional discrimination in its reasoning has, it is argued, hindered the pursuit of women's equality, especially within the realm of socioeconomic rights.[54] Relevant examples include unmarried women who are economically dependent on social assistance or on their partners in cohabitation or marriage-like relationships. While women alleging discrimination on the grounds of both marital status and gender have been among the most persistent claimants before the HRC,[55] that Committee has tended to focus on only a single discriminatory ground under Article 26 and given short shrift to the multiple and intersecting discriminatory grounds raised by the underlying facts in such cases.[56] Shreya Atrey contends that while most such cases display clear patterns of disadvantage created by the interwoven grounds of gender/sex, marital status, and poverty/class/socioeconomic status/

---

[48] *See, e.g.*, Niels Petersen, *The Implicit Taxonomy of the Equality Jurisprudence of the UN Human Rights Committee*, 34 LEIDEN J. INT'L L. 421 (2021).
[49] *See, e.g.*, HRC Views concerning Althammer v. Austria, CCPR/C/78/D/998/2001, ¶ 10.2 (2003).
[50] HRC GC No. 18, *supra* note 4, ¶ 13.
[51] Petersen, *supra* note 48, at 430.
[52] HRC Views concerning Prince v. South Africa, CCPR/C/91/D/1474/2006 (2007).
[53] Atrey, *supra* note 6, at 220.
[54] *Id.*
[55] *See, e.g.*, HRC Views concerning L.G. Danning v. Netherlands, CCPR/C/OP/2, at 205 (1987).
[56] Atrey, *supra* note 6.

reliance on social status, "intersectionality has fallen through the cracks of the Committee's discrimination jurisprudence."[57] She argues that these consistent failures evince a rather limited understanding of the root causes for women's equality.[58]

The HRC communications that are the focus of Atrey's criticisms, however, preceded the Committee's release of its GC 28 in 2000. That Comment noted that discrimination against women "may be intertwined with discrimination on other grounds . . . and that state parties should address ways in which any instances of discrimination on other grounds affects women in a particular way and include information on measures taken to counter these effects."[59] While this Comment implicitly embraces the concept of intersectional discrimination, it did not expressly adopt the concept of intersectional discrimination in the way that CEDAW Committee General Recommendation (GR) 28 did.[60] To date, under the individual communications procedure the Committee has only begun to acknowledge intersectional discrimination in a handful of times, almost exclusively in the context of state regulation of female religious dress such as headscarves.[61] Similarly, the HRC's post–GC 28 COs evince only occasional recognition and mention of systemic,[62] structural,[63] and intersecting forms of discrimination.[64]

6.2.4 Women's Property Rights

As is well known, the ICCPR does not address property rights as such. Express references to women's property rights have been mostly confined to the Committee's GCs and COs. In GC 28, the Committee made clear that states must "ensure that the matrimonial regime contains equal rights and obligations for both spouses with regard to the ownership or administration of property," and that, to do so,

> states should review the legislation to ensure that married women have equal rights in regard to their ownership and administration of such property, where necessary . . . and ensure that no sex based discrimination occurs in respect of the acquisition or loss of nationality by reason of marriage, of residence rights

---

[57] *Id.* at 233.
[58] *Id.* at 226–32.
[59] HRC GC No. 28, *supra* note 12, ¶ 30.
[60] GR 28 on the Core Obligations of States Parties, CEDAW/C/GC/28, ¶ 18 (2010).
[61] *See, e.g.*, HRC Views concerning Sonia Yaker v. France, CCPR/C/123/D/2747/2016 (2018).
[62] *See, e.g.*, HRC on Israel, CCPR/C/ISR/CO/5, ¶ 10 (2022).
[63] *Id.*
[64] *See, e.g.*, CO on Uruguay, CCPR/C/URY/CO/6, ¶ 6 (2022).

and of the right of each spouse to retain the use of his or her original family name and so on.[65]

The Committee had also previously affirmed that women "should also have equal inheritance rights to those of men when the dissolution of marriage is caused by the death of one of the spouses."[66]

Similarly, the Committee has emphasized the relevance of Article 16 (recognition as a person before the law) for gender equality, noting that women often see their right to be recognized as a person before the law curtailed because of sex or marital status.[67] Article 16 implies that "the capacity of women to own property, to enter into a contract or to exercise other civil rights cannot be restricted on the basis of marital status or any other discriminatory ground."[68] In practice, however, Article 16 has almost never been relevant to a Committee's decision on an individual communication concerning women's property rights, even where it was explicitly argued.[69]

In its COs, the Committee has consistently called out examples of women's inequality with respect to inheritance,[70] including as a result of failure to register customary marriages,[71] as a result of the devolution of property,[72] or other cases in such women do not inherit property on an equal footing with men,[73] or are not entitled to shares equal to those as men.[74] It has also criticized discriminatory laws of succession,[75] along with women's inequality with respect to marital property,[76] in the management of family assets,[77] rights of succession with respect to land permits and grants, the disposal of immovable property,[78] and in the appropriation of property from widows.[79] Its COs frequently signal out for criticism pervasive discrimination with respect to personal status laws affecting marriage, family, and inheritance.[80]

---

[65] HRC GC. No. 28, *supra* note 12, ¶ 25.
[66] HRC GC. No. 26: Continuity of Obligations, CCPR/C/21/Rev.1/Add.8/Rev.1, ¶ 26 (1997).
[67] HRC GC. No. 28, *supra* note 12, ¶ 19.
[68] Id.
[69] See, e.g., Views concerning Avellanal v. Peru, UN Doc. Supp. No. 40 (A/44/40), at 196 ¶ 7 (1988).
[70] See, e.g., HRC CO on Swaziland, CCPR/C/SWZ/CO/1, ¶ 24 (2017).
[71] HRC CO on Namibia, CCPR/CO/81/NAM, ¶ 9 (2004).
[72] HRC CO on Sri Lanka, CCPR/CO/79/LKA, ¶ 19 (2003).
[73] See, e.g., HRC CO on Burkina Faso, CCPR/C/BFA/CO/1, ¶ 15 (2016).
[74] Hum. Rts. Comm., Rep. of the Thirty-eight Session, ¶ 354, A/38/40 (Supp.) (1983).
[75] See, e.g., HRC CO on Kenya CCPR/C/KEN/CO/3, ¶ 7 (2012).
[76] See, e.g., HRC CO on Burkina Faso CCPR/C/BFA/CO/1, ¶ 15 (2016); HRC CO on Namibia CCPR/C/NAM/CO/2, ¶ 11 (2016).
[77] See, e.g., HRC CO on Congo CCPR/C/COD/CO/3, ¶ 11 (2006); HRC CO on Ghana, CCPR/C/GHA/CO/1, ¶ 11 (2016).
[78] See, e.g., HRC CO on Chile CCPR/C/CHL/CO/6, ¶ 12 (2014) (in the context of a matrimonial community property regime).
[79] See, e.g., HRC CO on Malawi CCPR/C/MWI/CO/1, ¶ 8 (2011).
[80] See, e.g., HRC CO on Burundi, CCPR/C/BDI/CO/2, ¶ 11 (2014).

By contrast, women's property rights are rarely the subject of individual communications before the HRC. In *Martínez de Irujo v. Spain*, the Committee refused to find a breach of Article 3 in conjunction with Article 26 where rules of hereditary succession to ranks and titles of nobility discriminated on the basis of sex.[81] The Committee decided the institution of nobility was not subject to the principles of equality or non-discrimination encompassed by the Convention. By contrast, in *Avellanal v. Peru*, the Committee found a breach of Article 14(1) in conjunction with Articles 3 and 26 where a provision in the Civil Code barred a married woman from suing her tenants for rent arrears because only husbands were entitled to represent matrimonial property before the courts.[82] Curiously, while the Committee found the author's claim of a breach of Article 16 (recognition as a person before the law) admissible, it did not rule on that point.[83]

6.2.5 Marital Status and Social Security

Early in its jurisprudence, the HRC established that while the Covenant did not require any state to enact legislation to provide for social security, when such legislation was adopted, it has to comply with the nondiscrimination guarantee in Article 26.[84] This flowed from the fact that Article 26 does not merely duplicate the guarantees already provided for an Article 2 but provides, as an independent right, the equal protection of the law. Article 26 is thus concerned with the obligations imposed on states with respect to their laws and their application.[85] The HRC supported interpretation of Article 26 in GC 18 stated that "the principle of nondiscrimination contained in article 26 is not limited to those rights which are provided for in the Covenant," as is the case with Article 2, but "prohibits discrimination in law or in fact in any field regulated and protected by public authorities ... Thus when legislation is adopted it must comply with the requirement that its content should not be discriminatory."[86]

Having clarified the role Article 26 plays within the Covenant, the Committee proceeded to strike down a provision that required married women to prove they were a "breadwinner" in order to receive benefits, a condition that did not apply to married men.[87] Crucial to this finding was the Committee's rejection of

---

[81] HRC Views concerning Isabel Hoyos Martinez de Irujo v. Spain, CCPR/C/80/D/1008/2001 (2004).
[82] Avellanal v. Peru, *supra* note 69, ¶ 7.
[83] Compare *id.* ¶ 7 to ¶ 11.
[84] *See, e.g.*, S.W.M. Broeks v. The Netherlands, *supra* note 5.
[85] *Id.* ¶ 12.3.
[86] HRC GC No. 18, *supra* note 4, ¶ 12.
[87] S.W.M. Broeks v. the Netherlands, *supra* note 5, ¶ 14.

the contention that the distinction in question was based on reasonable and objective criteria. The Committee opined that while "it appears on one level to be one of status (i.e. marriage)... is in fact one of sex, placing married women at a disadvantage compared with married men. Such a differentiation is not reasonable, and there seems to have been effective knowledge even by the state party by the enactment of a change in the law in 1985."[88] Petersen has argued that this illustrates the Committee's desire to combat gender stereotypes, which are often expressed in social benefits legislation.[89] As Atrey has pointed out, however, the Committee's decision to treat the claimant's assertion of sex, *and* social and marital status as simply "sex discrimination" effaced the intersectional nature of the discrimination at issue as it was specifically *married* women *in need of social benefits* because of their economic condition who were affected.[90] She argues that in that case, the Committee failed to recognize and address the structural disadvantages faced by women in marriage; a pattern that has continued in numerous claims brought against the Netherlands post-*Broeks* which have undermined the potential for Article 26 to advance substantive equality.[91]

Nonetheless, the HRC has found Article 26's protection against discrimination to apply at least in principle to many types of property interests. The HRC has found allegations of discrimination admissible with respect to: retirement pensions,[92] severance pay,[93] unemployment benefits,[94] disability pensions,[95] education subsidies,[96] employment,[97] veterans' pensions,[98] public health insurance,[99] survivors' pensions,[100] children's benefits,[101] and other property rights not mentioned in the Covenant.[102] At the same time, the HRC has been hesitant in upholding claims of direct or indirect discrimination whenever the claim of discrimination relates to social security legislation.[103] This is so even where

---

[88] *Id.*
[89] Petersen, *supra* note 48, at 432.
[90] Atrey, *supra* note 6, at 228.
[91] *Id.*
[92] HRC Views concerning Vos v. Netherlands, CCPR/C/66/786/1997 (1999).
[93] HRC Views concerning Orihuela Valenzuela v. Peru, CCPR/C/48/D/309/1988 (1993).
[94] *See, e.g.*, Zwaan-de-Vries v. Netherlands, *supra* note 5, ¶ 209.
[95] *See, e.g.*, Danning v. Netherlands, *supra* note 55; Vos v. Netherlands, *supra* note 92.
[96] *See, e.g.*, HRC Views concerning Waldman v. Canada, CCPR/C/67/D/694/1996, ¶ 10.6 (1999).
[97] *See, e.g.*, HRC Views concerning Bwalya v. Zambia, CCPR/C/48/D/314/1988, ¶¶ 6.6–6.7 (1993).
[98] HRC Views concerning Gueye et al. v. France, CCPR/C/35/D/196/1985 (1989).
[99] HRC Views concerning Sprenger v. the Netherlands, CCPR/C/44/D/395/1990 (1992).
[100] HRC Views concerning Pauger v. Austria, CCPR/C/44/D/415/1990 (1992); HRC Views concerning Hoofdman v. the Netherlands, CCPR/C/64/D/602/1994 (1998).
[101] HRC Views concerning Oulajin and Kaiss v. Netherlands, CCPR/C/46/D/406/1990 (1992).
[102] HRC Views concerning Haraldsson and Sveinsson v. Iceland, CCPR/C/91/D/1306/2004 (2007) (quota system unreasonably deprives authors of their property in fish stocks); HRC Views concerning Simuneck, Hastings, Tuzilova and Prochazka v. Czech Republic, CCPR/C/54/D/516/1992 (1995) (requirement of Czech citizenship and residency not a reasonable ground to deny compensation for previously confiscated property).
[103] ICCPR COMMENTARY, *supra* note 3, at 755.

the ground of distinction is as fundamental as gender, which, according to the Committee, places a heavy burden on the state party to explain the reason for the differentiation.[104] The Committee appears to consider distinctions made by the state in the context of social security legislation to be justifiable so long as a vague standard of reasonableness is met. Thus, the Committee has generally asked whether differentiations made in social security legislation were objective and reasonable,[105] as opposed to conducting "an impact analysis based on whether it impairs the recognition, enjoyment or exercise by all persons, on an equal footing, of all rights and freedoms," as it arguably strives to do according to the definition of discrimination it has adopted.[106]

In a number of cases the Committee considered the justifications offered by the Dutch government for differentiation in its social security legislation based on marital status to be reasonable and objective. *Danning* concerned a complaint concerning differences and disability benefits between married beneficiaries as opposed to those living in a common law marriage.[107] The Committee found in favor of the government, finding the differentiation based on objective and reasonable criteria because the decision to enter into a legal status by marriage lies entirely with the cohabiting persons. The Committee reasoned that by choosing not to enter marriage the claimant had not assumed the full extent of duties and responsibilities that married couples possess and consequently did not need to receive the full benefits provided for in Netherlands law for married couples.[108] *Danning* has been reaffirmed in the subsequent cases of *Hoofdman v. Netherlands* and *M.T. Sprenger v. Netherlands*, where distinctions between married and unmarried couples were found to be based on reasonable and objective criteria.[109]

Hoofdman suggests a certain reluctance by the Committee to second-guess the state even when its justifications lag behind social reality. The author unsuccessfully claimed that the denial of a widower's pension on the death of his partner with whom he cohabited constituted discrimination under Article 26 on the basis of his unmarried marital status.[110] The state relied on the fact that married and unmarried couples were subject to different sets of laws and regulations. In finding there had been no violation, the Committee did little more than recite its approach in *Danning*.[111] The dissent in *Hoofdman* argued, by contrast, that reasonable distinctions between married and unmarried couples can become

---

[104] HRC Views concerning Muller and Engelhard v. Namibia, CCPR/C/74/D/919/2000, ¶ 6.7 (2002).
[105] HRC Views concerning Cavalcanti Araujo-Jongen v. the Netherlands, CCPR/C/49/D/418/1990 (1993).
[106] Atrey, *supra* note 6.
[107] Danning v. Netherlands, *supra* note 55, at 205.
[108] *Id.* at ¶ 14.
[109] *See* discussion of Hoofdman v. Netherlands and Sprenger v. the Netherlands *infra*.
[110] Hoofdman v. Netherlands, *supra* note 100.
[111] *Id.* ¶ 11.4.

unreasonable over time when these become out of step with Dutch social reality.[112] The Concurring Opinion in *Sprenger* suggested by way of compromise that for purposes of Article 26 implementation, there was a difference between some Covenant rights that require immediate implementation and economic and social rights for which states may need time to achieve progress in implementation.[113] Some HRC members have expressed the view, in another Dutch case, that it is "for the legislature of each country, which best knows the socio-economic needs of the society concerned, to try to achieve social justice in the concrete context" and that for this reason, unless distinctions in social security legislation are "manifestly discriminatory or arbitrary, it is not for the Committee to reevaluate the complex socio-economic data and substitute its judgment for that of the legislatures of the States parties."[114]

As the authors of a Commentary on the ICCPR note, the Committee has not found many distinctions with respect to economic social and cultural rights to constitute Article 26 violations. As Sarah Joseph and Melissa Castan contend, this may be due to the fact that the HRC is more willing to defer to state parties' policies when dealing with complaints of discrimination in the economic field, as was recommended by Mr. Ando in a separate opinion in *Adam v. Czech Republic*.[115] It is noteworthy in this respect that other forms of differentiation in social security benefits have also led to findings of no violation. For example, differentiation was found to be neither unreasonable nor arbitrary in *Neefs v. Netherlands* when, as a result of sharing a household with his mother, the author received a lower level of social security benefit than if he had shared it with a nonrelative.[116] Similarly, no discrimination was found in *Snijders v. Netherlands* when a state-run medical insurance scheme adopted a user-pays approach to make it affordable, requiring those in residential care (such as the authors) to make personal contributions which were not payable by others.[117]

The distinctions that the HRC has made between successful and unsuccessful communications involving social security measures challenged under Article 26

---

[112] *Id.*

[113] Sprenger v. Netherlands, *supra* note 99 (concurring opinion) ("it is necessary to take into account that socioeconomic and cultural needs of society are evolving, so that legislation may well and often does lag behind developments. As such article 26 should not be interpreted as requiring absolute equality or nondiscrimination in that field at all times: instead it should be seen as a general undertaking on the part of the state to regularly review the legislation to ensure that it corresponds to the change in needs of society. In the field of civil and political rights the state party has to respect covenant rights such as fair trial immediately from the date of entry into do so without discrimination. But with regards to rights at a social economic it is generally understood that there may need some time for the progressive implementation of these rights.").

[114] Oulajin and Kaiss v. Netherlands, *supra* note 101 (Kurt Herdl et al. individual opinion).

[115] SARAH JOSEPH & MELISSA CASTAN, THE INTERNATIONAL COVENANT ON CIVIL AND POLITICAL RIGHTS: CASES, MATERIALS, AND COMMENTARY 1664 (3d ed. 2013).

[116] HRC Views concerning Neefs v. Netherlands, CCPR/C/51/D/425/1990 (1994).

[117] HRC Views concerning Snijders v. Netherlands, CCPR/C/63/D/651/1995 (1998).

are not altogether clear. Thus, while the Committee had found the distinctions between unmarried couples and married couples to be "reasonable and objective" in, for example, *Sprenger* and *Hoofdman*, it found the distinction between unmarried same-sex couples and married couples unsustainable in *Young v. Australia* and *X v. Colombia*.[118] *Young* was about the denial of a veteran's pension to a same-sex partner; *X v. Colombia* concerned the denial of a survivor's pension to a same-sex partner.

6.2.6 Forced Eviction

The HRC's jurisprudence on forced evictions is limited. Nonetheless, it has begun to identify the potential incompatibility of forced evictions with Article 17 (barring arbitrary or unlawful interference with privacy, family, home, or correspondence), sometimes in conjunction with Article 23 (protection of the family) and Article 27 (protecting ethnic, religious, or linguistic minorities of enjoy their own culture, practice their religion, or use their own language). While Article 26 is sometimes also raised by the authors of such communications, it is usually not taken up by the Committee.[119] By contrast with cases before the CESCR, communications grounded in forced evictions are not considered prima facie incompatible with the ICCPR.[120] By its terms, Article 17 protects only against "arbitrary" or "unlawful" interferences with one's home and family.[121]

The HRC has found that the term "family" is to be "given a broad interpretation to include all those comprising the family as understood in the society of the State party concerned."[122] A similarly wide concept of family has been adopted by the CESCR[123] and the CEDAW Committee.[124] In this regard, the Committee has

---

[118] HRC Views concerning Edward Young v. Australia, CCPR/C/78/D/941/2000 (2003); HRC Views concerning X v. Colombia, CCPR/C/89/D/1361/2005 (2007).

[119] *See, e.g.*, HRC Views concerning Vojnović v. Croatia, CCPR/C/95/D/1510/2006, ¶ 8.8 (2009); HRC Views concerning Georgopolous v. Greece, CCPR/C/99/D/1799/2008, ¶ 7.4 (2010).

[120] See *infra* section 6.2.6.

[121] According to the HRC, a review for arbitrariness ensures that even interference that is anticipated by the law must be in accordance with the provisions and objectives of the Covenant and thus reasonable under the circumstances. HRC GC No. 16: Article 17 (Right to Privacy), *reprinted in* Compilation of GCs and GRs Adopted by Human Rights Treaty Bodies, UN Doc. HRI/GEN/1/Rev. 9 (Vol. I), ¶¶ 2–4 (1988). *See also id.* ¶ 2.

[122] *See, e.g.*, HRC Views concerning Dauphin v. Canada, CCPR/C/96/D/1792/2008, ¶ 8.3 (2009). *See also* HRC GC No. 28, *supra* note 12, ¶ 27 ("in giving effect to recognition of the family in the context of Art. 23, it is important to accept the concept of the various forms of family, including unmarried couples and their children and single parents and their children, and to ensure the equal treatment of women in these contexts.").

[123] CESCR GC No. 4: The Right to Adequate Housing (Art. 11(1) of the Covenant), E/1992/23, ¶ 6 (1991); CESCR GC No. 5: Persons with Disabilities, E/1995/22, ¶ 30 (1994).

[124] GR No. 21 on Equality in Marriage and Family Relations, A/49/38, ¶ 13 (1994).

held that "permanent risk of forced eviction without secure and appropriate relocation option and without any clarity as to their prospects in terms of housing will amount to a clear interference with family life."[125]

The HRC has interpreted the term "home" to mean the place where a person resides or carries out her usual occupation.[126] A "home" is not limited to premises which are lawfully occupied or which have been lawfully established under domestic law; nor is it limited to traditional residences or fixed abodes.[127] It does not require the possession of legal title.[128] However, in the absence of any legal interest in the home, the individual must provide evidence of unchallenged occupation or that she has used it to carry out her usual occupation for a period of time.[129] While this does not require daily physical presence at the dwelling, an individual must demonstrate credible evidence of occupation of the home.[130] If the individual is voluntarily absent at the time of the alleged interference, it must be shown that ties to the home have not been severed.[131] Such proof can consist of the "presence of personal belongings or other signs of occupation that indicate it was claimed as a residence."[132] Where eviction occurs while the individual is physically absent, and has only recently occupied a dwelling in combination with its mere seasonal use, the dwelling is not sufficient to be a home within the meaning of Article 17.[133] In determining whether a dwelling constitutes a home within the meaning of Article 17, relevant factors include whether the authorities knew or should have known that the dwelling constituted an individual's residence;[134] or, in instances of informal settlements, whether the authorities tolerated or even implicitly accepted the settlement in question, such as by providing infrastructural support.[135] The duration a settlement was in existence as well as the individual's length of occupation can also be determinative,[136] as well as whether the authorities had decided not to take any measure to dislodge individuals from it.[137]

The requirement of legality and non-arbitrariness means that no interference can take place except in cases envisaged by the law. Any forced eviction

---

[125] HRC Views concerning I Elpida v. Greece, CCPR/C/118/D/2242/2013, ¶ 12.7 (2016).
[126] See HRC GC No. 16, *supra* note 121, ¶ 5.
[127] See, e.g., I Elpida et al. v. Greece, *supra* note 125, ¶ 12.3.
[128] HRC Views concerning Naidenova et al. v. Bulgaria, CCPR/C/106/D/2073/2011 (2012).
[129] I Elpida et al. v. Greece, *supra* note 125, ¶¶ 12.3–12.6.
[130] *Id.* ¶ 12.3.
[131] HRC Views concerning G.I. v. Greece, CCPR/C/126/D/2582/2015, ¶ 8.7 (2019).
[132] *Id.* ¶ 8.8.
[133] *Id.*
[134] *Id.*
[135] *Id.* ¶ 8.9.
[136] *Id.* ¶ 8.8.
[137] I Elpida v. Greece, *supra* note 125, ¶ 12.6.

must itself comply with the provisions, aims, and objectives of the Covenant[138] and has to be, "in any event, reasonable in the particular circumstances."[139] In *Georgopolous v. Greece*, the Committee found a forced eviction and demolition of a family's dwelling unlawful and arbitrary where the state party failed to adduce sufficient evidence to counter the author's allegations to that effect.[140] It also appeared to matter that in this case that the authors had "been born in the settlement from which they were evicted, had always lived there apart from for seasonal employment elsewhere, and had immediately contacted the municipal authorities to seek an administrative remedy after learning of their eviction."[141] In *Georgopolous*, the Committee held that Article 2(3)(a) obligates state parties to provide reparation, including compensation, to those affected by the forced eviction.[142] In a separate case arising from the same demolition orders, the Committee sided with the state party since, in that instance, the communicant could not prove the same length of residence.[143]

Evictions that are undertaken pursuant to national law can nonetheless be in violation of the Covenant if they are arbitrary. In *Vojnović v. Croatia*, the Committee found that loss of the family home as a result of termination of a lifetime tenancy against a backdrop of discrimination against Croatian Serbs was such an arbitrary interference.[144] Even though the revocation of residency had occurred legally, the Committee found the revocation arbitrary, given that both the author's initial abandonment of his tenancy and inability to travel back to defend his property interests was caused by duress and related to discrimination.[145] It also mattered that the author had informed the state party of his reasons for departing the property and had unjustifiably been prevented from participating in the court proceedings determining his tenancy rights.[146] In determining whether an interference with a home is arbitrary, the Committee will take into account the length of the settlement as well as whether a planned eviction decision had given due consideration to the consequences, including the risk of rendering the affected individuals homeless and the availability of satisfactory replacement housing.[147] The Committee has made clear that states should limit the use of forced eviction by considering all feasible alternatives and should

---

[138] HRC GC No. 15: The Position of Aliens Under the Covenant, *reprinted in* Compilation of GCs and GRs Adopted by Human Rights Treaty Bodies, UN Doc. HRI/GEN/1/Rev. 9 (Vol. I), ¶ 3 (1986).
[139] HRC GC No. 16, *supra* note 121, ¶ 4.
[140] HRC Views concerning Georgopolous v. Greece, CCPR/C/99/D/1799/2008, ¶ 7.3 (2010).
[141] G.I. v. Greece, *supra* note 131, ¶ 8.8 (distinguishing Georgopoulos et al. v. Greece).
[142] HRC Views concerning Georgopoulos et al. v. Greece, CCPR/C/99/C/1799/2008, ¶ 9 (2010).
[143] G.I. v. Greece, *supra* note 131, ¶ 8.8.
[144] HRC Views concerning Vojnović v. Croatia, CCPR/C/95/D/1510/2006, ¶ 8.7 (2009).
[145] *Id.*
[146] *Id.*
[147] *See, e.g.*, HRC Views concerning Naidenova et al. v. Bulgaria, CCPR/C/106/D/2073/2011, ¶¶ 14.2–14.7 (2012).

eviction be necessary—as where there is an urgent reason for it—guaranteeing alternative housing.[148] An individual's lack of property rights cannot serve as the only justification for the issuance of the eviction order.[149] In the absence of any pressing need to change the status quo, states must also take into account special circumstances, such as decades-old community life.[150]

Forcible evictions have also arisen in the HRC's COs. The HRC raised the problem with respect to displaced persons living in camps in Haiti who faced evictions without other solution being found, for example.[151] Evictions were also deemed a problem with respect to those living in informal settlements in Kenya who faced evictions without prior consultation and appropriate resettlement arrangements.[152] Other instances have involved mass house demolitions and forced evictions in Turkmenistan to make way for construction and development projects without adequate notice or provision for alternative accommodation;[153] evictions of Syrian refugees in Lebanon;[154] and in Italy against Roma, Sinti, and Camminanti communities.[155]

6.2.7 Remedial Approach

The ICCPR does not contain a provision for granting reparation or just satisfaction to victims of violations of the rights set forth in the Covenant. Its Optional Protocol simply states that the HRC, having considered the individual communications received under the Protocol, shall adopt its views and forward them to the parties concerned.[156] However, even the HRC's earliest responses to communications included recommendations that states provide redress for violations.[157] The HRC has invoked Article 2(3) as the legal basis for these remedies.[158]

Over time, the HRC has become more specific in indicating that states' duties to provide effective remedies include compensation and require the taking of steps to ensure that similar violations do not reoccur.[159] In 1981, the HRC opined

---

[148] *See, e.g.*, I Elpida v. Greece, *supra* note 125, ¶¶ 12.4 & 12.8.
[149] *Id.* ¶ 12.5.
[150] *Id.*
[151] HRC CO on Haiti, CCPR/C/HTI/CO/1, ¶ 18 (2014) (following the 2010 earthquake).
[152] HRC CO on Kenya, CCPR/C/KEN/CO/3, ¶ 21 (2012).
[153] HRC CO on Turkmenistan, CCPR/C/TKM/CO/2, ¶ 34 (2017).
[154] HRC CO on Lebanon, CCPR/C/LBN/CO/3, ¶ 37 (2018).
[155] HRC CO on Italy, CCPR/C/ITA/CO/6, ¶ 14 (2017).
[156] Optional Protocol to the International Covenant on Civil and Political Rights art. 5, Dec. 19, 1966, 999 U.N.T.S. 302 [hereinafter ICCPR Optional Protocol].
[157] Velaska David, *Reparations at the Human Rights Committee: Legal Basis, Practice and Challenges*, 32 NETHERLANDS Q. HUM. RTS. 14 (2014).
[158] HRC Views concerning Saldias de Lopez v. Uruguay, CCPR/C/13/D/52/1979, ¶ 14 (1981).
[159] *See, e.g.*, HRC Views concerning Weissman and others v. Uruguay, A/35/40 (Supp.), ¶ 17; HRC Views concerning Weisz v. Uruguay, CCPR/C/OP/1, ¶ 17 (1984).

in a communication concerning a Mauritanian law that discriminated against women with foreign spouses that the state should change its law for the first time.[160] In its GCs, the Committee has clarified that remedies should take into account the special vulnerability of certain categories of persons[161] and ought to make reparation to individuals whose Covenant rights have been violated.[162]

The HRC has affirmed that reparation within the meaning of Article 2(3) can involve restitution, rehabilitation, and measures of satisfaction, such as public apologies, public memorials, guarantees of nonrepetition, and changes in relevant laws and practices, as well as bringing to justice the perpetrators of human rights violations.[163] Beyond victim-specific remedies, the HRC often recommends that states take measures to avoid recurrence of the violations in question. As noted, this may require changes in laws or practices.[164] Restitution can involve the return of property[165] or the restoration of rights.

The most common means of redress in HRC jurisprudence is, however, compensation.[166] In this regard, the HRC has expressly requested reparation by way of material damages, including payment of the victims' fines and legal costs,[167] their loss of earnings,[168] as well as moral damages.[169] Though the Committee generally refrains from defining the amount of compensation or material damage due to victims, the HRC's recommendations have become a bit more specific over time.[170] For example, in a case involving a communicant's suspension from work in contravention of legal procedures, the HRC indicated that the state should provide compensation "comprising a sum equivalent to the payment of the arrears of salary and remuneration that he would have received from the time at which he was not reinstated to his post."[171] In a few other cases, the HRC has required the state to pay in a particular manner[172] or suggested the amount of money that ought to be paid.[173]

Generally, the HRC has not been as specific when it comes to its recommendations that states change their domestic laws.[174] In the typical case,

---

[160] HRC Views concerning Aumeeruddy-Cziffra and others v. Mauritius, CCPR/C/OP/1, ¶ 11 (1984).
[161] HRC GC No. 31[80], *supra* note 13, ¶ 15.
[162] *Id.* ¶ 16.
[163] *Id.*
[164] *Id.* ¶ [17.
[165] *See, e.g.*, HRC Views concerning Simunek et al. v. Czech Republic, CCPR/C/54/D/516/1992, ¶ 9 (1995).
[166] David, *supra* note 157, at 12.
[167] HRC Views concerning Wilson v. Philippines, CCPR/C/79/D/868/1999, ¶ 9 (2002).
[168] HRC Views concerning Adimayo M. et al. v. Togo, CCPR/C/51/D/422/1990, ¶ 9 (1994).
[169] HRC Views concerning Schedko v. Belarus, CCPR/C/77/D/886/1999, ¶ 12 (1999).
[170] David, *supra* note 157, at 21.
[171] HRC Views concerning Gedumbe v. Democratic Republic of Congo, CCPR/C/75/D/641/1995, ¶ 6.2b (2002).
[172] Wilson v. Philippines, *supra* note 167, ¶ 9.
[173] HRC Views concerning Tulzhenova v. Belarus, CCPR/C/103/D/1838/2008, ¶ 11 (2011).
[174] David, *supra* note 157, at 22.

the HRC simply states that the state party should amend, adjust, modify, or even simply review the law without further guidance as to what changes ought to take place.[175] Accordingly, some complain that such recommendations, no more specific than when they first appeared in the practice of the HRC in 1980, undermine the Committee's ability to address gross, systematic, and structural violations.[176] A particular example of the problem is illustrated by a large number of cases concerning the confiscation of property in the Czech Republic. In those cases, the HRC acknowledged that this was a reoccurring violation but simply recommended that the state party should "review its legislation to ensure that all persons enjoy both equality before the law and equal protection of the law."[177]

Criticisms of the HRC's remedial approach have been particularly pointed with regard to violations of Article 26, the ICCPR's autonomous requirement for nondiscrimination and the provision with the widest potential coverage since it extends to rights not specifically contained in the Covenant. As Velaska David points out, communications that rely only on Article 26—which some call "pure cases of discrimination"—generally avoid specific recommendations to award financial compensation.[178] Even when the damage from a finding of "pure" discrimination is financially accessible, the HRC in such cases tends simply to recommend an "effective or appropriate" remedy without further specification.[179] Moreover, guarantees of nonrepetition in such cases take the form of vague requests to states to prevent similar violations[180] or refer only in general terms to the need to review or amend domestic legislation.[181] In the past, the HRC has explicitly granted compensation to victims of "pure" discrimination rarely, as to compensate for the loss of an earned social benefit[182] or as an alternative to the restitution of property.[183]

---

[175] *See, e.g.*, HRC Views concerning Salgar de Montejo v. Colombia, CCPR/C/15/D/64/1979, ¶ 12 (1982); HRC Views concerning Karakurt v. Austria, CCPR/C/74/D/965/2000, ¶ 10 (2002); HRC Views concerning Mennen v. The Netherlands, CCPR/C/99/D/1797/2008, ¶ 10 (2010).

[176] David, *supra* note 157, at 29; CHERIF BASSIOUNI & WILLIAM SCHABAS, NEW CHALLENGES FOR THE UN HUMAN RIGHTS MACHINERY: WHAT FUTURE FOR THE UN TREATY BODY SYSTEM AND THE HUMAN RIGHTS COUNCIL PROCEDURES? 211, 213 (2011).

[177] *See, e.g.*, Simunek v. Czech Republic, *supra* note 165, ¶ 9.

[178] David, *supra* note 157, at 31.

[179] *See, e.g.*, Broeks v. Netherlands, *supra* note 5, ¶ 16; Avellanal v. Peru, *supra* note 69, ¶ 12. Complaints about the HRC's inconsistency in recommending financial recompense is not limited to cases alleging violations of Article 26. In the famous case of *Lovelace v. Canada*, the Indigenous woman who was deprived of her right to reside in her community's reserve because she married to a non-Indian man—a consequence not applicable to men who married non-Indian women—did not receive any remedy at all but merely a declaration that Canada had violated Article 27. HRC Views concerning Lovelace v. Canada, CCPR/C/13/D/24/1977 (1981).

[180] *See, e.g.*, Vos v. The Netherlands, *supra* note 92, ¶ 9.

[181] *See, e.g.*, Simunek v. Czech Republic 165, *supra* note, ¶ 9.

[182] *See, e.g.*, HRC Views concerning Pauger v. Austria, CCPR/C/65/D/716/1996, ¶ 12 (1999) (requesting the state to provide the author with a lump-sum payment calculated on the basis of full pension benefits).

[183] Simunek v. Czech Republic, *supra* note 165, ¶ 12.2.

There are signs, however, that the Committee's remedial practice with respect to "pure" violations of Article 26 may be evolving. It appears that the HRC is now including more specific and tailored remedial recommendations when violations are found in such cases. In *Mueller v. Namibia*, for example, the Committee recommended that the state refrain from enforcing a cost order or refund the respective amount of money.[184] In both *X v. Colombia* and *Young v. Australia*, the Committee specified that the remedy involved a "reconsideration of the request for a pension without discrimination on grounds of sex."[185] Shortly thereafter, in *L.N.P v. Argentine Republic*, the Committee specified that the "obligation to ensure that similar violations are not perpetrated in the future" required "guaranteeing access for victims, including victims of sexual assault, to the courts in conditions of equality."[186] Similarly, in *Elena Genero v. Italy*, which turned on a height requirement for firefighters that indirectly discriminated against women, the Committee considered that "full reparation" required "adequate compensation," that reconsideration be given to admitting the author as a permanent firefighter, and that the state amend its current law to prevent future violations.[187]

The Committee also issued very specific recommendations in *McIvor and Grismer v. Canada*, which concerned the discriminatory denial of Indian status impacting socioeconomic benefits to Full Nations members of matrilineal descent.[188] The Committee recommended that the state party was, "inter alia, to ensure that section 6(1)(a) of the 1985 Indian Act . . . is interpreted to allow registration by all persons including the authors who previously were not entitled to be registered under section 6(1)(a) solely as a result of preferential treatment accorded to Indian men over Indian women born prior to Apr. 17, 1985 and to patrilineal descendants over matrilineal descendants, born prior to Apr. 17, 1985; and to take steps to address residual discrimination within First Nations communities arising from the legal discrimination based on sex in the Indian Act."[189] This is exceptional for the HRC insofar as it prescribes exact steps needed to cure not just the author's rights violation but to "address residual discrimination" applicable to many others into the future. In so doing, the ICCPR appeared to move much closer to the ICESCR's and CEDAW's respective remedial approaches—which as discussed *infra*, usually attempt to go beyond particular remedies for the authors of the underlying communications.

---

[184] HRC Views concerning Mueller and Engelhard v. Namibia, CCPR/C/74/D/919/2000, ¶ 8 (2002).
[185] X v. Colombia, *supra* note 118, ¶ 9; Edward Young v. Australia, *supra* note 118, ¶ 12.
[186] HRC Views concerning L.N.P v. Argentine Republic, CCPR/C/102/D/1610/2007, ¶ 14 (2011).
[187] HRC Views concerning Elena Genero v. Italy, CCPR/C/128/D/2979/2017, ¶ 9 (2020).
[188] HRC Views concerning McIvor and Grismer v. Canada, CCPR/C/124/D/2020/2010 (2018).
[189] *Id.* ¶ 9.

6.3 ICESCR

6.3.1 The ICESCR's Equality Framework

Article 2(2) of the ICESCR requires its state parties to "guarantee" that they will permit the exercise of the rights in that treaty "without discrimination of any kind" and proceeds to list the same categories of barred discrimination as in the ICCPR's Article 2(1).[190] That nondiscrimination guarantee is supplemented by the ICESCR's Article 3's requirement that states "ensure the equal rights of men and women to the enjoyment of all economic, social and cultural rights" contained in that treaty. This clause, although seen as clarifying the obligation not to discriminate on the basis of sex that is already contained in the ICESCR's Article 2, provides further support for overlapping conceptions of equality between the ICESCR and CEDAW regimes.[191] As discussed *infra*, the ICESCR Commentary on Article 3 draws on a number of sources, particularly within CEDAW, to make affirmations that could easily have been made by the CEDAW Committee.[192]

The ICESCR's inclusion of "other status" within the barred categories under its Article 2 has also enabled its Committee to protect older persons. The Committee's GC 6 warns state parties that while age discrimination is not comprehensively prohibited, it is very rarely acceptable.[193] It urges special attention to older women, who, "because they have spent all or part of their lives caring for their families without engaging in a remunerated activity entitling them to an old-age pension," are faced with critical situations.[194] Those comments are

---

[190] Compare ICCPR, *supra* note 1, art. 2(1) to ICESCR, *supra* note 2, art. 2(2) (both affirming states' obligation not to discriminate "as to race, colour, sex, language, religion, political or other opinion, national or social origin, property, birth or other status").

[191] *See, e.g.*, BEN SAUL ET AL., THE INTERNATIONAL COVENANT ON ECONOMIC, SOCIAL AND CULTURAL RIGHTS COMMENTARY, CASES AND MATERIALS 177 (2014) [hereinafter ICESCR COMMENTARY] (noting the influence of the CEDAW Committee on the CESCR Committee's interpretation of Article 3); *id.* at 218 (discussing Article 3). Commonalities between the ICESCR's Article 3 and CEDAW are also suggested by some states' reservations. States like Bangladesh, Kuwait, and Qatar have all reserved on the ICESCR's Article 3 in order to "preserve" their constitutional or national laws. Qatar's reservation indicates that the intent is to avoid derogations from "Islamic Sharia with regard to inheritance and birth." Such reservations echo equally controversial reservations made by many states to CEDAW. *See* appendix 2.

[192] That Commentary draws on a number of soft law instruments to affirm, for example, that the unequal enjoyment of economic, social, and cultural rights contributes to women's economic dependence, denial of personal autonomy, and lack of empowerment—while impeding their ability to engage civil and political rights. ICESCR COMMENTARY, *supra* note 191, at 219–20 (discussing Article 3). It also affirms that states' obligations under Article 3 are immediate and not subject to progressive realization. *Id.* at 223.

[193] CESCR GC No. 6: The Economic, Social and Cultural Rights of Older Persons, E/1996/22, ¶ 12 (1995).

[194] *Id.* ¶ 20. The Committee also stresses that women without contributory pensions should, given their greater life expectancies, be the principal beneficiaries of noncontributory pension schemes. *Id.*

consistent with the CEDAW Committee's criticisms of state practices that harm older women, among the many other categories CEDAW embraces as part of its scrutiny over intersectional discrimination.[195]

While CEDAW does not indicate that state parties are permitted to make distinctions between the treatment accorded to aliens and those it takes with respect to states' own nationals, Article 2(3) of the ICESCR indicates that developing countries may determine to what extent they will guarantee the "economic" rights contained in the treaty to non-nationals. The ICESCR, like CEDAW, has no explicit limits on its territorial application.

6.3.2 Women's Equality and Property Rights

The ICESCR, unlike the ICCPR, contains a number of rights that are comparable to some of those that this book includes as property rights under CEDAW. The ICESCR's Article 6, which requires states parties to recognize the right to work, states that states must realize this right "under conditions safeguarding fundamental political and economic freedoms to the individual." Its Article 10(2) indicates that special protection should be extended to mothers during a reasonable period before and after childbirth and that "during such period working mothers should be accorded paid leave or leave with adequate social security benefits." Article 11(1) recognizes the right to "an adequate standard of living . . . including adequate food, clothing and housing." Article 11(2) recognizes, under the right to be free from hunger, the duty of states to undertake agrarian reforms that "achieve the most efficient development and utilization of natural resources." Finally, Article 15(1)(c) indicates that states recognize the right of everyone to benefit from material interests resulting from their scientific, literary, or artistic production.

Given the fact that the Optional Protocol for the ICESCR only entered into force in May 2013 and, as of March 2023, had only twenty-six states parties, the CESCR's other outputs, apart from individual communications, have had an outsized significance in the interpretation of the Convention.[196] The CESCR's GC 16 from 2005, addressing the equal rights of men and women, provides a

---

That Comment also suggests that state should "help elderly persons to continue to live in their own homes as long as possible," including through assistance with restoration and enabling continued access. *Id.* ¶ 33.

[195] *See, e.g.*, chapter 2, section 2.9.1.3. *See also* GR No. 35 on Gender-Based Violence against Women, Updating GR No. 19, CEDAW/C/GC/35, ¶ 12 (2017) (including age as a relevant category of intersectional discrimination).

[196] Optional Protocol to the International Covenant on Economic, Social and Cultural Rights, opened for signature Sept. 24, 2009, 2483 U.N.T.S. 3 [hereinafter ICESCR Optional Protocol].

roadmap for what appears to be an evolving interpretative convergence between that Committee and CEDAW's when it comes to protecting women and specifically their property rights. That GC begins by affirming that equal rights for men and women is a fundamental principle of international law enshrined not only in the ICESCR's own Articles 2 and 3 (which it views as "integrally related and mutually reinforcing"), but also in the UN Charter, the Universal Declaration of Human Rights, and the ICCPR's Articles 3 and 26.[197] This sets the stage for the implicit contention that this fundamental right to equality is, by now, a principle of general customary law applicable to all countries irrespective of whether they have ratified a particular human rights treaty and a residual rule for the interpretation of all human rights treaties. The Committee has even suggested that Article 3's equality guarantee is "non-derogable," suggesting that any attempt by a state to reserve on this obligation would be void for violating the ICESCR's object and purpose.[198]

GC 16 embraces the view that women's "lesser status" is the product of tradition and custom and is not only the result of overt or covert acts of discrimination through state action.[199] That Comment explains why the ICESCR's Committee, like CEDAW's, has adopted a more expansive view of the obligation of states to redress those structural realities. It indicates that states the need to address these structural disadvantages through positive state action and not merely a limitation on the state's own actions. Accordingly, the CESCR adopts the broad definition of discrimination found in CEDAW's Article 8 and emphasizes the need for states to attack stereotypical assumptions, including by private parties.[200] It defines direct and indirect discrimination in ways that are indistinguishable from those made under CEDAW,[201] emphasizing the need to go beyond formal equality (and gender neutral laws), to ensure that substantive equality is actually achieved by taking into account "existing economic, social and cultural inequalities."[202] It also indicates the need for governments to go beyond passing laws that respect the principle of equality and actually take concrete steps to give them effect.[203] Notwithstanding the ICESCR's Article 2's progressive realization clause, which may appear to limit the obligations imposed under the ICESCR,[204]

---

[197] CESCR GC No. 16: The Equal Right of Men and Women to the Enjoyment of All Economic, Social and Cultural Rights (Art. 3 of the Covenant), E/C.12/2005/4, ¶¶ 1–3 (2005).
[198] *Id.* ¶ 17.
[199] *Id.* ¶ 5.
[200] *Id.* ¶ 11; *see also id.* ¶ 19 (stating that the obligation to protect requires states to "take steps aimed directly at the elimination of prejudices, customary and other practices that perpetuate the notion of inferiority or superiority of either of the sexes").
[201] *Id.* ¶¶ 12 & 13.
[202] *Id.* ¶¶ 8 & 18.
[203] *Id.* ¶¶ 6–9.
[204] Under the ICESCR's Article 2(1), states need only "take steps . . . to the maximum of its available resources" to progressively realize these rights.

GC 16 emphasizes that Article 2(2)'s nondiscrimination guarantee is a "mandatory" duty on state parties subject to "immediate" state obligation.[205]

The ICESCR's GC 16 also indicates that the equal right of men and women to enjoy ICESCR rights imposes the three levels of obligations on states—duties to respect, protect, and fulfill—that both the ICESCR and CEDAW have long affirmed.[206] The CESCR's enumeration of the specific state obligations under that trifold framework mirrors those of the CEDAW Committee. GC 16 points out, for example, that states' duty to protect requires the monitoring of non-state actors who violate the equality of men and women.[207] The overlap with the CEDAW Committee's interpretations or applications is also evident with respect to GC 6's specific examples of how the obligation to give effect to substantive equality between men and women impacts all the substantive rights contained in the ICESCR. The CESCR affirms, for example, that social security and pension benefits need to take into account the differing impact of compulsory retirement age provisions on men and women.[208] It affirms that the ICESCR requires that states provide the mostly female victims of domestic violence with access to safe housing and redress for physical, mental, and emotional damage;[209] that states must ensure equal rights to marital property and inheritance upon the death of a husband;[210] and that the right to adequate housing requires "that women have a right to own, use or otherwise control housing, land and property on an equal basis with men," in addition to assurances that women have access to or control over the means of food production.[211]

The CESCR has been particularly vocal with respect to the rights contained in the Convention's Article 11 (adequate standard of living). The Committee's GCs criticize denials of equal rights between men and women with respect to adequate housing, food, education, health, and water.[212] It has also echoed the CEDAW Committee's oft-stated point that women "experience distinct forms of discrimination due to the intersection of sex with such factors as race, colour, language, religion, political and other opinion, national or social origin, property, birth, or other status, such as age, ethnicity, disability, marital, refugee or migrant status, resulting in compounded disadvantage."[213] As this example

---

[205] CESCR GC No. 16, *supra* note 197, ¶ 16 (reaffirming CESCR GC No. 3). This reflects the text of the ICESCR's Article 2(1) in which state parties "undertake to guarantee" (not just agree to "take steps . . . to achieving progressively") that the rights in the Convention will be exercised without discrimination.
[206] *Id.* ¶¶ 17–21.
[207] *Id.* ¶ 20.
[208] *Id.* ¶ 26.
[209] *Id.* ¶ 27.
[210] *Id.*
[211] *Id.* ¶ 28
[212] *Id.* ¶ 4 (citing portions of GCs 4, 7, 12, 11, 13, 14, & 15).
[213] *Id.* 6, ¶ 5 (citing, instead of CEDAW, the CERD Committee's GC 25 from 2000). Interestingly, GC 16 only cites to the CEDAW Committee in support of the need for states to adopt temporary

suggests, while the texts of neither CEDAW nor the ICESCR explicitly address "intersectional" discrimination, the reality that individuals have more than one identity and may therefore face what both the HRC and the ICESCR Committees recognize as "multiple" forms of discrimination is well established under both regimes.

6.3.3 The Right to Housing and Forced Evictions

For purposes of this book, comparisons between the CEDAW and ICESCR regimes' approach to the right to housing, affirmed, respectively, in ICESCR's Article 11 and CEDAW's Articles 14(2)(h), 15(4), and 16(1)(h), are especially pertinent. Early on, the CESCR took the lead in defining the components of the right to adequate housing, including the concept of "legal security of tenure."[214] It affirmed, in 1991, that

> the right to housing should not be interpreted in a narrow or restrictive sense which equates it with, for example, the shelter provided by merely having a roof over one's head or views shelter exclusively as a commodity. Rather it should be seen as the right to live somewhere in security, peace and dignity... Adequate shelter means... adequate privacy, adequate space, adequate security, adequate lighting and ventilation, adequate basic infrastructure and adequate location with regard to work and basic facilities all at a reasonable cost.[215]

From the start, the CESCR ignored the outdated terms of Article 11(1), which suggested that the right to an adequate standard of living (including housing) was limited to male-headed households. It affirmed that this right, like all others in the treaty, was subject to the bar on discrimination in Article 2(2), and therefore applied to women individually as well as female-headed households.[216]

"Adequacy" in terms of housing requires, in the Committee's view, evaluation of (1) legal security (which may include rentals but which "guarantees legal

---

special measures to "accelerate the equal enjoyment by women of all economic, social and cultural rights" (citing to CEDAW GR 25 as well as its own GC 13). *Id.* ¶ 35, n. 14.

[214] *See* Ingunn Ikdahl, *Property and Security: Articulating Women's Rights to Their Homes*, in WOMEN'S HUMAN RIGHTS: CEDAW IN INTERNATIONAL, REGIONAL AND NATIONAL LAW 268, 278 (Anne Hellum & Henriette Sinding Aasen eds., 2013).
[215] CESCR GC No. 4: The Right to Adequate Housing (Art. 11(1) of the Covenant), E/1992/23, ¶ 7 (1991).
[216] Compare Article 11 of ICESCR ("for himself and his family") to CESCR GC No. 4, *supra* note 215, ¶ 6.

protection against forced eviction, harassment and other threats"); (2) availability of services essential for health, security, comfort, and nutrition; (3) affordability (which includes housing subsidies for those unable to obtain housing given their income); (4) habitability (particularly to protect health); (5) accessibility (which includes full and sustainability access to housing resources for disadvantaged groups such as the elderly, the impoverished, or the disabled); (6) location (permitting access to employment, health-care, schools, child-care, and other social facilities); and (7) cultural adequacy (requiring housing that enables the expression of different cultural identities).[217] Although the need for states to provide nondiscriminatory access to "adequate" housing is not explicitly mentioned in CEDAW, the CEDAW Committee appears to have incorporated the essence of that obligation into CEDAW.[218] The CESCR's additional affirmation that housing needs to enable the fulfillment of all other human rights in the ICESCR and the ICCPR is, of course, also consistent with CEDAW's cross-reference to other "human rights and fundamental freedoms in the political, economic, social, cultural, civil or any other field."[219] GC 4's insistence that states have an obligation, subject to immediate effect, to collect relevant data on homelessness and inadequate housing mirrors the CEDAW Committee's oft-repeated recommendations to states to the same effect.[220]

The CESCR has forcefully defended its view that "instances of forced eviction are prima facie incompatible" with the ICESCR "and can only be justified in the most exceptional circumstances, and in accordance with the relevant principles of international law."[221] Six years after making that statement the Committee "clarified" it, adding considerable detail to what the requirements for security of tenure means, the procedural protections against eviction or displacement that it affords, and the many intersections between the right to housing and other fundamental rights, including under the ICCPR.[222]

---

[217] CESCR GC No. 4, *supra* note 215, ¶ 9. The CESCR has found that the provision of housing needs to be suitable to, for example, the cultural needs of vulnerable minorities such as Roma. *See, e.g.*, Eur. Comm. S.R., European Roma Rights Centre v. Portugal, Complaint No. 61/2010, ¶ 49 (2011).
[218] *See, e.g.*, Chapter 2, section 2.11.1.6. But note the critiques of *Cecilia Kell v. Canada* by Inniss, Hohmann, and Tramontana in chapter 3 at section 3.1.2 (criticizing the CEDAW Committee's failures to explicitly incorporate and apply the CESCR Committee's seven guarantees emerging from the right to housing).
[219] Compare CESCR GC No. 4, *supra* note 215, ¶ 9 to CEDAW, *supra* note 2, art. 1.
[220] Compare CESCR GC No. 4, *supra* note 215, ¶ 13 to, for example, chapter 2, section 2.6.2.8.
[221] CESCR GC No. GC 4, *supra* note 215, ¶ 18. *See also id.* ¶ 8(a) (indicating that tenure can take a variety of forms—from rentals to owner-occupation—but irrespective of form it needs to protect persons "from forced evictions, harassment and other threats" and that states must take "immediate measures aimed at conferring legal security of tenure").
[222] CESCR GC No. 7: The Right to Adequate Housing (Art. 11.1): Forced Evictions, E/1998/22 (1997).

CESCR GC 7 defines "forced evictions"[223] and describes the many types of situations in which they occur.[224] It also defines what "legal protection against forced eviction" entails. That Comment affirms that the state itself must refrain from forced evictions, enact laws to provide the greatest possible security of tenure to occupiers of houses and land, otherwise conform to the ICESCR's rights, control strictly the circumstances under which evictions may be carried out, and ensure accountability for state agents or private parties who engage in such acts.[225] It reiterates, consistent with the ICESCR's Articles 2(2) and 3, that states are under an additional obligation to protect groups particularly vulnerable to evictions, such as women, from this form of discrimination.[226] Consistent with Article 4's insistence that limitations on treaty obligations need to be "determined by law", and undertaken solely for the purpose of promoting the general welfare, GC 7 enumerates a number of procedural protections owed to those facing evictions.[227] The Committee also requires that states provide data on the number of persons evicted over the recent past, the numbers lacking legal representation against evictions, and relevant legislation.[228]

The CESCR's efforts to prevent threats to the security of land/tenure or housing through forced evictions have not been restricted to the issuance of GCs. A number of the individual communications brought before the CESCR have alleged failures to provide adequate housing or forced evictions. In the wake of the international financial crisis of 2008, Spain faced an extreme housing crisis, exacerbated by various municipalities' decisions to sell large swaths of public housing. One result was that the first View issued by the CESCR after the entry into force of the ICESCR's optional protocol in May 2013 addressed that crisis, as did numerous communications filed against Spain that together constitute a significant portion of the ICESCR's published Views.[229] The CESCR's Views relating

---

[223] *Id.* ¶ 3 (defining "forced evictions as the permanent or temporary removal against their will of individuals, families and/or communities from their homes and/or land which they occupy, without the provision of, and access to, appropriate forms of legal or other protection").

[224] *Id.* ¶ 5 (not only in heavily populated urban areas but also in connection with forced population transfers, internal displacement, relocations during armed conflict, mass exoduses, and refugee movements), ¶ 7 (undertaken in the name of development, as, for example, resulting from the clearing of land or "unbridled speculation in land").

[225] *Id.* ¶¶ 8–9.

[226] *Id.* ¶ 10.

[227] *Id.* ¶ 15 (namely, an opportunity for genuine consultation with affected parties, adequate and reasonable prior notice, information on the proposed eviction and the alternative purpose for which the land or housing is to be used, the presence of government representatives during the eviction (particularly when groups of affected persons are involved), access to legal remedies, and legal aid to those in need of it).

[228] *Id.* ¶¶ 19 & 21.

[229] *See* Press Release, CESCR, Spain Violated the Rights of a Woman Whose House Risks Being Auctioned (Sept. 18, 2015). As of Oct. 15, 2021, the CESCR reported that it had adopted only eleven Views under the Optional Protocol, including one in which no violation was found. Comm. Econ., Soc. & Culture Rts., Rep. on its Sixty-ninth and Seventieth Sessions, E/2022/22, E/C.12/2021/3, ¶ 81 (2021).

to the Spanish housing crisis set out states' obligations to respect, protect, and fulfill the right to adequate housing and avoid forced evictions with considerable lawyerly detail. Since these Views address comparable facts, only one will be addressed in detail.

In *López Albán v. Spain*, the Committee upheld the complaint of a mother of six who was evicted from a rental apartment and who had paid her rent to someone who she later discovered did not own the property instead of the bank that did.[230] The author of the communication, who had stopped paying rent once she discovered that the purported lessor did not own the property, was convicted by the Spanish courts of the minor offence of unlawful appropriation of property and ordered to pay a fine and surrender possession of the apartment. The Spanish courts determined that since the author was in a situation of actual and serious necessity, she was owed partial exemption, but that, since she was not destitute, it was not impossible for her to resolve the situation other than by illegally remaining in the apartment; accordingly, they upheld the order of eviction.[231] The CESCR upheld admissibility and found on the merits that Spain had violated the author's and her children's right under Article 11(1) of the Covenant since the eviction order proceeded without the assessment of proportionality required under the right to adequate housing and without taking into account the underlying situation of necessity but solely on the grounds that she was occupying the property without legal title.[232] It also issued interim measures requesting Spain to suspend the eviction of the author and her six children from the apartment.[233]

Along the way, *López* affirmed a number of points made in the CESCR's earlier GCs. It, along with other Views issued in the wake of the Spanish housing crisis, have made the right to housing and the need to avoid forced evictions more concrete under the ICESCR. In *López*, the Committee readily dismissed Spain's contention that since the underlying eviction was legal, the communication was inadmissible. The Committee affirmed that "even when evictions are justified" as for failures to pay rent, the relevant authorities need "to ensure that they are carried out in a manner warranted by a law that is compatible with the Covenant and that all the legal resources and remedies are available to those affected."[234] It affirmed that the right to adequate housing was a fundamental right that should be ensured irrespective of income since it was central to the enjoyment of all others in the Covenant and "inextricably linked" to those in the ICCPR;[235] that forced evictions are "prima facie" incompatible with the Covenant, can only be

---

[230] CESCR Views concerning López Albán v. Spain, E/C.12/66/D/37/2018 (2019).
[231] *Id.* ¶¶ 2.1–2.8.
[232] *Id.* ¶¶ 14–15.
[233] *Id.* ¶ 13.1.
[234] *Id.* ¶ 6.2 (noting that under the Covenant, it does not matter whether evictions are in accordance with national law).
[235] *Id.* ¶ 8.1.

justified in the most exceptional circumstances, and need to be carried out in accordance with laws that are compatible with the Covenant and general principles of reasonableness and proportionality;[236] and that evictions need to be a last resort when no alternative less injurious means are available, need to accord persons concerned access to an effective judicial remedy, must entail a real opportunity for "genuine and effective" prior consultation between the authorities and the persons concerned and not result in a situation for the person concerned that is itself a violation of the Covenant.[237]

The last prerequisite meant that states have a duty to provide alternative housing to persons in need, including as a result of an eviction. This means, according to the CESCR, that evictions should not result in homelessness or increased vulnerability to further human rights violations.[238] States must "take all appropriate measures, to the maximum of its available resources, to ensure that adequate alternative housing" is available.[239] In finding the author's eviction disproportionate given her vulnerable economic situation, the Committee refused to accept Spain's defense that had it allowed the author to remain in the apartment this would have violated the owner's right to property. The Committee responded that "the right to private property is not a Covenant right" and that even if states have a legitimate interest in ensuring protection for all rights under its national laws, that interest should not "conflict with the rights contained in the Covenant."[240] In a follow-up report, the Committee affirmed that states have an obligation to abide, in good faith, with interim measures issued by the Committee and that Spain's failure to abide by that request constituted a distinct violation of Article 5 of the Optional Protocol.[241]

A number of other cases directed at Spain, namely, *I.D.G.*,[242] *Ben Djazia*,[243]

---

[236] *Id.* ¶ 8.2
[237] *Id.* ¶ 8.3
[238] *Id.* ¶ 9.1.
[239] *Id. See also id.* ¶ 9.3 (affirming that adequacy includes legal security of tenure, availability of services, materials, facilities and infrastructure, affordability, habitability, accessibility, location which allows access to social facilities, and cultural adequacy).
[240] *Id.* ¶ 11.5.
[241] *Id.* ¶ 15; CESCR Follow-up Progress Rep. on Views concerning López Albán v. Spain, E/C.12/70/3 (2021).
[242] In CESCR Views concerning I.D.G. v. Spain, E/C.12/55/D/2/2014 (2015), the Committee upheld a claim by a female homeowner who failed to make mortgage payments during the financial crisis. State officials had attempted to serve notice of foreclosure but were unsuccessful and posted a notice on a court message board. By the time the homeowner learned of the foreclosure, it was too late to prevent it. The Committee found that when property is a residence, the same procedural protections apply as with respect to an eviction, including fair notice and legal aid if needed. It found the notice given insufficient. *Id.* ¶ 14.
[243] In CESCR Views concerning Ben Djazia v. Spain, E/C.12/61/D/5/2015 (2017), the communicant ceased paying rent after his unemployment payments ceased. When his rental contract ended, he was forced out and was provided only short-term inadequate housing by social services. *Id.* ¶¶ 3.1–3.3. The state justified refusing the communicant's repeated requests for social housing on the basis that he had been unhelpful in seeking either housing or work. *Id.* ¶¶ 4.4–4.5. The Committee

El Goumari,[244] and *El Ayubi*,[245] are consistent with the Committee's Views as expressed in *López*. All take the same views on what states must do to satisfy the right to "adequate" housing, as articulated in the ICESCR's GC 4, as well as states' substantive and procedural duties to ensure that evictions are lawful as laid out in GC 7. These cases, as well as others, illustrate the formidable obligations that the CESCR imposes upon states under the right to adequate housing.[246] The

found that forcing an occupant out of his home for failure to pay still qualifies as an eviction, thereby triggering the protections needed to prevent it from becoming an illegal forced eviction. *Id.* ¶¶ 11.1–11.6. It found Spain's rationale inadequate because government policies must pursue the aim of eventual full realization of the right to housing. *Id.* ¶ 17.5. The Committee noted the state had sold off large quantities of housing to an investment firm in order to balance the budget amidst a housing crisis, a retrograde step not consistent with implementing a general plan to progressively realize the right to housing especially for persons in vulnerable situations. *Id.* In two follow-up reports, the Committee criticized Spain's failure to comply with its recommendations. *See* CESCR Follow-up Progress Rep. on Views concerning Ben Djazia et al. v. Spain, E/C.12/70/3 (2021); CESCR Follow-up Progress Rep. on Views concerning I.D.G. v. Spain, E/C.12/66/3 (2019).

[244] In CESCR Views concerning El Goumari v. Spain, E/C.12/69/D/85/2018 (2021), the Committee addressed the eviction from a rental home for failure to pay rent of a couple with four minor children, two of whom had disabilities. After their eviction, the family was provided with a series of short-term accommodations that the state acknowledged suffered from overcrowding, poor sanitation, and lack of privacy. The family were then offered alternative housing that they considered even worse for a family of six. Although they found a home to rent, their precarious rental contract made it impossible to gain access to various social benefits. During her stay in one of the temporary housing units, one of the authors miscarried. *Id.* ¶¶ 2.1–2.13. The Committee found a violation, reiterating its views in *López Albán* and finding that the state had failed the proportionality analysis. *Id.* ¶ 10.3. The Committee noted that when adequate permanent housing is not possible, any temporary housing provided must nonetheless protect the human dignity of evicted persons, meet all safety and security requirements, take account of the right of members of a family not to be separated, and enable them to enjoy a reasonable level of privacy. *Id.* ¶ 9.3.

[245] El Ayubi v. Spain, E/C.12/69/D/54/2018 (2021) involved a couple who had been evicted from a home because the state sold the property to an investment fund. The couple then illegally occupied an unoccupied apartment left in poor condition and applied for social housing. They were denied housing because they were occupying property illegally. Although the couple then successfully applied for universal basic income and housing for their disabled son, a local court confirmed that as illegal occupants, they had no right for social housing and repeatedly refused applications for stays of eviction. *Id.* ¶¶ 2.1–2.13. The Committee found that the state violated Article 11 of the ICESCR by failing the proportionality analysis and failing to provide other alternatives less injurious to the right to housing. *Id.* ¶ 14.6. As in *López Albán*, the Committee affirmed that the conduct of those in need of housing, including those illegally occupying property out of necessity "cannot in itself be used by the State to justify denying his or her application." *Id.* ¶ 13.1. It added that the rules for accessing social housing "must avoid perpetuating the systemic discrimination and stigmatization of those in poverty." *Id.*

[246] *See also* CESCR Views concerning Walters v. Belgium, E/C.12/70/D/61/2018 (2021). Walters addressed a complaint from an elderly man whose lease was terminated and faced an order of eviction after being given six months' notice and monetary compensation. His request for housing, which included a request for an extra bedroom to enable his granddaughters to visit, was denied. *Id.* ¶¶ 2.1–2.17. The Committee found that Belgian law allowing lessors to terminate at will created an imbalance between the lessor's freedom to dispose of his or her property and the lessees' rights to housing as older persons. *Id.* ¶¶ 12.1–12.4. It noted that the rule permitting termination without cause enables lessors to terminate contracts in order to seek higher rent while older persons are disproportionately evicted. *Id.* ¶ 12.3. It stated that state laws needed to monitor the impact on vulnerable and marginalized groups such as older persons facing socioeconomic difficulty and include mechanisms for flexibility to avoid disproportionate impacts. *Id.* The Committee also noted that states must provide alternative accommodation to evicted persons to the maximum of their available resources and

CESCR's approach is also broadly consistent with that followed by the CEDAW Committee under comparable facts.[247]

Another CESCR View, in *Romero v. Spain*, suggests that broadly consistent approaches with respect to the right to housing as between the ICESCR and CEDAW regimes do not necessarily ensure identical outcomes.[248] The affirmations of states' obligations made by the CESCR in both its GCs and the Views surveyed earlier do not always lead to success for those who complain about violations of the right to housing. In *Romero*, the author of the communication, a Spanish national of Roma ethnicity and a single mother, began occupying without a license an apartment owned by a bank in 2015.[249] In 2016, she applied for social housing, but her application was closed due to improper documentation.[250] In 2017, the investment company which had bought the property pressed criminal charges on the minor offence of occupying the property of another without authorization. She was found guilty, with the court holding that exculpation was impossible because the defendant had not exhausted all other means for accessing property before resorting to an illegal occupation.[251] After multiple considerations before Spanish courts, a Madrid court reaffirmed the eviction order, noting that she had declined three housing proposals that the state had put forward.[252] Before the Committee, Spain argued, as it had in *López* and in other cases, that it needed to protect the underlying owner's property interests:

> The State party is of the view that article 11 of the covenant does not protect individual who are illegally occupying the property of another. The right to own property, individually or with others, is set forth in article 17 of the Universal Declaration of Human rights and article 33 of the State party's Constitution. Protecting property, considered internationally to be a fundamental human right, ensures that property owners are able to satisfy their basic needs; they must therefore be protected from arbitrary deprivation of their property. Accordingly, article 11 (1) of the Covenant cannot be used to sanction instances

---

that the author's request for housing that "would avoid breaking his existing social network" was not unreasonable, particularly for a state that "is among the countries with the highest per capital income in the world." *Id.* ¶ 12.6.

[247] *See* chapter 2, sections 2.11.1.6 (discussing GRs) and 2.11.2.1 (discussing Views issued in response to A.T. v. Hungary).
[248] CESCR Views concerning Romero v. Spain, E/C.12/69/D/48/2018 (2021).
[249] *Id.* ¶ 2.1; the reference to her Roma ethnicity is in ¶ 7.3 (where the author asserts that she was denied housing because she was discriminated against because of her Roma ethnicity even though she was a single mother with a recognized 35 percent disability).
[250] *Id.* ¶ 2.2.
[251] *Id.* ¶¶ 2.3–2.4.
[252] *Id.* ¶ 2.16.

where the property of others is unlawfully appropriated, as in the present case.[253]

In *Romero*, unlike the other cases against Spain, the CESCR accepted Spain's argument. It found that "[g]iven that the author was convicted of a minor offence of unlawful appropriation, the Committee considers that there were legitimate reasons for her eviction and that it could therefore be justified."[254] Noting that states "enjoy a degree of discretion when regulating matters such as the unlawful occupation of property and when deciding on judicial remedies aimed at protecting the peaceful enjoyment of property in a democratic society," the Committee deferred to the Spanish courts' determination that the eviction was proportionate, as was the offer of shared temporary accommodations which the author had turned down.[255] The Committee did not comment upon the allegation that the author had been discriminated against on the basis of her ethnicity. While it is unclear whether, faced with similar facts, the CEDAW Committee would reject a comparable claim, it seems unlikely that the allegations of intersectional discrimination made by Romero would go unremarked before that body.

6.3.4 Other Rights Relating to Property

While the CESCR has issued to date only two Views dealing with denials of social security, the one with a female communicant, *Trujillo Calero v. Ecuador*,[256] shares considerable common ground with CEDAW's Views on such rights.[257] The *Calero* case was a successful challenge to Ecuador's contributory pension scheme which allowed persons without formal employment to make social security payments. After 300 consistent payments, an individual who is over forty-five qualified for early retirement. The communicant participated in the scheme and was told that she was eligible once she quit her job. After doing so, however, the Social Security Institute determined that she was not eligible for early retirement after all since some of her payments were disqualified and by their calculation, she had made only 238 monthly contributions between 1972 and 2001.[258] The author alleged gender discrimination since the benefit scheme seemed primarily aimed at unpaid professional domestic workers and not women engaged in cleaning and care activities in their homes who made

---

[253] *Id.* ¶ 6.6.
[254] *Id.* ¶ 12.3.
[255] *Id.* ¶¶ 12.3–12.4 & 12.6.
[256] CESCR Views concerning Trujillo Calero v. Ecuador, E/C.12/63/D/10/201 (2018).
[257] *See* chapter 2, section 2.10.2.
[258] Turjillo Calero v. Ecuador, *supra* note 256, ¶¶ 2.1–2.10.

voluntary contributions even though they had no salary and may need to make retroactive contributions.[259]

The CESCR agreed with the author on a variety of grounds, including on the basis that she had relied on oral assurances from the agency that she qualified for early retirement under the scheme and that the agency had accepted contributions that it later found to be invalid.[260] Most relevant for purposes of comparisons to CEDAW, were the Committee's findings on the intersection of gender discrimination with the right to social security under the Covenant. The CESCR found that while everyone has the right to social security, states should give "special attention to those individuals and groups who traditionally face difficulties in exercising this right, such as women."[261] It recalled that the Covenant bars any discrimination, in law or in fact, that has the intention or effect of nullifying or impairing equal enjoyment or exercise of the right to social security and that it includes indirect discrimination "which appear neutral at face value, but have a disproportionate impact" on the exercise of Covenant rights.[262] States must ensure that men and women enjoy their economic rights on a basis of equality, that their policies "must take account of the economic, social and cultural inequalities experienced in practice by women," and must therefore at times "take measures in favour of women in order to attenuate or suppress conditions that perpetuate discrimination."[263] The Committee also affirmed that when reviewing their restrictions on social security, states must bear in mind the "persistence of stereotypes and other structural causes" that explain why women spend more time than men in unpaid work.[264] It also emphasized that one of the problems that the author faced was that Ecuador provided no alternative to its contributory scheme of old-age benefits and that this was inconsistent with Article 9 insofar as states should provide noncontributory old-age benefits because of the discriminatory impacts of relying solely on contributory schemes that implicitly benefit men.[265]

As reflected in the authorities cited in the *Calero* case, the CESCR has issued a number of GCs and COs that emphasize the significance of the right to social security when it intersects with the duty under the Covenant not to discriminate. The CESCR has treated nondiscrimination, including with respect to gender, as a core obligation under the Covenant's Article 9 right to social security.[266] It has

---

[259] *Id.* ¶ 3.5.
[260] *Id.* ¶¶ 16.1–16.4 (discussing the violation of the author's "legitimate expectations").
[261] *Id.* ¶ 13.1.
[262] *Id.* ¶ 13.2.
[263] *Id.* ¶ 13.3 (citing to, among other sources of authority, ¶¶ 7–12 of CEDAW's GR 29).
[264] *Id.* ¶ 13.4.
[265] *Id.* ¶ 14.2 (noting that noncontributory schemes must take into account "that women are more likely to live in poverty than men; that often they have sole responsibility for the care of children; and that it is more often they who have no contributory pensions").
[266] *See, e.g.*, ICESCR COMMENTARY, *supra* note 191, at 654–55 (noting that the reference to "everyone" in Article 9 has been treated as implicitly incorporating the right to nondiscrimination). This

indicated that the right is capable of being immediately enforced, as it was in the *Calero* case.[267] One of the Commentaries on the ICESCR argues that contrary to what the HRC had suggested in *Sprenger v. The Netherlands*, the right to nondiscrimination with respect to social security is not subject to progressive realization in the sense of permitting states to have discretion to deny vulnerable groups such as women the right to social security simply because the state has scarce resources.[268] It argues that the CESCR expects states to equitably distribute their resources, however scarce, across different groups rather than succumb to social prejudices that may lead to higher payments to fewer (and privileged) beneficiaries, citing in support the Committee's objection to a plan by Azerbaijan to increase the volume of social security benefits by decreasing the number of beneficiaries.[269]

The CESCR has been sensitive to the intersection of gender discrimination and the design of social security schemes in particular. CESCR GC 19 specifies a number of steps that states need to take to ensure that their social security schemes address women's realities and correct their inequalities.[270] That same sensitivity is reflected in a number of its critical COs—as where it has identified disproportionate impacts of welfare cuts in Canada on poor women, including the elderly and single mothers, and women victims of domestic violence; the lack of funding at Bosnian welfare centers for female heads of households and female victims of trafficking; or unequal employer-based insurance schemes which discriminate against those who work in the home or receive less than the minimum wage in places as different as Kenya and Japan.[271]

The CESCR's COs in response to domestic violence also share a number of commonalities with those canvassed in chapter 2, section 2.11.4. As under

---

is confirmed by the CESCR's GC 19, which indicates that rights to social security under Article 9 must be provided on a nondiscriminatory basis under Articles 2(3) and 3 of the Covenant. CESCR GC No. 19: The right to social security (Art. 9 of the Covenant), E/C.12/GC/19, ¶¶ 29–30 (2007). It is also indirectly affirmed by CESCR GC 20, ¶ 7 (indicating that the duty not to discriminate is "immediate" and "cross-cutting"). See CESCR GC No. 20: Non-discrimination in Economic, Social and Cultural Rights, E/C.12/GC/20 (2009).

[267] *See, e.g.,* ICESCR COMMENTARY, *supra* note 191, at 655–56. This is, of course, consistent with the CESCR's opinion that states' duties to "take steps" toward progressive realization anticipates the need for states to take "deliberate, concrete, and targeted" steps. *See* CESCR GC No. 3: The Nature of States Parties' Obligations (Art. 2, Para. 1, of the Covenant), E/1991/23, ¶ 2 (1990).
[268] ICESCR COMMENTARY, *supra* note 191, at 657.
[269] *Id.* at 657 (citing CESCR CO on Azerbaijan, E/C.12/1/Add.104, ¶ 22 (2004)).
[270] CESCR GC No. 19: The right to Social Security (Art. 9), E/C.12/GC/19 (2008) (noting the central importance of social security in protecting human dignity, reducing poverty, preventing social exclusion, and promoting social inclusion). That GC addresses challenges to gender equality with respect to social security posed by compulsory retirement age, schemes that link benefits to financial contributions, and other attributes that effectively discriminate against women. *Id.* ¶ 32.
[271] *See, e.g.,* ICESCR COMMENTARY, *supra* note 191, at 661 (citing COs directed at all those countries).

CEDAW, those reporting under the ICESCR have been urged to establish crisis shelters for safe lodging,[272] strictly enforce protection orders,[273] and provide remedies, including compensation to victims.[274]

6.3.5 Remedial Framework

Structurally, the CESCR's remedies are divided into remedies granted to the individual and recommendations addressed to the state party meant to prevent similar violations in the future and ensure nonrepetition.[275] As regards the latter two obligations, it usually recommends tailored suggestions, such as requests to: review, evaluate, or adopt legislation to prevent similar breaches;[276] ensure adequate access to justice;[277] "adopt" or "take measures to ensure" removal of identified procedural or substantive shortcomings that facilitated the breach in question;[278] and establish a protocol for complying with requests for interim measures.[279] As illustrated by the *López* case, in forced eviction cases, the Committee seeks to have states develop a procedural and normative framework that strikes an appropriate balance between the right to adequate housing and states' legitimate aims. Instead of simply recommending that the state party refrain from eviction or demanding the provision of alternate adequate housing, the Committee has used its recommendations to provide an increasingly comprehensive roadmap for evictions that would be compatible with the Covenant. It has emphasized the need for spaces, procedures, and judicial practices that allow the affected individuals to contest or prevent the occurrence of a forced eviction in the first place and compel the state to consider the particular vulnerabilities of persons, while also demanding that states implement comprehensive plans to guarantee the right to adequate housing for low-income persons.

As regards the individual, the CESCR recommends that the state party take steps to address the particular rights violation. Since most of these have addressed the right to adequate housing, this generally amounts to a recommendation that the state party reassess the author's state of necessity for adequate housing and their level of priority for receiving housing.[280] With one exception,[281] the

---

[272] *See, e.g.*, CESCR CO on Azerbaijan, E/C/12/1/Add.104, ¶ 49 (2004).
[273] *See, e.g.*, CESCR CO on Ukraine, E/C.12/UKR/CO/5, ¶ 42 (2008).
[274] *See, e.g.*, CESCR CO on Algeria, E/C.12/1995/17, ¶ 24 (1995).
[275] *See, e.g.*, Walters v. Belgium, *supra* note 246, ¶ 16.
[276] *See, e.g.*, *id.* ¶ 16 (a)–(b).
[277] *See, e.g.*, Ben Djazia v. Spain, *supra* note 243, ¶ 21(a).
[278] *See, e.g.*, I.D.G. v. Spain, *supra* note 242, ¶ 17(b) & (c).
[279] *See, e.g.*, López Albán v. Spain, *supra* note 230, ¶ 17(f).
[280] *Id.* ¶ 16(a).
[281] *See, e.g.*, Ben Djazia v. Spain, *supra* note 243, ¶ 20(a).

Committee appears not to mandate the grant of adequate housing; it requests a reassessment of the need for adequate accommodation, with a view to granting the author of the communication adequate housing.[282] The Committee regularly awards reimbursement for the legal costs incurred by the authors of communications.[283] It also awards, with very few exceptions,[284] financial compensation for the violations suffered (including with respect to forced evictions),[285] though it does not specify the amount of compensation due.[286] In more recent communications, the Committee has taken a broader view of the kind of harms that might flow from a violation. Thus, in *Calero*, it awarded adequate compensation for violations suffered during the period of denial "and for any other harm directly related to such violations,"[287] while in *S.C. and G.P. v. Italy*, it awarded compensation for "the physical, psychological and moral damages suffered,"[288] though this notably included a violation of Article 12 (enjoyment of physical and mental health) in conjunction with Article 3.

The CESCR's solicitude for individuals with respect to evictions has garnered praise for using procedural tools to advance substantively redistributive goals. In *I.D.G. v. Spain*, the Committee urged that the complainant's home not be sold unless and until she had been given reasonable opportunity to defend foreclosure proceedings, while also insisting that Spain amend its administrative and legislative processes to ensure that its foreclosure processes align with the decision of the Committee and GCs 4 and 7.[289] Stuart Wilson points out that while in that instance the Committee's recommendation were purely procedural, "[i]nsofar as it required adequate notice of foreclosure, in form of personal service unless practically impossible, [it provided] homeowner's facing foreclosure with a genuine opportunity to delay, suspend or resist [such] proceedings."[290] He argues that the Committee's remedial insistence on the creation of procedural speed bumps in the administrative process ultimately leads to a forced evictions process that has meaningful "redistributive effects, insofar as it can force bank/landlord to justify termination of a right of residence and allow court to consider fairness of termination."[291]

---

[282] *See, e.g.*, López Albán v. Spain, *supra* note 230, ¶ 16(a).
[283] *See, e.g.*, I.D.G. v. Spain, *supra* note 242, ¶ 16(b).
[284] CESCR Views concerning Rosario Gómez Limón Pardo v. Spain, E/C.12/67/D/52/20, ¶ 13 (2020) (noting that because the author's eviction has already been carried out, the adoption of the Committee's View constitutes a measure of satisfaction that provides appropriate reparation resulting in there being no need to recommend financial compensation).
[285] *See, e.g.*, Ben Djazia v. Spain, *supra* note 243, ¶ 20(b).
[286] *See, e.g.*, *id.*
[287] Trujillo Calero v. Ecuador, *supra* note 256, ¶ 22(b).
[288] CESCR Views concerning S.C. and G.P. v. Italy, E/C.12/65/D/22/2017, ¶ 13 (2019).
[289] I.D.G. v. Spain, *supra* note 242, ¶ 17.
[290] Stuart Wilson, *The Right to Adequate Housing*, in RESEARCH HANDBOOK ON ECONOMIC, SOCIAL AND CULTURAL RIGHTS 180, 190 (Jackie Dugard et al. eds., 2020).
[291] *Id.*

The CESCR continued to develop its procedurally focused remedial approach in *Ben Djazia v. Spain*, where it, *inter alia*, focused its recommendation on ensuring that tenants had appropriate appeal rights that would help ensure that a judge "might consider the consequences of eviction and its compatibility with the Covenant."[292] In that case, the Committee also recommended that evictions only be carried out following a "genuine consultation" with the affected individuals and after all steps were taken to ensure that the evicted have alternate housing.[293] It also urged the state party to develop a comprehensive plan to guarantee the right to adequate housing for low-income persons in keeping with GC 4.[294]

Although the CESCR's remedial approach has been developed largely in the course of communications raising the right to housing, its Views concerning the discriminatory denial of social security benefits in *Calero*, discussed earlier, suggest that it will adhere to the same approach in such cases. In that case, the Committee did not simply recommend the provision of benefits to which the author was entitled, it also recommended that "other equivalent social security benefits enabling her to have adequate and dignified standard of living bearing in mind the criteria of present views" be awarded, alongside compensation for violations suffered both during the period of denial and "for any other harm directly related to such violation."[295] Its more general recommendations issued in that case also sought to develop a legislative and normative framework that prevent reoccurrence.[296]

6.4 Conclusions

6.4.1 Blurring Distinctions, Emerging Commonalities

While comparisons between the CEDAW and the international investment regimes are marked by sometimes sharp differences (see chapter 5), the comparisons addressed in this chapter—among the CEDAW and the ICCPR and ICESCR regimes—are defined largely by commonalities. These three human rights regimes evince, over time, a growing interpretative convergence despite textual differences in the underlying three treaties. This unity within diversity is undergirded by the strikingly similar preambles of the two Covenants on the

---

[292] Ben Djazia v. Spain, *supra* note 243, ¶ 21(a).
[293] *Id.* ¶ 21(c).
[294] *Id.* ¶ 21(d).
[295] Trujillo Calero v. Ecuador, *supra* note 256, ¶ 22(a) & (b). The Committee also recommended, as usual, reimbursement for legal costs. *Id.* ¶ 22(c).
[296] *Id.* ¶ 23(a)–(f).

one hand (which are virtually identical) and that in CEDAW. All three preambles suggest a broadly consistent "object and purpose" that defines the human rights framework of analysis that they share. All three preambles emphasize more than once that the object and purpose of the respective treaty is to secure human dignity.[297] All three emphasize that all persons enjoy both dignity and rights equally.[298] All three proclaim that such fundamental rights include both civil and political as well as economic, social, and cultural rights.[299] All three suggest that both sets of rights are universally applicable and/or inherent to all human beings.[300] These premises—that human rights are owed to all equally because they are fundamental, inalienable, inherent, interdependent, and indivisible, as well as universally applicable—have come to define international human rights, and not only those applicable to women.[301]

These premises tell us not only what the three regimes are for but also, implicitly, what they are not. These human rights conventions seek to advance the rights of persons—and not corporations or businesses. They express commitments by states that accrue to the benefit of persons, particularly but not only, to those within a state's jurisdiction. By contrast to other treaties (including international investment agreements), these agreements are not designed to promote rights as a subsidiary goal in order to achieve short- or long-term goals such as economic security or the material wealth of nations.[302]

The three interpretative bodies, the HRC, the CESCR, and the CEDAW Committee have applied this human rights framework to overcome three obvious

---

[297] ICCPR, *supra* note 1, Preamble, ¶¶ 1 & 2; ICESCR, *supra* note 2, Preamble, ¶¶ 1 & 2; CEDAW, *supra* note 2, Preamble, ¶¶ 1 & 2.
[298] ICCPR, *supra* note 1, Preamble, ¶ 1 (recognizing applicability of "equal and inalienable rights"), ¶ 3 (need for "everyone" to enjoy rights); ICESCR, *supra* note 2, Preamble, ¶ 1 (recognizing applicability of "equal and inalienable rights"), ¶ 3 (need for "everyone" to enjoy rights). Virtually all of the sixteen paragraphs of CEDAW's preamble mention the need for equality, but *see especially* ¶ 1 (reaffirming faith in fundamental rights and "equal rights of men and women"), ¶ 2 (recognizing the "inadmissibility of discrimination" and proclaiming that "all human beings are born free and equal" and that "everyone" is entitled to rights "without distinction of any kind, including distinction based on sex"), ¶ 3 (stating that states parties to both Covenants are under the obligation to ensure "equal rights of men and women to enjoy all economic, social, cultural, civil and political rights"). CEDAW, *supra* note 2, Preamble.
[299] ICCPR, *supra* note 1, Preamble, ¶ 3; ICESCR, *supra* note 2, Preamble, ¶ 3; CEDAW, *supra* note 2, Preamble, ¶¶ 2–3 and art 1.
[300] ICCPR, *supra* note 1, Preamble, ¶ 4 (under the UN Charter all states need to promote "universal" respect and observance of human rights); ICESCR, *supra* note 2, Preamble, ¶ 4; CEDAW, *supra* note 2, Preamble, ¶ 2 (affirming all human beings "are born free and equal in dignity and rights" and that these apply to "everyone").
[301] *See, e.g.*, Ikdahl, *supra* note 214, at 287 (crediting the Vienna Declaration and Programme of Action). Ikdahl argues that this Declaration also contributed to the understanding that "indivisible" economic and social rights were binding and justiciable and were not merely policy objectives. *Id.*
[302] The preambles of the ICCPR and the ICESCR make no mention of such rationales, while CEDAW's preamble "recalls" that discrimination against women "hampers the growth of the prosperity of society" among other harms. CEDAW, *supra* note 2, Preamble, ¶ 7.

divergences in the underlying treaty texts.[303] First, as is suggested by their titles and their substantive provisions (apart from their preambles), the three treaties seem to address distinct rights. The ICCPR protects one set of rights, the ICESCR protects another, and CEDAW differs from both by protecting civil and political and economic, social, and cultural rights.[304] Second, the treaties ostensibly differ with respect to the duties each imposes on states. The ICCPR anticipates immediately applicable obligations on states "to respect and to ensure" its underlying rights, including to take steps to "adopt such laws or other measures as may be necessary to give effect" to the rights specified in that treaty.[305] The CEDAW also anticipates immediately applicable obligations on states but is far even more specific than is the ICCPR on what that entails for its states parties in terms of their general policies (Article 2(a)–(g)), measures in all fields including but beyond legislation (Article 3), authority to issue temporary special measures (Article 4), and affect social and cultural patterns of conduct (Article 5). States duties under the ICESCR are considerably less specific and less immediate. The ICESCR's text states that while states have a duty to "guarantee" that its underlying rights will be "exercised without discrimination" (Article 2(2)), states are otherwise only required "to take steps . . . to the maximum of its available resources, with a view to achieving progressively the full realization of the rights recognized in the present Covenant by all appropriate means" (Article 2(1)). A third ostensible difference is the target of concern. Both the ICCPR and the ICESCR appear, at first glance, to target actions or omissions by states, not by private actors. CEDAW, by contrast, makes it explicitly clear that states are obligated to "to take all appropriate measures to eliminate discrimination against women by any person, organization or enterprise" (Article 2(e)).

Over time, the HRC and the ICESCR Committee have blurred these three textual distinctions.

First, both committees have come to accept what is explicit in CEDAW: namely, that civil, political, economic, social, and cultural rights are, as suggested by the preambles of all three treaties, indivisible and deeply intertwined in fact—particularly when the underlying right, whatever its content, has been the subject of discrimination. The second ostensible difference—between the immediate effect of the ICCPR and CEDAW as opposed to the ICESCR's supposed focus on progressive realization—has been eroded in two ways: by the express text of the ICESCR's Article 2(2) and by how the CESCR has interpreted Article 2(1). As the CESCR has affirmed repeatedly, the ICESCR's requirement of nondiscrimination is subject to immediate effect under Article 2(2), as compared with the injunction

---

[303] For a summary of the ways that the CEDAW Committee has engaged in an evolutive interpretation of CEDAW, *see* chapter 4, section 4.1.

[304] CEDAW, *supra* note 2, art. 1.

[305] ICCPR, *supra* note 1, art. 2(1) & (2).

on states contained in Article 2(1), applicable to other ICESCR obligations, only requiring states to "take steps" towards "progressive realization." More subtly, the distinction between the two types of obligation has blurred over time thanks to the CESCR's evolving specificity on what state parties are actually required to do when taking steps—namely to use the "maximum" of their "available" resources, attempt in good faith to progress over time to achieve "full realization" of the underlying rights, and accomplish all of this through "appropriate" means (including but not only legislation).[306] The CESCR's attempts to guide states on what is expected of them even when discrimination is not alleged has further muddled distinctions between Article 2(1) and (2), thereby coming closer to CEDAW's demands of immediate application. Third, the HRC's interpretation that the ICCPR's duty to "ensure" includes making sure that states make the Covenant's rights effective even when the underlying actions are taken by private parties has helped generate a body of human rights law that indirectly extends to the actions of non-state actors, including businesses.[307] The CESCR's adoption of the "respect, protect, and fulfill" framework for interpreting states obligations under that Covenant has given rise to comparable effects. The result is that, to a considerable extent, all three regimes purport to create state obligations vis-à-vis non-state actors.

When read alongside the rest of this book, this chapter demonstrates that, to a considerable extent, all three human rights treaties have become vehicles to vindicate "indivisible" civil and political as well as economic, social, and cultural rights while advancing comparable (but not identical) due diligence obligations on their state parties to give immediate effect to both sets of rights at least with respect to the duty not to discriminate.

The evolving interpretations generated by their respective treaty bodies are making other distinctions among the three treaties less relevant. While chapter 5 was able to draw relatively sharp distinctions between the CEDAW and international investment regimes in terms of their respective definitions of protectable property interest, substantive obligations imposed on states, distinct approaches to barring discrimination, distinct territorial/jurisdictional scopes, distinct derogation or exception clauses, and distinct forms of enforcement,[308] such demarcations are far more difficult to make with respect to the human rights conventions addressed in this chapter.

Although neither the ICCPR nor the ICESCR formally protects "property" as such, they, along with CEDAW, attempt to protect a number of the same forms of assets addressed in chapter 2. All three regimes have addressed women's rights

---

[306] ICESCR COMMENTARY, *supra* note 191, at 137–72. *See also, e.g.,* CESCR GC No. 3, *supra* note 267, ¶¶ 10–12 (providing guidance based on a decade of examining state reports on the minimum core obligation entailed in utilizing the maximum available resources).
[307] *See, e.g.,* ANDREW CLAPHAM, HUMAN RIGHTS OBLIGATIONS OF NON-STATE ACTORS (2006).
[308] *See* chapter 5, sections 5.2–5.9.

to housing (including forced evictions), as well as women's equal rights to land, financial credit, family property, inheritance, and various forms of social and retirement benefits. All three have generated what this book characterizes as "property jurisprudence." Convergence of the three regimes with respect to protecting property rights has been encouraged by what the underlying treaties do not contain: none includes a distinct right to own all forms of private property and be compensated for denial of that right as a commodity. While the ICESCR comes closest when it protects intellectual property under Article 15(1)(c), its other property provisions identified in section 6.3, seek to protect nondiscriminatory access to such rights or underlying normative values (e.g., the value of one's work, the security underlying forms of social security, or the need to satisfy minimum needs, including those supplied by "adequate" housing). This distinguishes the three regimes' property jurisprudence from the protection of property under, for example, the European Convention of Human Rights or international investment agreements. A great deal of the relevant ECtHR and investor-state case law affirms international law's long-standing protections against the taking of private property by states without compensation, whether or not such expropriations are discriminatory.[309]

It is also difficult to draw sharp lines around how the ICCPR, ICESCR, and CEDAW regimes interpret states' duties not to discriminate. While the two Covenants do not define states' respective treaty obligations to bar discrimination, the HRC and the CESCR appear increasingly willing to interpret discrimination to include both direct and indirect discrimination, to require consideration of both substantive and not just formal equality, and to embrace states' obligations to bar discrimination by private actors and not just by the states themselves. This means that to the extent the three treaties protect some forms of property interests from discrimination, they purport to do so using the same concept.

All three treaties appear increasingly supple with respect to their territorial application as well. While the ICCPR does not clearly apply extraterritorially as do the CEDAW and the ICESCR, the HRC's interpretation that states need to respect and ensure the Covenant's rights not only within its territory but wherever the state exercises jurisdiction, expands the reach of that treaty.[310] Of course, for good or bad, the three regimes share a common approach to "enforcement"—namely, reliance on a number of identical outputs (COs, Views, GRs, or GCs), none of which are formally "binding" but all of which purport to be authoritative.

---

[309] *See, e.g.,* Ursula Kriebaum & August Reinisch, Property, Right to, International Protection (Apr. 2019), Oxford Public International Law, MPEPIL. *See also* chapter 5, at section 5.9.

[310] *See, e.g.,* HRC GC No. 31[80], *supra* note 13, ¶ 10 (ICCPR rights must be available to all individuals "in the territory of subject to the jurisdiction of the State Party").

6.4.2 Common Due Diligence Obligations?

Do the three regimes say the same things to states about what their respective duties are to affirm and protect women's equal property rights? As the discussion of applicable remedies at sections 6.2.7 and 6.3.5 suggest, the answer needs to be qualified: the CEDAW and ICESCR Committees' recommendations to states share more commonalities with each other than they do with the HRC when it comes to remedial recommendations issued in response to individual communications.

The Optional Protocols under the three treaties are broadly similar in authorizing communications that permit the respective treaty bodies to issue Views in response. Establishing such a mechanism under the ICCPR was not regarded as particularly controversial, at least with respect to Western states which had long recognized the justifiability of civil and political rights under national law. Accordingly, the Optional Protocol for the ICCPR was adopted and opened for signature as soon as the ICCPR itself was adopted and entered into force on March 23, 1976.[311] The communications procedures under the ICESCR and CEDAW proved more controversial and are of far more recent vintage. Although the ICESCR was adopted at the same time as the ICCPR, in 1966, it took far longer for an Optional Protocol to be established. The ICESCR's Optional Protocol, adopted in 2008, only came into force in May 2013.[312] The CEDAW Committee, while established alongside the treaty in 1979, did not gain authority to consider communications until December 22, 2000, when its Optional Protocol entered into force.[313] All three Protocols limit communications to persons under the jurisdiction of a state party.[314] (The CEDAW's Protocol is unusual insofar as it also permits parties to the Protocol to agree to give the Committee competence to pursue inquiries in cases where the Committee receives "reliable information against grave or systematic violations."[315])

Differences in how states view what is arguably the most intrusive form of "compliance" or "enforcement" for global human rights—individual communications—continues to be reflected in different rates of ratifications for the Optional Protocols of the ICESCR, the ICCPR, and CEDAW. The ICESCR continues to lag behind the others with only 26 ratifiers to its Optional Protocol, as compared to 117 for the ICCPR's and 114 for CEDAW's.

---

[311] ICCPR Optional Protocol, *supra* note 156, art. 9.
[312] ICESCR Optional Protocol, *supra* note 196.
[313] Optional Protocol to the Convention on the Elimination of All Forms of Discrimination against Women, Oct. 6, 1999, 2131 U.N.T.S. 83 [hereinafter CEDAW Optional Protocol].
[314] ICCPR Optional Protocol, *supra* note 156, art. 1; ICESCR Optional Protocol, *supra* note 196, art. 2; CEDAW Optional Protocol, *supra* note 313, art. 2.
[315] *Id.* art. 11.

A core difference between the ICCPR and the CEDAW and ICESCR regimes' respective remedial approaches under their communications procedures is that the latter two are more comprehensive and tailored to the facts and reasons that led to a finding of violation. In addition, by contrast to the HRC's approach, the CEDAW and ICESCR Committees divide their recommendations into two sections: one detailing the reparation due to the individual author of the communication and one detailing the steps the state party has to take in order to guarantee nonrepetition and prevent similar violations from occurring again in the future. As regards individual reparation, both the CEDAW Committee and CESCR tend to recommend that states award monetary compensation.[316] In many of the Views addressed in chapter 2, the CEDAW Committee recommended compensation commensurate with the gravity of the violations of the author's rights.[317] Over time, the CEDAW Committee has made it clear that compensation must be awarded for both material damages flowing from rights violations, such as loss of income or social security benefits,[318] as well as moral damages that the author suffered.[319] It has sometimes also recommended compensation for legal costs and expenses incurred by the author, while the CESCR has been more consistent in awarding such costs.[320] Both Committees are, nonetheless, inclined to delegate considerably to states with respect to the amount of awards, usually urging states to provide payments "as appropriate" without delineating specific amounts (as would be common in the international investment regime). This is consistent with the ICESCR's Optional Protocol, whose preamble repeats the text of the treaty's progressive realization clause, indicates that when examining communications the Committee shall consider the reasonableness of the steps taken by the state and that states "may adopt a range of possible policy measures for the implementation of the rights set forth in the Covenant."[321]

While the more general recommendations issued to states by the CEDAW Committee and CESCR under their respective Views share some structural

---

[316] See, e.g., CESCR GC No. 14: The Right to the Highest Attainable Standard of Health (Art. 12 of the Covenant), E/C.12/2000/4, ¶ 59 (2000) (recommending, with respect to violations of the right to health, that all victims be entitled to "adequate reparation, which may take the form of restitution, compensation, satisfaction, or guarantees of non-repetition").

[317] See, e.g., Views concerning Cecilia Kell v. Canada, CEDAW/C/51/D/19/2008, ¶ 11 (2012); Views concerning Elisabeth de Blok et al. v. Netherlands, CEDAW/C/74/D/104/2016, ¶ 9 (2019); Views concerning E.S. and S.C. v. Tanzania, CEDAW/C/60/D/48/2013, ¶ 9 (2015).

[318] Elisabeth de Blok et al. v. Netherlands, supra note 317, ¶ 9; View concerning D.S. v. Slovakia, CEDAW/C/65/D/66/2014 ¶ 8(a)(i) (2016); Views concerning Natalia Ciobanu v. Republic of Moldova, CEDAW/C/74/D/104/2016, ¶ 8(a)(ii) (2019).

[319] Cecilia Kell v. Canada, supra note 317, ¶ 11; D.S. v. Slovakia, supra note 318, ¶ 8(a)(iI); Ciobanu v. Moldova, supra note 318, ¶ 8(a)(iii).

[320] D.S. v. Slovakia, supra note 318, ¶ 8(a)(iii); Ciobanu v. Moldova, supra note 318, ¶ 8(a)(iv).

[321] ICESCR Optional Protocol, supra note 196, art. 8(4). No comparable language appears in CEDAW's Optional Protocol.

similarities, they evince somewhat different remedial approaches. The CESCR tends to recommend that states develop and adopt a variety of measures that are not merely legislative and emphasizes the need for states to provide adequate procedures and judicial practices that permit individuals to contest laws or judicial decisions, in particular in the context of forced evictions. CEDAW's recommendations to states included in its Views also go beyond legislative recommendations but tend to focus a bit less on specific changes to states' procedures. As might be expected of a Committee charged with addressing, among other things, prevailing cultural impediments to equality, that Committee is more intent on changing both the *legal-institutional* and *social landscape* that give rise to violations of Convention rights. Thus, alongside calls to review, repeal, and amend or otherwise changing offending legislative or administrative provisions that gave rise to violations, the CEDAW Committee in its Views (as well as COs) frequently recommends capacity training, as well as educational and awareness raising measures, for example.

Where intersectional discrimination is at issue, the CEDAW Committee's prescriptions for change are typically targeted to address it. In the case of forced eviction of pregnant Roma women discussed in chapter 2, for example, the Committee recommended the adoption and reinforcement of "effective policies, programmes and temporary special measures" (in accordance with Article 4(1) of the Convention and with GR 25) to combat intersecting forms of discrimination against Roma women and girls,[322] as well as "specific poverty alleviation and social inclusion programmes for Roma women and girls."[323]

The level of detail with respect to remedies that tends to appear in the CEDAW Committee and the CESCR's respective Views contrasts sharply with the terse statements that characterize the HRC's Views. While, as noted, the HRC has utilized its autonomous equality guarantee in Article 26 to bring violations of property rights as well as socioeconomic rights within the realm of the Covenant and has used its COs to criticize women's unequal access to property rights and resulting socioeconomic vulnerabilities, it has been less willing historically to uphold individual claims of violations of property or socioeconomic rights on the basis of the equality guarantee.[324] Moreover, while the HRC affirms, in principle, that discrimination embraces structural impediments and need to address the intersectional identities of those harmed, it has remained more unidimensional in its actual practice and likely to respond only to cases of formal and direct discrimination. As noted, critics have complained that its responses to individual

---

[322] Views concerning S.N. and E.R. v. North Macedonia, CEDAW/C/75/D/107/2016, ¶ 11 b) (2020).
[323] Views concerning L.A. et al. v. North Macedonia, CEDAW/C/75/D/110/2016, ¶ 9.8 b) (2020); S.N. and E.R. v. North Macedonia, *supra* note 322, ¶ 11 b).
[324] *See* discussion at *supra* section 6.2.7.

communications fail to recognize the indirect or intersectional forms of discrimination that often appear on the face of those communications. Fortunately, as section 6.2.7 indicates, the HRC's remedial approach appears to be evolving in its more recent practice.

The growing convergence with respect to how the Committees under the ICESCR and CEDAW see states' general due diligence obligations is also suggested in the two regimes' COs. The CESCR's COs frequently recommend, as do the CEDAW Committee's, that states take special affirmative steps to readdress women's inequality.[325] They urge states not only to refrain themselves from engaging in discrimination against women but to prevent private actors from doing so.[326] A number of the CESCR's COs emphasize the need for states to address the "multiple forms of discrimination" women face because they belong to racial, ethnic, and national minorities or encounter difficulties in accessing employment, social security, social services, housing, health, or education.[327] As does the CEDAW Committee, the CESCR calls on states to take measures to address traditional stereotypes or harmful cultural practices that encourage discrimination against women.[328] Its COs criticize states for social security schemes, for example, that in effect if not by intent, discriminate against women or inadequately address the needs of rural women, single mothers, or those who are elderly.[329] As in the CEDAW regime, CESCR COs may also recommend that states address the need for shelters to provide safe lodging for women facing domestic violence[330] or ask that states amend their civil codes or commercial laws to secure women's ability to own property, access credit, secure the benefits of bankruptcy, or enjoy property under inheritance.[331]

6.4.3 Toward Comparative International Property Rights Law

As noted in chapter 1, there are some twenty-one human rights treaties that extend protection to property rights broadly construed.[332] This chapter provides

---

[325] See, e.g., CESCR CO on Angola, E/C.12/AGO/CO/3, ¶ 18 (2008).
[326] See, e.g., CESCR CO on France, E/C.12/FRA/CO/3, ¶ 34 (2008).
[327] See, e.g., id. ¶ 13.
[328] See, e.g., CESCR CO on Chad, E/C.12/TCD/CO/3, ¶ 41 (2009) (requesting Chad to take more stringent measures, as through the use of media and education to eliminate traditional stereotypes regarding the status of women in the public and private spheres); CESCR CO on Nepal E/C.12/NPL/CO/2, ¶ 15 (2008) (expressing continuing concern over the persistence of practices such as deuki (dedicating girls to a god or goddess), badi (prostitution among the Badi caste), and chaupadi (isolating menstruating women)); CESCR CO on Nigeria, E/C.12/1/Add.23, ¶¶ 20 and 22 (1998) (expressing concern over polygamy as incompatible with the economic, social, and cultural rights of women).
[329] See, e.g., CESCR CO on Madagascar, E/C.12/MDC/CO/2, ¶ 20 (2009).
[330] See, e.g., CESCR CO on Lithuania, E/C.12/1/Add.96, ¶¶ 21 & 43 (2004).
[331] See, e.g., CESCR CO on Benin, E/C.12/1/Add.40, ¶ 11 (2002).
[332] See chapter 1, section 1.2, text and notes 46–47.

only a preliminary look at the two Covenants' respective treatment of property rights to enable preliminary comparisons with the CEDAW's jurisprudence described in chapter 2. It is hoped that the select comparisons made in this chapter will encourage a broader look at how CEDAW's jurisprudence compares with other regional and UN human rights regimes.

Research into comparative property jurisprudence under all human rights treaties, global and regional, remains at an incipient stage. It is clear from chapter 5 and the work of other scholars[333] that the international investment regime's conception of protectable property is likely to differ not only from the CEDAW Committee's jurisprudence but also from that of other regimes that adopt a human rights framing. These differences may emerge from the substantive rights relating to property within these treaties, such as human rights treaties that include rights to private property that do not rely on a showing of discrimination and/or incorporate customary international law norms on, for example, the compensation due for harms to property. Obvious examples of these are the European Convention of Human Rights and the Inter-American Convention of Human Rights—both of which anticipate appropriate compensation for government takings of property whether or not discrimination has occurred.[334]

Differences among human rights protections may also emerge not because of differences in the substantive rights included but because of how the respective human rights regimes have evolved over time. Christoph Scheruer and Ursula Kriebaum's relatively refined distinctions between the property-respective case law of the investment regime and the European Convention of Human Rights—which address issues such as whether both regimes protect claims for mere rights to performance or shareholder's rights, for example—are made possible by the relatively high number of publicly available investor-state arbitral awards and European Court of Human Rights (ECtHR) rulings addressing such issues.[335]

Much greater research on comparative international property law, even if limited to human rights regimes, is needed for cross-regime lessons to be drawn. Consider, for example, the case of the CERD. The text of that convention would suggest, at first glance, limited overlap with CEDAW's wide-ranging property jurisprudence as canvassed in chapter 2. The CERD addresses relevant rights only in its Article 5(d)(v)'s inclusion of "the right to own property alone as well as in

---

[333] *See, e.g.*, Christoph Schreuer & Ursula Kriebaum, *The Concept of Property in Human Rights Law and International Investment Law*, in HUMAN RIGHTS, DEMOCRACY AND THE RULE OF LAW: LIBER AMICORUM LUZIUS WILDHABER 743 (Stephan Breitenmoser et al. eds., 2017) (comparing the international investment regime to ECtHR jurisprudence). Ursula Kriebaum, *Property, Right to*, in ELGAR ENCYCLOPEDIA OF HUMAN RIGHTS 88 (Christina Binder et al. eds., 2022).

[334] *See, e.g.*, Tom Allen, *Compensation for Property Under the European Convention on Human Rights*, 28 MICH. J. INT'L L. 287 (2007); José E. Alvarez, *The Human Right of Property*, 72 U. MIAMI L. REV. 580 (2018).

[335] Schreuer & Kriebaum, *supra* note 333, at 748–58.

association with others" and Article 5(e)(iv)'s right to "social security and social services." The reference solely to property "ownership" would suggest that CERD has more in common with other regimes' protection of private property as commodity than with the CEDAW's focus with the normative values protected by property. However, the CERD's capacious bar on discrimination, which, long before CEDAW, embraced direct and indirect discrimination, *de facto* and *de jure*, means that there is considerable potential within that regime for property rights jurisprudence that draws lessons from or converges with that under CEDAW.[336]

There is considerable potential for linkages across the CERD and CEDAW regimes, since the right to property "in association with others" raises the collective dimensions of property rights also considered by the CEDAW Committee, as with respect to rights of Indigenous women,[337] and the CERD regime accepts the need for nondiscriminatory rights to inherit (as does the CEDAW regime).[338] In addition, as is suggested by the CERD Committee's adoption of GR 25 on the "gender-related dimensions of racial discrimination," that Committee accepts the proposition that racial discrimination "affects women in a different way, or to a different degree than men."[339] As is suggested by the CERD Commentary, this opens the door to consideration of intersectional discrimination within that regime, thereby enhancing the prospect of even greater cross-regime insights on the nuanced nature of the obligation not to discriminate contained in human rights treaties.

The incipient field of comparative international property law would obviously benefit by examining the jurisprudence generated by all regional human rights courts alongside the CEDAW's property jurisprudence. There are especially rich prospects to be mined for linkages between the European regime on human rights and CEDAW given the sheer volume of rulings issued by the ECtHR interpreting the European Convention on Human Rights' duties not to discriminate and that Convention's other rights, including property. Consider, as just one example, the ECtHR ruling in *Carvalho Pinto de Sousa Morais v. Portugal*.[340]

---

[336] On the CERD's definition of racial discrimination, see PATRICK THORNBERRY, THE INTERNATIONAL CONVENTION ON THE ELIMINATION OF ALL FORMS OF RACIAL DISCRIMINATION: A COMMENTARY 97–138 (2016) [hereinafter CERD COMMENTARY]. For examples of the CERD Committee's dismissals of a few communications based on discrimination with respect to social security and pensions, see *id.* at 375–76.

[337] See, e.g., CERD COMMENTARY, *supra* note 336, at 347–50 (discussing the overlaps between the CERD's GRs 23 and 34 and the case law on Indigenous peoples' property rights in the Inter-American Court of Human Rights).

[338] *Id.* at 351.

[339] CERD GR No. 25: Gender-Related Dimensions of Racial Discrimination, CERD/C/GC/25, ¶ 1 (2000). That GR affirmed the need for "a more systematic and consistent approach to evaluating and monitoring racial discrimination against women," *Id.* ¶ 3, as well as urged the collection of more data, disaggregated by gender within racial or ethnic groups, *Id.* ¶ 6.

[340] Carvalho Pinto de Sousa Morais v. Portugal, App. No. 17484/15, Eur. Ct. H.R. (2017).

In that case the ECtHR found a breach of Article 14 (nondiscrimination) and Article 8 (respect for private and family life) as a result of a ruling by the Portuguese Supreme Administrative Court. That court had reassessed a prior ruling awarding damages in the case of medical malpractice. Its reassessment led to a reduction in the nonpecuniary damages initially awarded in favor of the applicant, a female victim of medical negligence, which had led to the victim's inability to have sexual relations.[341] The Supreme Administrative Court justified its reduced award on the premise that the applicant was fifty years old at the time of the surgery and had two children, noting that this was "an age when sexuality was not as important as in younger years."[342] The ECtHR, over two dissents, found it relevant that the same court had affirmed in two prior cases involving men, one aged fifty-five and the second fifty-nine, that the inability not to have sexual relations affected their self-esteem and produced tremendous shock.[343] It noted that gender equality was now "a major goal for the member States of the Council of Europe and very weighty reasons would have to be put forward before such a difference in treatment could be regarded as compatible with the Convention . . . [R]eferences to traditions, general assumptions or prevailing social attitudes in a particular country are insufficient justification for a difference in treatment on the grounds of sex."[344] As a result, the ECtHR awarded the applicant 3,250 euros in respect of nonpecuniary damage in addition to legal costs.[345]

As is suggested by the two separate concurring opinions in *Carvalho*, by Judges Yudkivska and Motoc, much more could have been said about the "harmful clichés" and harmful gendered stereotypes that generated the applicant's complaint in the majority judgment.[346] Indeed, under the CEDAW Committee, one would expect that such a communication would have raised, in addition to nondiscrimination, the argument that Portugal had failed to modify stereotypes as demanded under CEDAW's Article 5. It is hard to imagine the CEDAW Committee agreeing with the dissenters in *Carvalho*, Judges Ravarni and Bošnjak, who took a more mechanistic view of what the applicant needed to prove. For those dissenters, the complaint failed because it did not prove disadvantageous treatment despite the harmful stereotypes on which the national court relied.[347] For the dissenters, it was important that the Supreme

---

[341] *Id.* ¶ 16. *See also id.* Ravarni, J. & Bošnjak, J., joint dissenting opinion, ¶ 34.
[342] *Id.* Majority Judgment, ¶ 49 (quoting the Supreme Judicial Court).
[343] *Id.* ¶¶ 23–24, 54–55.
[344] *Id.* ¶ 46.
[345] *Id.* ¶ 64.
[346] *Id.* Yudkivska, J. & Motoc, J., concurring Opinion.
[347] *Id.* Ravarni, J. & Bošnjak, J., joint dissenting opinion, ¶¶ 9–25.

Administrative Court had not explicitly relied on a harmful stereotype but had decided the case on the basis of age, not sex.[348]

If *Carvalho* is any indication, the ECtHR's judges might find the CEDAW Committee's examination of intersectional discrimination based on sexist stereotypes of some interest. That inquiry need not go in a single direction. It is possible that consideration of cases like *Carvalho* might inspire the CEDAW Committee's ongoing effort to clarify its interpretation of stereotypes and the evidence needed to prove them. It might inspire the Committee to resolve the question of whether such stereotypes can be presumed or need to be specifically proven; or whether they are discriminatory per se or are merely underlying causes of other discrete violations of the Convention.[349] *Carvalho* raises many other jurisprudentially rich inquiries, including whether the underlying complaint in that case could have been raised as a violation of property rights and if so, under which under which part of the CEDAW? Was the applicant's reduced nonpecuniary award for damages comparable to other possessions under Article 1, Protocol 1 of the ECHR, that is, comparable to other payments by private parties sanctioned by national courts that have been found to be discriminatory under that regime (such as employer contributory pensions)? Would a comparable claim, under CEDAW, constitute a kind of discriminatory social benefit and/or encompassed by the chapeau of CEDAW's Article 13? Or would such a communication be more appropriately handled as a simple case of denial of the equal protection of the law under CEDAW's Article 15(1)? Moreover, if discriminatory remedies by national courts violate gender equality as *Carvalho* indicates, should not the CEDAW Committee itself adhere to a more consistent approach to ensure that its own remedies do not reproduce harmful biases? Surely the response cannot be, as some international organizations have claimed, that the Committee itself, as a UN body, is not subject to the principle of equality?

Other ECtHR rulings raise questions about the standard and burdens of proof when authors claim that states failed to protect them from acts of domestic violence;[350] what constitutes a 'union' sufficient to trigger survivor's

---

[348] *Id.* ¶¶ 33–37.
[349] *See, e.g.*, Rikki Holtmaat, *The CEDAW: A Holistic Approach to Women's Equality and Freedom*, *in* WOMEN'S HUMAN RIGHTS, *supra* note 214, at 109 (suggesting that the Committee has been inconsistent on these points).
[350] Compare Eur. Ct. H.R., Guide on Article 14 of the European convention on Human Rights and on Article 1 of Protocol No. 12 to the Convention (Aug. 31, 2022), ¶¶ 99–100, https://www.echr.coe.int/Documents/Guide_Art_14_Art_1_Protocol_12_ENG.pdf [hereinafter ECtHR Guide] (discussing a number of ECtHR alleging failures by domestic authorities to take protective measures) to chapter 2, section 2.11.2 (describing CEDAW communications involving allegations of gender-based violence).

pensions;[351] what kinds of social benefits might be deemed protected possessions;[352] the interplay between access to justice and intersectional discrimination;[353] and what other kinds of assets merit protection at the intersection of the ECHR's Article 14 and Article 1 of Protocol 1.[354] All of these could benefit from comparisons with CEDAW's relevant jurisprudence. It is way past time for comparisons of how international law treats property rights to extend beyond the usual suspects: namely, rulings by investor-state arbitral tribunals and the ECtHR.

6.4.4 CEDAW's Added Value

This chapter's look at the ICCPR and ICESCR begins to suggest how times have changed from the conditions that motivated many to conclude CEDAW in the first place: namely, a time when women's rights were rarely addressed by the two principal UN human rights treaty bodies under the two Covenants—and, it was assumed, by precious few other international legal regimes. The interpretative efforts under the two Covenants surveyed here provide one response to the oft-expressed fear that the CEDAW regime would create a separate silo for women's rights.[355] As this chapter indicates, women's rights to equality generally, and to equal property rights in particular, are being addressed under the two Covenants and not only under CEDAW.[356]

The CEDAW Committee's broad definition of discrimination and the need to apply it to the intersecting identities of women appears to have entered into

---

[351] Compare ECtHR Guide, *supra* note 350, ¶ 183 (comparing Muñoz Diaz v. Spain to Şerife Yiğit v. Turkey) to GR 29, ¶¶ 16–24 (discussing various forms of recognized relationships for purposes of Article 16(1)(h)).

[352] Compare ECtHR Guide, *supra* note 350, ¶¶ 221–28 (discussing a number of ECtHR rulings on pension payments, unemployment benefits, disability benefits, housing benefits, parental leave allowances, child benefits, insurance covers, and social security or other payments) to chapter 2, section 2.10.2 (describing CEDAW communications relating to social benefits).

[353] *See, e.g.*, ECtHR Guide, *supra* note 350, ¶ 253 (discussing Moldovan and Others v. Romania involving the fillings of fellow Roma and the destruction of their homes and local authorities' refusal to award nonpecuniary damages).

[354] *Id.* ¶¶ 258–62 (discussing the ECtHR's extensive case law concerning violations of Article 14 taken together with the protection of property in Article 1, Protocol 1, including eligibility for tax relief on the purchase of a suitable property for a disabled child, obligation of a small landowners to become members of a hunting association, decrease in the nominal value of bonds, exclusion of certain landlords from allowances to terminate leases, alleged discrimination in disability benefits to a civilian).

[355] *See, e.g.*, Fleur Van Leeuwen, *"Women's Rights Are Human Rights!": The Practice of the United Nations Human Rights Committee and the Committee on Economic, Social and Cultural Rights*, in WOMEN'S HUMAN RIGHTS, *supra* note 214, at 249.

[356] For discussion of some of the other ways that CEDAW's jurisprudence has, over time, influenced the CESCR, *see* Meghan Campbell, *Like Birds of a Feather? ICESCR and Women's Socioeconomic Equality*, in FRONTIERS OF GENDER EQUALITY: TRANSNATIONAL LEGAL PERSPECTIVES 153 (Rebecca J. Cook ed., 2023).

the mainstream of the international bill of rights. Prompted in part by the principle of indivisible application of all international human rights, CEDAW's view of what it means to affirm equal rights for women, appears to be having an impact, whether explicitly acknowledged or not,[357] within other UN human rights treaties' expert committees, other human rights forums, including by UN Special Rapporteurs addressing a variety of subjects, and especially the right to housing, and regional human rights systems (including in Africa and Latin America).[358] While cause and effect is hard to prove, on at least some occasions the CEDAW Committee has alerted other UN human rights experts or bodies to pay heed to women's property rights and shown them ways to do so.[359]

When read alongside CEDAW's property jurisprudence, this chapter further undermines the complaint that international human rights regimes fail to address the root causes for women's economic subordination.[360] The CESCR, no less than the CEDAW Committee, has often addressed the underlying reasons for women's unequal status. It has done so, for example, in its GCs 4 and 7 as well as its Views in cases such as *Djazia* or *López Albán*, both of which contain assessments of the "root causes" of discrimination comparable to those issued on occasion by the CEDAW Committee.[361] Both the CESCR and the CEDAW Committee

---

[357] For one example of a human rights report that seems to have been deeply influenced by the CEDAW jurisprudence discussed in this book even though it does not cite to it, see the report by the Independent Expert on protection against violence and discrimination based on sexual orientation and gender identity, Victor Madrigal-Borloz (Independent Expert), Rep. of the Independent Expert on Protection Against Violence and Discrimination based on Sexual Orientation and Gender Identity, UN Doc. A/74/181, ¶ 4 (July 17, 2019) (discussing the "guiding principle" of intersectionality), ¶¶ 14–18 (discussing housing and forced eviction), ¶¶ 37–41 (discussing challenges faced by "women who are lesbian, bisexual, trans and gender diverse," including the burden of unpaid care work), ¶¶ 46–49 (challenges of older persons, including discriminatory pension schemes), and ¶ 67 (noting, as a desirable reform, social security legislation that extends benefits to those in same-sex marriages).

[358] The impact of CEDAW's jurisprudence on these other human rights forums is being increasingly recognized by scholars, *see generally* Hellum & Aasen, *supra* note 214 (see chapters by Andrew Byrnes, Fareda Banda, Rikki Haoltmaat, Simone Cusak, Cecilia M. Bailliet, Celestine Nyamu Musemi, Sandra Fredman, Fleur Van Leeuven, and Ingunn Ikdahl).

[359] *See, e.g.*, Leeuwen, *supra* note 355, at 265 (categorizing this as the CEDAW regime "whistleblowing" function). For a detailed account of the many interactions among the CESCR and CEDAW Committees and the work of Miloon Kothari as Special Rapporteur on the Right to Adequate Housing even in 2008, *see* Ikdahl, *supra* note 214, at 282–92 (noting how such interactions made evident specific types of "gendered" tenure insecurities). *See also id.*, at 288 (noting that these interactions were seldom cited in the reports of the Special Rapporteur and "leave the impression that the contact and cooperation with the CEDAW committee was more limited"). By contrast, the more recent reports by the Special Rapporteur on Adequate Housing, repeatedly cite to CESCR and CEDAW outputs. *See* Rep. of Special Rapporteur on Adequate Housing, Guidelines for the Implementation of the Right to Adequate Housing, UN Doc. A/HRC/43/43 (Dec. 26, 2019).

[360] Compare Leeuwen, *supra* note 355, at 261–62 (canvassing these concerns) to chapter 3, section 3.2 (canvassing the concerns of, for example, Susan Marks) and chapter 4, section 4.4.4 (suggesting that such criticisms, as applied to the CEDAW Committee, require more nuance).

[361] Compare chapter 4, section 4..4.4; *see also* GR No. 34 on the Rights of Rural Women, CEDAW/C/GC/34, ¶ 11 (2016) (noting that states need to "address the negative and differential impacts of economic policies, including agricultural and general trade liberalization, privatization and commodification of land, water and natural resources, on the lives of rural women and fulfillment of their rights").

highlight many of the underlying structural reasons preventing women from having adequate housing whether they are rural women, widows facing dispossession, or intersectionally discriminated women in refugee camps or informal urban settlements. The treaty breaches that both Committees identify—and the resulting recommendations for change they include in their outputs—implicate state or private action directed at the commodification of food markets; forced evictions caused by state-generated housing crises; or dispossessions of land, homes, goods, or government benefits prompted by religious or customary practices or unequal pay structures. Indeed, for some commentators, this jurisprudence, along with the work of a number of UN Special Rapporteurs, has provided a radical, even transformative, critique of fundamental concepts such as the need for "security" with respect to property.[362]

Apart from having a potential impact on the HRC and the CESCR, what does this chapter tell us about the added value of the CEDAW Committee's property jurisprudence?

The CEDAW Committee, unlike the HRC and the CESCR, presides over a regime specifically committed to three interrelated and inseparable goals: to ensure full equality of women within the law, to improve the *de facto* position of women in society by addressing structural changes embedded even within gender neutral laws and practices, and to modify gender-based stereotypes even in the 'private sphere' (such as the home).[363] Consistent with those goals, the CEDAW Committee's recommendations to states and remedies in response to communications anticipate political and legal changes to guarantee women's individual and collective rights, including property rights, and measures to provide social support and generate broader social and cultural change.[364] Its focus on achieving equality *in fact* means that the due diligence obligations it recommends seek to make it *feasible* in practice for women to exercise their full capabilities.

CEDAW's trifold women-focused goals explain why CEDAW's remedies to individuals who suffer harm may be both more comprehensive and more targeted to the particular intersectional discrimination that may have been at issue than under the HRC and, to a certain extent, under the CESCR. It is also why, consistent with the broad license to pursue by all the means identified in Article 2(a) to (g), the CEDAW Committee has often prescribed changes to both the legal-institutional *and* social landscape. The CEDAW Committee's asymmetrical focus on discrimination against women enables it to look

---

[362] Ikdahl, *supra* note 214, at 277–91 (discussing how CEDAW's jurisprudence, along with the reports of UN Special Rapporteurs on the right to adequate housing and the CESCR's outputs, have transformed the concept of tenure security).
[363] *See, e.g.*, Holtmaat, *supra* note 349, at 95.
[364] *Id.*

backward—to target the structural conditions that lead to present inequalities—but also to leap forward—to respond to the knock-on effects of failing to accord women their equal share of property. Its remedies and rationales for them indicate how property deprivations, whether as a result of the dissolution of unions or in the form of inheritance, have serious impacts on a woman's access to divorce, to support herself or her family, and to live in dignity as an independent person.[365] As is suggested by the Committee's GC 37 of 2018 on climate change and the gendered impact of disasters, the CEDAW Committee seeks to be proactive in anticipating new ways that ownership, access, use, disposal and inheritance of property, land, and natural resources will impact on women not as passive victims but as agents of change.[366] All of this suggests that the CEDAW Committee's remedial recommendations to states have encouraged unique perspectives on states' due diligence obligations to respect, protect, and fulfill women's rights to equality.

While it is now routine to credit the CEDAW regime with elevating the importance of intersectional discrimination, it may be that its singular contribution on that subject has not been sufficiently appreciated. Rikki Holtmaat argues that the Committee's emphasis on intersectionality is not merely about uncovering all the ways women are subordinated and making others (from governments to other human rights bodies) see them as well. It is about revealing, extolling, and protecting, as part and parcel of the principle of equality, a woman's "right to freedom to choose one's own identity, instead of being forced to adopt stereotyped and gendered self-images and roles."[367] On this view, one of the singular values that CEDAW brings to the table is to alert states to the need to protect individuals' agency and autonomy through fundamental changes to society to create more room for the freedom of women (and men) to decide their particular roles or identities.

As Holtmaat also argues, the CEDAW regime's asymmetric focus on discrimination against women makes visible five different forms of oppression: exploitation, marginalization, powerlessness, cultural (or other forms of) imperialism, and violence.[368] This awareness of the underlying ways women have been subordinated for centuries enables the CEDAW Committee to function as the guardian of a principle of equality that does not default to a male standard. The CEDAW Committee can serve as a beacon to others, including fellow human rights forums like the HRC and the ECtHR, alerting them to the risk of falling

---

[365] Ikdahl, *supra* note 214, at 273.
[366] *See, e.g.,* CHRISTINE CHINKIN & KEINA YOSHIDA, 40 YEARS OF THE CONVENTION ON THE ELIMINATION OF ALL FORMS OF DISCRIMINATION AGAINST WOMEN 17–20 (2020), https://eprints.lse.ac.uk/110306/1/Chinkin_40_years_of_the_convention_published.pdf.
[367] *Id.* at 96 (n. 7) & 113.
[368] *Id.* at 99.

into stereotypical thinking. This outlook also sets CEDAW apart even when it purports to address goals common to other human rights regimes.

When the CEDAW Committee makes recommendations to "economically empower" women by respecting their equal access to financial credit or social benefits, it means something a bit different than when that term is invoked by international financial institutions or even perhaps other human rights regimes.[369] While the CEDAW Committee, like all other human rights regimes, is well aware of the need to balance the right of some persons versus those of others, it seeks to make sure that any rebalancing is not taken on the backs of women. For the CEDAW Committee, the economic empowerment of individual women needs to be balanced against the interests of communities of women. In doing so, it is likely to deploy economic empowerment as a counterweight to the five forms of oppression historically imposed on women. This means, among other things, that individual economic empowerment must resist forms of imperialism— whether imposed from within a state (e.g., by religious or other groups that subordinate women) or forces outside it (e.g., by globalization pressures to commodify, privatize, deregulate). For the Committee, individual empowerment needs to give way when it is a weapon to exploit, marginalize, or disempower other women. This explains why the CEDAW Committee, as opposed to the HRC or the CESCR, is more apt to make recommendations criticizing, for example, the freedom of agri-businesses to exercise their power to acquire more property.[370] It may also explain why the CEDAW Committee sees "tenure security" from a variety of perspectives and is not likely to affirm that a woman's insecure tenure, which may be undermined by domestic violence, discriminatory inheritance laws, customs, or traditions, can be readily fixed simply by making sure she has title to the property.[371]

To be sure, as the next chapter addresses, the CEDAW Committee's property jurisprudence is a work in progress. Incorporating CEDAW into comparative international property law may generate insights in both directions—with some inuring to the benefit of the CEDAW Committee. Debates about what is the added value of CEDAW can surely be informed by more consistent efforts to compare the CEDAW Committee's jurisprudence with that generated by other UN human rights committees as well as interpretations suggested by other regional human rights instruments. While some claim that the CEDAW Committee's approach to discrimination, including intersectional discrimination, serves as a lesson to

---

[369] *See, e.g.*, Vasuki Nesiah, *Indebted: The Cruel Optimism of Leaning in to Empowerment*, in GOVERNANCE FEMINISM: AN INTRODUCTION 505 (Janet Halley et al. eds., 2019).

[370] *See, e.g.*, chapter 2, section 2.6.2.5 (describing COs addressing "land grabs" by foreign investors and other conflicts between development projects and gender equality).

[371] *See, e.g.*, Sandra Fredman, *Engendering Socio-Economic Rights*, in WOMEN'S HUMAN RIGHTS, *supra* note 214, at 231 (criticizing the gender neutrality in the CESCR GC 4 on the right to housing).

others on how to accommodate difference,[372] Celestine Nyamu Musembi and others may be right that the CEDAW Committee could learn much from the approach to legal pluralism suggested by instruments like the Maputo Protocol to the African Charter on Human and Peoples Rights.[373] Similarly, while Shreya Atrey argues that one of the benefits of the CEDAW Committee's approach to intersectionality is that it recognizes the need to prioritize those who suffer from multiple forms of discrimination, others may draw from other human rights regimes the lesson that it is best to resist such "hierarchies of oppressions" in favor of a "fluid" approach to intersectionality.[374]

---

[372] Ikdahl, *supra* note 214, at 276.
[373] Celestine Nyamu Musembi, *Pulling Apart? Treatment of Pluralism in the CEDAW and the Maputo Protocol*, in Women's Human Rights, *supra* note 214, at 183.
[374] Compare Shreya Atrey, *A Prioritarian Account of Gender Equality*, in Frontiers of Gender Equality, *supra* note 356, at 131 to Meghan Campbell, *CEDAW and Women's Intersecting Identities: A Pioneering New Approach to Intersectional Discrimination*, 11 Revista Direito GV. São Paulo 479 (2015).

7
Taking Women's Property Rights Seriously

7.1 Why CEDAW's Jurisprudence Is About "Property" and Is "Progressive"

As this book came together, a CEDAW expert expressed surprise at the scope of chapter 2. She noted that at least some of what that chapter (and this book) includes, such as social benefits, are not designated as "property rights" by the CEDAW Committee. She was curious (and politely skeptical) about how this book performed this "magic trick." The question raises profound questions about the topic of this book: What indeed are "property rights" and what makes what the CEDAW regime is doing "progressive"?

Property is a social and legal construct. Many have attempted to define it without success. A leading Property casebook widely used in the United States warns students that there are competing conceptions by "essentialists" who believe that there is a single "true" quality to what is properly seen as "property" and "skeptics" for whom property lacks any essential quality but can only be defined by other laws.[1] The leading essentialist, per this definition, is of course William Blackstone, who defined the right to property as "that sole and despotic dominion which one man claims and exercises over external things of the world, in total exclusion of the right of any other individual in the universe."[2] That casebook argues that most scholars are skeptical of the idea that property confers exclusive sovereign control over some external thing but holds a more "plastic" conception in which property consists of a "bundle of sticks" or entitlements, not all of which are necessary—not even the right to exclusively own or dispose.[3] Property theorists have not allowed definitional quandaries to stand in the way. All accept that, however defined, property is foundational to all forms of government. Each state (and even subdivisions within them) decides what constitutes "property" under its national (or even municipal) laws, including what may constitute "property" for purposes of applying constitutional provisions barring or qualifying takings of property by the state.[4]

---

[1] THOMAS W. MERRILL ET AL., PROPERTY PRINCIPLES AND POLICIES 17 (4th ed. 2022).
[2] *Id.* (quoting Blackstone).
[3] *Id.* at 17–18.
[4] *Id.* at 1165–1325.

Women's Property Rights Under CEDAW. José E. Alvarez and Judith Bauder, Oxford University Press.
© Oxford University Press 2024. DOI: 10.1093/oso/9780197751879.003.0007

The definitional quandary applies within international law. Although some have tried to delineate the contours of a general "international law of property," the default position is that property rights are defined by the applicable international law source, whether it be custom, treaty, general principle, or a mix of all three, and that these sources reveal definitional quandaries and indeterminacies.[5] As discussed in chapter 5, international investment agreements tend to avoid the definitional question in favor of a broad listing of tangible and intangible assets that constitute protected "investment" or "activities associated" with it—from the securing of finance to the conclusion of contracts related to such investments. As indicated in chapter 6, the most extensive regional case law on point, under the ECHR, embraces an expansive notion of "possessions" and has ignored, over time, certain distinctions that have emerged as between common law and civil law jurisdictions.[6]

CEDAW's text only mentions the word "property" twice—affirming women's rights to "administer" it in Article 15(2) and the right of "both spouses" to own, acquire, manage, administer, enjoy, and dispose of it in Article 16(1)(h). That text, literally applied, would mean that chapter 2 should not include anything other than direct applications of those two provisions. This would mean that this book would not address social or other forms of benefits, rights to housing in the course of domestic violence, inherited property outside of marriage, access to all forms of financial credit or intellectual property, or denials of effective remedies in court with respect to any of the preceding rights (whether or not financial recompense would be due for those failures). Further, since CEDAW's Article 14 (addressing rural women) contains no explicit mention of property, even the land and other related rights under it would not constitute "property rights."

---

[5] See, e.g., Koldo Casla, The Right to Property Taking Economic, Social, and Cultural Rights Seriously, 45 Hum. Rts. Q. 171 (2023)(engaging in comparisons among international human rights regimes' property protections and concluding that international law's definition of property is defined by "indeterminacy" and "polysemy"). For an attempt to distill a harmonious international law of property despite these differences, see John G. Sprankling, The International Law of Property (2014).

[6] The ECHR case law includes social benefits as possessions. See, e.g., Ursula Kriebaum & August Reinisch, Property, Right to, International Protection ¶¶ 34–47 (Apr. 2019), Oxford Public International Law, MPEPIL. The ECtHR has tended to ignore the formal classification of property under domestic law, including the fact that in several civil law jurisdictions, actual current possession "demarcates the province of the law of property." Michele Graziadei, The Structure of Property Ownership and the Common Law/Civil Law Divide, in Comparative Property Law Global Perspectives 71, 94 (Michele Graziadei & Lionel Smith eds., 2017). Accordingly, in German and Italian systems: "What cannot be possessed, namely brought under the physical control of a subject, cannot become the object of a property relationship in these legal systems, and belongs to other fields of the law, such as the law of obligations, or the law relating to intellectual property." Id. at 91. By contrast, in common law jurisdictions, a property relationship includes tangibles (such as land and "choses in possession") or intangibles ("choses in action"). Id. The term "property" as understood by common law lawyers is closer to the French notion of "bien," which means any asset capable of being included in a person's patrimony, regardless of whether it is, at present, only an intangible future possession. Id.

The legal coherence that most demand of international law (and probably the rule of law in general) would suggest that if CEDAW's property rights are to be so closely circumscribed as to exclude all of these things, there needs to be good reason for it.[7] The possibility that the CEDAW Committee is barred from considering anything other than Articles 15(1) and 16(1)(h) to be "property rights" because of the plain text of the Convention seems unlikely. As Fareda Banda has noted, "the Committee has not allowed itself to be constrained by its drafting."[8] As chapter 4's Lesson One demonstrates, the CEDAW Committee has gone far beyond the literal text of the Convention. It has, among other things, responded to intersectional discrimination (a concept not mentioned in the CEDAW's text); affirmed states' obligations to respect property rights beyond "spouses" in formal marriages despite the text of Article 16(1)(h); affirmed that states' obligations to bar discrimination require states to prevent domestic violence by, among other things, protecting women's rights to a secure home; found that women in urban (and not merely rural areas under Article 14) areas are entitled to adequate living conditions, including housing; and recommended to states that they ensure that private companies subject to their jurisdiction respect women's equality even when such companies act abroad. The idea that a treaty body capable of doing all of the preceding is legally disempowered from recognizing the deep interconnections between these rights by recognizing them as forms of property—or that such a step would go too far—is not convincing.

Legal coherence would demand, on the contrary, that those deep interconnections be recognized. It is coherent to recognize that social security or pension rights that many states include within legal estates for inheritance purposes be seen as (and not just treated as) no less a form of family property than other assets included in inheritance under Article 16(1)(h).[9] It makes sense that rights to land, forms of agricultural credit, loans, or other forms of credit (whether extended to rural women under Article 14 or to others, as under the chapeau of Article 13 or 13(b)) be included under the right to administer property in Article 15(2). And if the foregoing is correct, coherence would also demand that other forms of housing enjoyed through whatever form of tenure security—from ownership to tenancy at will—would be included within women's equal property rights. At a more conceptual level, if states insist on allowing women to be treated as property, it seems appropriate for the CEDAW regime to push back on this in

---

[7] *See, e.g.*, THOMAS FRANCK, THE POWER OF LEGITIMACY AMONG NATIONS 150–82 (1990) (discussing the role of coherence in legitimizing international law and eliciting compliance with it).

[8] Fareda Banda, *The Limits of Law: A Response to Martha C. Nussbaum*, in THE LIMITS OF HUMAN RIGHTS 267, 278 (Bardo Fassbender & Knut Traisbach eds., 2019). *See, e.g.*, GR No. 25 on Temporary Special Measures, HRI/GEN/1/Rev.7, ¶ 3 (2004) (describing CEDAW as a "dynamic instrument").

[9] Including pension rights, like all other assets that may be included in a person's patrimony, is also consistent with the broad interpretation of property applied by the ECtHR as well as the Inter-American Court of Human Rights. *See, e.g.*, Casla, *supra* note 5, at 180.

the most forceful way possible: namely, by challenging directly what is meant by property and property rights.

This is made easier by the fact that property is no more a legal term of art under CEDAW than it is under general international law. The Committee could continue to call social benefits and pensions "economic" benefits, for example, but it should recognize that the *naming* of states' obligations and of human rights matters. There are normative consequences to calling these forms of "property" and normative consequences in not doing so. Even a quintessential "property" issue such as the right to land can be seen not as only a self-standing right to property but as a unique concept grounded in the special relationship of Indigenous peoples to their lands, territories, and resources; a component of the right to food or water; a component part of each state's right to exercise economic self-determination or an individual's right to a livelihood or right to work.[10] The right to housing might be seen only as affirming privacy or other discrete benefits resulting from the individual possession of property, while the "right to adequate housing" as a form of property right implicates the duties of financial institutions to extend credit or avoid foreclosure, the obligations of landlords not to forcibly evict, the need for special measures to protect groups facing intersectional discrimination or homelessness due to poverty, and duties put on states to place "important limits on the hierarchies of power and processes of dispossession that sustain global capitalism."[11] How we characterize rights determines their normative scope.

Property is a foundational concept in all legal systems. Identifying CEDAW's interventions as making critical inroads in such a foundational concept is a promising gateway to requiring the changes in the "institutions, systems and structures that cause or perpetuate discrimination and inequality" required for the "transformational change" that CEDAW promises.[12] Property rights are foundational for a reason: the concept (however defined) intersects with multiple legal fields within national law, all of which provide additional possibilities for advancing women's equality by redefining the state's obligations to require

---

[10] *See, e.g.*, Olivier De Schutter, *The Emerging Right to Land*, 12 INT'L COMMUNITY L. REV. 303 (2010).

[11] Stuart Wilson, *The Right to Adequate Housing*, in RESEARCH HANDBOOK ON ECONOMIC, SOCIAL AND CULTURAL RIGHTS AS HUMAN RIGHTS 180, 181 (Jackie Duggard et al. eds., 2020).

[12] *See, e.g.*, Simone Cusak & Lisa Pusey, *CEDAW and the Rights to Equality and Non-discrimination*, 14 MELB. J. INT'L L. 54, 64 (2013). *See also* Nehal Bhuta, *Recovering Social Rights*, IILJ Working Paper 2023/1 (recovering the intellectual history of what today we call international economic and social rights and their connections to arguments for redefining the role of the state to enable transformative social change to promote greater equality). Unlike those who see international human rights regimes as beholden to neo-liberal political economy, Bhuta argues that many of those responsible for incorporating social rights in the Universal Declaration of Human Rights saw these as tools to redefine the state as a "public power that must organize the economy in order to ensure a "society of equals' "). *Id.*, at 2–3.

genuine equality among all persons.[13] Identifying CEDAW's jurisprudence as dealing with "property" enables a new kind of family or marital law more resistant to patriarchy, for example.[14] In addition, seeing CEDAW's embrace of economic, social, and cultural rights as redefining the very concept of property makes it easier to bring contracting rules (such as the requirement of spousal consent to sales of land or mortgages) or diverse tenure systems within CEDAW's principle of equality—while also having an impact on what it means for women to ensure "tenure security" in the first place and what is required of states to protect that right over time.[15]

Categorizing the jurisprudence addressed in chapter 2 as "property rights" enables us to see the forest from the trees. As Stuart Wilson argues with respect to certain changes in South Africa law that resemble some of CEDAW's jurisprudence, legal outcomes that enable squatters to avoid forced evictions challenged "the very nature and purposes of South African property law."[16] Restrictions on forced eviction undermine, he argues, the "ownership" model of structuring property relationships and expand the spaces for "property outsiders" to "reshape the terms on which property is distributed."[17] As this suggests, seeing cases like the North Macedonia cases discussed in chapter 2 as not being merely about "rights to housing" but as being about property rights enables insights that might otherwise remain less visible. The deceptively simple affirmation that Roma women on the brink of homelessness have equal rights to rooms of their own, has, as Wilson argues in a different context, repercussions for common law of property's "complex structure of status hierarchies that overwhelmingly privilege the powers and rights of owners over things, and other people with subordinate rights, or no rights at all."[18] These hierarchies, Wilson points out, "privilege one form of ownership over another, as in the case of mortgagors and mortgagees. The pattern is everywhere the same, however: a pattern of domination and

---

[13] *See, e.g.*, Bhuta, *supra* note 12; Ingunn Ikdahl, *Property and Security: Articulating Women's Rights to Their Homes*, in WOMEN'S HUMAN RIGHTS: CEDAW IN INTERNATIONAL, REGIONAL AND NATIONAL LAW 268, 284 (Anne Hellum & Henriette Sinding Aasen eds., 2013) (noting how protecting women's equal rights to housing require addressing diverse regulatory issues in multiple fields).

[14] *See, e.g.*, Ruth Halperin-Kaddari, *Parenting Apart in International Human Rights Family Law: A View from CEDAW*, 22 JERUSALEM REV. LEGAL STUD. 130 (2020) (introducing a "new field of family law" based in part on CEDAW's jurisprudence). *See also* Ruth Halperin-Kaddari, *Human Rights Treaty Bodies as Standard-Setting Mechanisms: The Case of Family Law*, in STRENGTHENING HUMAN RIGHTS PROTECTIONS IN GENEVA, ISRAEL, THE WEST BANK AND BEYOND 82 (Joseph E. David et al. eds., 2012).

[15] *See, e.g.*, Ikdahl, *supra* note 13, at 284–85 & n. 57.

[16] STUART WILSON, HUMAN RIGHTS AND THE TRANSFORMATION OF PROPERTY 7 (2021).

[17] *Id.* Wilson argues that requirements that bar evictions that lead to homelessness, insistence that terminations of leases be fair, requirements that creditors attempting to execute against defaulting debtors propose alternatives, and demands that any termination of rights to housing be subject to a proportionality analysis are all novel limitations on a property insider's ordinary common law right to dispossess an outsider. *Id.*

[18] *Id.* at 127.

control by reference to status. That status is membership of a pre-social common law category that affords its members privileged rights."[19] Those debating the CEDAW regime's contribution to transformational change need to consider the consequences of naming what the CEDAW Committee does.

As is suggested by many of the critiques surveyed in chapter 3, a number of scholars resist associating "property rights" with CEDAW precisely because they fear the normative consequences. As indicated in chapter 3, a number of critical scholars argue that property rights hinder social justice for women and bolsters international law's colonialist legacies.[20] Gabriele Wadlig forcefully articulates these concerns.[21] Like others, she contends that the very concept of "property" is connected, inescapably, to ideas of leading figures in the West such as John Locke and Blackstone, and therefore attempts to protect "property rights" inescapably "naturalize" private individual property, along with the proposition that equal property rights, must entail equal rights to alienate it.[22] While Wadlig acknowledges that the concept of property under international law has expanded beyond individualized property to include, for example, the rights of Indigenous peoples "to own, develop, control and use their communal lands, territories, and resources,"[23] she suggests that this imposes an inappropriate "reductive view" of the actual relationships to land held by non-Western peoples.[24]

Under this view, property is a historically shaped concept that *necessarily* affirms "the 'Western' concept of property (based on exclusion and alienability) as the 'norm' and the 'othering' of ways to relate to land that do not conform to this."[25] The "language of property is not neutral—and can never

---

[19] *Id.* The broader ramifications of the CEDAW Committee's emerging jurisprudence on the due diligence obligations imposed on states relating to forced evictions is further demonstrated in its Views concerning X v. Cambodia, CEDAW/C/85/D/146/2019 (2023) and discussed at notes 141–142 in chapter 5. In that case, the Committee noted with apparent approval the communicant's contention that "forced evictions are not a gender-neutral phenomenon" (*id.* ¶ 3.2) and considered the un-remedied threats faced by the communicant to constitute discriminatory harassment against a human rights defender. See *id.* ¶ 8 (vi) (recommending that Cambodia provide training to its judicial institutions to "raise awareness of the human rights of rural women and women human rights defenders").

[20] *See, e.g.*, Maria Mies, Patriarchy and Accumulation of a World Scale: Women in the International Division of Labor (2014) (arguing that private property hinders rather than promotes social justice for women); Poul Wisborg, *Human Rights Against Land-Grabbing? A Reflection on Norms, Policies, and Power*, 26 J. Agric. Environ. Ethics 1199, 1202 (2013) (expressing skepticism about treating rights to land as human rights).

[21] Gabriele Wadlig, The International (Un)Making of "Tenure Security," 27–41 (2022) (J.S.D. Dissertation, New York University) (on file with author).

[22] *Id.* at 29–31. But *see* Bhuta, *supra* note 12, at 22–35 (arguing that natural rights, including to property, were not always associated with "possessive individualism" but were instead part and particle of, for example, English radical thought that combined the "natural right of self-property" (ownership over one's self as the sine qua non of liberty) with a challenge to the justice of enclosure and unconstrained private property accumulation).

[23] Wadlig, *supra* note 21, at 36 (quoting International Convention on the Elimination of All Forms of Racial Discrimination (CERD), and GR XXIII).

[24] *Id.* at 36–37.

[25] *Id.* at 38.

be."[26] Wadlig argues that given property's historical baggage—including the socially constructed "whiteness" of property in former slave-holding countries like the United States[27]—it is naive to assume that such legacies can be overcome.[28] Her arguments resonate deeply with the subject of this book given longstanding feminist critiques of what Mary Wollstonecraft called "the demon of property."[29]

Ronald Sackville makes the same kind of argument from the opposite end.[30] He argues that social benefits are not properly regarded as property rights *because they are distinct from the essence of private property*. A property right, he argues, "describes a right enforceable by appropriate legal remedies to exclude other persons from the object."[31] Those seeking to enhance entitlements to social benefits by transforming a right to a revenue stream into a right to material things, namely property, do "violence" to the concept of property.[32] Entitlements to social security, he contends, need to addressed like all other government entitlements. They need to be secured through laws that establish appropriate bureaucratic procedures that permit the independent review of such claims to ascertain that qualified claimants receive the payments to which there are entitled.[33] Whereas Wadlig criticizes property because, in her view, it cannot escape Blackstone's concept of "despotic" exclusive possession, for Sackville that is the one virtue of property that should not be undermined by confusing it with radically different things like entitlements for social benefits that are best handled through administrative, not property, law.

It is hard to recognize the CEDAW Committee's treatment of the entitlements surveyed in chapter 2 in these descriptions of traditional property law. As chapter 6 indicates, the CEDAW Committee does not treat social benefits as subject only to administrative law or procedural rules to secure equal treatment. It has recommended that states take these benefits as seriously as all the other property rights it addresses—and accordingly recommends that states reform

---

[26] *Id.* at 39.
[27] *See, e.g.*, Cheryl Harris, *Whiteness as Property*, 106 HARV. L. REV. 1721 (1993).
[28] Wadlig, *supra* note 21, at 30.
[29] Mary Wollstonecraft, *A Vindication of the Rights Of Women*, *in* THE WORKS OF MARY WOLLSTONECRAFT (Janet Todd & Marilyn Butler eds., 1989). *See also* Lena Halldenius, *Mary Wollstonecraft's Critique of Property: On Becoming a Thief from Principle*, 29 HYPATIA 942 (2014). The concern is understandable given how property rights have been used to advance the commodification of women. *See generally* Patricia Crawford, *Women and Property: Women as Property*, 19 PARERGON 151 (2002) (discussing the relationship between women's rights to property in early modern England and the status of women in that society). For a survey of the many scholars who have conflated the idea of property with exclusive and private ownership whether in the course of condemning this "natural right" or praising it, *see, e.g.*, Casla, *supra* note 5, at 192–94.
[30] Ronald Sackville, *Property, Rights and Social Security*, 2 U.N.S.W. L.J. 246 (1978).
[31] *Id.* at 250.
[32] *Id.* at 248 & 252.
[33] *Id.* 252–66.

the legal-institutional, social, and cultural structures that make women either ineligible to receive such benefits or less "worthy" to receive the same amounts as men. If Sackville's views are taken seriously, the CEDAW Committee should adjust its remedial approach to conform to his rigid demarcation of legal categories. As this suggests, Sackville's insistence that social benefits are not "property" may have a normative consequence: it slots these entitlements into administrative law, thereby circumscribing from the outset CEDAW's liberating possibilities.

Despite their different rationales, Wadlig and Sackville agree on one thing: "property" cannot be anything other than what scholars like Locke and Blackstone said it was.

That is precisely what the CEDAW's jurisprudence challenges. As chapters 4 through 6 indicate, the CEDAW regime avoids many of the criticisms directed at traditional conceptions of property and international legal regimes closely associated with them (such as the international investment regime). CEDAW's property rights do not depend on ownership or what Blackstone considered its one essential feature: "despotic" exclusive possession. The Committee's fluid approach to protecting tenure security—an entitlement that the Committee addresses only when needed to secure women's equality—recognizes the right to exclude others only when that is needed to protect the security of individual women, the family unit, or the rights of others.[34] While CEDAW is not the only regime to recognize that the right to property does not have to include the right to exclude others, it is unique in insisting that the deployment of that particular stick in property's bundle of entitlements needs to be justified on the basis of women's equality.

CEDAW does not treat property as the traditional civil right of individuals that Wadlig criticizes and Sackville applauds. The CEDAW Committee's jurisprudence presumes that the Convention's property-respecting rights interact with and need to be consistent with the other civil, political, economic, social, and cultural rights specifically contained (or incorporated by reference) in the Convention. The CEDAW Committee does not mark these rights out from others as being exclusively about private commodities belonging to individuals competing in the market. Consistent with the CESCR's approach to the right to adequate housing, the CEDAW Committee is not exclusively focused on protecting traditional rights to buy or sell one's own property and therefore evict others. It concentrates on changing existing property rules in order to enable women's equal rights to adequate housing. As Stuart Wilson points out is

---

[34] Ikdahl, *supra* note 13, at 282–84. *See, e.g.*, chapter 2, section 2.11.2 (discussing communications involving allegations of gender-based domestic violence).

the case under the ICESCR, CEDAW's relevant jurisprudence reinforces and provides additional protection to the rights of groups made vulnerable by discrimination "to keep hold of residential property in the face of acts of dispossession."[35] The CEDAW Committee repeatedly affirms that equal rights to contract, to housing, to economic and social benefits, to borrow money or possess, enjoy, and dispose of land, or to inherit property are as important to human dignity as are rights to an adequate standard of living or health but goes further still. It criticizes states when they put traditional private property interests, along with the country's economic priorities, ahead of women's equality. It criticizes "development" efforts that essentialize the value of private property and its commodification.[36]

Contrary to Wadlig's fears and Sackville's recommendations, the CEDAW Committee does not demand that states adopt property regimes inspired by Western models. Its property jurisprudence cannot be easily dismissed as yet another paternalistic (or hegemonic) effort to export the laws and practices of "the West"—along with its conception of property—onto the "other."

The Committee's jurisprudence ignores Blackstone's script for property in other ways. That jurisprudence protects the private sphere in many respects: it affirms individuals' equal rights to conclude private contracts, administer personal private property, or make an application for credit. But it also punctures that sphere by insisting that family members and market actors treat women equally, even if this requires challenging stereotypes prevalent in the home or in the marketplace. It imposes equal property rights as public obligations for states—as when it affirms equal rights to pensions (whether supplied under state funds or based on employers' contributions) or when it maintains that states must provide adequate shelters for those victimized by domestic violence. It affirms equal rights to all forms of property whether or not these result from discriminatory laws issued by the state or whether denials of such rights result from stereotypes that lead male relatives to seize the property of a widow. In all these ways, the Committee's demands increase the regulatory burdens on states by compelling them to act in the sacrosanct "private" sphere (such as the family). What the Committee demands from CEDAW's states parties

---

[35] Wilson, *supra* note 11, at 180. As Wilson points out, traditional property rights, by contrast, are often enforced by extinguishing the housing rights of existing occupiers. *Id. See also* Casla, *supra* note 5 (arguing in favor of recognizing the social function of property by embedding it in economic, social, and cultural rights). For examples of the CEDAW Committee's expressed concerns with the gendered impact of forced evictions across its various outputs, see chapter 2, sections 2.6.1.2 (discussing GR 34 on rural women); 2.6.2.5 and 2.7.1.2 (discussing specific COs); and 2.7.2.1 (describing the Committee's Views in the North Macedonia cases).

[36] *See, e.g.*, chapter 2, section 2.6.2.5 (describing COs addressing the harmful impact of certain development projects).

resembles the transformational states originally sought by English Radicals or French Jacobins (as described by Nehal Bhuta) or the governments defending "non-absolutist" forms of property (praised by Koldo Casla), rather than the governmental servants of the "morality of the market" denounced by Jessica Whyte.[37]

The Committee's attention to private property's negative externalities and how these impact women differently due to intersectional discrimination makes its jurisprudence an unlikely tool to advance "neo-liberalism" as that term is most commonly defined.[38] Unlike investor-state arbitrators who largely ignore the negative externalities of property ownership when asked to enforce property's traditional bundle of entitlements, CEDAW's interpreters scrutinize those entitlements and attach them to CEDAW's protections only to countermand formal or substantive discrimination against women.[39] The Committee, unlike the World Bank's efforts to promote "gender equality," does not treat women's equality as subsidiary to, and rendered necessary by, the need to promote economic globalization.[40] Nor does the Committee elevate land titling as an all-purpose solution to achieve "tenure security."[41]

Nor is CEDAW's property jurisprudence principally directed at protecting the rights of individual private property holders.[42] Its interpretation of property rights may protect the rights of groups or collectivities such as Indigenous, Roma, or rural women. Further, when the Committee faces a choice of whether to favor those with government-sanctioned titles to land over those without such entitlements, it does not necessarily favor the former or individual private rights to property over a collective's.[43] The Committee may rule in favor of group rights

---

[37] Compare Bhuta, *supra* note 12, and Casla, *supra* note 5, to Jessica Whyte, THE MORALS OF THE MARKET (2019).

[38] Compare chapter 3, section 3.2, at text and notes 111–123 (critiques of human rights regimes as tools to advance "neo-liberalism") to chapter 4, section 4.2 (arguing that CEDAW's property jurisprudence does not advance the specific elements of neo-liberalism as these are most commonly defined).

[39] See chapter 5, section 5.11 (comparing how "property" is protected under the CEDAW and international investment regimes).

[40] *See, e.g.*, Poul Wisborg, *Transnational Land Deals and Gender Equality: Utilitarian and Human Rights Approaches*, 20 FEMINIST ECON. 24 (2014) (noting the tendency for institutions like the World Bank to pay uneven attention to the gender consequences of transnational land deals justified on utilitarian grounds); Diane Elson, *Gender Justice, Human Rights, and Neo-Liberal Economic Policies*, in GENDER JUSTICE, HUMAN RIGHTS, AND NEO-LIBERAL ECONOMIC POLICIES 78 (Maxine Molyneux & Shahra Razavi eds., 2002) (contrasting neo-liberal policies of institutions like the World Bank, grounded in economic efficiency, with discourses based on human rights).

[41] *See, e.g.*, Ikdahl, *supra* note 13, at 284–85.

[42] Compare, for example, Martti Koskenniemi, *The Effect of Rights on Political Culture*, in THE EU AND HUMAN RIGHTS 99, 114–15 (Philip Alston, 2000) (asserting that rights are "inescapably individualist"; "rights always occupy the perspective of the single individual . . . .").

[43] For an example in which the CEDAW Committee ignored the absence of formal legal title, *see* X v. Cambodia, discussed at *supra* note 19 and also in chapter 5, at notes 141–142.

and the groups' rules—as where Indigenous or customary norms may recognize women's right to access and enjoy agricultural land without the formality (and possible hindrances) of title.[44]

The CEDAW regime does not focus on the protection of property as material objects or on the value of possessing such objects as such. It does not protect an abstract right to non-interference with property and is likely to impose proportionally different burdens on, for example, private and corporate landlords or owners of commercial versus residential property.[45] To be sure, the Committee, while not as narrowly intent on compensating individuals for property dispossessions as are investor-state arbitrators, affirms that persons are ordinarily owed compensation when they are deprived of possessions in violation of the principle of equality.[46] However, CEDAW's remedies typically extend beyond compensating injured individuals and attempt to respond, proactively, through recommendations that seek to prevent comparable future violations of the Convention. As described in chapter 6, the CEDAW Committee's remedial recommendations encompass a wide gamut of noncompensatory actions that would not be considered in venues that remedy only violations of individual private property by compensating persons on the basis of fair market value.[47]

All of this inspires a "progressive" sensibility about why property matters. Under CEDAW, property rights are worth protecting not because they are commodities worth having but because they protect values worth protecting—that is, because they are intrinsic to protecting and advancing women's inherent dignity, agency, and autonomy. For all these reasons, there are fewer reasons to fear embracing the term "property" in this regime and many reasons for progressives to embrace CEDAW's property jurisprudence.

---

[44] X v. Cambodia, *supra* note 43, seems to be an example of such a case insofar as the Committee upheld the rights of the commune's farmers despite the absence of title. But *see* chapter 3, section 3.2, at text and notes 100–104 (discussing Musembi's criticisms of the CEDAW Committee's 'abolitionist' approach to cultural norms).

[45] Compare Casla, *supra* note 5, at 203–04.

[46] Notably, even an organization as critical of private property as FIAN accepts the need for an entitlement to the right to tenure so long as this is defined as "non-discriminatory, equitable and sustainable access to, and use and management of land and natural resources for all rural people." This includes "the right to restitution and return to the lands and natural resources of which rural people were arbitrarily or unlawfully deprived." FIAN International, *The Human Right to Land* (Position Paper Nov. 2017), https://www.fian.org/fileadmin/media/publications_2017/Reports_and_Guideli nes/FIAN_Position_paper_on_the_Human_Right_to_Land_en_061117web.pdf.

[47] *See generally* the remedies typically provided under the international investment regime (as described at chapter 5, section 5.9.1) and those resulting from a human rights approach (described in chapter 6, sections 6.2.7 and 6.3.5). *See also* chapter 6, section 6.4.4 (addressing CEDAW's arguable "added value" as compared to other human rights regimes).

7.2 Why CEDAW's Property Jurisprudence Remains a Work in Progress

7.2.1 Flawed Outputs

CEDAW's property jurisprudence lacks systemization. As suggested by efforts to "re-write" *Kell v. Canada*,[48] even the most lawyerly of CEDAW's outputs, its quasi-judicial Views, often lack the lawyerly exposition sought by those expecting stable, consistent, and coherent guidance on what Convention rights mean or fully articulated signposts that enable accurate predictions of likely interpretations into the future. Contrasts, fair or not, can be drawn between the Committee's relatively laconic issued Views in response to individual communications and the more legally detailed rulings issued in comparable cases by investor-state arbitrators or judges on regional human rights courts. Some charge that the Committee's Views are inconsistent in adhering to its own GRs, including on matters such as the meaning and import of intersectional discrimination.[49]

Comparable critiques extend to the Committee's other outputs. The issues picked up by COs in response to state reports vary, as do their depth of analyses of critical issues, such as the existence or impact of intersectional discrimination.[50] Committee members do not always probe deeply into a state's claims over succeeding state reports that it has complied with the Committee's criticisms by passing new laws. Its dialogues with reporting states may not seriously engage or interact with those representing the state even in the limited time for such interactions. The Committee's criticisms of states and prescriptions for change often err on the side of being "constructive" to avoid being castigated as "confrontational." The result are frequently vague recommendations that fail to address in any detail serious gaps between the states' laws and realities on the ground or fall short in addressing the underlying structural causes for unequal treatment.[51]

---

[48] *See* chapter 2, section 3.1.2, text and notes 41–53 (discussing the scholarly effort to rewrite the Views issued in *Kell v. Canada*).

[49] *See, e.g.*, Loveday Hodson, *Gender Equality Untethered?*, in FRONTIERS OF GENDER EQUALITY: TRANSNATIONAL LEGAL PERSPECTIVES 175, at 184–87 (Rebecca J. Cook ed., 2023) (arguing that the Committee's expressed approach to intersectional discrimination has been unevenly applied in responding to individual communications and identifying shortcomings in, for example, the Views issued in *A.T. v. Hungary*).

[50] *See, e.g.*, Meghan Campbell, *CEDAW and Women's Intersecting Identities: A Pioneering New Approach to Intersectional Discrimination*, 11 REVISTA DIREITO GV. SÃO PAULO 479, 494–99 (2015) (discussing discrepancies in the consideration of intersectional discrimination among the Committee's COs responding to different state reports).

[51] For general criticisms of the Committee's interactions with states along these lines, *see, e.g.*, Yvonne Donders & Vincent Vleugel, *Universality, Diversity, and Legal Certainty: Cultural Diversity in the Dialogue Between the CEDAW and States Parties*, in THE RULE OF LAW AT THE NATIONAL AND INTERNATIONAL LEVELS: CONTESTATIONS AND DEFERENCE 321 (Machiko Kanetake & André

A salient example relating to property rights emerges from China's periodic state reports. China, like forty-eight other state parties to the CEDAW that have not ratified its Optional Protocol, is exposed to the Committee's scrutiny only through the state reporting system. This means that the Committee's COs are the regime's sole tool for protecting the property rights of women in the world's most populous country. Like many countries, China's periodic reports are not always filed in timely fashion. The Committee's Concluding Observations for China, published in November 2014, responded to China's combined seventh and eight periodic reports, for example.[52] While on that occasion the Committee challenged China's level of compliance on a number of issues, its COs paid scant attention to the property provisions that are the subject of this book with two exceptions: continued allegations that rural Chinese women face severe restrictions on access to land and discriminatory property deprivations in connection with martial property.

With respect to these issues, this is all that the Committee had to say:

... the Committee remains concerned that a high proportion of women in rural areas are still left without contracted land (¶ 42)

The Committee calls upon the State party to eliminate all barriers restricting women's access to land, particularly in rural areas, and ensure that the mediation and settlement of such disputes affords women effective remedies (¶ 43)

... the Committee is concerned about the decision of the Supreme People's Court regarding the interpretation of the marriage law that in cases of divorce or inheritance title to property reverts back to the original investor, a decision which has the effect of indirectly discriminating against women and depriving them of titles to property (¶ 44).

The Committee's response to unequal access to family property was as succinct as it was with respect to rural Chinese women's unequal access to land. It declared that China should

[T]ake effective measures to ensure that women fully enjoy their property rights regardless of their marital status, in line with article 16 of the Convention and the Committee's general recommendation No. 29 on the economic consequences of marriage, family relations, and their dissolution (¶ 49).[53]

Nollkaempereds, 2016). *See also* chapter 4, section 4.4.4 (addressing criticisms that the CEDAW Committee fails to address "root causes").

[52] CO on China, CEDAW/C/CHN/CO/7–8 (2014).
[53] *Id. See also* chapter 2, at text and notes 244, 413–414 (discussing the CO on China from 2014).

The Committee's Concluding Observations issued on May 30, 2023, in response to China's ninth report, essentially repeated the same concerns with rural women's access to land expressed nine years before.[54] While the Committee praised China for amending its Law on the Protection of Rights and Interests of Women, which covers, among other things, rights to property, as well as for ostensibly prohibiting all forms of domestic violence in its Anti-Domestic Violence Law,[55] it alluded only indirectly to the lack of effective enforcement of either when it acknowledged the bias of Chinese judges "who apply gender stereotypes and give little weight to women's testimony, evidence and claims," while in some cases dismissing "up to 80% of women's domestic violence claims in divorce proceedings."[56]

There is no mystery about why millions of Chinese women face severe constraints with respect to securing equal access to rural land—although one has to read between the lines of the Committee's COs to find the answer. Access to Chinese agricultural land, although formally governed by China's Property Law in 2007, is controlled not by that law—which provides for formal equality between men and women with respect to land contract disputes and with respect to compensation in cases of expropriation—but by the male leaders of agricultural cooperatives who apply cultural norms that effectively limit control of such lands to men.[57] Similarly, the reasons why Chinese rural women face endemic discrimination with respect to securing equal rights to family property when a marriage dissolves, only indirectly addressed by the Committee's cryptic observations on point,[58] have been addressed by Ke Li, among others.[59] Based on empirical data on the numbers of divorce petitions and claims in China and field research involving a substantial number of interviews with women seeking divorces, lawyers charged with assisting them, and judges handling the cases in two rural townships carried out from January 2010 through May 2011, Ke explains how, despite the passage of an ostensibly progressive Marriage Law in 2001, the property rights of rural Chinese women seeking a legal separation from their spouses, often in cases in which they allege domestic abuse, are severely undermined at every stage of the process, from the initial consultation with attorneys to state

---

[54] CO on China, CEDAW/C/CHN/CO/9 (2023), at ¶¶ 47–48.

[55] *Id.*, at ¶ 4(a) & (e).

[56] *Id.*, at ¶ 15. *See also id.*, ¶ 25 (noting that "a small percentage of all domestic violence reported to the police result in restraining orders").

[57] *See, e.g.*, Li Ke, *Land Dispossession and Women's Rights Contention in Rural China*, 5 CHINA L. & SOC'Y REV. 33 (2020).

[58] *See, e.g.*, CO on China, CEDAW/C/CHN/CO/9 (2023), ¶ 59 ("The Committee notes with concern that family courts rarely take incidents of gender-based violence into consideration of alimony payments ... which may have a negative impact on women and their children ....").

[59] LI KE, MARRIAGE UNBOUND: STATE LAW, POWER, AND INEQUALITY IN CONTEMPORARY CHINA (2022); XIN HE, DIVORCE IN CHINA: INSTITUTIONAL CONTROLS AND GENDERED OUTCOMES (2021); ETHAN MICHELSON, DECOUPLING GENDER INJUSTICE IN CHINA'S DIVORCE Courts (2022).

mediations and judicial proceedings.[60] Ke documents how, at every turn—and consistent with national data on point—women confront a legal system that favors keeping marriages intact, consistent with Communist Party concerns with social stability and sagging birth rates.

Ke provides evidence on how women are first discouraged from filing for divorce and when they persist discouraged from pursuing their equal rights to property even by their own lawyers, who fail to convert their property claims into written requests, and by mediators or judges who resist addressing them.[61] She reports that women, unlike men, are most likely to be denied a divorce when they first initiate the process and are encouraged to enter into settlements where their husbands routinely extract marital property waivers in exchange for consents to divorce.[62] Her empirical data shows how, when women manage to secure divorces, judge-ordered or mediated cases most often result in no decision on property partition and that, in the few cases when property partition is addressed, women rarely prevail.[63] More disturbing still is that nothing changes when the women present evidence of serious and ongoing spousal abuse. Allegations of violence, Ke reports, are not raised during mediation sessions or trials:

> No investigations were conducted within or without courtrooms. The overall pattern was remarkably consistent: not a single case in the sample generated a court decision that expressly identified a husband as a perpetrator ... not a single case demanded a violent, abusive spouse pay damages to his victim, although the Marriage Law decrees otherwise. Everywhere I looked in my data collection, I could not find any indication of judicial attempts to address violence against women.[64]

These conclusions are consistent with those of many others who point out that despite laws against marital rape, that crime is not prosecuted except in the rare

---

[60] KE, *supra* note 59, at 8–13.
[61] *Id.* at 232–38.
[62] *Id.* at 238–39.
[63] *Id.* at 239.
[64] *Id.* at 241. This is consistent with the work of others who document that, despite improvements in formal Chinese legislation aimed at combating violence against women and sexual harassment in the workplace, women victimized by either domestic violence or workplace harassment face significant obstacles in obtaining legal remedies. In one study, of eighty-three sexual harassment cases identified, only six resulted in formal suits against the harassers and the handful who prevailed "often receive little, if any, compensation for their suffering." AARON HALEGUA, U.S.-ASIA L. INST., WORKPLACE GENDER-BASED VIOLENCE AND HARASSMENT IN CHINA: HARMONIZING DOMESTIC LAW AND PRACTICE WITH INTERNATIONAL STANDARD (2021). *See also* Xin He, *Why Don't Chinese Divorce Courts Better Protect Women?*, 1 USALI PERSPECTIVES 22 (May 13, 2021), https://usali.org/usali-perspectives-blog/why-dont-chinese-divorce-courts-better-protect-women.

instance when the marriage has been effectively dissolved.[65] A country in which husbands are still essentially free in fact (if not in law) to rape their wives—a fact that is not addressed by the Committee's COs—is not a place from which one can expect equality with respect to division of marital property.[66]

Neither China's reports to the CEDAW Committee nor the Committee's responses addresses the causes of these manifest violations of equality, evincing stark gaps between the formal law and its implementation. The Committee's diplomatically expressed concerns with women's "access to justice" fall far short of giving effect to its own principal GRs on point, 34 and 39; they do not do justice to the many women who have faced grave harm and even death given the Chinese legal system's callous disregard for women seeking divorce under threat of domestic violence.[67]

Another example of relatively anodyne COs responding to circumstances that resemble those in China is the Committee's 2020 response to Pakistan's fifth periodic report.[68] The Committee's report starts promisingly enough, by denouncing Pakistan's continued failure to withdraw its declaration declaring CEDAW subject to "the provisions of the Constitution of the Islamic Republic of Pakistan."[69] But anyone looking for pointed inquiries and challenges directed at a state whose parallel justice systems grants women belonging to distinct ethnic and religious groups distinct rights and access to justice with respect to marriage and family relations is bound to be disappointed. Only those familiar with NGO and scholarly reports on point will know that much like China, the Pakistani legal system effectively does not prosecute marital rape, is otherwise largely indifferent to serious allegations of domestic abuse when it comes to authorizing divorce, affirms men as the legally ordained breadwinner of the family, and regularly exposes divorced women to the threat of total destitution.[70] In response to these grim realities,

---

[65] See, e.g., Shichao Sun & Zhitao Zhang, *A Study on the Route of Criminalization of Marital Rap*, 32 J. HUBEI U. POLICE 90 (2019); Huoliang Wang, *Legislative Review of Marital Rape Was Written into the Anti-Domestic Violence Law*, 31 J. HUBEI U. POLICE 122 (2018); *U.N. Population Fund, Research on Gender-based Violence and Masculinities in China: Quantitative Findings* (Nov. 2013), https://china.unfpa.org/en/publications/research-gender-based-violence-and-masculinities-china-quantitative-findings.

[66] See, e.g., Hannah Feldshuh, *Marital Rape: A Crime Left Unseen and Unspoken in the Chinese Legal System*, THE DIPLOMAT (Dec. 8, 2018), https://thediplomat.com/2018/12/marital-rape-a-crime-left-unseen-and-unspoken-in-the-chinese-legal-system/. Of course, China is not the only state that fails to prosecute this crime. See, e.g., *Marital Rape Is Not a Crime in 32 Countries. One of Them Is India*, NEWS 18, https://www.news18.com/news/india/marital-rape-is-not-a-crime-in-32-countries-one-of-them-is-india-4130363.html (last visited Mar. 29, 2023). *See also* Iqra Saleem Khan, *Consent in Marriage: A Radical Feminist Analysis of Pakistani Law*, 26 WM. & MARY J. OF RACE, GENDER & SOC. JUST. 671 (2020) (describing the absence of prosecutions for marital rape in Pakistan).

[67] Compare chapter 2, sections 2.11.1 (discussing the GRs relevant to gender-based violence) and 2.11.2 (discussing the Communications addressing gender-based violence).

[68] CO on Pakistan, CEDAW/C/PAK/CO/5 (2020).

[69] *Id.* ¶ 9. *See also* appendix 2.

[70] *See also* Saleem Khan, *supra* note 66, at 671.

the Committee's COs blandly express "concern" with Pakistan's parallel justice systems and urges the state to ensure that these do not discriminate against women.[71] With respect to the many blatant violations of CEDAW's Article 16(1)(h), the CO notes with concern "that in case of non-consensual divorce, only women petitioners are required to prove grounds for divorce in court, and that the support to be provided in the event of divorce is not harmonized for the different religious groups."[72] The Committee recommends, by way of response, that Pakistan "ensure that the family laws of the different religious communities provide for financial protection for women upon divorce in the form of equal levels of marital support and equitable shares in matrimonial property" and "amend or repeal all discriminatory provisions in laws that provide for unequal rights of women with respect to marriage, divorce, guardianship, inheritance and property."[73]

The Committee's COs on Pakistan are generally consistent with concerns expressed in its GR 16 that "identity-based personal status laws and customs perpetuate discrimination against women" and that "the preservation of multiple legal systems is in itself discriminatory against women."[74] But the Committee's laconic paragraphs on these issues in its report on Pakistan—the sheer absence of detail on the dire impact these personal status laws are having on the security and even the right to life of Pakistani women—suggest a less than fulsome application of GR 16. As Rangita de Silva de Alwis and Indira Jaising point out, personal status laws, whether based on Muslim, Christian, or Hindu traditions, customs, or religious rules, drafted by male hierarchies that did not involve women's participation, play a substantial role in creating a "second sex" with direct consequences on, among other things, women's equal property rights.[75] Although other COs are more fulsome in responding to underlying problems by reporting states,[76] the inconsistency among the CEDAW's COs indicates why

---

[71] CO on Pakistan, *supra* note 68, ¶¶ 19, 20(a), & 49.

[72] *Id.* ¶ 49(d).

[73] *Id.* ¶ 50(d) & (e).

[74] GR No. 16 on Unpaid Women Workers in Rural and Urban Family Enterprises, A/46/38, ¶ 15 (1991).

[75] Rangita de Silva de Alwis & Indira Jaising, *The Role of Personal Laws in Creating a "Second Sex,"* 48 N.Y.U. J. INT'L L. & POL. 1085 (2016).

[76] One such example may be the Committee's 2017 response to Kenya's eighth periodic report. *See* CO on Kenya, CEDAW/C/KEN/CO/8 (2017). That report canvassed, among other things, the Committee's concerns with Kenya's Marriage Act of 2014, criticizing the requirement to prove contribution to marital property given challenges to proving the existence of or quantifying nonmonetary contributions, the removal of spousal consent for transactions relating to marital property, intestate succession rules that directly discriminate against women and girls, rules that render widows' inheritance rights void upon remarriage, and discrimination against women married under Islamic law (including the right of men to divorce their wives unilaterally and to withhold divorce certificates to extract concessions). *Id.*, at ¶ 50. The report made recommendations with respect to each of these problems. *Id.* ¶ 51. While that report still falls short of recognizing numerous realities on the ground (compare, *e.g.*, Julian Nnoko-Mewanu & Najma Abdi, *Securing Women's Property Rights in Kenya*, DAILY NATION (Mar. 7, 2020), https://www.hrw.org/news/2020/03/07/securing-womens-prope

critics contend that the Committee is superficial, and more reactive than disciplined, in its treatment of at least some state reports.

7.2.2 Substantive Lacunae

Complaints about the Committee's GRs underlie the more general charge that the Committee has not taken full advantage of its ability to fill in or systematize its jurisprudence through this vehicle.[77] The substantive lacunae relevant to property are substantial.

The jurisprudence surveyed in chapter 2 does not provide a coherent explanation of when or whether the extensive property rights specially accorded CEDAW's Article 14 to "rural women" should be understood as applying to non-rural women,[78] whether Article 14 or other parts of the Convention are the best places to locate the Committee's rationale for intersectional discrimination, what specific remedies are owed by states when they violate particular property rights violations,[79] or whether, if compensation is due, when the sums due should be left to governments to decide.[80] The Committee has not resolved the tension between according individual remedies to communicants simply because some communications were deemed admissible and led to a result on the merits, and the possible adverse impact such remedies may have on other women in the same state facing comparable discrimination who are not accorded the same remedy given limited state resources.

The Committee has not clarified under the right to housing precisely when a reasonable eviction turns into a "forced" one.[81] Nor has it identified precisely

rty-rights-kenya), it identifies more of the relevant legal shortcomings that either the Pakistan or China reports.

[77] *See, e.g.*, Catherine Briddick, *Unprincipled and Unrealized: CEDAW and Discrimination Experienced in the Context of Migration Control*, 22 INT'L J. DISCRIMINATION & L. 224 (2022) (criticizing the CEDAW Committee's GRs for their opacity, omissions, and inconsistencies, particularly as applied to discriminatory migration policies).

[78] For example, while in the North Macedonia cases discussed in chapter 2, section 2.7.2.1, the Committee appeared to extend the right to adequate housing in Article 14(2)(h) to Roma women in an urban setting, it has not suggested that the protection of the intellectual property interests of Indigenous and rural women, presumed to be included in Article 14(2)(g), extends to all forms of women's intellectual property rights. *See generally* chapter 2, section 2.8.

[79] This is not to imply that other human rights treaty bodies have necessarily generated clearer or more coherent jurisprudence with respect to remedies. *See generally* chapter 6, sections 6.2.7 and 6.3.5.

[80] *See, e.g.*, chapter 5, section 5.10, particularly at text and notes 151–155 (comparing the likely forms of relief available to individuals under the investment and CEDAW regimes).

[81] The few mentions of objectionable evictions discussed in chapter 2 do not clarify if an eviction becomes prima facie wrongful under CEDAW when the state fails to ensure public housing or rental assistance to intersectionally discriminated women. The North Macedonia cases, discussed in chapter 2, section 2.7.2.1, suggest that the absence of notice and the relative rarity of such evictions in

what types of unions or families are entitled to the protections of Article 16(l)(h) or why states should be accorded deference on whether to initially recognize some unions before the Committee can address their discriminatory impact on, for example, LGBTQ+ persons.[82] The Committee has also not overcome the general problem that a treaty that specifically targets discrimination "against women" (in both title and text) seems ill-suited to advance the rights of anyone other than cis-gendered women or girls.[83] Although the Committee has made some inroads in expanding CEDAW to embrace members of LGBTQ+ communities, these efforts have been uneven and lack coherence.[84] At a time when in some parts of the world identifying as LGBTQ+ continues to risk a death sentence—never mind a threat to one's property rights—CEDAW's mixed messages on this kind of intersectional discrimination threatens its credibility on much else.[85]

Moreover, despite the Committee's revisitations of the topic throughout all its outputs, uncertainties exist about when, exactly, distinctions relating to property interests based on sex amount to wrongful discrimination. Although it is possible to infer, particularly from recommendations it issues to states, that the CEDAW Committee sees its mission as advancing certain key goals that may yield insights on that question, these are not usually articulated in a systemic, clear, and consistent way throughout its outputs and are the product of scholarly speculation.[86] The Committee has not articulated a clear position or preference among possible theoretical frameworks to answer that question. Is denying women equal property rights objectionable because or to the extent that it denies

---

North Macedonia were relevant to upholding the individuals' claims. One might compare the HRC's relatively richer jurisprudence on the procedural requirements required in cases of forced eviction, as summarized in chapter 6, section 6.2.6, under the ICCPR's Article 17(1)'s explicit guarantee against "arbitrary" or "unlawful" interference with the home or family.

[82] *See* chapter 2, section 2.4.3.8.
[83] *See* chapter 3, section 3.1.2, at text and notes 24–27. Tensions among states about whether the CEDAW regime should address discrimination directed at sexual orientation date back at least to the Beijing Conference. *See, e.g.*, Dianne Otto, *Lesbians? Not in My Country: Sexual Orientation at the Beijing World Conference on Women*, 20 ALTERNATIVE L.J. 288 (1995).
[84] GR No. 29 on Economic Consequences of Marriage, Family Relations and Their Dissolution, CEDAW/C/GC/29 (2013), for example, interprets Article 16(1)(h)'s protections for the property of both "spouses" to include family property of non-heterosexual couples. *Id.* at ¶ 24. But anyone searching chapter 2 for specific discussions of the particular problems faced by LGBTQ+ persons with respect to social and economic benefits or generally with respect to the right to housing, for example, will come up empty-handed. Compare, *e.g.*, Rep. of the Independent Expert on Protection Against Violence and Discrimination Based on Sexual Orientation and Sexual Identity, A/74/181 (July 17, 2019), ¶¶ 14–18 (discussing LGBTQ+ persons and housing), ¶¶ 37–41 (discussing women who are lesbian, bisexual, trans, and gender diverse).
[85] *See generally* Daniel Del Gobbo, *Queer Rights Talk: The Rhetoric of Equality Rights for LGBTQ+ Peoples, in* FRONTIERS OF GENDER EQUALITY, *supra* note 49, at 68.
[86] Compare chapter 6, section 6.4.4, at text and notes 363–364 (discussing Holtmaat's articulation of CEDAW's goals).

them equal opportunity?[87] Because when states discriminate against women's property interests, they send the message that women (or particular groups of women) do not merit being treated as equals and are therefore second-class citizens?[88] Or is the problem not only that such discrimination sends detrimental expressionist messages but produces a state of affairs in which women actual suffer from lower social status relative to others?[89]

Given the Committee's geographically and disciplinarily diverse membership, one would not expect it to back any *one* of these theories. A Committee that is as pluralist as CEDAW's is more likely to be sympathetic to what Sophie Moreau describes as a "pluralist" answer: discriminating against women's property interests is wrong for all of these reasons. That response is also to be expected given the diverse rationales suggested by the Convention's preamble as well as the outputs surveyed in chapter 2.

However, even if we cannot reasonably take the Committee to task for failing to back one of these philosophical approaches, one might still expect that its applications of the equality principle to be clearer about a distinction that cuts across all of these approaches: namely, whether distinctions among property rights are wrongful under CEDAW only when they fail to treat people as each other's equals (equality) or whether they are also wrong because they fail to provide women or certain women enough of a basic good (sufficiency). Sufficiency-based views posit that discrimination is objectionable when it leaves some people or groups without enough of some good that matters (and implicitly, once they have enough, any further inequalities between them and others ceases to matter). While the text of CEDAW—and specifically its suggestion that women should be treated like men—suggests that the Convention foregrounds equality, a number of the Committee's interpretations in chapter 2 indicate that the Committee is also concerned with sufficiency.

The Committee's interpretations of the diverse economic and social benefits contained in Articles 11, 13, and 14 provide examples. As described in chapter 2, CEDAW obligates states to redress discrimination against women with respect to everything from contribution-based social security schemes paid by employers

---

[87] Compare JOSEPH FISHKIN, BOTTLENECKS: A NEW THEORY OF EQUAL OPPORTUNITY (2016). This seems implied by CEDAW's ¶ 8 of the preamble (stating that inequality interferes with the "full development" of women's "potentialities").

[88] Compare DEBORAH HELLMAN, WHEN IS DISCRIMINATION WRONG? (2011); Elizabeth Anderson, *What Is the Point of Equality*, 109 ETHICS 287 (1999). This might be suggested by CEDAW's preamble, ¶ 1's reference to the need to affirm the "dignity and worth" of the human person as well as ¶ 7's reference to equality as an obstacle to women's equal "participation" in the "political, social, economic and cultural life of their countries."

[89] A leading piece propounding this "subordination" thesis is Cass Sunstein, *The Anti-Caste Principle*, 92 MICH. L. REV. 2410 (1994). The idea is arguably implied by CEDAW's preamble, ¶ 7, which connects equality to respect for human dignity and declares that respect for both enables the growth of the prosperity of society and family.

to nonemployment related benefits that may be paid by the state such as maternity benefits and noncontributory pensions. The Committee's interpretations of the states' obligations often evince a concern for whether women secure *sufficient* benefits, whether or not those benefits are extended to men.[90] In these cases, the Committee seems to be suggesting that the principle of equality—or more accurately substantive equality—requires states to extend an adequate floor of social protection to women as a whole or to distinct groups of women.[91] The Committee's recommendations that women receive certain benefits not comparable to those extended to men or not extended to anyone at all under the existing law of some states—relating to pregnancy or based on income earned outside the formal sector, for example—collapse distinctions between the equality and sufficiency frameworks.[92] As Beth Goldblatt argues, the Committee has not defined whether protectable social benefits under CEDAW anticipate minimum entitlements to "social assistance for all groups of women facing economic insecurity."[93] The Committee's practice on economic/social benefits surveyed in chapter 2 does not indicate how far the Convention goes in demanding from

---

[90] *See, e.g.*, in chapter 2, section 2.10 (describing GRs addressing rights to social benefits). Concerns for the sufficiency of women's social benefits seem apparent in the Committee's insistence that states include women's unenumerated work in social security payments; make sure that economic benefits to migrant workers include consideration of the contributions they make to their home countries, caregiving, and domestic work; consider the impact of gender-based discriminations in employment throughout women's lives; adequately address the special needs of female heads of household; and redress the impact of intersectional discrimination (as with respect to refugees or rural women). In these instances, the Committee goes beyond ensuring that social/economic benefits extended to men are made equally available to women. The Committee also treats the duty not to discriminate as requiring some forms of social protection even to those, like refugees, who may not be entitled to any under existing national law. The Committee's recommendations in these respects are consistent with those who see social security as a rights-based entitlement that is vital to addressing the feminization of poverty and other negative impacts of "neo-liberal economic policies on women in the developing world." *See, e.g.*, BETH GOLDBLATT, DEVELOPING THE RIGHT TO SOCIAL SECURITY—A GENDER PERSPECTIVE 2 (2016). *See generally* GENDERING WELFARE STATES (Diane Sainsbury ed., 1994).

[91] While the Committee has not articulated a theoretical account explaining the right to substantive equality, its recommendations directed at achieving that goal would appear to have much in common with, for example, Sandra Fredman's definition of the term. *See, e.g.*, Sandra Fredman, *Challenging the Frontiers of Gender Equality: Women at Work, in* FRONTIERS OF GENDER EQUALITY, *supra* note 49, at 38 (defining the right to substantive equality as a multidimensional principle requiring attention to redressing disadvantage; addressing stigma, stereotyping, prejudice, and violence; facilitating voice and participation; and transforming structures and accommodating difference).

[92] The kind of scrutiny for substantive equality exercised by the CEDAW Committee in a case like *Ciobanu v. Republic of Moldova* (chapter 2, section 2.10.2.3) is inconceivable as a matter of contemporary constitutional law in a country like the United States. Such an outcome would be transformational for a country whose Supreme Court does not apply the strictest form of constitutional scrutiny to cases of sex discrimination and does not consider substantive equality (or "substantive due process") to be required by the US Constitution. *See generally* FEMINIST JURISPRUDENCE CASES AND MATERIALS 19–101 (Cynthia Grant Bowman et al. eds., 5th ed. 2018).

[93] GOLDBLATT, *supra* note 90, at 71. Compare chapter 2, section 2.10.3.8 (discussing the Committee's Concluding Observations that demonstrate its concern with those who are denied any social security benefits and the connections to the feminization of poverty).

states fundamentally redistributive "benefits" that would seriously address the impoverishment of women.

The Committee could fill such interpretative gaps. Sophia Moreau, for example, has proposed a tripartite framework that embraces the equality and sufficiency frames and that could help provide structure to the Committee's capacious property jurisprudence (as well as to how it applies the bar on discrimination more generally). She argues that wrongful discrimination consists of actions that distinguish among people in ways that subordinate them socially, deny some deliberative freedoms to which they have a right, or leave some without access to a "basic good."[94]

It would not be difficult to apply her tripartite division to the jurisprudence described in chapter 2. Discrimination against the property rights of rural or Indigenous women, for example, wrongfully elevates the social standing of certain groups over others consistent with her first form of discrimination. Denials of the rights of women to have equal access to family property upon dissolution of a marriage deprives them from making choices about their lives, consistent with the second form. And either of those actions (as well as many others suggested by chapter 2's sad litany of property rights violations) may also be wrongful when they restrict access to a good that is necessary for persons to be, and to be seen as, a full and equal participant in society —consistent with Moreau's third discrimination frame and definition of "basic goods."[95]

Moreau's trifold distinctions might also be used to fill another interpretative void: the CEDAW Committee's failure to articulate a clear theory about when or why the particular identities or roles of women constitute wrongful intersectional discrimination.[96] While the Committee has identified a number of identities

---

[94] Sophie Moreau, *Faces of Gender Inequality*, in FRONTIERS OF GENDER EQUALITY, *supra* note 49, at 19. Moreau defines social subordination as a "state of affairs in which one social group has a standing or status that is lower than that of another." *Id.* at 21. Subordinated social groups generally have less *de facto* authority, receive less obedience or deference, are subjected to stereotypes, and less benefited by structural accommodations. *Id.* at 23. Denials of deliberative freedoms prevent people from making choices about their lives, such as being able to work without their gender being an issue or deciding whether to have children. Such denials fail to show respect people's autonomy. *Id.* at 26. Basic goods are those where access to it "is necessary in order for this person to be a full and equal participant in her society" and where access to the good "is necessary in order for this person to be seen by others as well as herself as a full and equal participant in her society." *Id.* at 27.

[95] Moreau, *supra* note 94, at 27. This seems consistent with much of the Committee's work to advance gender equality with respect to, for example, rights to housing (chapter 2, section 2.7) or access to justice (chapter 2, section 2.5). The Committee's Views in the North Macedonia cases (chapter 2, section 2.7.2.1) emphasize the need to rectify, through access to adequate housing, the intersectional discrimination imposed on Roma women who were pregnant or had young children, for example. Similarly, many of the Committee's COs in chapter 2, section 2.7.3 (addressing the need for equal treatment with respect to safe, secure, and affordable housing for older, Indigenous, or disabled women, migrants, refugees and asylum seekers, low-income persons, as well as those suffering in the wake of natural disasters) suggest Moreau's third frame for discrimination: denials of access to basic goods.

[96] *See, e.g.*, Amanda Barbara Allen Dale, Intersectional Human Rights at CEDAW: Promises Transmissions and Impacts (Aug. 23, 2018) (PhD dissertation, Osgoode Hall Law School),

or roles that can be considered in determining whether intersectional discrimination exists—and has been lauded for naming harms that are often "hidden, camouflaged or normalized" and adding to these over time[97]—it has not clearly explained why distinctions directed at particular identities among women violate the Convention. Nor has it clearly indicated whether some forms of intersectional discrimination matter more than others— including for purposes of deciding suitable remedies. The Committee has not explicitly suggested that distinctions made partly or wholly on the basis of race, for example, might be particularly problematic or worth priority attention or whether that would be unwise or legally problematic (or both). The Committee could indicate, but has not, that a state that is violating both its CEDAW and Convention on the Elimination of All Forms of Racial Discrimination (CERD) obligations commits a graver breach that merits a particular level of financial recompense to those harm. Shreya Atrey has argued in favor of prioritizing among some intersectional forms of discrimination, suggesting that the CEDAW Committee has implicitly endorsed this approach.[98] She sees GR 37's emphasis on particular groups of women who are especially threatened by climate change as an example of the Committee's emerging efforts to prioritize attention and remedies for those under the gravest threat.[99]

Quite apart from distinguishing among those most gravely impacted by intersectional discrimination, the CEDAW Committee has not given guidance about whether certain forms of property deprivation matter more than others. One justification for distinguishing among violations of CEDAW is suggested, for example, by its Optional Protocol—which authorizing inquiries only for "grave or systematic" violations of the Convention. Of course, distinctions among human rights appear in other contexts, such as the International Covenant on Civil and Political Rights (ICCPR)'s identification of certain of its provisions as "non-derogable" even in cases of public emergencies or the Convention against Torture and Other Cruel, Inhuman and Degrading Treatment or Punishment's distinctions with respect to torture as compared to cruel, inhumane, and degrading treatment.[100] As those distinctions suggest, some human

---

https://yorkspace.library.yorku.ca/xmlui/bitstream/handle/10315/35582/Dale_Amanda_BA_ 2018_PhD.pdf?sequence=2&isAllowed=y (discussing interpretative gaps and uncertainties in CEDAW's use of intersectional discrimination); *see also* chapter 4, section 4.4.2.

[97] Rebecca J. Cook, *Many Paths to Gender Equality, in* FRONTIERS OF GENDER EQUALITY, *supra* note 49, at 2.

[98] Such distinctions might find support from some of the Committee's prior practice—as where it highlights, in making recommendations, that the state appears to be in violation of both the CEDAW and another human rights treaty. See Shreya Atrey, *A Prioritarian Account of Gender Equality, in* FRONTIERS OF GENDER EQUALITY, *supra* note 49, at 64–65.

[99] *Id.* at 64–65.

[100] Compare ICCPR, Article 4(2) (barring derogations even in such cases of the right to life; the bans on torture or cruel, inhuman or degrading treatment, slavery or slave-trade in all its forms,

rights violations might be regarded as more serious or "fundamental" because of their greater impact on the human person, either as a category or as applied. Yet another possible justification for prioritizing among rights is suggested by recommendations that states criminalize certain human rights violations (such as sex trafficking) precisely because these are particularly serious or comparable to other actions that trigger the use of national criminal law.[101]

Given these examples, it would not be unreasonable for the Committee to opine that depriving a woman who is facing the threat of domestic violence or viable threats of being trafficked safe housing is a more serious or grave breach of CEDAW that merits, for example, lesser deference to states. That example also raises another interpretative gap in CEDAW's general as well as property jurisprudence: its failure to articulate with clarity what kind of deference states are owed and whether that standard should vary depending on whether intersectional discrimination is present or particular rights under CEDAW are at issue.[102]

Moreau's tripartite approach—indicating that distinctions are discriminatory when they constitute or result in social subordination, interference with deliberative freedoms, and/or denial of basic benefits—could be used to clarify any or all these issues. Her tripartite distinctions could also be useful to provide guidance on issues that have not been addressed under CEDAW's existing outputs. Determining that one or more of her three harms are triggered when, for example, single women in India are denied rental housing could enrich CEDAW's now limited jurisprudence on the threats to property rights that single women face in many parts of the world.[103]

Lawyers advising prospective communicants, states drafting their periodic reports, and NGOs reacting to state abuses could all benefit from interpretative clarifications on any of these matters—particularly in the form of cross-cutting

---

imprisonment for failure to fulfill a contractual obligation, and a number of other rights in the ICCPR); Convention on Torture and Other Cruel Inhuman or Degrading Treatment or Punishment, Articles 4–9 (imposing various obligations on states with respect to its requirement that torture (but not other matters addressed in that treaty) must be made a criminal offense).

[101] *See, e.g.*, G.A. Res. 52/98 (Dec. 12, 1997) (calling on states to criminalize trafficking crimes).

[102] Compare chapter 2, sections 2.10.2.1, 2.10.2.2, and 2.10.2.3 (discussing the Committee's undefined references to "large" or other "margin of appreciation" or "margin of discretion" in *Nguyen v. The Netherlands, Blok v. The Netherlands,* and *Ciobanu v. Moldova*). *See also* Briddick, *supra* note 77, at 230–32 (complaining that the CEDAW Committee applied an inconsistent and "overly wide" margin of appreciation when addressing states' actions to control migration).

[103] *See, e.g.*, Damien Cave, *For Single Indian Women, Renting Is Complicated*, N.Y. TIMES, Jan. 18, 2023, at A4; Meng Chen & Fangfang Yu, *A Home of One's Own? Gendered Homeownership in Urban China*, 20 CHINA REV. 143 (2020); Wen Jing Deng & Joris Hoekstra, *Why Women Own Less Housing Asserts in China? The Role of Intergenerational Transfers*, 34 J. HOUSING & THE BUILT ENV'T 1 (2019). *See generally* SANDY TO, CHINA'S LEFTOVER WOMEN: LATE MARRIAGE AMONG PROFESSIONAL WOMEN AND ITS CONSEQUENCES (2015).

discursive GRs on point. Leaving these basic questions unresolved (or only the subject of scholarly speculation gleaned from the language of some COs) undermines the predictability and stability of the law—as well as the Committee's credibility as a consistent treaty interpreter. They also encourage criticisms that rights discourse, here as elsewhere, deploys overly indeterminate language leading to outcomes dictated by preexisting political preferences.[104]

It is particularly discouraging to women's rights advocates that, irrespective of the quality or quantity of its work products, the CEDAW regime is encountering growing resistance to its work products, amidst a much broader populist backlash against human rights within authoritarian and even some states touted as democracies.[105] NGOs and scholars complain that even once "progressive" states are backsliding—as with respect to reporting on gender-based violence or failing to take measures that the Committee has recommended for years with respect to protective orders and provision for adequate shelters.[106] Others point to a more subtle from of backsliding: a growing number of governments are using gender-neutral language to describe deeply gendered phenomena, resulting in poor data and, worse still, poor government policies. Ruth Halperin-Kaddari and Marsha Freeman contend that when governments report the number of shelters available to "domestic violence survivors" or report on "partner homicides," "family killings," "violence between spouses or partners," or "battered family members," these gender-neutral terms conceal the fact that the vast majority of the victims are female—and that state responses such as providing shelters need to be available to them.[107] Amid such backlash, particularly, but not only by, authoritarian states, the CEDAW Committee's interpretative silences or ambiguities may make it easier for future CEDAW Committees, perhaps composed of some members more amenable to state preferences, to roll back the more progressive aspects of prior Committees' jurisprudence.

---

[104] *See, e.g.*, Koskenniemi, *supra* note 42, at 111–13 (noting, for example, the indeterminacy of the Strasbourg Court's "margin of appreciation"); 110–11 (arguing that policy dictates whether exceptions to rights apply); 106–07 (discussing the selectivity of rights discourse which protects certain principles of economic freedom as fundament rights but not, for example, immigration challenges), 107–10 (discussing the role of public policy in resolving conflicts among rights, including with respect to women's rights, when to emphasize formal equality and when it is necessary to resort to "reverse discrimination" to achieve substantive equality).

[105] *See, e.g.*, Ruth Halperin-Kaddari & Marsha A. Freeman, *Backlash Goes Global: Men's Groups, Patriarchal Family Policy, and the False Promise of Gender-Neural Laws*, 28 CANADIAN J. WOMEN & L. 165, 172–77 (2016) (describing the "global backlash" against women's rights in the United Nations' political bodies over recent years).

[106] *See generally* Conny Roggeband & Andrea Krizsán, *Democratic Backsliding and the Backlash Against Women's Rights: Understanding the current challenges for feminist politics* (UN Women, Discussion Paper No. 35, 2020).

[107] Halperin-Kaddari & Freeman, *supra* note 105, at 183–93 (describing problematic laws and data-collection policies in Western European states such as The Netherlands, Norway, the United Kingdom, and Finland, but also in Armenia, Lithuania, Canada, Lebanon, Tuvalu, and Bahrain).

7.2.3 Institutional Constraints and Challenges

There are many possible explanations for the deficiencies in the CEDAW outputs discussed in the prior sections 7.2.1 and 7.2.2. With respect to the inconsistency of COs or their laconic contents, it is important to keep in mind that the state reporting process does not erase differences among states. The contrast between the Committee's anodyne language and even praise for China's ostensibly "progress" and stark Chinese realities on the ground may be the predictable product of inadequate shadow reports by NGOs from outside that country who struggle to secure information in a challenging environment and the absence of internal civil society organizations that are independent of the Chinese Communist Party.[108] Flaws in these COs may also reflect choices made by the CEDAW Committee to emphasize China's progress in passing new laws or to avoid the hard work of assessing whether China's laws are given effect on the ground. They may, on the contrary, simply reflect the fact that the Committee simply ran out of time during state reporting sessions, particularly if Article 16 issues are left to the end of Geneva sessions subject to, as noted in chapter 2, time constraints and word limits. With respect to Pakistan, some of the same factors may be in play in addition to one more: the trepidation some Committee members may feel when it comes to addressing, head-on, direct conflicts between women's rights and religious traditions.

Connections might also between drawn between perceived flaws in the Committee's outputs and its interdisciplinary composition. While the Committee's array of disciplinary expertise has been lauded as enabling it to address the complexity of women's subordination,[109] the composition of the Committee may have downsides. Some insiders suggest that one cannot expect lawyerly or deeply analytical work-products if lawyers are not closely involved throughout the drafting process for all of the Committee's outputs, from Views to GRs to COs to Reports on Inquiries. With respect to COs, some blame other factors over which the Committee has little control such as the word limits imposed on its COs, the tendency of states to delay their reports and forward

---

[108] Compare CO on China, CEDAW/C/CHN/CO/9 (2023), ¶ 17 (noting the "limited participation of civil society organizations"). Even outside of China, human rights NGOs evince uneven attention to property rights. The Human Rights Watch March 2021 Submission on China's periodic report for the 80th CEDAW Pre-Session, for example, did not address property rights issues in China. Human Rights Submission to CEDAW, Mar. 2021. *See generally* UN TREATY BODY DATABASE, https://tbinter net.ohchr.org/_layouts/15/treatybodyexternal/SessionDetails1.aspx?SessionID=2470&Lang=en (last visited Mar. 29, 2023).

[109] *See, e.g.*, Andrew Byrnes, *The Convention on the Elimination of All Forms of Discrimination against Women and the Committee on the Elimination of Discrimination against Women: Reflections on Their Role in the Development of International Human Rights Law and as a Catalyst for National Legislative and Policy Reform* 4 (U.N.S.W.L., Research Paper No. 2010-17, 2010), https://papers.ssrn.com/sol3/papers.cfm?abstract_id=1595490.

multiple state reports all at once, the lack of support by sufficient UN staff, or the temporal constraints imposed on how the Committee conducts its sessions in Geneva.

The Committee's own operating procedures—not always transparent—and the ways it engages with NGOs might also bear scrutiny. The quality of the Committee's GRs may be the byproduct of the fact that at least the initial drafts of GRs are produced by particular Committee members with distinct skills, goals, or levels of ambition. There is little transparency on how topics are generated for GRs, when or why a "follow-up" to a GR is produced, or whether the production of GRs over time reflects intentional priorities that correspond to the most serious challenges to women's equality around the world. It seems striking that only as this book is going to press is the Committee getting around to drafting a GR on the meaning of stereotypes—a critical cross-cutting issue that may explain much of what is going on in places like China and Pakistan. These flaws might also be attributed to the Committee's practice of leaving the initiative for suggesting suitable GR topics to individual Committee members who may choose topics based on their own interests or the loudest NGO voice in the room. The thin reasoning of some GRs may also reflect the difficulty of cobbling together a consensus acceptable to all the Committee.[110]

Comparable complaints about the uneven quality of Views are sometimes explained in terms of authorship: that is, by which committee member is assigned to write the initial draft. The lack of consistency among Views in terms of depth of analysis may reflect distinct views among Committee members on what Views *are for*. Some members may believe that these should produce, case by case, a result that is fair to the individual communicant given the particular matrix of factors, including distinct forms of intersectional discrimination.[111] Others might be more inclined to use Views—and not only GRs—more ambitiously to reach for more clarifying general interpretations of the Convention or of underlying principles.[112]

More fundamental are concerns that supranational human rights scrutiny is invariably superficial and lacks context. Notwithstanding the CEDAW Committee's efforts to respond to and interact with international civil society, it faces complaints that it, like other Geneva-based human rights bodies staffed

---

[110] In this respect, the capacity of members of the Committee to file dissents to Views may enable those outputs to probe more deeply and also to evolve over time in response to such dissents. For a dissent that suggests such possibilities, see the dissenting opinion in *Nguyen v. Netherlands* (described in chapter 2, section 2.10.2.1).

[111] *See, e.g.*, Loveday Hudson, *supra* note 49, at 195 (noting that transformative intersectional analysis demands attention to contextual factors "that [do] not always sit comfortably alongside the strive for legal clarity").

[112] Compare the inclusion of the ICESCR's seven housing guarantees in the rewritten *Kell v. Canada* View discussed in chapter 3, section 3.1.2, at text and notes 41–53.

by and served by "elite cadres" of professionals, is disconnected from local, on-the-ground actors (assuming that these exist and are permitted to function independently of government). For human rights critics like Stephen Hopgood only the latter are seriously interested in solving particularized societal injustices (including stark forms of growing inequalities).[113]

7.3 Does CEDAW's Property Jurisprudence Matter?

Underlying many of the criticisms of the CEDAW regime is the worry that the CEDAW Committee's rhetoric does nothing to address the stark disparities in wealth and access to property that women face. Underlying many of the general criticisms of international human rights regimes and of CEDAW is the sense that their creators—states—have purposely made them, as Sam Moyn says, "powerless."[114] Some may believe that, as Moyn suggests is true of international human rights regimes in general, CEDAW's property efforts are the equivalent of putting a "Band-Aid" on a "charnelhouse."[115] The CEDAW Committee's nonbinding sources of *non-authority* are thin reeds against the formidable structural forms of subordination that underlie the property deprivations targeted by the Convention. The problem, say compliance skeptics, is that the Committee's outputs do not legally compel states or private actors to comply.[116]

There is a substantial literature addressing how or whether international law, international human rights regimes, and CEDAW specifically, achieves implementation, compliance, and effectiveness.[117] It would require a separate book—and distinct empirical tools and methods—to engage with that literature. It is outside the scope of this book to gauge whether or how CEDAW's property jurisprudence affects the actions of states and/or private actors over time. While such

---

[113] *See generally* STEPHEN HOPGOOD, THE ENDTIMES OF HUMAN RIGHTS (2013). Hopgood begins his book-length critique of international human rights by distinguishing those elites engaged in Human Rights (in capital letters) from "on the ground" activists intent on advancing human rights (lower case). *Id.* vii–xii.

[114] Samuel Moyn, *A Powerless Companion: Human Rights in the Age of Neoliberalism*, 77 LAW & CONTEMP. PROBS. 147 (2014). Indeed, Moyn, among others, argues that one alternative to Western-styled neoliberalism, namely state-led efforts to reduce poverty as practiced in China, has "sometimes done a better job than actual human rights movements." *Id.* at 168.

[115] *Id.* at 169.

[116] *See, e.g.*, RHODA E. HOWARD-HASSMANN, IN DEFENSE OF UNIVERSAL HUMAN RIGHTS 42 (2018) (citing critics who see human rights regimes as evincing a "moral emptiness" or emphasizing principles over enforceable law).

[117] For an example of the range of views on CEDAW's impact, compare Martha C. Nussbaum, *Women's Progress and Women's Human Rights, in* THE LIMITS OF HUMAN RIGHTS 231 (Bardo Fassbender & Knut Traisbach eds., 2019) (suggesting that CEDAW has a real but limited legal significance) to Fareda Banda, *The Limits of Law: A Response to Martha C. Nussbaum, in* THE LIMITS OF HUMAN RIGHTS, *supra* note 8, at 267 (contesting Nussbaum's view of "modest progress").

a research agenda should be encouraged, a word of warning is necessary: those looking for demonstrable proof that states have changed their behavior *because* of the CEDAW Committee's recommendations—that is, demonstrable evidence that "but for" that Committee's outputs states' behavior would have been different—would probably be looking for the wrong thing in the wrong place.

Consider a common example sometimes touted to demonstrate "effectiveness." The CEDAW Committee earns praise when its criticisms of states' reservations to CEDAW are followed by partial or complete withdrawals of such reservations.[118] It is difficult, however, to establish clear links between the CEDAW Committee's "dialogues" with state parties to convince them to withdraw their objectionable reservations to the Convention's provisions relating to property and states' withdrawals of such reservations.[119] As appendices 2 and 3 indicate, state parties' to CEDAW have most frequently made reservations that relate to the subject of this book, namely, the property-relating provisions within Articles 11, 13, 14, 15, and 16 (which frequently overlap with reservations to the overreaching duties of states not to discriminate under Article 2). The number and broad content of such reservations are a testament to the challenge that the principle of equal property rights poses to states' gendered preferences. As shown by appendix 3, of the original thirty-four state parties that made such reservations, twelve had, by 2022, partially or wholly withdrawn those reservations after one or more interactions with the Committee, including critical COs issued in response to their state reports. While it would be easy to credit the Committee with these positive developments, there are simply too many other factors that may have intervened to produce these results. It would require even more intrusive (and probably still inconclusive) inquiries to determine, in any case, whether the withdrawals of relevant reservations made any difference to the underlying state laws or practices—much less to the lives of women in these jurisdictions.

It is, of course, true that the enforcement tools *contained in CEDAW* are starkly different from those available to regional human rights courts, investor-state arbitrations, or national courts applying international law. However, assessments of the impact of the Committee's jurisprudence need to consider what happens outside Geneva—that is, the direct or indirect incorporation of CEDAW through national courts when interpreting local laws and even constitutions, as well as the work of many other forums that rely on CEDAW but do not involve

---

[118] *See generally* Siobhán Mullally, *CEDAW Reservations and Contested Equality Claims*, in FRONTIERS OF GENDER EQUALITY, *supra* note 49, at 88–107.

[119] *Id.* 93–100 (discussing the "reservations dialogue" between the Committee and reserving states). Apart from critical comments on states' reservations in COs, the Committee has made a number of general statements against reservations to the Convention, *see, e.g.*, CEDAW Comm., Statement on Reservations to the Convention on the Elimination of All Forms of Discrimination against Women, A/53/38/Rev.1, at 47–50 (1998).

the application of binding international law as such, including those seeking to implement the United Nations' Sustainable Development Goals to advance women's equality.[120] Those who are skeptical of the impact of CEDAW's jurisprudence given the continuing global gender gap on wealth and property need to consider the effects of that jurisprudence on millions of women when even just one national Supreme Court decides to directly incorporate that jurisprudence to interpret national law (as has happened innumerable times since CEDAW was concluded).[121]

More generally, it is shortsighted to equate international legally binding adjudicative rulings with international law "compliance."[122] As a substantial literature on how or when states implement, comply with, or give effect to international law demonstrates, there is no one-to-one correspondence between on the ground legal impact and "hard" or "binding" judicial remedies.[123] One should not presume that formally binding arbitral or judicial rulings are necessarily more "effective" at eradicating or reducing discriminatory practices than the subsequent practice of UN treaty bodies delegated with the power to interpret human rights when that practice interacts, over time, with civil society efforts to enforce it.[124]

Nor is it clear that courts, national or international, authorized to issue binding rulings in response to individual cases are more significant in *developing* international legal norms than UN treaty bodies like the CEDAW Committee—whose outputs extend beyond responding to individual cases and include opportunities to opine on what the law generally means (as through GRs, COs in response to state reports from virtually all nations, and more in-depth Reports on Inquiries

---

[120] On the SDGs, *see, e.g.*, UN WOMEN, PROGRESS ON THE SUSTAINABLE DEVELOPMENT GOALS: THE GENDER SNAPSHOT 2022 (2022); Marieme S. Lo, *Gender Equality and the Sustainable Development Goals: Discursive Practices in Uncertain Times*, *in* FRONTIERS OF GENDER EQUALITY, *supra* note 49, at 108. On the use of CEDAW and its jurisprudence in national courts, INTERNATIONAL WOMEN'S RIGHTS CASES (K. Adams et al. eds., 2005); ASIA PAC. F. ON WOMEN, L. & DEV., A DIGEST OF CASE LAW ON THE HUMAN RIGHTS OF WOMEN (ASIA PACIFIC) (2003); GLOBAL JUSTICE CENTER, CEDAW CASE BANK (June 6, 2017), https://globaljusticecenter.net/publications/advocacy-resources/751-cedaw-casebank; Vijaya Nagarjan & Archan Parashar, *Gender Equality in International Law and Constitutions: Mediating Universal Norms and Local Differences*, *in* THE PUBLIC LAW OF GENDER 170 (Kim Rubenstein & Katharine G. Young eds., 2016); Christopher McCrudden, *Why Do National Court Judges Refer to Human Rights Treaties? A Comparative International Law Analysis of CEDAW*, 109 AM. J. INT'L L. 534 (2015). For an in-depth account of a specific national court case, *see, e.g.*, Naina Kapur, *Breathing Life into Equality: The Vishaka Case*, *in* FRONTIERS OF GENDER EQUALITY, *supra* note 49, at 305.

[121] *See supra* note 120.

[122] *See* Robert Howse & Ruti Teitel, *Beyond Compliance: Rethinking Why International Law Really Matters*, 1 GLOBAL POL'Y 127 (2010). It is also important to consider the costs imposed by legally binding compliance tools. *See* chapter 5, section 5.11 (comparing the remedies available under CEDAW to those for investor-claimants under the international investment regime).

[123] *See generally* BETH SIMMONS, MOBILIZING FOR HUMAN RIGHTS (2009); NINA REINERS, TRANSNATIONAL LAWMAKING COALITIONS FOR HUMAN RIGHTS (2021).

[124] *See generally* TREATIES AND SUBSEQUENT PRACTICE (Georg Nolte ed., 2013).

into systematic human rights violations in particular countries). And even if we presume that legally binding rulings under a particular bilateral international investment agreement or a regional human rights treaty tend to lead to compliance by states on the losing end of such judgments, these rulings bind only the parties to such suits. In a system lacking hierarchically superior courts, it is the persuasive value of the legal interpretations themselves combined with the perceived legitimacy of the body that issues them that matters.[125] Indeed, one answer to the charge that resorting to legal rights (as under the CEDAW) "depoliticizes" what ought to stay in the political realm is to contest the premise that the turn to rights necessarily deflects politics or removes such contestations from political struggles.[126] CEDAW's interpretative efforts on property rights, as well as everything else, have political consequences and are deployed as such by both women's rights activists and their opponents.

Human rights regimes like CEDAW's are discursive forums in which levels of compliance, implementation, or effectiveness need to be defined and assessed in different ways.[127] Many factors enter into whether the interpretations of international law, whether issued by the CEDAW Committee, the UN Human Rights Committee, or, for that matter, the US Supreme Court, prove to be more or less persuasive or worthy of emulation. None of these is formally "authoritative" for purposes of determining international law of general application. All of them, depending on context and other factors—such as the use put to them by transnational civil society—can be more or less impactful. How, when, or why international law protects "property" is not the exclusive preserve of any single international legal regime. Those who dismiss all these efforts, including CEDAW's, as powerless rhetoric need to do better than rely on impressions and anecdotes.

7.4 Beyond *A Room of One's Own*

Virginia Woolf's *A Room of One's Own* famously drew direct connections between a woman's needs for basic personal space and possessions and her capacity for autonomy and self-expression.[128] Woolf contended that certain "necessities,"

---

[125] *See, e.g.*, Helen Keller & Leena Grover, *General Comments of the Human Rights Committee and Their Legitimacy*, in UN HUMAN RIGHTS 128 (Helen Keller et al. eds., 2012) (arguing that the HRC's legal legitimacy, premised on its delegated authority to interpret the ICCPR, is not enough to secure its normative legitimacy).

[126] *See, e.g.*, chapter 4, section 4.3, at text and notes 106–108 (discussing the possibility that "rights talk" can lead to political contestations instead of shutting these down).

[127] *See, e.g.*, Howse & Teitel, *supra* note 122. Nina Reiners's focus on the impact of what she calls "transnational lawmaking coalitions" is one example of why measuring human rights "compliance" by a single measure, such as whether the CEDAW Committee's outputs are "authoritative," is simplistic. REINERS, *supra* note 123.

[128] VIRGINIA WOOLF, A ROOM OF ONE'S OWN (1929).

namely, a room with a key and lock as well as some money of her own, were essential to enable women to become authors or artists (and, implicitly, much else).[129] As Woolf made clear in reflecting on the probable fate of Shakespeare's fictional sister, Judith, the impediments that women have long faced in patriarchal British society extended to much more than denials of private space and money. Among the many "contrary instincts" facing any woman brave enough to aspire to make a literary contribution, Woolf identified impediments to securing basic education, active discouragement from pursuing goals apart from marriage and motherhood, denials of access to many public and professional spaces, and myriad gendered prejudices. On Woolf's account, lack of access to a metaphorical (as well as a real) room of one's own embodied countless inequalities between men and women imposed by economic, cultural, or societal structures.

CEDAW's property jurisprudence repeatedly calls out the "contrary instincts" women face. It has much in common with Woolf's indictment of patriarchy. Both the CEDAW Committee and Woolf draw connections between equal rights to property and other economic, social, and cultural rights. Both see "material security" as deeply connected to autonomy, agency, and dignity. Both draw attention to the stereotypes that stand in the way of women's equality. At the same time, as this book indicates, the CEDAW regime seeks to protect far more than ownership of property and far more than a right to a room of one's own.

Criticisms of *A Room of One's Own* are instructive as they echo some of those lobbed at CEDAW. The African American author, Alice Walker, for example, asked her readers to imagine the plight of women enslaved in America who did not even "own" their own bodies and might have had artistic aspirations, the high hurdles faced by the formerly enslaved in America who were not permitted to read or write, or the intense effort it took their descendants, like successful author Zora Hurston, to overcome the exceedingly high "contrary instincts" they faced.[130] Walker implicitly questions the premise that Woolf's fictional Judith, a privileged woman living in a developed nation filled with bourgeois comforts made possible, at least in part, by the United Kingdom's colonist wealth, should be seen as a universal stand-in for women everywhere. Her criticisms echo those targeting CEDAW's "essentialist" woman and its "Western" biases, including its inclusion of property rights.

The meaning and value of Woolf's "Room" varies with the observer and context. Jesok Song, writing about reactions to *A Room of One's Own* in South Korea over recent decades, describes the transformations of a play based on it

---

[129] *Id.* at 4, 44, & 88. Woolf suggested that the amount of money needed was "500 a year." *Id.* at 88.
[130] Alice Walker, *In Search of Our Mother's Gardens, in* WITHIN THE CIRCLE: AN ANTHOLOGY OF AFRICAN AMERICAN LITERARY CRITICISM FROM THE HARLEM RENAISSANCE TO THE PRESENT 401, 404–06 (Angelyn Mitchell ed., 1994).

depending on contemporary developments in that country.[131] In the early 1990s, Song writes, the play based on Woolf's essay served as an indictment of a particular kind of patriarchy that resonated with an oppositional political movement and then engaged in ending South Korea's military dictatorship.[132] Later, in the wake of the country's turn to electoral democracy, the rise in human and women's rights movements locally, and other forms of environmental and consumer activism, the play became a vehicle for extolling "inner harmony for individual women, rather than a collective confrontational approach to the status quo."[133] At that time, according to Song, Woolf's focus on the need for spatial autonomy gained new currency in a society with restive young women searching for privacy and independence with no interest in marriage but confronted with discriminatory housing and loan-lending systems that made such space unavailable to them.[134] In the wake of the Asian Debt Crisis (1997–2003), as the ideal of "independent entrepreneurialism" came to be associated with democracy itself, the message in *Room* reverberated within a free-wielding neo-liberal economy that demanded self-sufficient, independent, and employable citizens. Woolf's ideal of self-governed women not dependent on the state and able and willing to care for themselves now served, according to Song, the cause of the neo-liberal South Korean state.[135]

While this book distances CEDAW's property jurisprudence from the most commonly accepted definitions of "neo-liberalism," the changing perceptions of the canonical *A Room of One's Own* over time suggest a cautionary note. It is difficult to say how the work in progress that is CEDAW's property jurisprudence will evolve over time or how perceptions of it will change. A core premise of this book is that if, as Molière might suggest, the CEDAW Committee has been speaking "property" for years without knowing it, that is not a bad thing.[136] Property rights, as defined by and for women, may be essential to the transformational change needed to enable half the world's population to secure equality.

---

[131] Jesok Songs, "*A Room of One's Own*": *The Meaning of Spatial Autonomy for Unmarried Women in Neoliberal South Korea*, 17 GENDER, PLACE AND CULTURE 131 (2010).
[132] *Id.* at 131.
[133] *Id.* at 132.
[134] *Id.* at 135–37.
[135] *Id.* at 141.
[136] MOLIÈRE, LE BOURGEOIS GENTILHOMME (1670) (Fr.).

Afterword

E. Tendayi Achiume, Alicia Miñana Professor of Law, UCLA School of Law, Former UN Special Rapporteur on Racism, Racial Discrimination, Xenophobia and Related Intolerance

There really is no question that the contemporary status of the property rights of women reflects the systemic and globally subordinate position of women. What is far more contested, is what role property rights, including through human rights regimes, should and can play in disrupting the subordinate status of women. It is in this fraught, high-stakes debate that *Women's Property Rights Under CEDAW* intervenes, combining rich empirical data with deft and productively provocative theoretical analysis. As a detailed study of how the CEDAW Committee's human rights jurisprudence addresses "male/female property gaps," the authors' descriptive and analytical contributions cannot be overstated. Their forensic treatment of the work the Committee is actually doing facilitates the authors' granular evaluation of jurisprudence that has been critiqued by some on general, abstracted terms unmoored from the concrete output of the Committee. The authors also present a nuanced and wide-ranging account of theories of property, accounting for hegemonic as well as critical and non-Western perspectives.

The ambition of the project extends beyond meticulously rendering the CEDAW Committee's property jurisprudence legible. The authors examine how the Committee's jurisprudence fares relative to the rather damning critique that liberal and critical feminists have leveled broadly at CEDAW's framework, and specifically at its approach to property and the human rights of women. The authors conclude that the Committee's property jurisprudence is " 'progressive' insofar as it seeks to protect substantive ends related to property . . . while limiting private property rights when these threaten women's lives and well-being." They also argue that CEDAW's property jurisprudence does not privilege or advance an ideological agenda in favor of the individualization, formalization, and commodification of property.

The authors convincingly show that the staunch neoliberal property rights agenda advocated by the likes of Hernando de Soto and fellow travelers is a far cry from the Committee's overall approach. In some areas, the Committee has brought to the fore of its critique the range of neoliberal economic and political structures that form part of the foundations of gendered and other forms of subordination. The Committee seems not, however, to have been capable of fashioning remedies or recommendations that plausibly disrupt these framing structures (e.g., neoliberal extractivism, patriarchal customary practices and beliefs). Among the constraints the Committee faces is the very structure of the international human rights framework. Other constraints included the gendered (and racialized) nature of liberal "rule of law" institutions and procedures. For example, the Committee's seeming faith in criminalization is in tension with what mobilization of the criminal justice framework means in practice for rural, or urban, or racially/ethnically marginalized women. In some cases, remedies the Committee relies upon to address discrimination are themselves deeply gendered and racialized, highlighting very real limits.

On the question of remedies, whereas the Committee's jurisprudence reveals a commitment to intersectional inclusivity in its analysis of petitions and country conditions, especially where rural and Indigenous women are concerned, that commitment is less evident in the crafting of remedies. In its work on rural, Indigenous, and older women, for example, the Committee's analysis of their vulnerabilities is intersectional, but its remedial frameworks fail sufficiently to internalize the underlying thrust of intersectional analysis.

Overall, it is significant that the Committee's framing of the role of property and property rights in shaping gendered subordination reflects the perspectives of liberal and critical feminists. But in the absence of remedial frameworks capable of disrupting the power hierarchies often at the forefront of feminist critique, the Committee's noteworthy, and in some cases impressive, jurisprudence remains fundamentally constrained along many of the axes articulated by liberal and critical feminists. In other words, what we see in the Committee's jurisprudence, as presented by the authors, is by no means a resounding refutation of feminist concerns with the emancipatory limits of property and human rights jurisprudence. Rather, it is—as the authors point out—a more complicated picture that nonetheless makes clear the material differences that fundamentally constrained frameworks can make in the lives of individuals and groups subject to systemic oppression. Even for those attuned to the CEDAW framework's myriad constraints, the authors' analysis demonstrates this framework remains a site of underappreciated value.

Even if one disagrees with particular conclusions or evaluations the authors advance in relation to feminist critique of CEDAW, it will be difficult to find a reader who is not compelled by what, in my view, should be taken to be the central evaluative insights of this book. First, that the Committee's jurisprudence is significantly more complex and even more progressive than many well-known feminists critiques of the CEDAW framework have grappled with. The second and related insight is the clear demonstration of the fact that notwithstanding the very real limits feminist and other critical scholars have attributed to the international human rights framework as a whole with respect to undoing systemic national and transnational subordination of women and others, there is concrete but not fully explored potential within this flawed framework, even assessed from the perspective and goals of feminists, liberal, critical, or otherwise.

Although the authors do not analyze inputs and knowledge produced in dialogues, consultations, or other exchanges through which the Committee conducts its work, it is likely that that the Committee operates with keen awareness of the most salient critiques of the CEDAW framework. An important area for further research would include exploring the extent to which CEDAW's progressive jurisprudence is a *product* in some meaningful part of feminist pushback and critique as opposed to being a counter or a refutation of that critique. Future research might also examine the Committee's treatment of race and racialization in its property jurisprudence, as distinct from analysis of its treatment of rural and Indigenous women. Notwithstanding the overlaps among race, ethnicity, and indigeneity, critical scholars have articulated analytically distinct relationships between race and property in law that operate transnationally and that warrant careful attention.

The value of this book's jurisprudential analysis extends even beyond the specific purposes to which the authors put it and provides an invaluable resource to researchers, activists, policymakers, educators, and students whose work is specifically on gender, property, and human rights, or more broadly, on human rights monitoring and implementation mechanisms. Even broader still, this book is of value to theorists of property of all stripes, and, by placing human rights and international investment regimes in conversation, the authors model the generative encounters that are possible between seemingly far-flung fields.

APPENDICES

The CEDAW Committee's Output Engaging with Property Rights

APPENDIX 1

RELEVANT CEDAW PROVISIONS

CEDAW

Article 11

1. States Parties shall take all appropriate measures to eliminate discrimination against women in the field of employment in order to ensure, on a basis of equality of men and women, the same rights, in particular:
   (e) The right to social security, particularly in cases of retirement, unemployment, sickness, invalidity and old age and other incapacity to work, as well as the right to paid leave;
2. In order to prevent discrimination against women on the grounds of marriage or maternity and to ensure their effective right to work, States Parties shall take appropriate measures:
   (b) To introduce maternity leave with pay or with comparable social benefits without loss of former employment, seniority or social allowances;

Article 13

States Parties shall take all appropriate measures to eliminate discrimination against women in other areas of economic and social life to ensure, on a basis of equality of men and women, the same rights, in particular:

(a) The right to family benefits;
(b) The right to bank loans, mortgages, and other forms of financial credit;

Article 14

2. States Parties shall take all appropriate measures to eliminate discrimination against women in rural areas in order to ensure, on a basis of equality of men and women, that they participate in and benefit from rural development and, in particular, shall ensure to such women the right:
   (c) To benefit directly from social security programmes;
   (g) To have access to agricultural credit and loans, marketing facilities, appropriate technology and equal treatment in land and agrarian reform as well as in land resettlement schemes;
   (h) To enjoy adequate living conditions, particularly in relation to housing, sanitation, electricity and water supply, transport and communications.

Article 15

1. States Parties shall accord to women equality with men before the law.
2. States Parties shall accord to women, in civil matters, a legal capacity identical to that of men and the same opportunities to exercise that capacity. In particular, they shall give women equal rights to conclude contracts and to administer property and shall treat them equally in all stages of procedure in courts and tribunals.

Article 16

1. States Parties shall take all appropriate measures to eliminate discrimination against women in all matters relating to marriage and family relations and in particular shall ensure, on a basis of equality of men and women:
   (h) The same rights for both spouses in respect of the ownership, acquisition, management, administration, enjoyment, and disposition of property, whether free of charge or for a valuable consideration.

APPENDIX 2

STATE RESERVATIONS TO PROPERTY-RELATING CEDAW PROVISIONS

Article 2	Art. 11(1)(e) Right to social security	Art. 11(2)(b) Paid maternity leave or other comparable social benefits	Art 13(b) Bank loans, mortgage, other forms of financial credits	Art. 15 Equal capacity in contracts and administer property	Art. 16(1)(c) Same rights and obligation during marriage and its dissolution	Art. 16(1)(h) Same rights to ownership, acquisition, management of property
Algeria	Malta	Australia	Malta	Algeria (4)	Algeria	Algeria
Bahamas (a)	Monaco	Micronesia	UK	Bahrain (4)	Bahrain	Bahrain
Bahrain	Singapore	Singapore	Ireland*2004	Malta	Bangladesh	Egypt
Bangladesh	UK	UK		Niger (4)	Egypt	India
Egypt		Cook		Qatar (1)(4)	India[5]	Iraq
Iraq (f)(g)		Islands*2007		Switzerland (2)	Iraq	Israel
Lesotho		New Zealand,		Syrian Arab	Israel	Malta
Libya		and Niue*2003		Republic (4)	Jordan	Mauritania
Micronesia (f)				UAE (2)	Lebanon	Micronesia
Morocco[1]				Belgium*1998	Libya	Singapore
Niger (d)(f)				France*1986	Malaysia	Switzerland
Qatar (a, hereditary)				(2)(3)	Maldives	UAE
Syrian Arab Republic					Malta	Brazil*1994
Singapore (a–f)					Mauritania	Bahamas*2011
UAE[2] (f)					Micronesia	France*1986
Cook Islands (f) *[3]2007					Niger	Malaysia*1998
DPRK[4] (f)*2015					Oman	Tunisia*2014
					Qatar	
					Singapore	
					Syrian Arab Republic	
					UAE	
					Brazil*1994	
					France*1986	
					Morocco*2011	
					ROK[6]*1991	
					Tunisia*2014	
					Turkey*1999	

[1] Morocco technically it does not have a reservation on Article 2, rather it has a declaration that indicates it will accept Article 2 to the extent that it does not: (1) prejudice the constitutional rules regaling the rules of succession to the throne, and (2) does "not conflict with the provisions of the Islamic Shariah, which has laws that confer different rights to men and women.

[2] UAE – United Arab Emirates.

[3] (*) reservation withdrawn.

[4] DPRK – Democratic People's Republic of Korea.

[5] India doesn't have a reservation against Article 16, rather it has a declaration stating that "India declares that it shall abide by and ensure these provisions in conformity with its policy of non-interference in the personal affairs of any Community without its initiative and consent."

[6] ROK – Republic of Korea.

APPENDIX 3

WITHDRAWN STATE RESERVATIONS TO PROPERTY-RELATING CEDAW PROVISIONS

State	Reservation(s)	Timeline of Reservation Withdrawal[7]	Year of Withdrawal
Bahamas	Art. 16(1)(h): The inheritance law of the Bahamas, which were governed by primogeniture, did not permit women to inherit from a person who died intestate.[8]	Combined Initial, Second, Third, and Fourth Periodic Report – 2009: "In 2002 . . . a new Inheritance Law was enacted which now permits men and women to inherit equally. The Bahamas can now consider removing the reservation to Article 16(h)."[9] Reply to List of Issue – 2010: In response to the Committee's question on whether the Bahamas wished to withdraw its reservation Bahamas indicated that its withdrawal was under consideration.[10] Response – 2011: Bahamas withdrew its reservation after the submission of initial report and before the constructive dialogue.	2011
Belgium	Art. 15(2): On the provision of equal legal capacity and ability to exercise such capacity, specifically regarding capacity "to conclude contracts and to administer property."	Constructive Dialogue – 1989: Belgium indicated that its reservation to Art. 15(2) was "purely theoretical" because it was "based on transitional measures that had ceased to have any effect."[11] Constructive Dialogue – 1996: "Reservation to Art. 7 and 15 would be withdrawn, since a new law had been adopted to enable women to exercise royal powers and change in the Constitution had rendered void the reservation relating to marriage law."[12] Response – 1998: Belgium withdraws its reservation.	1998

---

[7] https://tbinternet.ohchr.org/_layouts/15/TreatyBodyExternal/Countries.aspx.

[8] Consideration of reports submitted by states parties under Article 18 of the Convention on the Elimination of All Forms of Discrimination against Women, Combined initial, second, third, and fourth periodic reports of states parties, Bahamas.

[9] *Id.*

[10] Responses to the list of issues and questions with regard to the consideration of the combined initial to fourth periodic report, Bahamas.

[11] Report on the Committee on the Elimination of Discrimination Against Women, General Assembly forty-fourth session, 56–57, https://tbinternet.ohchr.org/_layouts/15/TreatyBodyExternal/Countries.aspx.

[12] Report of the Committee on the Elimination of Discrimination against Women (Fifteenth session) General Assembly Official Records · Fifty-first Session Supplement No. 38 (A/51/38).

State	Reservation(s)	Timeline of Reservation Withdrawal[7]	Year of Withdrawal
Brazil	Art. 16(1)(c) & (h): Brazilian's Civil Code differentiated the rights of women and men in the ownership, acquisition, management, administration, enjoyment, and disposition of property.[13]	Initial Report – 2003: Noted the influence that the Vienna Conference of Human Rights (1993), the Vienna Human Rights Declaration, and the Beijing Platform of Action—urging countries to withdraw reservations contrary to the object and purpose of the CEDAW—had on Brazil's withdrawal decision. Combined Initial 1st–5th Periodic Reports – 2003: Noted Brazil's withdrawal of Art. 16 reservations along with its passage of domestic laws ensuring the "rights and duties of spouses during marriage."[14]	1994
Cook Island	Art. 11(2)(b): "On the provision of maternity leave." Art. 2(f) & Art. 5(A): "With regard to inheritance of chiefly titles; and in general, as regards recruitment and service of women in the armed forces."	Initial Report – 2006 (September): Committee highlighted Cook Island's reservations and recent advancements regarding inclusion of women in armed force employment. Response – 2007 (April): Cook Island indicates willingness to withdraw reservations. Constructive Dialogue – 2007 (July): Government notifies committee of its withdrawal prior to dialogue.	2007
France	Art. 15(2), Art. 16(1)(c), & Art. 16(1)(h): Only husbands granted legal power to legally administer and dispose of common property and act as administrator of minor children's property.[15]	Initial Report – 1986: France indicated that in "the future, wives, in the same way as husbands, will be able to administer and dispose of common property alone," and legitimately administer minor children's property.[16] Constructive Dialogue – 1987: France indicated it had withdrawn its reservations.	1986

---

[13] Consideration of reports submitted by states parties under Article 18 of the Convention on the Elimination of All Forms of Discrimination against Women, Combined initial, second, third, fourth, and fifth periodic reports of states parties, Brazil.

[14] *Id.*

[15] Consideration of reports submitted by states parties under Article 18 of the Convention, Initial reports of states parties, France.

[16] Consideration of reports submitted by states parties under Article 18 of the Convention, Initial reports of states parties, France.

State	Reservation(s)	Timeline of Reservation Withdrawal[7]	Year of Withdrawal
Ireland	Art. 13(b): On the provision of economic equity in "bank loans, mortgages, and other forms of financial credit."	Constructive Dialogue – 1989: Ireland indicated that citizens could utilize the courts for any grievances relating to equality on bank loans, mortgages, and other forms of financial credits, and therefore specific legislation was not necessary. Fourth and Fifth Periodic Review – 2003: When acceding CEDAW, there was no specific legislation expressly regulating the obligations of private individuals to accord equality in the areas covered by Art. 13(b) and (c). Response – 2004: Prior to constructive dialogue and following its enactment of the Equal Status Act in 2004, Ireland withdrew its reservation to Arts. 13(b) and (c).	2004
New Zealand[17] (NZ)	Art. 11(2)(b): "On the provision of maternity leave."	Initial Report – 1987: Committee emphasized NZ's advancements and shortcomings in maternity leave legislation. Fourth Periodic Report – 1998: NZ indicates it has no foreseeable plans to withdraw reservation. Fifth Periodic Report – 2002: NZ enacts the Paternal Leave and Employment Protection Act and indicates willingness to assess its provisions to reach compatibility under CEDAW. Response – 2003: Before constructive dialogue, NZ formally withdrew its reservation.	2003
Malaysia	Art. 16(1)(h): Because family law is governed by civil, Islamic, and customary laws, this limits the autonomy, rights, and decision-making powers of wives, who must obey and act according to their husbands wishes.[18]	Combined Initial and Second Periodic Report – 2004: "Following the Beijing Conference [Fourth World Conference on Women] (1995), steps were taken to review Malaysia's reservations," including Art. 16(1)(h). This resulted in its withdrawal in 1998.[19]	1998

---

[17] https://tbinternet.ohchr.org/_layouts/15/TreatyBodyExternal/Countries.aspx

[18] Consideration of reports submitted by states parties under Article 18 of the Convention on the Elimination of All Forms of Discrimination against Women, Combined initial and second periodic reports of states parties, Malaysia.

[19] Consideration of reports submitted by states parties under Article 18 of the Convention on the Elimination of All Forms of Discrimination against Women, Combined initial and second periodic reports of states parties, Malaysia.

State	Reservation(s)	Timeline of Reservation Withdrawal[7]	Year of Withdrawal
Morocco	Art. 16(1)(c): "Considerable discrimination [against women] in the areas of marriage, conjugal relations, divorce and the custody of children."	Concluding Observations – 1997: Recommended withdrawal of reservations and highlighted the "considerable discrimination against women in Morocco, particularly in the field of family law." Constructive Dialogue – 2003: Morocco indicated it "must strike a balance between international law and Shariah," particularly in the issue of family law. "Therefore the Government established a commission consisting of women, religious leaders, and other representatives of civil society to discuss ways of changing the family law and modifying traditional attitudes." Morocco indicated possible withdrawal. Concluding Observations – 2003: Committee urged Morocco to expedite its withdrawal process. Third & Fourth Periodic Review – 2006: Following Morocco's revisions to its Family Code, it released a statement announcing its reservation withdrawal. Response – 2011: Morocco withdrew its reservation.	2011
Republic of Korea (ROK)	Art. 16(1)(c): Continuation of patriarchal family system, including "sharing of property between divorced couples" and the "family headship system."[20]	Initial Report – 1986: Korean family and property law still has some contradictory provisions with CEDAW. Concluding Observations – 1987: Urge ROK to consider a withdrawal. Response – 1993: ROK withdrew its reservation following its Family Law revisions made in 1990. Concluding Observations – 1998: "Ratification of the Convention had impacted significantly on the lives of Korean women. The comments of the Committee members on the second report in 1993 had provided substantial guidance in implementing women's policies, particularly in respect to women's participation in decision-making and the elimination of gender-discriminatory laws relating to citizenship."[21]	1991

---

[20] CEDAW, Initial Report of States Parties, Republic of Korea.
[21] Report of the Committee on the Elimination of Discrimination against Women (eighteenth and nineteenth sessions), General Assembly Official Records Fifty-third session Supplement No. 38 (A/53/38/Rev.1).

State	Reservation(s)	Timeline of Reservation Withdrawal[7]	Year of Withdrawal
Tunisia	Art. 16(1)(c): The Personal Status Code (PCS) establishes the husband as the "head of the family." Art. 16(1)(h): "No interference with [the PCS's laws concerning the] acquisition of property by succession."	Combined Initial and Second Periodic Report – 1993: Stated that the current PCS violated CEDAW's provisions; committee urged withdrawal. Sixth Periodic Report – 2009: Although it still faced shortcomings, Tunisia stated that it had "constantly and progressively adapted its legislation" to increase gender equality in "matrimonial and family rights."[22] It further indicated that it such efforts were made with the aim at bringing its "domestic law more closely in line with the Convention's standards and provisions."[23] Response: 2011 – Tunisia's government approved the withdrawal. 2014 – Tunisia officially withdrew its reservation.	2014
Turkey	Art. 16(1)(c): Husbands given the "right to the family home," considered "head of the family," and therefore "made all decisions regarding it."[24]	Initial Report – 1990: Turkey had established a committee in Parliament to review the Civil Code and propose to change the necessary provisions that discriminate against women. Second & Third Periodic Report (Combined): Turkey communicated efforts to withdraw its reservations. The Committee continued recommending it to expedite the process. Response – 1991: Turkey made changes to its Constitution, Legislation, and Civil Code and subsequently withdrew its reservation.	1999

---

[22] Consideration of reports submitted by states parties under Article 18 of the Convention on the Elimination of All Forms of Discrimination against Women, Combined fifth and sixth periodic reports of states parties, Tunisia.

[23] Written replies from the Government of Tunisia to the list of issues and questions (CEDAW/C/TUN/Q/6) with regard to the consideration of the combined fifth and sixth periodic reports (CEDAW/C/TUN/5–6).

[24] Committee on the Elimination of Discrimination against Women ninth session summary record of the 161st meeting held at Headquarters, New York, on Monday, January 29, 1990, at 3 p.m.

APPENDIX 4

THE CEDAW COMMITTEE'S GENERAL RECOMMENDATIONS ADDRESSING PROPERTY RIGHTS

- Comm. on the Elimination of Discrimination against Women, General Recommendation No. 12: Violence against Women, U.N. Doc. A/44/38 (Eighth session, 1989)
- Comm. on the Elimination of Discrimination against Women, General Recommendation No. 16: Unpaid Women Workers in Rural and Urban Family Enterprises, U.N. Doc. A/46/38 (Tenth session, 1991)
- Comm. on the Elimination of Discrimination against Women, General Recommendation No. 17: Measurement and Quantification of The Unremunerated Domestic Activities of Women and Their Recognition in the Gross National Product, U.N. Doc. A/46/38 (Tenth session, 1991)
- Comm. on the Elimination of Discrimination against Women, General Recommendation No. 19: Violence against Women, U.N. Doc. A/47/38 (Eleventh session, 1992)
- Comm. on the Elimination of Discrimination against Women, General Recommendation No. 21: Equality in Marriage and Family Relations, U.N. Doc. A/49/38 (Apr. 12, 1994)
- Comm. on the Elimination of Discrimination against Women, General Recommendation No. 23: Political and Public Life, U.N. Doc. A/52/38 (Sixteenth session, 1997)
- Comm. on the Elimination of Discrimination against Women, General Recommendation No. 26 on Women Migrant Workers, U.N. Doc. CEDAW/C/2009/WP.1/R. (Dec. 5, 2008)
- Comm. on the Elimination of Discrimination against Women, General Recommendation No. 27 on Older Women and Protection of Their Human Rights, U.N. Doc. CEDAW/C/GC/27 (Dec. 16, 2010)
- Comm. on the Elimination of Discrimination against Women, General recommendation No. 29 on Article 16 of the Convention on the Elimination of All Forms of Discrimination against Women (Economic Consequences of Marriage, Family Relations and Their Dissolution), U.N. Doc. CEDAW/C/GC/29 (Oct. 30, 2013)
- Comm. on the Elimination of Discrimination against Women, General Recommendation No. 30 on Women in Conflict Prevention, Conflict and Post-Conflict Situations, U.N. Doc. CEDAW/C/GC/30 (Nov. 1, 2013)
- Comm. on the Elimination of Discrimination against Women, General Recommendation No. 32 on the Gender-Related Dimensions of Refugee Status, Asylum, Nationality and Statelessness of Women, U.N. Doc. CEDAW/C/GC/32 (Nov. 14, 2014)
- Comm. on the Elimination of Discrimination against Women, General Recommendation No. 33 on Women's Access to Justice, U.N. Doc. CEDAW/C/GC/33 (Aug. 3, 2015)
- Comm. on the Elimination of Discrimination against Women, General Recommendation No. 34 on the Rights of Rural Women, U.N. Doc. CEDAW/C/GC/34 (Mar. 7, 2016)

- Comm. on the Elimination of Discrimination against Women, General Recommendation No. 35 on Gender-Based Violence against Women, Updating General Recommendation No. 19, U.N. Doc. CEDAW/C/GC/35 (July 26, 2017)
- Comm. on the Elimination of Discrimination against Women, General Recommendation No. 37 on Gender-Related Dimensions of Disaster Risk Reduction in the Context of Climate Change, U.N. Doc. CEDAW/C/GC/37 (Mar. 13, 2018)
- Comm. on the Elimination of Discrimination against Women, General Recommendation No. 38 (2020) on Trafficking in Women and Girls in the Context of Global Migration, U.N. Doc. CEDAW/C/GC/38 (Nov. 20, 2020)
- Comm. on the Elimination of Discrimination against Women, General Recommendation No. 39 (2022) on the Rights of Indigenous Women and Girls, U.N. Doc. CEDAW/C/GC/39 (Oct. 31, 2022)

APPENDIX 5

THE CEDAW COMMITTEE'S VIEWS ON COMMUNICATIONS ADDRESSING PROPERTY RIGHTS

Property Rights in Marriage and Family Relations

- Comm. on the Elimination of Discrimination against Women, Views under Article 7(3) of the Optional Protocol concerning Communication No. 19/2008, Cecilia Kell v. Canada, U.N. Doc. CEDAW/C/51/D/19/2008 (Feb. 28, 2012)
- Comm. on the Elimination of Discrimination against Women, Views under Article 7(3) of the Optional Protocol concerning Communication No. 048/2013, E.S. and S.C. v. United Republic of Tanzania, U.N. Doc. CEDAW/C/60/D/48/2013 (Mar. 2, 2015)

Adequate Housing and Property Rights

- Comm. on the Elimination of Discrimination against Women, Views under Article 7(3) of the Optional Protocol concerning Communication No. 110/2016, L.A. et al. v. North Macedonia, U.N. Doc. CEDAW/C/75/D/110/2016 (Feb. 24, 2020)
- Comm. on the Elimination of Discrimination against Women, Views under Article 7(3) of the Optional Protocol concerning Communication No. 107/2016, S.N. and E.R. v. North Macedonia, U.N. Doc. CEDAW/C/75/D/107/2016 (Feb. 24, 2020)

Social Benefits

- Comm. on the Elimination of Discrimination against Women, Views under Article 7(3) of the Optional Protocol concerning Communication No. 3/2004, Ms. Dung Thi Thuy Nguyen v. The Netherlands, U.N. Doc. CEDAW/C/36/D/3/2004 (Aug. 29, 2006)
- Comm. on the Elimination of Discrimination against Women, Views under Article 7(3) of the Optional Protocol concerning Communication No. 36/2012, Elisabeth de Blok et al. v. The Netherlands, U.N. Doc. CEDAW/C/57/D/36/2012 (Mar. 24, 2014)
- Comm. on the Elimination of Discrimination against Women, Views under Article 7(3) of the Optional Protocol concerning Communication No. 104/2016, Natalia Ciobanu v. Republic of Moldova, U.N. Doc. CEDAW/C/74/D/104/2016 (Dec. 17, 2019)
- Comm. on the Elimination of Discrimination against Women, Views under Article 7(3) of the Optional Protocol concerning Communication No. 131/2018, V.P. v. Belarus, U.N. Doc. CEDAW/C/79/D/131/2018 (June 28, 2021)

Gender-Based Violence and Property Rights

- Comm. on the Elimination of Discrimination against Women, Views under Article 7(3) of the Optional Protocol concerning Communication No. 2/2003, Ms. A.T. v. Hungary (Jan. 26, 2005)
- Comm. on the Elimination of Discrimination against Women, Views under Article 7(3) of the Optional Protocol concerning Communication No. 5/2005, Şahide Goekce v. Austria, U.N. Doc. CEDAW/C/39/D/5/2005 (Aug. 6, 2007)
- Comm. on the Elimination of Discrimination against Women, Views under Article 7(3) of the Optional Protocol concerning Communication No. 006/2005, Fatma Yildirim (deceased) v. Austria, U.N. Doc. CEDAW/C/39/D/6/2005 (Aug. 6, 2007)
- Comm. on the Elimination of Discrimination against Women, Views under Article 7(3) of the Optional Protocol concerning Communication No. 20/2008, V.K. v. Bulgaria, U.N. Doc. CEDAW/C/49/D/20/2008 (July 25, 2011)
- Comm. on the Elimination of Discrimination against Women, Views under Article 7(3) of the Optional Protocol concerning Communication No. 103/2016, J.I. v. Finland, U.N. Doc. CEDAW/C/69/D/103/2016 (Mar. 5, 2018)
- Comm. on the Elimination of Discrimination against Women, Views under Article 7(3) of the Optional Protocol concerning Communication No. 065/2014, S.T. v. Russian Federation, U.N. Doc. CEDAW/C/72/D/65/2014 (Apr. 8, 2019)

Land Rights

- Comm. on the Elimination of Discrimination against Women, Views under Article 7(3) of the Optional Protocol concerning Communication No. 146/2019, X. v. Cambodia, U.N. Doc. CEDAW/C/85/D/146/2019 (Jun. 7, 2023)[1]

---

[1] This communication, adopted on May 19, 2023, was not presented as part of chapter 2 because the research for that chapter ended on March 15, 2023. It is nonetheless discussed in footnotes to some of the later chapters.

APPENDIX 6

THE CEDAW COMMITTEE'S INQUIRY REPORTS ADDRESSING PROPERTY RIGHTS

- Comm. on the Elimination of Discrimination against Women, Report of the Inquiry concerning Canada under Article 8 of the Optional Protocol, U.N. Doc. CEDAW/C/OP.8/CAN/1 (Mar. 30, 2015)
- Comm. on the Elimination of Discrimination against Women, Report of the Inquiry concerning South Africa under Article 8 of the Optional Protocol to the Convention, U.N. Doc. CEDAW/C/ZAF/IR/1 (May. 14, 2021)

Select Bibliography

Books, Book Chapters, and Dissertations

ALVAREZ, JOSÉ E., THE BOUNDARIES OF INVESTMENT ARBITRATION: THE USE OF TRADE AND EUROPEAN HUMAN RIGHTS LAW IN INVESTOR STATE DISPUTES (Huntington: Juris 2018).

ALVAREZ, JOSÉ E., *The Once and Future Foreign Investment Regime, in* LOOKING TO THE FUTURE: ESSAYS ON INTERNATIONAL LAW IN HONOR OF W. MICHAEL REISMAN 607 (Mahnoush H. Arsanjani et al. eds., Leiden/Boston: Martinus Nijhoff 2011).

ALVAREZ, JOSÉ E., THE PUBLIC INTERNATIONAL LAW REGIME GOVERNING INTERNATIONAL INVESTMENT (The Hague: AIL-Pocket 2011).

ANGHIE, ANTONY, IMPERIALISM, SOVEREIGNTY AND THE MAKING OF INTERNATIONAL LAW (Cambridge: Cambridge University Press 2005).

ATUAHENE, BERNADETTE, WE WANT WHAT'S OURS: LEARNING FROM SOUTH AFRICA'S LAND RESTITUTION PROGRAM (Oxford: Oxford University Press 2014).

BANDA, FAREDA, *The Limits of Law: A Response to Martha C. Nussbaum, in* THE LIMITS OF HUMAN RIGHTS 267 (Bardo Fassbender & Knut Traisbach eds., Oxford: Oxford University Press 2019).

BARBARA, AMANDA & DALE, ALLEN, INTERSECTIONAL HUMAN RIGHTS AT CEDAW: PROMISES TRANSMISSIONS AND IMPACTS (Aug. 23, 2018) (PhD dissertation, Osgoode Hall Law School), https://yorkspace.library.yorku.ca/xmlui/bitstream/handle/10315/35582/Dale_Amanda_BA_2018_PhD.pdf?sequence=2&isAllowed=y.

BAXI, UPENDRA, THE FUTURE OF HUMAN RIGHTS (3d ed., Oxford: Oxford University Press 2012).

BONNITCHA, JONATHAN ET AL., THE POLITICAL ECONOMY OF THE INVESTMENT TREATY REGIME (Oxford: Oxford University Press 2017).

BOWMAN, CYNTHIA GRANT ET AL. EDS., FEMINIST JURISPRUDENCE CASES AND MATERIALS (5th ed., St. Paul: West 2018).

BOYLE, ALAN & CHINKIN, CHRISTINE, THE MAKING OF INTERNATIONAL LAW (Oxford: Oxford University Press 2007).

BUTEGWA, FLORENCE, *Using the African Charter on Human and People's Rights to Secure Women's Access to Land in Africa, in* HUMAN RIGHTS OF WOMEN: NATIONAL AND INTERNATIONAL PERSPECTIVES 495 (Rebecca J. Cook ed., Philadelphia: University of Pennsylvania 2012).

CAMPBELL, MEGHAN, WOMEN, POVERTY, EQUALITY: THE ROLE OF CEDAW (Oxford: Hart 2018).

CHARLESWORTH, HILARY & CHINKIN, CHRISTINE, *Between the Margins and the Mainstream: The Case of Women's Rights, in* THE LIMITS OF HUMAN RIGHTS 205 (Bardo Fassbender & Knut Traisbach eds., Oxford: Oxford University Press 2019).

CHARLESWORTH, HILARY & CHINKIN, CHRISTINE, THE BOUNDARIES OF INTERNATIONAL LAW (Manchester: Manchester University Press 2000).

SELECT BIBLIOGRAPHY

CHINKIN, CHRISTINE, *The Convention on the Elimination of All Forms of Discrimination against Women*, in HANDBOOK ON GENDER IN WORLD POLITICS 318 (Jill Steans & Daniela Tepe-Belfrage eds., United Kingdom: Elgar 2006).

CLAPHAM, ANDREW, HUMAN RIGHTS OBLIGATIONS OF NON-STATE ACTORS (Oxford: Oxford University Press 2006).

COOK, REBECCA J., ED., FRONTIERS OF GENDER EQUALITY: TRANSNATIONAL LEGAL PERSPECTIVES (Philadelphia: University of Pennsylvania Press 2023).

DAVIS, ANGELA Y., WOMEN, RACE & CLASS (New York: Knopf Doubleday Publishing Group 1981).

DONDERS, YVONNE & VLEUGEL, VINCENT, *Universality, Diversity, and Legal Certainty: Cultural Diversity in the Dialogue Between the CEDAW and States Parties*, in THE RULE OF LAW AT THE NATIONAL AND INTERNATIONAL LEVELS: CONTESTATIONS AND DEFERENCE 321 (Machiko Kanetake & André Nollkaemper eds., Oxford: Hart 2016).

DUPUY, PIERRE-MARIE, *Unification Rather than Fragmentation of International Law? The Case of International Investment Law and Human Rights Law*, in HUMAN RIGHTS IN INTERNATIONAL INVESTMENT LAW AND ARBITRATION 45 (Pierre-Marie Dupuy et al. eds., Oxford: Oxford University Press 2009).

ELSON, DIANE, *Gender Justice, Human Rights, and Neo-Liberal Economic Policies*, in GENDER JUSTICE, HUMAN RIGHTS, AND NEO-LIBERAL ECONOMIC POLICIES 78 (Maxine Molyneux & Shahra Razavi eds., Oxford: Oxford University Press 2002).

ELY, JAMES W., THE GUARDIAN OF EVERY OTHER RIGHT: A CONSTITUTIONAL HISTORY OF PROPERTY RIGHTS (3d ed., Oxford: Oxford University Press 2007).

FREDMAN, SANDRA, COMPARATIVE HUMAN RIGHTS LAW (Oxford: Oxford University Press 2018).

FREDMAN, SANDRA, *Engendering Socio-Economic Rights*, in WOMEN'S HUMAN RIGHTS: CEDAW IN INTERNATIONAL, REGIONAL AND NATIONAL LAW 217 (Anne Hellum & Henriette Sinding eds., Cambridge: Cambridge University Press 2013).

FREEMAN, MARSHA A. ET AL. EDS., THE UN CONVENTION ON THE ELIMINATION OF ALL FORMS OF DISCRIMINATION AGAINST WOMEN: A COMMENTARY 51 (Oxford: Oxford University Press 2012).

GOLDBLATT, BETH, DEVELOPING THE RIGHT TO SOCIAL SECURITY—A GENDER PERSPECTIVE (Abingdon: Routledge 2018).

GRAZIADEI, MICHELE, *The Structure of Property Ownership and the Common Law/Civil Law Divide*, in COMPARATIVE PROPERTY LAW GLOBAL PERSPECTIVES 71 (Michele Graziadei & Lionel Smith eds., United Kingdom: Elgar 2017).

HALPERIN-KADDARI, RUTH, *Human Rights Treaty Bodies as Standard-Setting Mechanisms: The Case of Family Law*, in STRENGTHENING HUMAN RIGHTS PROTECTIONS IN GENEVA, ISRAEL, THE WEST BANK AND BEYOND 82 (Joseph E. David et al. eds., Cambridge: Cambridge University Press 2012).

HE, XIN, DIVORCE IN CHINA: INSTITUTIONAL CONTROLS AND GENDERED OUTCOMES (New York: NYU Press 2021).

HEATHCOTE, GINA, FEMINIST DIALOGUES ON INTERNATIONAL LAW: SUCCESS, TENSIONS, FUTURES (Oxford: Oxford University Press 2019).

HENNEBEL, LUDOVIC & TIGROUDJA, HELENE, THE AMERICAN CONVENTION ON HUMAN RIGHTS: A COMMENTARY (Oxford: Oxford University Press 2022).

HOLTMAAT, RIKKI, *The CEDAW: A Holistic Approach to Women's Equality and Freedom*, in WOMEN'S HUMAN RIGHTS: CEDAW IN INTERNATIONAL, REGIONAL AND NATIONAL

LAW 95 (Anne Hellum & Henriette Sinding Aasen eds., Cambridge: Cambridge University Press 2013).

HOPGOOD, STEPHEN, THE ENDTIMES OF HUMAN RIGHTS (Ithaca: Cornell University Press 2013).

HOWARD-HASSMANN, RHODA E., IN DEFENSE OF UNIVERSAL HUMAN RIGHTS (Various: Polity Press 2018).

IKDAHL, INGUNN, *Property and Security: Articulating Women's Rights to Their Homes*, in WOMEN'S HUMAN RIGHTS: CEDAW IN INTERNATIONAL, REGIONAL AND NATIONAL LAW 268, 284 (Anne Hellum & Henriette Sinding Aasen eds., Cambridge: Cambridge University Press 2013).

INNISS, LOLITA BUCKNER ET AL., *Cecilia Kell v. Canada*, in FEMINIST JUDGMENTS IN INTERNATIONAL LAW 333 (Loveday Hodson & Troy Lavers eds., London: Bloomsbury Press 2019).

JOSEPH, SARAH & CASTAN, MELISSA, THE INTERNATIONAL COVENANT ON CIVIL AND POLITICAL RIGHTS: CASES, MATERIALS, AND COMMENTARY (3d ed., Oxford: Oxford University Press 2013).

KE, LI, MARRIAGE UNBOUND: STATE LAW, POWER, AND INEQUALITY IN CONTEMPORARY CHINA (Redwood City: Stanford University Press 2022).

KELLER, HELEN & GROVER, LEENA, *General Comments of the Human Rights Committee and Their Legitimacy*, in UN HUMAN RIGHTS TREATY BODIES 128 (Helen Keller et al. eds., Cambridge: Cambridge University Press 2012).

KENNEDY, DAVID, THE DARK SIDES OF VIRTUE: REASSESSING INTERNATIONAL HUMANITARIANISM (Princeton: Princeton University Press 2004).

KLEIN, NAOMI, THE SHOCK DOCTRINE: THE RISE OF DISASTER CAPITALISM (New York: Metropolitan Books/Henry Holt 2007).

KOSKENNIEMI, MARTTI, *Rocking the Human Rights Boat: Reflections by a Fellow Passenger*, in THE STRUGGLE FOR HUMAN RIGHTS: ESSAYS IN HONOUR OF PHILIP ALSTON 51 (Nehal Bhuta et al. eds., Oxford: Oxford University Press 2022).

KOSKENNIEMI, MARTTI, *The Effect of Rights on Political Culture*, in THE EU AND HUMAN RIGHTS 99 (Philip Alston ed., Oxford: Oxford University Press 2000).

KOTZ, DAVID M., THE RISE AND FALL OF NEOLIBERAL CAPITALISM (Cambridge: Harvard University Press 2015).

LACEY, NICOLA, *Feminist Legal Theory and the Rights of Women*, in GENDER AND HUMAN RIGHTS 13 (Karen Knop ed., Oxford: Oxford University Press 2004).

LEEUWEN, FLEUR VAN, *"Women's Rights Are Human Rights!": The Practice of the United Nations Human Rights Committee and the Committee on Economic, Social and Cultural Rights*, in WOMEN'S HUMAN RIGHTS: CEDAW IN INTERNATIONAL, REGIONAL AND NATIONAL LAW 242 (Anne Hellum et al. eds., Cambridge: Cambridge University Press 2013).

MACKINNON, CATHARINE A., ARE WOMEN HUMAN? AND OTHER INTERNATIONAL DIALOGUES (Cambridge: Belknap Press 2006).

MASON, KAREN O. & CARLSSON, HELEN M., *The Development Impact of Gender Equality in Land Rights*, in HUMAN RIGHTS AND DEVELOPMENT: TOWARDS MUTUAL REINFORCEMENT (Philip Alston & Mary Robinson eds., Oxford: Oxford University Press 2015).

MCLACHLAN, CAMPBELL ET AL., INTERNATIONAL INVESTMENT ARBITRATION: SUBSTANTIVE PRINCIPLES (2d ed., Oxford: Oxford University Press 2007).

MERRILL, THOMAS W. ET AL., PROPERTY PRINCIPLES AND POLICIES (4th ed., St. Paul: West 2022).
MERRY, SALLY & LEVITT, PEGGY, *The Vernacularization of Women's Human Rights*, in HUMAN RIGHTS FUTURES (Stephen Hopgood et al. eds., Cambridge: Cambridge University Press 2017).
MIES, MARIA, PATRIARCHY AND ACCUMULATION OF A WORLD SCALE: WOMEN IN THE INTERNATIONAL DIVISION OF LABOR (London: Bloomsbury Press 2014).
MIÉVILLE, CHINA, BETWEEN EQUAL RIGHTS: A MARXIST THEORY OF INTERNATIONAL LAW (London/Boston: Brill 2006).
MILL, JOHN STUART, *The Subjection of Women*, in ESSAYS ON SEX EQUALITY 125 (Alice S. Rossi ed., Chicago University of Chicago Press 1970).
MOHANTY, TALPADE, FEMINISM WITHOUT BORDERS: DECOLONIZING THEORY, PRACTICING SOLIDARITY (Durham: Duke University Press 2003).
MOYN, SAMUEL, THE LAST UTOPIA: HUMAN RIGHTS IN HISTORY (Cambridge: The Belknap Press of Harvard University Press 2010).
MUSEMBI, CELESTINE NYAMU, *Pulling Apart? Treatment of pluralism in the CEDAW and the Maputo Protocol*, in WOMEN'S HUMAN RIGHTS: CEDAW IN INTERNATIONAL, REGIONAL AND NATIONAL LAW 183 (Anne Hellum & Henriette Sinding Aasen eds., Cambridge: Cambridge University Press 2013).
NAGARJAN, VIJAYA & PARASHAR, ARCHAN, *Gender Equality in International Law and Constitutions: Mediating Universal Norms and Local Differences*, in THE PUBLIC LAW OF GENDER (Kim Rubenstein & Katharine G. Young eds., Cambridge: Cambridge University Press 2016).
NESIAH, VASUKU, *Indebted: The Cruel Optimism of Leaning in to Empowerment*, in GOVERNANCE FEMINISM: AN INTRODUCTION (Janet Halley et al. eds., Minneapolis: University of Minnesota Press 2018).
NOWAK, MANFRED, U.N. COVENANT ON CIVIL AND POLITICAL RIGHTS: CCPR COMMENTARY (3d ed., Oxford: Oxford University Press 2019).
NUSSBAUM, MARTHA C., *Women's Progress and Women's Human Rights*, in THE LIMITS OF HUMAN RIGHTS 231 (Bardo Fassbender & Knut Traisbach eds., Oxford: Oxford University Press 2019).
ORFORD, ANNE, READING HUMANITARIAN INTERVENTION: HUMAN RIGHTS AND THE USE OF FORCE IN INTERNATIONAL LAW (Cambridge: Cambridge University Press 2003).
OTTO, DIANNE, *Disconcerting "Masculinities": Reinventing the Gendered Subject(s) of International Human Rights Law*, in INTERNATIONAL LAW: MODERN FEMINIST APPROACHES 105 (Doris Buss & Ambreena Manji eds., London: Bloomsbury Press 2005).
OTTO, DIANNE, *Gendering the Right to Social Security in the Era of Crisis Governance: The Need for Transformative Strategies*, in WOMEN'S RIGHTS TO SOCIAL SECURITY AND SOCIAL PROTECTION 215 (Beth Goldblatt & Lucie Lamrche eds., London: Bloomsbury Press 2014).
OTTO, DIANNE, *Lost in Translation: Re-scripting in the Sexed Subjects of International Human Rights Law*, in INTERNATIONAL LAW AND ITS OTHERS 318 (Anne Orford ed., Cambridge: Cambridge University Press 2006).
PAHUJA, SUNDHYA, DECOLONISING INTERNATIONAL LAW: DEVELOPMENT, ECONOMIC GROWTH AND THE POLITICS OF UNIVERSALITY (Cambridge: Cambridge University Press 2011).

PATEMAN, CAROLE, THE SEXUAL CONTRACT (Stanford: Stanford University Press 1988).
PLEHWE, DIETER ET AL. EDS., NINE LIVES OF NEOLIBERALISM (London/New York: Verso Books 2020).
REHOF, LARS A., GUIDE TO THE TRAVAUX PRÉPARATOIRES OF THE UNITED NATIONS CONVENTION ON THE ELIMINATION OF ALL FORMS OF DISCRIMINATION AGAINST WOMEN (London: Brill 1993).
REINERS, NINA, TRANSNATIONAL LAWMAKING COALITIONS FOR HUMAN RIGHTS (Cambridge: Cambridge University Press 2021).
REINISCH, AUGUST, *Expropriation*, in THE OXFORD HANDBOOK OF INTERNATIONAL INVESTMENT LAW (Peter Muchlinski et al. eds., Oxford: Oxford University Press 2008).
REINSICH, AUGUST & SCHREUER, CHRISTOPH, INTERNATIONAL PROTECTION OF INVESTMENTS: THE SUBSTANTIVE STANDARDS (Cambridge: Cambridge University Press 2020).
RITTICH, KERRY, *Social Rights and Social Policy: Transformations on the International Landscape*, in EXPLORING SOCIAL RIGHTS: BETWEEN THEORY AND PRACTICE 107 (Daphne Barak-Erez & Aeyal M. Gross eds., London: Bloomsbury Press 2007).
RITTICH, KERRY, *The Properties of Gender Equality*, in HUMAN RIGHTS AND DEVELOPMENT: TOWARDS MUTUAL REINFORCEMENT 87 (Philip Alston & Mary Robinson eds., Oxford: Oxford University Press 2005).
ROBERTS, ANTHEA, IS INTERNATIONAL LAW INTERNATIONAL? (Oxford: Oxford University Press 2019).
ROSE, CAROL M., *Property's Relation to Human Rights*, in ECONOMIC LIBERTIES AND HUMAN RIGHTS (Jahel Queralt & Bas van der Vossen eds., Various: Routledge 2019).
SAUL, BEN ET AL., THE INTERNATIONAL COVENANT ON ECONOMIC, SOCIAL AND CULTURAL RIGHTS COMMENTARY, CASES AND MATERIALS (Oxford: Oxford University Press 2014).
SCHABAS, WILLIAM A., THE EUROPEAN CONVENTION ON HUMAN RIGHTS: A COMMENTARY (Oxford: Oxford University Press 2015).
SCHEFER, KRISTA N., INTERNATIONAL INVESTMENT LAW: TEXT, CASES AND MATERIALS (3d ed., United Kingdom: Elgar 2020).
SCHREUER, CHRISTOPH & KREIBAUM, URSULA, *The Concept of Property in Human Rights Law and International Investment Law*, in HUMAN RIGHTS, DEMOCRACY AND THE RULE OF LAW: LIBER AMICORUM LUZIUS WILDHABER 743 (Stephan Breitenmoser et al. eds., Baden-Baden: Nomos Publishers 2017).
SCHULZ, PATRICIA ET AL. EDS., THE UN CONVENTION ON THE ELIMINATION OF ALL FORMS OF DISCRIMINATION AGAINST WOMEN AND ITS OPTIONAL PROTOCOL: A COMMENTARY (2d ed., Oxford: Oxford University Press 2022).
SEN, AMARTYA, DEVELOPMENT AS FREEDOM (Oxford: Oxford University Press 1999).
SHELTON, DINAH, REMEDIES IN INTERNATIONAL HUMAN RIGHTS LAW (3d ed., Oxford: Oxford University Press 2015).
SIMMONS, BETH, MOBILIZING FOR HUMAN RIGHTS: INTERNATIONAL LAW IN DOMESTIC POLITICS (Cambridge: Cambridge University Press 2009).
SIMPSON, A.W. BRIAN, HUMAN RIGHTS AND THE END OF EMPIRE BRITAIN AND THE GENESIS OF THE EUROPEAN CONVENTION (Oxford: Oxford University Press 2001).
SORNARAJAH, MUTHUCUMARASWAMY, THE INTERNATIONAL LAW ON FOREIGN INVESTMENT (2d ed., Cambridge: Cambridge University Press 2004).

SORNARAJAH, MUTHUCUMARASWAMY, *The Neo-Liberal Agenda in Investment*, in REDEFINING SOVEREIGNTY IN INTERNATIONAL ECONOMIC LAW (Wenhua Shan et al. eds., London: Bloomsbury Press 2005).

SOTO, HERNANDO DE, THE MYSTERY OF CAPITAL: WHY CAPITALISM TRIUMPHS IN THE WEST AND FAILS EVERYWHERE ELSE (New York: Basic Books 2000).

SOTO, HERNANDO DE, THE OTHER PATH: THE INVISIBLE REVOLUTION IN THE THIRD WORLD (New York: Basic Books 1989).

SPRANKLING, JOHN G., THE INTERNATIONAL LAW OF PROPERTY (Oxford: Oxford University Press 2014).

SWEBERG, RICHARD, TOCQUEVILLE'S POLITICAL ECONOMY (Princeton: Princeton University Press 2009).

TAMALE, SYLVIA, DECOLONIZATION AND AFRO-FEMINISM (Québec: Daraja Press 2020).

TAYLOR, PAUL M., A COMMENTARY ON THE INTERNATIONAL COVENANT ON CIVIL AND POLITICAL RIGHTS: THE UN HUMAN RIGHTS COMMITTEE'S MONITORING OF ICCPR RIGHTS (Cambridge: Cambridge University Press 2020).

THORNBERRY, PATRICK, THE INTERNATIONAL CONVENTION ON THE ELIMINATION OF ALL FORMS OF RACIAL DISCRIMINATION: A COMMENTARY (Oxford: Oxford University Press 2016).

TIMMER, ALEXANDRA & HOLTMAAT, RIKKI, *Article 5*, *in* THE UN CONVENTION ON THE ELIMINATION OF ALL FORMS OF DISCRIMINATION AGAINST WOMEN AND ITS OPTIONAL PROTOCOL: A COMMENTARY 221 (Patricia Schulz et al. eds., 2d ed., Oxford: Oxford University Press 2022).

TZOUVALA, NTINA, CAPITALISM AS CIVILISATION: A HISTORY OF INTERNATIONAL LAW (Cambridge: Cambridge University Press 2020).

UPHAM, FRANK, THE GREAT PROPERTY FALLACY: THEORY, REALITY AND GROWTH IN DEVELOPING COUNTRIES (Cambridge: Cambridge University Press 2018).

WADLIG, GABRIELE, THE INTERNATIONAL (UN)MAKING OF "TENURE SECURITY" (2022) (J.S.D. Dissertation, New York University) (on file with author).

WALDRON, JEREMY, THE RULE OF LAW AND THE MEASURE OF PROPERTY (Cambridge: Cambridge University Press 2012).

WALKER, ALICE, *In Search of Our Mother's Gardens*, *in* WITHIN THE CIRCLE: AN ANTHOLOGY OF AFRICAN AMERICAN LITERARY CRITICISM FROM THE HARLEM RENAISSANCE TO THE PRESENT 401 (Angelyn Mitchell ed., Durham: Duke University Press 1994).

WALSH, JANET, *Women's Property Rights Violations in Kenya*, *in* HUMAN RIGHTS AND DEVELOPMENT: TOWARDS MUTUAL REINFORCEMENT 133 (Philip Alston & Mary Robinson eds., Oxford: Oxford University Press 2005).

WHYTE, JESSICA, THE MORALS OF THE MARKET: HUMAN RIGHTS AND THE RISE OF THE MARKET (New York: Verso Books 2019).

WILSON, STUART, HUMAN RIGHTS AND THE TRANSFORMATION OF PROPERTY (Capetown: Juta & Company 2021).

WILSON, STUART, *The Right to Adequate Housing*, *in* RESEARCH HANDBOOK ON ECONOMIC, SOCIAL AND CULTURAL RIGHTS 180 (Jackie Dugard et al. eds., United Kingdom: Elgar 2020).

WOLLSTONECRAFT, MARY, *A Vindication of the Rights of Women*, *in* THE WORKS OF MARY WOLLSTONECRAFT (Janet Todd & Marilyn Butler eds., Various: Routledge 1989).

WOOLF, VIRGINIA, A ROOM OF ONE'S OWN (New York: Harcourt, Brace and Co. 1929).

Articles and Working Papers

Allen, Tom, *Compensation for Property Under the European Convention on Human Rights*, 28 Mich. J. Int'l L. 287 (2007).
Alston, Philip, *Does the Past Matter? On the Origins of Human Rights*, 126 Harv. L. Rev. 2043 (2013).
Alston, Philip, *Resisting the Merger and Acquisition of Human Rights by Trade Law: A Reply to Petersmann*, 4 Eur. J. Int'l L. 815 (2002).
Alvarez, José E., *ISDS Reform: The Long View*, 36 ICSID Rev. Foreign Inv. L.J. 1 (2021).
Alvarez, José E., *The Human Right of Property*, 72 U. Miami L. Rev. 580 (2018).
Alvarez, José E., *The International Law of Property*, 112 Am. J. Int'l L. 771 (2018).
Alwis, Rangita de Silva de & Jaising, Indira, *The Role of Personal Laws in Creating a "Second Sex,"* 48 N.Y.U. J. Int'l L. & Pol. 1085 (2016).
Anderson, Elizabeth, *What Is the Point of Equality*, 109 Ethics 287 (1999).
Anghie, Antony, *Legal Aspects of the New International Economic Order*, 6 Human. J. 154 (2015).
Arato, Julian et al., *The Perils of Pandemic Exceptionalism*, 114 Am. J. Int'l L. 627 (2020).
Atrey, Shreya, *Fifty Years On: The Curious Case of Intersectional Discrimination in the ICCPR*, 35 Nordic J. Hum. Rts. 220 (2017).
Barnett, Randy, *The Right to Liberty in a Good Society*, 69 Fordham L. Rev. 1603 (2001).
Bhuta, Nehal, Recovering Social Rights, IILJ Working Paper 2023/1.
Borchard, Edwin, *The Minimum Standard of the Treatment of Aliens*, 33 Am. Soc'y Int'l L. Proc. 51 (1939).
Briddick, Catherine, *Unprincipled and Unrealised: CEDAW and Discrimination Experienced in the Context of Migration Control*, 22 Int'l J. Discrimination & L. 224 (2022).
Briddick, Catherine, *When Does Migration Law Discriminate Against Women?*, 115 Am. J. Int'l L. Unbound 356 (2021).
Brooks, Rosa Ehrenreich, *Feminist Justice, at Home and Abroad: Feminism and International Law: An Opportunity for Transformation*, 14 Yale J.L. & Feminism 345 (2002).
Búrca, Gráinne de, *Human Rights Experimentalism*, 111 Am. J. Int'l L. 277 (2017).
Byrnes, Andrew, *The Convention on the Elimination of All Forms of Discrimination against Women and the Committee on the Elimination of Discrimination against Women: Reflections on Their Role in the Development of International Human Rights Law and as a Catalyst for National Legislative and Policy Reform* (U.N.S.W.L., Research Paper No. 2010-17, 2010), https://papers.ssrn.com/sol3/papers.cfm?abstract_id=1595490.
Campbell, Megan, *The Austerity of Lone Motherhood: Discrimination Law and Benefit Reform*, 41 Oxford J. Legal Stud. 1197 (2021).
Campbell, Meghan, *CEDAW and Women's Intersecting Identities: A Pioneering New Approach to Intersectional Discrimination*, 11 Direito GV L. Rev. 479 (2015).
Casla, Koldo, *The Right to Property Taking Economic, Social, and Cultural Rights Seriously*, 45 Hum. Rts. Q. 171 (2023).
Charlesworth, Hilary et al., *Feminist Approaches to International Law*, 85 Am. J. Int'l L. 613 (1991).
Chen, Meng & Yu, Fangfang, *A Home of One's Own? Gendered Homeownership in Urban China*, 20 China Rev. 143 (2020).

Chimni, Bhupinder S., *Customary International Law: A Third World Perspective*, 112 AM. J. INT'L L. 1 (2018).

Crawford, Patricia, *Women and Property: Women as Property*, 19 PARERGON 151 (2002).

Creamer, Cosette D. & Simmons, Beth A., *The Proof Is in the Process: Self-Reporting Under International Human Rights Treaties*, 114 AM. J. INT'L L. 1 (2020).

Cusack, Simone & Pusey, Lisa, *CEDAW and the Rights to Non-Discrimination and Equality*, 14 MELB. J. INT'L L. 54 (2013).

David, Velaska, *Reparations at the Human Rights Committee: Legal Basis, Practice and Challenges*, 32 NETHERLANDS Q. HUM. RTS. 14 (2014).

Deere, Carmen Diana, *Women's Land Rights, Rural Social Movements, and the State in the 21st-century Latin American Agrarian Reforms*, 17 J. AGRARIAN CHANGE 258 (2016).

Deere, Carmen Diana & León, Magdalena, *Consensual Unions, Property Rights, and Patrimonial Violence against Women in Latin America*, 29 SOC. POL. 608 (2022).

Deng, WenJing & Hoeckstra, Joris, *Why Women Own Less Housing Asserts in China? The Role of Intergenerational Transfers*, 34 J. HOUSING & THE BUILT ENV'T 1 (2019).

Durkee, Melissa, *Interpretive Entrepreneurs*, 107 VA. L. REV. 431 (2021).

Feldshuh, Hannah, *Marital Rape: A Crime Left Unseen and Unspoken in the Chinese Legal System*, THE DIPLOMAT (Dec. 8, 2018), https://thediplomat.com/2018/12/marital-rape-a-crime-left-unseen-and-unspoken-in-the-chinese-legal-system/.

Gaddis, Isis et al., *Women's Legal Rights and Gender Gaps in Property Ownership in Developing Countries*, 48 POPULATION & DEV. REV. 331 (2022).

Gallaher, Rovina, *Redefining CEDAW to Include LGBT Rights*, 29 S. CAL. INTERDISC. L.J. 637 (2020).

Gomtsyan, Suren & Gomtsyan, David, *What Do the Decisions of ECtHR Tell About Property Rights Across Europe?* (Tilburg L. & Econ. Center Discussion Paper, Paper No. 09, 2016), https://ssrn.com/abstract=2762522.

Greif, Elisabeth, *Upward Translations—The Role of NGOs in Promoting LGBTI* Human Rights under the Convention on All Forms of Discrimination against Women (CEDAW)*, 4 PEACE HUM. RTS. GOVERNANCE. 9 (2020).

Halldenius, Lena, *Mary Wollstonecraft's Feminist Critique of Property: On Becoming a Thief from Principle*, 29 HYPATIA 942 (2014).

Halperin-Kaddari, Ruth, *Parenting Apart in International Human Rights Family Law: A View from CEDAW*, 22 JERUSALEM REV. LEGAL STUD. 130 (2020).

Halperin-Kaddari, Ruth & Freeman, Marsha A., *Backlash Goes Global: Men's Groups, Patriarchal Family Policy and the False Promise of Gender-Neutral Laws*, 28 CANADIAN J. WOMEN & L. 165 (2016).

Hannum, Hurst, *The Status of the Universal Declaration of Human Rights in National and International Law*, 25 GA. J. INT'L & COMP. L. 287 (1996).

He, Xin, *Why Don't Chinese Divorce Courts Better Protect Women?* 1 USALI PERSPECTIVES 22 (May 13, 2021), https://usali.org/usali-perspectives-blog/why-dont-chinese-divorce-courts-better-protect-women.

Hernández-Truyol, Berta E., *Unsex CEDAW? No! Super-Sex It!*, 20 COLUM. J. GENDER & L. 195 (2011).

Hodson, Loveday, *Women's Rights and the Periphery: CEDAW's Optional Protocol*, 25 EUR. J. INT'L L. 561(2014).

Howard-Hassmann, Rhoda E., *Reconsidering the Right to Own Property*, 12 J. HUM. RTS. 180 (2013).

Howse, Robert & Teitel, Ruti, *Beyond Compliance: Rethinking Why International Law Really Matters*, 1 GLOBAL POL'Y 127 (2010).

IGLP Law and Global Production Working Group, *The Role of Law in Global Value Chains: A Research Manifesto*, 4 LONDON REV. INT'L L. 57 (2016).

Kanetake, Machiko, *María de los Ángeles González Carreño v. Ministry of Justice*, 113 AM. J. INT'L L. 586 (2019).

Kapur, Amrita, *"Catch-22": The Role of Development Institutions in Promoting Gender Equality in Land Law—Lessons Learned in Post-Conflict Pluralist Africa*, 17 BUFF. HUM. RTS. L. REV. 75 (2011).

Kapur, Rana, *The Tragedy of Victimization Rhetoric: Resurrecting the "Native" Subject in International/Postcolonial Feminist Legal Politics*, 15 HARV. HUM. RTS. L.J. 1 (2002).

Ke, Li, *Land Dispossession and Women's Rights Contention in Rural China*, 5 CHINA L. & SOC'Y REV. 33 (2020).

Kelkar, Govind, *The Fog of Entitlement: Women's Inheritance and Land Rights*, 49 ECON. & POL. WKLY. 51 (2014).

Khan, Iqra Saleem, *Consent in Marriage: A Radical Feminist Analysis of Pakistani Law*, 26 WM. & MARY J. OF RACE, GENDER & SOC. JUST. 671 (2020).

Kriebaum, Ursula & Reinisch, August, PROPERTY, RIGHT TO, INTERNATIONAL PROTECTION (Apr. 2019), Oxford Public International Law, Max Planck Encyclopedia of Public International Law (MPEPIL).

Landau, David, *The Reality of Social Rights Enforcement*, 53 HARV. INT'L L.J. 190 (2012).

Levy, Leonard W., *Property as a Human Right*, 5 CONST. COMMENTARY 169 (1988).

Marks, Susan, *Human Rights and Root Causes*, 74 MOD. L. REV. 57, 76 (2011).

McCrudden, Christopher, *Why Do National Court Judges Refer to Human Rights Treaties? A Comparative International Law Analysis of CEDAW*, 109 AM. J. INT'L L. 534 (2015).

Merrills, Thomas A., *Incomplete Compensation for Takings*, 11 N.Y.U. ENVTL. L.J. 110 (2002).

Moyn, Samuel, *A Powerless Companion: Human Rights in the Age of Neoliberalism*, 77 L. & CONTEMP. PROB. 147 (2014).

Murdoch, Jim, *Unfulfilled Expectations: The Optional Protocol to the Convention on the Elimination of All Forms of Discrimination against Women*, 1 EUR. HUM. RTS. L. REV. 26 (2010).

Musembi, Celestine N., *De Soto and Land Relations in Rural Africa: Breathing Life into Dead Theories about Property Rights*, 28 THIRD WORLD Q. 1457 (2007).

Mutua, Makau W., *Savages, Victims, and Saviors: The Metaphor of Human Rights*, 42 HARV. INT'L L.J. 201 (2001).

Nnoko-Mewanu, Julian & Abdi, Najma, *Securing Women's Property Rights in Kenya*, DAILY NATION (Mar. 7, 2020), https://www.hrw.org/news/2020/03/07/securing-womens-property-rights-kenya).

Olomojobi, Yinka, *Women's Right to Own Property* (Dec. 16, 2015) (unpublished working paper), https://ssrn.com/abstract=2716902.

Orford, Anne, *Feminism, Imperialism and the Mission of International Law*, 71 NORDIC J. INT'L L. 275 (2002).

Otto, Dianne, *Lesbians? Not in My Country: Sexual Orientation at the Beijing World Conference on Women*, 20 ALTERNATIVE L.J. 288 (1995).

Pauwelyn, Joost, *The Rule of Law without the Rule of Lawyers? Why Investment Arbitrators Are from Mars, Trade Adjudicators from Venus*, 109 AM. J. INT'L L. 761 (2015).

Petersen, Niels, *The Implicit Taxonomy of the Equality Jurisprudence of the UN Human Rights Committee*, 34 LEIDEN J. INT'L L. 421 (2021).

Pipes, Richard, *Private Property, Freedom and the Rule of Law*, HOOVER DIGEST (Apr. 30, 2001), https://www.hoover.org/research/private-property-freedom-and-rule-law.

Powell, Catherine, *Gender Indicators as Global Governance: Not Your Father's World Bank*, 17 GEO. J. GENDER & L. 777 (2016).

Rierson, Sandra L., *Race and Gender Discrimination: A Historical Case for Equal Treatment Under the Fourteenth Amendment*, 1 DUKE J. GENDER L. & POL'Y 89 (1994).

Rose, Carol, *Property and a Keystone Right?*, 71 NOTRE DAME L. REV. 329 (1996).

Rosenblum, Darren, *Unsex CEDAW, or What's Wrong with Women's Rights*, 20 COLUM. J. GENDER & L. 98 (2011).

Rubio-Marín, Ruth & Sandoval, Clara, *Engendering the Reparations Jurisprudence of the Inter-American Court of Human Rights: The Promise of the Cotton Field Judgment*, 33 HUM. RTS. Q. 1062 (2011).

Sackville, Ronald, *Property, Rights and Social Security*, 2 U.N.S.W. L.J. 246 (1978).

Salacuse, Jeswald, *The Treatification of International Investment Law: A Victory of Form over Life? A Crossroad Crossed?*, 3 TRANSNAT'L DISP. MGMT. 3 (2006).

Schutter, Olivier de, *The Emerging Right to Land*, 12 INT'L COMMUNITY L. REV. 303 (2010).

Schutter, Olivier de et al., *Commentary to the Maastricht Principles on Extraterritorial Obligations of States in the Area of Economic, Social and Cultural Rights*, 34 HUM. RTS. Q. 1084 (2012).

Simm, Gabrielle, *Queering CEDAW? Sexual Orientation, Gender Identity and Expression and Sex Characteristics (SOGIESC) in International Human Rights Law*, 29 GRIFFITH L. REV. 374 (2021).

Simma, Bruno, *Foreign Investment Arbitration: A Place for Human Rights?*, 60 INT'L & COMP. L.Q. 573 (2011).

Simma, Bruno, *Self-Contained Regimes*, 16 NETHERLANDS Y.B. INT'L L. 111 (1985).

Simma, Bruno & Desierto, Diane A., *Bridging the Public Interest Divide: Committee Assistance for Investor-Host State Compliance with the ICESCR*, 10 TRANSNAT'L DISP. MGMT. 1 (2013).

Slaughter, Joseph R., *Hijacking Human Rights: Neoliberalism, the New Historiography, and the End of the Third World*, 40 HUM. RTS. Q. 735 (2018).

Song, Jesok, *"A Room of One's Own": The Meaning of Spatial Autonomy for Unmarried Women in Neoliberal South Korea*, 17 GENDER, PLACE & CULTURE 131 (2010).

Sun, Shichao & Zhang, Zhitao, *A Study on the Route of Criminalization of Marital Rape*, 32 J. HUBEI U. POLICE 90 (2019).

Thobani, Sunera, *Reviewing Feminism without Borders: Decolonizing Theory, Practicing Solidarity*, 20(3) HYPATIA 221–24 (2005).

Vandevelde, Kenneth, *Investment Liberalization and Economic Development: The Role of Bilateral Investment Treaties*, 36 COLUM. J. TRANSNAT'L L. 501 (1998).

Waldron, Jeremy, *How Law Protects Dignity*, 71 CAMBRIDGE L.J. 200 (2012).

Wang, Huoliang, *Legislative Review of Marital Rape Was Written into the Anti-Domestic Violence Law*, 31 J. HUBEI U. POLICE 122 (2018).

Whyte, Jessica, *Powerless Companions or Fellow Travelers? Human Rights and the Neoliberal Assault on Post-Colonial Economic Justice*, 2(2) RADICAL PHILOSOPHY 13–29 (June 2018).

Wisborg, Poul, *Human Rights Against Land Grabbing: A Reflection on Norms, Policies, and Power*, 16 J. AGRIC. ENVTL. ETHICS 1199 (2013).

Wisborg, Poul, *Transnational Land Deals and Gender Equality: Utilitarian and Human Rights Approaches*, 20 FEMINIST ECON. 24 (2014).

Index

For the benefit of digital users, indexed terms that span two pages (e.g., 52–53) may, on occasion, appear on only one of those pages.

absolute rights, 28
access to justice
   civil and political rights, 73, 74–77
   COs and, 350–51
   gender-based violence, 153, 157, 158–59
   GRs and, 350
   housing rights, 100–1
   international investment agreement, 246
   intersectional discrimination, 328–29
   introduction to, 8–9, 13–15, 16
   marriage and family, 42–43, 47, 55–56, 57–58, 61, 65
   re-engendering property rights, 211–12
   remedial framework, 314
   states obligations, 142, 145
African Charter on Human and Peoples' Rights, 15, 179, 333–34
afro-feminism, 177–79
agricultural land as livelihood source, 90
alien property rights, 24–25, 240, 256, 257–58, 259–60
all appropriate measures requirement, 3–4, 22, 23–24, 78, 95, 125, 128, 144, 156–57, 160, 199–200, 308, 317–18, 373, 374
Alston, Philip, 184–85
Alwis, Rangita de Silva de, 351–52
American Convention on Human Rights, 13–15
American Declaration of the Rights and Duties of Man (American Declaration), 11–15, 20
Amnesty International, 177, 211
Article 2 (CEDAW), 189
Article 7 (CEDAW), 73–74
Article 9 (CEDAW), 74
Article 11 (CEDAW), 116, 373
Article 13 (CEDAW), 78, 95, 109, 116, 337–38, 373
Article 14 (CEDAW), 78, 95, 106, 109, 116, 195, 216–18, 227–28, 250–51, 337–38, 352, 374
Article 15 (CEDAW), 47, 74–76, 245–46, 337–38, 374
Article 16 (CEDAW), 47, 245, 337–38
Article 6 (DEDAW), 22

Articles on the Responsibility of States for Internationally Wrongful Acts, 257–58
Asian Debt Crisis (1997–2003), 366–67
asylum rights, 73, 74, 102–3, 229
autonomy of women, 16–17, 109, 111–12
Avellanal v. Peru, 289

battered women, 55, 57, 147, 202–3, 359
Beijing Platform for Action, 24–25, 205
Ben Djazia v. Spain, 316
bilateral international investment agreements, 24–25, 364–65
bilateral investment treaties (BITs), 235–38. *See also* US-Argentina BIT; US Model BIT
Blackstone, William, 335, 341, 342, 343–44
Briddick, Catherine, 170
Byrnes, Andrew, 170–71

Cambell, Meghan, 230–32
Canada, Inquiry Reports, 153–55, 188–89
Carvalho Pinto de Sousa Morais v. Portugal, 326–28
Cecilia Kell v. Canada, 54–59, 171–73, 189, 199, 219–25, 346
CEDAW Committee overview. *See also* critiques of CEDAW Committee; property jurisprudence of CEDAW
   authority to interpret Convention, 33–35
   human rights conventions, 8–9, 12–13, 165, 317, 319
   introduction to, 26–27, 28–29
   jurisprudential tools of, xix–xx, 6–7
   normative outputs, 8, 32
   procedures and outputs on property rights, 35–46
Charlesworth, Hilary, xv, 1, 163–70
Charter of Economic Rights and Duties of States, 24–25
Chinkin, Christine, 1, 163–70
citizenship, 76
citizenship certificates, 76, 197
civil codes, 63–64, 72, 204–5, 324

civilizing mission, 29, 175, 177, 182–83, 191–92, 275–77
civil rights
  COs, 76–95, 288
  introduction to, 9–10, 16, 27, 32
  property rights as, 73–77, 342–43
civil society
  communications and, 219–20
  COs and, 43–45
  GRs and, 36, 37
  human rights and, 361–62, 364–65
  Inquiry Reports and, 42
  land rights and, 16–17
  organizations, 360
  property jurisprudence of CEDAW, 35
  remedial processes and, 271–72
  role in constructive dialogue, 45
  submissions to CEDAW Committee, 43–44
climate change, 82, 111
Committee on Economic, Social and Cultural Rights (CESCR), 281
communications of CEDAW Committee
  civil society and, 219–20
  due diligence and, 147–51, 152, 154, 156–57
  follow-up procedures, 46
  gender-based violence, 146–53, 384
  housing rights, 97–101, 198–99, 383
  introduction to, 31, 32
  overview of, 38–41, 383–84
  property rights in marriage and family relations, 54–63, 383
  social benefits, 119–39, 383
Community Court of Justice of Economic Community of West African States (ECOWAS), 16
comparative property law, 28, 325
Comprehensive and Progressive Trans-Pacific Partnership (CPTPP), 237–38
Concluding Observations (COs) under CEDAW
  for China, 347–51
  civil and political rights, 76–95, 288
  civil society and, 43–45
  on divorce, 350–52
  divorce and, 63, 350–52
  domestic violence and, 188–89
  due diligence and, 42–43, 159, 160–61
  economic empowerment, 112–15
  equal treatment requirements, 42
  financial credit, 42–43, 112–15
  follow-up procedures, 46
  gender-based violence, 159–61
  gender equality and, 284–85, 288

housing rights, 42–43, 101–9
intellectual property rights, 42–43, 108–9
interpretation authority, 33–35
introduction to, 31, 32, 42–45
land rights, 87–95
overview of, 42–45
for Pakistan, 350–52
poverty/economic precarity, 189
procedures and outputs on property rights, 35–46, 187–88
property rights in marriage and family relations, 63–73
social benefits, 42–43, 132–39
conflict situations, 94–95, 104–5
constructive dialogues, 33, 34, 43–45, 222–23, 376
Convention on the Elimination of Racial Discrimination (CERD), 15, 285, 325–26, 356–57
Convention Relating to the Status of Refugees, 20
Convention Relating to the Status of Stateless Persons, 20
COVID-19 pandemic, 103, 104
critiques of CEDAW Committee
  feminist critiques, 163–73, 190–96, 370–71
  gender binary and, 167–68
  intersectionality and, 215–18
  marginalization and, 218–19
  neo-liberalism and, 209–13
  property jurisprudence and, 42–228
  public/private divide, 214–15
  structural change and, 225–28
  supranational security and, 228–33
  Third World women and, 168–69, 173–74
cultural heritage, 107–8
cultural relativism, 209
cultural rights, 9–10, 31, 32, 185–86, 338–39, 342–43, 366. *See also* Indigenous women and girls; intellectual property rights; International Covenant on Economic, Social and Cultural Rights,
customary international law, 24–25, 141, 218–19, 238–39, 246, 247, 325
customary marriages, 69, 288

David, Velaska, 298
Declaration on the Elimination of Discrimination against Women (DEDAW), 20–22
de facto equality, 203, 214–15, 225, 226–27, 271–72
de facto unions, 49, 69–70, 72, 204–5
de jure equality, 6, 191, 200, 214–15, 225, 251, 325–26

despotic dominion over private property, 6, 335
development. *See also* land rights;
  neo-liberalism
  development projects, 81, 84, 86, 87–88, 91–92, 101, 104, 205–6, 243–44, 296
  economic development, 1–2, 7–8, 11, 16–17, 84, 85, 86, 114, 180–81, 192–93, 198–99, 202–3, 210–11, 235–36, 243–44, 265–66, 277
  housing rights, 104
  right to, 79, 316
  rural development, 79, 92, 189, 203, 273–74, 374
  sustainable development, 114, 223–24, 363–64
  Sustainable Development Goals, xix, 24–25, 363–64
  World Bank, 2–3, 7–8, 11, 183, 275–76, 344
dignity, 1–2, 12–13, 19, 110, 126, 131, 172–73, 177–78, 190, 191–92, 223–24, 235–36, 304, 316–17, 331–32, 342–43, 345
disability benefits, 13–15, 135, 136–37, 291
disabled women/girls/daughters, 36–37, 126, 127–28, 188–89
discrimination against women
  defined, 23–24
  elimination of discriminatory provisions, 71–73
  entitlement provisions, 199–200
  under ICCPR, 285–87
  under ICESCR, 303
  intersectional forms of, 71
  property rights in marriage and family relations, 38, 47–54
  protection from, 26
  socioeconomic discrimination, 215–16
discriminatory denials of property rights, 8–10
discriminatory laws, 41, 48–49, 79–80, 82, 130, 288, 343–44
disenfranchisement of women, 27, 51, 52, 59, 68, 78–79, 87–89, 94, 101, 102, 114–15, 119–20, 135, 137–38, 154, 187–88
divorce
  child maintenance following, 156
  COs on, 63, 350–52
  domestic violence concerns, 158, 348, 350
  equal distribution, 65
  fault-based divorce, 50
  financial impact of, 48–49, 331–32, 348–49, 350–51
  GRs and, 53–54
  protection of property, 49–50, 53–54, 65–68, 71–73, 77, 156, 187–88, 207, 225–26, 227, 347

tangible/intangible assets, 65, 66
unremunerated domestic work, 67, 75, 117
domestic violence
  battered women, 55, 57, 147, 202–3, 359
  COs and, 188–89
  divorce and, 158, 348, 350
  interventions in, 145
  marital rape, 349–51
  partner homicides, 359
  rights of battered spouses, 202–3
domestic workers, 135
due diligence
  common obligations, 321–24
  communications and, 147–51, 152, 154, 156–57
  COs and, 42–43, 159, 160–61
  discrimination by private actors, 252–53
  financial credit and, 256–57
  gender-based violence, 139–40, 143–44, 160
  GRs and, 107, 143–44
  housing rights and, 172
  ICCPR *vs.* ICESCR, 321–24
  Indigenous women's rights, 85, 87, 146
  non-state actors and, 282–84
  state actors and, 319

East African Court of Justice, 16
Economic and Social Council (ECOSOC), 165
economic benefits of property rights, xx, 4–5, 16–17, 23–24, 117, 221, 299
economic development, 1–2, 7–8, 11, 16–17, 84, 85, 86, 114, 180–81, 192–93, 198–99, 202–3, 210–11, 235–36, 243–44, 265–66, 277
economic empowerment
  access to, 109–11, 112–15
  COs, 112–15
  criticism of, 208
  financial credit and, 109–15
  GRs and, 36–37
  intellectual property rights and, 108
  by international financial institutions, 333
  by international law, 25
  intersectionality and, 114–15
  introduction to, 10, 32, 36–37, 108
  land rights of women and, 93
  protection of, 27, 193
  social security rights benefits and, 137
economic harm, 142, 261–62, 270
economic rights, 5, 32, 49, 65, 69–70, 170, 184–85, 211–12, 282, 286–87, 301, 312, 323–24
economic security, 52–53, 62, 128, 193, 202, 317
economic violence, 139–40, 156, 159–60

effective protection requirement, 23–24, 147–48, 158
Elena Genero v. Italy, 299
Elisabeth de Blok et al. v. The Netherlands, 123–25
entitlement provisions, 199–200, 341
entrepreneur/entrepreneurship, 10, 24–25, 108, 109, 110–11, 112–15, 180, 198–99, 200, 203–4, 205–6, 208, 238, 249, 265–71, 275, 366–67
equality
    de facto equality, 203, 214–15, 225, 226–27, 271–72
    de jure equality, 6, 191, 200, 214–15, 225, 251, 325–26
    formal equality, 6, 9–10, 51–52, 164–65, 167, 169, 187–88, 190–91, 210–12, 213–14, 222, 228–29, 268, 302–3, 320, 348–49
    substantive equality, 9–10, 51, 80, 81–82, 93–94, 105, 178, 188–89, 190–91, 202–3, 207, 211–12, 220–21, 225–26, 230–31, 251, 256, 268–70, 273–75, 289–90, 302–3, 354–56
    transformative equality, 170–71, 172–73
equality before the law provision, 53–54, 194, 281–82, 284, 289, 298
equal property rights, 5–6, 8–9, 19, 23, 27–28, 29, 68, 214–15, 226–27, 228, 235–36, 278–79, 321, 329, 337–38, 340, 343–44, 351–52, 353–54, 363
equal treatment requirements
    COs and, 42–43
    for employees, 122–23
    GRs and, 60, 187–88, 225–26
    under international law, 23
    interpretations of, 21–22, 190–91
    land rights, 374
    male bias, 199–200
    measure of, 177–78
    neutral laws or practices, 227
    obligation on states, 246, 250–51, 265–67, 346
    property jurisprudence and, 203, 204
    rural women's rights, 78, 106, 109
    social benefits and, 341–42
E.S. and S.C. v. United Republic of Tanzania, 59–63, 187–88
ethic of rights, 163–64, 213–14
European Convention for the Protection of Human Rights (ECHR), 13–15, 230–31, 328
European Court of Human Rights (ECtHR), 4–5, 6–7, 13–15, 16, 240–41, 243–44, 325, 326–28

European human rights systems
    European Convention for the Protection of Human Rights, 13–15, 230–31, 328
    European Court of Human Rights, 4–5, 6–7, 13–15, 16, 240–41, 243–44
extractive industries, 79, 81, 85, 91–92, 146, 205–6

fair and equitable treatment (FET), 247–48
family relations. *See* marriage and family relations property rights
feminism/feminists
    afro-feminism, 177–79
    critiques of CEDAW Committee, 163–73, 190–96, 370–71
    as equal rights activists, xv
    liberal feminism, 27, 169, 173
    socialist feminism, 173–74
    Third World feminism, 27, 173
FIAN International, 2–3
financial credit
    access to microcredit, 114
    access to services, 112–14
    climate change, 111
    COs and, 42–43, 112–15
    due diligence, 256–57
    economic empowerment, 109–15
    GRs and, 36–37, 109–15
    introduction to, 32
    older women's rights, 110
    rural women's rights, 110–11
    trafficking in women and girls and, 111–12
follow-up procedures
    communications of CEDAW Committee, 46
    Concluding Observations (COs) under CEDAW, 46
    Inquiry Reports under CEDAW, 45–46
    Optional Protocol, 45–46
forced eviction, 293–96, 304–11
formal equality, 6, 9–10, 51–52, 164–65, 167, 169, 187–88, 190–91, 210–12, 213–14, 222, 228–29, 268, 302–3, 320, 348–49
Fourth World Conference on Women (1995), xix
free and informed consent, 60, 81, 86, 87, 91, 107
free market, 174–75, 181–82, 193, 196, 203, 204, 206, 222, 274–75
full equality, 190–91, 331
full protection and security (FPS), 247–48

gender-based violence
    communications of CEDAW Committee, 146–53, 384
    COs, 159–61

domestic violence interventions, 145
due diligence obligations, 160
in family relations, 142
GRs, 140–46
housing rights, 145
Inquiry Reports, 153–59
intersectional discrimination, 145–46
introduction to, 32
land rights, 145
by private actors, 143–44
protection and eviction order, 42–43, 157, 159, 160–61
shelter, 161
trafficking in women and girls, 142–43
gender binary, xv, 167–68
gender equality
African continent and, 177–78, 210
Article 16 issues over, 214–15, 228–29
COs and, 284–85, 288
ECtHR and, 326–27, 328
land rights and, 2–3, 26
neoliberal co-optation of, 176–77
role of states in, 93
supranational security and, 228–33
World Bank and, 7–8, 11, 183, 275–76, 344
gender gap
in land and housing, xix
property jurisprudence of CEDAW, 363–64
subordination of women, 164–65, 219–25, 360–61, 369–71
wealth and property, 25
General Agreement on Tariffs and Trade (GATT), 237–38
General Recommendations (GRs) under CEDAW
civil society and, 36, 37
defense of women's equality in, 170
divorce and, 53–54
due diligence and, 107, 143–44
economic empowerment, 36–37
equal treatment requirements, 60, 187–88, 225–26
financial credit, 36–37, 109–15
gender-based violence, 140–46
housing rights, 36–37, 95–97
intellectual property rights, 36–37, 105–9
interpretation authority, 33–35
intersectional discrimination on property rights for women, 52–54
introduction to, 31, 32
land rights, 36–37, 77–95
marriage and family relations property rights, 38, 47–54

OHCHR and, 37
overview of, 36–38, 381–82
procedures and outputs on property rights, 35–46
property rights of women under CEDAW, 73–77
social benefits, 36–37, 115–19
transparency of, 361
generational rights, 194
Georgopolous v. Greece, 294–95
Goldblatt, Beth, 354–56
good governance, 174–75, 181, 210–11, 247, 275–76
GR 12, 140–41
GR 16, 116–17
GR 17, 117
GR 19, 141, 142, 143, 144
GR 21, 47–52, 109–10, 187–88
GR 23, 73–74
GR 26, 117
GR 27, 52–54, 95–97, 110, 117, 118
GR 28, 142, 252–53
GR 29, 47–52, 117, 119, 142, 206–7
GR 32, 74
GR 33, 74–76, 77, 142
GR 34, 78–82, 95–97, 106–8, 110–11, 117–18, 199–201, 206
GR 35, 141–43, 144
GR 37, 82, 95–97, 111
GR 38, 111–12, 118
GR 39, 82–87, 106–8, 112, 118, 216
Grismer v. Canada, 299

Halley, Janet, 168–69
Halperin-Kaddari, Ruth, 359
Hayek, Friedrich, 211
Heathcote, Gina, 176–77
Hohmann, Jessie, 171–72
Holtmaat, Rikki, 332–33
Hoofdman v. Netherlands, 291–92
housing/housing rights
communications addressing, 97–101, 198–99, 383
conflict situations and, 104–5
COs and, 42–43, 101–9
development projects, 104
due diligence, 172
economic precarity and, 103
forced eviction, 293–96, 304–11
gender-based violence, 145
gender gap in, xix
GRs and, 36–37, 95–97
under ICESCR, 304–11

housing/housing rights (*cont.*)
  intersectional discrimination, 101–3
  introduction to, 10–11, 32
  poverty/economic precarity, 103
  rural women's rights, 95–97
  temporary special measures, 105
human rights. *See also* civil rights; Office of the High Commissioner for Human Rights; political rights; Universal Declaration of Human Rights
  civil society and, 361–62, 364–65
  committees, 16, 175–76, 219, 254–55, 281, 333–34, 365
  conventions, 8–9, 12–13, 165, 317, 319
  criticism of, 173–86, 190–96
  international human rights, 11, 27–28, 173–86, 190–96
  regional system, 8, 12–13, 115–16, 232, 253–54, 261–62, 326–27, 329–30, 333–34, 346, 363–65
  treaties, 8–9, 12–16, 19–20, 24–25
  universal, 27, 209
  UN treaty bodies, xx, 7–8, 35, 175–76, 242, 253–54, 264–65, 281, 329
  violations, xviii, 38, 42, 75, 85, 135, 144, 154–55, 205–6, 230, 250–51, 297, 308, 357–58, 364–65
Human Rights Committee (HRC), 16, 254–55, 281, 365

identity documents, 76, 197
I.D.G. v. Spain, 315
Indigenous women and girls
  due diligence over, 85, 87, 146
  financial credit, 112
  land rights of, 82–87, 91–92
  social benefits, 117–18
  vulnerabilities of, 226
informal employment, 117–18
informal sector social security rights, 133–34
inheritance rights, 16–17, 21, 62, 69, 72–73, 195, 288
Inniss, Lolita Buckener, 171–72
Inquiry Reports under CEDAW
  on Canada, 153–55
  civil society and, 42
  follow-up procedures, 45–46
  gender-based violence, 153–59
  introduction to, 31, 32
  Optional Protocol and, 41–42
  overview of, 41–42, 385
  on South Africa, 155–59
Institute for Liberty and Democracy, 181

intellectual property rights
  COs and, 42–43, 108–9
  economic empowerment and, 108
  GRs and, 36–37, 105–9
  introduction to, 27, 32
  seed rights, 32, 36–37, 105–6, 108–9
Inter-American Court of Human Rights, 6–7
  American Convention on Human Rights, 13–15
  American Declaration of the Rights and Duties of Man, 11–15, 20
International Court of Justice (ICJ), 195–96
International Covenant on Civil and Political Rights (ICCPR)
  CEDAW's added value to, 329–34
  comparisons with the CEDAW's jurisprudence, 324–29
  due diligence obligations, 321–24
  equality framework, 281–85
  forced eviction and, 293–96
  generational rights, 194
  Human Rights Committee, 16, 254–55, 281, 365
  human rights distinctions, 357–58
  meaning of discrimination against women under, 285–87
  premise overview, 316–20
  property rights of women under, 10, 12–13, 16, 287–89
  protection of property under, xvi
  remedial/reparative approach under, 296–99
  social benefits under, 289–90, 298, 328–29, 333
  social security rights and, 289–93
  standard for discrimination, 165–66
International Covenant on Economic, Social and Cultural Rights (ICESCR)
  CEDAW's added value to, 329–34
  Committee on Economic, Social and Cultural Rights, 281
  comparisons with the CEDAW's jurisprudence, 324–29
  due diligence obligations, 321–24
  equality framework, 300–4
  forced eviction and, 304–11
  generational rights, 194
  housing rights under, 304–11
  other rights under, 311–14
  premise overview, 316–20
  property rights of women under, 10, 12–13, 301–4
  protection of property under, xvi
  remedial/reparative approach under, 314–16
  standard for discrimination, 165–66

INDEX   403

international division of labor, 173–74
international human rights, 11, 27–28, 173–86, 190–96
international investment agreement (IIA)
    approaches to derogation, 256–58
    approaches to discrimination, 249–52
    defining protected property, 244–46, 336
    distinct enforcement remedies, 258–65
    hypothetical comparisons, 265–80
    introduction to, 235–38
    jurisprudence constante, 241–42, 254–56
    relative prominence of, 238–44
    sources of authority, 253–56
    state obligations, 247–48
    territorial and judiciary scope, 252–53
international investment agreements (IIAs), 203–4
International Labor Organization (ILO), 20, 115–16, 134, 139
international law of property, xv, 10–11, 238, 242, 336
international property law, xx, 6–8, 28, 173–86, 325–27, 333–34
intersectional discrimination
    critiques of CEDAW Committee and, 215–18
    economic empowerment and, 114–15
    gender-based violence, 145–46
    housing rights, 101–3
    land rights, 71
    self-employed women, 137–39
Investment Disputes between States and Nationals of Other States (ICSID), 240–41, 244, 263–64
investor-state dispute settlement (ISDS), 238, 253, 258, 265, 277–78

Jaising, Indira, 351–52
J.I. v. Finland, 152
jurisprudence constante, 241–42, 254–56
justice rights, 74–76, 77

Ke Li, 348–49
Kennedy, David, 179–81
Koskenniemi, Martti, 11–12, 185–86
Kriebaum, Ursula, 28

L.A. et al. v. North Macedonia, 97–101, 189
Lacey, Nicola, 169, 213–14
land dispossession, 80, 81
land grabbing, 2–3, 42–43, 53, 87–88, 91–92, 226–27
land/land rights
    agricultural land as livelihood source, 90

    civil society and, 16–17
    conflict situations and, 94–95
    COs, 87–95
    decision-making process, 92–93
    development projects, 81, 84, 86, 87–88, 91–92, 101, 104, 205–6, 243–44, 296
    dispossession, 80, 81
    economic empowerment, 93
    elimination of discriminatory legislation, 93
    equal treatment requirements, 374
    extractive industries, 79, 81, 85, 91–92, 146, 205–6
    free and informed consent, 60, 81, 86, 87, 91, 107
    gender-based violence, 145
    gender equality and, 2–3, 26
    gender gap in, xix
    GRs and, 36–37, 77–95
    of Indigenous women and girls, 82–87, 91–92
    intersectional discrimination, 71
    introduction to, 32
    land acquisition, 81, 91
    land dispossession, 80, 81
    land grabbing, 2–3, 42–43, 53, 87–88, 91–92, 226–27
    mega-projects, 91, 205–6
    poverty/economic precarity, 90
    registration, 89
    rural women's rights, 78–82, 88–89
    temporary special measures, 94
    tenure security, 105, 333, 337–39, 342, 344
    visibility and awareness of, 93
land registration, 89
Landsea, 16–17
LGBTQ+ persons, 167, 191, 215–16, 352–53.
    See also same-sex relationships
liberal feminism, 27, 169, 173
Liberté sans Frontieres (LSF), 177
L.N.P v. Argentine Republic, 299
Locke, John, 17–19
López Albán v. Spain, 307–8

MacKinnon, Catherine, 1, 228
male bias, 199–200
marginalization issues, 72, 78, 99, 132–33, 142, 154, 155, 165, 168–69, 171–72, 188–89, 214, 218–19, 332–33, 369–70
marital rape, 349–51
Marks, Susan, 219
marriage and family relations property rights.
    See also divorce
    assets of women, 19, 67, 187–88, 225–27

marriage and family relations property
	rights (*cont.*)
  communications of CEDAW Committee,
	54–63, 383
  control over, 64
  COs, 63–73
  customary marriages, 69, 288
  decision-making supremacy of
	husband, 63–64
  de facto unions, 49, 69–70, 72, 204–5
  in different types of family relations, 69–71
  disabled women/girls/daughters, 36–37, 126,
	127–28, 188–89
  discrimination, 286–87, 289–93
  elimination of discriminatory
	provisions, 71–73
  equal division of, 65
  GRs and, 38, 47–54, 109–10
  intersectional forms of discrimination, 71
  intestate succession and inheritance, 68–69
  introduction to, 32
  joint ownership of, 64
  maternity leave benefits, 121, 123, 124–25,
	188–89
  ownership, 57, 59
  polygamy, 49, 53, 69, 72, 179
  recognition and distribution of, 66–67
  same-sex relationships, 49, 69, 93, 195, 292–93
  separation of, 67–68
  survivorship benefits, 118–19, 136
  widowhood, 15, 50, 51–53, 59, 60–61, 68–69,
	77, 88, 136, 142, 202, 214, 217–18, 230,
	288, 291–92, 343–44
Martínez de Irujo v. Spain, 289
maternity leave, 123–25, 137
maternity leave benefits, 121, 123, 124–
	25, 188–89
Merry, Sally, 209
microcredit access, 114
migrant workers, 117, 135, 139–40, 193
Mohanty, Chandra Talpade, 173–74
moral codes, 178–79, 209–10
Moreau, Sophia, 356–58
most-favored-nation (MFN) treatment, 236,
	249–50, 259–60
Moyn, Samuel, 177, 185, 210, 362
Ms. A.T. v. Hungary, 147–49
Ms. Dung Thi Thuy Nguyen v. The Netherlands,
	120–23, 232–33
M.T. Sprenger v. Netherlands, 291–92
Mueller v. Namibia, 299
Murdoch, Jim, 169–70
Musembi, Celestine Myamu, 179, 209–10, 333–34

Natalia Ciobanu v. Republic of Moldova, 125–29
national treatment (NT), 236
Neefs v. Netherlands, 292
neo-liberalism
  criticisms of, 29, 174–75, 180–86, 210
  property jurisprudence of CEDAW
	Committee, 196–209
  re-engendering property rights, 209–13
New International Economic Order (NIEO),
	24–25, 205
non-accumulation clause, 120–23
nonbinary gender, xv
non-state actors, 10–11, 86, 96, 141, 144, 152,
	156–57, 160, 228, 256, 282–84, 318–19
normative outputs of CEDAW Committee, 8, 32

Office of the High Commissioner for Human
	Rights (OHCHR), 33, 37, 38–41
older women's rights, 110, 118–19, 129–32
Optional Protocol
  communications and, 38–41
  follow-up procedures, 45–46
  GRs and, 38
  Inquiry Reports and, 41–42
  interpretation authority, 33–34
Orford, Anne, 173–74, 183–85, 196
Otto, Dianne, 168–69
ownership
  marriage and family relations property
	rights, 57, 59
  property ownership, 28, 62–64, 73–74, 76,
	101, 112–13, 197, 229, 344
  registered owner, 56–57
  sole owner, 55

partner homicides, 359
Pateman, Carol, 177–78
pension benefits, 118–19, 129–32, 136
pension rights, 13–15, 67, 337–38
Permanent Court of International Justice
	(PCIJ), 259
personal assistant rights, 125–29
personal status laws, 48–49, 60, 63, 76, 204–5,
	214, 288, 351–52
perspectival claims, 212
Pipes, Richard, 17–18
political rights
  COs, 76–95
  introduction to, 27, 32
  property rights of women under
	CEDAW, 73–77
  women in politics, 73–74
polygamy, 49, 53, 69, 72, 179

poverty/economic precarity, 90, 103, 189
powerless companion, 177, 191–92
Pre-Sessional Working Group, 43–44
property deprivations, 16, 331–32, 347, 357–58, 362
property disenfranchisement of women, 27, 51, 52–53
property grabbing, 52, 79, 142, 159–60, 203–4, 205–6
property jurisprudence of CEDAW
    alien property rights, 24–25, 240, 256, 257–58, 259–60
    civil and political rights, 73–77
    in context, 11–20
    contrary instincts in women's rights, 365–67
    despotic dominion over, 6, 335
    discriminatory denials, 8–10
    economic benefits of, xx, 4–5, 16–17, 23–24, 117, 221, 299
    economic empowerment and, 10
    equal property rights, 5–6, 8–9, 19, 23, 27–28, 29, 68, 214–15, 226–27, 228, 235–36, 278–79, 321, 329, 337–38, 340, 343–44, 351–52, 353–54, 363
    equal treatment requirements, 203, 204
    flawed outputs, 346–52
    government regulation of, 203–9
    GRs and, 73–77
    importance of, 362–65
    institutional constraints and challenges, 360–62
    introduction to, xv–xvi, 27–29, 31–32
    neo-liberalist definitions and, 196–209
    origins of, 20–22
    progressive nature of, 335–45
    property deprivations, 16, 331–32, 347, 357–58, 362
    property provisions, 23–26
    realities and challenges, 1–11, 369–71
    state reservations to, 375–76
    substantive lacunae, 352–59
    titling private property, 197–201
    violations, 39, 42, 54, 57, 139–40, 352, 356
property ownership, 28, 62–64, 73–74, 76, 101, 112–13, 197, 229, 344
prosperity, 183–84, 191–92, 203.
    See also wealth
protection and eviction order, 42–43, 157, 159, 160–61
Protocol to the European Convention for the Protection of Human Rights and Fundamental Freedoms, 20

re-engendering human rights, 7–8, 273–74
re-engendering property rights
    battered spouses, 202–3
    binary arguments, 209–13
    CEDAW's interpretation, 190–96
    introduction to, 187–90
    property jurisprudence and neo-liberalism, 196–209
    titling private property, 197–201
    universalizing concepts, 209–13
refugee status rights, 74
regional human rights system, 8, 12–13, 115–16, 232, 253–54, 261–62, 326–27, 329–30, 333–34, 346, 363–65
relative rights, 247
remedial/reparative approaches, 296–99, 314–16
rights talk, 180, 210, 212, 213–14
Roma women, 100–1, 195
Romero v. Spain, 310–11
A Room of One's Own (Woolf), 365–67
Rosenblum, Darren, 168–69
rule of law
    delimited conceptions of, 174–75
    gendered and racist nature of, 369–70
    goals of neo-libertarians and, 205
    independent national courts and, 230
    property rights of women and, 17–19, 29
    regional human rights system, 232
rural development, 79, 92, 189, 203, 273–74, 374
rural women's rights
    economic empowerment and, 114–15
    equal treatment requirements, 78, 106, 109
    financial credit, 110–11
    free and informed consent, 60, 81, 86, 87, 91, 107
    housing rights, 95–97
    industrial farming, 106–8
    intellectual property rights, 106–8
    land rights, 78–82, 88–89
    self-employed women, 137–39
    social benefits, 117–18
    tenure security, 105, 333, 337–39, 342, 344

Sackville, Ronald, 341–42
Şahide Goekce v. Austria, 150
same-sex relationships, 49, 69, 93, 195, 292–93.
    See also LGBTQ+ persons
SC and others v. Secretary of State for Work and Pensions, 230–31
seed rights, 32, 36–37, 105–6, 108–9
self-determination rights, 83, 85, 86–87, 164–65, 186, 197–98, 202, 205–6, 338

self-employed women
  intersectional discrimination, 137–39
  maternity benefits, 137
  maternity leave, 123–25, 137
  non-accumulation clause, 120–23
  pension benefits, 136
  rural women's rights, 137–39
  social security rights, 135–36
  survivorship benefits, 136
  temporary special measures, 137
  unemployment benefits, 136–37
shadow reports, 43–45, 232, 360
shelter, 161
Simplified Reporting Procedure, 43–44
Slaughter, Joseph, 186
S.N. and E.R. v. North Macedonia, 97–101
Snijders v. Netherlands, 292
social benefits
  CEDAW Committee and, 27
  communications of CEDAW Committee, 119–39, 383
  COs and, 42–43, 132–39
  disability benefits, 13–15, 135, 136–37, 291
  equal treatment requirements, 341–42
  GRs and, 36–37, 115–19
  under ICCPR, 289–90, 298, 328–29, 333
  Indigenous women and girls, 117–18
  informal employment, 117–18
  introduction to, 32
  maternity leave, 123–25, 137
  maternity leave benefits, 121, 123, 124–25, 188–89
  pension benefits, 118–19
  property rights of women, 4–5
  rural women's rights, 117–18
  survivorship benefits, 118–19
  trafficking in women and girls, 118
  unemployment benefits, 134, 136–37, 290–91
  Universal Credit, 230–31
  unpaid care work, 116–17
social contract theory, 17–18
socialist feminism, 173–74
social security rights
  in informal sector, 133–34
  marital status and, 289–93
  self-employed women, 135–36
  women domestic workers, 135
socioeconomic discrimination, 215–16
Song, Jesok, 366–67
South Africa, Inquiry Reports on, 155–59
Sprenger v. The Netherlands, 312–13
S.T. v. Russian Federation, 153
Standard Reporting Procedure, 43

statelessness, 74
State Reporting/State Party Reports. *See also* civil society
  constructive dialogues, 33, 34, 43–45, 222–23, 376
  Pre-Sessional Working Group, 43–44
  reporting cycles, 34, 42
  shadow reports, 43–45, 232, 360
  Simplified Reporting Procedure, 43–44
  Standard Reporting Procedure, 43
subordination of women, 164–65, 219–25, 360–61, 369–71
substantive equality, 9–10, 51, 80, 81–82, 93–94, 105, 178, 188–89, 190–91, 202–3, 207, 211–12, 220–21, 225–26, 230–31, 251, 256, 268–70, 273–75, 289–90, 302–3, 354–56
supranational security, 228–33, 275, 361–62
survivorship benefits, 118–19, 136
sustainable development, 114, 223–24, 363–64
Sustainable Development Goals, xix, 24–25, 363–64
S.W.M. Broeks v. Netherlands, 282
systematic violations, 41, 158–59, 321, 357–58

Tamale, Sylvia, 177–79, 210
temporary special measures, 94, 105, 137
tenure security, 105, 333, 337–39, 342, 344
Third World feminism, 27, 173
Third World women, 168–69, 173–74
titling private property, 197–201
trafficking in women and girls, 111–12, 118, 142–43
Tramontana, Enzamaria, 171–72
transformational equality, 171–72, 214, 222–23, 226
transformational equality for women, 171–72, 214, 222–23, 226
transformative equality, 170–71, 172–73
Trujillo Calero v. Ecuador, 311–13
Tzouvala, Ntina, 175

UN Charter, 301–2
UN Commission on the Status of Women (CSW), 1–11, 20, 165
UN Convention on the Elimination of All Forms of Discrimination against Women (CEDAW)
  Article 2 (CEDAW), 189
  Article 7 (CEDAW), 73–74
  Article 9 (CEDAW), 74
  Article 11 (CEDAW), 116, 373
  Article 13 (CEDAW), 78, 95, 109, 116, 337–38, 373

Article 14 (CEDAW), 78, 95, 106, 109, 116, 195, 216–18, 227–28, 250–51, 337–38, 352, 374
Article 15 (CEDAW), 47, 74–76, 245–46, 337–38, 374
Article 16 (CEDAW), 47, 245, 337–38
unemployment benefits, 134, 136–37, 290–91
UN General Assembly, xix, 20, 23, 24–25
UN human rights treaty bodies, xx, 7–8, 35, 175–76, 242, 253–54, 264–65, 281, 329
United Nations Commission on International Trade Law (UNCITRAL), 263
Universal Declaration of Human Rights (Universal Declaration, UDHR), 11–13, 20, 301–2
  jurisprudence under, 281
  property rights of women, 26
  rule of law and, 18
universal human rights, 27, 209
Universal Human Rights Index, 42–43
unpaid care work, 116–17
unremunerated domestic work, 67, 75, 117
UN Security Council, xix
UN Women, 1–2
Urbaser v. Argentina, 279
US-Argentina BIT, 245–46, 247–48, 257–58, 270, 275–76
US-Mexican Claims Tribunal, 239–40
US Model BIT, 237–38, 245, 258, 276–77

Vienna Conference on Human Rights (1993), 11
V.K. v. Bulgaria, 151–52
Vojnović v. Croatia, 295–96
voting rights, 73–74
V.P. v. Belarus, 129–32

Wadlig, Gabriele, 340, 341
Waldron, Jeremy, 18–19

wealth, 1–2, 25, 112, 176–77, 181–82, 183–84, 203, 222, 223–24, 254, 317, 362, 363–64, 366. *See also* prosperity
Whyte, Jessica, 177, 210–12
widowhood, 15, 50, 51–53, 59, 60–61, 68–69, 77, 88, 136, 142, 202, 214, 217–18, 230, 288, 291–92, 343–44
Wilson, Stuart, 315, 342–43
Wollstonecraft, Mary, 340–41
women. *See also* discrimination against women; gender-based violence; Indigenous women and girls; rural women's rights; self-employed women
  autonomy of, 16–17, 109, 111–12
  battered women, 55, 57, 147, 202–3, 359
  disabled women/girls/daughters, 36–37, 126, 127–28, 188–89
  disenfranchisement of, 27, 51, 52, 59, 68, 78–79, 87–89, 94, 101, 102, 114–15, 119–20, 135, 137–38, 154, 187–88
  older women's rights, 110, 118–19, 129–32
  rights regime, 167, 168–69, 211–12
  Third World women, 168–69, 173–74
  trafficking in women and girls, 111–12, 118, 142–43
  transformational equality for, 171–72, 214, 222–23, 226
  UN Women, 1–2
Woolf, Virginia, 365–67
World Bank, 2–3, 7–8, 11, 183, 275–76, 344
Wright, Shelly, 163–64

X v. Cambodia, 292–93, 299

Yildirim v. Austria, 150–51
Young v. Australia, 292–93, 299